Reader's Digest

COMPLETE
GUIDE
to the
BIBLE

Reader's Digest

COMPLETE
GUIDE
to the
BIBLE

AN ILLUSTRATED
BOOK-BY-BOOK COMPANION
TO THE SCRIPTURES

The Reader's Digest Association, Inc.
Pleasantville, New York / Montreal

COMPLETE GUIDE TO THE BIBLE

Designed and Edited by Gardner Associates

Editorial Director: Joseph L. Gardner
Art Editor: Howard P. Johnson
Picture Editor: Laurie Platt Winfrey
Associate Picture Editor: Robin J. Sand
*Associate Editor and Principal Contributing
    Writer:* Stephen M. Miller
Research Editor: Josephine Reidy
Art Researchers: Christopher Deegan,
    Robert Melzak
Contributing Writers: Charles Flowers, Larry L. Lyke,
    Judith H. Newman, Thomas L. Robinson, Carol Weeg
Cartographer: Bette Duke
Copy Editor: Felice Levy
Indexer: Cynthia Crippen
Proofreader: James R. Gullickson
Technical Adviser: Justin Gardner

Project Staff for Reader's Digest

Editor: Gayla Visalli
Senior Art Editor: Judith Carmel

Reader's Digest General Books

*Editor-in-Chief, Books and
    Home Entertainment:* Barbara J. Morgan
Editor-in-Chief, U.S.General Books: David Palmer
Executive Editor: Gayla Visalli
Managing Editor: Christopher Cavanaugh
*Editorial Director, History, Religion,
    and Reference Books:* Edmund H. Harvey, Jr.
*Design Director, History, Religion,
    and Reference Books:* Irene Ledwith

Board of Consultants

David Noel Freedman
Professor of Hebrew Biblical Studies
University of California, San Diego

Theodore Hiebert
Professor of Old Testament
McCormick Theological Seminary, Chicago

Walter T. Wilson
Assistant Professor of New Testament
Emory University, Atlanta

Address any comments about *Complete Guide to the Bible* to
Editor-in-Chief, U.S. General Books, Readers Digest,
260 Madison Avenue, New York, NY 10016.

To order additional copies of *Complete Guide to the Bible*,
call 1-800-846-2100.
You can also visit us on the World Wide Web at
http://www.readersdigest.com

The credits and acknowledgments that appear on pages 435-438 are
hereby made a part of this copyright page.

Printed in the United States of America

The scripture quotations contained herein are from the New Revised
Standard Version of the Bible, copyright ©1989, by the Division
of Christian Education of the National Council of the Churches of
Christ in the United States of America. Used by permission.
All rights reserved.

Library of Congress Cataloging in Publication Data
Complete Guide to the Bible.
        p.   cm.
    ISBN 0-7621-0073-7
    1. Bible--Introductions.   I. Reader's Digest Association.
BS475.2.C63   1998
220.6' 1--dc21   98-6836
                                                                  CIP

ABOUT THIS BOOK

s the richest work of faith, history, and literature ever written, the Bible is the cornerstone of many family libraries. It is a book that is read again and again, studied, savored, and shared by young and old alike. Yet, reading the Bible can present problems. The stories are complex; the characters numerous; the settings distant in time and place. Some of the language—even in modern translations—is difficult to understand. To get the most out of this incomparable volume a reader needs assistance. Complete Guide to the Bible offers such help to a layperson.

A virtual road map to the Old and New Testaments (and the Apocrypha, or deuterocanonical books included in Roman Catholic and Orthodox Bibles), this new book from Reader's Digest conducts the reader on a page-by-page tour of the Bible—from Genesis through Revelation. How the Bible was preserved in the form known today is explained in brief essays on the Old Testament (pages 10-11), the Apocrypha (pages 262-263), and the New Testament (pages 310-311). Each biblical book is introduced with a summary and pertinent information about its historical period and authorship. For example, the introduction to Genesis explains that it and the following three books in the Old Testament took shape over the course of centuries—its remarkable stories first passed down from generation to generation by word of mouth, then compiled by different editors, perhaps beginning in the time of King David about 1000 B.C. The introduction to the Gospel According to Mark reveals that, in all probability, it was the first of the four gospels, written about the time Rome destroyed Jerusalem and its temple in A.D. 70. Yet, the reader will learn, the oldest book in the New Testament, according to most scholars, is Paul's first letter to the Thessalonians, penned some 20 years earlier.

Following these introductions are selected quotations that present principal events, persons, and themes—chapter by chapter—of the biblical book. "Now a new king arose over Egypt, who did not know Joseph" (Ex 1:8) sets up the dramatic and momentous confrontation between Pharaoh and Moses that resulted in the Israelites'

escape from bondage, the Exodus. "There was once a man in the land of Uz whose name was Job" (Job 1:1) introduces the main character of one of the Bible's most profound and disturbing books. "For I am not ashamed of the gospel; it is the power of God for salvation to everyone who has faith" (Rom 1:16) leads into Paul's theological masterpiece, his Letter to the Romans. Each summary and commentary of a book of the Bible is illustrated with photographs of biblical sites and artifacts, as well as beautiful works produced over the centuries by skilled and pious artists who sought to interpret Bible stories.

Throughout are box features that explain ancient customs and provide background historical information. Maps trace the journeys of the patriarchs, the conquest of Canaan, and the missionary travels of Paul, among other subjects. Genealogies and dynastic charts help sort out the descendants of Jacob, the rival kings of Judah and Israel, and the Seleucid rulers in the time of the Maccabees. Such features and maps help relate Bible stories to events in the history of the ancient Near East, the lands stretching from the Persian Gulf and the basin of the Tigris and Euphrates rivers through Canaan to Egypt— what historians refer to as the Fertile Crescent.

All biblical quotations are from the New Revised Standard Version. Ellipses (. . .) are used to indicate omissions within the quote, though not at the beginning or end. The abbreviations used for the books of the Bible are given on page 434, along with a comparison of the Hebrew, or Jewish, Bible with what Protestants and Catholics call the Old Testament and how their two versions differ.

Here, in summary and with answers to innumerable questions, is the Bible in all its splendor and complexity. Because Complete Guide to the Bible is organized in the same way, it is the ideal companion. Through these pages the reader will more clearly follow the inspiring story of God's benevolence toward his creation, his tender concern for a chosen people, the Jews, and his infinite love in sending his only son, Jesus, to redeem an errant humankind.

THE EDITORS

CONTENTS

THE APOCRYPHA   262

THE NEW TESTAMENT   310

Illustrations:

Cover: A 19th-century Nativity scene.

Frontispiece: *All Saints Before God the Father* from the Book of Hours of Catherine of Cleves, c. 1435

About This Book: *The Archangel Michael,* a stained glass window by Edward Burne-Jones (1833-1898)

Contents: *Return of the Spies,* a 13th-century stained glass window from Canterbury Cathedral
Daniel in the Lions' Den, from an 11th-century Spanish Bible
Jesus' Entry into Jerusalem, a 6th-century ivory plaque

Opposite: *Angels* by Hans Memling (c. 1430-1498)

Reader's Digest

COMPLETE
GUIDE
to the
BIBLE

THE OLD TESTAMENT

The creation of the world as depicted in a late-12th-century French Bible

Long centuries before the first Hebrew writer traced a word on a sheepskin scroll, storytellers were preserving the epic history of the Israelites. Tales of the creation, Noah and the Flood, the Tower of Babel, and Abraham's long trek to Canaan were passed from generation to generation by word of mouth. The storytellers may have been family elders, community leaders, or perhaps humble herdsmen with extraordinary gifts for memory and recitation. The greatest of them may have been able to memorize a poetic tale thousands of lines long.

In cultures throughout the ancient Near East, such tribal bards were a cherished breed who safeguarded the identity and collective memory of their peoples. Among the Hebrews, storytellers were held in high re-

gard, for they spoke not only a nation's history, but the story of God's relationship with his chosen people. Their accounts grew so familiar and sacred that listeners expected them to be told the same way each time.

No one knows when stories of the Bible began the transition from spoken to written word. Moses, however, is the first Hebrew that the Bible identifies as a writer. After the Israelites of the Exodus crossed the Red Sea, they fought off an attack by the Amalekites. To commemorate this first battlefield victory, God told Moses to "write this as a reminder in a book and recite it in the hearing of Joshua" (Ex 17:14), the Israelite commander who later led his people in the conquest of Canaan. Whether these written words were perceived by the Israelites as sacred, the Bible does not say. But writings that followed in the next months and years certainly were. When Moses descended from Mount Sinai with the Ten Commandments, he held in his hands "the writing of God, engraved upon the tablets" (Ex 32:16). Then, while the Israelites camped at the foot of the mountain, God gave Moses a detailed set of rules for the Hebrews to live by. This, the Mosaic Law, is woven into the stories of Exodus, Leviticus, and Numbers, then summarized in Deuteronomy. "Moses wrote down this law, and gave it to the priests" (Deut 31:9). Since at least that time, the Israelites knew they were the guardians of divinely inspired writings.

The Five Books of Moses

According to ancient Jewish tradition, Moses wrote the first five books of the Bible, including the patriarchal stories of Genesis that took place at least hundreds of years before he was born. Though none of the five books identifies its writer, Moses' authorship went unchallenged until the 17th century. Yet, even in ancient times, students of scripture detected evidence suggesting that Moses may not have been the sole author of the five-book collection known as the Pentateuch. The most obvious clue is that Deuteronomy ends with a description of the lawgiver's death and burial.

The English philosopher Thomas Hobbes, in the 1600s, became the first on record to declare that Moses probably did not write most of the five books. Theologians rallied behind this bold statement by compiling a large body of evidence suggesting that many divinely guided prophets and priests had a hand in the writing. For instance, they argued, the Pentateuch's repeated phrase "to this day" seems an obvious reference to a time long after the events took place—probably to the period when editors pulled together a wide array of sources primarily about Moses and compiled what became known as the Five Books of Moses. Work on these books—the earliest history of the Hebrews—likely began in earnest after Israel solidly established itself as a nation, during the reign of King David, which began about 1000 B.C. While the Pentateuch was being shaped into its final form, palace scribes and temple priests recorded the continuing history of their nation. Musicians wrote psalms of praise and grief; sages gathered nuggets of wisdom for the young; prophets spoke the word of God. Many of these spoken and written words began to find their way into the liturgy of worship and inevitably became embraced by the people as the remaining books of the Hebrew, or Jewish, Bible.

Rediscovering the Law

How and when this wealth of remembrance and revelation became the sacred Jewish scriptures remains a mystery. One milestone, however, was the day a high priest found a long-forgotten scroll during the renovation of Solomon's 350-year-old temple about 620 B.C. The scroll may have been some version of Deuteronomy, a summary of Jewish laws in the Pentateuch, for the priest called it "the book of the law" (2 Kgs 22:8). King Josiah ordered that the scroll be read publicly to all the Hebrew elders. He then launched a vigorous nationwide reform in which he deposed pagan priests and destroyed idolatrous shrines.

A second milestone in the development of the Hebrew Bible came about 160 years later, when a new Jewish nation began to rise from the ashes of horrifying defeat. Returning from exile in Babylon, a meager community of Jews gathered amid Jerusalem's charred ruins. There, a priest named Ezra read to the assembly "the book of the law of Moses" (Neh 8:1). This suggests that Ezra read the five books traditionally ascribed to Moses—or at least the scattered sections containing Jewish laws. The returned exiles would have had a compelling reason to believe the words: Mosaic Law ends with the warning that if the Israelites disobey, God will send invaders and "scatter you among all peoples, from one end of the earth to the other" (Deut 28:64). That is exactly what had happened—and what the returning exiles feared could happen again.

Divisions of the Bible

Jews divide their Bible into three sections: the Law, or Torah; the Prophets; and the Writings (see page 434). Scholars believe that the Jews accepted their current scriptural canon in stages, beginning with the Law shortly after their tragic exile to Babylon. Perhaps Ezra's reading, about 458 B.C., formalized this initial stage. Over the next several centuries, the people also came to revere the eight books of the Prophets: Joshua, Judges, Samuel, Kings, Isaiah, Jeremiah, Ezekiel, and the Twelve (the Minor Prophets combined in a single scroll). By about 180 B.C., the author of the deuterocanonical book of Sirach shows that the Prophets were regarded as authoritative: He speaks repeatedly about the books of the Law and the Prophets, along with

"other books." Still later, by about A.D. 100, Jews accepted the 11 books of the Writings: Psalms, Proverbs, Job, Song of Solomon, Ruth, Lamentations, Ecclesiastes, Esther, Daniel, Ezra-Nehemiah (on one scroll), and Chronicles (1 and 2 Chronicles on a single scroll).

Early in the first Christian century, before the Jewish canon was firmly established, Jesus described Israel's scriptures as "the law of Moses, the prophets, and the psalms" (Lk 24:44), implying that not all the Writings had been acknowledged. But perhaps the strongest evidence that the Hebrew Bible evolved gradually lies in the story of the Septuagint, the ancient Greek translation of Hebrew scriptures. Septuagint means "seventy," taking its name from the 70 Jewish scholars who, in the mid-200s B.C., translated the Pentateuch into Greek, the common language of the day. Over the next two centuries, other respected Jewish books were gradually added until the Septuagint included all of today's Hebrew Bible—and more. The additional books, written between about 300 B.C. and A.D. 70, later became known as the Apocrypha (see page 262).

People of the Book

When Rome crushed the Jewish revolt in A.D. 70, destroying Jerusalem and the temple, it also exterminated the sacrificial system on which the Jewish faith was built. Without the temple—which has never been rebuilt—there could be no sacrifices and no priesthood. The Jews turned to their scriptures and, as never before, became a people of the Book—that is, the Hebrew Bible. The problem was that the Book had many disputed texts and many versions of those texts. So the Jews set out to decide which texts and versions were authoritative, eventually settling on 24 books. (Christians later divided these same 24 books into 39, splitting the books of Samuel, Kings, Ezra-Nehemiah, and Chronicles into two each, and the Minor Prophets into 12.) The oldest complete copy of the Hebrew Bible is the Leningrad Codex of 1008, copied by scribes called Masoretes. This and other early Masoretic texts became the authoritative editions on which most modern translations of the Old Testament are based.

The famous Dead Sea Scrolls, the library of an isolated desert community overrun by Romans in A.D. 68, contain sacred manuscripts 1,000 years older than the Masoretic texts, including fragments or entire scrolls from every Old Testament book except Esther. Among this ancient cache, discovered in 1947, is a scroll of Isaiah copied about 100 B.C. This Hebrew text, like that of other sacred writings found in caves not far from the shore of the Dead Sea, has proved remarkably similar to the traditional Masoretic texts—a strong indication that Jewish scriptures were becoming standardized by the first century B.C. and that later scribes preserved these sacred words with remarkable care and reverence.

A word meaning "origin," Genesis presents a sweeping history of the period from God's creation of the earth to the beginning of the Israelites' 400-year-long sojourn in Egypt. It is the first of the so-called "Five Books of Moses"—Genesis, Exodus, Leviticus, Numbers, and Deuteronomy—also known as the Pentateuch, a Greek term for a work divided into five scrolls. Jews refer to these five books of the Hebrew Bible as the Torah, or "law."

The Pentateuch took shape over the course of centuries—first in stories, songs, and sayings passed from generation to generation in order to preserve the experiences and traditions of the Israelites. In time, these were written down—perhaps as early as King David's reign (c. 1005-965 B.C.), but compiled in the form known today only during the Babylonian exile (586-538 B.C.). The first four books stem from two separate literary sources, apparently merged by a third and edited by a fourth. Deuteronomy is generally attributed to another writer or group of writers, who are also responsible for the books of Joshua through 2 Kings, with the exception of Ruth.

Genesis contains four distinct sections: primordial history (chapters 1-11) and three cycles dealing with the Israelites' ancestors—Abraham (chapters 12:1-25:18); Jacob (25:19-36:43); and Joseph and his brothers (37-50). Significantly, the book ends with the word "Egypt," which puts God's chosen people in the land where they will become enslaved. With equal significance, the final word in Deuteronomy—and thus the final word also of the Pentateuch—is "Israel," for the remainder of the Old Testament is the story of that nation's long and troubled residence in the promised land.

But the Old Testament is more than the history of a relatively small and politically vulnerable kingdom at the crossroads of three continents, Europe, Africa, and Asia. By relating creation of the world to the ancestors of Israel, through whom "all the families of the earth shall be blessed" (Gen 12:3), Genesis immediately and emphatically establishes that the Bible is to be the record of God's infinite power, wisdom, and compassion. It is no less than the compelling account of the Creator's ongoing relationship with the capstone of his creation: humankind.

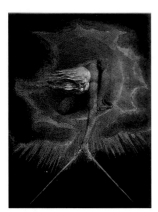

God, the architect of the universe, as depicted by English artist and poet William Blake (1757-1827)

In the beginning when God created the heavens and the earth, the earth was a formless void and darkness covered the face of the deep, while a wind from God swept over the face of the waters. GEN 1:1-2

*M*ajestic and poetic, the opening words of the Bible establish God's mastery of the storm-swept emptiness from which he would call forth the vast wonders of the universe. He did this in six days. Seeing "everything that he had made . . . was very good" (Gen 1:31), God then rested on the seventh day—a pause still observed in the Jewish sabbath.

Scholars point to two independent traditions preserved in the biblical creation story, as indicated by two Hebrew names for the Creator. *Elohim*, translated as "God" in verses 1:1 through 2:3, is actually a plural noun but in the Old Testament takes a singular verb to stress that there is but one true Deity. *YHWH* (for *Yahweh*) *Elohim*, translated as "the Lord

God," is introduced in verse 2:4. The two terms, of course, refer to the same Supreme Being.

In solemn words and rhythmic, repetitive phrases, the first creation narrative divides God's work into two sets of three. The first three days are ones of separation: light from darkness, water below from water above, sea from land upon which vegetation springs forth. The story of the second three days describes what has been created: sun and moon, creatures of the sea and birds of the air, creatures of the earth—up to and including "humankind in our image" (Gen 1:26) with dominion over all the others. Readers will note that Day 1 is linked to Day 4 (light to the sun and moon), Day 2 to Day 5 (water and air to fish and birds), and Day 3 to Day 6 (land to the animals and humans that move upon it).

The second creation narrative, distinguished by a flowing literary style, presents quite a different order of events. Here the Lord God created "man from the dust of the ground, and breathed into his nostrils the breath of life," set him in "a garden in Eden," and, seeing that he was lonely, made woman from "one of his ribs" (Gen 2:7, 8, 21). The first man names the woman Eve, Hebrew for "life-bearer." His own name, Adam, which can be translated as "man" or "human being," is a play on the word 'adamah, meaning "soil" or "ground."

Of the four rivers that flowed out of Eden, a word meaning "delight," the Tigris and the Euphrates are still known by the names given in Genesis. All attempts to identify Pishon and Gihon have failed. Since those two names can be translated as "gusher" and "bubbler," it is possible that they were minor tributaries of the first two. All four streams may have converged at or near a lush plain at the head of the Gulf of Persia.

Now the serpent was more crafty than any other wild animal that the Lord God had made. GEN 3:1

Initially Adam and Eve enjoy a carefree life of intimacy with God—restricted only by their Creator's command not to eat "of the tree of the knowledge of good and evil" (Gen 2:17) that he had planted in the middle of the garden. But the wily serpent insinuates to the woman that God's prohibition prevents her from being godlike. She eats the forbidden fruit and persuades her husband to partake of it also. At once the previously innocent couple are aware of their nakedness, clothe themselves in fig leaves, and hide from the Lord God. The tradition that the forbidden fruit was an apple dates from early Christian times and perhaps came about because of the similarity between the Latin words *malus* ("bad") and *malum* ("apple").

God's punishment is swift and severe. The serpent is condemned to crawl on its belly, loathed for all time by humankind; Eve is told that she will

The creation of Eve, the temptation by the serpent, and the expulsion from Eden appear on this triptych panel by Dutch artist Hieronymous Bosch (c. 1450-1516).

suffer the pains of childbirth and be subject to her husband; Adam is forced to toil for his food. Worse, humans will die: "You are dust, and to dust you shall return" (Gen 3:19). But before expelling the pair from the garden, God shows his continuing benevolence by providing them with garments of animal skin. The cherubim he places as guards to the garden apparently are the half-human, half-animal figures that also appear in Babylonian mythology and not the angelic figures of much later Christian art.

Although Judaism did not hold Adam responsible for the sins of humanity, the apostle Paul did: "Sin came into the world through one man," he wrote, "and death came through sin" (Rom 5:12). But Jesus offered resurrection: "For as all die in Adam, so all will be made alive in Christ" (1 Cor 15:22). The early church father Augustine used the story of the temptation and fall in Genesis 3 to propound the Christian doctrine of original sin.

Cain rose up against his brother Abel, and killed him. GEN 4:8

Adam and Eve's great sin of disobedience is followed in the biblical narrative by a shocking act of violence: the murder of their son Abel by his elder brother, Cain. As God had severed his intimate relationship with humanity for the parents' transgression, now Cain is forced to part from his family as punishment for fratricide.

The brothers bring offerings to the Lord—the farmer Cain, products of the soil; the shepherd Abel, young of his flock. When God looks with favor on Abel's offering but not his, Cain lures his brother into a field and commits the bloody deed. As the Lord had sought their father in the garden following Adam's disobedience, he now seeks Abel through his brother—getting only the abrupt and insolent answer: "Am I my brother's keeper?" (Gen 4:9). Again, the Lord's punishment is immediate and devastating: The ground, polluted by Abel's blood, will no longer yield crops to Cain; the murderer is banished. But once again, God shows his mercy. He gives the fugitive a distinguishing mark—possibly a skin blemish or a tattoo. This was not a stigma, as in the English idiom "mark of Cain," but rather a sign that God would shield the murderer from acts of vengeance.

This story is often used to explain the hostility between shepherds and farmers in ancient societies. And the fact that the first murderer is the first to build a city reveals the antiurban bias in Genesis, later expressed in the Tower of Babel and Sodom and Gomorrah stories. But more important are the two themes introduced here, themes that will reappear in the remaining chapters of Genesis. First is the strife between brothers; second is God's mysterious rejection of an elder for a younger son. Both themes are initially echoed in the Jacob-Esau narrative beginning at Genesis 25:22.

Cain slaying his brother Abel, an enamel on gilded copper plaque made about 1180 for an Austrian abbey

This is the list of the descendants of Adam. GEN 5:1

After a few brief verses devoted to Cain and his descendants, the first biblical genealogy is presented: the ten generations spanning 1,656 years from Adam to Noah on the eve of the Flood. Here and later in Genesis, a genealogy is used to set off one narrative sequence from another.

Scholars point out that the great ages attributed to Adam's descendants should be considered in the context of prevailing traditions in the ancient Near East, in which ancestors were often said to have lived for tens of thousands of years. Viewed from another perspective, even the extraordinary longevity given for Methusaleh—all of 969 years—is comparatively brief. A thousand years, according to Psalms 90:4, were but a single day in the sight of the Lord.

A fragment of ancient mythology survives in Genesis 6:4. The Nephilim—according to one authority, a term meaning "fallen ones"—were offspring of celestial beings who mated with women. They later appear as giants in the land of Canaan, in comparison to whom the Israelite spies "seemed like grasshoppers" (Num 13:33).

And the Lord was sorry that he had made humankind on the earth, and it grieved him to his heart. GEN 6:6

Within ten generations, humankind once again proved itself unworthy of God's great benevolence. The thoughts of men turned to evil; the earth was filled with corruption and violence. And so God decided to destroy his creation—sparing only the righteous Noah, his wife, their three sons (Shem, Ham, and Japheth), and their sons' wives.

Following the Lord's detailed instructions, Noah builds an enormous ark. In this curious vessel—from its description, little more than a buoyant box—Noah's family seeks refuge from the great Flood that God calls down upon the earth. On board, they have two of every animal and bird (or in Genesis 7:3 seven pairs of clean animals and seven pairs of each bird and a pair each of unclean animals).

The torrents cease after 40 days, and at the end of 150 days "the ark came to rest on the mountains of Ararat" (Gen 8:4)—long identified with twin peaks in eastern Turkey near the borders with Armenia and Iran. This location and the record of frequent floods in the Tigris-Euphrates basin point to a Mesopotamian origin for the Noah story. Indeed, universal flood stories are fairly common in Mesopotamian mythology, some of

A BABYLONIAN NOAH?

Discovered and published in 1872, the epic of Gilgamesh caused a sensation, for it seemed to duplicate—and perhaps even contradict—the Flood story in Genesis. Written about 2700 B.C., the poem tells of Babylonian gods who decide to flood the earth because noisy humans are keeping them from sleep. One god warns a man named Utnapishtim, instructing him to build a gigantic, cube-shaped boat and load it with his family, his possessions, and all species of animal in order to escape the impending disaster.

The storm erupts with such force that even the gods are terrified. After a weeklong deluge, the boat bumps to a halt on a mountain peak and Utnapishtim—like Noah—sends birds to find dry land. The first two return, but the third, a raven, does not. On this signal, the hero releases all the animals and then—again like Noah—offers a sacrifice. For this act of piety, Utnapishtim is rewarded with eternal life. The critical difference between the two stories, of course, is God's benevolent concern for an erring humankind in the Bible. In Gilgamesh, self-centered gods betray no such emotion, regarding humans merely as troublesome pests.

them dating back to the third millennium B.C. Perhaps the most striking parallel to Noah is in the Babylonian epic of Gilgamesh, preserved on tablets unearthed among the ruins of Nineveh in the 19th century.

To learn if the waters have subsided, Noah sends out first a raven, then a dove that on its second flight brings back an olive leaf. Aware that they have survived the disaster, Noah and his family disembark, bring out the animals, and make a sacrifice to God. Pleased by the offering, the Lord promises never again to destroy his creation and restores the normal seasons. And humankind, previously vegetarian, is permitted to eat meat. Finally, and most important, the Creator renews his covenant with humanity and places a rainbow in the sky as a sign of the renewal.

In a revealing postscript to the Flood story, Noah is described as the first vintner—and apparently the first to overindulge in wine. For his disrespect in looking on "the nakedness of his father" (Gen 9:22) while he is drunk, Ham, through his son Canaan, is cursed, doomed to be a slave of his two brothers, Shem and Japheth. That the curse endured is revealed by Joshua's condemnation of Canaan's descendants, the deceitful Gibeonites: "You shall always be slaves, hewers of wood and drawers of water"

(Josh 9:23). The Flood story concludes with a list of the descendants of Noah's three sons—the so-called "Table of Nations" that apparently reflects what was known about the peoples of the eastern Mediterranean region at the time Genesis was compiled.

"Come, let us build ourselves a city, and a tower with its top in the heavens." GEN 11:4

For the fourth time, humanity sins against the Lord, demonstrating its unworthiness by setting out to build a tower in the land of Shinar. This act of pride is used to explain the diversity of languages, for God punishes the builders by confusing (Hebrew: *balal*) the words in which people speak. It also explains humankind's geographic dispersal, for an angry Lord "scattered them abroad over the face of all the earth" (Gen 11:8). The land of Shinar has been identified as the Tigris-Euphrates basin, where ancient civilizations such as that of Babylon built stepped pyramids known as ziggurats. Such temple-towers provided worshipers a place between heaven and earth to meet their gods. By having the builders in Shinar say, "Come, let us make bricks, and burn them thoroughly" (Gen 11:3), the writer reveals his

In the detail (left) from mosaics decorating San Marco cathedral in Venice, Italy, Noah takes pairs of birds aboard the ark; above, Turkey's Mount Ararat, the purported landing place of the ark after floodwaters had receded.

Sumerian ziggurats, like this one in ruins at a site in Iraq 30 miles northwest of Ur, no doubt inspired the Tower of Babel story. The tower under construction in the 17th-century Armenian manuscript illustration at left appropriately pierces the clouds.

knowledge of Mesopotamian construction methods. In the Israelite homeland, stone, not brick, was the common building material.

The so-called primeval history of Genesis ends with the Tower of Babel and the dispersal of humankind across the earth. The remaining chapters of the book (12 through 50) are devoted to the history of the ancestors of Israel, a chronicle divided into three segments: Abraham (and the transitional figure of Isaac), Jacob, and Joseph and his brothers—the progenitors of the 12 tribes of Israel. Once again, a genealogy marks the break between narratives, the ten generations from Noah to Abraham (Abram) echoing the ten generations from Adam to Noah.

Now the Lord said to Abram, "Go from your country and your kindred and your father's house to the land that I will show you." GEN 12:1

With this call God shifts his concern to a single people, promising Abram a land, numerous progeny, and a special relationship with the Lord that will be of benefit to all humanity. To the genealogies that punctuate the earlier chapters of Genesis are now added itineraries. The remaining chapters range across the vast panorama of the ancient Near East, stretching from Mesopotamia down through the promised land of Canaan to Egypt (see maps opposite and on page 25).

Earlier, Abram, his barren wife Sarai, and his nephew Lot had set out with Abram's father, Terah, on a migration from Ur of the Chaldeans to the land of Canaan. They got only as far as Haran when Terah died. Archaeologists have identified Ur as a site on the Euphrates River in southern Iraq, and speculate that the family's travels were part of mass population shifts in Mesopotamia during the first half of the second millennium B.C.—that is, about 2000 to 1800 B.C. Haran, elsewhere called Paddan-aram, was most likely in southern Turkey near the border with Syria.

As the Lord has directed him, Abram continues the journey, entering Canaan, where he pauses to build altars at Shechem and between Bethel and Ai, three cities in the central highlands that will play important roles in Israelite history. But the clan continues south into Egypt because of a famine. This is the first mention of famine in the Old Testament. Such periodic food shortages were a constant threat to life in the ancient Near East. Famine took Jacob's family to Egypt and Naomi's family to Moab in the book of Ruth, and gave King David an excuse to hand over Saul's descendants for execution (2 Sam 21:1-14). Egyptian inscriptions and paintings reveal that refugees from famine frequently sought provisions in the land of the Nile.

In Egypt, Sarai's beauty puts her in jeopardy when Pharaoh takes her for his harem. But the Lord afflicts Pharaoh for taking another man's wife—though Abram had told Sarai to pose as his sister. Nonetheless, Abram is rewarded for his white lie. Pharaoh releases Sarai and sends the wanderers back north laden with generous gifts of livestock and slaves.

The main trajectory of the Abraham cycle begins with Sarai's barrenness and leads to the birth of Isaac. It is an account of a family's survival among threats and tensions. But a second trajectory is the Abraham-Lot narrative: the tale of family territory.

Then Abram said to Lot, "Let there be no strife between you and me, and between your herders and my herders, for we are kindred." GEN 13:8

Back in the land of Canaan, Abram realizes that there is not enough room for both his herds and those of Lot and offers his nephew a choice of territory. From the heights of Bethel can be seen the entire Jordan River valley, even to the southern shore of the Dead Sea. Lot selects the well-watered valley and settles near Sodom, one of the five cities of the Plain. Abram moves on to Hebron, another highland city that figures prominently in Israelite history.

Some time later an alliance of four kings attacks the cities of the Plain and takes Lot into captivity. Abram, the peaceful pastoralist, is forced into action to rescue his nephew. Historians have long puzzled over the names of the attackers, identifying only the kingdoms of Shinar (Babylon) and Elam and a Hittite king named Tidal.

For his brave military exploit, Abram is blessed by King Melchizedek of Salem. Melchizedek is one of the most baffling figures in the Bible. In Genesis he is presented as the monarch of Salem (Jerusalem) and "priest of God Most High" (Gen 14:18)—that is, El Elyon, a Canaanite deity. And he is identified in Psalms 110:4 as the priest in whose succession King David is ordained, seeming to indicate that the Israelites retained some of the pagan traditions of their predecessors in the land of Canaan. But a New Testament reference makes Melchizedek a supernatural being: "without father, without mother, without genealogy having neither beginning of days nor end of life" (Heb 7:3). His origins and eternal life suggest that Melchizedek was an angelic being, one somehow foreshadowing the divinity of Jesus.

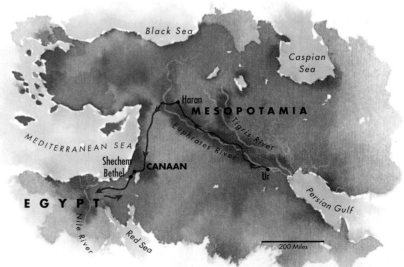

Abraham setting out for Canaan, by James Tissot (1836-1902)

THE MIGRATION OF ABRAHAM

As God turns his attention from the whole of humankind to a single man, Abram (later Abraham), Genesis becomes the story of people on the move. Joining his father, Terah, on a migration from Ur northwestward up the Euphrates River, Abram reaches Haran. There—after Terah's death—he first receives God's promise of a homeland and numerous offspring through whom all nations will be blessed. In obedience to God's summons, Abram sets off on the journey south to Canaan. Though the land is already occupied, Abram pauses to build altars to the Lord at Shechem and between Bethel and Ai. But the patriarch does not linger in the promised land, for a famine forces him to continue south to Egypt for food. After a misunderstanding with Pharaoh over his wife, Sarai, Abram returns to Canaan to pitch his tents near Bethel.

The 800-mile arc that Abram traversed is known as the Fertile Crescent. It stretched from the well-watered land between the Tigris and Euphrates rivers in what is now Iraq north and west into southern Turkey and then south through Canaan to Egypt's lush Nile River valley. Beginning about 3000 B.C., perhaps a thousand years before Abram, the region gave birth to a number of the world's first civilizations: Sumeria, Assyria, Babylonia, and Egypt. It was later the birthplace of three great religions: Judaism, Christianity, and Islam.

Black Sea

Caspian Sea

Haran

MESOPOTAMIA

MEDITERRANEAN SEA

Euphrates River

Tigris River

Shechem
Bethel **CANAAN**

Ur

EGYPT

Persian Gulf

Nile River

Red Sea

200 Miles

Salt formations at the southern end of the Dead Sea remind observers of the fate of Lot's wife. The 13th-century stained glass window at left shows her turned into a pillar of salt as she looks back at the destruction of Sodom and Gomorrah.

tuous encounters were Moab and Ben-ammi, ancestors of Israel's hostile neighbors the Moabites and the Ammonites.

Now Sarai, Abram's wife, bore him no children. GEN 16:1

As the years pass and Sarai continues to be childless, Abram grows troubled because the Lord's promise of progeny is unfulfilled. But at this point Sarai takes matters into her own hands. She offers Abram her Egyptian slave Hagar as a surrogate mother, and Hagar at last gives Abram a son, Ishmael ("God has heard"). According to custom in the ancient Near East, the child born of such a liaison is Sarai's legitimate offspring. Other surrogate mothers in the Old Testament are the maids Zilpah and Bilhah, whose sons by Jacob are considered the children of their mistresses, his wives Leah and Rachel

Some 13 years later, when Abram is 99 and Sarai is 90, the Lord renews his covenant with the patriarch—giving him a new name, Abraham ("ancestor of a multitude") in keeping with the repeated promise of numerous descendants. But after Abraham laughs at news that his aged wife (renamed Sarah, "princess") will bear a child, the Lord names the unborn son Isaac ("he laughs").

As a sign of the renewed covenant, the Lord orders Abraham and all the males of his household to be circumcised. Henceforth, male infants are to be circumcised eight days after birth. Western Semitic peoples practiced circumcision at least as early as the third millennium B.C., perhaps as a marriage or fertility rite or simply for the sake of cleanliness. Starting with Abraham, circumcision gives the Israelites a cultural and religious identity. Any uncircumcised male is to be "cut off from his people" (Gen 17:14).

Before the birth of Isaac, there is an interjected story of Abraham's sojourn in the Negeb. At Gerar he once more puts his wife in jeopardy by telling the local ruler Abimelech that she is his sister. But here it is revealed—as it had not been in the account of a similar event in Egypt (Gen 12:10-20)—that Abraham's deception is at least a half-truth, for Sarah is his father's daughter by another woman. Although such marriages were later forbidden (Lev 18:9,11; 20:17), they were still possible at the time of King David.

Literary scholars call such repeated narratives as the wife-sister story about Abraham "doublets"; when Isaac later passes off his wife, Rebekah, as his sister (Gen 26:6-11), the story becomes a "triplet."

The story of Lot is brought to a dramatic conclusion in Genesis 18:16-19:38. God has determined to destroy Sodom and Gomorrah for their great wickedness. In the first biblical example of an expostulation, or dispute, with God (others occur in Job, Jeremiah, Amos, Jonah, and Habakkuk), Abram intercedes on behalf of the sinful inhabitants. But he fails to find even ten righteous men for whose sake the cities could be spared. After angels alert Lot to the impending catastrophe, he sets out to escape with his wife and two daughters. In one of the most enduring images of the Old Testament, Lot's wife turns back to look at the rain of fire and sulfur over the two cities and is transformed into a pillar of salt.

Digging southeast of the Dead Sea, archaeologists have found several settlements of what was apparently once a fertile agricultural region. They appear to have been destroyed in an earthquake about 2350 B.C., some four centuries before the earliest dates proposed for Abraham but late enough for such a catastrophic event to have been remembered in his lifetime. Even today, salt-encrusted tree stumps rising from the Dead Sea's fetid waters remind visitors of the fate of Lot's wife.

In an unsavory addendum to this tale of destruction, Lot's two daughters—believing their father to be the last man on earth—get him drunk and seduce him into having sexual relations with them so that they can bear children. The offspring of these inces-

Sarah conceived and bore Abraham a son in his old age. GEN 21:2

As his biography is preserved in Genesis, Isaac serves mainly as a link between the longer Abraham and Jacob cycles; he is a passive figure in contrast to the other two more active patriarchs. Yet there are four independent stories about Isaac.

The first story involves an intricate play on words. Sarah sees Hagar's teenage son, Ishmael, "playing with her son Isaac" (Gen 21:9) on the day the child's weaning is being celebrated. Furious, she calls upon Abraham to drive away the slave and her son. The harshness of Sarah's demand can perhaps be explained by comparing the Hebrew name Isaac (*yishaq*) with the verb for "playing" (*mesaheq*). Another translation of the verse could have the slave's child "Isaacking"—or attempting to take the place of Isaac.

At any rate, Abraham sends Hagar and Ishmael into the desert, where they are spared almost certain death by the fortuitous appearance of an angel. In time, Hagar finds Ishmael an Egyptian wife and he fathers 12 sons and a daughter who grows up to marry his nephew Esau. The descendants of Ishmael, by tradition, are the bedouins of the Negeb desert. They first appear in the biblical narrative as the traders who spare Joseph from death by taking him into slavery in Egypt.

The sacrifice of Isaac, as depicted in a bronze plaque by Filippo Brunelleschi (1377-1446) for the baptistery doors in Florence, Italy

"Take your son, your only son Isaac, whom you love, and go to the land of Moriah, and offer him there as a burnt offering." GEN 22:2

In the second story concerning Isaac, God once again commands Abraham to expose a son to death. But before the terrible price of obedience to the Lord's will can be paid, an angel of the Lord again intervenes, revealing to Abraham a trapped ram that is to be substituted for Isaac. Human sacrifice was abhorred by the later Israelites and specifically condemned in their religious law (Lev 18:21; 20:2-5). But the ghastly custom continued to be practiced by some of their

neighbors—for example, King Mesha of Moab (2 Kgs 3:26-27)—and even the apostate kings of Judah, Ahaz (2 Kgs 16:3) and Manasseh (2 Chr 33:6). It is clear in this story, however, that God never intended the sacrifice of Isaac to be carried out.

The land of Moriah, to which the Lord sends Abraham for the sacrifice, is unknown. The only other use of the name in the Bible is the Mount Moriah in Jerusalem where Solomon builds his temple (2 Chr 3:1).

"Go to my country and my kindred and get a wife for my son Isaac." GEN 24:4

After the death and burial of Sarah at Hebron, Abraham sends a trusted servant to upper Mesopotamia to find a bride for Isaac so that his heir will not marry a Canaanite woman. The bride found is Rebekah, granddaughter of Abraham's brother Nahor. The servant's chance encounter of Rebekah at a well that leads to her marriage with Isaac is echoed in Genesis 29 (Jacob and Rachel) and Exodus 2 (Moses and Zipporah). By now settled in the Negeb, a semiarid region south and east of the Dead Sea, Isaac happily accepts Rebekah as his wife when the servant returns with her on camelback.

The camels mentioned in this story long posed a problem for historians, who were doubtful that the beasts had been domesticated so early. However, recent archaeological evidence has confirmed that camels were used for food and transportation in eastern Iran as early as 2700 B.C. and could well have been introduced through Arabia to lands bordering the Mediterranean Sea by Abraham's time.

In the fourth and final independent story about Isaac, the Lord commands him not to go to Egypt during a famine. And thus, alone of the patriarchs, Isaac never leaves his homeland. Instead, he moves to Gerar near the Mediterranean coast, an area ruled by King Abimelech of the Philistines—incidentally, an anachronism since the

Abraham sending Hagar and their son Ishmael into the wilderness; a painting by Sebastiano Ricci (1660-1734)

*Rebekah drawing water
for the camels of Abraham's
servant and accompanying him back to
Canaan to marry Isaac; two late-12th-
century mosaic panels from
the cathedral of Monreale, Italy*

Philistines did not settle in this area until much later. Isaac's attempt to pass off Rebekah as his sister, not his wife, was foiled when the king "looked out of a window and saw him fondling his wife Rebekah" (Gen 26:8). Isaac retreats to Beer-sheba in the Negeb after a quarrel with Abimelech's men over wells, such scarce water supplies being critical to survival in most parts of the ancient Near East.

Abraham took another wife, whose name was Keturah.
GEN 25:1

Before he departs the biblical narrative, Abraham takes a second wife. But the patriarch's offspring by Keturah (who is called his concubine in 1 Chronicles 1:32) receive gifts in lieu of land and are eventually sent eastward to the desert country. Keturah's sons were the ancestors of such Arabic tribes as the Midianites. Moses married the daughter of a Midianite priest, and the Israelites of the Exodus encountered Midianites during their years of wandering in the wilderness. Abraham's first two sons, Ishmael and Isaac, join to bury their father in the cave at Machpelah at Hebron, purchased many years earlier as Sarah's last resting place.

The Hittites from whom Abraham purchased the family burial place are identified as "sons of Heth," one of the sons of Canaan (Gen 10:15; 1 Chr 1:13). Throughout Genesis the Hittites are listed among the peoples inhabiting Canaan who must be driven out in order for the Israelites to settle there. Scholars disagree about whether the biblical Hittites are linked to the people of an extensive second-millennium B.C. kingdom in central Turkey. Except for mention of them in the Bible, little if anything was known of the Turkish Hittites until archaeological excavations in the first half of the 19th century.

Isaac prayed to the Lord for his wife, because she was barren; and the Lord granted his prayer, and his wife Rebekah conceived. GEN 25:21

The compelling story of Jacob and Esau—second of the three cycles dealing with the ancestors of Israel—repeats themes and incidents that appear earlier in Genesis. But the underlying motif, one that occurs again and again, is deception.

Conflict between brothers, first introduced in the Cain-Abel story, here takes place even before the birth of Jacob and Esau, as the twins struggle within Rebekah's womb. In answer to the woman's cry of pain, the Lord announces that she is carrying two nations, "the one shall be stronger than the other, the elder shall serve the younger" (Gen 25:23). As he had done in accepting Abel's sacrifice but not Cain's, God inexplicably bestows his favor on a younger son. Although Esau is the firstborn, Jacob immediately thereafter emerges from his mother's womb, grasping his elder brother's heel. The extraordinary occurrence accounts for his name, which can mean either "he takes by the heel" or "he supplants."

As the twins grow, differences between them emerge. Esau, a hunter, is his father's favorite. Jacob, a quiet tent dweller, is loved by his mother. Returning one day from the field, the famished Esau is tricked into selling his birthright as an elder son to Jacob for bread and a stew the latter had cooked.

When Isaac was old and his eyes were dim so that he could not see, he called his elder son Esau. GEN 27:1

With the connivance of his doting mother, Jacob repeats the deception of his brother in order to win the aged Isaac's blessing of the firstborn. At Rebekah's bidding, he kills two kids from the flock

MARRIAGE CUSTOMS IN BIBLE TIMES

In the ancient Near East it was acceptable for a man to marry more than once and to have concubines—lower status women or slaves who provided children and served the household. The size of a man's harem was a symbol of his prosperity.

Though a number of prominent men in the Old Testament had several wives, God clearly favored monogamy by creating Adam and Eve who devoted themselves to each other and "become one flesh" (Gen 2:24). Ominously, the first man to take a second wife was a descendant of the murderous Cain. Throughout scripture, men with multiple wives generally produced not only the desired offspring but families in which bitter rivalries erupted. By the time of the prophets, polygamy had become rare—except among royalty. When used as an analogy for God's covenant with Israel, marriage in the Old Testament is described as a monogamous relationship.

Rabbis in New Testament times continued to permit polygamy in special cases, such as prolonged infertility of a first wife; but the practice disappeared in the Middle Ages.

Deceived by his wife and younger son, Isaac bestows his blessing on Jacob instead of the firstborn Esau; a painting by Jean-Baptiste Jouvenet (1644-1717).

for a tasty stew, covers his smooth hands with skins from the kids, and dresses in Esau's clothing. And so, bringing the dish to his father, Jacob poses as his elder brother. Though the voice is Jacob's, Isaac says, the hairy hands and the smell of the garments are Esau's, and he bestows the blessing. Isaac's words (Gen 27:28-29, 39-40) suggest a tribal or even national blessing rather than a personal one. Jacob's poetic blessing of his own 12 sons (Gen 49:1-28) is clearly bestowed on the 12 tribes of Israel.

Once given, such a blessing could not be revoked, nor could Isaac offer Esau anything other than servitude to his younger brother when Esau learns that he has once more been tricked. Enraged, he vows to kill Jacob. But Rebekah finds a ploy to put her favored son beyond reach of his elder brother.

Then Isaac called Jacob and blessed him, and charged him, "You shall not marry one of the Canaanite women."
GEN 28:1

Esau had married outside the clan, two Hittite women who "made life bitter for Isaac and Rebekah" (Gen 26:35). Now Rebekah uses this unhappy situation to persuade Isaac to send their son to Paddan-aram to find a wife from among her own family and, incidentally, to escape Esau's wrath.

En route north, Jacob stops for the night, takes a stone for a pillow, and falls asleep. In a dream that night, he sees angels ascending and descending a ladder—the Hebrew word might better be translated as "ramp" or "stairway." The Lord appears in the dream to repeat the threefold blessing first bestowed on Abraham and confirmed to Isaac at Gerar: the land of Canaan, numerous offspring, and—through him and his descendants—a blessing to "all the families of the earth" (Gen 28:14).

Awakening from his dream, Jacob makes of his stone pillow a sacred pillar, names the place Bethel, "house of the Lord," and pledges to give back to the Lord a tenth of whatever good fortune God grants him. This story establishes the antiquity of Bethel as a cultic center. King Jeroboam I of Israel later sets up golden calves for worship at Bethel and at Dan (1 Kgs 12:25-33). It also confirms the practice of tithing, first mentioned in Abraham's award of a tenth of his spoils of battle to King Melchizedek of Jerusalem (Gen 14:17-20). Strict regulations for tithing were later to be spelled out in Deuteronomy 12, 14, and 26, where a tenth of grain,

His head on a pillow of stone, Jacob sleeps as angels ascend a ladder to God in heaven; an illustration from a 15th-century German Bible.

Then Jacob went on his journey, and came to the land of the people of the east. GEN 29:1

Arriving in Paddan-aram, Jacob meets his cousin Rachel at a well—just as Abraham's servant had found Rebekah. When he learns that she is the daughter of his mother's brother, Laban, Jacob kisses Rachel and she runs to tell her father the news of her cousin's arrival. Jacob offers to serve seven years for Rachel's hand, but on the wedding night Laban tricks his nephew by substituting the apparently less comely elder sister, Leah, for the bride. The meaning of the Hebrew word describing Leah's eyes is uncertain. It has been translated as "weak" or "dull" (Semitic peoples favored women with dark, sparkling eyes) and even "lovely," suggesting that they were her one good feature. Because women were brought to the bridal chamber heavily veiled, it was apparently easy enough for Laban to deceive Jacob.

To win Rachel, Jacob serves another seven years and six years beyond that, during which time he contrives to cheat Laban out of his flocks. The resulting hostility of Laban and his sons forces Jacob—now with two wives, two concubines (the maids Zilpah and Bilhah), eleven sons, and a daughter—to flee.

Marriage to sisters was later forbidden by Israelite law (Lev 18:18); at this time, however, it was still permissible. According to custom, the sons of the

wine, oil, and firstborn of the flocks was to be set aside for the Lord.

If the stone pillar Jacob erected at Bethel before resuming his journey northward was anything like the seven-foot megaliths of the period, he must have been a man of exceptional strength. And indeed, in the very next episode, he proves that strength by removing the large stone covering a well, an endeavor that generally required a team effort.

Having removed the well covering so that Rachel can water her father's flock, Jacob greets his cousin and future wife with a kiss; in this 19th-century painting, the other shepherds tactfully avert their eyes from the intimate scene.

concubines were considered off-spring of their mistresses, the legitimate wives Leah and Rachel. The naming of Jacob's sons by their mothers—for example, Reuben ("See, a son"), Simeon (*shama*, "heard"), Judah (*hodah*, "praise"), Naphtali (*niphtal*, "wrestled"), Issachar (*sakar*, "hire"), Zebulun (*zabal*, "honor"), and Joseph ("he adds")—relies on intricate rhymes or puns that can fully be understood only in the original Hebrew.

Laban catches up with the fugitives on the border of Canaan, where he and his son-in-law make a covenant of peace and go their separate ways. The "household gods" (Gen 31:19) Rachel had stolen from her father and concealed from his search by sitting on them most likely were small cultic objects revered by pagan peoples; there is no reason to suppose that she had adopted her husband's monotheism. Indeed, before settling in Bethel, Jacob must charge his family "to put away the foreign gods that are among you" (Gen 35:2).

Scholars see a cyclical pattern in this extended narrative: Jacob's arrival in Haran; his contracts with Laban to marry Rachel; Laban's deception of Jacob; the birth of Jacob's children; Jacob's deception of Laban; his dispute with Laban over the contracts; his departure. Framing the cycle is Laban's kiss of welcome to his nephew and his kiss of farewell to his daughters and grandchildren.

Sitting on the camel saddle that contains her father's stolen household gods, Rachel foils Laban's search. Giovanni Battista Tiepolo (1696-1770) gave the scene a baroque setting more appropriate to his native Italy than Canaan.

Jacob sent messengers before him to his brother Esau in the land of Seir, the country of Edom. GEN 32:3

Because of strife between his foreign wives and his parents, Esau had moved southeast of the Dead Sea to Edom. Now, as he returns to Canaan, Jacob worries that his elder brother will seek vengeance for the long-ago theft of his birthright and the parental blessing. To Jacob's surprise and relief, Esau greets him with a kiss and the two brothers are at long last reconciled. Yet Jacob, perhaps wisely in view of the protracted history of family disputes, declines his brother's request to join him in Edom. Instead, he moves his clan to Shechem, the place where Abraham had built his first altar in Canaan.

The 400 men Esau brings with him to the encounter was a standard number for a military unit and therefore reason enough for Jacob to fear his brother's approach. Mahanaim, the place where Jacob hears that his brother is coming, is derived from either the word for "camp" or "gift." Jacob not only plies his brother with gifts but bows to him seven times. Such a greeting would have been more suitable for an appearance before a monarch than for a reunion with a brother, no matter how much Jacob desired a reconciliation.

Real violence awaits the family in their new home, for at Shechem Jacob's only daughter, Dinah, is raped by a local prince. When the man offers to marry Dinah, her brothers appear to agree—on the condition that the prince and all the males of the city first be circumcised. But on the third day, when the Shechemites "were still in pain" (Gen 34:25), Simeon and Levi murder all the men of Shechem. It is an offense for which the two will later pay a heavy penalty, their descendants denied tribal space in Israel.

Jacob was left alone; and a man wrestled with him until daybreak. GEN 32:24

En route to what he fears will be an unpleasant meeting with Esau, Jacob takes the precaution of sending his family across a river while he waits alone through the night. That night a mysterious stranger tests his strength but cannot prevail. Not until the stranger has blessed and given him a new name does Jacob release his hold.

The new name, Israel, can be translated as "the one who strives with God." Among those who have vacillated over identifying the stranger is the prophet Hosea: "In his womb he [Jacob] tried to supplant his

During a nightlong contest Jacob pits his strength against a divine opponent; a painting by Eugène Delacroix (1798-1863) from a Paris church.

brother, and in his manhood he strove with God. He strove with the angel and prevailed" (Hos 12:3-4). The name that Jacob gave the place of the struggle, Peniel, draws on the phrase *panim 'el panim*, meaning "face-to-face," for Jacob was convinced that he had "seen God face to face, and yet my life is preserved" (Gen 32:30).

God said to Jacob, "Arise, go up to Bethel, and settle there." GEN 35:1

As directed, Jacob seeks a new home for his family and at Bethel erects an altar to God—as his grandfather, Abraham, had done earlier. This verse is further support for the Israelites' claim to Bethel as one of their most sacred sites. Once more, God appears to Jacob to confirm his name change and to repeat the promise made to Abraham and Isaac: "Be fruitful and multiply; a nation and a company of nations shall come from you" (Gen 35:11). But on the way to Ephrath (Bethlehem), the beloved Rachel dies giving birth to Jacob's twelfth and last son, Benjamin.

Joseph thrown into a well by his jealous brothers; a 13th-century stained glass roundel from Canterbury Cathedral in England

Esau and Jacob meet one last time, to bury their father, Isaac. To conclude the cycle, Esau's descendants are listed (Gen 36:1-43). The passage identifies them with the Edomites, later Israel's hostile neighbors southeast of the Dead Sea.

Now Israel [Jacob] loved Joseph more than any other of his children, because he was the son of his old age. GEN 37:3

This simple statement of parental favoritism introduces the final, and most complex, of the narrative cycles pertaining to the Israelites' ancestors: Joseph and his brothers.

Like the Jacob-Esau story immediately preceding it, the Joseph narrative starts with a father deceived by offspring through an article of clothing—a deception that leads to a 20-year separation. The climax of Joseph's story, again mirroring that of Jacob-Esau, is the reconciliation of estranged brothers and the easing of family strife.

Joseph, the first son of Jacob's beloved wife Rachel, enters the story as a tattletale—giving his father "a bad report" (Gen 37:2) of his half brothers, with whom he had been herding sheep. Next he is a braggart, infuriating his brothers and even his father with tales of dreams foretelling that one day they will be forced to pay obeisance to him. He is sent back to the grazing fields by his father, but cannot find his brothers. Joseph's wanderings in search of his brothers would have taken him some 60 miles north of the family home at Hebron and over some rough mountain terrain to the valley of Dothan. The fact that the brothers had moved on from their original pasturage near Shechem no doubt reflects the hostility of that city following the revenge Simeon and Levi had wrought on its inhabitants for the rape of their sister Dinah.

Now, by flaunting the special robe Jacob had given him and recounting dreams in which his family is shown subordinate to him, Joseph intensifies the jealousy his father's blatant favoritism had aroused among his ten elder brothers. The offensive robe—sometimes translated as "a coat of many colors"—was likely a long-sleeved, heavily ornamented tunic of the type later worn by royalty (2 Sam 13:18). When Joseph appears so dressed in the fields where they are tending their flocks, the brothers decide to kill him. But Reuben convinces them to strip Joseph of his robe and throw him into an empty cistern, thinking to return later to rescue his younger brother from certain death.

Having second thoughts about the murder of their 17-year-old brother, Judah persuades the others to sell Joseph to slave traders en route to Egypt. The mention of both Ishmaelites and Midianites in this account may represent two different traditions melded together by the editors of Genesis. The former were descendants of Ishmael, Abraham's son by the slave Hagar; the latter were his descendants by his second wife, Keturah. The "twenty pieces of silver" (Gen 37:28) the brothers received for Joseph was the proper price for a male slave between the ages of five and twenty (Lev 27:5).

With Joseph's robe dipped in goat's blood as evidence, the brothers convince Jacob that his favorite is dead, devoured in the fields by a wild beast. Refusing to be comforted by his family, Jacob tears his clothing, puts on sackcloth, and declares that he will "go down to Sheol [the underworld] to my son, mourning" (Gen 37:35).

Judah went down from his brothers and settled near a certain Adullamite whose name was Hirah. GEN 38:1

The interpolated story of Judah, his three sons, and his daughter-in-law Tamar has certain similarities to the narrative it interrupts: deception, failure to recognize a family member, reconciliation after true identity is revealed.

Behind this lurid story is the Israelite practice of levirate marriage. As specified in Deuteronomy 25:5-10, Judah was obligated to give his second son, Onan, in marriage to Tamar on the death of her husband, Judah's firstborn son, Er. But any child born of that union would be Er's and not Onan's. For refusing the obligation to consummate his marriage with Tamar, Onan is struck dead by the Lord. Then, apparently fearing a curse attached to Tamar because of the two deaths, Judah withholds his youngest son, Shelah, from marriage to her. It is at this point that the widow

JOURNEYS OF THE PATRIARCHS

The descendants of Abraham did not settle down easily in the promised land. Isaac, the son of Abraham's old age, was born to Sarah somewhere in the desert between Gerar and Beer-sheba. With the exception of the journey with his father to Moriah (possibly Jerusalem), he spent his entire life in the arid corner of the northwestern Negeb—scarcely venturing more than 50 miles from his birthplace. After the death of his mother, Isaac dwelt at Beer-lahai-roi, an oasis on the caravan route to Egypt and the place where Sarah's pregnant maid Hagar was comforted by an angel after her mistress had driven her into the desert. It was likely to Beer-lahai-roi that Isaac's bride, Rebekah, was brought by Abraham's trusted servant. The couple's twin sons, Esau and Jacob, may also have been born there. Seeking water for his flocks, Isaac moved to Gerar, but, after quarrels with the ruler there, he settled in Beer-sheba.

Unlike his father, Jacob traveled widely—first to his mother's homeland, Haran, to find a bride. En route, he dreamed of angels on a heavenly ladder at Bethel. Returning to Canaan with two wives, two concubines, twelve offspring, and large flocks, Jacob wrestled with a mysterious stranger at Peniel. After building an altar at Shechem and clashing with the local inhabitants over the rape of his daughter, Jacob proceeded south to Mamre (Hebron). There, his long estranged brother Esau joined him to bury Isaac in the cave of Machpelah. It was from Hebron that the pampered Joseph set out to search for his elder brothers, finding them at Dothan. First dumped in a cistern to die, Joseph was sold to slave traders who took him to Egypt. Years later, driven by famine, the brothers and then Jacob followed Joseph to Egypt, settling there as guests. It would be 400 years before his descendants returned to the promised land.

MEDITERRANEAN SEA

To Haran

Dothan

Shechem

Jordan River

Peniel

Bethel
Ai

Jerusalem

Mamre (Hebron)

Dead Sea

Gerar

To Egypt

N E G E B

Beer-sheba

Zoar

Beer-lahai-roi?

—— Wanderings of Isaac
—— Wanderings of Jacob
—— Wanderings of Joseph

20 Miles

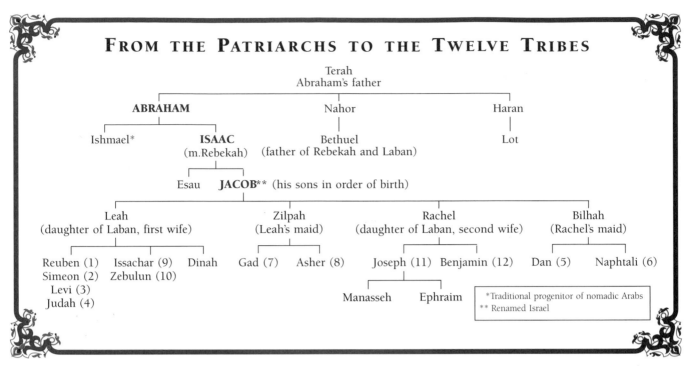

FROM THE PATRIARCHS TO THE TWELVE TRIBES

Terah
Abraham's father

ABRAHAM | Nahor | Haran

Ishmael* | **ISAAC** | Bethuel | Lot
(m.Rebekah) (father of Rebekah and Laban)

Esau **JACOB**** (his sons in order of birth)

Leah | Zilpah | Rachel | Bilhah
(daughter of Laban, first wife) | (Leah's maid) | (daughter of Laban, second wife) | (Rachel's maid)

Reuben (1) Issachar (9) Dinah | Gad (7) Asher (8) | Joseph (11) Benjamin (12) | Dan (5) Naphtali (6)
Simeon (2) Zebulun (10)
Levi (3)
Judah (4)

Manasseh Ephraim

*Traditional progenitor of nomadic Arabs
** Renamed Israel

---

tricks her father-in-law into having sexual relations with her by posing as a cult prostitute.

What is perhaps more interesting to Christian readers is the link to Jesus. Tamar, who gives birth to twin sons after her encounter with Judah, is one of four women mentioned in Matthew's genealogy of Jesus. Like the other three—Rahab, Ruth, and Uriah's wife, Bathsheba—Tamar has an unusual or irregular marital status. Scholars suggest that Matthew included these women's names as background and explanation for Mary's pregnancy out of wedlock.

Joseph fleeing the unwanted amorous advances of Potiphar's wife; one of the biblical frescoes in the Vatican loggia by Raphael (1483-1520)

Now Joseph was taken down to Egypt, and Potiphar, an officer of Pharaoh . . . bought him from the Ishmaelites. GEN 39:1

Because he retains the Lord's favor, Joseph prospers in his land of captivity—rising to become overseer of Potiphar's household. And so, in this chapter, the youthful egotist is transformed into a righteous man of substance, for "the Lord was with Joseph" (Gen 39:2). But unlike earlier chapters of Genesis, in which God appears to his chosen ones, divine providence remains hidden in the Joseph cycle.

Despite the preference he has earned, Joseph's descent—to the empty cistern, to slavery in Egypt—is not complete. When he spurns the advances of Potiphar's wife, the woman claims that the Hebrew slave tried to rape her. Her designation of Joseph as "a Hebrew" (Gen 39:14) is clearly derogatory; the term is generally used in the Bible by Egyptians and Philistines to contrast themselves to the Israelites. But "Hebrew" was used by such other people of the ancient Near East as the Baylonians, Assyrians, and Hittites to denote people of a lower social class rather than members of a particular national group. The name Potiphar appears in Egyptian sources as Pa-di-pa-re, meaning "he whom Re [the sun god] has given." It is nearly identical to the name of Joseph's father-in-law, Potiphera, although the two are different characters.

Ancient literature has a number of tales similar to the one of Potiphar's wife. An Egyptian version dating to 1225 B.C., but no doubt much earlier, has been found. In the biblical narrative Joseph is thrown in prison for his alleged offense. If Potiphar had truly believed his wife, some commentators suggest, the punishment would have been death.

Pharaoh dreamed that he was standing by the Nile, and there came up out of the Nile seven sleek and fat cows. GEN 41:1

*I*n prison the Lord again intervenes and Joseph is given charge of the other prisoners. The resilient slave successfully interprets the dreams of the royal cupbearer and baker, who have been incarcerated for having offended Pharaoh. In a clever play on words, Joseph tells each that "Pharaoh will lift your head" (Gen 40:13, 19). The cupbearer, says Joseph, will be restored to favor within three days; the baker, however, will be beheaded. And so it comes to pass.

Although Joseph had asked the cupbearer to remember him when he was back at court, the man forgets to do so for two years—until "all the magicians of Egypt and all its wise men" (Gen 41:8) are unable to explain Pharaoh's dreams of the seven fat and seven lean cows and a similar one about seven plump ears of grain and seven lean ones. Told of the young Hebrew who had correctly decoded the cupbearer's dream, Pharaoh summons Joseph from prison.

Joseph explains that the dreams foretell seven years of plenty to be followed by seven years of famine. Greatly impressed, Pharaoh makes Joseph overseer of all Egypt, gives him a new name (Zaphenath-paneah, "God speaks, he lives"), and awards him the daughter of a priest of On—the city later called Heliopolis because it was the center of sun worship. Joseph is just 30 years old. This episode, down to the details of Pharaoh arraying Joseph in fine linen garments and giving him a signet ring and a gold chain to wear about his neck, reveals the biblical writer's exceptional knowledge of Egyptian customs.

By storing food in the seven years of plenty, Joseph is ready for the famine that—as he had predicted—comes in the eighth year. Not only is he able to feed all Egypt, Joseph can also accommodate strangers coming from afar "because the famine became severe throughout the world" (Gen 41:57).

Now a powerful official of Pharaoh in Egypt, Joseph is reunited with the brothers who sold him into slavery; one of a series of tapestries depicting the Joseph story from Genesis in the Palazzo Vecchio in Florence, Italy.

When Jacob learned that there was grain in Egypt, he said to his sons, ". . . go down and buy grain for us there, that we may live and not die." GEN 42:1-2

*A*ngry at young Joseph's dream presuming that their sheaves of grain would bow to his, the elder brothers had long ago asked, "Are you indeed to reign over us?" (Gen 37:8). Now, with Joseph in a position of power in Egypt, they get their answer.

Appearing at the Egyptian court to buy grain, the brothers prostrate themselves before Pharaoh's overseer. Though he knows them at once, they fail to recognize the brother they had sold into slavery 20 years earlier. Their mistake is understandable, given that Joseph would have been clean-shaven, dressed in court robes, and obviously wielding great power. Moreover, Joseph speaks to them through an interpreter. But maintaining his disguise was not easy for

Joseph brings his sons Ephraim and Manasseh for the blessing of his aged father, Jacob; a detail from a painting by the Dutch master Rembrandt (1606-1669).

Joseph, who "turned away from them [his brothers] and wept" (Gen 42:24). Only rarely does the Bible reveal such inner feelings of one of its characters.

Before he finally makes himself known to his brothers, Joseph puts the sons of Jacob to a series of tests. He forces them to return to Canaan and bring back the youngest brother, Benjamin, then contrives to have Benjamin accused of theft, for which he will be detained in Egypt. It is impossible to overlook Jacob's continuing insensitivity toward the older brothers. Told that he must send Benjamin with them on their second journey to Egypt, he wails in self-pity, "He alone is left. If harm should come to him . . . you would bring down my gray hairs with sorrow to Sheol" (Gen 42:38).

Ancient historians confirm that Egyptians declined to eat with foreigners, so Joseph continues his masquerade during the second visit by having his brothers served a meal apart from himself. The silver cup that Joseph has hidden as a trap in Benjamin's sack as the brothers again leave for the north was not an ordinary drinking cup. Rather, it was one used for divinations. Prophecies were made by studying the surface patterns of liquids inside the cup or marks made by drops running down its sides. Mosaic Law forbade such divination (Lev 19:26; Deut 18:10), and Isaiah proclaimed an oracle against Egyptians for such practices (Isa 19:3).

Arrested on their way home for possession of the cup, the brothers are once more brought before Joseph. Judah offers himself as a hostage, saying that their father will die if they return without Benjamin. Coming from the brother who hatched the plot to sell Joseph into slavery, Judah's offer is all the more remarkable. Historians say that his pledge to protect

Benjamin reflects the later period in Israelite history when the powerful tribe of Judah sheltered such weaker tribes as that of Benjamin.

In response to Judah's eloquent plea, ending "For how can I go back to my father if the boy is not with me? I fear to see the suffering that would come upon my father" (Gen 44:34), Joseph at last relents.

Then Joseph said to his brothers, "Come closer to me. . . . I am your brother, Joseph, whom you sold into Egypt." GEN 45:4

Like the Jacob-Esau cycle, the story of Joseph and his brothers ends with a family reconciliation. To weather the remaining five years of famine, Joseph settles Jacob, his brothers, and all their herds and flocks in Goshen, lush grazing land in the Nile Delta. It was the beginning of the Israelites' 400-year residency in Egypt.

En route to Egypt, Jacob stops at Beer-sheba to offer sacrifices to the Lord and for a final time receive God's promise that he will be the father of a great nation. "I myself will go down with you to Egypt," says the Lord, "and I will also bring you up again" (Gen 46:4)—a prediction of the end of the Israelites' exile. A concluding genealogy gives the number of settlers as 70, including Jacob, Joseph, Joseph's two sons, and all the other grandchildren. The list marks the transition from a family narrative to the collective history of an entire people in the book of Exodus.

Two clues in the Joseph cycle help establish the likely time for the Israelites' arrival in Egypt. Joseph is allowed to "ride in the chariot of his [Pharaoh's] second-in-command" (Gen 41:43). Later he tells his family to "settle in the land of Goshen, and you shall be near me" (Gen 45:10). About 1700 B.C., Hyksos invaders seized control of Egypt, introducing the horse and chariot and establishing their headquarters in the delta—the only time an Egyptian capital was located there. Moreover, these Semitic interlopers would no doubt have been more sympathetic to Israelite settlement than native Egyptians. Finally, the Hyksos capital of Avaris or Tanis is known in Hebrew as Zoan. Twice in Psalms the Israelite residency in Egypt is located "in the fields of Zoan" (Ps 78:12, 43).

When Joseph tells his brothers not to be "angry with yourselves, because you sold me here" (Gen 45:5), the purpose of the entire cycle is revealed: God sent Joseph to Egypt to preserve the clan.

"Your two sons, who were born to you in the land of Egypt . . . are now mine; Ephraim and Manasseh shall be mine, just as Reuben and Simeon are." GEN 48:5

Before the famine, Joseph's Egyptian wife had given birth to two sons: Manasseh and Ephraim. Their names were drawn from Hebrew words meaning "made to forget" and "to be fruitful."

By adopting his grandsons as his own, Jacob ensures that these two half tribes of Israel will have equal status with the other 11 tribes when they return to the land of Canaan. For a final time in Genesis, a younger son is given preference over an elder, as the aged and infirm Jacob switches hands to give the more desirable right-handed blessing to Ephraim. It is the tribe of Ephraim, not Manasseh, that will be dominant in northern Israel.

Then Jacob called his sons, and said, "Gather around, that I may tell you what will happen to you in days to come." GEN 49:1

*I*n a long poem, obviously dating from the time of King David, when the tribe of Judah had achieved preeminence, Jacob establishes the character of the tribes and reflects upon the past.

By sleeping with his father's concubine Bilhah, Reuben has forfeited the prerogatives of the firstborn. For their violence in seeking revenge for the rape of

Dinah, Simeon and Levi are also passed over. Thus the fourth son, Judah, gains the ascendancy; certainly his role in the Joseph narrative is a critical one. One by one, the others are told what lies ahead for their descendants—not all of it positive.

Having concluded his forecast, Jacob "drew up his feet into the bed, breathed his last, and was gathered to his people" (Gen 49:33). Joseph has the body embalmed and, with Pharaoh's permission, he and his brothers take the patriarch's body back to Canaan for burial in the cave in the field at Machpelah. There Jacob is put to rest alongside the other patriarchs and their wives—all save his beloved Rachel, who had been buried en route to Bethlehem after giving birth to Benjamin.

Realizing that their father was dead, Joseph's brothers said, "What if Joseph still bears a grudge against us?" GEN 50:15

A story that contains so much trickery and so much strife between brothers ends with a final deception. Bearing a false report of their father's deathbed wish that Joseph forgive them for the wrong they did him so many years ago, the brothers once more approach Pharaoh's powerful overseer. All weep as Joseph explains, "God intended it for good, in order to preserve a numerous people" (Gen 50:20).

The Israelites' long sojourn in Egypt and their eventual release, which will be recounted in the book of Exodus, is foreshadowed in the Abraham cycle (Gen 12:10-20). Because of famine, the first patriarch goes down to Egypt, Pharaoh is afflicted for taking Sarai into his harem, and the clan is sent back north with gifts from the Egyptian ruler. Genesis, at least as far as the three cycles concerning the Israelites' ancestors, has come full circle.

The step pyramid of Zoser at Saqqara (left) was about a thousand years old at the time the Israelites arrived in Egypt; in a panel from a tomb at Beni Hasan dating to about 2000 B.C., Semitic nomads in striped tunics are shown entering Egypt.

*E*xodus continues the dramatic saga of Jacob's family begun in Genesis. At the close of that book, Jacob has settled his clan in Egypt where his long lost son Joseph has risen to a position of power. As Exodus begins, some 400 years later, Jacob's family of 70 children and grandchildren has multiplied to thousands, and these Israelites, or Hebrews, are no longer guests. They are slaves, forced to build entire cities to the glory of the Egyptian king.

This turn of events propels the memorable episode from which the book takes its name, Exodus, from the Greek word for "exit." Through a spectacular show of invincible power, God liberates the Israelites, then leads them out of Egypt. Later, at Mount Sinai, God forges the people into a nation united by a covenant that he establishes with their leader, Moses. The covenant is most succinctly expressed in the Ten Commandments but is fully developed into a code of laws covering everything from worship to everyday conduct. This comprehensive agreement requires the Israelites to express their devotion to God by obeying his laws. In return, God vows to protect and bless them and lead them home to the promised land of Canaan.

These two events of deliverance and covenant-making, pivotal in Jewish history, form the two major sections of Exodus. Chapters 1-18 tell of Israel's liberation; chapters 19-40 describe the Israelites' sojourn at Sinai, where they receive God's laws. The stories of Exodus are part of the five-volume account of Israel's emergence as a nation, which begins in Genesis and continues through Leviticus, Numbers, and Deuteronomy.

Israelites forced to work on an Egyptian building project, from a 14th-century Spanish manuscript

Now a new king arose over Egypt, who did not know Joseph. EX 1:8

*J*acob's extended family stays in Egypt so long that everyone from the immigrant generation dies. A new king comes to the throne, one who does not seem to realize how much Egypt owes Joseph for his interpretation of a previous Pharaoh's dream that helped the country survive a seven-year famine.

Instead of feeling indebted to Joseph and Joseph's people, the king feels only threatened. The immigrants have grown so numerous that the king considers them a serious threat to national security.

It is uncertain when this takes place. The Egyptian ruler is not named. But references to a "new king" and to the Israelites building cities such as Rameses suggest the story unfolds at the beginning of the 19th dynasty, founded by Rameses I (c. 1293-1291 B.C.) and continued by his son Seti I (1291-1279) and grandson Rameses II (1279-1212). Rameses II, in particular, was famous for his building projects.

Whoever the worried king is, he decides to curb the proliferation of Israelites by imposing on them the arduous task of field labor as well as making mud bricks for public buildings and monuments. One Egyptian scroll from the time of Rameses II says that the ten men in a work gang had a daily quota of 2,000 bricks. An earlier record written on the wall of a tomb describes such workers as "dirtier than pigs . . . simply wretched through and through."

The oppression does not stop the growth of the Israelites. "The more they were oppressed, the more they multiplied" (Ex 1:12). And so the Egyptian king takes the drastic action of ordering two Hebrew midwives to kill newborn boys—an order that the women disobey. When the king demands an explanation for such insolence, the midwives lie, saying that the Hebrew women are of hardy stock, and that they often deliver before the midwives arrive. Thus, the Hebrew population continues to grow.

Taking even more drastic measures, the king appeals to the Egyptian citizens, ordering them to do what the midwives obviously refused to do. The method of execution is to be drowning: "Every boy that is born to the Hebrews you shall throw into the Nile" (Ex 1:22). Ironically, the river that cuts a fertile swath through the desert and provides a source of life for the Egyptians is to become the instrument of death for the Hebrews.

Now a man from the house of Levi went and married a Levite woman. The woman conceived and bore a son. EX 2:1-2

*L*evi was one of Jacob's 12 sons—the one whose descendants would later become priests and religious support staff, first for the tent tabernacle in the wilderness, then for the temple in Jerusalem. The Levite husband and wife, not named until Exodus 6:20, are Amram and Jochebed. Their child is Moses.

The story of the miraculous survival of the infant Moses is remarkably similar to folktales about other leaders of the ancient Near East who were destined for greatness. More than 30 such stories exist, including one about Sargon of Akkad (2600 B.C.) and another about Cyrus II of Persia (550 B.C.).

Technically, the mother of Moses obeys the king's command. She casts her child into the Nile River. But shrewdly, she waits until he is three months old and, when she sets him adrift, it is in a waterproofed basket woven from papyrus reeds. The Hebrew term used to describe this basket is a rare word that appears only here and in the story of Noah's ark, another rudderless vessel under God's watchful care.

Gently and ever so carefully, Jochebed places the basket containing her son among some reeds along the banks of the Nile. The reeds block the basket and keep it from floating downstream. As Jochebed slips away, leaving Moses to whatever fate God has in store for him, she also leaves a young guardian, Miriam, the older sister of Moses. The girl stands within sight of her brother's basket, yet far enough away to dissociate herself from the child when he is found.

What happens next suggests that Jochebed's actions were part of a desperate, risky scheme. The king's daughter comes to bathe in the privacy of the reed-choked riverbank. There she sees the basket and sends her maid to retrieve it. When the princess looks inside, Moses is crying. "This must be one of the Hebrews' children" (Ex 2:6), she says, filled with pity. Immediately, as though rehearsed, young Miriam is at the side of the princess, offering the

services of a Hebrew nurse who can feed and care for the seemingly abandoned child.

The nurse, of course, is Jochebed. In a humorous twist to the story, she is paid to take care of her own son. This she does until he no longer needs constant supervision and can live in the palace. There, Moses grows up with all the benefits of Egyptian royalty, but with a deep and abiding attachment to his enslaved people. Once, when Moses sees an Egyptian beating a Hebrew, he kills the man. For this act, at about 40 years of age, Moses exchanges the life of royalty for the life of a fugitive condemned to die.

Moses flees east to the land of Midian, somewhere on the Sinai Peninsula or perhaps in northern Arabia, near the Red Sea. There, he comes to the defense of the seven daughters of a Midianite priest named Jethro (also called Reuel or Hobab), who are being prevented from watering their father's flocks by hostile shepherds. In return for the favor, Jethro gives his daughter Zipporah in marriage to Moses. After Moses takes up the quiet life of a shepherd, the couple has two sons, Gershom and Eliezer.

The Midianites, Arabic-speaking descendants of Abraham by his second wife, Keturah, first appear in the biblical narrative as the slave traders who take Joseph to Egypt. Jethro reappears at Mount Sinai, returning Zipporah and her sons to Moses, who apparently had sent them home during his trials with Pharaoh. Hearing what God has done for the Israelites, Jethro avers, "Now I know that the Lord is greater than all gods" (Ex 18:11), makes a burnt offering, and shares a sacrificial feast with Aaron.

In depicting the scene of Pharaoh's daughter discovering the infant Moses, Orazio Gentileschi (1563-1647)
gave the royal party clothing of his own period and put them in a woodland setting quite unlike the Nile valley.

God speaking to Moses from the burning bush; one of many Old Testament scenes Raphael (1483-1520) painted for a gallery in the Vatican

The angel of the Lord appeared to him [Moses] in a flame of fire out of a bush. EX 3:2

The most momentous experience in the life of Moses takes place while he is alone, shepherding his flock near Mount Sinai, also called Horeb. He sees a thornbush glowing in what appears to be the flames of a fire, yet the bush is not consumed. When he walks over to investigate, he is astonished to hear his name called out twice from the bush.

"Here I am," Moses replies. "Come no closer!" the voice warns. "Remove the sandals from your feet, for the place on which you are standing is holy ground" (Ex 3:4, 5). Indeed, it was customary in the ancient Near East to show respect for a sacred place by removing one's shoes before entering.

The power manifested within the bush is first identified only as "the angel of the Lord." Sometimes this phrase refers to an angelic messenger of God and other times—as here—it refers to God himself. God tells Moses, by now 80 years old, that he is to return to Egypt, order the king to free the Israelites, and lead them back to Canaan. En route, they are to worship on the mountain where Moses is standing.

Quickly, Moses reveals that he would rather lead sheep than people. For in short order, he identifies what he thinks are three solid arguments against choosing him as the solitary person to confront Pharaoh: He is no one of influence; the Israelites will not believe he is on a mission from God; and he is not an eloquent speaker.

To the first argument God replies, "I will be with you" (Ex 3:12). As further assurance, God reveals his name, which incorporates the Hebrew verb "to be" and emphasizes his abiding presence. This name, often translated "I AM WHO I AM," is a variation of the sacred Hebrew name for God: *Yahweh.*

As to the second argument—that the Israelites will not believe him—God promises to grant Moses miraculous powers to convince both the Hebrews and the Egyptian king, who God warns will stubbornly resist. God creates for Moses two miracles: He turns the shepherd's staff of Moses into a snake and back to a staff again, then turns the hand of Moses white with leprosy and back to health again. God also says that Moses will receive the power to turn the Nile into blood.

God counters the third argument—that Moses is not eloquent—by allowing Aaron, Moses' older brother, to be spokesman for the reluctant leader.

"Thus says the Lord, the God of Israel, 'Let my people go.'" EX 5:1

Using the miraculous signs that God has given him, Moses convinces the Israelite elders that he has been sent by the Lord. Buoyed by such speedy success, Moses and Aaron arrange an audience with Pharaoh—probably the infamous and vain Rameses II, a compulsive builder who had his own name inscribed on monuments of previous kings. Boldly, the Hebrew brothers announce that the God of Israel has ordered his people to make a pilgrimage into the wilderness to celebrate a religious festival. Pharaoh, himself considered one god among the many worshiped in Egypt, sneers that he has never heard of this god.

Any confidence that Moses may have experienced as he first approached the king seems now to have evaporated. He makes no commands. He issues no threats. He shows no miraculous signs. Instead, he pleads as a feeble subject to a powerful king. The festival will take no more than three days, Moses says. And if they do not go, God will "fall upon us with pestilence or sword" (Ex 5:3). Suspecting a ruse to rob Egypt of its cheap labor, Pharaoh concludes that the Israelites have too much time on their hands. Instead of using government-supplied straw, a binding agent that strengthens mud bricks, they will have to gather and chop the straw themselves—while producing just as many bricks as before.

The burden proves impossible. When Hebrew supervisors plead their case before Pharaoh, he refuses to relent. Devastated by this disastrous outcome, Moses turns to God and complains, "Why did you ever send me?" (Ex 5:22).

The Egyptians shall know that I am the Lord, when I stretch out my hand against Egypt and bring the Israelites out from among them. EX 7:5

At God's command, Moses and Aaron return for a second audience with Pharaoh. When the king asks to see proof that they come in the name of God, they employ the first sign that God gave Moses at the burning bush: They throw down a staff and it turns into a snake. Pharaoh is unimpressed; he has probably seen similar feats. The ancients reportedly had the ability to hypnotize snakes, making them rigid and sticklike. In fact, when Pharaoh beckons his court magicians, they come out carrying what appear to be staffs. When they throw them down, the staffs become snakes. Aaron's staff, however, swallows up the Egyptian magicians' snakes.

Pharaoh remains stubbornly resistant about releasing the Israelites, even for a three-day pilgrimage. This sets the stage for a nearly yearlong string of ten more signs, or plagues, the first nine of which follow a cycle of natural disasters still common in the Middle East. But the Bible suggests that the cycle was intensified by God.

In the first plague, the Nile River turns blood red and fish die, making the water foul smelling and undrinkable. This occasionally happens in late summer and early autumn when heavy flooding dumps tons of red dirt into the river, along with oxygen-robbing algae from nearby swamps.

Next come frogs, which may have abandoned the river to escape whatever killed the fish—perhaps the bacteria-laden algae. Eventually the frogs die, too, possibly from the same infestation that killed the fish. Plagues three and four are gnats (or mosquitoes) and flies, which may have bred in stagnant pools left by the Nile as it receded in the autumn.

The fifth plague is a disease striking all Egyptian livestock but mysteriously sparing animals belonging to the Israelites. To begin the sixth plague, Moses throws kiln soot into the air. Afterward, Egyptians

Returning to Egypt with his wife and sons, Moses greets Aaron; a 14th-century Jewish seder manual.

and their animals break out in boils—possibly from tiny anthrax organisms carried by the river and animals. The disease attacks livestock and humans and produces burning, pus-filled blisters that form soot-black scabs. Untreated, it can be fatal.

The seventh plague, hail, destroys flax and barley crops growing in winter, about January. Then comes

Moses and Aaron appear before Pharaoh to demand that he allow the Israelites to leave Egypt; one of a series of biblical paintings by French artist James Joseph Jacques Tissot (1836-1902).

an invasion of locusts, blown in by the prevailing east winds that strike Egypt in March or April. The ninth plague—three days of darkness—may have been the result of dirt and sand swept in by the hot khamsin wind. It can arrive anytime between March and May.

For many months, Pharaoh remains intransigent. Several times he says he will let the people go if Moses only stops a particular plague. But each time Moses complies, Pharaoh reverts to his unyielding position.

By means of these first nine plagues, God demonstrates his power not only over nature but also over the many Egyptian gods. By polluting the Nile, God shows himself stronger than Hapi, the river god. He also humbles the gods and goddesses of livestock, earth, sky, sickness, and the protector from locusts and other pests. With the ninth plague, he overwhelms one of Egypt's most powerful deities, Ra, the sun god.

Gradually, these accumulating horrors—which do not harm the Hebrews—wear down the resistance of the Egyptians. With one final, tragic horror, all remnants of Egyptian national pride will suddenly disintegrate.

The Lord said to Moses and Aaron in the land of Egypt: This month shall mark for you the beginning of months.
EX 12:1-2

What is about to take place—the tenth and most terrifying plague, commemorated as Passover—is so important that the month in which it occurs will become the first month of the Hebrew religious calendar. This is Abib, later called Nisan, occurring in late March and early April. God warns Moses that at midnight on the beginning of Abib 15, when the moon is full, he will pass through Egypt and kill the firstborn in each family, human as well as livestock.

Moses gives the Hebrews detailed instructions that serve two purposes. The first is to ward off "the destroyer" (Ex 12:23). At God's order, the Israelites are to

Five of the ten plagues that God inflicted on Egypt (from top): frogs, flies, boils, hail and lightning, and locusts; from a 15th-century German Bible

daub blood from a sacrificed sheep or goat onto the frame around the door of their home. "When I see the blood, I will pass over you, and no plague shall destroy you when I strike the land of Egypt" (Ex 12:13), the Lord says.

The second purpose is to inaugurate a festival to commemorate the liberation of the Israelites—one that has become the oldest perennial ceremony in Jewish history. "This day shall be a day of remembrance for you," God tells Moses. "Throughout your generations you shall observe it as a perpetual ordinance" (Ex 12:14).

Moses gives the people specific instructions for the observance. At dusk on the 14th of Abib, each family is to kill a year-old lamb or goat that has no defects; this animal should be the most perfect specimen they can find. After they brush some of the animal's blood on the door frame, they are to roast the animal over a fire, then eat it with yeastless bread (quick to make because it does not have to rise) and bitter herbs, such as endive or chicory, native to Egypt. These herbs are possibly intended to remind the people of the bitter slavery they have endured.

The Hebrews are to eat in a spirit of anticipation and haste, sandals on and ready to leave at a moment's notice.

In the years to come, this Passover meal will begin the weeklong Festival of Unleavened Bread, a continuation of the Exodus celebration. But in this inaugural year of the rite, the people will have to forego the extended celebration. For by morning on the 15th of Abib, they will be making a hasty exit out of Egypt, headed east toward the forbidding Sinai wilderness.

At midnight the Lord struck down all the firstborn in the land of Egypt. EX 12:29

Just as Moses had warned, the Lord launches the tenth and final plague at midnight. Homes with the divinely instituted mark of blood smeared onto the door frames are passed over. But every other home in Egypt becomes a target. God strikes down the first-

*To ward off the tenth plague, death of
every firstborn, Hebrews mark their doorposts
with blood; a 12th-century enamel plaque.*

of value: clothing, jewelry, silver, gold. "And so they plundered the Egyptians" (Ex 12:36) as effectively as an army would plunder a defeated foe.

After 430 years in a foreign land, the Israelites are headed home, northeast toward Canaan. Together they number about 600,000 men, plus women, children, and vast herds. If this figure is correctly interpreted, the total migration would have involved more than 2 million people, a highly unlikely number. Experts in Hebrew linguistics, however, say that "thousand" can also mean "group." In this case, the Hebrews would have numbered 600 extended tribal families, totaling perhaps 20,000 people.

The Lord went in front of them in a pillar of cloud by day . . . and in a pillar of fire by night. EX 13:21

As the crowd of Israelites depart, they are led not by scouts familiar with the territory or even by Moses, who has lived and traveled on the Sinai Peninsula, a barren triangle of land about 230 miles north to south and 150 miles wide at its northern end along the Mediterranean coast. They are led by God himself, concealed by a cloud in daytime and fire at night. The divine pillar remains in front of the marching people, in a manner similar to the burning brazier carried before an army in ancient times.

Throughout Israel's early history, the presence of God is often associated with fire, clouds, and smoke. He first appears to Moses in the fire of a thornbush. He later covers Mount Sinai with clouds and smoke as he descends upon it in fire. When the Israelites build their tent worship center in the wilderness, the cloud settles on it and God's glory fills it. Centuries later, when they build and dedicate a permanent temple in Jerusalem, a divine cloud fills the sacred place.

born of every family, from Pharaoh's oldest son to the firstborn of the livestock.

Pharaoh, his officials, and all Egyptians are suddenly awakened: "There was a loud cry in Egypt, for there was not a house without someone dead" (Ex 12:30). Over the past several months the citizens of Egypt had suffered through ten plagues. For all they knew, the plagues would continue endlessly until the God of Israel had killed every Egyptian. The desperate Pharaoh tells Moses to take his people away.

Following instructions from Moses, the Israelites go to their Egyptian neighbors and ask for anything

THE PASSOVER SEDER

Since the time of Moses, Jews the world over have celebrated the Exodus each spring by eating a Passover meal. The holiday—on the 15th of Abib (March/April)—is called Passover because God "passed over" Israelite homes daubed with a sacrificial lamb's blood as he killed the firstborn of each Egyptian household. The horrifying event convinced Pharaoh to free the Israelite slaves. The ceremony surrounding the meal is called a seder, Hebrew for "order of service," because it is rich in tradition and symbolism.

On the family table at Passover are foods that link the celebrants to their ancestors. The sacrificial lamb is symbolized by a lamb shank; slavery by bitter herbs such as horseradish; tears of slaves by a saltwater dip; mortar for Egypt's building projects by a mixture of chopped nuts, apples, cinnamon, and wine; and the Israelites' hasty departure by unleavened bread. Throughout the meal, family members read from a prayer book called the Haggadah, which recounts the compelling story behind their gathering.

*A ceramic seder plate shows the foods associated
with Passover: bitter herbs, lamb, unleavened bread.*

ROUTE OF THE EXODUS

Although the book of Exodus contains a number of clues, it is impossible to retrace the route of the Israelites on their flight from Egypt with any degree of accuracy. The land of Goshen, where Jacob's extended family originally settled, has been identified as the fertile grazing land in the Nile River's delta. Rameses, one of the supply cities Jacob's enslaved descendants were forced to build, was likely the Hyksos capital also known as Avaris or Tanis. Succoth, the Israelites' first stop, is a word meaning "booths"; it may refer to the tents the refugees pitched near a swampy region known as the Bitter Lakes. None of the other place-names—Etham, Pi-hahiroth, Migdol, Baal-zephon—can be located; they were probably Egyptian frontier outposts. Indeed, the prophets Jeremiah and Ezekiel both name Migdol as an Egyptian frontier town.

One thing is virtually certain: The body of water miraculously parted for the Israelites was not the Red Sea, as the Hebrew has been mistranslated. The Hebrew term yam suph means "sea of reeds"; it could be any of the shallow lakes or marshy areas between the Nile Delta and the Sinai Peninsula.

Following the drowning of their pursuers, the Israelites could have taken any of several routes through the forbidding Sinai Peninsula. Only the northern route along the Mediterranean Sea is unlikely, because it would have taken the refugees to the land of the warlike Philistines—a destination God blocked for fear it would discourage the Israelites. If they had turned northeast through the Wilderness of Shur, two peaks en route to the Negeb could have been Mount Sinai. The central caravan route would have taken them directly to Ezion-geber. Again, the names in the biblical account are only tantalizing clues. Marah means "bitter"; its water was undrinkable. Elim offered 12 springs, but Rephidim—where the Israelites withstood an attack by the Amalekites—had no water at all.

The traditional route is along the shore of the Gulf of Suez through the wilderness of Sin to 7,500-foot Jebel Musa, Arabic for "Mountain of Moses"—long identified as the biblical Mount Sinai. An oasis there would have provided the Israelites with a comfortable resting place as God summoned Moses to

At last relenting, Pharaoh lets Moses lead his people out of Egypt; a 13th-century stained glass window from Canterbury, England.

the peak to give him the laws of his covenant with the people. After nearly a year at Mount Sinai, the Israelites broke camp to follow God in his pillar of cloud. Of the many names of the itinerary in Numbers 33, the only one known today is Ezion-geber, a site at the head of the Gulf of Aqaba. From there the Israelites moved north to the oasis of Kadesh-barnea, on the threshold of the promised land of Canaan. But it would take another 40 years for them to reach that destination.

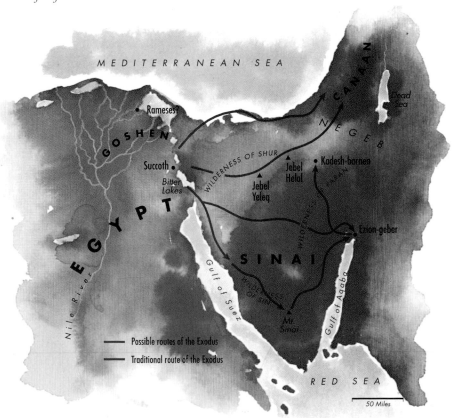

MEDITERRANEAN SEA

CANAAN

NEGEB

Dead Sea

Rameses?

GOSHEN

WILDERNESS OF SHUR

Kadesh-barnea

Jebel Helal

EGYPT

Succoth

Bitter Lakes

Jebel Yeleq

WILDERNESS OF PARAN

Ezion-geber

SINAI

Gulf of Suez

WILDERNESS OF SIN

Gulf of Aqaba

Nile River

Mt. Sinai

—— Possible routes of the Exodus

—— Traditional route of the Exodus

RED SEA

50 Miles

God does not lead the Hebrews along the shortest route to Canaan—the coastal road protected by Egyptian fortifications that archaeologists confirm existed in the days of Rameses II. "If the people face war," God explains to Moses, "they may change their minds and return to Egypt" (Ex 13:17). So God leads the Israelites into the barren wilderness between the Gulf of Suez and the Gulf of Aqaba.

The route remains a mystery, not for lack of reference points identified in the story, but because the location of these places is no longer known. The Hebrews set out from Succoth and camp at Etham, at the edge of the wilderness. But both sites remain uncertainties, as do the landmarks for their next campsite "in front of Pi-hahiroth, between Migdol and the sea, in front of Baal-zephon" (Ex 14:2). It is here, along the banks of a body of water, that the Israelites are overtaken by the pursuing Egyptian chariot corps. Pharaoh has again changed his mind about releasing the slaves, and is leading his charioteers on a mission to bring them back.

When the Israelites catch sight of the Egyptians storming toward them, they become terrified because they are trapped between the charging army and water too deep to cross. It is unknown which body of water blocked their advance. An early Greek translation of the Hebrew incorrectly interpreted the name of the site as the Red Sea. But the Hebrew language simply calls it the reed sea, perhaps one of many lakes just north of the Red Sea, such as the reed-choked Bitter Lakes or Lake Timsah farther north.

Panicked, the people ask Moses, "Was it because there were no graves in Egypt that you have taken us away to die in the wilderness?" (Ex 14:11). But Moses tells the people to have faith in the God who has gotten them this far.

With the Israelites safely across the Red Sea, Moses stretches out his hand, and the Lord—appearing in a pillar of cloud—releases the parted waters to drown Pharaoh's army; a scene from an Italian book of hours dated 1546.

The Lord drove the sea back by a strong east wind all night, and turned the sea into dry land; and the waters were divided. EX 14:21

At God's command, Moses lifts his staff and stretches it toward the sea—in the direction that the people are to go. As the divine pillar of cloud moves from the point position to the rear guard, halting the Egyptian pursuit, a strong east wind begins blowing. Hot and dry, it blows in from the Arabian desert all night long. Before dawn, the wind has produced a path across the sea for the refugees.

Pharaoh, obsessively intent on capturing the former slaves, orders his charioteers to give chase. They charge down the beach and into the sea bottom, but the wheels of their heavy war wagons apparently become hopelessly mired in mud.

At daybreak, Moses stands on the opposite bank and stretches out his hand toward the sea. The water surges back into place, killing the chariot corps that had ventured onto the path. This marks a turning point for the Hebrews. No longer are they fugitives, for no one remains to chase them. Decimated, Pharaoh's army no longer poses a threat. As Moses had promised, this is the last that his generation sees of the despised Egyptians.

Exhilarated at witnessing such an unprecedented miracle of deliverance, Moses leads the people in a song of praise to God. The psalm begins with one of the oldest couplets in Hebrew poetry: "I will sing to the Lord, for he has triumphed gloriously; horse and rider he has thrown into the sea" (Ex 15:1). The language of verses 8 to 10 appears to draw on ancient Near Eastern traditions of a divine battle against the hostile forces of a sea god and is echoed in Psalms 77:16-19 and 114:3-5.

When the song is finished, Miriam, the older sister of both Moses and Aaron, and well into her eighties or beyond, grabs a tambourine and begins dancing as she sings the couplet like a repeating chorus—an encore for God's glory. Inspired by Miriam's joyous spirit, the Hebrew women seize tambourines and join the chorus, dancing along the seashore.

The Lord said to Moses, "I am going to rain bread from heaven for you." EX 16:4

Exactly one month after the Exodus had begun, the Israelites are out of food and deep in the barren wilderness of Sin, possibly in the southwestern Sinai Peninsula. "You have brought us out into this wilderness to kill this whole assembly with hunger" (Ex 16:3), they bitterly complain to Moses.

Again, Moses calms the people with assurance that God has not brought them this far only to abandon them. In the evening, Moses says, they will eat their fill of meat. And in the morning, they will fill up on "bread from heaven."

That evening, migrating quail cover the landscape. It is springtime, and the quail are returning home to Europe and western Asia after wintering in Africa. These small, plump birds, excellent for eating, are not strong fliers. When they land, exhausted, they are easy prey for hungry animals and hunters. Egyptians used to preserve these brown birds for year-round eating by drying them in the sun or pickling them in jars. During the early 1900s these Middle Eastern quail were killed by the millions. As a result, flocks today are much smaller.

The next morning, after the dew has evaporated, the Israelites are mystified to discover that lying on the ground is "a fine flaky substance, as fine as frost . . . . white, and the taste of it was like wafers made with honey" (Ex 16:14, 31). The Hebrews simply called it *manna*, meaning "What is it?"

Each morning they collect just enough for each person in their family—about a half-gallon container per person. On Friday mornings they collect a double portion, because they will not find any on Saturday, the sabbath. This substance will serve as the people's staple food during their entire 40-year sojourn in the wilderness. To remind future generations of how God cares and provides for his chosen people, Moses orders that a single helping of the manna be preserved in a sealed jar. Aaron will later store it in the ark of the covenant, the gold-covered chest that holds the Ten Commandments.

The biblical description of manna makes it sound like it could be the secretion of two types of desert insect that feed on the sap of tamarisk trees. The sticky droplets they secrete, which dry quickly in the desert sun, are so sweet they are called honeydew.

In the barren wilderness, God sustains the Israelites by sending manna; in this 16th-century painting the hungry people gather the bread from heaven.

The Lord summoned Moses to the top of the mountain, and Moses went up. EX 19:20

Three months after the Israelites leave Egypt, they arrive at the base of Mount Sinai, where Moses had earlier encountered God in a burning bush. The specific location is uncertain, but many have suggested Jebel Musa (Arabic for "Mountain of Moses"), a 7,500-foot-high granite peak that towers over other mountains in the south Sinai range. Additional suggestions include some mountains half as high in the central Sinai Peninsula.

Whatever the mountain, the Hebrews set up camp in the plain below it. They remain there for nearly a year—long enough to accumulate the laws and experiences reported in the remainder of Exodus, all of Leviticus, and through Numbers 10:10. It is here that God offers to embrace them with the covenant he had made with Abraham, Isaac, and Jacob hundreds of years earlier: "I will establish my covenant between me and you, and your offspring after you . . . . I will be their God" (Gen 17:7-8).

Moses tells the people that if they are willing to enter into this binding agreement that requires them to obey God, then God will treat them as a "treasured possession" (Ex 19:5). The people eagerly agree to his offer.

In an astonishing, unprecedented move, God decides to reveal the heart of the covenant—the Ten

Moses receiving the Ten Commandments from God, as depicted in the 13th-century psalter of Ingeburg of Denmark

Commandments—in a speech to Moses that the entire assembly will hear. He explains to Moses that he is doing this "in order that the people may hear when I speak with you and so trust you ever after" (Ex 19:9). God wants the Hebrews to know that the laws they will soon learn about are his laws—not an assortment of rules created by Moses, a man.

The people have two days to prepare to meet God. As part of the spiritual purification, they wash their clothes and abstain from sexual relations. During this time, they are not to set foot on the mountain, under penalty of death.

At dawn on the third day, Moses leads the people to the foot of Mount Sinai, the peak of which is shrouded in a thick cloud. Thunder and lightning fill the sky with majestic power as God descends to the

top of the mountain in a fire. The ground shakes violently, and a mysterious trumpet blasts so loudly that the people become frightened.

God summons Moses onto the mountain and tells him to warn the people not to look at their God or to come any closer to the mountain, otherwise they will die. After Moses delivers this message, God speaks in a thundering voice that fills the plain. "I am the Lord your God, who brought you out of the land of Egypt," he begins; ". . . you shall have no other gods before me" (Ex 20:1).

With this, he has delivered the first of the Ten Commandments, the fundamental laws of Judaism on which other Jewish laws are based. The first three commandments deal with humanity's relationship to God: Worship only God; do not make idols; do not misuse God's name. The remaining seven involve relationships between human beings: Rest on the seventh day of the week; honor your parents; do not murder, commit adultery, steal, lie, or crave what belongs to someone else. As a hint of women's status, the last commandment includes a wife, slaves, and livestock among the belongings not to be coveted.

When God is finished, the people are thoroughly terrified. They ask Moses to serve as their intermediary in the future, receiving God's instruction and delivering it to them. This is a role that Moses accepts. He returns to the mountaintop, where he remains in seclusion with God for 40 days. There he receives instructions for building the tabernacle and scores of detailed religious and ethical laws. To mark the conclusion of his lawgiving, God presents Moses with a copy of the covenant—by tradition, the Ten Commandments—written on a pair of stone tablets with his own finger. Though later replaced, this cultic object becomes enshrined within the ark of the covenant as the Israelites' most sacred possession, the loss of which brings disaster.

From atop a forbidding peak in the Sinai Peninsula, Moses brought the Ten Commandments from God to the Israelites waiting below.

*These are the ordinances that you shall
set before them.* EX 21:1

When Moses returns to Mount Sinai, God gives him the first several score of what will eventually become a body of more than 600 meticulous laws that are preserved in the remainder of the Pentateuch, the five books of the Bible traditionally attributed to Moses.

The initial corpus of laws—the full collection—is incredibly diverse, covering issues of worship and everyday living. There are laws concerning annual religious observances, violence, property, restitution, even how to treat slaves, who in this ancient setting typically were perceived as having no rights at all. For example, the law requires that if a master knocks out the tooth of a slave, as compensation, the slave must be set free.

This is not the first set of laws in ancient society; it is only one of many. The Code of Hammurabi, laws created by the 18th century B.C. founder of the Babylonian empire, was several hundred years old when Moses first climbed Mount Sinai. Yet there are distinctions to Israel's law. Hammurabi's code, for example, favored the powerful upper class, requiring lesser penalties from them. It also permitted vicarious punishment. For example, if a man accidentally but negligently killed the son of another, then he could be punished by watching the execution of his own son. Israel's law, however, banned vicarious punishment and furthermore required the same punishment for rich and poor alike.

*I will set your borders from the Red Sea to the sea of
the Philistines, and from the wilderness to the Euphrates.*
EX 23:31

One of the most compelling benefits of the Israelites' covenant with God is the gift of a homeland, a pledge repeated in Exodus 33:1-3. This is not a new promise, but the renewal of an old one. For after Abraham had arrived in Canaan and walked throughout the territory, the Lord told him, "To your offspring I will give this land" (Gen 12:7).

God promises to give the Israelites land as far south as the Red Sea, as far west as the Mediterranean coast, where the Philistines lived, and as far north as the Euphrates River, in what is now northern Syria. This territory will include the wilderness of the Negeb Desert, in what is today southern Israel. No eastern boundary is mentioned, but many have assumed it to be the port city of Elath at the northeastern tip of the Red Sea, in the Gulf of Aqaba.

*Israelites carrying the ark of the covenant;
a 19th-century stained glass window*

These boundaries—Elath in the south, the Euphrates in the north, the Mediterranean in the west—in reality represent the kingdom of Israel at the height of its power, during the reigns of David and Solomon. The eastern boundary projected beyond the Jordan River, into what is now Jordan.

But God's promise of this land is conditional. The Hebrews have to obey him. In particular, they are to make no treaties with the Canaanites living there, but are to drive them out. The Lord also vows that once the Israelites arrive in the promised land of Canaan, they will be blessed and multiply.

*Have them make me a sanctuary,
so that I may dwell among them.*
EX 25:8

People throughout the ancient Near East were accustomed to worshiping their gods at temples and shrines. The remains of several Egyptian temples date to the time of Rameses II, most likely the stubborn king with whom Moses had to contend. The Israelites were certainly familiar with such holy places, but they had none of their own. God's instructions to Moses change that.

Because it is not practical for the Israelites to build a permanent temple while they are sojourning in the Sinai, God gives Moses detailed instructions for an exquisitely crafted tent worship center known as the tabernacle. This "tent of meeting" (Ex 27:21) will provide the people with a portable shrine they can take wherever they go. God tells Moses to collect from the people a voluntary offering of all the supplies needed to build and furnish the tabernacle: gold, silver, bronze, gemstones, yarn dyed in the royal colors of blue, purple, and crimson, fine linen, animal skins, hardwood, oil for lamps, and spices for incense and anointing oil.

The sacred tent, always pitched in the center of the camp, stands 45 feet long by 15 feet wide and 15 feet high. It is made with four layers of cloth and animal hide draped over a gold-plated frame. The two outer layers are of fine leather and ram hide to provide waterproofing. Next comes a layer of woven goat hair. Then, forming the interior ceiling and walls, is a layer of fine linen decorated with cherubim.

Only priests can enter this sacred tabernacle, through a screen curtain of yarns, fine twisted linen, and embroidery. Inside, another curtain separates the tent into two sections. In the larger front room, called the holy place, are gold furnishings: a seven-branched, oil-burning lamp that provides the only source of light; a small altar on which to burn fragrant incense offerings; and a table for 12 loaves of bread, put out fresh each week to symbolize the 12 tribes of Israel and their devotion to God.

In the smaller back chamber, called the most holy place, the Hebrews keep the ark of the covenant, a gold-covered chest that holds two stone tablets containing the Ten Commandments. The lid of this most sacred Hebrew relic is fashioned of solid gold and topped with two winged cherubim. This lid, also known as the "mercy seat," symbolizes the earthly throne of God. "There I will meet with you," God tells Moses, ". . . I will deliver to you all my commands for the Israelites" (Ex 25:22).

Outside the sacred tent is a courtyard, 50 yards long and 25 yards wide, surrounded by a wall of curtains seven feet high, with a single entrance that always faces the rising sun. It is to this courtyard that the Israelites come when they want to worship God by offering sacrifices of gratitude or to atone for sin. For this purpose, they slaughter and burn sacrificial animals on the most dominant object in the courtyard: a bronze-plated altar equipped with a grating. Nearby is a large bronze basin, where the priests come to purify themselves by washing before making a sacrificial offering.

Whenever the Hebrews break camp, they disassemble this worship center, load it onto four large wagons, and take it with them. The single exception is the holy ark of the covenant. Instead of traveling as sacred baggage, this holy symbol of God's presence is carried with gold-covered poles by priests who lead the entire assembly.

Then bring near to you your brother Aaron, and his sons with him, from among the Israelites, to serve me as priests.
EX 28:1

Before the Exodus, Israelite clan leaders served as priests for their extended families. Abraham, Isaac, and Jacob each built altars and offered sacrifices to God. But during the Hebrews' 11-month encampment at the foot of Mount Sinai, God assigns this responsibility to Aaron and his four sons. The priesthood becomes the exclusive privilege of Aaron's descendants—but only those with no deformity or disfiguring blemish. Priests have to be as free of defect as the sacrificial animals they bring to God.

In a weeklong service of ordination, filled with dramatic sacrifices, anointing with oil, and other emotive rituals, Aaron is commissioned the chief priest, and the only one permitted to enter the most holy room of the tabernacle; his sons become ministering priests. Each man wears garments uniquely designed for the priesthood. All five wear long linen tunics held in place by royal blue sashes. Covering their heads are turbans.

As high priest, Aaron has magnificent vestments to wear while officiating inside the sacred tent. Over his checkered linen tunic he wears a brilliant blue robe edged with golden bells that ring with each barefooted step he takes onto the sacred ground of the tabernacle. Over his chest he wears a breastplate studded with 12 gemstones, each engraved with the name of one of the 12 sons of Jacob, symbolizing that he ministers on behalf of all Hebrews. Attached to his turban is a golden plate inscribed "Holy to the Lord" (Ex 28:36). As priests, only Aaron and his sons can bring the body or blood of sacrificial animals to the altar; only they can enter the sacred tent.

The priests are assisted by men who, like Aaron and Moses, are descended from Jacob's son Levi. The Levites earned this privilege by remaining loyal to God when many in the Sinai camp worshiped a golden calf. These priestly assistants become caretakers not only of the tabernacle, but also later of the Jerusalem temple. They maintain the religious facility and serve as musicians, guards, treasurers, and butchers who help to prepare the sacrifices.

And they shall know that I am the Lord their God, who brought them out of the land of Egypt that I might dwell among them. EX 29:46

These closing verses of chapter 29 form a beautiful and sensitive summary of the entire book, taking the reader full circle, back to God's introduction to Moses at the burning bush, followed by his first words to the full assembly at Mount Sinai.

Up to this point in the story, God has repeatedly revealed in dramatic miracle after miracle that he is the Lord and is present among the Hebrews. But after they receive God's law at Mount Sinai, and are sealed into a covenant relationship with him, it becomes primarily their responsibility to prove the relationship. The Israelites are to accomplish this by what

The ark of the covenant rendered in stone; from the ruins of a 4th-century synagogue at Capernaum in Galilee

Moses dispensing the law to the people of
Israel, as depicted on a 16th-century Italian plate

they do—in the way they live in obedience to his laws and in the distinctive way they worship, meticulously observing the prescribed rituals.

Year after year, generation after generation, Jews have celebrated Passover as a way of commemorating the seminal event in their history, expressed in these summary words. During the spiritual crises throughout the succeeding decades and centuries, from the time of Joshua through the prophets and beyond, this statement has endured as a rallying cry, urging the people to have faith in the miracle-working God who dwells among his chosen people.

The people gathered around Aaron, and said to him,
"Come, make gods for us." EX 32:1

For 40 days and 40 nights—a common way of saying "for a long time"—Moses remains on Mount Sinai, receiving instructions about building the tabernacle and ordaining Aaron and his sons. Meanwhile, at the foot of the mountain the future high priest of Israel is busy making an idol.

The people, apparently afraid that Moses has been killed, insist that Aaron make gods who will lead them out of the desert. Revealing his enormous deficiency as their leader, Aaron quickly gives in to the crowd. He collects gold earrings from the people, which they likely have taken as booty from Egypt, and molds them into the image of a calf. To the Hebrews, the idol probably resembled

Bronze idols like this bull were
worshiped by many of Israel's neighbors.

Apis, the Egyptian god of sexual fertility. This would explain the sexual implications behind the description of the revel that follows.

Aaron, however, may have intended the idol as only a representation of God, or perhaps as a pedestal for him, similar to the cherubim on the ark of the covenant. Some ancient figurines depict the Canaanite god Baal standing on the back of a calf. Further evidence of this interpretation comes when Aaron presents the calf to the people; he announces, "Tomorrow shall be a festival to the Lord" (Ex 32:5). Furthermore, when the people come, they bring sacrifices that God has requested for himself. But even if Aaron intended the calf to symbolize the God of Israel, and even if the people accepted it as such, they have broken the second of the Ten Commandments: "You shall not make for yourself an idol" (Ex 20:4).

Warned by God of what is happening below, Moses quickly descends the mountain, carrying the newly inscribed stone tablets bearing the Ten Commandments. When he sees the calf and the dancing revelers, he furiously flings down the tablets, shattering them as a symbol of the broken covenant. When he confronts Aaron, all he gets is the absurd explanation that the people demanded a god and that Aaron collected some gold and "threw it into the fire, and out came this calf!" (Ex 32:24).

Moses burns the calf, grinds it to powder, mixes it with water, and orders the Israelites to drink it. This may have been a trial by ordeal, in which Moses believed that God would punish the guilty by making them sick. A short time later a plague sweeps through the camp as punishment for this sin. But God stops short of annulling the covenant.

This, the Israelites' first community-wide sin against God, is just the beginning of what will become many centuries of similar sins. Yet each time the people repent, God mercifully forgives them. Only after they persistently refuse to repent of idolatry do they meet with the staggering disaster that destroys them as a nation and scatters them as slaves and refugees throughout the Near East. But even then, when the punishment is complete and the repentance genuine, the Lord graciously brings his people home.

Thus the Lord used to speak to Moses
face to face as one speaks to a friend.
EX 33:11

Moses—the first and most revered of the Old Testament prophets—is unique among those who received and delivered messages from God.

God himself explains the difference, while rebuking Aaron and Miriam for their jealous presumption that they are their brother's equal because God has delivered messages through them also. "When there are prophets among you," God says, "I the Lord make myself known to them in visions; I speak to them in dreams. Not so with my servant Moses; he is entrusted with all my house. With him I speak face to face" (Num 12:6-8). The point is that God speaks directly to Moses, not through an angelic intermediary or through the distancing medium of a dream.

That Moses does not literally see the face of God becomes clear when Moses asks to see the Lord in all his glory. God replies, "you cannot see my face; for no one shall see me and live" (Ex 33:20). God does, however, permit Moses a fleeting glance of his back. Such encounters with God leave the face of Moses shining. When Moses returns from Mount Sinai with the stone tablets replacing the earlier ones he had shattered, his face is shining so radiantly that the people are afraid to approach him. After future meetings with God, Moses takes to wearing a veil. This allows the people to look at him when he delivers God's message.

Then the cloud covered the tent of meeting, and the glory of the Lord filled the tabernacle. EX 40:34

The closing chapters of Exodus report that Moses leads the people in a covenant renewal ceremony, then begins to implement the divine regulations and instructions that God had given him earlier.

On the first day of the second year of the Israelites' liberation from bondage in Egypt, the people erect the tabernacle. As soon as everything is made ready, and all the furnishings are in place, God descends, settling upon the tabernacle as a cloud and filling it with his glory. As long as the cloud remains upon the tabernacle, the people camp. But when the cloud lifts and begins to move away, the Hebrews break camp and follow.

Several centuries later, when the tent sanctuary has been replaced by Solomon's magnificent temple in Jerusalem, the Lord again assures his people that he dwells among them: "A cloud filled the house of the Lord, so that the priests could not stand to minister because of the cloud; for the glory of the Lord filled the house of the Lord" (1 Kgs 8:10-11).

After another several centuries, the prophet Ezekiel has a devastating vision of God leaving the temple, just before he allows the Babylonians to invade and defeat the nation for its perpetual idolatry: "The glory of the Lord went out from the threshold" (Ezek 10:18). But Ezekiel, prophesying from exile in Babylon, also foresees a restored Israel, with a rebuilt temple to which God returns: "As the glory of the Lord entered the temple by the gate facing east, the spirit lifted me up, and brought me into the inner court, and the glory of the Lord filled the temple" (Ezek 43:4-5).

Events of Exodus, including Moses receiving the Ten Commandments and smashing them to the ground as the people worship a golden calf, are shown in this painting for the Vatican's Sistine Chapel by Cosimo Rosselli (1439-1507).

A ram was among the male animals specified for sacrifices; this one is from a 14th-century German stained glass window.

*T*he Israelites camped near Mount Sinai for nearly a year. During that time God delivered through Moses a system of laws for the people to live by. Because those laws were to be administered by priests—all from the tribe of Levi—the book containing them has become known as Leviticus, meaning "related to Levites." In ancient times this part of the five books traditionally attributed to Moses was simply called the Priests' Manual.

While Exodus gives the Israelites directions for building the tent worship center known as the tabernacle, Leviticus gives them laws for worshiping there. Included are regulations about when and how to offer sacrifices, the ordination ceremony for priests, laws about the kinds of animals that can and cannot be eaten, rituals for the annual day of atonement, and laws for everyday living to preserve the moral and ritual purity of the people so they can live in the presence of God.

Behind all of these laws and rituals is the people's conviction that they worship a holy God who has pitched his sacred tent among them. Because God is with them, in the tabernacle at the center of the camp, and because his covenant with them makes Israel the earthly representation of God's kingdom, the Israelites must live as a people who are holy—set apart for God's purpose. "Sanctify yourselves therefore, and be holy," God tells the Israelites, "for I am holy" (Lev 11:44). By carefully observing the rules in Leviticus, the people maintain their holiness in the generations to come—and they find forgiveness when they fail.

Lay your hand on the head of the burnt offering, and it shall be acceptable in your behalf as atonement for you. LEV 1:4

*T*he laws of sacrifice, preserved in the book of Leviticus, convey the message that God cannot ignore sin. There is a price to pay for disobedience. In the beginning, when God created Adam and Eve, he revealed what that price would be: "You shall die" (Gen 2:17). But as an act of mercy, God now establishes a sacrificial system that allows an animal to substitute for a sinner.

The intricate sacrificial system that God gives his people is not a set of rituals for placating an angry deity or for currying favor, as was the case in many ancient religions. Instead, it gives the people a merciful means of forgiveness and a graphic reminder of the deadly seriousness of sin. When the Israelites lay their hands on the head of a sheep—an act symbolizing the atonement that the animal will make for their sin—and when the people see the life drain out of the animal through the flow of bright red blood, then smell the meat burning on the altar, the life-and-death seriousness of sin becomes vividly real. Anything less than such a sacrifice would make sin seem inconsequential and devalue God's holiness.

The burnt offering, in which the entire animal is consumed in fire, is one of the most important rituals among the Israelites. Unlike other sacrifices, no part of the animal is kept for a sacred meal. The sacrifice becomes a symbol of the worshiper's complete surrender to God. It also serves as an act of atonement for sin, or as a voluntary expression of worship and devotion.

The Israelites can offer any of three male animals. People who can afford it sacrifice a bull; others offer a ram or—poorer people—a dove or pigeon.

Before entering the tabernacle courtyard, worshipers bathe to purify themselves from any uncleanliness. When they reach the altar, in front of the tent sanctuary, they lay their hands on the head of the animal to identify with it and to express their understanding that the animal is about to die for them, making atonement for their sins.

Leading the bull or ram to the north side of the altar, the worshiper cuts the throat of the animal—or, in the sacrifice of a bird, pinches off its head, producing a quick death. As the lifeblood drains out, the priest catches some of it in a small basin, then splashes it on all four sides of the altar, signifying that the life belongs to God. For among the Israelites, blood symbolizes life. When worshipers pour out the blood of an animal, they pour out its life. "The life of the flesh is in the blood," God explains to Moses; "and I have given it to you for making atonement for your lives on the altar" (Lev 17:11).

The worshiper skins the bull or ram, giving the hide as payment to the officiating priest, then cuts the carcass into sections. Later in Israel's history, priests and their assistants do the butchering out of a desire to make sure the ritual is done properly. As the worshiper looks on, the priest washes the animal's legs and entrails, which contain dirt or excrement that can contaminate the altar. Then the priest carefully places all the carcass pieces on the wood of the altar. If the offering is a bird, the priest removes the crop, which contains the food waste, then lays the animal on the wood. When the fire is ignited, the meat burns and fills the courtyard with the strong smell of an acceptable sacrifice, vividly described as a "pleasing odor to the Lord" (Lev 1:9).

When anyone presents a grain offering to the Lord, the offering shall be of choice flour. LEV 2:1

*A*nimals are not the only offerings burnt on the altar. Though grain does not bleed, and therefore has no atoning power to remove sin, it is a gift of worship and an expression of gratitude that God considers acceptable. Grain offerings sometimes are made at the same time as animal sacrifices.

Israelites bring their grain offerings in various forms: flour, whole roasted kernels, ovenbaked loaves, toasted on a griddle much like pancakes, or deep-fried. But in each case, the offering is suppose to be made from the worshiper's best grain.

In some ancient Near Eastern religions, offerings of grain, vegetables, and fruit were believed to nourish the gods. This is not the case among the Israelites. They are to burn only a handful of the grain offering. The rest becomes the property of the priests, who eat it in payment for their ministry.

If the offering comes in the form of flour or roasted kernels, the priest mixes a handful of it with some oil and frankincense, an expensive and fragrant gum resin tapped from several kinds of trees that grow in Arabia and eastern Africa. If the offering comes in a cooked form, the priest tears off a small piece for burning, then mixes it with oil but—perhaps as a concession to the poor—not frankincense.

Baked grain offerings are not to be mixed with yeast or fruit syrup (called honey), both of which fer-

Animal sacrifices to the gods were common in many ancient cultures; here Sargon II of Assyria (721-705 B.C.) offers a gazelle.

ment. But all grain offerings—cooked or not—are required to include salt, a preservative. In the ancient Near East, people would often seal a contract by eating a meal seasoned with salt. The salt symbolizes that the covenant will be a long-lasting one. For the Israelites, the "salt of the covenant" (Lev 2:13) represents the eternal nature of the covenant between God and his chosen people.

If the offering is a sacrifice of wellbeing, if you offer an animal . . . you shall offer one without blemish. LEV 3:1

*T*he only sacrifice that worshipers can eat is the offering of well-being, also called the peace offering, communion offering, shared offering, or fellowship offering. The various names for this sacrifice grow out of a Hebrew word that is hard to translate, but that seems to come from a root word meaning "complete, sound, whole, healthy." A familiar Hebrew term from this same root is *shalom,* a popular Hebrew greeting that means "peace" or "wholeness." The offering of well-being, then, may symbolize the peace between God and humanity, and perhaps the inner peace that individuals experience when they know that all is well between them and the Lord.

This offering does not atone for sins. It is given in praise, for any number of reasons. It can express gratitude for surviving illness or a great ordeal. It can accompany a promise made to God. Or it can simply express a person's devotion.

The worshiper may offer a male or a female bovine, sheep, or goat—as long as the animal has no obvious defects, such as broken bones, scars, or disease. The animal needs to be of top quality, an offering fit for a holy God. Once slaughtered, the sacrifice is divided among God, priests, and worshiper. Burned on the altar are the kidneys, part of the liver, and the layer of fat beneath the animal's skin, as well as fat covering the organs. The breast and right thigh are given to the priests for them and their families to eat. The rest of the animal goes to the worshiper, who holds a banquet for family and friends with his portion. This meal celebrates the special relationship between God and Israel, in much the same way that other ancient Near Eastern banquets sealed and sustained contractual agreements between groups of people.

ISRAEL'S INHERITED PRIESTHOOD

Moses and Aaron, who wears the 12 gemstones symbolizing the 12 tribes, worship at the portable ark of the covenant.

In the days of Abraham, Isaac, and Jacob, family elders led the worship by building altars on which they made animal sacrifices to God. But when the Israelites were freed from slavery in Egypt several hundred years later, they made the Exodus in numbers large enough to comprise a nation. So, while they camped at Mount Sinai, God gave their leader, Moses, an extensive set of instructions and laws to organize them into one people. He also created an intricately detailed system of worship—and a priesthood to administer it.

God appointed Aaron and his four sons as priests. They alone could officiate at sacrificial ceremonies in the newly erected tent worship center. Entering the priesthood became the exclusive privilege of Aaron's descendants. Yet not everyone born into the priesthood met the additional, stringent requirements. Priests had to be as free of physical defects as the animals they offered. Disqualified were the blind, crippled, or disfigured—and men who had married a divorcee, a prostitute, or a foreign woman.

The priesthood survived for more than a millennium, until Roman soldiers destroyed Herod's temple in A.D. 70. With no place to offer sacrifices, there was no need for priests. Modern descendants of Aaron bear the name Cohen or Kohen (Hebrew for "priest") or related names such as Kahane. According to a 1997 study, men descended from priests bear genetic markers different from those of other Jews.

If anyone of the ordinary people among you sins unintentionally . . . you shall bring a female goat without blemish as your offering. LEV 4:27-28

The sin offering—also known as the purification offering—allows the Israelites to atone for any unintentional sins that offend the holiness of God and defile his tabernacle in the heart of the camp. These sins include any inadvertent breach of law, such as speaking rash, harmful words in the heat of anger, touching the carcass of a ritually unclean animal, or shirking the duty of testifying at a trial. There is no ritual, however, that atones for sins deliberately committed against God. But premeditated sins against others, such as stealing, are often dealt with through a combination of sacrificial rituals, punishment, and restitution if possible.

The first step to finding forgiveness for an unintentional sin is to confess it to God. The type of ritual that follows depends on who commits the sin. The most elaborate rituals are reserved for the high priest and the entire nation. This is because only the high priest, who represents the entire community before God, has access to the most sacred precincts of the tabernacle. For this reason, the priest is required to sacrifice a young bull and to use its blood to purify the inside of the sacred tent. This blood is important because "under the law almost everything is purified with blood, and without the shedding of blood there is no forgiveness of sins" (Heb 9:22).

The priest sprinkles some of the animal's blood at the entrance of the sacred back room, where the ark of the covenant is kept. The ark, containing the Ten Commandments, represents the earthly throne of God. Next, the priest daubs blood on the four raised projections, or horns, of the incense altar inside the tent. Then he pours the rest at the base of the main altar outside, in the tabernacle courtyard. Finally, the priest burns on the altar the bull's fat, kidneys, and part of the liver. The rest of the carcass is hauled outside the camp and burned, symbolizing that the sacrificed animal has absorbed the sin.

Civic rulers must sacrifice male goats, while ordinary citizens may sacrifice female goats or lambs. The poor may offer a pair of doves or pigeons, and the desperately poor may bring a handful of flour.

In the New Testament book of Hebrews, the writer portrays Jesus as the ultimate and final sin offering—the one whose blood cleanses sin and whose body, like that of the bull and other sin offerings, is destroyed "outside the camp" (Heb 13:13).

Restore what you took by robbery or by fraud . . . you shall repay the principal amount and shall add one-fifth to it. LEV 6:4-5

When an Israelite commits a sin for which he can make amends—such as robbery or withholding offerings he is supposed to take to the tabernacle—he can find forgiveness by doing three things: confessing the sin to a priest, paying back the lost principal plus a 20 percent fine, and sacrificing a ram in what is called a reparation or guilt offering. The ram's value must match the silver or shekel amount established by the priest—a value that may vary, depending on the severity of the offense.

The law regarding this sacrifice includes a mystifying phrase about people sinning "unintentionally in any of the holy things of the Lord" (Lev 5:15). This may refer to misuse of any sacred object belonging to the tabernacle, rendering the object unholy. For example, a worshiper might accidentally touch a sacrificial utensil that only priests can touch, or mistakenly take home a portion of sacrificial meat reserved for the altar or for the priest. Centuries after Moses, King Uzziah committed such a sin when he violated the sacred precincts of the temple by going inside the sanctuary to burn an offering of incense—a rite reserved for priests. The king was instantly struck with leprosy, a disease he suffered for the rest of his life (2 Chr 26:16-21).

Other sins requiring reparation include cheating people out of money, lying about a deposit or anything else entrusted to someone, or finding some property that belongs to another, then refusing to acknowledge the rightful ownership. By confessing the sin, paying back the principal and fine, then offering the ram as a sacrifice, the priest is enabled to "make atonement on your behalf before the Lord, and you shall be forgiven" (Lev 6:7).

He [Moses] poured some of the anointing oil on Aaron's head . . . to consecrate him. LEV 8:12

After the tabernacle and priestly garments are completed according to the specifications God has given Moses (Ex 35-40), Aaron and his four sons are ordained as the first priests of Israel. They become the nation's religious leaders, responsible for sacrifices and other sacred rituals established by God. The terms ordination and consecration translate a picturesque Hebrew phrase that literally means "fill your hands." For once inducted into the priesthood, the men fill their hands with sacrifices by raising parts of the offerings to the sky in a symbolic gesture of giving them to the Lord and by carefully arranging the carcass on the altar. As priests, they also have the right to "fill their hands" with specified portions of meat in payment for their services.

The ordination ceremony, described in remarkable detail in Leviticus 8, takes a full seven days. Seven is

Perhaps at an oasis like this, the Israelites camped while Moses ascended Mount Sinai to receive the laws of the covenant from God; they were forbidden to approach the sacred peak under pain of death.

a number used often in Old Testament rituals because it symbolizes completion. It was on the seventh day, of course, that God rested after finishing the work of creation. Moses begins the ceremony by gathering sacrifices he will need and by calling the Israelites to assemble in front of the entrance to the tabernacle. There Moses bathes Aaron and his sons with the sacred water that the priests will later use to wash sacrifices. Then he dresses the men in their priestly uniforms.

Next Moses sprinkles anointing oil on the tabernacle, altar, and all the furnishings—consecrating them as holy and for use only in the service of God. Then Moses pours oil on the head of Aaron, Israel's first high priest. The imagery of this moment is so powerful that a psalmist will later compare something "very good and pleasant" to "the precious oil on the head, running down upon the beard, on the beard of Aaron, running down over the collar of his robes" (Ps 133:1-2).

Climaxing the rituals, Moses offers three sacrifices: first, a bull as a purification offering to cleanse the altar; then a ram as a burnt offering to signify complete surrender to God; and finally a second ram as an offering of well-being, which Aaron and his sons eat in celebration of their ordination. Moses takes some of the blood of this final sacrifice and daubs it on the right earlobes, thumbs, and big toes of each man. Why he does this is uncertain. In similar ancient Near Eastern rituals, people considered themselves protected by the rite of smearing blood on their most vulnerable areas: head, arms, and legs. But the Israelite ritual may have symbolized that the priests are devoted to God, head to toe.

For the rest of the week, Aaron and his sons remain inside the tabernacle, perhaps praying and receiving instructions from Moses. On the eighth day

they emerge from the tabernacle as fully ordained priests who initiate a tradition of sacrificial worship that will endure for more than a millennium—until Rome destroys the temple in A.D. 70, ending the sacrificial system with its accompanying priesthood.

These are the creatures that you may eat. LEV 11:2

God gives Moses a list of the kinds of animals—from land, sea, and sky—that the Israelites may and may not eat. Animals considered ritually clean, and permitted as food, include those that have split hoofs and chew the cud (swallow their food, then bring it back up and chew it a second time). Such animals include cattle, sheep, and goats. Land animals excluded are camels, which chew the cud but do not have cleft hoofs, badgers and hares, which do not have cleft hoofs though they appear to chew the cud, and pigs, which have cleft hoofs but do not chew the cud.

Edible animals from the water must have scales as well as fins. Everything else is excluded from the Israelite menu, including all shellfish such as shrimp, crab, and oyster. Regarding birds, the law identifies only prohibited fowls, such as carrion-eating vultures, hawks, and owls. Among those missing from the list and presumed edible are quail, chickens, and doves. Most insects are considered unclean, and forbidden as food, but not all. The Israelites can eat locusts, grasshoppers, and crickets.

The carcass of any animal is considered unclean—even an animal permitted as food. If Israelites touch it, they instantly become ritually unclean, meaning they cannot enter the tabernacle courtyard to offer sacrifices to God. To remove this ritual defilement, the individuals have to wash not only themselves but their clothing, then wait until evening. At sundown they are again considered ritually clean. The same cleansing procedure holds true for most household utensils or clothes that come into contact with the carcass of an unclean animal, such as a mouse or a lizard. One exception is when the carcass falls into a clay container, which can absorb the impurity; in that case, the container must be destroyed.

God's rationale behind these dietary laws remains a mystery. Some scholars suggest that the rules—still obeyed by many observant Jews—protect Israel from disease. Others speculate that God arbitrarily chooses which animals will be clean and unclean because he is interested primarily in teaching the Israelites to obey him and to understand that even in everyday life there are objects and behavior that are holy and acceptable, and some that are not. Another possible explanation is that these dietary regulations serve as a badge of distinction, in the same way that sabbath observance visibly marks Jewish people as different from others.

In the New Testament, Jesus and the apostles after him declare that God has established a new covenant that renders the dietary laws obsolete. Nothing going into people renders them unclean, Jesus explains. "It

For making an unauthorized offering—"unholy fire before the Lord" (Lev 10:1)—Aaron's sons Nadab and Abihu are consumed by fire rained from heaven; their punishment is depicted in this 15th-century German Bible illustration.

Unblemished rams are brought for sacrifice to God in this detail from the famed ceiling fresco of the Vatican's Sistine Chapel, painted about 1515 by Michelangelo.

is what comes out of a person that defiles. For it is from within, from the human heart, that evil intentions come: fornication, theft, murder, adultery, avarice, wickedness, deceit, licentiousness, envy, slander, pride, folly" (Mk 7:20-22).

If a woman conceives and bears a male child, she shall be ceremonially unclean seven days. LEV 12:2

Awoman is considered ritually unclean for a week after the birth of a son, two weeks after the birth of a daughter, and throughout her menstruation. During this time, she usually stays inside because anything she touches also becomes unclean. If a neighbor accidentally bumps into her, the neighbor has to wash and wait until evening before worshiping God at the tabernacle.

This impurity is caused not by sin, but by the discharge of blood, implying a lack of wholeness that renders a person unfit to approach the sacred tent of God. After the week or two of uncleanness is over, the woman still cannot take part in religious ceremonies for another 33 days if she has given birth to a son or 66 days if she has had a daughter.

The Bible does not explain why a woman is unclean for twice as long if she has a daughter. Some suggest that the extension for daughters is based on the fact that a son was more highly regarded among Israelites as well as other ancient peoples.

When the one-month or two-month purification waiting period has ended, the woman takes two sac-rifices to the tabernacle: a young lamb as a burnt offering and a pigeon or a dove as a purification offering. If she can not afford a lamb, she may use a bird for each of the two offerings. When the priest has sacrificed the animals on her behalf, "she shall be clean" (Lev 12:8).

Joseph and Mary, according to Luke, strictly adhered to the regulations in Leviticus after the birth of Jesus. Their offering of a pair of turtledoves or pigeons revealed their humble status (Lk 2:21-24).

When a person contracts a leprous disease, he shall be brought to the priest. LEV 13:9

Priests do more than sacrifice animals. Another of their jobs is to identify people with skin disease and order the individuals to live in isolation outside the camp until the symptoms disappear. This is a priestly responsibility because chronic skin disorders render a person ritually unclean, and unfit to live in the presence of a holy God or to eat the sacred food of a well-being sacrifice. In addition, this person can render others unclean with a single touch.

The illness that the priest is looking for is not necessarily Hansen's disease, the modern medical term for leprosy. The Hebrew term for "leprous disease" covers a wide range of skin ailments. The many symptoms described in Leviticus 13—"white swelling in the skin," "raw flesh," "itching," "a reddish-white diseased spot"—can fit vitiligo, psoriasis, eczema, and skin cancer, to name a few such disorders.

This shall be an everlasting statute for you, to make atonement for the people of Israel once in the year for all their sins. LEV 16:34

The holiest and most solemn day on the Jewish lunar calendar arrives in late September or early October. It is known as the Day of Atonement, Yom Kippur in Hebrew. No matter what day of the week it falls on, the people stop their work and turn to prayer and fasting, in repentance for the sins of their nation.

On this day, the high priest performs a complex series of rituals to atone for his own sins and those of the nation, as well as to purify the sanctuary and the altar that have been contaminated by these sins.

The rituals start with the priest bathing in the sacred water used to wash sacrifices, then dressing in a plain white tunic and turban. He sacrifices a bull for his own sins and a goat for the sins of the nation. With blood from each animal, he enters the holiest room in the sanctuary—the place where the Israelites keep the ark of the covenant, the symbol of God's earthly throne and presence. There he splashes the blood of the animals on the lid of the ark to ritually cleanse it. Then he returns to the courtyard outside to sprinkle blood on the altar.

Next, in a unique and emotional ritual, he lays both hands on the head of a second goat, known as a scapegoat, symbolically transferring to it the sins of the nation. As the Israelites watch, the animal is led out of the camp and set free deep in the desert, carrying with it the sins of the people.

The New Testament presents Jesus as both high priest and sacrificial offering: a sinless priest who atones for all of humanity, and the ultimate and final sacrifice necessary "to bear the sins of many" (Heb 9:28).

You shall be holy, for I the Lord your God am holy. LEV 19:2

The first 16 chapters of Leviticus deal with matters of special interest to priests: details about sacrifices, ordination of priests, and laws about ritual impurity. Most of the remaining chapters, however, set forth everyday regulations of deep interest to all Israelites: laws about sexual practices, religious holidays, and many other moral and religious issues. These chapters, 17-26, comprise what is some-

times called the Holiness Code, since the main theme is that the Israelites must be holy because God is holy.

For Israel, "holy" does not mean perfect. It means set apart—reserved for God's purposes. Out of all the nations on earth, Israel has been chosen by God to demonstrate who he is and what he is like. The people of Israel maintain their holiness, or unique relationship with God, by complying with the laws he has given them through Moses.

Both the adulterer and the adulteress shall be put to death. LEV 20:10

Chapter 20 identifies many of the same sexual offenses listed in chapter 18, but adds the punishments required to maintain the holiness of Israel. Though the punishments vary according to severity of the infraction, most offenses draw the death penalty. These include incest, adultery, homosexuality, and bestiality (for which the animal is also killed).

The method of execution is not identified, but likely involved stoning or shooting with arrows—methods specified for other capital offenses (Ex 19:13).

Only one sexual offense listed here is deemed offensive enough to require a specific and painful execution. If a man marries a mother and her daughter, all three "shall be burned to death" (Lev 20:14). This is the same punishment the Lord demands when a priest's daughter becomes a prostitute (Lev 21:9). The Bible does not explain why these offenses require such an extreme measure, which denies the offender a speedy death and proper burial. Burning is, however, one of the more radical methods that the Israelites use to eliminate impurity.

For a couple who engages in sex while the woman is menstruating, or a brother and sister who gaze licentiously at each other's nakedness, their punishment is to be "cut off from their people" (Lev 20:18), probably meaning banishment. If a man has sex with his aunt or takes his brother's wife for his own, God will punish them by making them childless.

Because these offenses are intentional, and sacrifices cleanse only unintentional impurities, the Israelites must carry out the appropriate punishment for each in order to maintain holiness within the community.

Moses accepting the Ten Commandments (top) and ordaining his brother Aaron as priest; a 12th-century German stained glass window

No descendant of Aaron the priest who has a blemish shall come near to offer the Lord's offerings. LEV 21:21

Only male descendants of Aaron can serve as priests, but not all of them can meet the rigorous qualifications. Priests have to be as physically whole and free of defect as the animals they offer to God in sacrifice. Aaron's descendants can be disqualified from the priesthood if they are blind, crippled, disfigured in the face or limbs, hunchbacked or dwarfed, have unusual colors or spots in their eyes, have crushed testicles, or suffer from an obvious skin disorder. Though these men are disqualified from offering sacrifices on the altar, they are not banished from the tribe of Levi or forced to make their living in nonpriestly professions. They are able to remain in the service of the tabernacle, performing tasks other than offering sacrifices.

Because priests provide a critical link between God and the Israelites, instructing the people in God's ways, they not only have to meet rigorous physical qualifications, they have to live by higher moral standards. The high priest has to live by the highest criteria of all. Most priests can marry only a virgin or a widow, but no one who has been divorced, a prostitute, or "defiled" (Lev 21:7), perhaps meaning raped or having been a cult prostitute from another religion. The high priest can marry only a virgin.

Another higher standard for the priesthood involves funerals. Because merely coming near a corpse produces ritual uncleanness, which takes a week to purge, most priests are not permitted to attend the funeral of anyone except immediate family members. Even for family, priests cannot express their grief in any ways customary in the ancient Near East: cutting their hair, beards, or skin. This would temporarily disfigure them, leaving them less than whole. The high priest cannot attend the funeral of even close relatives, except possibly his wife.

These lofty standards are intended to preserve the holiness of priests, so the Israelites will respect them as authentic servants of God who are always at their post, willing and able to minister on behalf of anyone who needs them.

Six days shall work be done; but the seventh day is a sabbath of complete rest . . . you shall do no work. LEV 23:3

Each week, from sundown on Friday to sundown on Saturday, the Israelites are to observe the sabbath by resting. On this day their thoughts turn to God who, after creating the heavens and earth in six days, "rested on the seventh day" (Gen 2:2).

In the seventh year there shall be a sabbath of complete rest for the land. LEV 25:4

When the Israelites arrive in Canaan, they are to give the land a rest every seventh year. They cannot plant crops, prune vineyards, or even harvest untended grapes, but they can eat anything

FESTIVALS OF THE LORD

The Jewish calendar *is filled with joyous festivals and holy days as specified in Leviticus 23. Some commemorate God's miraculous intervention on Israel's behalf in years past. Others express the Lord's continuing provision for his chosen people. The annual celebrations, in the order in which they fall, are as follows:*

Passover is celebrated on the 14th day of the first month of the Jewish year, Nisan (roughly equivalent to mid-March to mid-April). It is a remembrance of Israel's liberation from bondage in Egypt after the Lord struck down all of Egypt's firstborn but passed over the Israelites. As Israelites did on that first Passover night, future generations are to kill a lamb and eat it.

Festival of the Unleavened Bread is a weeklong celebration that begins on the 15th of Nisan. Israelites recall their hasty departure from Egypt by not eating bread made with yeast. On the first and last day of the festival they refrain from working.

Festival of the First Fruits celebrates the beginning of the barley and flax harvests; it takes place after the last sabbath of the preceding festival and thus also in March or April. People bring their grain offerings to the tabernacle.

Festival of Weeks, later known as Pentecost (from the Greek word for "fifty" because it comes 50 days after the Festival of the Unleavened Bread), celebrates the wheat harvest in May or June. People offer more grain.

Festival of Trumpets, Rosh Hashanah in Hebrew, is a day of worship, rest, and sacrifices, when trumpets are blown to present the people to God. This takes place on the first day of Tishri (September/October), the most solemn month of the year. After the Exodus, this becomes New Year's Day for the Jews.

Day of Atonement, Yom Kippur in Hebrew, falls on the tenth of Tishri; it is a day of nationwide repentance for sins.

Festival of Booths, or Tabernacles, is a weeklong thanksgiving celebration at the end of harvest, starting on the 15th of Tishri. Future generations are to camp out in huts or tents to recall Israel's years of wandering in the wilderness after the Exodus.

that grows in the wild. This practice not only allows the soil to naturally replenish itself, in a land management technique similar to crop rotation, it reminds the Israelites that the land is not theirs to do with as they please. It belongs to God.

How faithful the Hebrews were in obeying this law is unknown, but evidence from history shows they were observing the sabbatical year a millennium later, during the second-century B.C. Maccabean revolt. Jewish defenders of Beth-zur surrendered to Syrian attackers because the town did not have provisions to withstand a siege "since it was a sabbatical year for the land" (1 Macc 6:49). And according to first-century historian Josephus, Julius Caesar granted tax exemption to Israel during the seventh year, "since they neither take fruit from trees nor do they sow."

Every seventh sabbatical year the Israelites are to blow trumpets on the Day of Atonement and proclaim the following year, the 50th year, a year of jubilee. But celebrating two years in a row—the seventh sabbatical year and the year of jubilee—

In this imposing sculpture made about 1515 for the tomb of Pope Julius II in Rome, Michelangelo has captured the strength and religious fervor of Moses.

proved an economic burden. And thus the religious authorities sought to condense and equate the two years. There is some evidence that a year of jubilee was celebrated in the days of King Hezekiah (727-698 B.C.; Isa 37:30-32) and King Zedekiah (596-586 B.C.; Jer 34:8-22). The end of the Babylonian exile may also have been celebrated by a jubilee (539-538 B.C.; Isa 61:1).

If you follow my statutes . . . I will give you your rains in their season, and the land shall yield its produce.
LEV 26:3-4

Legal codes as well as treaties in the ancient Near East often included blessings for those who followed the rules and curses for those who broke them. The Code of Hammurabi, the earliest known complete set of laws, which governed Babylon several centuries before Moses, concludes with blessings and curses. And the Treaty of Esarhaddon, a Babylonian ruler many centuries after Moses, also contains them. Likewise, the Holiness Code of Leviticus ends with blessings and curses that urge the Israelites not to break their covenant with God.

If Israel remains faithful, God promises to send four blessings: rain when it is needed, peace, fertility in families and fields, and his presence: "I will walk among you, and will be your God, and you shall be my people" (Lev 26:12).

If, however, Israel starts ignoring its covenant obligations, God warns that the nation will face a series of five curses that escalate in severity. If the first-tier punishment does not convince Israel to return to covenant loyalty, God will resort to the next level of reproof—and so on up. The five curses are a plague of terror, fever, and wasting away; drought; an onslaught of wild animals; defeat in war, followed by lethal disease and famine; then near annihilation and exile: "You I will scatter among the nations, and I will unsheathe the sword against you; your land shall be a desolation, and your cities a waste" (Lev 26:33).

Mercifully, God does not stop here. If the exiled survivors confess their sins, God says he will remember his covenant with Abraham, Isaac, and Jacob. After the land has enjoyed an extended sabbath rest, God will bring his people home.

In the centuries that follow, the Jews abandon the covenant time and time again, and for their transgressions, they suffer a string of disasters including drought and multiple invasions and defeats. Then in 586 B.C., Babylon destroys all that remains of the Jewish nation and forces most of the survivors into exile. But even then, the Lord does not abandon his chosen people. About 50 years later, after Persia conquers Babylon and frees the captives held there, the first group of Jews returns home to repair the walls of Jerusalem, rebuild the temple, and restore the nation. God has kept his promise: "I will not spurn them, or abhor them so as to destroy them utterly and break my covenant with them; for I am the Lord their God" (Lev 26:44).

For 40 years the Israelites linger in the desert—mostly near the oasis of Kadesh-barnea on the southern border of Canaan. The book of Numbers tells what happens during those years, from the time Moses and his generation leave Mount Sinai until the next generation arrives on the eastern banks of the Jordan River, ready to claim the promised land.

The English title of the book comes from the numbering, or census, of each generation. God first orders a counting of all able-bodied men as the Israelites prepare to break camp at Mount Sinai. A generation later, when Israel is on the verge of invading the land of Canaan, God orders a second census. The Hebrew title of the book, however, is Bemidbar, "In the Wilderness," since this is where the dramatic stories unfold.

Numbers can be divided into three main sections. The first takes place at Mount Sinai, where God organizes the Israelites for their march into Canaan (Num 1:1-10:10). The second takes place in the desert south of Canaan, after God condemns the people to roam there for 40 years (Num 10:11-21:35). God metes out this stern sentence after Israel refuses to trust him enough to proceed with the invasion; the Israelites had become terrified when their spies returned from Canaan and reported the land to be full of walled cities and huge people. The third part takes place on the plains of Moab, as a younger and braver generation prepares to follow Joshua across the Jordan River (Num 22:1-36:13).

Numbers is the fourth book in the five-volume history of Israel's birth as a nation. These five books, Genesis through Deuteronomy, are traditionally attributed to Moses, though clues in the text suggest that other writers and editors also contributed. For example, it would have been out of character for Moses to pen words such as these: "Moses was very humble, more so than anyone else on the face of the earth" (Num 12:3). Yet some of the material is quite ancient and possibly dates from the days of Moses.

The Israelite spies returning with grapes from Canaan; one of a series of enamel on gilded copper plaques made in the late 12th century for an Austrian monastery

---

Take a census of the whole congregation of Israelites, in their clans, by ancestral houses, according to the number of names, every male individually. NUM 1:2

The Israelites have been camping at the base of Mount Sinai for nearly a year, receiving the laws recorded in Exodus and Leviticus. Now God decides it is time for them to march to Canaan. In what amounts to a military roll call, the Lord orders a census of all men age 20 and up who are able to fight in battle. This census excludes men from the tribe of Levi, who are responsible for maintaining the tabernacle and the nation's system of worship. To keep the number of tribes at 12, Joseph's two sons—Ephraim and Manasseh—are each counted as a separate tribe.

The census produces staggering results. It reveals there are more than 600,000 fighting men. Since the encampment also includes wives, children, and the elderly, the entire Israelite population would be more than 2 million. Most scholars say this is an unrealistic number. They argue that the desert could not have sustained that many people, nor could the Canaanite city-states, with an estimated population of only 200,000, have resisted them. Yet southern Canaanite forces initially repel the invaders.

Various theories attempt to solve the mystery of the huge numbers. Some experts in Hebrew linguistics say that "thousand" can also mean "group." In that case, the Israelites would have numbered 600 extended families, or clans, totaling perhaps 20,000. Others suggest that scribes who later preserved the numbers on new scrolls got confused by various categories and merged the numbers. For example, they might not have realized the difference between trained warriors and untrained militia. So they could have interpreted 45 warriors or officers in Reuben's family as units of thousands, then added them to 1,500 untrained militia. The result: 46,500 when the actual number may have been a mere 1,545.

Whatever the Israelite population, it had become large enough in Egypt that a troubled Pharaoh once observed, "Look, the Israelite people are more numerous and more powerful than we" (Ex 1:9). And as they reached the east bank of the Jordan River, a Moabite king described them as a "horde" that has "spread over the face of the earth" (Num 22:4, 5).

The Israelites shall camp each in their respective regiments, under ensigns by their ancestral houses. NUM 2:2

God tells Moses how to set up camp. In the center is the tent tabernacle, with its single entrance always facing east, toward the rising sun. Priests and the remainder of the Israelites camp around the tabernacle, much like Egyptian commanders and their soldiers around the king's tent, and like pilgrims around a shrine during sacred festivals.

In the Israelite camp, every tribe knows exactly where to set up its tents. Priests and other tabernacle workers camp just outside the shrine. Beyond this ring of tents are those of the 12 tribes—all facing the tabernacle. Each tribe has its own flag, perhaps with a motto reflecting the tribal blessing in Genesis 49 and the color of the jewel representing the tribe on the priest's breastplate.

Camped in the position of greatest honor, along the eastern entrance to the tabernacle, are the three tribes of Judah, Issachar, and Zebulun. It is from the tribe of Judah, one of Jacob's sons with Leah, that David and Jesus both descend. Across the camp, west of the tabernacle, are the tribes from Jacob's sons with Rachel, Ephraim and Manasseh (Joseph's two sons), along with Benjamin. North of the tabernacle are Dan, Asher, and Naphtali. To the south are the final three tribes, Reuben, Simeon, and Gad.

If any man's wife goes astray and is unfaithful to him . . . then the man shall bring his wife to the priest. NUM 5:12, 15

Before breaking camp at Mount Sinai, God gives Moses some additional laws. Among these are harsh instructions for dealing with women suspected of adultery. The regulations focus only on women because a wife's infidelity—if it leads to the birth of a son—could bring an inheritance into question, with another man's offspring gaining the husband's property.

The law requires that if a husband suspects his wife of infidelity, he is to bring her to the priest at the tabernacle. In the sacred precincts, the woman endures a trial by ordeal. The priest dishevels her hair, typically a mourning ritual that may symbolize the anguish of the occasion. Then he prepares a drink made from holy water used in sacrificial rites mixed with dust from the sanctuary floor. This dust apparently signifies the holiness of God, who dwells in the tabernacle—holiness being incompatible with sin. The woman takes an oath that if she is guilty of adultery, the drink will make her sick. If she is not guilty, it is believed that she will be unaffected.

When either men or women make a special vow, the vow of a nazirite . . . they shall separate themselves from wine and strong drink. NUM 6:2-3

Some Israelites take an extraordinary vow of devotion to God to express their gratitude to him or to seek his help. Ancient Jewish writings indicate that the vow can last for as few as 30 days or it can endure for a lifetime. The parents of Samson, Samuel, and John the Baptist invoked this vow on behalf of their unborn sons, thereby dedicating the children to a lifetime of service to God. By taking the vow of a nazirite (from a Hebrew word meaning "consecrated one"), people make three promises that place them or their child on a plane of holiness comparable to the one held by priests.

First, the vow requires abstinence from fermented beverages and from eating any grape products. It is uncertain why the vow forbids all grape products, including raisins. Perhaps this is meant as a protest against pagan religions that offered raisin cakes and grape juice as food for the gods.

Second, the vow requires avoidance of any contact whatsoever with a corpse—including that of an im-

The prescribed order of encampment of Israel's 12 tribes around the enclosed tent worship center gives the place of honor east of the entrance to Zebulun, Judah, and Issachar.

mediate family member. For nazirites, even accidental contact with a dead person renders the vow invalid. If a person dies unexpectedly in their presence, for example, the vow must be renewed after a week of purification rituals.

Finally, those who take the nazirite vow shave their heads, then leave their hair uncut for the duration of the vow. Long hair becomes the distinguishing mark of a nazirite. When the period of the vow ends, the devotee cuts the hair and burns it on the tabernacle altar. Hair offerings were common in other ancient religions, since many believed that hair—much like blood—was a living part of a person and that it mystically contained some of the person's essence. In this sense, it qualified at least partially as a human sacrifice. But the Israelites probably think of the burned hair quite differently. They likely consider the altar's fire as an appropriate way to dispose of something consecrated to God, so it cannot be defiled.

The practice of nazirite vows apparently continued throughout Jewish history, until Romans destroyed the temple in A.D. 70. The apostle Paul was under a vow during his missionary travels (Acts 18:18).

The Lord bless you and keep you; the Lord make his face to shine upon you, and be gracious to you. NUM 6:24-25

Priests not only conduct sacrifices, they bless the people. The Israelites, like people in other ancient cultures, believed that spoken blessings release power that improves a person's future. Perhaps the most familiar blessing in the Bible is the beautiful prayer that God tells Aaron and his sons to use; it is a prayer that will serve as a benediction for worship services throughout Jewish history.

The wording is quite ancient, and three times employs the Israelite name for God: Yahweh, translated as "the Lord." Aaron asks that God turn his face and lift up his countenance toward the people—expressions that invite God to show his concern and love for Israel. Aaron also prays that God grant the people "peace" (Num 6:26), using the Hebrew word *shalom*. This is a broad term that means far more than protection from war. Shalom means well-being in every area of life, physical and spiritual. It means peace with others, with oneself, and with God.

Take the Levites from among the Israelites and cleanse them. NUM 8:5

Earlier in the story of the Exodus, when Moses comes down from Mount Sinai and catches many of the people worshiping a golden calf, he cries out, asking who is on God's side. His own extended family—the tribe of Levi—answers the call, and in so doing dedicate themselves and their descendants to God's service. The Lord appoints Aaron and his sons as priests, then chooses the Levites from other families in the tribe to serve as their assistants.

Before leaving Mount Sinai, God tells Moses to consecrate and purify the Levites for the sacred du-

CODE OF HAMMURABI

Topping the black basalt stele preserving his famous law code is this scene of Babylon's Hammurabi standing before the sun god Shamesh.

Several hundred years before Moses presented Israel with a pair of stone tablets inscribed with the Ten Commandments—the foundation for some 600 more explicit laws he received from God later—a Babylonian king engraved his laws on an eight-foot stele (above). The monarch, Hammurabi (c.1792-1750 B.C.), believed his ordinances would bring "justice to the land."

The oldest known complete set of laws, the Code of Hammurabi covers a wide range of criminal and civil cases, including adoption, property rights, and damages for personal injury. Some of the Babylonian laws are quite similar to Israelite statutes. If an upper-class man destroyed the eye of another aristocrat, he lost his eye—echoed in "eye for eye, tooth for tooth" (Ex 21:24). But Hammurabi's code stipulated only a financial penalty for destroying the eye of an ordinary citizen. The Mosaic Law is not only more egalitarian but also more compassionate. The son of a guilty Babylonian could be executed for his father's crimes; Israelite children could not (Deut. 24:16). Perhaps the most important distinction between the two sets of laws lies in the issues tackled. Hammurabi's code deals only with secular problems; Israelite law covers both secular and religious realms, showing that God rules both.

God in a pillar of light guides the Israelites on their journey through the awesome wilderness to the promised land; a detail from a painting by William West (1801-1861).

ties they will perform. These honored men, ages 25 to 50, purify themselves by shaving all the hair from their bodies and washing their clothes. The Israelite masses lay their hands on the selected men, symbolizing that the Levites will take the place of the nation's firstborn sons, who were previously the ones designated to serve the Lord.

The main duty of the Levites is to care for the tabernacle and all its equipment. They disassemble the sacred shrine when it comes time to break camp. Then they load it onto wagons and carry it through the desert. Whenever the Levites reassemble and pitch the sacred tent, they form a human buffer between the people and the holiness of the tabernacle.

In this way, they guard the shrine from being defiled by outsiders and by any ritually unclean Israelites. In other religions of the day, images of protector gods were placed at the temple entrances to ward off demons. Israelites, however, are concerned about humans who may desecrate the sacred precincts and provoke the wrath of God upon the entire nation.

The Israelites set out by stages from the wilderness of Sinai. NUM 10:12

Eleven months after the Israelites arrive at Mount Sinai, and 19 days after they take a census of their able-bodied men, the cloud of God's presence lifts from the tabernacle, and the people rise to follow it toward Canaan. The distance is probably about 300 miles, and should have taken even a huge group of refugees no more than three or four months.

A group of Levites leads the march, carrying the ark of the covenant, which represents the earthly throne of God. The 12 tribes follow in four divisions of three tribes each. They are arranged in the order that they camp around the tabernacle. The three tribes that camp east of the tabernacle form the first division, led by Judah. Next comes a group of Levites carrying the disassembled tabernacle. Following them are three more tribes led by Reuben, then another group of Levites carrying the tabernacle furnishings, and yet another division of tribes led by Ephraim. Serving as a rear guard is the final division of three tribes, led by Dan. This arrangement protects the tabernacle from raiders, and gives the Levites carrying the tent some time to assemble it in the camp before the furnishings arrive.

As the ark sets out on the first day's march, and on every march thereafter, Moses recites a prayer expressing his confidence that God travels ahead of the people: "Arise, O Lord, let your enemies be scattered, and your foes flee before you" (Num 10:35).

The first leg of the march requires three days, followed by at least two more stops before the Israelites arrive for an extended stay at Kadesh-barnea in the wilderness of Paran in northeastern Sinai.

The Lord said to Moses, "Gather for me seventy of the elders of Israel . . . . they shall bear the burden of the people along with you." NUM 11:16-17

As the journey begins, the Israelites start complaining about their hardships, especially the lack of food. Moses, who has led this rebellious and complaining mass of people for over a year, becomes utterly frustrated. "I am not able to carry all this people alone, for they are too heavy for me," he tells God. "If this is the way you are going to treat me, put me to death at once" (Num 11:14-15).

God instructs Moses to select 70 tribal leaders to help him. How these men will help is not stated. But during the Exodus, tribal elders administer justice, lead military units, and direct work crews. When the 70 gather for their first meeting, God gives them some of the same spirit he has given Moses. In response, the men suddenly begin prophesying. Their outburst of prophecy is a one-time event to confirm for them and the Israelites that God has accepted them as helpers of Moses.

A wind went out from the Lord, and it brought quails from the sea and let them fall beside the camp. NUM 11:31

Among the various complaints of the people is that they are tired of manna, a white flaky substance that falls with the dew and tastes like wafers made with honey. The people crave meat.

God becomes angry at their ingratitude and vows that they will eat meat "until it comes out of your nostrils and becomes loathsome to you" (Num 11:20). "Loathsome" is the translation of a Hebrew word that appears only here. In the context, it suggests violent vomiting.

Wind pushes inland a massive flock of migrating quail—small, plump birds excellent for eating. Quail are not strong fliers, unable to cover long distances without a tail wind. If the wind decreases or blows against them, they are forced to land and spend a day or more regaining their strength. As they recuperate, they are easy prey. In ancient times, Egyptians would snatch them up and dry them in the sun or pickle them in clay pots to eat throughout the year.

Exhausted quail descend on the Israelites, covering the landscape for miles around. The Israelites scramble to harvest the birds, working furiously all day, all night, then all the next day. They collect enough quail for each person to have at least six bushels. What the Israelites cannot eat right away, they dry to eat later as quail jerky.

Miriam and Aaron spoke against Moses because of the Cushite woman whom he had married. NUM 12:1

Complaining among the Israelites is not limited to the rank and file. A power struggle erupts in the family of Moses when his older sister and brother, Miriam and Aaron, decide that Moses made a mistake by marrying a Cushite. The woman is probably Zipporah the Midianite. Though Cush often refers to Ethiopia, it also identifies a place in northern Arabia, and is used synonymously with Midian (Hab 3:7).

Miriam, a prophetess, and Aaron, the high priest, add to their complaint that God does not speak exclusively through Moses; he speaks through them as well. The Lord hears this and immediately calls the three together. Appearing in a pillar of cloud, God reminds Miriam and Aaron that he speaks through them and through other prophets only in visions and dreams. "Not so with my servant Moses . . ." God says. "With him I speak face-to-face" (Num 12:7-8). The phrase "face to face" more literally means "mouth to mouth," implying that God speaks directly to Moses instead of using an intermediary or appearing during a vision.

When the cloud of God's presence leaves, Miriam's skin turns leprous white. She recovers only after living outside the camp for a week. The Bible does not say why Aaron escapes punishment. Perhaps Miriam instigated the power struggle.

"Send men to spy out the land of Canaan, which I am giving to the Israelites." NUM 13:2

During harvesttime late in the summer, the Israelites arrive at Kadesh-barnea on the southern border of Canaan. Here, they set up camp. Moses selects one leader from each of the 12 tribes to form a scouting party. Their assignment is to reconnoiter the land of Canaan and bring back information about the people living there and the defenses of their cities.

When the scouts return, 40 days later, only two of them recommend invasion: Caleb and Joshua. The other ten agree that the land is fertile, but argue that many cities are fortified and the people "are of great size. . . . to ourselves we seemed like grasshoppers, and so we seemed to them" (Num 13:32-33).

Fear grips the Israelites, and they refuse to go any farther. God is furious that in spite of all that the Israelites have seen him do for them, they still do not trust him. He sentences the entire nation of adults, ages 20 and older, to spend 40 years in the wilderness—one year for each day of the scouts' mission. Among this generation, God rules, only Caleb and Joshua will live to reach the promised land.

Bearing a huge cluster of grapes like those still grown in Israel (inset), the spies turn back from Canaan's fortified cities in this scene by Julius Schnorr von Carolsfeld (1794-1872).

The Israelites are devastated. Again they take matters into their own hands, ignoring Moses' warning not to invade. A coalition of Canaanites and nomadic Amalekites from the desert in south Canaan easily repel the invaders and chase them back across the border into the wilderness.

The earth opened its mouth and swallowed them up . . . everyone who belonged to Korah and all their goods.
NUM 16:32

As harsh reality settles in on the Israelites and they realize they will never see the promised land, discontentment with Moses and Aaron intensifies, erupting into a verbal confrontation. In a narrative that evidently melds two separate traditions, three men challenge their authority. Korah, a Levite and member of the same tribe as that of Moses and Aaron, seems to want the Levites to do more than assist the priests. Joining Korah are two descendants of Reuben, the oldest of Jacob's 12 sons. The Reubenites may feel that their tribe should be the dominant one—not the tribe of Judah, descended from Jacob's fourth son.

Together, the three malcontents gather a following of 250 respected Israelites, then en masse take their complaints directly to Moses and Aaron. Korah demands to know why the two brothers exalt themselves as leaders since "all the congregation are holy" (Num 16:3). The Reubenites charge that Moses has not honored his promise to bring the Israelites into "a land flowing with milk and honey" (Num 16:14).

God punishes the rebels in a horrifying spectacle. The ground opens, the leaders and their entire families fall in, and the ground closes. The remaining 250 men are consumed by fire, perhaps lightning. Remarkably, the Israelites verbally assault Moses and Aaron on the very next day, accusing them of killing "the people of the Lord" (Num 16:41). Again, God's punishment is swift and terrifying. Thousands die as a plague strikes the camp.

To settle the matter of who should be the rightful leader of worship, Moses asks the tribal chiefs to give him their staffs, with names inscribed. Moses places these 12 staffs in the sacred tent, along with Aaron's staff. By the next morning, only Aaron's staff has produced blossoms and ripe almonds. Moses orders the staff kept with the ark of the covenant, "as a warning to rebels" (Num 17:10).

Assemble the congregation . . . and command the rock before their eyes to yield its water. NUM 20:8

At the end of Israel's 40 years in the wilderness, the people are still camped at the oasis of Kadesh-barnea, where Miriam dies and is buried. The water that feeds the oasis has dried up, and the new generation of Israelites are engaging in a custom that their parents had established and perfected: "The people quarreled with Moses" (Num 20:3). The new generation insists on knowing why Moses brought them out of Egypt, to die in such a wretched place.

As usual, Moses takes the criticism to God, who instructs him to assemble the people and command a rock to release its water. With Aaron standing beside him, an enraged Moses rebukes the entire congregation: "Listen, you rebels, shall we bring water for you out of this rock?" (Num 20:10). He strikes the rock twice with his staff, and water bursts out.

In the process of performing this miracle, however, Moses and Aaron do something terribly wrong. The Bible does not say exactly what it is—only that it shows disrespect for God's holiness. Perhaps the two sinned in the way they expressed their anger or in not giving God credit for the miracle. As punishment, neither Moses nor Aaron will lead the Israelites into the land of promise.

The two, however, will at least get the nation headed on a course toward the invasion, from east of the Jordan River. The most direct route to the site

Parched Israelites lap at the water flowing from the rock Moses has struck; a wall painting from Florence's Palazzo Vecchio.

is through Edom, a land inhabited by descendants of Jacob's twin brother Esau. Moses asks for permission to pass through peacefully, but the Edomites deny the request and send soldiers to guard the border. Rather than fight distant relatives, Moses turns the Israelites south, on a long and treacherous bypass around Edom. Somewhere along the way, on a hilltop near the border of Edom, Aaron dies. The nation pauses for 30 days of mourning, and Aaron's son Eleazar replaces him as high priest.

The Lord sent poisonous serpents among the people, and they bit the people, so that many Israelites died. NUM 21:6

As the people trek through the rugged wasteland south of the Dead Sea, they complain one last time, in an unusually bitter attack on both God and Moses. "There is no food and no water," they grumble, "and we detest this miserable food" (Num 21:5), referring to the manna the Lord continues to provide each day.

God unleashes a plague of poisonous snakes, more literally translated "fiery snakes," perhaps an indication of the searing pain that their venomous bite produces. Many Israelites die before the people come to Moses, repent, and plead with him to ask God to remove the snakes. God instructs Moses to make a bronze image of a snake and to set it on a pole: "Everyone who is bitten shall look at it and live" (Num 21:8). The bronze snake that Moses created may have been preserved and kept at the temple in Jerusalem, for it later became an object of worship among the Jews. King Hezekiah eventually destroyed the image (2 Kgs 18:4).

Jesus, referring to his crucifixion, compares himself to the healing image of the snake: "Just as Moses lifted up the serpent in the wilderness, so must the Son of Man be lifted up, that whoever believes in him may have eternal life" (Jn 3:14-15).

"God said to Balaam,". . . you shall not curse the people, for they are blessed." NUM 22:12

Bypassing Edom, Moses and the Israelites turn north, into what is now Jordan. They defeat armies sent to intercept them, and quickly capture much of the land immediately east of the Jordan River—as far north as the Sea of Galilee. The king of Moab, a nation east of the Dead Sea, sends for Balaam, a famous seer who lives near the Euphrates River in northern Mesopotamia. The king wants to hire Balaam to curse the Israelite invaders. The ancients believed that just as a spoken blessing can release positive power that improves the future of an individual or a nation, a curse could release negative power that causes harm to the target.

To relieve the curse of poisonous snakebites, the Lord instructs Moses to erect a bronze serpent; a painting by Peter Paul Rubens (1577-1640).

Though offered a rich fee, Balaam initially refuses because of a warning from God. But after a second invitation from the Moabites, Balaam receives God's approval of the mission—told, however, to speak only the words that he receives from the Lord. As further warning, God sends an angel with a drawn sword to block Balaam's path. Only Balaam's donkey can see the angel. The irony is clear: God permits a beast to see what a seer cannot. When his donkey halts, Balaam strikes it. God then allows the animal to speak and Balaam to see the angel, who again warns the seer to proclaim only the words of God.

When Balaam arrives in Moab and it comes time to speak the curse, he shocks the Moabite king by blessing Israel and cursing Moab.

The people began to have sexual relations with the women of Moab . . . and bowed down to their gods. NUM 25:1-2

While camped at Shittim, a Moabite city opposite Jericho, many Israelite men accept the invitation of local women to engage in sexual rites and eat sacrificial meals in honor of the Canaanite rain god Baal, who is believed to provide fertility in field, flock, and family.

God responds by sending a plague that kills thousands of Israelites. At the Lord's command, Moses or-

*Visible only to Balaam's donkey, an angel of the Lord halts the journey
of the Mesopotamian seer who has been summoned by the king of Moab to curse the
invading Israelites; Hans Bol set the scene in his own 16th-century Netherlands.*

ders the immediate execution of all tribal leaders who have taken part in the orgy. Yet in blatant defiance, a household leader from the tribe of Simeon marches a Midianite woman right past Moses and into his own tent. Phinehas, son of the high priest Eleazar and grandson of Aaron, grabs a spear and follows. With a single thrust, he stabs them both. In recognition of this act of zeal, God lifts the plague.

The daughters of Zelophehad came forward. . . . and they said, "Our father died in the wilderness . . . . Give to us a possession among our father's brothers." NUM 27:1-4

The time is approaching for Israel to claim the land of promise. So Moses orders a census of the new generation to determine its strength and to help assign land. Despite the hardships, plagues, and battles that the people have endured over the past 40 years, their numbers remain surprisingly stable. The tally shows 601,730 able-bodied men ages 20 and older, compared with 603,550 in the first census. Simeon's tribe has suffered the greatest loss, cut to nearly one-third of its previous size. But the tribe of Judah, leader among the 12 tribes, has grown.

In preparing to divide up the land, Moses establishes a system that will preserve the tribal bound-aries. Keeping the land in the tribe starts with keeping it in the family. For this reason, a father passes his land on to his sons, not to his daughters. For if a daughter marries outside the tribe, any land she has will become the property of her husband.

The five daughters of Zelophehad, an Israelite who died in the wilderness and who produced no sons, complain. Moses takes the matter to God, who establishes the right of women to inherit property. The only restriction is that the women marry within their own tribe. In accordance with this decree, Zelophehad's daughters marry their cousins.

The Lord said to Moses, "Take Joshua . . . have him stand before Eleazar the priest and all the congregation, and commission him in their sight." NUM 27:18-19

God invites Moses to climb a mountain and gaze across the Jordan River into Canaan. He reminds the elderly lawgiver that he cannot ford the Jordan with the Israelites because of the sin he committed earlier. So Moses asks God to give Israel a new leader "so that the congregation of the Lord may not be like sheep without a shepherd" (Num 27:17).

Affirming that "the spirit" is in Joshua, the Lord instructs Moses to give Joshua some authority so the people will begin obeying him. Moses complies in a public ceremony by ritually laying hands on Joshua, designating him as heir. Eleazar confirms the choice by consulting with the Urim and Thummim, dice-like objects that give "yes" or "no" answers to questions. From this point on, Joshua serves as Israel's military commander in the conquest of Canaan.

Moses said to the people, "Arm some of your number for the war, so that they may go against Midian." NUM 31:3

In one of his last acts, Moses declares war on the Midianites for their role in the apostasy that took place at Shittim in Moab. The story of the battle is an ancient one, evidenced by the fact that there is no mention of Midian's camel calvary, which becomes a formidable weapon during the time of the judges. A force of a thousand conscripts from each tribe easily defeats the Midianites, slaughtering five kings and all the males and taking the women and children as captives and their livestock as booty. Another victim of the massacre is Balaam, killed for the role he had played in instigating the women of Moab and Midian to seduce and corrupt the men of Israel.

With the defeat of Midian, the Transjordan is firmly in control of the Israelites. The tribes of Reuben and Gad realize that this area is prime grazing territory for their large flocks and ask for permission to settle there. Moses allows them and half of Manasseh to claim the eastern land—as long as they help the other nine and a half tribes capture Canaan.

This shall be your land with its boundaries. NUM 34:12

At God's command, Moses identifies the geographical boundaries of what will become the nation of Israel. Moses does this by citing carefully designated landmarks then familiar to the people, though some are now a mystery.

The southern boundary plunges as deep as Kadesh-barnea, the oasis where the Israelites spent so many years. The Mediterranean, or Great Sea, marks the western boundary. To the north, Israel's boundary extends well beyond the Sea of Galilee—apparently even farther north and east than Damascus. The eastern boundary follows the Jordan River to the Dead Sea, but does not include the Transjordanian lands already claimed by three of the tribes.

Moses orders the Levites not to cluster themselves into a single tribal region. Instead, these priests and their assistants are to scatter themselves among 48 towns throughout the nation. The land outside these towns will serve as pastures for their livestock as well as gardens. Six of these towns will be designated as cities of refuge—places where people accused of manslaughter can escape from vengeance-seeking relatives of the dead person and receive a trial. Well-spaced throughout the land, three of these cities are to be located in Canaan and three more east of the Jordan. An Israelite living in the allotted territory will be within about a day's journey of protection.

THE HUMBLE DONKEY

About a thousand years before camels were tamed, the donkey began serving humans. The animal's surefooted brawn relegated it to hard and tedious labor. It hauled sacks bulging with grain, pulled plows and carts, and turned millstones to crush olives into oil and loosen grain kernels.

Because donkeys are more comfortable to ride than camels and easier to mount than horses, they were favored for transportation. Some of the Bible's most memorable scenes involve people riding donkeys—for example, Balaam's remarkable talking beast. Mounted on a donkey, Abigail met her future husband, David. And Solomon rode on a donkey to his coronation. Though the Bible does not say that Joseph and his pregnant wife Mary rode a donkey to Bethlehem or on their later escape to Egypt with the infant Jesus, they are usually so depicted.

The Bible's most famous scene with a donkey is of Jesus riding one into Jerusalem—to fulfill Zechariah's prophecy of the messianic king's arrival. Mounted on horses in wartime, kings preferred donkeys in peace—which makes Jesus' humble mount the perfect symbol for the heavenly king who promised, "Peace I leave with you; my peace I give to you" (Jn 14:27).

In this 12th-century English Bible illumination, the Joshua chosen by God to lead the Israelites to victory in Canaan is depicted as a knight of that era's Crusades.

DEUTERONOMY

On the border of Canaan Moses reviews the law he had received from God on Mount Sinai; shown here in a 15th-century Bible.

The Israelites pitch camp near the eastern banks of the Jordan River, and await orders to ford the stream and begin the conquest of Canaan. Moses does not join them; he will die outside the promised land. But before he does, he gathers the people and speaks to them for one last time. His words, preserved in the book of Deuteronomy, remind the people of the great miracles God has done for them. Moses also reviews many of the laws God has given, and he pleads with the Israelites to obey—or suffer the tragic consequence of losing the land.

Because Moses repeats many of the laws, including the Ten Commandments, this book became known as Deuteronomy, from a Greek phrase meaning "repeated law" or "second law." In the Hebrew Bible, however, it is called Debarim, "Words," abbreviated from the opening phrase of the book: "These are the words that Moses spoke."

Deuteronomy, last of the five books traditionally attributed to Moses, is written in the distinctive and lofty style of an authoritative yet warm speech, much like the instructions of contemporary Egyptian rulers to their successors. In his last words, Moses urges the Israelites to worship one God, live in one land as one specially chosen people, and worship at one sanctuary rather than follow the Canaanite custom of worshiping at hilltop altars throughout their homeland.

The writing style is quite different from that of the other four books of Moses. This, and the message that emphasizes the horrors that will afflict Israel if the people disobey God, has led scholars to conclude that the book was compiled and edited by historians interested in tracing the emergence and fall of Israel. Their work is called the Deuteronomic History: the books of Deuteronomy, Joshua, Judges, 1 and 2 Samuel, and 1 and 2 Kings. Though some of Deuteronomy may come from Moses, as the text frequently claims, much comes from other sources. Another writer, for example, added the final paragraph about the death of Moses. Also, the text repeats the phrase "to this day," referring to a time after Moses.

Deuteronomy has enjoyed special reverence among both Jews and Christians through the centuries. Because the book is a thorough summary of the covenant relationship between God and Israel, rabbis called the book "five-fifths of the law." The New Testament quotes the book frequently, most notably when Jesus identifies the greatest commandment: "You shall love the Lord your God with all your heart, and with all your soul, and with all your mind" (Mt 22:37, quoting Deut 6:5).

The Lord our God spoke to us at Horeb, saying, "You have stayed long enough at this mountain. Resume your journey." DEUT 1:6-7

Forty years after the Israelites begin the Exodus, they arrive at a plain near the eastern banks of the Jordan River. Here they secure the territory and set up camp. This will become their staging area for the invasion of Canaan. It will also become the site of perhaps the most important speech in the history of the Jewish people: the final words of Moses, addressing the assembled masses.

Most of the generation of Israelites who witnessed the miracles of the Exodus and who received the covenant laws at Mount Sinai have died during the long desert trek. Now, as the next generation stands on the verge of claiming the inheritance God has promised the descendants of Abraham, Moses reviews what the earlier generation experienced—starting with their departure from Mount Sinai at the Lord's command.

In the first three chapters of Deuteronomy, Moses tells of reaching the southern perimeter of Canaan and of sending scouts to explore the land. He relates the report that the men brought back, the people's fear and unwillingness to invade, and God's sentencing the entire nation to wander 40 years in the desert. Moses then reminds the people that after they served their time, God brought them into the Trans-jordan. En route to the staging area for their invasion, they have enjoyed astonishing victories over defenders who refused to grant them peaceful passage through the land. Moses explains that these victories, east of the Jordan River and stretching from the Dead Sea in the south to the Sea of Galilee in the north, confirm that God is already doing in the Transjordan what he will also do for them in Canaan.

So now, Israel, give heed to the statutes and ordinances that I am teaching you to observe, so that you may live to enter and occupy the land that the Lord, the God of your ancestors, is giving you. DEUT 4:1

Before reviewing the laws God gave the Israelites at Mount Sinai, Moses stresses the importance of heeding them. If the people obey, they will win the promised land. If they disobey, it is implied, they will suffer the fate of their parents—to die without ever reaching their promised homeland.

Moses reminds this new generation of a recent event confirming that God punishes disobedience. A devastating plague struck the Israelites and killed thousands after some of the people accepted the invitation of Midianite and Moabite women at Shittim opposite Jericho to engage in an orgy of sexual rites and sacrificial meals in honor of the Canaanite fertility god Baal.

On the other hand, compliance with God's laws will draw favorable attention from other nations, who will declare Israel a wise and discerning people. More important, the Israelites will retain God's favor and as a result will receive so many blessings that they will gratefully proclaim, "What other great nation has a god so near to it as the Lord our God is whenever we call to him?" (Deut 4:7).

I am the Lord your God, who brought you out of the land of Egypt . . . you shall have no other gods before me. DEUT 5:6-7

Moses reminds the Israelites of the awesome and terrifying day at Mount Sinai, also called Horeb, when God spoke in a thundering voice that all could hear: "You approached and stood at the foot of the mountain while the mountain was blazing up to the very heavens, shrouded in dark clouds. Then the Lord spoke to you out of the fire. You heard the sound of words but saw no form; there was only a voice" (Deut 4:11-12). Thus, God delivered the Ten Commandments—the spiritual and moral bedrock on which all Jewish laws are built.

The first three commandments deal with humanity's relationship to God: Worship God alone, make no idols, and treat God's name with respect. The rule about idols prohibits the Israelites from making images of any deity, including God. This rule distinguished Judaism from most ancient religions, which commonly portrayed their gods in animal or human form. The law regarding God's name orders the Israelites not to use his sacred name in any irreverent way, such as swearing a dishonest oath, conjuring dead spirits, or performing magic.

The remaining seven commandments involve more practical issues of daily living, especially relationships with other people: Do not work on the sabbath, honor your parents, do not murder, commit adultery, steal, lie, or crave what belongs to someone else. The commandment that most clearly distinguished Israelites from other peoples is the law that prohibits working from sunset on Friday through sunset on Saturday. People of other faiths could most easily identify an Israelite by watching what he did—or did not do—during those 24 hours.

Violations of the Ten Commandments, from left to right and top to bottom, are portrayed in this wall painting by Lucas Cranach (1472-1553); the artist linked his patrons' coats of arms with an arch superimposed over the graphic scenes.

By the time God finishes speaking, the Israelites are so terrified by their dramatic encounter with the Deity that they plead with Moses to serve as their intermediary, to receive and deliver the rest of God's laws. It is a request that God grants.

Hear, O Israel: The Lord is our God, the Lord alone. You shall love the Lord your God with all your heart, and with all your soul, and with all your might. DEUT 6:4-5

These sacred words, repeated daily in the prayers of observant Jews in biblical times, summarize the Jewish faith into a single command: Love God. Jews call this directive the Shema, from the Hebrew word that begins the section, "Hear." Jesus later identifies this injunction as the single greatest commandment in scripture (Mt 22:36-38). Essentially, these words restate the first of the Ten Commandments. In place of the negatively phrased mandate against worshiping other gods, Moses offers a positive one, urging the people to worship God alone and to love him with all their "heart" (mind), "soul" (a person's entire essence), and strength.

You must utterly destroy them [the Canaanite nations]. Make no covenant with them and show them no mercy. DEUT 7:2

Moses reminds the Israelites that the land they are about to invade is occupied not by one united people, but by many separate kingdoms or city-states. The task of the Israelites is to purge the land of its occupants, and to do this as completely as the Flood purged the sinful people of Noah's day—and for much the same reason: "because of the wickedness of these nations" (Deut 9:5).

The Israelites are to take no prisoners—men, women, or children. To the Israelites who serve God as his chosen people, this is a holy war, not just a territorial conflict. It is holy because God has judged the Canaanites and has sentenced them to death; the Israelites are to carry out that sentence.

Flanked by Aaron and Joshua, Moses speaks to the assembled Israelites. This rare and remarkably well-preserved pottery sculpture, dated about 1000 B.C., was found in the Sinai desert.

If Israel spares anyone, Moses explains in issuing God's edict, the Canaanite survivors will eventually return to their religious roots and "turn away your children from following me, to serve other gods" (Deut 7:4). Annihilation of the Canaanites is not only to punish wickedness, but to protect God's holy people from being seduced into breaking the first and most important of the Ten Commandments: fidelity to the Lord alone.

In the years of conquest that follow, this is exactly what happens. The Israelites invade and secure much of the land, often destroying the entire populations of cities. But Israel stops short of displacing all the Canaanites, and idolatry eventually gains a foothold among God's people. One reason that many Israelites are drawn to the worship of Baal, Canaan's god of fertility in field, flock, and family, is because the Canaanites are good farmers and herders. Some Israelites apparently conclude this is because Baal is blessing them, so they began to worship Baal alongside God—or Baal exclusively. Another more primal attraction of Canaanite religion is that it involves sexual rites with cult priests and priestesses. These ritual orgies are attempts to convince Baal to bless the worshiper with abundant crops, flocks, and children.

Over the next several centuries, God tries unsuccessfully to convince Israel to honor the covenant obligations summarized in Deuteronomy. He sends prophets with warnings, punishing famines, and brutal invaders. But eventually he resorts to doing to the Israelites what they were supposed to do to the Canaanites: remove them from the land. The Babylonians carry out God's sentence against his rebellious people in 586 B.C., defeating the nation, leveling Jerusalem, and exiling many of the inhabitants.

The Lord your God is not giving you this good land to occupy because of your righteousness; for you are a stubborn people. DEUT 9:6

Moses warns that once the Israelites capture Canaan and begin prospering, they must not say to themselves, "My power and the might of my own hand have gotten me this wealth" (Deut 8:17). Nor should they fool themselves into believing that God gave them this bountiful land as a reward for their righteousness.

The Israelites will inherit Canaan for two reasons, Moses says, neither of which has anything to do with their worthiness. Israel will conquer the land because of the wickedness of the Canaanites and because of the promises God made first to Abraham: "To your descendants I will give this land" (Gen 15:18).

Every good thing that the Israelites are about to receive will come from God as a generous and undeserved gift. God will provide the battlefield victories. He has already prepared the land, supplying the refugee nation of Israel with well-developed cities, furnished houses, cisterns for storing water, vineyards, and even mature olive groves that usually take seven years of cultivation before yielding a crop.

If you will diligently observe this entire commandment . . . then the Lord will drive out all these nations before you, and you will dispossess nations larger and mightier than yourselves. DEUT 11:22-23

Several centuries before the time of Moses, when God first promised Abraham that his descendants would receive the land, there was no mention of any conditions. Now, as Moses publicly reviews the covenant that God established with Abraham's descendants at Mount Sinai, it becomes clear that there are conditions. The covenant is a formal and binding contract between God and Israel. If the Israelites want to conquer Canaan and partake of its bounty, they must obey God's laws that are outlined in the agreement. In return for Israel's obedience, God pledges to protect and bless the nation.

Deuteronomy is structured much like ancient treaties between a ruler and his subjects. A preamble sets the context of the treaty (Deut 1:1-5). A brief history reviews the relationship between the two parties (Deut 1:6-4:43). Rules identify the subjects' obligations (Deut 4:44-26:19). Subjects are asked to accept the treaty (Deut 27:1-26). Blessings identify the ruler's obligations to the obedient subjects (Deut 28:1-14). Curses reveal the price of disobedience (Deut 28:15-68). And the treaty ends with a short summary (Deut 29:1-30:10).

There are striking parallels between what happens in Deuteronomy and what is reported in the vassal treaties of Esarhaddon, an Assyrian king who lived in the seventh century B.C. In both, the entire population is assembled—young and old. And in both, subjects take the vow of loyalty not only for themselves but for future generations as well.

Seek the place that the Lord your God will choose out of all your tribes as his habitation to put his name there. DEUT 12:5

Canaanites worshiped a pantheon of gods on hilltops throughout the land. The sites were apparently chosen to get the worshipers as close as possible to their celestial deities such as Baal, the god who sends rain to water the crops on which the people and their flocks depend. But Moses orders the Israelites to demolish every Canaanite shrine, breaking down sacrificial altars, smashing pillars that may have been erotic fertility emblems, and burning sacred poles that were possibly carved with images of gods. The Israelites are then to set up their own sanctuary at a single location that God selects. This practice of worshiping God at a central location will further distance Israel from Canaan's pagan customs.

When the Israelites settle in Canaan, they erect their tabernacle sanctuary at Shiloh in the central highlands. Several centuries later, Solomon builds a magnificent temple in the capital city of Jerusalem.

In spite of these attempts to protect the spiritual integrity of Israel, Canaanite influences manage to survive. Amazingly, the laws of God are apparently

OBEYING THE LAW

For his bar mitzvah at age 13, a Jewish boy reads from the scriptures at the temple's western wall in Jerusalem.

Moses tells the Israelites *to teach God's laws to their children and to "bind them as a sign on your hand, fix them as an emblem on your forehead, and write them on the doorposts of your house" (Deut 6:8-9). Some Jews take this quotation figuratively, believing that Moses means the people are to thoroughly learn the law. Others take it literally. They place tiny scrolls of selected scriptural passages such as the Ten Commandments in small black leather boxes called tefillin (phylacteries), which they wear on their forehead and forearms (see above). They also put at the entrance of their homes a miniature scroll of such scriptures in a box called a mezuzah ("doorpost"). Each time a person enters or leaves, he brushes the mezuzah with his fingers or kisses it.*

Many Jewish men wear a prayer shawl called the tallith, in keeping with the law to "make tassels on the four corners of the cloak with which you cover yourself" (Deut 22:12). God explained that these tassels would be a visual reminder of the law. Jesus criticized Jewish leaders for showing off their piety by making their phylacteries wide and their tassels long (Mt 23:5).

Jewish men of some orthodox communities refuse to trim their beards or long locks of hair left dangling in front of their ears. They are observing the command, "You shall not round off the hair on your temples or mar the edges of your beard" (Lev 19:27).

lost for a time. In about 620 B.C., as the temple is being renovated, a priest discovers the lost book of the law—probably Deuteronomy. The priest immediately takes the book to the king, Josiah. As the law is read aloud, Josiah tears his clothes in grief, realizing that Israel has broken its covenant with God. The king assembles the leaders of the nation and reads the book to them, in a covenant renewal ceremony. He then orders the high priest to remove from the temple "all the vessels made for Baal, for Asherah, and for all the host of heaven" (2 Kgs 23:4). The king also orders the destruction of hilltop shrines and pagan worship facilities throughout the country. This nationwide religious reform, however, is lamentably short-lived. Josiah's son and successor, Jehoahaz, "did what was evil in the sight of the Lord, just as his ancestors had done" (2 Kgs 23:32).

If anyone secretly entices you . . . saying, "Let us go and worship other gods". . . . your own hand shall be first against them to execute them. DEUT 13:6, 9

God announces the first and most important of the Ten Commandments by telling the Israelites, "You shall have no other gods before me" (Deut 5:7). Out of this fundamental command emerges other laws revealing that God considers idolatry the most serious threat facing his people. He orders the death penalty for any Israelite who tries to convince others to embrace pagan gods. Even prophets whose predictions come true are to be executed if they lead people away from the Lord.

Anyone found guilty of proselytizing on behalf of pagan gods is to be executed by stoning. This method requires the involvement of the entire community in purging a sin that threatens to contaminate their holiness, endanger their status as the chosen people, and render them unfit to serve God. The prophet Elijah, centuries later, will invoke this extreme penalty by ordering the Israelites to execute the 450 false prophets of Baal after he defeats them in a contest on Mount Carmel to bring an end to the drought that has devastated the land (1 Kgs 18:20-40).

If entire Israelite cities abandon the Lord in favor of pagan gods, they are to be treated as Canaanites: "Put the inhabitants of that town to the sword, utterly destroying it and everything in it—even putting its livestock to the sword" (Deut 13:15). All buildings are to be burned and left as a perpetual ruin, never to be rebuilt. For generations, the desolate shell will serve as a horrifying memorial to idolatry. Yet as the story of Israel continues, even deterrents as severe as these prove unable to prevent the people from rejecting God time and time again. For such blatant and persistent disobedience, the entire nation of Israel will become a sprawling heap of charred ruins.

You are a people holy to the Lord your God; it is you the Lord has chosen out of all the peoples on earth to be his people. DEUT 14:2

Moses describes the Israelites as holy. He does not mean that the people are morally perfect. They are not—as their defiant misbehavior during the Exodus demonstrated. What he does mean is that God has set them apart from other nations to use for his purposes. The prophet Isaiah will later describe God's ultimate purpose for Israel: "I will give you as a light to the nations, that my salvation may reach to the end of the earth" (Isa 49:6).

By obeying the law, Israelites maintain their holiness and are permitted to continue their sacred partnership with God. Moses reviews a variety of the laws, to illustrate how to live the holy life. For example, God's people are not to cut their bodies or hair when mourning the death of a loved one. These

A traditional seder table, with the proper table settings, foods, and prayers, is depicted in this contemporary stained glass window from a synagogue in London, England.

are rituals associated with pagan worship rites; at the contest on Mount Carmel, the prophets of Baal cut themselves in the hope of drawing the attention of their god. Moses also discusses laws about what meat to eat, tithing as a resource for the priestly class and the poor, and writing off all debts every seventh year.

Observe the month of Abib by keeping the passover for the Lord your God, for in the month of Abib the Lord your God brought you out of Egypt by night. DEUT 16:1

The month of Abib, later called Nisan, is about a 30-day period spanning the end of March and the beginning of April. The early Israelites mark time by the changes in the moon, with each new moon signaling the start of a month. Moses reminds the Israelites of the three pilgrimage festivals they are to observe in Canaan: "Three times a year all your males shall appear before the Lord your God at the place that he will choose" (Deut 16:16). This place later becomes the temple at Jerusalem.

Passover, known also as the Festival of the Unleavened Bread, is a weeklong observance that begins on the full moon at mid-month in Abib. During this early springtime festival, the Israelites commemorate their escape from Egypt after the Lord's messenger "passed over" Hebrew homes but killed all Egyptian firstborn. The festival's alternate name comes from the last meal that the Israelites ate before leaving: roast lamb and bread cooked without yeast. According to the Gospel of Luke, Jesus' parents went each year to Jerusalem to celebrate Passover; at age 12, Jesus was separated from them and later found discoursing with teachers in the temple (Lk 2:41-51).

The second pilgrimage festival is Shavuot (Hebrew for "weeks"). It is held in late May or early June to mark the end of the grain harvest. The name comes from the instruction to observe it seven weeks after the grain harvest begins. In New Testament times the feast became known as Pentecost (Greek for "fiftieth," since seven weeks is about 50 days). Observing Pentecost in Jerusalem after Jesus' death, the disciples were "filled with the Holy Spirit" (Acts 2:4).

Succoth (Hebrew for "booth"), also known as the Festival of Booths or Tabernacles, is the year's final pilgrimage observance. It is a weeklong thanksgiving celebration at the conclusion of harvesttime, near the end of September. The Israelites are to camp out in huts to recall their years of wandering. During each celebration, every man is to bring a gift in proportion to his blessing. No one should "appear before the Lord empty-handed" (Deut 16:16).

Appoint judges and officials throughout your tribes in all your towns that the Lord your God is giving you, and they shall render just decisions for the people. DEUT 16:18

Deuteronomy is passionate about justice: "Justice and only justice, you shall pursue" (Deut 16:20). Moses identifies this as a condition for conquering and holding onto the promised land.

The Israelites are to select judicial officials to serve in all the towns and throughout the tribal territories. These judges are to be impartial and honest, accepting no bribes. Cases too difficult for local judges— such as those involving death, assault, or property rights—are handled by a high court tribunal made up of priests and regional judges.

A single witness is not enough to convict someone of a capital offense; there must be at least two witnesses. And if an accusing witness proves to be lying, that witness is to suffer the punishment intended for the defendant. Whatever the punishment—for the lying witness or for the convicted defendant—it should be commensurate with the crime: "life for life, eye for eye, tooth for tooth, hand for hand, foot for foot" (Deut 19:21).

Six cities of refuge are to be set up throughout the 12 tribes. People accused of killing someone can flee to one of these cities to escape vengeful relatives of the victim. There the accused is to receive a fair trial. If found innocent, the person can remain in the city, protected from anyone who may not agree with the verdict. If found guilty, the person is turned over to relatives of the victim for execution.

Deuteronomy also calls on all the people to follow God's lead and look out for the welfare of the powerless: orphans, widows, travelers, and the poor. Prophets later explain that God's judgment against Israel, which will culminate in the fall of the nation and the exile of the survivors, is partly attributable to the prevailing spirit of injustice. Isaiah says Hebrew rulers "turn aside the needy from justice . . . rob the poor of my people of their right, that widows may be your spoil, and that you may make the orphans your prey! What will you do on the day of punishment?" (Isa 10:2, 3).

When you have come into the land that the Lord your God is giving you . . . you may indeed set over you a king whom the Lord your God will choose. DEUT 17:14, 15

The Israelites initially have no king. They are led by individuals chosen by God: Moses, Joshua, then a succession of judges—one of whom is Gideon, who refuses to become king by saying, "the Lord will rule over you" (Judg 8:23). Deuteronomy, however, anticipates a time when the people will insist on a king. Moses says that God will allow this, with severe restrictions. Israel's king will not be like the kings of other nations. The king of Israel must not enjoy absolute power but be subject to God's law, like any other Israelite. Nor should the king amass wealth for himself or acquire many wives. Kings who honor these restrictions are promised a long dynasty.

Centuries later, the Israelites ask the prophet Samuel to choose for them "a king to govern us, like other nations" (1 Sam 8:5). Reluctantly, but at God's command, Samuel does as he is asked. But he predicts that the people will get what they asked for: a monarchy like others, which wallows in wealth and power at the expense of its citizens. The Israelite king

Three scenes from the Israelites' years of wandering are depicted in this illustration from the renowned Lambeth Bible, produced in Canterbury, England, about 1150: Moses receiving the law from God (top right); the ark carried on the march to Canaan (center); worship at the portable tent tabernacle (bottom).

most famous for his wealth, harem, and heavy taxation is Solomon. When he dies, the northern part of the nation secedes, leaving Solomon's son and successor, Rehoboam, with only a rump kingdom.

The Lord your God has chosen Levi out of all your tribes, to stand and minister in the name of the Lord. DEUT 18:5

The extended family of Moses—the tribe of Levi—is not assigned any block of territory in Canaan. The Levites are to serve God as priests and worship assistants, and live off the sacrifices and offerings brought to the tabernacle, and later to the temple. Though some of the animal and grain sacrifices are consumed in the fire on the altar, much becomes the property of the Levites.

Not all Levites live near the worship center in Canaan. Many reside in the 48 cities designated for them, which are scattered throughout the territory assigned the other tribes. Family groups eventually organize themselves to take turns ministering at the sanctuary, serving in shifts of up to a week at a time.

When you come into the land that the Lord your God is giving you, you must not learn to imitate the abhorrent practices of those nations. DEUT 18:9

The "abhorrent practices" condemned by Moses are magical arts that the Canaanites and other ancient cultures used to discover or manipulate the future: child sacrifice, sorcery, witchcraft, spells, the consultation of dead spirits, and the interpretation of naturally occurring events as omens.

When a king needed to make an important decision, such as whether to go to war, he consulted a seer. This influential adviser could employ any number of techniques to discern an answer. He might study the alignment of stars and planets, the pattern of birds in flight, the way an arrow falls, or the shape and markings on the liver of a sacrificed sheep. The prophet Ezekiel reports that when the king of Babylon has a choice to make, he "shakes the arrows, he consults the teraphim [idols], he inspects the liver" (Ezek 21:21).

Before the Exodus, Moses confronted seers and magicians in the palace of Egypt's king. Though Moses did not deny the power of the mystical arts, he clearly demonstrated that God's power is greater. If Israelites want to know the future, God says, they should turn to prophets: "I will raise up for them a prophet like you [Moses] . . . I will put my words in the mouth of the prophet" (Deut 18:18).

When you go out to war against your enemies . . . you shall not be afraid of them; for the Lord your God is with you. DEUT 20:1

When pitted against larger, better equipped armies, the Israelites are to remember that the God who leads them is the same God who freed them from Egypt against seemingly impossible odds. Unarmed in the desert, fleeing Hebrews of the Exodus needed do no more than watch as God opened and then closed a path through the sea and drowned their pursuers. And now, before each battle, a priest is to encourage the troops by reminding them that this God "goes with you, to fight for you against your enemies, to give you victory" (Deut 20:4).

Officers address the men, excusing those who are afraid or who have a new house, vineyard, or bride. The size of the army is not as important as the spirit of bravery and the devotion of the soldiers to the task before them.

Canaanite cities are to be utterly destroyed as a sacrificial offering to God: "You must not let anything that breathes remain alive" (Deut 20:16). This is to punish Canaan for its wickedness and to protect Israel from adopting any harmful Canaanite customs. Enemies outside Canaan are spared annihilation. Moses instructs the Israelites to offer terms of peace when they approach these enemy fortifications. If the offer is rejected, the Israelites are to kill only the men. Women, children, and all enemy possessions become the property of Israel as spoils of war.

WANDERINGS OF THE HEBREWS

Arriving at the oasis of Kadesh-barnea, the Israelites were on the threshold of the promised land. To find the best invasion route, Moses sent 12 spies, one from each tribe, north into Canaan. In obedience to God's command that they avoid the land of the bellicose Philistines on the Mediterranean coast, the spies would have taken a desert caravan route through Hormah to Hebron in the central highlands. Apparently, the reconnaissance covered the full extent of their inheritance, from the wilderness of Zin in the Negeb north to "Rehob, near Lebo-hamath" (Num 13:21), possibly just beyond present day Damascus, Syria. After noting the inhabitants and their well-fortified cities, the spies stopped to gather grapes at the Wadi Eschol, a name meaning "cluster," and returned to the encampment.

The Israelites panicked at the spies' report of people so large they made their group seem like grasshoppers and even talked of replacing Moses with a leader who would take them back to Egypt. For such cowardice and failure to believe in his protection, God condemned the people to 40 years of wandering, a year for every day of the spies' mission. Of the present generation, only Caleb and Joshua, who disputed the bad report of their colleagues, would be allowed to enter the promised land. The remaining ten spies were struck dead by a plague. Next, the Israelites further disobeyed God by launching a hasty invasion that ended in humiliating defeat.

Blocked by the Philistines to the west and deterred from invading Canaan directly from the south, the Israelites had only one option: a strike at central Canaan from east of the Jordan River. Scholars argue about the route they would have taken, for there are two different accounts in Numbers, and the story is repeated with variations in Deuteronomy. According to Numbers 20-21 (possibly echoed in Deuteronomy 2), the Edomites and Moabites east of the Dead Sea refused permission for a peaceful passage through their territories. And thus, the Israelites looped back through the desolate wilderness of Paran as far south as Ezion-geber on the Gulf of Aqaba and then marched north to the plains of Moab. But in Numbers 33 it is reported that the wanderers headed directly east from Mount Hor to Zalmonah and Punon.

From Punon, the Israelites would have reached the broad eastern plateau overlooking the Dead Sea and a famous caravan route called the King's Highway. Crossing several deeply eroded river canyons, the Israelites finally reached their destination. Before dying, Moses ascended Mount Nebo for a view east and north of the promised land—a haven he would never reach for a single act of disobedience in an otherwise exemplary life.

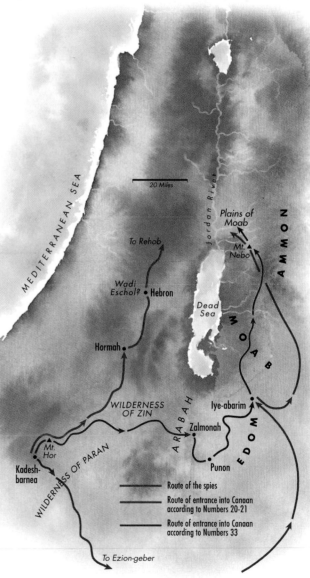

Route of the spies
Route of entrance into Canaan according to Numbers 20-21
Route of entrance into Canaan according to Numbers 33

Pausing at Kadesh-barnea (left), the Israelites pondered their next move. God had blocked them from entering Canaan through Philistine territory on the Mediterranean coast, and the report of the spies discouraged a march north. Two different routes to the plains of Moab, from which they would eventually launch their invasion, are given in the book of Numbers.

When the Israelites surround a walled city and lay siege to it, they are prohibited from cutting down fruit trees for fuel. The fruit will feed them in years to come, long after the battle is won.

When someone is convicted of a crime punishable by death and is executed, and you hang him on a tree, his corpse must not remain all night upon the tree. DEUT 21:22

The corpses of people executed for particularly atrocious crimes, such as murder, were sometimes placed on public display—probably to degrade the criminal and to deter others from committing similar crimes. Executioners hung the body on a tree or impaled it on a stake; the Hebrew phrase for "hang him on a tree" can mean either. Such criminals were seen as suffering from the condemnation and judgment of God—they were "under God's curse" (Deut 21:23) for defiling the promised land with sin. Even so, their bodies were not to be left out overnight, but were to be buried on the day of the execution.

The apostle Paul quoted Deuteronomy 21:23 to explain that when Jesus hung on the cross, he took upon himself the sins of humanity, "becoming a curse for us—for it is written, 'Cursed is everyone who hangs on a tree'" (Gal 3:13).

Throughout Deuteronomy 21-25, Moses reviews a wide collection of rules that the Israelites are to observe in Canaan. These include laws about female captives, inheritance, lost property, interest on loans, vows made to God, marriage, kidnaping, justice and compassion for the poor, and using honest weights when measuring goods being bought or sold.

Although some of the laws are like those of law codes in neighboring cultures, there are substantial differences. For instance, laws in surrounding regions dealt only with secular issues. But biblical laws cover both religious and secular realms—showing that God rules in both domains.

If you obey the Lord your God: Blessed shall you be in the city, and blessed shall you be in the field. DEUT 28:2-3

As in other ancient treaties between ruler and subject, the covenant between God and Israel contains a list of benefits that the people will enjoy if they comply with the agreement they have made.

Moses briefly identifies several blessings, followed by explanations. He says God promises to bless the entire nation, city dwellers and farmers alike. This nationwide blessing includes fertility in the field, flock, and family—the very domain of the Canaanite god Baal. But the blessing extends far beyond this, to embrace all the daily tasks of life. This is the meaning behind the phrases "when you come in" and "when you go out" (Deut 28:6).

Rising above the plains east of the Jordan River and the Dead Sea, the rugged mountains of Moab offered the aged Moses a glimpse of the promised land he was forbidden to enter as well as a final resting place.

Not only will there be prosperity in the land, there will be protection from invaders. In a vivid image of Israel routing the enemy, Moses says attackers "shall come out against you one way, and flee before you seven ways" (Deut 28:7).

Particularly enticing for these nomadic people who have spent the last 40 years in the barren desert is the promise of abundant rain: "The Lord will open for you his rich storehouse, the heavens, to give the rain of your land in its season" (Deut 28:12).

If you will not obey the Lord your God . . . then all these curses shall come upon you. DEUT 28:15

Like other ancient treaties, God's covenant with Israel also includes a list of the dreadful consequences for disobedience. These begin by reversing the same short list of blessings in Deuteronomy 28:3-6, then adding a long and graphic explanation—much longer than the explanation of blessings. The content and even the order of the curses in 28:23-35 is parallel to those in a seventh-century B.C. treaty of the Assyrian king Esarhaddon.

Moses says that in place of rain, God will send dust and blistering drought. Enemies will invade, and when Israel tries to defend itself, the Hebrew soldiers "shall go out against them one way and flee before them seven ways" (Deut 28:25). The people will suffer from terrifying diseases: madness, blindness, leprosy, and "the boils of Egypt, with ulcers, scurvy, and itch, of which you cannot be healed" (Deut 28:27). Starvation will turn gentle people into cannibals who eat their own children. The cities, vineyards, and furnished houses of Canaan that God has given to Israel will be taken back and given to savage invaders. As for the Hebrews who somehow manage to survive, "the Lord will scatter you among all peoples, from one end of the earth to the other" (Deut 28:64).

Moses says that "the next generation . . . will wonder, 'Why has the Lord done this to this land? What caused this great display of anger?' They will conclude, 'It is because they abandoned the covenant of the Lord'" (Deut 29:22, 24-25).

The curses take several hundred years to achieve the worst that they threaten. Israel divides into two nations after the reign of Solomon, in about 928 B.C. About 200 years later, in 722 B.C., Assyrians defeat the northern nation of Israel, exile many Hebrew survivors, and resettle the land with other people. In less than a century and a half, in 586 B.C., Babylonians conquer the southern nation of Judah and exile its people. The Jewish nation ceases to exist.

The Lord said to Moses, "Your time to die is near; call Joshua and present yourselves in the tent of meeting, so that I may commission him." DEUT 31:14

After Moses finishes speaking, he performs several final, important tasks before dying. He writes the law he has just reviewed and gives it to the priests. Ancient treaties between ruler and sub-

Assisted by angels, the Lord places Moses in his unmarked grave; a scene from the renowned 15th-century Nuremberg Bible.

ject are preserved in writing, with a copy kept at the sanctuary or temple. For Israel, this means keeping the law with the chest that holds the Ten Commandments inside the tent tabernacle.

Next, Moses brings Joshua to the tabernacle, as God has ordered. There, Joshua is commissioned to lead the Israelites into Canaan. Moses is not permitted to go into the promised land because of an unspecified sin he committed when he was providing the thirsty Israelites with water from a rock. Then Moses recites for the assembly a song that contrasts the faithfulness of God with the rebelliousness of the people. Finally, he gives the tribes of Israel a last blessing, as a dying father might bless his children with prayers of encouragement, hope, and warning—as an elderly Jacob so long ago blessed his 12 sons, the progenitors of the 12 tribes Moses has led to the threshold of the land of promise.

"Happy are you, O Israel!" Moses sings to those who will soon cross into Canaan. "Who is like you, a people saved by the Lord, the shield of your help and the sword of your triumph!" (Deut 33:29).

Moses was one hundred twenty years old when he died; his sight was unimpaired and his vigor had not abated. DEUT 34:7

Israel's great lawgiver climbs a hilltop and gazes across the Jordan River—permitted by the Lord to see Israel's future territory as far north as Galilee, south to the Negeb, and west to the Mediterranean Sea. After beholding all this, Moses dies and is buried somewhere in the plains of Moab, in what is now Jordan. The burial site is kept secret, perhaps so the Israelites will not turn it into a shrine where people come to worship and seek mystical power.

The gripping epitaph for Moses, added later, comes at the end of the five books traditionally attributed to him: "Never since has there arisen a prophet in Israel like Moses, whom the Lord knew face to face. He was unequaled for all the signs and wonders that the Lord sent him to perform" (Deut 34:10-11).

A dramatic epic of conquest that reveals many fascinating details about warfare in the ancient Near East, the book of Joshua above all is a profound spiritual document. It explains the divine foundations of the nation of Israel.

After 40 years of wandering in the desert wilderness, a loose federation of tribes pauses at the eastern border of the promised land of Canaan. How can these weary nomads overpower the defenders of long-established hilltop cities? Will Joshua, previously in the shadow of the divinely appointed Moses, be able both to lead the Israelites and retain the confidence of the Lord, who has chosen him as Moses' successor? The answers become dramatically clear as Joshua follows God's advice and oversees a series of stunning victories.

Yet setbacks occur whenever he or his people ignore or defy the divine will. The moral is fundamental: Obedience to the Lord brings victory and the fulfillment of his enduring promise, but disobedience brings punishment swift and sure. When Canaan is finally in Israelite hands, after years of battles and negotiations with the inhabitants, Joshua is principally concerned that the new nation never forget its origins. The future will be peaceful as long as the Israelites remain faithful to their covenant with God. If they fail to do so, catastrophe will inevitably follow.

Drawing upon a wide variety of written and spoken sources, priestly scribes wrote the book of Joshua around 560 B.C., or about six centuries after the events described. A sorrowful Israel was enduring the Babylonian captivity, but the book could have been written in either Babylon or Judah. In Jewish tradition, Joshua is considered the first of the Former Prophets, the series of books that spans national history from the invasion of Canaan up to the disaster of exile in Babylon. Perhaps intended as a sequel to the Pentateuch, the first five books of the Bible, Joshua is known as a Deuteronomic book because it incorporates many ideas from the same source as Deuteronomy. Clearly, the writers want to show that Israel was established by the will of God despite the frequent failings of the Israelites themselves. All of the promises made in Genesis and Exodus are fulfilled, and the land of Canaan is given into the hands of the chosen people, often with astonishing demonstrations of divine intervention.

Historically, the occupation of Canaan was much more complicated and prolonged than this book suggests, though archaeologists have uncovered some evidence of a destruction in central Canaan during the period proposed for Joshua, from about 1250 to 1200 B.C. Still, the writer is using historical materials to affirm a spiritual lesson during a period of national crisis: The God who founded the nation must be continually honored if the nation is to survive.

The Israelites carrying the ark of the covenant across the Jordan, from the 15th-century baptistery doors in Florence, Italy, by Lorenzo Ghiberti

---

Now proceed to cross the Jordan, you and all this people, into the land that I am giving to them, to the Israelites. JOSH 1:2

Joshua begins in the midst of a national crisis. Moses, the greatest of all Israel's leaders, has just died. He alone has stood face-to-face with God and received from him the laws that are to govern the nation. Now, gathered just east of the Jordan River and gazing eagerly westward at the hill country beyond, the people surely wonder whether their new leader, Joshua, is worthy of the huge task of claiming the land first promised to their patriarchal ancestors, Abraham, Isaac, and Jacob. They must follow the Lord's will in all things and also conquer the well-defended, walled cities of the Canaanites.

Immediately, the Lord lays both fears to rest. He makes Joshua his confidant and also his commander in chief. The promise of a national home is renewed, although the actual territory described in Joshua 1:4 will never be completely captured by Israel.

Already, the Reubenites, Gadites, and half the tribe of Manasseh have settled on lands just east of the Jordan. As God wills, Joshua orders their 40,000 men

Rahab helping Joshua's spies escape from Jericho; a 14th-century manuscript illumination

Israelite victories over the Amorites and now believe that the Lord of Israel is invincible. She wants to save her beloved family from certain death. The two spies promise to protect them all.

The spies escape down a rope lowered from her window. The city walls are casement type—that is, two separate walls perhaps 15 feet apart. Simple houses like Rahab's were built on planks laid across this space. This position will be advantageous for her later on, for she is told to suspend a "crimson cord" (Josh 2:18) from her outside window as a sign that she and her family should be spared. Whatever Rahab's motives, her deliverance shows that God is not solely the Israelites' national deity. People of all races and nations will be welcomed if they choose to obey his will.

The waters of the Jordan flowing from above shall be cut off. JOSH 3:13

The crossing of the Jordan is the first miracle to affirm that Joshua's mission is divinely inspired. Snowmelt from the north and recent spring rains have swollen the river to flood stage. The intruders have access to neither bridges nor boats.

But Joshua, following specific directions from the Lord, tells the people to walk a respectful 2,000 cubits (1,000 yards) behind the ark of the covenant, which is carried toward the Jordan by priests. The day before, the Israelites had sanctified themselves for the challenges to come; in other words, they had ritually purified themselves for the holy work of the Lord. War was to serve the aims of their religion.

As soon as the feet of the priests touch the water, the flooded river miraculously stops flowing, and the

to join with the other Israelite tribes in the national war of conquest. Here, as in the number 600,000 given for the Israelites leaving Egypt, the figure is perhaps an exaggeration. The Hebrew term *'elep,* usually translated "thousand," can also mean "section" or "unit." If 40,000 actually means 40 troop units, as some experts believe, the total of the eastern forces would be 400. Whatever their number, the Israelite forces gather at Shittim, the Hebrew word for the acacia trees that grow in these desert lands.

Joshua son of Nun sent two men secretly from Shittim as spies. JOSH 2:1

Many times, the story of Joshua offers glimpses of ancient military tactics. For example, he chooses to attack tiny hilltop Jericho, only about ten acres in area, because it controls the entire Jordan valley, including numerous fords across streams and the mountain passes leading to the central highlands of Canaan. In preparation, he sends two spies into town to learn about its defenses and, even more important, the mood of its people.

The spies go at night to the house of the prostitute Rahab, probably a good place to hear local gossip. But the king of the city has spies, too. When his men come to arrest the strangers, Rahab hides them under a pile of flax already heaped up on her roof. The three-foot stalks of this plant had to be dried in the sun before the fibers could be woven into linen. She deftly deceives the king's men, telling them that the spies took off before the city gates were closed for protection at nightfall.

Why does Rahab betray her own town? As she explains, the people of Jericho have heard about

Normally a shallow, meandering stream, the Jordan River overflows its banks in spring—as it did at the time the Israelites were preparing to invade Canaan.

In this scene by 15th-century French miniaturist Jean Fouquet, the Israelites carry the ark around a city reminiscent of the artist's homeland.

Before war begins, it is important to renew Israel's covenant with the Lord. During the years in the desert, circumcision has not been practiced, but only circumcised men will be allowed to participate in the Passover celebration, the first held in the promised land. By this time, the Israelites had adopted bronze tools, but the Lord specifies flint knives for the operation, perhaps to honor tradition. After the circumcision, the troops are truly warriors for the Lord, who says, "Today I have rolled away from you the disgrace of Egypt" (Josh 5:9). The men rest until they are healed, for great military trials await them.

There is another change of historic significance. The day after Passover, the miraculous manna never again falls from heaven. As part of the traditional feast, the Israelites have eaten food produced in the recent spring harvest. From now on, after decades of nomadic life, they must learn to grow crops, store food, and build permanent settlements. Their way of life will never again be the same.

Meanwhile, as Joshua makes final preparations for the attack on Jericho, a mysterious armed stranger appears. He reveals himself as the angel who commands the Lord's army and orders Joshua to take off his sandals, because the ground where they stand is holy. The incident recalls Moses' encounter with God at the burning bush, and thus reaffirms that Joshua is his mentor's legitimate successor as leader of Israel.

riverbed becomes completely dry. A similar phenomenon occurred as recently as 1927, when an earth tremor caused parts of the Jordan's soft limestone banks to slide into the watercourse, blocking it for a time. Here, the event is believed to be divine intervention, recalling the miraculous parting of the Red Sea 40 years earlier. Once again, the entire nation crosses safely to the other side. The new general's leadership reflects that of Moses.

God tells Joshua to choose 12 men, one from each tribe, to pick up one stone each from the middle of the river and set them up as a memorial on the western bank, where they will camp that night. (A different tradition is recalled in verse 9, where the memorial is established in the riverbed.) The priests bring the ark out of the watercourse, and the river flows freely to flood heights again. The place where they camp, Gilgal, meaning "circle of stones," was considered a sacred site long before, perhaps because of stones arranged to form a kind of solar calendar to help predict changes in the agricultural year. Here and elsewhere, the Israelites are skillful in adapting pagan shrines to their own religious purposes.

Then all the people shall shout with a great shout; and the wall of the city will fall down flat. JOSH 6:5

*I*n the stirring first battles of conquest, the Lord takes an active part, instructing his earthly lieutenant in sound military strategy and also performing miracles to assure victory.

Jericho has barred its gates to prepare for the usual siege warfare. But instead of attacking immediately, the Israelite warriors, preceded by seven priests carrying the ark, march around the watchful town for six days in a row. The priests blow continually on the sacred rams' horns, producing an ominous low note, but the circling warriors remain frighteningly silent.

On the seventh day, as the Lord commands, the Israelites tramp around Jericho seven times as the priests blow their horns. Some commentators see this as the climax of a kind of psychological warfare that erodes the will of the besieged. In addition to the clamor, seven was considered a magical number in many cultures of the ancient Near East. More literal historians have suggested that the din might have covered the noise made by sappers, or soldiers delegated to undermine the foundations of the walls while the inhabitants of the town are distracted. In any event, after a long blast upon the horns, the Israelites give a great shout all at once. The walls of the city collapse in rubble, just as God has promised, and the invaders storm in joyfully.

In this geologically fragile area, part of the Great Rift stretching down through East Africa, earthquakes are frequent. It is possible that more than one settlement at Jericho was destroyed by seismic activity over the centuries. In this story, however, the disaster occurs only because the people of God follow divine instructions to the letter.

The Israelites are also ordered to destroy the town completely and kill all of its people, a frequent practice in many ancient cultures. Experts suggest that this total destruction, called *cherem*, arose as protection from the influence of an enemy's idolatrous religion or from epidemics associated with war. God forbids anyone to take any booty, perhaps to prevent undisciplined looting. All useful or valuable metal objects are to be handed over to the national treasury.

An important theme of the book of Joshua is the injunction to keep one's word, whether to the Lord or to other human beings. Thus, as his spies have promised, Joshua saves Rahab and her family before torching the city. They will live with the victorious Israelites thereafter.

Joshua then pronounces a curse on anyone who would ever try to rebuild Jericho—a curse fulfilled in the days of King Ahab (1 Kgs 16:34). This particular kind of curse appears nowhere else in the Old Testament and may mean that the ancient Hebrews believed the very site to be unhealthy or demonically possessed. Archaeologists have found evidence there of a water snail that carries the parasite that causes schistosomiasis, a dreaded intestinal disease.

"Ah, Lord God! Why have you brought this people across the Jordan at all, to hand us over to the Amorites so as to destroy us?" JOSH 7:7

Flush with this easy victory and convinced of the Lord's continuing support, Joshua becomes overconfident. To conquer and resettle central Canaan, he focuses on the small town of Ai, a name meaning "ruin." Situated about 2,500 feet above sea level on a ridge in the central mountain region, Ai looks like an easy target to the Israelite spies, who advise their leader he need send up no more than 3,000 soldiers.

But the 3,000 chosen for the mission meet with unexpected disaster. Not only are the men

For taking spoils at Jericho, Achan is stoned to death along with his family and livestock.

shamefully chased off, but 36 are killed on the spot. This is by no means a small number to the loose-knit tribes of Israel, fitfully making their way through a strange land, especially if their numbers are much smaller than the figures used by the scribes.

In despair, Joshua rips his clothing and falls down before the ark, the place where God can be approached most directly. The distraught general tries to blame the Lord, who impatiently orders him to "Stand up!" (Josh 7:10) and get on with the task of leadership. The military defeat is divine punishment because someone has disobeyed the ban on taking booty. In effect, the whole nation has disobeyed God because of the act of one person, and the whole nation must suffer until the wrong is punished.

To discover the culprit Joshua has the Israelites pass in front of him by tribes, by tribal clans, and by families within the clans. Guilt or innocence is probably determined by casting lots, perhaps the sacred dicelike Urim and Thummim.

The finger of God points indelibly toward Achan, a member of the tribe of Judah. He confesses that he could not resist stealing and hiding silver that weighs 200 shekels (about 5 pounds), a bar of gold weighing 50 shekels (1.25 pounds), and a lovely cape made in Shinar, an old name for Babylon. For breaking the covenant with the Lord, the sinner is stoned to death in the Valley of Achor, meaning "trouble" in Hebrew. Then Achan's body, his booty, his entire family, his farm animals, and all of his other possessions are burned to ashes. A mound of stones is set up as a memorial of this divinely ordained punishment. After the Lord's wrath cools, his people again take up the challenge of conquering Canaan.

"Stretch out the sword that is in your hand toward Ai; for I will give it into your hand." JOSH 8:18

This time, Joshua takes directions from God before trying to subdue Ai. In a plan that involves the entire Israelite army, the enemy will be lured into an ambush, a tactic that shows military sophistication.

By nightfall, thousands of troops are in hiding on a ridge to the west of Ai. The first number given in this account is 30,000, later altered to 5,000. Because of the terrain, the latter figure or even a smaller number is more probable. Meanwhile, Joshua ostentatiously makes camp with the main body of his troops at the edge of a valley north of the town.

On the morning of battle, the king of Ai confidently marches toward the visible detachment of Israelites, who flee in apparent

THE CONQUEST OF CANAAN

From Abel-shittim on the plains of Moab, Joshua launched his invasion of Canaan, crossing the Jordan River to camp at Gilgal and then quickly capturing strategic Jericho. After leveling Ai, he defeated an Amorite (or western Canaanite) coalition led by Jerusalem that attacked Israel's ally, Gibeon. Pursuing the defeated enemy to Azekah, Joshua effectively cut Canaan in two and thus successfully concluded the central campaign of the Israelite conquest. In the swift southern campaign, Joshua took Makkedah (site unknown), Libnah, Lachish, Eglon, Hebron, and Debir.

The Israelites' victories alarmed King Jabin of Hazor, a major political and commercial center north of the Sea of Galilee. He summoned not only his fellow Canaanites but also the non-Semitic Hittites, Perizzites, Jebusites, and Hivites to meet at the waters of Meron. The gathered forces, "in number like the sand on the seashore" (Josh 11:4), included horse-drawn chariots. Instructed by the Lord, Joshua overcame the enemy's tactical advantage by a sudden attack in which he hamstrung the horses and burned the chariots.

This circular stone tower is among the ancient ruins unearthed at Jericho.

confusion. Delighted, the king orders all of his men to join him in excited pursuit, leaving his city unprotected. When the Lord gives the word, Joshua wheels round and lifts his sword high in the bright sunlight. This signal alerts his troops lying in ambush. They quickly emerge from hiding, storm Ai, and burn the entire city to the ground.

With horror, the king and his subjects realize that they are hopelessly trapped. The supposedly fleeing Israelites turn and advance on them, while the troops formerly in ambush approach from the rear. All of the enemy forces are swiftly slaughtered, except the king, who is taken prisoner. But Joshua continues to raise aloft his sword of victory—perhaps the sickle-shaped one at that time used as a symbol of kingship in Egypt and Mesopotamia—until all the civilians of the town are also slain. The king is then killed and his body is hung from a tree until sunset as a warning to all the peoples of Canaan.

Now that the campaign is again successful, Joshua pauses to erect an altar of unhewn stones on Mount Ebal. Not coincidentally, this site is very important to the strategy of controlling the hill country of Canaan. According to historians, the Shechem pass to the central highlands between Mount Ebal to the north and Mount Gerizim to the south may have been acquired through peaceful negotiations. It does not appear in the stories of battle.

As Israelites and friendly Canaanites gather round, burnt offerings are offered to the Lord in thanksgiving for his guidance and protection. Either on the stones of the altar or on plaster, a traditional medium for recording terms of a treaty, Joshua inscribes a part of the law Moses received from the Lord, in all probability the Ten Commandments.

Recalling the covenant God made with Moses on Mount Sinai, he reads aloud from the ancient Levitical book of laws that is the basis for the book of Deuteronomy. In the days that precede the building of the temple at Jerusalem, such a gathering, often bringing together pilgrims from afar for a ceremonial feast, is considered to be the congregation of worshipers of the Lord.

But when the inhabitants of Gibeon heard what Joshua had done to Jericho and to Ai, they on their part acted with cunning. JOSH 9:3-4

The stunning conquests of the Israelites frighten some of the neighboring kings, who form a military alliance against the invaders. But the people of Gibeon, a village six miles northwest of Jerusalem, save themselves with a ruse. Appearing before Joshua at Gilgal in rags and carrying moldy bread and torn wineskins, they claim to be travelers from afar. In other words, they offer no obstacle to Joshua's territorial ambitions and seek only peace. Foolishly, the Israelites neglect to ask the Lord's advice about this motley delegation. Peace is made with the emissaries and an oath is sworn.

Three days later, the Israelites learn that they have been tricked. A brief march reveals that the Gibeonites actually have four settlements very nearby, and all are critical to gaining access to Jerusalem from the northwest. Following traditional military tactics, Joshua would have crushed them as part of his overall strategy of occupation.

But if the incident shows once again that humans ignore God's counsel at their peril, it also affirms the necessity of keeping one's word. Joshua and the leaders of the congregation cannot break their oath to allow the Gibeonites to live. To do so would risk the Lord's wrath. Evidently, as this story suggests, Gibeon and no doubt other parts of Canaan were peacefully brought under Israelite control.

Nonetheless, an angry Joshua curses the Gibeonites, perhaps because they have lied. From then on, they are responsible for supplying firewood and water for the Israelites' altar of worship, wherever it may be established. According to some biblical interpreters, however, the enslavement of the Gibeonites did not actually take place until the reign of Solomon several centuries later.

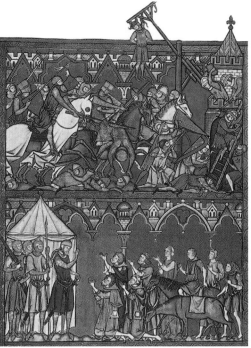

The king of Ai hung as a warning (top) and the Gibeonites seeking peace; two scenes from a mid-13th-century illuminated manuscript

And the sun stood still, and the moon stopped, until the nation took vengeance on their enemies. JOSH 10:13

Whatever their ethics, the Gibeonites almost immediately benefit from the treaty with the Israelites. Jerusalem's Amorite king feels understandably threatened by this new alliance and invites four other Amorite kings to join him in attacking the Gibeonites. Incidentally, this is the first time the scriptures use the actual name "Jerusalem" (Josh 10:1) for this ancient city.

Suddenly, little Gibeon is portrayed as a large city with fully trained warriors, but only because the sixth-century scribes are imagining cities as large and wealthy as those of the heyday of Israel's monarchy.

Once again, Joshua sensibly remembers to consult the Lord, who promises victory. After an exhausting all-night march, mostly up winding hill pathways, the Israelites meet their assembled enemies at Gibeon. There is a rout. Frightened by the spirit of God, the Amorites try to flee southward to safety, but the Israelites cut them down in great numbers. Then the Lord pummels them with a burst of hailstones, an unusual event in that region, generally limited to the winter months.

As the bloody slaughter continues, Joshua prays for sufficient time to vanquish the Amorites, using an image borrowed from ancient poetry: "Sun, stand still

Flanked by Mount Ebal and Mount Gerizim, modern Nablus is on the site of ancient Shechem, sacred to Israel from the time of Abraham.

at Gibeon, and Moon, in the valley of Aijalon" (Josh 10:12). This elevated language is most probably a way of celebrating the Lord's intervention, not necessarily a description of a supernatural event. Indeed, God has arranged the day so that there is time enough to destroy virtually all of the enemy forces, except those few who manage to escape and find sanctuary in designated cities of refuge.

The victory is complete. The terrified kings hide together in a cave at Makkedah, whose location is not known today, but they are soon brought out and forced to kneel down. Israelite warriors put their feet upon the royal necks, an ancient sign of victory often seen in the triumphal sculpture of Assyria and Egypt. Then the monarchs are killed and suspended from five trees until nightfall.

All of these actions are taken with one end in mind: to intimidate anyone in the land of Canaan who may be thinking of standing in the way of Israelite conquest. The bodies of the kings are thrown into the very cave where they had hidden and the entrance is sealed with large stones. Such a pile of stones was still there for all to see when the book of Joshua was written.

Joshua took Makkedah on that day, and struck it and its king with the edge of the sword. JOSH 10:28

After the crushing defeat of the Amorite league, Joshua seems to progress through the southern part of Canaan with little resistance, perhaps a triumph of propaganda as well as military might. The roll call of cities includes fortresses of the Shephelah, the region of low foothills between the Judean highlands and the plains near the Mediterranean. Israel's adversaries from the east would take this same route of invasion in the centuries to come.

Makkedah, Libnah, Lachish, Eglon, Hebron, Debir—all are quickly conquered and their peoples slaughtered by the sword. "So Joshua defeated the whole land, the hill country and the Negeb and the lowland and the slopes" (Josh 10:40).

In fact, neither the Bible nor archaeology agrees to the letter with this inclusive summary. Hebron and Debir, two important walled cities, are taken only later by Caleb and his younger brother Othniel, according to Joshua 15:13-17 and Judges 1:10-13. Historians believe that the other cities mentioned became part of Israel only during the monarchy.

To this point in the biblical story, however, Joshua has indeed accomplished the conquest of major cen-

Under a sun halted in the sky, Joshua defeats the Amorites at Gibeon; a 17th-century English stained glass window.

ters throughout the central and southern regions of Canaan, laying the groundwork for his successors' conquests in the decades to come.

They came out, with all their troops, a great army, in number like the sand on the seashore. JOSH 11:4

Finally, the Israelites turn their attention toward the north, where yet another coalition of kings has joined together in self-defense under the leadership of King Jabin of Hazor. He has probably heard that Joshua renewed the Lord's covenant at Mount Ebal and has enjoyed unprecedented success on the battlefield. Interestingly, four non-Semitic nations join his confederacy —the Hittites, the Perizzites, the Jebusites, and the Hivites—perhaps because Hazor's influence was so great during this period.

No previous battle in Joshua has involved chariots, but this great force includes many such horse-drawn military vehicles. Because of the rough countryside, it is likely that they were lightweight and collapsible for easy transportation from one level battlefield to another. They carried only two men, the armed soldier and his driver. The Israelites would not gain access to this technology until the reign of King David some 200 years later.

The foes' apparent tactical advantage proves worthless, however, since God is directly involved in the conflict. He orders Joshua to have his troops hamstring the horses—that is, make them lame by cutting the great tendons at the back of their hind legs. Then the Israelites put the disabled, foundering chariots to the torch. Yet again, a league of strong and battle-hardened enemies is resoundingly defeated, fleeing in different directions in panic.

Joshua himself slays King Jabin, then orders the people of Hazor massacred and burned, along with everything else in their town. Ordinarily, any city built atop a hill would not be razed because the site was ideal for well-defended occupation, but Hazor is perhaps punished for being especially resistant to the Israelite advance. In the other defeated towns, the remaining citizens are also killed, but the Lord allows the Israelites to seize their livestock and other possessions as the spoils of war. All towns built on mounds are set aside for resettlement.

Listing many more defeated enemies, including the famously strong giants known as Anakim, the chroniclers report that "Joshua took the whole land, according to all that the Lord had spoken to Moses" (Josh 11:23). If the Israelites seem brutal in victory to some readers, their massacres do effectively cleanse the cities of pagan religion and clear the way for God's people. These actions are taken in obedience to the will of the Lord.

The conquest is actually incomplete at this point, and many battles and skirmishes have proved inconclusive. But the major themes of the book are affirmed: At this juncture, Joshua has proved himself worthy of leading the Israelites under God. He has become Moses' rightful successor by ensuring the settlement of Canaan as the land of promise. He has conquered many strategically important cities for his people, given them lands for pasturage and crops after years of nomadic wandering, and brought them into a period of hard-won and negotiated peace.

Now these are the kings of the land, whom the Israelites defeated, whose land they occupied. JOSH 12:1

Chapter 12 sums up the Israelite victories. The first six verses recall the lands taken under Moses, the rest list the kings defeated by Joshua. This record is a prelude to the important work of the next lengthy section of the book, the distribution of those lands among the tribes of Israel by lot. From a practical point of view, this discussion provides the information that would be available to later cultures in the form of a map.

God has promised the land to his people if they obey him, he has fulfilled his promise by defeating their enemies, and now he determines how the land is to be distributed by the casting of sacred lots. When the process begins, Joshua is "very old and advanced in years" (Josh 13:1), a description suggesting that even the partial conquest and settlement of Canaan has been the grueling work of decades.

Even in the beginning, the Lord's promise is said to include land that would never really become an integral part of Israel in biblical times. Philistia (Josh 13:2) is held only briefly during the reigns of Kings David and Solomon, and Phoenicia (Josh 13:5-7) never comes under the control of the Israelites.

In addition, there are frequent explanations for areas that remain unoccupied by the invaders, beginning with Joshua 13:13: "Yet the Israelites did not drive out the Geshurites or the Maacathites; but Geshur and Maacath live within Israel to this day." Such inconsistencies are necessary to explain historical realities in the days the book of Joshua was written, but they are not allowed to distract the reader from the overriding celebration of tribal settlement.

Caught in the cave where they were hiding, the five defeated Amorite kings are hanged by Joshua; an early-15th-century French manuscript illumination.

"Allot the land to Israel for an inheritance, as I have commanded you." JOSH 13:6

The allotments are eventually divided among 12 tribes, even though the Levites receive no land. According to Moses, their inheritance is not land but the right to perform sacrifice and spread the teachings of the law. To fulfill their obligations to the Lord, the Levites must be dispersed throughout the lands of all of the other tribes. To retain the division of 12, however, the tribe of Joseph is split into Manasseh and Ephraim, tribes named for his two sons by his Egyptian wife Asenath.

Previously, Moses assigned the inheritances of two and a half tribes east of the Jordan—the Reubenites, Gadites, and half the tribe of Manasseh. He also promised Caleb, as the 85-year-old former spy now reminds Joshua, the land this stalwart soldier scouted out 45 years earlier. Joshua acts on the promise of his predecessor, ceding Hebron to Caleb. Evidently still competent on the battlefield, the elderly veteran has to conquer this area for himself.

As the land is given out, it is clear that the tribe of Judah receives the prime property, which is specifically described in Joshua 15:1-63. A very human anecdote puts this great panorama into the perspective of daily life in ancient times. Caleb, probably a Kenizzite, whose clan seems to be allied with Judah, gives his daughter in marriage to his younger brother, Othniel, who has seized some land in the Negeb. The young woman returns home to ask her father for water to go with this land and make it habitable, and he gives her "the upper springs and the lower springs" (Josh 15:19). Considering the nature of the terrain, the "springs" are probably cisterns that capture and store scarce rainwater in the arid climate.

As the long tally of the inheritance of Judah comes to a close, an important exception stands out. Although Jerusalem is assigned to the Judahites, the tribe is unable to drive out the Jebusite natives, who continued to "live with the people of Judah in Jerusalem" (Josh 15:63). But in Joshua 18:27, Jerusalem (called Jebus) is assigned to Benjamin. In fact, Jerusalem was not conquered until the time of David (2 Sam 5:6-7).

Meanwhile, one tribe is not satisfied. On the only occasion in which Joshua is shown functioning as a judge of Israel, the Joseph tribe, which is split in two, complains that it needs two lots to accommodate all of its people. Joshua agrees, but the land he gives them will require the clearing of forests and more fighting. The tribe complains about the might of the nearby Canaanites, who "have chariots of iron" (Josh 17:16), meaning chariots covered with protective iron plates. Still, the final conquest of their assigned territories becomes their own responsibility.

The last seven tribes are assigned their inheritances at Shiloh, where the tent of meeting has been set up. Previously in the book of Joshua, the Israelite congregation has assembled at Gilgal and Shechem, but Shiloh, about 20 miles north of Jerusalem, is apparently now the principal sanctuary. It will be the seat of the tabernacle for about another 100 years, or until its destruction by the Philistines around 1050 B.C.

The allocation of territories ends with Joshua's personal inheritance, the hill town of Timnath-serah, or "remaining portion" in Hebrew, 17 miles southwest of Shechem.

Then the Lord spoke to Joshua, saying, "Say to the Israelites, 'Appoint the cities of refuge, of which I spoke to you through Moses.'" JOSH 20:1

After the 12 tribes have been given their lands in accordance with God's plan, two very important exceptions are made: the cities of refuge and the Levitical cities.

The first are set up to ensure that accused murderers will be protected from vengeance killings until given a fair trial. Three cities of refuge are designated west of the Jordan and three east of the river. Anyone seeking asylum will be subject to a strict system of justice. The cities of refuge are already considered shrines because they are chosen from among the Levitical cities.

The Levitical cities, 48 in all, are dispersed throughout the conquered land on the average of four to a tribe. The Levites are to live with their families in these walled towns with nearby pasturage for their livestock. Nonetheless, the cities remain the property of the tribes who own them, and other people might live among the Levites. In addition to houses and pasturage, the Levites are compensated for their priestly functions by tithes from worshipers.

After the allotment of the cities, Joshua summons the eastern tribes and bids them farewell in words that mirror his speech to them at the beginning of the task of conquest, when he reminded them of their covenant with God. In both cases, he speaks more diplomatically than forcefully, perhaps because the Transjordanian tribes are only loosely federated with the rest of Israel.

The Israelites heard that the Reubenites and the Gadites and the half-tribe of Manasseh built an altar at the frontier. JOSH 22:11

Indeed, an unfortunate dispute soon emphasizes the mutual distrust between east and west. When the Transjordanian tribes build an altar to God, the Israelites are so disturbed that they gather in Shiloh to consider launching a war against their eastern brethren for apparent apostasy.

Erecting the secondary altar is considered an act of rebellion, since the law prohibits more than one designated place of worship. Burnt offerings are to be given "only at the place that the Lord will choose in one of your tribes" (Deut 12:14). Moreover, the Israelites still feel the shame and guilt of having succumbed earlier to the worship of Baal of Peor, a god of the Moabites. Finally, the sin of Achan is a very recent memory, a strong reminder that the sin of one person can bring punishment on an entire people. In other words, if the Transjordanian tribes are practicing idolatry, all of Israel will be made to suffer.

The priest Phinehas, grandson of Moses' brother Aaron, crosses the Jordan with ten leaders, one from each of the western Israelite tribes, to confront the easterners. Horrified, the accused deny any taint of rebellion against Israel or blasphemy against the Lord. They have built an altar only as a witness to their descendants, in case future generations on both sides of the river forget their shared covenant with the Lord. In fact, there may have been a belief in ancient Israel that only the west side of the Jordan was actually the promised land. Being isolated, the eastern tribes apparently are afraid of losing their connection to the wellsprings of the national religion.

A potentially disastrous situation is averted when Phinehas and his delegation accept this explanation. To some observers, the story reveals a Levitical obsession with control of the worship services. In any event, the Deuteronomic point is dramatically underscored for the reader: The God of Israel is officially worshiped in one place only, where the rituals are performed by the designated priestly class of Israel, the tribe of Levi.

Joshua summoned all Israel, their elders and heads, their judges and officers, and said to them, "I am now old and well advanced in years." JOSH 23:2

It is perhaps to that very place, the sanctuary at Shiloh, that Joshua goes to deliver his final speech to the Israelite congregation toward the close of his long, tumultuous life.

To the tribes from both sides of the river, he reaffirms the divine promises that have propelled their successful conquest of new lands for settlement. At the same time, he warns them strongly against intermarriage because of the danger of being corrupted by pagan religion.

Lest the people forget why they have prevailed in this new land, Joshua stresses that the war of occupation has been a holy war. It was the superhuman strength of the divine warrior, the Lord, who guaranteed final victory.

And Joshua warns that the lesson of war is also the rule of conduct for peace. If the people turn from their solemn covenant with the Lord, they will be punished: "You shall perish quickly from the good land that he has given to you" (Josh 23:16).

*Then Joshua gathered all the tribes of Israel
to Shechem.* JOSH 24:1

Finally, in a gathering of the congregation at sacred Shechem that reflects the earlier meeting at Mount Ebal, Joshua unites the tribal federation of Israelites into the nation of Israel. That is the name by which the 12 tribes will be collectively known from now on in the scriptures.

For the benefit of all tribes, whether descended from Abraham or incorporated into the tribal federation during the conquest of Canaan, Joshua recalls the promises of the Lord from the time of the patriarchs as well as the fulfillment of those promises down to the present.

But each person is given the opportunity to choose to serve the Lord and put away idolatry as a free moral act: "Choose this day whom you will serve" (Josh 24:15). The people say that they will serve God, but their leader is not satisfied with this ready answer. Again and again he reminds them that their decision is deadly serious. Once they agree to worship God, they will be profoundly punished for disobeying his laws. Over and over, the people swear that they do indeed understand the consequences.

As a witness to their new covenant with the Lord, Joshua sets up a special stone beside an oak tree in this ancient shrine. It is as if God's presence resides within the stone, actually hearing the oaths taken by the congregation.

Sometime afterward, the general who has followed God's will in settling the Israelites in Canaan dies at age 110 and is buried on his own land in the rugged hill country allotted to his tribe, Benjamin. Joseph died at the same age, which was considered the ideal life span in ancient Israel. And now, Joseph's remains, which had been carried with the Israelites from Egypt, are buried at Shechem.

The book of Joshua ends with the death of the high priest Eleazar, son of Aaron and father of his successor Phinehas. Both the political and the religious leaders of one generation pass from the stage, and the new nation of Israel faces the challenges of the future in new hands. Never again will it experience such steadfastness of purpose as in the age of Joshua's skillful, God-fearing leadership.

DIVISION OF THE PROMISED LAND

Though much of the promised land had yet to be secured, the Lord instructed the aged Joshua to allot territory to nine and a half tribes—Reuben, Gad, and half of Manasseh having already received land east of the Jordan River. Judah, the dominant tribe at the time the book of Joshua was compiled, was given the prime territory south of Jerusalem (still apparently in the hands of the Canaanites). Simeon was given only a handful of towns at the edge of the Negeb within Judah's allotment and, indeed, was eventually absorbed by its powerful neighbor. Dan, unable to hold its assigned territory in central Canaan, soon migrated north of the Sea of Galilee. Its allotment was divided among Judah, the small tribe of Benjamin, the dominant northern tribe of Ephraim, and perhaps the Philistines, who remained contentious adversaries on the Mediterranean coast.

It is virtually impossible to trace the tribal borders on a map with any degree of precision. The towns listed in Joshua 13-19 as given to one tribe may appear in Joshua 20-21 as allotted to another. Moreover, Joshua 13-19 seems to combine two lists, one of towns and another of borders. For example, only borders are given for Ephraim and Manasseh, whereas only the towns of Simeon are listed. Issachar's border is incomplete, and the territory of the two and a half tribes east of the Jordan is but vaguely described. Many scholars believe that the tribal areas listed in Joshua are actually administrative districts from a later period, perhaps that of David or Solomon. At any rate, the struggle for the promised land was by no means over at the death of Joshua—as the book of Judges vividly reveals.

The judge Ehud kills Moab's King Eglon with a quick sword thrust; a 14th-century stained glass window.

A collection of ancient stories written down and edited with religious intent in about the middle of the eighth century B.C., the book of Judges is a disturbing work. Although 12 "judges," or leaders, of Israel are shown triumphing over the pagan enemies of the emerging nation, their influence does not last past their deaths. In other words, without strong leadership, the Israelites invariably abandon the Lord, even though he has brought them from Egyptian bondage to the promised land of Canaan. Instead, they turn to the colorful fertility gods of their new neighbors.

But why are there so many pagans still in Canaan? Obviously, the great victories of the book of Joshua were confined to certain cities and regions, principally in the central highlands. Many Canaanite tribes are still firmly entrenched, desert warriors from the eastern deserts prove to be skillful raiders, and the Philistines invade the land from the Mediterranean seacoast. The struggles covered in the book of Judges—possibly stretching from about 1200 to 1020 B.C.—represent a confused, trying time for the Israelite tribes and their leaders. In the end, a horrendous civil war almost destroys one of the original 12 tribes. According to the archaeological record, these centuries were definitely a time of continuing conflict and disorder, including the complete destruction of many cities.

Many of the so-called judges are the heroes of individual tribes or clans rather than all of Israel, and none offers the kind of sustained, enlightened spiritual leadership of Moses or Joshua. Competent leaders alternate with highly flawed ones. Toward the end of the book, ungodly actions are common yet again. For example, the tribe of Dan fails to hold onto its patrimony, turns to idolatry, and massacres harmless citizens. The tribe of Benjamin defends crimes against nature and the law. As the editor hints, the Israelites will not gain unity and righteousness as a nation that follows God's will until the monarchy is established.

After the death of Joshua, the Israelites inquired of the Lord, "Who shall go up first for us against the Canaanites, to fight against them?" JUDG 1:1

The Israelites' invasion is incomplete in southern Canaan, mostly because the established residents have strong defensive walls around their cities and more advanced weapons than the invaders. But the Israelites are stubbornly determined to continue their conquest, in part because each tribe has been assigned a particular area as its God-given property.

The editor of Judges begins with military activities in the Jerusalem area. Beforehand, the Israelites asked the Lord's will by casting lots. Probably, this ritual was preceded by prayer. Then small stones with different inscriptions were shaken together in a pottery jar. The stone that was drawn out by hand or jiggled out first on the ground indicated the divine answer.

In this case, the tribe of Judah is chosen to renew the assault. To the writer of Judges, the Lord's response, "I hereby give the land into his hand" (Judg 1:2), means that the outcome of the battle is a fore-gone conclusion. Judah invites the lesser tribe of Simeon to join with it, for the two are descended from blood brothers. In later generations, the Simeonites are absorbed into the larger tribe.

The battle in Judges 1:4 is somewhat puzzling to biblical historians. The site of Bezek has not been determined, but it might be between Shechem and Jerusalem or near Gezer. Nor is much known about the Perizzites. They had resided in Canaan since the days of the patriarchs, and their name suggests that they lived in unwalled cities or in the countryside. Finally, the number "ten thousand" is unclear. In an ancient census, the word translated as "thousand" could stand for a unit of 5 to 14 fighting men.

The Israelites destroy Jerusalem. But because King David will have to conquer the city again in the future, the Canaanites must have actually retained the city or regained control during the tumultuous years covered by the book of Judges.

From the heights of Jerusalem, the Israelites launch a campaign to acquire the central highlands of Canaan down to Hebron 20 miles to the south.

Then Caleb said, "Whoever attacks Kiriath-sepher and takes it, I will give him my daughter Achsah as wife."
JUDG 1:12

The believably naturalistic story of the marriage of Caleb's daughter was previously told of in Joshua 15:13-19.

The Hebrew in this version suggests that Othniel could be either Caleb's nephew or a younger brother. Later in Judges, he will emerge as the first model "judge," or leader of the people.

Since the word "urged" (Judg 1:14) can be translated as "nagged," it seems clear that Achsah believes she has a right to the springs at Upper Gulloth and Lower Gulloth. Ordinarily, her father's gift of land to her husband would be sufficient for her dowry. But Othniel has to win the land by fighting for it; therefore, the wells might be considered the dowry. The writer names them as if they are well known, but "gulloth" may simply mean "basins."

The descendants of Hobab the Kenite, Moses' father-in-law, went up with the people of Judah from the city of palms into the wilderness of Judah. JUDG 1:16

As the conquest continues, the Kenites, who were nomadic metalworkers, join with the Israelites. Hobab may have been Moses' son-in-law, according to an alternate translation. Experts disagree, too, about "the city of palms." Usually, the phrase applies to Jericho, but here it might indicate a town to the south near the Dead Sea.

The results of the campaign are mixed. Many enemy towns are captured, and archaeological digs in recent years show that many new Hebrew towns were soon built in the region. Still, a few Canaanite city-states, including Acco and Megiddo, could not be overthrown, nor could Philistia be conquered.

In verse 22, the house of Joseph takes the stage from Judah and moves against Bethel, which means "house of God." According to some commentators, this story may echo the fall of Ai in Joshua 7:1-5. The towns were very close to each other.

After success at Bethel, there follows a list of failures. Many of these Canaanite cities had such strong fortifications that they could not be breached until the time of King David. Gezer, an ancient city first mentioned in Egyptian writing around 1400 B.C., resists until the time of Solomon. The tribe of Dan fares the worst. The Danites are literally driven back into the hills, anticipating their ignominious behavior at the end of Judges.

"But you have not obeyed my command. See what you have done!" JUDG 2:2

Suddenly, the story skips forward in time. God's presence, venerated in the book of Joshua at the Israelites' camp at Gilgal, has moved to Bochim, which may have been situated between Gilgal and Bethel. Bochim means "weepers," for the people have reason to weep bitterly there.

God's messenger from heaven, an angel, sternly reminds them that the Lord freed them from Egyptian bondage and fulfilled his ancient promise to give them the land of Canaan. But they have defaulted on their part of the bargain. Evidently, in the years since the first conquests, the Israelites have allowed the subdued Canaanites to continue their pagan ways. As punishment, the Lord will allow the enemy and their religion to become powerful adversaries in the future.

Then the Israelites did what was evil in the sight of the Lord and worshiped the Baals; and they abandoned the Lord. JUDG 2:11-12

The new generation born since Joshua's day has not only forgotten the ways of God, it has enthusiastically embraced the worship of idols.

The Canaanite storm god Baal was the most important. He may have been especially tempting to the Israelites, now a nation of farmers, because he controlled the weather and ensured fertility. The plural "Baals" may refer to idols attached to local shrines. Similarly, the "Astartes" were local manifestations of the Canaanite goddess of fertility. Under other

The undulating hill country stretching from central Canaan to the Mediterranean Sea was the locale of many struggles led by the judges of Israel.

names, she was worshiped throughout the ancient Near East, from Egypt to Babylon.

The writer of Judges next explains the pattern that will be repeated again and again throughout his story.

First, the Israelites do "evil"—that is, they turn from the Lord to paganism. Second, they are divinely punished by being given over to their enemies, who plunder and enslave them. Third, the people cry out in their hardship, at last turning back to God to ask for deliverance.

Fourth and finally, the Lord raises up judges to lead and rescue them. These judges, as will become apparent throughout the book, are not lawyers or jurists. They come from a variety of backgrounds but they have two things in common: The Lord is with them, and they quickly demonstrate their extraordinary talent for leadership. But unfortunately, as the writer warns, the people abandon the Lord as soon as the judge dies. The cycle begins again: apostasy, oppression, prayer, and rescue.

Judging Israel from beneath a palm tree, Deborah orders Barak into battle against King Jabin of Hazor.

And he sold them into the hand of King Cushan-rishathaim of Aram-naharaim. JUDG 3:8

The cycle of judgeship stories begins with Othniel, who was a member of a clan allied with the tribe of Judah; all the other judges come from the ten northern tribes.

The Israelites worship the Canaanite idols, and God punishes them with slavery. The land of Aram-naharaim was probably in northern Syria or western Mesopotamia. The name of its king might mean something like "double trouble of the two rivers."

Although Othniel's story is briefly told, he is clearly the editor's ideal judge. Verse 10 sums up his basic virtues and achievements: He is blessed by God, makes judicious decisions, leads the people into battle, and thereafter governs the nation. During his lifetime, the Israelites are faithful to God, and "the land had rest forty years" (Judg 3:11), a phrase first used here to denote a generation.

And the Lord strengthened King Eglon of Moab against Israel, because they had done what was evil in the sight of the Lord. JUDG 3:12

Once Othniel dies, the Israelites backslide again. This time, they are invaded by King Eglon, whose name could mean "fat calf" in ancient Hebrew. His Moabites, who live just east of the Dead Sea, join forces with the Ammonites to the north and the Amalekites, fierce nomads from the Negeb Desert who despise the Israelites. They defeat and occupy Israelite territory, capturing strategic Jericho.

The second judge comes from the tribe of Benjamin and makes a strong contrast with Othniel. Not only is Ehud left-handed, like an unusual number of his tribesmen, but he is a violent loner of a hero. Clearly, he does the work of the Lord, but the Bible does not note that "the spirit of the Lord" blesses his actions as it does those of other judges.

Charged with leading the delegation that delivers tribute to Eglon, Ehud hides a short sword at his right thigh. As the Israelites head homeward, he suddenly turns back at "the sculptured stones near Gilgal" (Judg 3:19). Some experts believe these were boundary stones at the edge of Moabite land. Others think they are the stones Joshua set up as a memorial to the time when the flooded Jordan River miraculously stopped flowing to let the Israelites cross into Canaan.

Ehud cleverly gains entrance to the king's private rooftop chamber, a kind of cool summer parlor, by claiming to have a secret message, perhaps suggesting a message from God. Eglon impatiently orders his courtiers out of the room. But once they leave, Ehud draws out his concealed sword with his left hand and stabs the overweight monarch deep in the belly. The description is intentionally grotesque, perhaps a writerly revenge. The king dies instantly.

Ehud leaves quickly, locking the doors behind him. For some time, the cowed Moabites dare not disturb their king. His own arrogance has helped give Ehud the time he needs to escape.

Emboldened by the assassination, Ehud sounds the ram's horn trumpet, calling together the Israelite troops. Their first tactic is to seize "the fords of the Jordan" (Josh 3:28), thereby preventing the enemy forces occupying Canaan from fleeing to safety in the east. Thus cut off and surrounded, the Moabites are slaughtered to the last man. There is peace for 80 years—though Shamgar, possibly a mercenary, delivers Israel by single-handedly slaying 600 Philistines.

At that time Deborah, a prophetess, wife of Lappidoth, was judging Israel. JUDG 4:4

After Ehud, the cycle recurs. Jabin, misidentified as king of all Canaan, was more likely the local Canaanite king of Hazor, an important trading center some nine miles to the north of the Sea of Galilee. His army commander, Sisera, has a non-Semitic name that suggests he could have been a Philistine. The oppressors' 900 chariots, almost as many as the Egyptian empire of that period would field in a major battle in the area, could easily crush the poorly armed Israelites on a level battlefield. At this time, the newcomers had not yet acquired military chariots.

After the oppression has lasted for about half a generation, Israel's Deborah takes action. A charismatic woman respected for her wisdom and prophetic gifts, she commands Barak, the nation's military commander, to take his troops up to Mount Tabor and prepare to ambush Sisera's mighty forces.

Sisera falls for Deborah's ruse. He races toward Tabor across the Esdraelon plain to the northern pass guarded by the large cities of Megiddo and Taanach. But this is the same spot where streams converge to form the Kishon, a river that can rise to produce muddy, swampy ground. The account is not clear, but the Lord somehow intervenes, throwing the Canaanite forces into a panic. The Israelites recognize that they prevail only because God is with them.

Now Sisera had fled away on foot to the tent of Jael wife of Heber the Kenite. JUDG 4:17

*I*n the confusion, proud Sisera is forced to run away on foot while his terrified warriors are massacred. Exhausted, he manages to reach an encampment of the nomadic Kenites, who are at peace with King Jabin. But Sisera cannot know that Jael, the wife of the chief of the Kenites, is faithful to the God of Israel.

Jael deceptively offers hospitality, inviting the defeated general into her tent to rest. When he asks only for a little water, she gives him milk, perhaps because some forms of goat's milk cause drowsiness.

As her guest sleeps, Jael seizes a mallet and pounds a tent peg through his skull and into the ground, killing him instantly. She would have been especially handy with these simple tools because women in those times were responsible for setting up and taking down the tents of the nomads.

As the defeated general Sisera sinks into sleep, the heroine Jael drives a tent peg into his head; a painting by Artemisia Gentileschi (1597-c. 1651).

The Israelites did what was evil in the sight of the Lord, and the Lord gave them into the hand of Midian seven years. JUDG 6:1

*B*ut Deborah's great victory is followed by only a generation of peace. This time, the apostasy of the Israelites coincides with an important cultural advance in the deserts east of the Jordan River. The Midianites and other nomadic tribes have learned to tame the camel. The reference to their invasions of Israel is the first known written account of camel raids. Neither the Israelites nor anyone else knows how to defend against troops mounted on camelback.

The Midianites and the Amalekites appear on the horizon in the beginning of the growing season. They set up their tents and put their herds to pasture, steal the harvest, and return to their oases only when the land has been laid bare.

Desperate for relief, the Israelites call out to the Lord. Thus begins the story of Gideon, one of the greatest of all biblical figures.

For the first time in Judges, the Lord is shown speaking directly with one of his people. First, an angel prepares the way at Ophrah, a village of the tribe of Manasseh. An oak there was considered a sacred spot for the receiving of oracles. Gideon, who is secretly threshing wheat so that the enemy will not steal it, seems impatient with the angel's message, "The Lord is with you" (Judg 6:12). If that is true, he wonders aloud, why is Israel oppressed? At that point, God himself speaks up, though he remains invisible, and commissions Gideon to

The Kishon River's swampy banks became a trap for Sisera's chariots; the two-man battle carriages should have given the Canaanites a great advantage.

rescue the nation. The amazed and grateful Gideon builds an altar to the Lord of Israel. That night, God tells him to destroy his father Joash's altar to Baal. Wealthy enough to have power over ten servants, Gideon orders them to help him tear down the Canaanite pagan altar, including a sacred pole that was always to be found at these fertility shrines. This pole will be used to fuel the sacrificial fire of a seven-year-old bullock to be burnt as an offering on the Lord's altar. Ironically, Gideon is convinced of the might of the Lord, yet he performs these actions during the night to avoid notice.

His fear is not unfounded. The next day, the furious townspeople demand he be put to death for dishonoring Baal. But Joash, as head of the family, takes full responsibility for his son's actions. He also recognizes that he has been wrong to forsake the worship of God and threatens execution of anyone defending Baal. "If he is a god, let him contend for himself," Joash says with scorn (Judg 6:32).

From that day forward, Gideon is also known as Jerubbaal, a name suggesting that Baal will have to contend with him. This name might have originated with the head of a Manasseh clan at Shechem who was a zealous follower of the God of Israel.

At this point, the nomadic tribes return on their annual invasion to the Jezreel valley, Canaan's most tempting area for plunder. Dedicated now to the Lord's work, in fact possessed with the divine spirit, Gideon calls on the warriors of his tribe and three Galilean tribes to fight the invaders.

"In order to see whether you will deliver Israel by my hand, as you have said, I am going to lay a fleece of wool on the threshing floor." JUDG 6:36-7

Then Gideon seems to have second thoughts. He asks God to back up the promise of victory with more proof. First, Gideon asks that a fleece left on the dry ground be soaked with dew the following morning. This happens and was, in fact, a phenomenon well known to ancient fishermen who lived on desert, unwatered islands in the Near East.

Gideon then asks for the reverse. The next morning, the fleece is completely dry and the ground wet with dew. This is clearly a supernatural event.

Then Jerubbaal (that is, Gideon) and all the troops that were with him rose early. JUDG 7:1

Having gathered his forces, Gideon sets up camp in the southeastern end of the Jezreel valley at the spring of Harod just below Mount Gilboa.

Then the Lord makes clear that the victory to come must be seen by the world as divine intervention. Gideon's 32,000 men are too great a number because they could perhaps drive out the Midianites by sheer force without the help of God.

Following God's instructions, Gideon tells anyone who feels frightened to return home. That cuts his army down to 10,000, which is still too large for the Lord's purposes. Next, Gideon is ordered to have his men drink water from the spring and eliminate anyone who kneels and brings water in his hands to his mouth rather than bending to drink "as a dog laps" (Judg 7:5). Does the method of drinking indicate whether a soldier is alert? Or is this merely a convenient way of winnowing down to the smallest number? To most experts, the meaning here is debatable, but the Lord's end is achieved. The army is now no more than 300 strong.

While everyone else heads homeward, this small band collects all of their pottery jars and trumpets. That very night, following God's command, Gideon and his young personal attendant and armor-bearer Purah, which can mean "boy" or "lad," sneak northward to the outskirts of the Midianite camp below the hill of Moreh, an extinct volcano opposite Gilboa. The Lord sees that Gideon's confidence has to be renewed yet again, for the tiny Israelite force is about to attack a huge armed encampment protected by formidable camel troops.

Moving silently in the darkness, Gideon and Purah come upon a couple of sentries chatting nervously. One tells of a dream in which a barley cake falls on a Midianite tent, presumably the tent of the chieftain or tribal leader, and causes it to collapse. Like the Hebrews, the Midianites and other ancient peoples believed that dreams were messages from divine powers. Immediately, the other sentry interprets the dream to mean that God will help Gideon defeat the entire Midianite army.

When Gideon heard the telling of the dream and its interpretation, he worshiped. JUDG 7:15

Astounded, for this is the word of the Lord coming through the mouth of a pagan, Gideon prostrates himself on the ground. Assured of success, he returns to camp and rouses his men, dividing them into three separate companies. Each man is given a trumpet and a pottery jar with a torch hidden inside. The soldiers approach the enemy camp after the sentries of the first watch are replaced. The night was customarily divided into three watches.

Then, in one of history's most famous military ruses, the three tiny groups take up three separate positions around the sleeping Midianites. Apparently unarmed, they will rely upon an act of psychological warfare. At a given signal, they all give a mighty blast on their trumpets and smash open their jars, revealing the torches burning inside. To the Midianites, suddenly roused from deep sleep by this din, it looks as if they are completely surrounded by a great army. From all sides they hear the terrifying shout, "A sword for the Lord and for Gideon!" (Judg 7:20).

In the confusion and the darkness of night, the Midianites flail around wildly, killing each other, not knowing who is friend or foe. Then the surviving forces split apart in panic, and stampede leaderless toward the supposed safety of their homelands in the desert highlands to the east of the Jordan River.

STRUGGLES OF THE JUDGES

Israel was besieged by enemies during the chaotic period described in the book of Judges. Having seized Jericho, the Moabites extracted a tribute from the Israelites until Ehud killed their king. Judging Israel from beneath a palm near Bethel, Deborah charged Barak with the task of defeating Jabin, the Canaanite king of Hazor; he was crushed in swampy waters near Megiddo. A generation later, desert raiders from east of the Jordan threatened the Jezreel valley. Summoned by the Lord, Gideon routed the invaders near Endor and drove them back across the Jordan. His son Abimelech briefly ruled as king at Shechem.

Jephthah's triumph over the Ammonites at Abel-keramim was followed by tragedy upon his return to Mizpah. Fulfilling a vow, he was forced to kill his daughter who came to welcome him. Samson's dramatic exploits took place mainly in the Philistine cities on the Mediterranean coast.

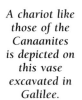

A chariot like those of the Canaanites is depicted on this vase excavated in Galilee.

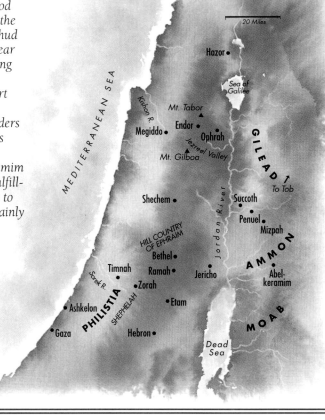

Then Gideon sent messengers throughout all the hill country of Ephraim. JUDG 7:24

As the rout continues, Gideon sends word on his own, without seeking the Lord's advice, to the tribe of Ephraim. The tribesmen respond quickly enough to regain territory and kill two Midianite captains named Oreb, meaning "raven," and Zeeb, meaning "wolf." Rather than thank Gideon for their prizes, the Ephraimites are annoyed. Members of a tribe proud of its preeminence among the other tribes of the central highlands, they resent being left out of the original attack, which would have yielded more glory and also more spoils.

But Gideon flatters them with a proverb that he either invents on the spot or retrieves from folk wisdom for the occasion, suggesting that killing the captains is more glorious than anything he has done. The Ephraimites are appeased, and Gideon recommences his pursuit of the escaping Midianites, who are adept at vanishing into the rocky hills and valleys of the desert.

By this time, Gideon's tiny band of Manassehites is exhausted and hungry. Still, they cross the Jordan, hoping to receive aid from the Israelite tribes east of the river. Unfortunately, the eastern tribes did not always sympathize with the aims of their relatives who had settled west of the Jordan.

In this case, the people of Succoth, a settlement in the river valley, refuse to help, sneering at Gideon's explanation that he is chasing after two Midianite kings. "Do you already have in your possession the hands of Zebah and Zalmunna?" (Judg 8:6), they sneer. The question refers to the ancient custom of chopping off a defeated enemy's hands. Gideon angrily promises revenge and forges on to the nearby town of Penuel, meaning "face of God," where the people also deny his men food. Again, he threatens reprisal but first leads his men eastward on the caravan route. Surprising the enemy to the east of the Dead Sea at Karkor, he captures the two kings mentioned in the taunts at Succoth, and the Midianite armies flee farther eastward. Not even dreaming that Gideon would pursue them so obstinately, they had failed to set out sentries.

He caught a young man, one of the people of Succoth, and questioned him. JUDG 8:14

The enemy of the nation disposed of, a coldly angry Gideon retraces his steps and plans his revenge. Outside Succoth, he finds out the names of the town's 77 elders from a captured youth. Then he enters the town and confronts these leaders, who probably belong to a governing council of all of the heads of families in the area. Reminding them of their own words, he displays the captured kings. Without mercy, he puts the elders of Succoth to death, most probably by some means of torture that is not clearly explained. At Penuel, he kills the able-bodied men and tears down the town fortress.

Then the Israelites said to Gideon, "Rule over us, you and your son and your grandson also." JUDG 8:22

For all of his hesitations, Gideon shows himself to be an organized and skillful military leader, and it is clear to everyone in Israel that he has been blessed by God. He has saved the tribe of Manasseh and a portion of the tribe of Issachar from perhaps the worst disaster yet faced by the Israelites.

Naturally, the people ask him to rule over them and even establish a family dynasty. He refuses, reminding the Israelites that only God can lead them. Then he makes a strange request. He asks his soldiers to contribute the gold earrings from their Midianite spoils to the making of an ephod, or priestly

In these 13th-century manuscript illuminations, an angel calls Gideon and kindles his sacrificial fire (top); Gideon destroys his father's idols and summons Israel to battle (center); Gideon's troops rout the Midianites (bottom).

garment with a hollow breastplate to hold ritual dice for divining the future. Apparently, the ephod was also an item of veneration, for the Israelites worship before Gideon's ephod at Ophrah. In other words, God's people return to idolatry even before their judge has died because he has fallen into error.

Still, there is peace for another generation until Gideon dies at a ripe age, the father of many sons.

They gave him seventy pieces of silver out of the temple of Baal-berith with which Abimelech hired worthless and reckless fellows, who followed him. JUDG 9:4

Abimelech, one of Gideon's 70 sons (most likely a symbolic rather than an actual number), was born to a Canaanite concubine in Shechem. Only half-Hebrew, Abimelech did not share his father's distaste for hereditary kingship. Drawing on the nationalistic feelings of the Shechemites, he argues that he is a preferable ruler to any of the other possible heirs. The city's ruling elite gives him part of the treasure stored in the local temple to Baal. He uses the funds to hire thugs and leads them to Ophrah to kill his potential rivals. After this slaughter, he is acknowledged king of Shechem near an especially sacred spot, a famous oak.

But Gideon's youngest son, Jotham, has escaped alive. Standing boldly atop Mount Gerizim, he shouts down to the town below a parable that is a direct challenge to the upstart Abimelech.

In this tale, various trees gather together to proclaim a king, but they are refused by their first three choices. All have more important things to do: The olive produces oil for sacrifice and the anointing of guests and kings; the fig yields a beloved fruit basic to the ancient diet; and the vine, which symbolizes the bounty of Israel, produces libations for the gods and happiness for human beings.

But the bramble, a useless weed, agrees to take the throne. Still, its promise to provide shade to the other mighty trees is obviously ridiculous, and it admits that fire is often generated in its dry branches, making it a very risky sort of protector.

Leaving no room for misinterpretation, Jotham explains to the lords of Shechem exactly what the story means: They have chosen a bramble as king. His listeners must have reacted violently because Jotham flees to an unknown village named Beer. This name, which means "well," was a common one in Canaan.

Abimelech ruled over Israel three years. JUDG 9:22

Only three years after the usurper's bloody triumph, there is strife in Shechem. God causes the split by sending an evil spirit to work a kind of poetic justice: Both the king and the leaders who supported him will be punished.

For their part, the Shechemites who defect begin robbing caravans that ply the principal trade route through Manasseh. Aside from causing chaos in his territory, these raids may have deprived Abimelech

MINOR JUDGES

The book of Judges names 12 leaders who helped deliver the Israelites from their enemies in Canaan and kept them faithful to the covenant with the Lord during the period between Joshua and Saul, Israel's first king. Because the Hebrew word somewhat misleadingly translated as "judge" stems from a verb that can also mean "decide," "govern," or "deliver," the elite 12 are not to be regarded as jurists in the modern sense. Rather, they were prophets like Deborah, military commanders like Gideon, or bold heroes like Samson. In addition, there were six so-called minor judges about whom the Bible has little to say.

Shamgar is perhaps a later addition in Judges 3:31; his non-Semitic name suggests he may have been a convert. Tola and Jair appear only in Judges 10:1-5. The first dwelled in the hill country of Ephraim and governed for 23 years. The second, a man of Gilead who ruled 22 years, had 30 sons, each of whom rode a donkey and had his own town. The remaining three minor judges, filling the gap between Jephthah and Samson, are briefly identified in Judges 12:8-15. Ibzan judged Israel for seven years from Bethlehem, most likely not the southern town of Jesus' birth but rather the Bethlehem in Galilee. He was rich and influential enough to marry off all 30 of his daughters and find wives for his 30 sons. The Zebulunite Elon judged for ten years and was followed by another northerner, Abdon. He led Israel for eight years and had 40 sons and 30 grandsons, each of whom owned a donkey.

The dearth of information about the six has fueled speculation that their names were added to fill chronological gaps in the biblical narrative or to round out the number of judges to 12, one for each tribe.

of the protection money travelers often paid to a ruler. Like the bramble, he offered no shade.

In a dramatic confrontation, the depth of rebellious feeling in Shechem is made clear during the festival to celebrate new wine. Drinking in the temple to Baal, the lords of Shechem make fun of Abimelech. By nightfall, Abimelech's troops set up an ambush outside Shechem. The next morning, they soundly defeat the rebels.

Still, Abimelech, the bramble of the parable, is not satisfied. The next day, his men divide into three companies and hide in the fields. When the Shechemites come out to work their land, the troops rise up and kill them all. Then they rush into Shechem, slaughter the people there, and destroy the town. The

phrase "sowed it with salt" (Judg 9:45) might mean simply that vengeful Abimelech cursed the city. The tower of Shechem, possibly a fortification at Bethmillo, is put to the torch, and 1,000 men and women are burned alive inside.

Abimelech seems to grow even hungrier for blood. He leads his men to the city of Thebez, about 12 miles northeast of Shechem, and captures everything but the stone defensive tower. As he approaches to burn it to the ground, a woman inside hurls a heavy millstone onto his head. His skull crushed, his life rapidly ebbing away, the unworthy ruler asks his armor-bearer to kill him with a sword, "so people will not say about me, 'A woman killed him'" (Judg 9:54). The usurper is punished for the murder of his half brothers; Shechem pays for supporting him.

After Abimelech, Tola son of Puah son of Dodo, a man of Issachar, who lived at Shamir in the hill country of Ephraim, rose to deliver Israel. JUDG 10:1

In the years that follow, two more men will judge Israel: Tola and Jair.

After the judgeship of Jair, the Hebrews once again abandon God. As punishment, they are afflicted for 18 years both by the Philistines, their traditional enemies from the Mediterranean shore, and the Ammonites, descendants of Lot from east of the Jordan River. More is said of the Philistines in the saga of Samson. Now, the focus is on the Ammonites.

It is time to find a new judge.

Now Jephthah the Gileadite, the son of a prostitute, was a mighty warrior. JUDG 11:1

One of the most unlikely heroes of Israel is Jephthah, whose great personal virtues overcame his unfortunate background. His story is the only one in Judges to unfold entirely in the lands east of the Jordan River, here called Gilead.

The son of a prostitute, he was driven from his father's house by his half brothers. They are certainly not compassionate human beings in this account, but they are merely following the custom of the time: An illegitimate son could not inherit family property.

In Tob, most likely a more distant eastern town, Jephthah becomes the leader of a band of outlaws who live by raiding. Evidently, his fame as a skilled warrior spreads homeward, for the elders of Gilead ask him to help them fight against the Ammonites, who are claiming the territory.

Then Jephthah initiates the only attempt at negotiations with foreigners in the entire book of Judges. In correspondence with the king of the Ammonites, he recalls the history of the tribes of Israel to make a basic point: God gave the land in dispute to the Israelites three centuries ago (a clearly exaggerated figure for the period since the invasion of Canaan). The Ammonites have not complained before; why should they now? Moreover, their god, Chemosh, has given them land of their own. The king is unmoved.

Then the spirit of the Lord came upon Jephthah, and he passed through Gilead and Manasseh. JUDG 11:29

Jephthah tries to ensure success in the campaign he launches against the Ammonites by making an extreme vow. It is as if he cannot resist using his skills at diplomacy, even with the Lord. He promises to show gratitude for victory by making a burnt offering of "whoever" first comes out of his house to greet him when he returns to his home in Mizpah.

Some scholars think this might be an intentional reference to human sacrifice, which was condemned by but not unfamiliar to the Hebrews. But most believe that he actually meant "whatever." In the typically humble houses of this period, the family's animals would have stayed within the walled courtyard. Jephthah was probably offering to sacrifice whatever lamb or young goat came stumbling out of the enclosure first.

Instead, after thrashing the Ammonites, he returns home only to shrink in horror as his only child, his beloved daughter, races out to celebrate his triumph. She dances and sings joyously in the traditional way women of those times greeted conquering heroes.

Tearing his clothes in grief, he tells her about his vow. She immediately understands that he has no choice but to kill her in a ritual sacrifice. Since it was a disgrace for a Hebrew woman to die without children, however, she asks for two months' respite to mourn her fate with friends in the desert mountains. Verse 40 describes a feast of lamentation that is mentioned nowhere else in the scriptures. Perhaps it was observed only in the region of Gilead. Wisely, the writer does not include the details of the horrifying sacrifice. But the story reinforces a theme repeated throughout the book of Judges: The word of the Lord or of a human being must always be kept.

The men of Ephraim were called to arms, and they crossed to Zaphon and said to Jephthah, "Why did you cross over to fight against the Ammonites, and did not call us to go with you?" JUDG 12:1

As in the days of Gideon, the Ephraimites try to benefit from another's victory. They cross the Jordan to complain to Jephthah that they have been insulted by not being asked to participate in the rout of the Ammonites. They threaten revenge, but Jephthah, the former outlaw, is not as conciliatory to the Ephraimites as Gideon had been.

Unaware of her father's pledge to sacrifice whoever first greeted him on his return from battle, Jephthah's daughter rushes to welcome the victor; a detail from a 17th-century painting.

At the major ford of the Jordan occurs one of the most fascinating stories of the Old Testament. Although Ephraimite stragglers are trying to return to their homelands west of the river, Jephthah's men ask them to say the word "shibboleth." The meaning of this password, which could be "brook," "ears," or "twig," is not important. Since there was no "sh" sound in the Ephraimite dialect, the fugitives could say only "sibboleth." This is a dead giveaway of their origins, and they are immediately slaughtered by the angry Gileadites.

After this unfortunate intertribal conflict, Jephthah serves as judge for six years. Three judges whose lives are not recorded in any detail follow: Ibzan, Elon, and Abdon.

There was a certain man of Zorah, of the tribe of the Danites, whose name was Manoah. His wife was barren, having borne no children. JUDG 13:2

The seven episodes of the compelling story of Samson show little if any signs of an editorial hand, perhaps because these tales were so familiar and beloved throughout Israel by the time Judges was compiled in the form known today.

The contradictory hero is seen in all of his complexity—arrogant, passionate, vengeful, stubborn, lusty, but in the end dedicated to the will of the Lord. The historical background is also complicated. The non-Semitic Philistines had appeared on the southeastern Mediterranean coastal plain between 1200 and 1180 B.C., but they apparently coexisted with the Israelites at first. If there were armed raids, there was also intermarriage and mutual trade. Still, hostilities could flare up, and the Philistines would remain a problem until King David's reign.

Before Samson's birth, according to Judges 13:1, the Israelites turned from God. Consequently, the Philistines have been allowed to exploit them for 40 years, again the round number used to signify the passage of a generation.

Samson's mother, who is unnamed, is barren until the angel of the Lord appears to announce that she will have a son. But she must agree to raise the boy as a nazirite. This sect of very pious men and women live by three basic rules: no alcohol, no cutting of hair, and no contact with the dead.

After the angel repeats the message to the woman's husband, Manoah, the prophecy is fulfilled. Samson is born in Zorah, a town on the border between Judah and Dan, and the Lord is with him.

*Once Samson went down to Timnah, and at Timnah
he saw a Philistine woman.*   JUDG 14:1

When next seen, Samson is a grown man in
love. According to the custom of the day, his
parents, especially his father, are supposed to approve
and arrange a marriage. Unfortunately, Samson's parents do not agree with his choice of a Philistine
woman. They do not understand, the editor points
out, that God is preparing an excuse for Samson to
attack Israel's Philistine oppressors.

After their son stubbornly insists, Samson's parents
accompany him to Timnah. Along the way, inspired
by the Lord, the unarmed young man rips a lion in
two. He keeps this act secret from his mother and father. On a later trip, he discovers a hive of honeybees in the lion's carcass, eats some of the sweet
honey, and takes some to his parents without telling
them where it came from. Bees would not choose to
live in decaying flesh, nor could they produce so
much honey so rapidly. This story is a narrative device to set up the famous riddle that follows.

Samson's father apparently arranges a special kind
of ancient Near Eastern marriage: The wife will live
with her parents, and Samson will visit from time to
time. As the traditional seven-day marriage feast
begins, the Philistines appoint 30 local young men to
act as his groomsmen. Perhaps they are actually meant
to keep Samson in check, since the Israelite is obviously strong and self-confident. Nor does he seem
particularly friendly when he proposes a very expensive bet. If they can answer his riddle, he will give
each of them two fine garments. If they fail, he will
expect a total of 60 garments from the lot of them.

The riddle is clear from previous events, but impossible to solve otherwise: "Out of the eater came
something to eat. Out of the strong came something
sweet" (Judg 14:14).

The groomsmen are stumped. Angry at having to
pay such a steep price, they tell Samson's wife they
will burn her to death in her father's house if she does
not discover the solution. Terrified, she wheedles the
truth out of him. At the very last possible moment,
the Philistine young men foil the Israelite stranger
with the correct answers of "honey" and "a lion."

Samson instantly realizes that he has been betrayed
by his new wife. Feeling the power of the Lord, he
goes to one of the five major Philistine cities,
Ashkelon, kills 30 men there, and seizes their garments to pay off the bet. He goes home in anger, leaving his wife, who is soon given to the best man from
the ill-fated wedding.

*Samson said to them, "This time, when I do mischief to
the Philistines, I will be without blame."*   JUDG 15:3

After calming down, or perhaps driven by his
passionate nature, Samson decides to return to
visit his wife. He brings a kid, perhaps a traditional
gift for visiting the spouse in this kind of marriage,
but also the fee for a prostitute (Gen 38:17). The
woman's father informs Samson that she has been
given away and offers her younger sister instead.

This insult plays right into Samson's hands. In revenge, he ties burning torches to the tails of 300
foxes and sends them running through the Philistine
fields, destroying their essential grain crops. The
Philistines cannot punish him because he has been
wronged. Instead, they burn his wife and her father
to death. Now Samson takes revenge, striking down
many Philistines "hip and thigh" (Judg 15:8). The
phrase "hip and thigh" may be a term used to describe ancient wrestling. Quite possibly, wrestlers vied
with each other as added entertainment when the
stories of Samson were told in public.

*On this page from a 13th-century German Bible,
scenes from Judges are paired with New Testament events.
Jephthah's daughter greeting her father (top left)
is followed by the women at the tomb learning of Jesus'
resurrection (second left). The angel appearing to
Samson's mother (third right) is paired with Gabriel
announcing Jesus' birth to Mary (bottom right).*

Then the Philistines came up and encamped in Judah, and made a raid on Lehi. JUDG 15:9

After this slaughter, Samson hides out in Etam, an unidentified spot in Judah's territory. When the Philistines raid the town of Lehi, the Judahites, weakened by decades of oppression, decide to deliver up the Danite hero to the enemy. Samson agrees to be bound with two new ropes and handed over.

As soon as the Philistines spot the bound Samson, they rush toward him, shouting with glee. At that moment, the spirit of the Lord possesses Samson, creating a surge of superhuman strength. The ropes virtually melt away. Samson picks up the jawbone of a donkey recently killed and slays a huge number of the enemy single-handedly. If the reference is literal, it is likely that a fresh jawbone would be less brittle and heavier than one left in the open for a time. It is also possible that Samson used a kind of common sickle made from a jawbone with teeth fashioned of flint.

After this deed, as Samson feels faint with thirst from the physical effort of killing so many opponents, he communicates directly with God for the first time in the saga. He asks rather brazenly for water, and God responds by causing a spring to gush up from a rocky cleft. Perhaps connected to this divine favor, he is installed as judge of Israel for 20 years, or something like half a generation.

Samson slaying the lion used in a riddle to trick the Philistines; a 14th-century stained glass window

After this he fell in love with a woman in the valley of Sorek, whose name was Delilah. JUDG 16:4

In one of the most famous love stories of all time, blind lust and betrayal are the principal actors. Delilah, probably a Philistine though she had a Semitic name, lived perhaps 13 miles southwest of Jerusalem in a valley known for its fine grapes. When it becomes known that she is intimate with the Israelite strongman, the chieftains who control the five major Philistine cities promise her an enormous bribe to betray her lover, a total of 5,500 pieces of silver. She does not need long to ponder this offer.

Three times she asks Samson the secret of his strength, so that he can be overpowered. Three times he invents a preposterous but presumably magic enslavement—binding with seven unprocessed gut bowstrings, binding with "new ropes" that might be willow boughs, and weaving seven locks of his hair into a loom. Each time, however, Samson bursts free when the Philistines come out of hiding to seize him.

Finally, the determined Delilah nags him until "he was tired to death" (Judg 16:16), and he reveals the truth: His strength resides in his hair, never shaved because of the nazirite vow. Delilah senses that she has finally earned her money. She calls the chieftains

and asks to be paid immediately. As Samson sleeps, she has a man shave his head, and his great strength ebbs away. The Philistines are able to seize him at last. Delirious with triumph, they gouge out his eyes, take him south to Gaza in shackles made of bronze, and set him to the humiliating work of pulling a millstone in prison. "But the hair of his head began to grow again after it had been shaved" (Judg 16:22).

Now the lords of the Philistines gathered to offer a great sacrifice to their god Dagon, and to rejoice. JUDG 16:23

In Gaza there was a famous temple to Dagon, who had been worshiped in the ancient world since the 25th century B.C. A grain god and Baal's father, he was the chief divinity of the Philistine town Ashdod.

At a festival honoring Dagon, the Philistines become drunk, demanding that Samson be brought out as cruel entertainment. Sightless and pale, the former hero looks exhausted. He asks his attendant to lead him to the two huge pillars that support the great stone roof so that he can lean against them to rest. Then he suddenly stands tall, crying out to the Lord to help him get revenge for his blinding, and pushes the pillars apart, causing the temple to collapse. He and the pagan worshipers are crushed to death.

With Samson's death, the epic of Israel's heroic judges ends—though judges continued to guide Israel through the time covered in 1 Samuel.

There was a man in the hill country of Ephraim whose name was Micah. JUDG 17:1

Chapters 17 and 18 give historical background for the migration of the Danites to the north and explain why they have a Levite sanctuary of their own.

A young man named Micah returns money he has stolen from his mother. Since she had promised the sum to God, he is afraid of being cursed. His mother is so overjoyed that she has a silversmith make an image to be placed in a shrine with an ephod, the garment worn by a priest, and some teraphim, perhaps small images or objects revered as household gods. Micah installs one of his sons as priest but soon replaces him with a Levite who wanders by. Meanwhile, the Danites have neither found peace with their neighbors nor been able to defend their land in the south. They send five spies northward to seek a new tribal homeland.

On the way, they stop at Micah's house and ask the Levite if their mission will be successful. The young priest tells them that the Lord has given his blessing. Indeed, they find at Laish, which means "lion," a peaceful community of people living among great plenty. They return, gather a force of men, and head back north to conquer the city. Along the way, they turn aside to steal Micah's idol, ephod, and teraphim and convince the priest to join with them. They reach unprotected Laish, put its innocent population to the sword, and rename the city Dan. There they set up the stolen idol.

A certain Levite, residing in the remote parts of the hill country of Ephraim, took to himself a concubine from Bethlehem in Judah. JUDG 19:1

Another chaotic story involves a prosperous Levite from the hill country of Ephraim. When he angers his concubine, she returns to her father's house in Bethlehem. Four months later, the Levite seeks her out. The woman is pleased to have a reconciliation, and the happy pair head homeward.

Toward nightfall, the Levite refuses to stay in Jebus, or Jerusalem, because it is still a Canaanite city at this time. But when he seeks lodging among the Benjaminites living in Gibeah, a few miles to the north, he is turned away. Only an old man, also from Ephraim, will take in the stranded travelers.

In a horrifying twist of the tale, rowdies in the Benjaminite town bang on the old man's door, demanding to have unlawful sexual relations with the stranger. The host offers his virgin daughter and the Levite's concubine instead, but the men persist. When they threaten to kill the Levite, he sends out his concubine, who is ravished throughout the night and left dead. To rouse the men of Israel to take revenge for this outrage, the Levite cuts his concubine's corpse in 12 pieces and sends them to the 12 tribes—a bizarre call to arms echoed by Saul in Samuel 11:7.

The Israelite tribes meet at Mizpah, vowing to act in unison. They urge that the guilty men be turned over for execution as the law requires. But the Benjaminites refuse, successfully repelling two assaults upon their town Gibeah. On the third day, the Lord intervenes, and the Benjaminites are drawn out of their city into ambush. The city is destroyed and many of the Benjaminites are killed.

But the Israelites had compassion for Benjamin their kin. JUDG 21:6

After the destruction of Gibeah, some 600 Benjaminite men still survive in exile. The Israelites realize that the tribe may die out because the Benjaminite men cannot intermarry with other tribes. At Mizpah, everyone had vowed not to let his daughters take husbands from among the renegades.

The solution is bloody, but effective. Only one city, Jabesh-gilead, had refused the summons to join with the Israelites against Gibeah. The Israelites kill every man and woman in the city, except for 400 virgins. These young women are given to the surviving Benjaminites. In a second story, the Benjaminites are allowed to capture women dancing in the vineyards during a harvest festival at Shiloh. Thus, the oath at Mizpah is not broken because the men steal their wives instead of seeking permission to marry.

Benjamin will survive, and the rest of Israel returns to their tribal lands. But the editor ends the book of Judges on a note that has been repeated throughout these last five chapters: "In those days there was no king in Israel; all the people did what was right in their own eyes" (Judg 21:25). The entire future of the nation is in gravest doubt.

Powerless after the treacherous Delilah has his long locks shaved, Samson is seized by the Philistines; a detail from a painting by Anthony Van Dyck (1599-1641).

RUTH

*O*ne of the shortest books in the Old Testament, Ruth is a masterpiece of world literature, beautifully written and profoundly moving. The books immediately preceding it, Joshua and Judges, deal with the grand sweep of Israelite history. In contrast, Ruth is the story of a single family—though one that has an enormous impact on subsequent events in the Bible. For the faithful heroine Ruth gives birth to Obed, the grandfather of King David. And David, as specified in two gospels, those of Matthew and Luke, is a royal ancestor of Jesus.

Although set in the time of the judges, Ruth must have been written after the reign of David—most likely, between 950 and 700 B.C. However, some scholars suggest a post-exilic date (the sixth century B.C. or even later), arguing that the story is a reaction against Ezra's decree (Ezra 9-10; Neh 13:23-29) that the returning Israelites must divorce their foreign wives. Its placement in Christian Bibles between Judges and 1 Samuel was established by the Septuagint, the translation of the Hebrew Bible into Greek that was begun in the third century B.C. and completed by the first century B.C. In most editions of the Hebrew Bible, Ruth is included among the Writings, placed between Song of Solomon and Lamentations.

Ruth follows Naomi home to Bethlehem.

In the days when the judges ruled, there was a famine in the land, and a certain man of Bethlehem in Judah went to live in the country of Moab, he and his wife and two sons. RUTH 1:1

*W*ithin six verses, the author skillfully sets the stage for the dramatic tale: Fleeing a famine in Judah, Elimelech takes his wife, Naomi, and their two sons to Moab, an often hostile land east of the Dead Sea. Elimelech soon dies, as do both sons after marrying the Moabite women Orpah and Ruth.

Hearing that the famine has ended, Naomi sets off for home, telling her daughters-in-law that they need not accompany her. Orpah turns back but—in one of the Bible's most eloquent passages—Ruth tells Naomi, "Where you go, I will go" (Ruth 1:16). This introduces the major theme of the book, *chesed*, a Hebrew word meaning "loyalty" or "faithfulness."

The women of Bethlehem can scarcely believe that Naomi has returned. Saying that she had gone away "full" but is returning "empty" (Ruth 1:21), the childless widow gives herself a new name, one that reflects the bitterness of her losses. For Naomi means "pleasant," whereas Mara—the name she has chosen—means "bitter."

Now Naomi had a kinsman on her husband's side, a prominent rich man, of the family of Elimelech, whose name was Boaz. RUTH 2:1

*T*he introduction of Naomi's kinsman Boaz leads to the second major theme of the book of Ruth: family continuity. It is Boaz—through his levirate marriage to Ruth—who ensures that Elimelech's line will not be be allowed to die out.

Ruth meets Boaz when poverty drives her to glean the fields for leftover grain. According to Mosaic Law (Lev 19:9, 23:22; Deut 24:19), harvesters were required to leave some grain for the poor. By chance, Ruth comes to work behind the reapers in the field belonging to her deceased father-in-law's distant relative Boaz. Her diligence is noted by Boaz, who also knows of her loyalty to Naomi and extends his protection to her.

Ruth seems ignorant of the family connection with Boaz, but that evening Naomi explains the relationship and encourages her daughter-in-law to continue working her kinsman's field, Thus, Ruth gleans through the barley and wheat seasons, while the resourceful Naomi hatches a plot that will salvage the family's fortunes.

Naomi her mother-in-law said to her, "My daughter, I need to seek some security for you, so that it may be well with you." RUTH 3:1

*W*hen first she goes to Boaz's field, Ruth is searching for food. She returns, seeking a husband—carefully coached by Naomi.

There is a hint of sexual intimacy in Naomi's instructions that Ruth approach Boaz when he has eaten and drunk and is resting. Turning over in his sleep, Boaz is startled to find Ruth lying at his feet. But when she asks him to "spread your cloak over your servant" (Ruth 3:9)—a phrase meaning "take me for your wife"—he mentions an obstacle. There is a closer kin, a man with first claim to her. Vowing to marry Ruth if the other man declines to honor his duty, Boaz sends her away before her indiscretion is discovered but rewards her with a generous portion of barley.

LEVIRATE MARRIAGE

In **agreeing to marry Ruth,** *Boaz is apparently conforming to a Mosaic Law stipulating that a childless widow can claim her brother-in-law as husband (Deut 25:5-10). The practice was called levirate marriage from the Latin word* levir, *"brother-in-law."*

Yet Boaz was not Ruth's brother-in-law but only a man Naomi described as "one of our nearest kin" (Ruth 2:20)—in Hebrew, go'el, *"one with the right to redeem." Such a close relative was required to take responsibility for a family that had lost its head of household. This included buying back, or redeeming, property that had been sold. Boaz agrees not only to redeem property being sold because of Elimelech's death but also to marry the young widow so that she will not be separated from her inheritance.*

The union of Boaz and Ruth differs from levirate marriage in another key point. Their firstborn, Obed, is not called the child of Ruth's deceased husband, Mahlon—as the law requires—but is listed in biblical genealogies as Boaz's son.

Another example of levirate marriage occurs in Genesis 38. At the death of Judah's eldest son, Er, the widow Tamar is given to the second son, Onan. But when Onan refuses to accept the obligation, he is punished by death. Judah's procrastination in marrying Tamar to a third son, Shelah, leads to the encounter between the widow and her father-in-law that produces twin sons.

And so Boaz gains a wife "to maintain the dead man's name" (Ruth 4:10). In sanction of the union, the elders of the city beseech the Lord to make Ruth the instrument of building up the house of Israel— the role previously played by Jacob's wives, Rachel and Leah. Heeding their plea, God bestows a son on Ruth and Boaz: Obed, the grandfather of King David.

There is some scholarly argument over the refrain of the women: "A son has been born to Naomi" (Ruth 4:17). Some say "son" should read "grandson"; others that the child was more than a biological grandson but rather a replacement for the two sons she had lost, Mahlon and Chilion. At any rate, Naomi is restored to center stage, the focus of the story at the end as she was at the beginning.

Now these are the descendants of Perez.   RUTH 4:18

The brief genealogy that concludes the book of Ruth is perhaps a later addition to the original story. It traces the ancestry of King David back through nine generations to Perez, first of the twins born to the widowed Tamar following her clandestine encounter with her father-in-law, Judah. Evidence that the book of Ruth acquired its present form after the time of King David, the genealogy perhaps draws upon the one found in 1 Chronicles 2:5-15, though with some variations in spelling.

Ruth's son Obed is mentioned in both New Testament genealogies of Jesus (Mt 1:5 and Lk 3:32). Placing the Moabite woman Ruth among the ancestors of Jesus is confirmation that the Messiah was sent for the redemption of all peoples, not just the Israelites.

No sooner had Boaz gone up to the gate and sat down there than the next-of-kin, of whom Boaz had spoken, came passing by.   RUTH 4:1

In biblical times, the traditional meeting place was at the city gate, where farmers and merchants would pass in and out of a city as they went about their business. And so it was natural for Boaz to wait there for the kinsman who had a prior claim to the widow Ruth.

With ten elders of the city as witnesses to the discussion, Boaz tells the unnamed kinsman of his opportunity to buy back, or redeem, family property that Naomi is selling. The man appears interested—until he learns that the purchase also means acquiring a wife (perhaps he already had one). In line with the ancient custom of removing footgear to conclude a transaction, the kinsman takes off his sandal. He realizes that marrying Ruth would jeopardize his own acquisition of property, for any child born of that marriage—not he—would inherit the land.

As Ruth had done centuries earlier, women in Israel today glean the wheat fields, carefully gathering their sheaves from what the harvesters have left behind.

1 SAMUEL

*I*n a span of little more than a century, from about 1085 B.C. to about 970 B.C., a loose confederation of Hebrew tribes was consolidated into a well-organized and powerful monarchy centered on its religious and political capital, Jerusalem. This emergence of a national identity for Israel is covered in the books of 1 and 2 Samuel.

The narrative focuses on three great figures: Samuel, the last of the judges, who also functioned as a prophet and a priest; Saul, the first king of Israel; and David, the greatest of the nation's monarchs. Samuel's story begins with his miraculous birth and overlaps with that of Saul, who is introduced in 1 Samuel 9. Saul's story continues to the end of 1 Samuel, but early on he is overshadowed by David, who makes his first appearance in 1 Samuel 16. David is the main character through the last half of 1 Samuel and throughout 2 Samuel.

Actually, 1 and 2 Samuel were originally a single book written in Hebrew over a long period of time. They were first divided into two books when the Hebrew Bible was translated into Greek between the third and first centuries B.C. The name Samuel only highlights the first main character in the narrative and does not indicate the author of the whole, who is never identified. As might be expected in a work that incorporates detailed narratives from such a long and important period, many hands have contributed to the story. The earliest extensive portion to be compiled was evidently the account of David's rise to the throne, written probably in the time of his son and successor, Solomon. Numerous shorter stories were incorporated into the whole, sometimes overlapping with traditions already in place. Such overlaps account for a number of puzzling twists in the narrative. David, for example, becomes Saul's beloved armor-bearer in 1 Samuel 16, but in the next chapter Saul does not know who David is (1 Sam 17:55-58). Work on the narrative was probably not finished until the entire series of historical works from Joshua to 2 Kings (called the Former Prophets in the Hebrew Bible) was completed in the period after the Babylonian exile.

The great theme of the whole work is the rule of God among his people, Israel. Everyone, whether ordinary citizen or judge or king, is subject to God's rule and is sustained by God's care. The Lord both protects his people and disciplines them when they are unfaithful. Though 1 and 2 Samuel have much historical content, their main point is religious, and God is the dominant character in the narrative throughout.

As a boy, Samuel was sent to serve the Lord at the shrine of Shiloh. In this English stained glass window, the priest Eli undertakes Samuel's religious education.

In due time Hannah conceived and bore a son. She named him Samuel, for she said, "I have asked him of the Lord."
1 SAM 1:20

*T*he story begins with the miraculous birth of Samuel to a childless woman named Hannah, one of the wives of Elkanah, a man of the tribe of Ephraim. Hannah is childless because "the Lord had closed her womb" (1 Sam 1:5). Similar miraculous births are well known from Genesis (the births of Isaac to Sarah, Jacob and Esau to Rebekah, and Joseph to Rachel), from Judges (the birth of Samson), and from the Gospel of Luke (the birth of John the Baptist to Elizabeth). Such births portend the great significance of the children who are born.

Here, the narrative vividly shows the pain suffered by a childless woman in a society in which her status in the household and thus her self-esteem were dependent on having children. In a polygamous household with its inevitable rivalries among the wives (like those experienced by Sarah and Rachel), even the love of Hannah's husband, Elkanah, cannot make up for the scorn of the second wife Peninnah.

Israel's worship in those days was centered in Shiloh, a town belonging to the tribe of Ephraim, about 20 miles north of Jerusalem. There, the ancient tabernacle had been set up in the time of Joshua and converted into a more or less permanent shrine (Josh 18:1). Elkanah went to the shrine every year with his wives. On one of those visits, Hannah's pain so overflows as she weeps and prays that she vows to God that, if he will give her a son, she will dedicate him to the Lord as a lifelong "nazirite"—one devoted to God who would neither drink wine nor cut his hair—such as Samson was supposed to have been.

When God indeed blesses her with a child, Hannah keeps her vow. She nurses young Samuel until he is weaned (perhaps at age three) and then brings him to the shrine at Shiloh and presents him to Eli, the patriarch of the priests. She celebrates this fulfillment of her hopes in a poetic prayer of worship on the theme of God's power over all things and his mercy toward even the most lowly. The prayer seems to portray Hannah as a prophet, since it refers to Israel's king as though he already existed. Some suggest that only 1 Samuel 2:1 represents Hannah's prayer, which has been supplemented by a psalm from a later time. In any case, this beautiful prayer serves as the model of praise and thanksgiving that the virgin Mary draws upon to celebrate the future birth of her child Jesus in Luke 1:46-55.

Now the sons of Eli were scoundrels; they had no regard for the Lord or for the duties of the priests to the people.
1 SAM 2:12

As Samuel grows up in the service of God at Shiloh, it becomes more and more clear that he is needed to replace Hophni and Phinehas, the sons of Eli who have already taken over the duties of their aged and nearly blind father. These two are described as "scoundrels" (literally "sons of Belial") who use the priesthood for profit and pleasure. The narrative gives colorful details of the traditional practices of handling the distribution of sacrifices and the ways in which Eli's sons manipulate them. Typically, part of the fat and a small portion of meat from a large sacrificial animal is burned as an offering to God. The remainder is boiled for a feast of thanksgiving by the person or family offering the sacrifice, and a portion is given to the priests. Eli's sons demand to have their portions before the sections offered to God are removed and they want the meat raw (perhaps for resale) rather than cooked for use in a feast of celebration. Furthermore, they treat the women who serve in various ways at Shiloh as though they are members of a private harem.

Eli becomes aware of the gross abuses that his sons are committing but he cannot control them and warns the two of the Lord's punishment. By contrast, the narrative describes the positive growth and progress of Samuel "ministering before the Lord" (1 Sam 2:18) and the blessings that come to Hannah as she bears other children.

The future consequences of the sins of Eli's house are revealed in a prophecy given to Eli by an unnamed "man of God" (1 Sam 2:27). Because of their flagrant abuses, both of Eli's sons will die on the same day—a prediction soon fulfilled during the battle of Aphek (1 Sam 4:11). Later their descendants will be killed, though one will escape—a forewarning of the slaughter of the priests at Nob (1 Sam 22:18-20). But the Lord will "raise up for myself a faithful priest" (1 Sam 2:35). This, as it turns out, is Zadok (1 Kgs 2:35). It is he who will found a permanent priestly dynasty parallel to the royal dynasty of the descendants of David.

Now the Lord came and stood there, calling as before, "Samuel! Samuel!" And Samuel said, "Speak, for your servant is listening."
1 SAM 3:10

The result of the faithlessness exemplified by Hophni and Phinehas is the near silence of divine revelation in Israel. The narrative emphasizes that "the word of the Lord was rare in those days; vi-

Scenes from a late-12th-century Bible: Hannah praying at Shiloh and telling Eli her woes (left, bottom); Hannah presenting her son to Eli (right, top); God appearing to Samuel (right, center); Samuel annointing Saul (right, bottom)

sions were not widespread" (1 Sam 3:1) in order to introduce a new period marked by the faithfulness and prophetic power of Samuel. The account shows that Eli himself is personally faithful to his calling but is spineless in not stopping the blasphemies of his sons. As he grows ever more aged and blind, the priestly service at Shiloh becomes more corrupt.

The text provides a beautiful and poignant account of God calling the young Samuel (traditionally about 12 years old) to his service as a prophet. Being a prophet for God is never easy, and the very first message that Samuel has to convey is one of horror for his beloved mentor, Eli. Throughout his life Samuel often has to speak words of judgment and punishment on people and leaders who have failed in their service to God. From his calling, Samuel learns to listen to God with childlike honesty and to speak God's message with fearless clarity.

Samuel is sleeping in the Shiloh temple near the Holy of Holies, where the ark of the covenant symbolizes God's presence. As dawn nears, marked by the phrase "the lamp of God had not yet gone out" (1 Sam 3:3), a clear voice calls his name. Samuel is immediately awake but runs to Eli since he has never experienced a revelation from God before. Twice more the call comes with the same result, until the reality of what is happening finally penetrates even Eli's slow perception. At Eli's instruction, Samuel at last responds to God's call with a readiness to listen. The message is dreadful: All the evil prophesied against Eli's house is about to be fulfilled and cannot be expiated by a sacrificial offering. But when morning comes, the boy overcomes his fear and reports everything to the priest. Eli is experienced enough to recognize that

this is indeed a message from God: "Let him do what seems good to him" (1 Sam 3:14).

From that point on, Samuel grows increasingly into his role as a prophet of the Lord, one recognized throughout Israel. His very existence is a message of hope that God has not forsaken his people.

In those days the Philistines mustered for war against Israel, and Israel went out to battle against them.
1 SAM 4:1

*T*he 40-year service of Eli as priest and judge at Shiloh ends in abject disaster. Israel is relatively divided and disorganized, as it had been throughout the period of the judges, subject to domination by various outside powers. The Philistines, who had invaded Canaan from the Mediterranean and settled along the southern coast at about the same time that Israel arrived from east of the Jordan, are in a period of strength, organized under five city-states, each with its own ruler. The Philistines remain the primary foe of Israel throughout the time of Saul and David, their strength aided by the fact that they have mastered the use of iron weapons far in advance of the Israelites, who continue to use primarily bronze.

When the Philistines muster their forces at the town of Aphek about 22 miles east of Shiloh, militias from the various tribes of Israel, led by the elders of Israel, encamp at nearby Ebenezer. In the first skirmishes the Israelites are soundly defeated with severe losses. As they regroup, the elders attribute their defeat to God and try to enlist his support by bringing the ark of the covenant with them onto the battlefield. Hophni and Phinehas bring the sacred chest, described as "the

For having brought the captured ark to the temple of Dagon, the Philistines of Ashdod are cursed with a plague. Nicholas Poussin painted the scene about 1630.

ark of the covenant of the Lord of hosts [armies] who is enthroned on the cherubim" (1 Sam 4:4). The cherubim were evidently represented as winged bulls, with their wings symbolizing God's throne and presence. If the Israelites can draft the Lord into their army, they feel, they cannot lose the battle.

God, however, refuses to be drafted. Though the Philistines, who understand what the Israelites are trying to do, are fearful, the next encounter brings devastating defeat for the Israelites. Hophni and Phinehas are both killed, and the holy ark is captured. One soldier runs marathon-like to Shiloh and tells blind, old Eli about his sons and the ark. Eli had anticipated the fate of his sons, but when he hears about the loss of the ark, the most sacred and precious possession of the Israelites, he falls backward, breaks his neck, and dies. When Phinehas's pregnant wife learns the news, she goes into labor. The childbirth proves fatal for her, but before she dies, she names her new, orphaned son Ichabod, signifying, "The glory has departed from Israel" (1 Sam 4:21).

To rid their land of plague, the Philistines return the ark to the Israelites along with offerings of golden mice and tumors. The stricken city of Ashdod is at left in this mid-13th-century French Bible illumination.

Then the Philistines took the ark of God and brought it into the house of Dagon and placed it beside Dagon.
1 SAM 5:2

God refuses to be forced to fight for Israel, but he has lost none of his power. When the Philistines lead the ark in triumph southward to one of their chief cities, Ashdod, they think they can deliver the God of Israel as a prisoner of war to their own god Dagon, lord of grain and harvest. But the morning after the ark is placed in Dagon's temple, Dagon's statue is found facedown on the ground. The Philistines hurriedly set the image back up, but by the next morning it has again fallen, and this time Dagon's head and hands are broken off, symbolizing the utter powerlessness of the pagan idol.

In contrast to Dagon's broken hands, "the hand of the Lord was heavy upon the people of Ashdod" (1 Sam 5:6). A plague of tumors afflicts them, evidently accompanied by an onslaught of mice (or perhaps rats). This combination has often suggested to historians that bubonic plague may have broken out, though another tradition suggests that the "tumors" were merely hemorrhoids.

In any case, the people of Ashdod quickly decide to let another city share the glory of conquest over the God of Israel and ship the ark off to Gath. With it comes the plague, and panic seizes the new host city. Again the ark is moved, this time to Ekron, where the cry arises to send the ark home.

The Philistines, like the Egyptians of the Exodus, are stubborn and refuse to admit defeat for seven months. Some believe the coming of the plague is just a coincidence, having nothing to do with the ark or Israel's God. In returning the ark, however, the Philistine priests devise a way to test if the God of Israel is indeed involved. They dispatch the ark homeward with a "guilt offering" (1 Sam 6:3) as reparation—five golden tumors and five golden mice, symbolizing the plague. But they put the ark on a new cart pulled by cows who have never before been yoked and have just been separated from their young calves. If such cows head for Israelite territory rather than home to their calves, that is sign enough for the Philistines that Israel's God is behind the entire disastrous sequence of events.

Sure enough, the cows head directly for the nearest Israelite town of Beth-shemesh. There, startled Israelite farmers harvesting wheat rejoice to see the ark returning to them. When the ark stops by a huge stone in the field of a man named Joshua, Levites from the town set the ark high on the stone and sacrifice the cows to God. Centuries later, when the books of Samuel were written, the great stone was still pointed out as a memorial to this momentous demonstration of God's power.

The people of Israel said to Samuel, "Do not cease to cry out to the Lord our God for us, and pray that he may save us from the hand of the Philistines." 1 SAM 7:8

The holiness of God means that no one can take him for granted, neither Philistine nor Israelite. Some of the men of Beth-shemesh think that now that they have the ark back, God as well as the ark symbolizing his presence are at their disposal. They open the holy ark to look inside, and 70 of them are instantly struck dead.

Grief and fear seize the people, and they are terrified to have God's presence so powerfully among them without the mediation of a priest. "Who is able to stand before the Lord, this holy God?" they cry. "To whom shall he go so that we may be rid of him?" (1 Sam 6:20). Shiloh has evidently been destroyed in the aftermath of Israel's defeat at Aphek, and thus the ark cannot be brought back there.

An interim solution is found in nearby Kiriath-jearim, where a man named Abinadab provides space for a sanctuary, and his son Eleazar is consecrated as custodian of the ark. The arrangement becomes semipermanent, extending until the time of David. The people do not feel endangered by the ark, but ultimately they mourn because it is shut up with a caretaker, and God's presence seems less vivid among them.

In the meantime, Samuel leads the people in a period of reform and renewal. He challenges them to put away their Canaanite gods—the Baals and the Astartes—and he assembles them at the hilltop town of Mizpah for a community rite of fasting and confession.

The Philistines see this big religious gathering as a perfect opportunity to attack and do maximum damage. The people beg Samuel to cry to God for help rather than try to force God to help them. In a spirit of repentance and sacrifice, Samuel prays, and God indeed delivers Israel by stampeding the approaching Philistines with peals of thunder.

In celebration of this deliverance, Samuel sets up a large stone and names it Ebenezer ("stone of help"), the name of the Israelite encampment at the time the Philistines captured the ark. The irony of the old name is transformed into reality as Israel humbly turns to God for help: "Thus far the Lord has helped us" (1 Sam 7:12). Samuel's leadership and the people's change of heart bring a period of strength and security to Israel. The Philistines draw back from challenging Israel, and even the Amorites (or western Canaanites) remain peaceful.

Then all the elders of Israel gathered together and came to Samuel at Ramah, and said to him, "You are old and your sons do not follow in your ways; appoint for us, then, a king to govern us, like other nations." 1 SAM 8:4-5

Though Samuel became well known early in life as a prophet and continued to fulfill some of Eli's functions as a priest for Israel, he led the people primarily in a judicial role. Year by year, he followed a circuit from his home in Ramah to Bethel, Gilgal, Mizpah, and back to Ramah. He perhaps functioned as a court of appeals, deciding cases that could not be handled by the town elders. The entire circuit, however, lay in central Canaan in the territory of Ephraim and Benjamin. For many Israelites it was a long and dangerous journey to visit Samuel.

As Samuel grows old, his sons Joel and Abijah help by serving as judges in Beer-sheba far to the south. Like Eli's sons, however, they are unworthy of their father's trust, and their corrupt practices cause the people to fear for the future when Samuel is gone. They also fear for the future of their loose tribal confederacy, which has proven weak in the face of its many foreign enemies and has so often descended into near anarchy.

The tribal elders come to Samuel at Ramah and urge him to change the government before it falls under the control of his sons and to appoint a king who can both unite the tribes and govern them. Samuel is insulted by their rejection of his type of government. Answering his prayer, God urges Samuel not to take the request personally—it is God, not Samuel they are rejecting as ruler—and to grant the people's request while warning them of the dangers of a monarchy.

Samuel obeys. He issues dire warnings that anticipate many of the abuses of kingship for which Solomon was condemned—especially conscripted labor and military service, confiscation of property, and taxes. "You shall be his slaves" (1 Sam 8:17), he warns, but the people long for united government and military leadership like other nations of the ancient world. Although the Lord again commands Samuel to grant their request for a king, he dismisses the petitioners without acting.

After proving his leadership by his victory over Nahash the Ammonite (top), Saul is confirmed as king of Israel and Samuel offers a sacrifice to the Lord (bottom, left and right); scenes from a mid-13th-century French Bible.

THE SHRINE AT SHILOH

*Ruins at Shiloh, Israel's early
worship center in the central highlands*

Nestled among hills *overlooking a
fertile plain 30 miles north of Jerusalem,
the village of Shiloh served as Israel's first permanent worship center—one that endured for
centuries, through the time of the judges. After
his victories, Joshua gathered the tribes at Shiloh
to apportion their conquests and there set up the
tent tabernacle to house the ark of the covenant.*

*What the shrine looked like remains a mys-
tery, though in time the tent seems to have been
replaced by some kind of structure. In Samuel's
day, the "house of the Lord" had "doors" (1 Sam
3:15). After defeating the Israelites at Aphek,
the Philistines apparently destroyed Shiloh.
Excavations at the 12-acre site confirm that
the town was leveled in about 1050 B.C., a few
decades before Israel anointed its first king, Saul.*

*"Tomorrow about this time I will send to you a man from
the land of Benjamin, and you shall anoint him to be ruler
over my people Israel. He shall save my people from the
hand of the Philistines." 1 SAM 9:16*

God has to intervene to move Samuel to designate a king, telling him that on the morrow he
will send him a man of the tribe of Benjamin who is
to be God's chosen ruler and military leader. The next
day on the way to a sacrifice, Samuel meets a tall,
handsome young man named Saul son of Kish, a
wealthy Benjaminite. He has been traveling for days
in search of some lost donkeys. "Here is the man"
(1 Sam 9:17), God tells Samuel. Samuel immediately
introduces himself, informs Saul that his lost donkeys have been found, and invites him to be guest
of honor at the sacrificial banquet that evening.

The next morning before sending Saul on his way,
Samuel pours a vial of olive oil over his head, say-

ing, "The Lord has anointed you ruler over his people Israel" (1 Sam 10:1). Although Saul is wealthy,
handsome, and head and shoulders taller than most
other men, he is self-effacing and shy. He hardly
knows what to make of Samuel's statements, but
Samuel promises him that he will experience the
power of God's spirit. Just as Samuel had predicted,
Saul is on his way home when he meets a band of
prophets and falls into a prophetic frenzy.

Soon the private anointing of Saul is confirmed
publicly. Samuel gathers the people at Mizpah and
castigates them for their desire for a king, but then
goes through a rite of casting lots in order to allow
God to select the king. From tribe to clan to family,
the lot narrows the choice to one person, Saul. The
candidate does not want the public role, however,
and has to be sought as he hides among the baggage
animals. As he is brought forth, many praise the
choice of such a princely looking man, but some
"worthless fellows" (1 Sam 10:27) express discontent
with the choice.

*"See, it is the king who leads you now; I am old and
gray, but my sons are with you. I have led you from my
youth until this day." 1 SAM 12:2*

Distrust of Saul is overcome only when his actions show him to be a credible leader.
Though twice designated by God as king, Saul has
little idea of how to rule. Instead, he returns to the
simple life of farming around his home in Gibeah, a
few miles north of Jerusalem. But events elsewhere
soon change his course.

King Nahash of the Ammonites is rampaging
through Israelite territory east of the Jordan, gouging
out the right eye of everyone who falls under his control. When he besieges the Israelite town of Jabesh-
gilead, the citizens send a desperate call for help to
their compatriots across the river. When the message
finally arrives in Gibeah, Saul is coming in from
plowing. After "the spirit of God came upon Saul" (1
Sam 11:6), he kills two oxen, cuts them up, and
sends pieces throughout Israel as a challenge to unite
in the defense of Jabesh-gilead.

The people accept the king's summons. Thousands
of soldiers march on Jabesh-gilead, defeat the Ammonite forces, and destroy the threat to Israel. Now,
support for Saul becomes nearly universal. The people assemble at Gilgal to officially designate Saul as
king and offer a sacrifice to the Lord. Still convinced
that choosing a king is wicked and unwise, Samuel
delivers his farewell address and retires.

*Saul said, "Bring the burnt offering here to me, and the
offerings of well-being." And he offered the burnt offering.
1 SAM 13:8-9*

The opening verse of 1 Samuel 13 is a good example of the many problems found in the two
books. The Hebrew text was damaged in many places
as it was handed down over the centuries. In 13:1 at

least two words are missing from a sentence telling how old Saul was when he became king and how long he reigned. Since he had an adult son, he was perhaps 40 years old. The best guess for the length of his reign is 22 years.

Whatever the date, Saul immediately sets out to organize Israel's militias to oppose the Philistines, who are expanding into traditional Israelite territory. He establishes two garrisons, one commanded by his son Jonathan at Gibeah and the other under his own command at Michmash about six miles to the northeast. Between them is a Philistine outpost at Geba. Though Jonathan quickly defeats the Philistines at Geba, Saul is unready to meet the enemy with untrained soldiers—many of whom desert in the face of overwhelming odds. It is at this point that Saul commits a fatal error.

As previously instructed, Saul goes to Gilgal to await Samuel, who will offer a sacrifice to seek God's favor in battle. Samuel had promised to arrive in seven days, but the desertions mount as the king awaits Samuel. After the seventh day and with a Philistine attack imminent, Saul offers the sacrifice himself. At that moment, Samuel arrives, learns what Saul has done, and issues a dire prediction: "Your kingdom will not continue" (1 Sam 13:14).

Having protected his father's sheep from lions and bears (top), David has no fear as he goes out to meet the giant Goliath.

When Saul had taken the kingship over Israel, he fought against all his enemies on every side . . . . He did valiantly, and struck down the Amalekites, and rescued Israel out of the hands of those who plundered them.   1 SAM 14:47-48

Though the narrative of 1 Samuel focuses primarily on the tragic wrongs done by Saul in contrast to the accomplishments of the noble David, some passages reflect Saul's positive impact on the history of Israel. His were days of hard fighting and life spent in a rough-hewn fortress. He had neither palace, nor harem, nor government bureaucracy. And he repeatedly defeated the numerous enemies surrounding his infant nation. Nonetheless, Saul continued to reveal his fallibility.

After another bold stroke by Jonathan against a Philistine outpost leads to panic in the enemy camp, the king hesitates before pursuing his advantage. And joy over Saul's subsequent victory is partially spoiled by a foolish oath he has made to execute anyone who eats before the Philistines are totally defeated. Unaware of his father's oath, Jonathan takes some honey for strength. Saul is ready to execute his own son until the people refuse to allow such a travesty: "As the Lord lives," they cry, "not one hair of his head shall fall to the ground; for he has worked with God today" (1 Sam 14:49).

The word of the Lord came to Samuel: "I regret that I made Saul king, for he has turned back from following me, and has not carried out my commands."
1 SAM 15:10-11

Though he has many positive accomplishments, Saul's failures overshadow them all, especially his inability to realize that the king must be obedient to the word of God as communicated by his prophet. The last straw comes when Saul fails to scrupulously fulfill a mission of holy war. When Israel had escaped from Egypt, the Amalekites had attacked and tried to destroy them in the desert. After God swore to "blot out the remembrance of Amalek," Moses promised that "the Lord will have war with Amalek from generation to generation" (Ex 17:14, 16). Samuel sends Saul to fulfill those vows by utterly destroying every living thing—"man and woman, child and infant, ox and sheep, camel and donkey" (1 Sam 15:3)—in the city of Amalek. Nothing is to be taken as booty; everything belongs to God and is "devoted to destruction, to sacrifice to the Lord" (1 Sam 15:21).

After his successful attack on the Amalekites, Saul allows his people to keep the best of the animals they find, ostensibly for sacrifice, and permits the Amalekite king, Agag, to live. Samuel confronts Saul, who tries to justify his actions as perfectly proper and well-intentioned. Samuel will allow no such excuses: "Surely, to obey is better than sacrifice" (1 Sam 15:22). Brushing off the king's offer of repentance, Samuel kills Agag and departs, never in his life to see Saul again.

"How long will you grieve over Saul? I have rejected him from being king over Israel. Fill your horn with oil and set out; I will send you to Jesse the Bethlehemite, for I have provided for myself a king among his sons."   1 SAM 16:1

A new story begins with the introduction of God's choice for Saul's replacement. In obedience to the Lord's command, Samuel sets out to find and anoint a new ruler. But fearing Saul's jealous anger, he pretends his sole purpose for traveling to Bethlehem is to make a special sacrifice.

As Samuel looks over Jesse's seven sons, he is impressed. The eldest seems to be a perfect candidate for king. But God warns Samuel not to be swayed by external appearances. And so, one by one, Samuel examines each son, but none meets God's criteria. Finally, Samuel asks if there is yet another son. The youngest, who is "keeping the sheep" (1 Sam 16:11), is sent for—a ruddy, handsome youth named David, with beautiful eyes and a heart that can satisfy God.

As David approaches, the Lord instructs Samuel, "Rise and anoint him; for this is the one." The gift of God's spirit that had prepared Saul for kingship now "came mightily upon David from that day forward" (1 Sam 16:12-13).

At the same time, God's spirit departs from Saul only to be replaced by a tormenting mood of despondency. Ironically, Saul's depression provides the catalyst that brings Saul and David together and begins their love-hate relationship. One of Saul's servants suggests music to lift the king's spirits, and another servant happens to be acquainted with David, a man "skillful in playing, a man of valor, a warrior, prudent in speech" (1 Sam 16:18). David is summoned and makes such an impression by his music and valor that "Saul loved him greatly, and he became his armor-bearer" (1 Sam 16:21). From this point on, the story of David dominates the narrative of 1 and 2 Samuel, though it is entwined with Saul's story until the end of 1 Samuel.

And there came out from the camp of the Philistines a champion named Goliath, of Gath, whose height was six cubits and a span.   1 SAM 17:4

The well-known story of David and Goliath in 1 Samuel 17 offers an independent account of how Saul comes to know David. The contents imply an earlier time, for Saul does not recognize David, called a valiant warrior and made the king's beloved armor-bearer in the previous chapter.

The setting is one of Saul's many confrontations with the Philistines, this time with the two armies facing each other across the valley of Elah, some 15 miles west of Bethlehem (see map, page 115). The Philistines' secret weapon is a nearly ten-foot-tall giant named Goliath of Gath, who is so formidable in his heavy armor that not even Saul, tallest of the Israelites, will face him. Every day Goliath challenges any Israelite to single combat, with freedom or slavery resting on the outcome. (The earliest Greek translation and a text found among the Dead Sea Scrolls gives Goliath's height as "four cubits and a span"—about six feet, nine inches—unusually tall, but scarcely superhuman.)

Bringing food to his three eldest brothers in the army, David sees the giant. Goliath's defiance infuriates David, who is confident that God can give victory over any Philistine. David volunteers to fight Goliath, telling the king how he has "killed both lions and bears" with his bare hands; "this uncircumcised Philistine shall be like one of them, since he has defied the armies of the living God" (1 Sam 17:36), he says.

Against all expectations, Saul allows this youth to fight Goliath with the fate of his whole kingdom at stake. David rejects Saul's battle armor and takes only his familiar sling, itself a powerful weapon widely used in ancient warfare. Excellent slingers could propel heavy three-inch stones at up to 150 miles per hour with deadly accuracy.

The blustering Goliath is insulted to have his challenge answered by such an inexperienced youth. But David returns his disdain with a promise to cut off Goliath's head and show that "the Lord does not save by sword and spear; for the battle is the Lord's" (1 Sam 17:47).

The lithe David runs straight at Goliath and, with a single throw, fells the giant with a stone to the forehead. He unsheathes the giant's great sword and beheads him as the exultant Israelites flood across the valley to destroy the Philistine army. A relieved Saul asks Abner, his army commander, whose son the stripling is. His inquiry is answered when David appears to present Saul with the head of Goliath.

And the women sang to one another as they made merry, "Saul has killed his thousands, and David his ten thousands."   1 SAM 18:7

David immediately forms a permanent friendship with the king's son Jonathan, one that survives overwhelming obstacles. Jonathan seals their friendship covenant with a gift of his own armor and weapons. As David quickly becomes the most famous soldier in Saul's army, women sing that his exploits surpass even those of the king.

Such songs kindle Saul's fears, for Samuel has predicted that he will be supplanted. Once, when David is playing the lyre for the despondent king, Saul throws his spear at him, but David eludes the attempted murder.

Women with tambourines greet King Saul on his return from defeating the Philistines, but save their highest praise for David with his trophy, Goliath's head.

Melancholy King Saul appears about to use his spear against his lyre player and potential rival, David.

Still, Saul appoints David commander over a thousand troops, and David compiles an unbroken string of successes in battle. After reneging on his promise to give David his eldest daughter, Merab, in marriage, Saul begins seeking deceptive ways to rid himself of his potential rival. Hoping David will be killed, the king offers him another daughter, Michal, if David will kill 100 Philistines. When David returns with proof of his slaughter, Saul reluctantly accepts the young man as his son-in-law. But his fear and hatred of David only increase.

Jonathan told David, "My father Saul is trying to kill you; therefore be on guard tomorrow morning; stay in a secret place and hide yourself."   1 SAM 19:2

*J*onathan's friendship for David is greater than his loyalty to his father. When Saul orders his servants to kill David, Jonathan defends him so effectively to his father that Saul rescinds the order and recalls David to his service. But even after David wins another victory over the Philistines, the jealous king again tries to kill the young man with a spear while he is playing the lyre.

Next, Saul sends men to murder David as he leaves home in the morning. Michal foils her father's plot by putting an idol in his place in bed and pretending that David is sick while her husband escapes out the bedroom window. When Saul accuses her of treachery, she says David had threatened her life.

Meanwhile, David flees to Samuel at Ramah. Undeterred, Saul sends three groups of agents to arrest him but, when each party approaches the place, "the spirit of God came upon the messengers of Saul" and they were stopped by "a prophetic frenzy" (1 Sam 19:20). Saul himself tries to arrest David there, but a prophetic frenzy seizes him as well, and the king

strips off his clothes and lies naked on the ground all day and night. Saul's nakedness symbolizes how the king has stripped away all who have been closest to him: Samuel, Jonathan, Michal, David, even God.

David leaves Ramah and meets secretly with Jonathan, who still hopes for a reconciliation between his father and his friend and can hardly believe his father will kill David. "There is but a step between me and death" (1 Sam 20:3), David tells Jonathan. In order to clarify the situation, they arrange for Jonathan to test Saul's attitudes at a festival beginning the next day. Jonathan will then signal David in hiding as to whether it is safe for him to return home.

When the festival banquet is set, Jonathan offers excuses for David's absence, but Saul berates his son and even throws a spear at him. Jonathan recognizes that the situation is hopeless and informs David the next day that he must flee. With tears the two friends part, promising to maintain their friendship even to succeeding generations.

Everyone who was in distress, and everyone who was in debt, and everyone who was discontented gathered to him; and he became captain over them. Those who were with him numbered about four hundred.   1 SAM 22:2

*H*aving found it impossible to remain in the king's service, David becomes an outlaw leader and, in the eyes of many, a rival king. At first David is filled with uncertainty and is alone. He goes to the relatively new sanctuary at Nob, just east of the future city of David, Jerusalem. Nob has evidently replaced Shiloh as a religious center after the Philistines destroyed the earlier shrine. Ahimelech, the leading priest, is easily intimidated by the famous warrior, as David pretends to be on a secret mission for Saul in order to get food (the sacred bread) and a weapon (Goliath's sword).

David next goes to the Philistines at Gath, but quickly realizes his danger when the people speak of him as an Israelite king who has killed tens of thousands of their compatriots. Again using deception, David feigns madness and escapes back to Judah, where he finds broad popular support. His brothers and various discontented men join him at the cave of Adullam, where they form a private army.

Meanwhile, Saul learns of David's exploits and begins to see conspiracies all around him. When Doeg, one of Saul's Edomite servants, reports David's visit to Nob, Saul accuses Ahimelech of treason and orders his own men to execute all the priests. Saul's Israelite soldiers are afraid to kill priests of God, but Saul is undeterred. His fear of conspiracies is greater than his fear of the Lord, and he orders Doeg the Edomite to slaughter all the priests and their families who live at Nob. Only Abiathar, the son of Ahimelech, escapes alive and goes to David. Feeling guilty for causing this disaster, David promises protection to Abiathar. "Stay with me," he assures Abiathar, "for the one who seeks my life seeks your life; you will be safe with me" (1 Sam 22:23). Thus, David has in his entourage the heir to the high priesthood of Israel, while Saul becomes ever more alienated from the religious leaders of the people.

"This very day your eyes have seen how the Lord gave you into my hand in the cave; and some urged me to kill you, but I spared you."
1 SAM 24:10

Even as an outlaw, David continues his role as the scourge of the Philistines. When the Philistines attack the town of Keilah, he consults God, using the Urim and Thummim that Abiathar has brought in the sacred ephod, or priestly vestment, and convinces his reticent men to take on the mighty Philistines. David's relatively small band is able to drive out the Philistines and gain a great deal of booty. But when Saul hears that David is in Keilah, he decides to attack. The people of Keilah feel trapped between the king and the local hero. David knows that the town will not protect him from Saul, and he escapes into the wilderness of Ziph south of Hebron, where he receives reassurance from Jonathan.

The people of Ziph try to betray David to Saul, but he moves south to Maon with Saul in hot pursuit. The Philistines unintentionally help David by at-

Michal helps her husband David escape King Saul's wrath by lowering him from their bedroom window.

tacking Israel, so that Saul has to return home while David moves into the barren hills around the Dead Sea.

After the Philistines withdraw, Saul returns with 3,000 soldiers to pursue David, whose men hide in the cave-riddled hills around En-gedi. At a place appropriately called "rocks of the wild goats," David and his men are deep in a cavern when Saul enters the front of the cave to relieve himself. His men urge David to seize the opportunity God has given him to kill his enemy, but David, in respect for "the Lord's anointed" (1 Sam 24:6), simply gets close enough to cut off a piece of Saul's robe.

As Saul departs, David calls to him from afar, protesting his innocence and holding up the robe fragment to show that he means no harm to the king. Saul is touched by this display, admits David's innocence, and calls off his pursuit. But David's action also confirms the king's suspicion that David is indeed the one who will take the kingdom from him.

There was a man in Maon, whose property was in Carmel. The man was very rich; he had three thousand sheep and a thousand goats. 1 SAM 25:2

An era ends with the death of Samuel, the last of Israel's judges. Henceforth, kings and their rivals battle for supremacy.

In Judah, David's private army offers farmers, ranchers, and towns protection from Philistines and other raiding tribes. In return, David expects the wealthy people of the region to help supply the needs of his soldiers. When David sends men requesting support from a rancher named Nabal, the response is an insulting rejection. David is so incensed that he prepares to attack Nabal with 400 men.

Learning what has happened, Nabal's wife Abigail immediately assembles supplies for David's men and goes to meet him. Her apology and plea for mercy are so eloquent and moving that David abandons any thought of revenge and thanks Abigail for saving him from bloodguilt. When Abigail reports the incident to her churlish husband, he evidently has a stroke and soon dies. Hearing of Nabal's death, David sends for Abigail and asks her to marry him. His marriage to her and to Ahinoam, another woman of the south, helps consolidate his control of the region.

Saul soon returns to his pursuit of David, and the Ziphites again try to betray the fugitive. But now David is much more experienced. He infiltrates Saul's camp at night along with a trusted compatriot named Abishai. They could easily have assassinated Saul, but David simply takes Saul's spear and jug of water and leaves. In the morning David speaks from afar with Saul and his commander, Abner. Again, the king is touched that his rival has passed up an opportunity to kill him and renounces his dogged chase.

Fleeing the anger of the jealous king, David gathered his clan in the cave of Adullam, southwest of his native Bethlehem.

To make up for her husband's refusal of hospitality, the beautiful Abigail appears before the outlaw leader David, wearing an improbable crown in this painting.

David said in his heart, "I shall now perish one day by the hand of Saul; there is nothing better for me than to escape to the land of the Philistines; then Saul will despair of seeking me any longer within the borders of Israel, and I shall escape out of his hand." 1 SAM 27:1

In spite of Saul's temporary change of heart, David knows that he cannot escape Saul's pursuit forever. He decides to try an alliance with the Philistines again, this time from a position of strength, in the hope that Saul will give up his persecution. Achish, the king of Gath, assigns to David and his 600 men a border town called Ziklag. David and his men are able to settle their wives and children there in some comfort, far superior to the fugitive life to which they have been accustomed. Saul apparently decides that David poses little threat as a potential king of Israel while he is among the arch-enemy Philistines. Though still obsessed, the king maintains his tenuous truce with David.

For 16 months, David uses Ziklag as a base for raiding not Israelite villages but towns of the hostile Amalekites and other tribes far to the south. His men utterly destroy the population of the villages they raid so that no report can seep back to Gath, and David falsely reports to Achish that he is plundering Israelite villages in southern Judah. The massive booty from these raids mounts up, thus increasing the resources of David's private army. Achish believes David's reports, thinking that the fugitive has finally burned all his bridges with Israel and no longer retains any loyalty to the land of his birth.

A hard test confronts David, however, as the Philistines, long suppressed by Saul, mass their forces for a major assault on Israel, hoping to regain their lost dominance of the region. When Achish calls on David to march with him against Saul, David chooses to go along with Achish for the present.

Then Saul said to his servants, "Seek out for me a woman who is a medium, so that I may go to her and inquire of her." 1 SAM 28:7

As armies from the Philistines' five city-states assemble near the town of Shunem in the Jezreel valley far north of their traditional territory, Saul is filled with dread and despondency. It is obvious that the Philistines are ready for a massive attack and that his forces gathered at Mount Gilboa are inadequate to resist. The only thing that could have given Saul comfort was the clear assurance that God would continue to favor the cause of Israel. But Saul has forfeited the means of learning such a divine message: "The Lord did not answer him, not by dreams, or by Urim, or by prophets" (1 Sam 28:6).

Samuel had been Saul's only trustworthy link to God, and now Samuel is gone—unless Saul can reach him through a medium. Although the king himself has outlawed mediums, he now seeks one in the village of Endor, just a few miles northeast of the Philistine camp. In disguise, he goes to the medium at night, but she senses a trap. Only by swearing that no harm will come to her can the king persuade her to do her work.

When Saul requests to see Samuel, the aged prophet appears rising like "a divine being coming up out of the ground" (1 Sam 28:13). The medium is frightened by the apparition and realizes that the inquirer is the king, as Saul bows before Samuel. Angry that his rest in death has been disturbed, Samuel demands to know the reason he has been summoned. When Saul confesses his confusion and foreboding, Samuel only confirms the worst: God has become Saul's enemy, far more fearsome than the Philistines. The kingdom has been torn from Saul and given to David. The Philistines will defeat Israel; Saul and his sons will be dead by morning. Initially Samuel's words sap all of Saul's waning strength, but soon the certainty of an end to his troubles allows the king to regain his composure, eat a meal, and renew his strength for his final battle.

Achish replied to David, "I know that you are as blameless in my sight as an angel of God; nevertheless, the commanders of the Philistines have said, 'He shall not go up with us to the battle.'"   1 SAM 29:9

The time of decision is quickly approaching for David. Will he actually go into battle with the Philistines against the Israelites? Such a deed of betrayal may alienate him forever from leadership in Israel. Achish trusts him completely, and David cannot reject the invitation to join the Philistine army without causing himself difficulties. Fortunately, David is blessed with a reputation that the rest of the Philistine commanders simply cannot tolerate. He is known as a slayer of Philistines, a man not to be trusted. Achish has to send David and his troops home. Thus, David can protest his faithfulness and at the same time escape the onus of either betraying Achish or fighting in a war against Israel.

When David returns to Ziklag, however, he finds that the Amalekites have taken revenge for some of his raids by burning the town and making off with all the women and children. Though David's men are near exhaustion and so distressed and bitter about the situation that some want to stone their leader, God tells David that he should pursue the Amalekites in order to rescue the captives.

Aided by an Egyptian slave that the Amalekites had abandoned in the desert because he was sick, David's men find the Amalekites celebrating the great spoils they have captured. They destroy the Amalekites and rescue all the captives along with all the spoils. David marches back in triumph, sharing what has been taken among all his men and sending substantial gifts to the elders of the tribe of Judah in all the areas where his band had stayed.

So Saul and his three sons and his armor-bearer and all his men died together on the same day.   1 SAM 31:6

Meanwhile, far to the north, disaster overtakes Saul and the armies of Israel. As the Philistine onslaught drives the Israelite forces before it, one Israelite commander after another falls. Jonathan is killed, as are two of his brothers, Abinadab and Malchishua. Saul's most promising heirs are gone.

Saul is in the thick of the fighting on Mount Gilboa and, unfortunately, his famous stature makes him an easy target for archers to spot. Despite his shield and heavy armor, Saul is severely wounded by a volley of arrows. Knowing the ignominy that will go with being taken alive, Saul commands his armor-bearer to draw a sword and run him through. But the armor-bearer cannot bring himself to kill his king. Saul has to fall on his own sword to bring death, and the armor-bearer follows suit.

Everywhere, the Israelites flee before the victorious Philistines. Towns are abandoned to the invaders, and by the end of the day the Philistines control nearly all of the central region of Israel. When they find Saul's body the next day, enemy soldiers behead the corpse, hang up his armor in a temple of Astarte, and tie his body to the walls of Beth-shan as food for vultures. The people of Jabesh-gilead hear of this indignity, however, and they remember how years ago Saul had marshaled all of Israel to save their city. Without hesitation, the warriors of Jabesh-gilead set out on an all-night march to Beth-shan. They boldly rescue the headless corpse of the fallen king and the bodies of his three sons from the walls and bring them to their own city for cremation. After burying the bones, they mourn Saul with seven days of fasting. Thus, the tragic story of Israel's first king comes to an end.

After his sons are killed in battle with the Philistines on Mount Gilboa (above), King Saul falls on his own sword to avoid capture (inset, stained glass window from Chartres Cathedral in France).

David is hoisted aloft to be crowned by a Grecian goddess in this unlikely scene from a 10th-century Byzantine manuscript.

*T*he break between 1 and 2 Samuel is an artificial division into two parts of what was originally a single work. At the end of 1 Samuel, the fortunes of Israel have reached a low point, with Saul and his most promising heirs killed in battle and much of the emerging nation at the mercy of the Philistines. But 2 Samuel marks David's swift transition from outlaw to king and the beginning of a dramatic rise in Israel's national dreams. Samuel and the ideal of a simple confederation of tribes led by circuit riders serving as prophets, priests, and judges fade into the past. The ideal of a prosperous Israel led by a powerful king and triumphant over all enemies is the dominant vision.

Saul had been king, but the narrative of 1 Samuel never suggests that he showed ambition in organizing the nation. He remained more a chieftain over diverse tribes than the master of a united government. He seemed to have no aspirations as a builder and never created a national capital or religious center. He was a warrior whose home was the rough fortress of Gibeah, not a palace.

The potential for the unity of Israel is left for David to develop, and 2 Samuel is the story of his reign. In a pattern that is not uncommon in the biographies of powerful kings, the narrative describes first the struggle of David to establish his kingdom, then the years of greatest power and prosperity, and finally a troubled period of challenges to the king's power and the perhaps inevitable struggle for succession.

Saul and Jonathan, beloved and lovely!
In life and in death they were not divided;
* they were swifter than eagles,*
* they were stronger than lions.* 2 SAM 1:23

*T*he final irony in the tragic story of King Saul is that the chief voice in mourning and memorializing Saul's life is the man whom Saul considered his archenemy, David.

David learns of the deaths of Saul and Jonathan and the defeat of Israel from a young Amalekite who, remarkably enough, had been with Saul's army. He brings David the crown he had removed from the king's head as well as Saul's armlet. Aware of the well-known antagonism between Saul and David, the young man colors his report of taking the crown by adding the erroneous claim that he himself had dealt the coup de grâce to the dying monarch. He had found Saul wounded and convulsing, he says, and at the king's request had put him out of his misery.

David is in an awkward position. Though he himself had almost been drawn into the Philistines' battle against Saul, he has always in the past held that the person of "the Lord's anointed" (1 Sam 24:6)—a role that he is to play in the future—is sacrosanct, and he had refused to harm

Saul. The king had also been his father-in-law and the father of Jonathan, David's dearest friend. Thus, even though Saul's death clearly relieves him of his most persistent adversary, David is sincere when he rends his clothes and mourns and fasts at the news of the two deaths.

The Amalekite is also unfortunate in that David has just come from destroying Amalekites, and this man's claim to have killed the king is intolerable. The bearer of bad news pays with his life for his lie.

In his grief at the death of Saul and especially at the death of Jonathan, David writes a beautiful lament that would later evidently be called "The Song of the Bow" and be included in an ancient anthology known as the Book of Jashar. Considered by many scholars as one of the most ancient poetic works in the Bible, the lament generously celebrates Saul and his sons as the glory of Israel and expresses David's profound sense of loss over Jonathan:

"How the mighty have fallen in the
  midst of the battle!
Jonathan lies slain upon your high
  places.
I am distressed for you, my brother Jonathan;
  greatly beloved were you to me;
your love to me was wonderful,
  passing the love of women"
(2 Sam 1:25-26).

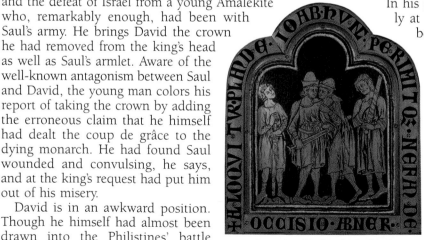

Avenging his brother's death and eliminating a rival, David's commander Joab kills Abner, who has switched his allegiance from Saul; a 12th-century plaque.

Then the people of Judah came, and there they anointed David king over the house of Judah.   2 SAM 2:4

Bible readers often think that the split between the northern kingdom of Israel and the southern kingdom of Judah began only in the time of Rehoboam, after the death of Solomon. In fact, the division first becomes a major problem immediately after the death of Saul. David is a hero of Judah, one of the largest and most powerful tribes, which dominates the entire south of Canaan. Support for Saul against David has come primarily from the northern tribes, of which Ephraim is paramount. After Saul's death, David consults the Lord's will through the Urim and Thummim and goes directly to Hebron, the largest city of Judah. There, the leading men of the tribe anoint him king over Judah.

Meanwhile, Abner, Saul's commander and right-hand man, who had escaped the slaughter on Mount Gilboa, supports the one surviving son of Saul and helps anoint him king over all the northern tribes in the city of Mahanaim east of the Jordan River. The new king is Ishbaal (or Esh-baal, 1 Chr 8:33), meaning "man of the Lord." But because the word "baal" later came to be closely identified with the pagan god, the word "bosheth," meaning "shame," was substituted for it in historical records. Thus, in the original Hebrew of 2 Samuel, Saul's heir is called Ish-bosheth.

Warfare and competition between north and south break out immediately. David seems to have tried to build positive relationships with some in the north by sending official praise to Jabesh-gilead for rescuing the bodies of Saul and Jonathan while also informing them of his new role as king of Judah. But soon Abner musters northern troops and marches south. Joab, David's commander, meets Abner's troops at Gibeon. First they test each other through a battle of 12 champions from each side. After all 24 die in the duel, a full battle erupts, and David's forces drive back the northern troops. In the pursuit that follows, however, the fleeing Abner turns to kill Joab's brother Asahel.

There was a long war between the house of Saul and the house of David; David grew stronger and stronger, while the house of Saul became weaker and weaker.   2 SAM 3:1

Ishbaal is on the throne, but Abner holds the power, and both men know it. When Abner presumes to take one of Saul's royal concubines, considered a severe insult, Ishbaal tries to confront his commander but soon regrets having done so. Abner is enraged and swears to Ishbaal that he will deliver the northern tribes to David. Abner immediately makes overtures to David and begins discussing the overthrow of Ishbaal with the tribal elders, even to the point of convincing the men of Benjamin—Saul's fellow tribesmen—to support his action.

When Abner approaches him, David makes only a single demand—the return to him of his wife Michal, Saul's daughter. After she helped David escape her father's wrath, Saul had given her to another man, Paltiel. Now she is returned to David, though her new husband follows her weeping. Michal's return strengthens David's claim to succeed the dynasty of Saul.

While Joab is absent, David meets with Abner and agrees on a process for reuniting the 12 tribes, this time under his rule. While north and south are weakened by war, the Philistines benefit greatly in consolidating their control over central Canaan. Union will benefit both sides of the intertribal conflict. After concluding the negotiations, Abner departs. Joab returns, still bent on avenging Asahel's death and distrustful of David's agreement with a potentially powerful rival. On a pretense of peace, Joab meets with Abner and instead murders him in cold blood.

David is outraged at Joab's rash vengeance, for it puts him immediately under suspicion with the northern tribes of having betrayed Abner. The agreement they had negotiated is in severe danger. Only by publicly condemning Joab and by an elaborate display of mourning for Abner does David convince the north that he is not responsible for the murder.

They anointed David king over Israel. David was thirty years old when he began to reign, and he reigned forty years.   2 SAM 5:3-4

Abner's plan for overthrowing Ishbaal, however, is accomplished by other means. At the death of Abner, Ishbaal might have acted boldly to secure an advantage. Instead, his courage fails and the northern tribes realize that he is a hopeless leader. Two of Ishbaal's own captains from the tribe of Benjamin decide to bring the dynasty of Saul to an end. They ride up to Ishbaal's house in Mahanaim where, though a war is going on, no soldiers appear to be guarding the king's residence. They enter Ishbaal's bedchamber while he is taking his noon nap, assassinate and behead him, and escape—all apparently without attracting any notice.

After assassins bring the head of Ishbaal, Saul's son and successor, to David (top), he is anointed king; two scenes from a 13th-century illuminated Bible.

The captains carry the head south to David in Hebron. With bravado, they claim God's sanction for their murder: "The Lord has avenged my lord the king this day on Saul and on his offspring" (2 Sam 4:8). David has no tolerance for the treasonous murder of a king, however, and has the two captains immediately executed.

Soon, elders from all the tribes rally to support David at Hebron. They affirm their common kinship, remembering God's promise to David: "It is you who shall be shepherd of my people Israel, you who shall be ruler over Israel" (2 Sam 5:2). They fulfill the promise by making a covenant with David and anointing him king of all Israel.

The year is about 1000 B.C. Finally, the events God had initiated through Samuel when he anointed David in secret more than 15 years earlier come to fruition. David is only a few years past 30, having already spent several years as king of Judah in Hebron. Now he must serve in a new role as ruler of a reunited, but still weakened, Israel.

So David and all the house of Israel brought up the ark of the Lord with shouting, and with the sound of the trumpet.   2 SAM 6:15

The first order of business for David in uniting his kingdom is to establish a national capital independent of any of the tribes. He had already, during his days on the run from Saul, established a force of soldiers loyal to him alone. Now he chooses a city that belongs neither to Judah nor Ephraim nor any other tribe. The choice falls on the fortified city known as Jebus (Judg 19:10-12), soon to be renamed Jerusalem. The city belongs to the Jebusites, a Canaanite people who have never been driven out and have lived for centuries surrounded by the Israelites. It is the last substantial town in Canaanite control, but the location is ideal—a high ridge on the border between Judah and Benjamin.

The Jebusites think their fortifications so invulnerable that they taunt David, but his forces soon find a weak spot and use a water shaft leading to a spring outside the walls to enter and conquer the city.

No sooner has David taken the city than he begins building. He concentrates on the section known as the stronghold of Zion, which he calls the city of David. Drawing on help from a foreign ally, King Hiram of Tyre, he builds a beautiful palace of cedar to symbolize the solidity of his kingdom.

The Philistines become agitated over the bold independence of their former ally, and decide to show David that they are still in control by marching against Jerusalem from the west. After seeking divine guidance, David soundly defeats their forces. When they regroup and attack again, David is guided by God to crush the Philistines, drive them back into their own territory, and break their control on Canaan.

The creation of a new capital city is complete, however, only when David succeeds in bringing the sacred ark of the covenant into the city. Saul failed

Raphael's fresco of David's triumphal entry into Jerusalem; the original city of David is in the foreground of the aerial view at left, looking north to present-day Jerusalem.

as king because he broke away from Israel's prophet and priests and disobeyed God. David, by contrast, wants to support and enhance Israel's faith in every way he possibly can.

The first attempt to bring the ark from its exile in Baale-judah (another name for Kiriath-jearim) fails because of the fear engendered when Uzzah, one of the attendants, reaches out to steady the ark and dies when he touches the holy object. A second attempt three months later becomes a great celebration. Dancing before the ark dressed in the garb of a priest, David leads it into the city and sets it up inside a tent similar to the tents that held the ark in previous generations. David serves as a royal priest and offers elaborate sacrifices of celebration, and all the people share in the vast feast he provides.

David's wife Michal, however, shows that she has lost her former love for David by expressing contempt for his role in this celebration. David defends the fact that he "danced before the Lord" (2 Sam 6:21), but evidently never again treats Michal as his wife.

Your house and your kingdom shall be made sure forever before me; your throne shall be established forever.
2 SAM 7:16

By honoring God in the restoration of a united nation, David takes on a unique role in Israel's history. He establishes a royal dynasty that becomes not only part of the history of Israel but also part of its religion, its understanding of God, and its future.

Since its original construction, the ark of the covenant has been a portable shrine, kept in an elaborate tent, in part symbolizing that Israel's God can never be contained in one location. As David becomes more secure in his new national capital, it seems to him less appropriate that the ark of God should be kept in lodgings so far inferior to his own. He asks advice from the prophet Nathan, who at first indicates that David can proceed with any plan he desires to house the ark.

God, however, corrects Nathan and sends him back to David. God has not "lived in a house" (2 Sam 7:6) since he first delivered Israel from Egypt, nor does he desire David to build one for the ark now. God will, however, let the king's son build it. David's position of greatness and power is due to God's blessing and protection. Now God will complete that blessing by making a house for David, that is, establishing his dynasty as the permanent royal dynasty of Israel. Though some of his descendants may sin and be punished, God will never withdraw his loving support: "I will establish the throne of his kingdom forever" (2 Sam 7:13).

David responds to these promises in a beautiful prayer that celebrates God's graciousness to Israel: "You established your people Israel for yourself to be your people forever; and you, O Lord, became their God" (2 Sam 7:24). David concludes by beseeching the Lord to fulfill his promises. These promises to David and his descendants establish the foundation

ISRAEL'S DREADED ENEMY: THE PHILISTINES

David at war with his troublesome foes, the Philistines, as depicted on a 14th-century stained glass window

Israel's most feared neighbors for nearly 200 years were the Philistines, who invaded Canaan about the same time the Israelites did. The Philistines were concentrated along the southern coast, in a league of five cities: Ashkelon, Ashdod, Gath, Gaza, and Ekron. As the Israelites expanded west from the Jordan River into the central highlands, the Philistines pressed east from the fertile coastal plains. When the two clashed, the Philistines usually won because they could forge iron weapons—a secret they guarded from the Israelites, who were still using softer bronze. Another Philistine advantage lay in their ability to fight as a single force. In contrast, Israel's 12 tribes initially lacked a unifying leader.

The Philistines were part of a massive wave of refugees, called the Sea Peoples, driven from their homelands in the Aegean region by unknown forces, perhaps famine. The prophet Amos said the Philistines were from Caphtor, Hebrew for Crete, an island south of Greece. Repelled from an invasion of Egypt, the Philistines turned to Canaan.

King Saul died in battle with the Philistines, but David—the shepherd boy who killed the Philistine champion Goliath—ended their dominance of the region. Because the only surviving documents about them are from their enemies, the Philistines acquired a reputation as uneducated brutes. Yet, ironically, the land still bears their name: Palestine, derived from the word a Greek historian used to identify the Philistines' descendants.

for the later belief in a Messiah ("anointed one") who will reestablish David's throne and kingdom after the destruction of 586 B.C.

So David reigned over all Israel; and David administered justice and equity to all his people. 2 SAM 8:15

The lengthy and successful story of David ruthlessly building an empire is summarized in 2 Samuel 8-10. Under the judges, Israel was often beset by foreign troops; now Israel turns the tables and makes vassals of the surrounding nations. The more powerful empires of Egypt and Assyria, which will later dominate Israel's history, are temporarily weak and virtually leaderless, leaving room for David's expansion far beyond the traditional boundaries of the 12 tribes.

David first subdues the Philistines and Canaanites, thus securing the internal territory of Israel against challenge. Next he turns to Moab. Earlier friendly relations degenerate into a fierce war in which, apparently, two of every three captured Moabite soldiers are executed. South of the Dead Sea, David defeats the forces of Edom with great slaughter, which the vanquished will remember for generations. David also takes on the Aramean or Syrian

Playing his lyre on a palace balcony, David ogles a rather decorous Bathsheba in this 16th-century painting.

peoples to the east and north of Israel. Largely using infantry, David is able to defeat armies strengthened with large chariot forces. Everywhere, David's military genius meets with success until his empire stretches from the Euphrates River in the north to the borders of Egypt and the Gulf of Aqaba in the south.

Such extensive conquests require a larger governmental structure. David creates a small but functional cabinet with himself in firm control. He has an official record keeper and secretary in addition to the key positions that are held by Joab as commander of the army and by Zadok and Abiathar as the chief priests. David also maintains a personal bodyguard of foreign soldiers, primarily Philistine mercenaries, who are loyal only to him. Curiously, he names his sons priests.

David asked, "Is there still anyone left of the house of Saul to whom I may show kindness for Jonathan's sake?" 2 SAM 9:1

David's ferocity in war is balanced by personal kindness and even tenderness. He never forgets the covenant he had made with Jonathan years earlier when Jonathan helped him escape Saul's jeal-

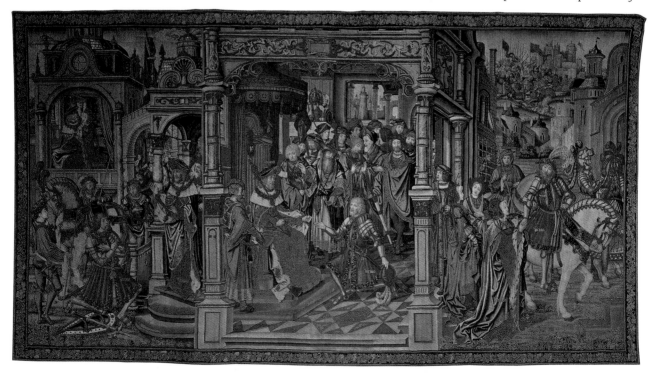

As shown on a 16th-century tapestry from Brussels, David commits adultery with Bathsheba (upper left), summons her husband Uriah (left), and gives him a letter for Joab (center). Bathsheba bids farewell to Uriah (right), perhaps knowing that David's letter will lead to her husband's death on the battlefield (upper right).

ous rage. Though most of Saul's descendants have perished, David inquires now whether any remain "to whom I may show the kindness of God" (2 Sam 9:3).

As it happens, Jonathan's young son Merib-baal (whose name was later recorded as Mephibosheth), had been severely injured and left permanently crippled at the time of Jonathan's death on Mount Gilboa (2 Sam 4:4). When David learns about Mephibosheth from a former servant of Saul's family, he immediately arranges to bring the young man to his court and offers him lifelong support.

When David tries to show kindness to other nations, however, the reputation he bears for his conquests creates distrust of his motives. He sends ambassadors to the Ammonites to express condolences on the death of their king, but the Ammonite leaders think the ambassadors are spies and grossly insult them. David responds by sending Joab with a large army to besiege their capital city of Rabbah (modern Amman, Jordan). The Ammonites retaliate by hiring a mercenary army that attacks Joab from the rear. Joab shows his great skill as a military commander by defeating the enemy on both fronts.

This defeat rouses Aramean rulers farther north to try to stop Israel's seemingly inexorable advance. But David leads his army against them and gains dominance in the entire Aramean territory.

It happened, late one afternoon, when David rose from his couch and was walking about on the roof of the king's house, that he saw from the roof a woman bathing; the woman was very beautiful. 2 SAM 11:2

Everything is going well for David, the empire builder—so well that he no longer has to lead troops into battle himself. He can remain at home in the spring, the time that for years has meant a foray into some new area for conquest or expansion. Now David can send Joab to renew the siege of the Ammonite city of Rabbah.

With his troops in the field and little to do, David walks late one afternoon along the parapets of his palace overlooking much of the city, and there below him he sees a beautiful woman bathing. David already has many wives, but he is used to power and having whatever he wants. He inquires about the woman and learns that she is called Bathsheba and is the daughter of one of his personal guards and the wife of another, a soldier named Uriah the Hittite. The husband is with David's troops at Rabbah. David sends for Bathsheba, who comes to the palace and commits adultery with the king.

When Bathsheba becomes pregnant, David tries to avoid the potential disgrace by calling Uriah home, supposedly to bring news from the front, so that he can sleep with his wife and claim paternity of the child. Uriah is more honorable than David, however. He knows that, as a soldier for Israel on a mission of war, he is expected to stay away from women, and he flatly refuses to go home to his wife even when David tries to get him drunk.

After Nathan tells him of the Lord's anger, David prostrates himself as Bathsheba ponders the fate of their son.

Caught in the web of his sin, David sinks even further. Too much a coward to face his wrong, he instigates a murder. He has Uriah take to Joab the orders for his own destruction. Uriah is ordered into an especially dangerous attack on the walls of Rabbah, from which Joab—as instructed—withdraws support. Uriah is killed along with several other soldiers, who pay with their lives for David's sin.

When the news of Uriah's death is brought back to Jerusalem, Bathsheba makes the required lamentations over her husband and then marries David. The coconspirators seem to have gotten away with adultery and murder.

Thus says the Lord: I will raise up trouble against you from within your own house. 2 SAM 12:11

Nothing, however, is hidden from God. Soon the prophet Nathan asks to speak to the king and tells him a parable about a wealthy man who has taken and killed the pet lamb of his impoverished neighbor in order to feed a guest. David's well-honed sense of justice fires his anger against the man who has committed such an outrage. "You are the man!" (2 Sam 12:7), Nathan replies. God has given David everything he can desire and more; yet David has "despised the word of the Lord" and has struck down Uriah "with the sword of the Ammonites" (2 Sam 12:9) and taken his wife.

The punishment will fit the crime. Nathan predicts that the violence of the sword will plague David's family, his own wives will be taken from him, and the child of Bathsheba will die. David admits his sin and is filled with penitence, but the judgment is

Feigning illness, David's son Amnon lures his half sister Tamar into his bedroom to seduce her; Dutch artist Jan Steen (1626-1679) included Amnon's eager accomplice, Jonadab.

irrevocable. When Bathsheba's baby is born, he quickly becomes ill. For seven days David fasts and prays for the child until he dies. Then David rises, refreshes himself, and worships God; there is no longer any reason to fast and weep. "Can I bring him back again?" (2 Sam 12:23), the king asks.

David and Bathsheba are chastened and drawn closer together by the experience. Their next child is Solomon, who is given the personal name Jedidiah, meaning "beloved of the Lord."

There is a footnote to the final conquest of Rabbah in 2 Samuel 12:31. Not only does David gain much booty and a heavy gold crown from the Ammonite king; he also begins to conscript labor from the conquered peoples.

David's son Absalom had a beautiful sister whose name was Tamar; and David's son Amnon fell in love with her.
2 SAM 13:1

The fulfillment of the family violence predicted by Nathan breaks out between the sons and a daughter of different mothers in David's large and self-indulgent household. David's eldest son Amnon, the crown prince, becomes obsessed with a tormented love for his beautiful half sister Tamar, who is the full sister of Absalom. A clever friend, Jonadab, helps Amnon concoct a plan to get Tamar in his room alone. It even involves using King David to order Tamar to prepare some food for Amnon, who pretends to be ill and confined to his chambers.

When Tamar arrives with the food, Amnon rapes his virgin sister, and then throws her out as if she has defiled herself and become something hateful. Tamar tells her story to Absalom, who calms her and waits for an opportunity to take revenge.

Two years pass before Absalom invites all the sons of David to a sheepshearing celebration. When Amnon is drunk, Absalom's servants attack and kill him. All the other sons of David flee the scene, and rumors spread that they have been killed. David is thrown into despair, bewailing the news until more accurate reports of the murder reach him. Absalom escapes to the home of his mother's father, the king of Geshur, just east of the Sea of Galilee, and remains there for three years. David is soon reconciled to the death of Amnon, but he mourns the absence of Absalom day after day.

Absalom sent secret messengers throughout all the tribes of Israel, saying, "As soon as you hear the sound of the trumpet, then shout: Absalom has become king at Hebron!" 2 SAM 15:10

After three years Joab uses an elaborate scheme to convince David to recall Absalom from Geshur. He asks a woman to take a mournful tale to the king, apparently for his judgment, but actually to make David see the injustice of leaving Absalom in self-enforced exile. The scheme works, and David recalls Absalom but refuses to see him for two more years. By this time Absalom has no remaining loyalty to his father, but finally forces Joab to take his cause to the king again. David agrees to see Absalom; when he does, he kisses him and restores him to full favor at court.

Absalom immediately begins to take advantage of his position as well as his famous beauty and outgoing personality to systematically convince the people that they will be better off if he is king: "So Absalom stole the hearts of the men of Israel" (2 Sam 15:6). He even gains the support of some senior advisers of the king and arranges to have his coup d'état proclaimed in Hebron, where David had been anointed king over Judah and later over all Israel.

David recognizes what is happening only when it is almost too late. Now it is he who has to flee the capital before Absalom's forces can take the city. But David is ever the fighter. Even in apparent defeat, he leaves behind spies and agents to plant false advice in Absalom's inexperienced ears. David refuses to take the ark of the covenant in flight with him, since he

hopes God will allow him to return in triumph. The faithful priests Zadok and Abiathar arrange for their sons to take messages to David before he crosses the Jordan River into friendly territory.

When King David came to Bahurim, a man of the family of the house of Saul came out whose name was Shimei son of Gera; he came out cursing. He threw stones at David and at all the servants of King David. 2 SAM 16:5-6

David's withdrawal from Jerusalem is nonetheless an ignominious experience. A servant he encounters convinces him that even Mephibosheth, Jonathan's son, has betrayed him. Another man, a Benjaminite named Shimei, curses David ferociously and throws stones at him, crying, "The Lord has avenged on all of you the blood of the house of Saul in whose place you have reigned . . . . for you are a man of blood" (2 Sam 16:8). When one of David's soldiers wants to kill Shimei, David refuses to allow

DAVID: WINNING AND KEEPING HIS KINGDOM

En route to his control of a unified Israel, David had to contend with both the hostile Philistines and an envious King Saul, who maintained his tenuous control of the kingdom from a residence at Gibeah. After his stunning defeat of the Philistine giant Goliath in the valley of Elah, David joined the court and eventually was given Saul's daughter Michal in marriage. But he was soon forced to flee the king's jealous rage—stopping first at the shrine of Nob, then gathering an outlaw band at the cave of Adullam southwest of his native Bethlehem. David's victory over the Philistines at Keilah further enraged the king, who pursued him through the wilderness of Ziph south of Hebron to En-gedi on the Dead Sea. In a cave there, David spared the life of his royal adversary. Next, from a base at Ziklag given him by the Philistine king of Gath, David made war on the Amalekites of the Negeb. Spared the choice of fighting his fellow Israelites, David sat out the battle in the Jezreel valley, in which the Philistines killed Saul and his sons on Mount Gilboa.

After ruling as king of Judah at Hebron for seven and a half years, David was anointed king of all Israel. Among his first acts was capturing Jebusite Jerusalem, making it his capital and bringing the ark of the covenant to it from its temporary home at Kiriath-jearim. In time, he expanded his kingdom to the border of Egypt in the south and to the Euphrates River in the north.

Toward the end of his 33-year reign at Jerusalem, David had to deal with the revolt of his own son Absalom. While fleeing to Mahanaim east of the Jordan, David directed the forces that defeated Absalom in the forest of Ephraim, possibly near Rogelim. A second rebel, the Benjaminite Sheba, was pursued north of the Sea of Galilee and killed at Abel of Beth-maacah.

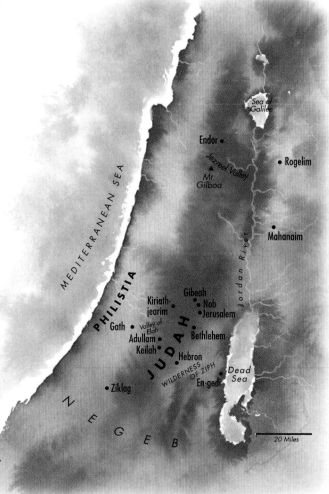

Fleeing defeat by his father's soldiers, Absalom is caught in tree branches and killed by Joab; a scene from the renowned 15th-century Nuremberg Bible.

him to do so: "My own son seeks my life; how much more now may this Benjaminite!" (2 Sam 16:11).

But the plans that David has set in motion before fleeing Jerusalem prove effective. He has left behind a respected courtier named Hushai to counteract the influence of Absalom's principal adviser Ahithophel, whose counsel is valued "as if one consulted the oracle of God" (2 Sam 16:23). Hushai then effectively convinces Absalom that he has forsaken David to support the new king whom God and the people have chosen, and thus the crafty Hushai gains Absalom's confidence.

The decisive moment comes when Ahithophel advises Absalom to allow him to pursue David immediately: "I will strike down only the king," he says, "and I will bring all the people back to you as a bride comes home to her husband" (2 Sam 17:2-3). Such a plan may well have proved disastrous for David. But Hushai convinces Absalom to delay until he can assemble a larger force and gain a more glorious victory over all of David's forces. The delay, communicated to David through Zadok and Abiathar, gives the king's forces time to recross the Jordan and organize for battle. Meanwhile, Ahithophel, whose counsel has been rejected by the foolish Absalom, goes home and hangs himself. He has backed a man unworthy of his oracular wisdom.

The king ordered Joab and Abishai and Ittai, saying, "Deal gently for my sake with the young man Absalom."
2 SAM 18:5

Though Absalom imagines that his forces, drawn from all of Israel, will overwhelm David's limited army, his inexperienced troops cannot even begin to match the battle-hardened, well-led soldiers that remain faithful to David. The king divides his troops into thirds under Joab and his brother Abishai and under his Philistine commander Ittai the Gittite. At first David proposes to go with them into battle, but the commanders refuse. This battle is about the person of the king, and victory will count for nothing if

David is lost. Thus David remains in the city of Mahanaim while his troops march forth to meet those of Absalom in the forest of Ephraim. As they depart, David publicly orders his commanders to treat Absalom gently if they capture him, an order that certainly sends mixed signals concerning David's resolve to suppress this treasonous rebellion.

David's commanders are able to drive Absalom's forces into the forest, where they cannot maintain even rudimentary order and are overwhelmingly defeated. The forest itself becomes an ally of David and "claimed more victims that day than the sword" (2 Sam 18:8). Absalom himself is being pursued by David's soldiers when his mule passes under a low tree and his head is caught and wedged between the branches. The mule keeps going while Absalom is left dangling by his head, injured but still alive. Told of Absalom's predicament, Joab comes immediately to run three spears through the young man's heart. His corpse is buried in a forest pit under a heap of stones.

Messengers are dispatched back to David to report the victory, though Joab knows full well that David will not react well to news of his son's death. Indeed, nothing seems to matter to David except the fate of Absalom, and when he learns of the death, he mourns inconsolably, "O my son Absalom . . . . Would I had died instead of you, O Absalom, my son, my son!" (2 Sam 18:33).

David returns to Jerusalem, grateful but chastened. Absalom's many supporters are in confusion about what to expect from the king, but his every action shows his intention to reunite the people. He even pardons Shimei the Benjaminite, who had cursed him and thrown stones at him, and promises to replace Joab with Amasa, the commander of Absalom's troops. In spite of David's conciliatory attitude, however, deep divisions still run through the nation, splitting the people in the north from those in the south.

Now a scoundrel named Sheba son of Bichri, a Benjaminite . . . . sounded the trumpet and cried out, "We have no portion in David, no share in the son of Jesse! Everyone to your tents, O Israel!" 2 SAM 20:1

Before David reaches Jerusalem, a new rebel leader named Sheba takes advantage of the rift between north and south to lead the ten northern tribes in rejecting the reestablishment of David's rule. The cry that he raises, reflecting the northern belief that David and his house belong too closely to Judah, is almost precisely the same as the cry raised 50 years later when the north rebels against Solomon's son Rehoboam (1 Kgs 12:16).

As promised, David calls on Amasa to gather troops for an attack on Sheba, but Amasa delays in fulfilling the command, and David turns to Abishai. As Abishai pursues Sheba northward, he is joined by Joab and David's personal guards. Joab has never tolerated a military rival. And so when Amasa comes to join the troops at Gibeon, Joab gives him a kiss of greeting while stabbing him in the belly and disemboweling him. Amasa is left lying in a field while soldiers follow Joab north to the town of Abel of Beth-maacah near the city of Dan, where Sheba is safely ensconced.

Joab besieges the city with a ramp and battering ram. Abel's situation seems hopeless until "a wise woman" of the city calls for negotiation with Joab. She quickly learns that Joab does not want to destroy the city but simply wants to have Sheba. The woman agrees to a bargain: "His head shall be thrown over the wall to you" (2 Sam 20:16, 21). The people of Abel consent to the woman's plan; they decapitate Sheba, toss his head over the wall, and thereby save their city from a destructive siege.

In the following list of David's cabinet officers there is one notable addition: Adoram as the minister "in charge of the forced labor" (2 Sam 20:24), an office that was to prove significant in later years. It is also noteworthy that David has a personal priest who is not from the tribe of Levi.

Now there was a famine in the days of David for three years, year after year. 2 SAM 21:1

The final four chapters of 2 Samuel seem to contain accounts of events from various periods during David's reign. These were added at the end of the narrative without any attempt to place them in their appropriate chronological sequence.

David's anguish at the death of his son Absalom is captured in this colored engraving by Gustave Doré (1832-1883).

The first is the strange and powerful story of a famine that grips the land for three years. David seeks guidance from the Lord, who tells him that the famine is caused by "bloodguilt on Saul and on his house, because he put the Gibeonites to death" (2 Sam 21:1), even though Israel has had a covenant with the Gibeonites since the time of Joshua not to destroy them (Josh 9:3-27). Curiously, 1 Samuel does not indicate when Saul may have committed such a wrong. Though Saul is dead and his family replaced on the throne by David, the bloodguilt is believed to pollute the land and has to be expiated by some corresponding offering of blood.

David allows the Gibeonites, who are one of the Canaanite peoples, to define what expiation is needed in order for them to bless Israel. They demand that they be allowed to impale seven sons of Saul "before the Lord at Gibeon on the mountain of the Lord" (2 Sam 21:6). Amazingly, though seven sons of Saul are not available, the narrative records that David turns over to the offended Gibeonites two sons of Saul by his concubine Rizpah and five grandsons to be summarily executed.

Even more remarkable is the devotion of Rizpah. She cannot stop the sacrifice of her sons, but she protects the bodies from scavengers day and night for six months until David hears of her devotion and retrieves the bones of Saul, Jonathan, and all those impaled at Gibeon and buries them in the land of Benjamin. Thus the famine comes to an end.

The second half of 2 Samuel 21 describes wars with the Philistines and perhaps fits chronologically after 2 Samuel 5. Here four different Philistine giants are listed—one with six fingers on each hand and six toes on each foot. Remarkably enough, the famous Goliath is listed as being killed by an Israelite warrior named Elhanan from Bethlehem. Whether Elhanan is an otherwise unknown name for David, or whether this represents a tradition about the death of Goliath that conflicts with the well-known story of David's battle with the giant, is never dealt with in the narrative of 1 and 2 Samuel.

David spoke to the Lord the words of this song . . . . The Lord is my rock, my fortress, and my deliverer, my God, my rock, in whom I take refuge, my shield and the horn of my salvation. 2 SAM 22:1-3

The psalm in 2 Samuel 22 is specifically associated with the period when David was fleeing from Saul. The poem is also included with a few variations as Psalm 18 in the book of Psalms. In the first section (2 Sam 22:2-20), the psalmist—presumably David—praises God for rescuing him from the danger of death and uses an image of a thunderstorm to describe the power of God. In the second part (2 Sam 22:21-31) he reflects on God's faithfulness to those who are righteous and keep his commands. In the concluding section (2 Sam 22:32-51) he celebrates how God has strengthened him to conquer his enemies and deliver him from strife.

Another psalm in 2 Samuel 23 is described as "the last words of David" and "the Oracle of David" (2 Sam 23:1). The psalm likens a just ruler to the rising sun while the godless are like useless thorns to be thrown away.

The narrative in 2 Samuel 23:8-39 seems to continue that of 2 Samuel 21. It presents a list of David's leading warriors during the wars with the Philistines, celebrating first the exploits of the mightiest of David's warriors, known as "the Three": Josheb-basshebeth, Eleazar son of Dodo, and Shammah son of Agee. Their adventures include invading a Philistine garrison in Bethlehem in order to get David a drink of water from his hometown well. Next come the exploits of "the Thirty," led by Abishai, the brother of Joab, and Benaiah, who was given command of David's personal bodyguard.

When David saw the angel who was destroying the people, he said to the Lord, "I alone have sinned, and I alone have done wickedly." 2 SAM 24:17

The story of a census and plague in 2 Samuel 24 should probably be closely associated with the description of David's expanding empire in 2 Samuel 8. The account begins with the remarkable statement that God is angry with Israel and "incited David against them, saying, 'Go, count the people of Israel and Judah'" (2 Sam 24:1). The same incident is recorded in 1 Chronicles 21:1 but attributes the in-citement to Satan. David calls for a census of the men available for combat throughout the land of Israel. Although he strenuously objects to such an action, Joab carries out the king's order.

When the census is completed, David realizes the greatness of his sin and appeals to God to take away his guilt. Through the prophet Gad, David is given a choice of punishments: a three-year famine, a three-month series of defeats, or a three-day pestilence. David chooses the last and shortest of the three. During the three days of punishment that follow, 70,000 die until God decides to halt the destroying angel just before he strikes the capital, Jerusalem. David is allowed to see the angel as he stops at the threshing floor of Araunah the Jebusite, just north of the city of David, and God commands David to build an altar on that spot.

When David approaches Araunah, the man offers to give the place to David, but the king insists on paying for the threshing floor in full: "I will not offer burnt offerings to the Lord my God that cost me nothing" (2 Sam 24:24), he says. The location David purchases that day for 50 shekels of silver (about 24 ounces) later becomes the site of the famous temple that his son and successor Solomon constructs (1 Chr 22:1). The end of 2 Samuel is another artificial break in the biblical narrative. The concluding events of David's 40-year reign and the struggle for succession between two of his sons are the subjects of the opening chapters of the following book, 1 Kings.

Old and infirm, David is persuaded by Bathsheba to designate their son Solomon as heir;
Cornelis de Vos (1584-1651) depicted the king on his deathbed transferring crown and scepter.

The two books now known as 1 and 2 Kings were originally an uninterrupted history, ascribed to the prophet Jeremiah. Drawn from many different sources, including court records dating to the time of King David, this history of the Israelite monarchy is also a deeply religious text. The unnamed editor and commentator, pondering the four centuries of chaos and idolatry in Israel between David's death around 965 B.C. and the fall of Jerusalem in 586 B.C., aims to prove that the tragedies of the Israelites arise from a single cause: God is punishing them for abandoning the true faith and turning to the pagan gods of the alien peoples who surround them.

After the climactic days of Solomon's spiritual leadership and worldly glory, the story becomes a grim account of the dissolution of God's chosen people. The first book begins with Solomon's success in building a great and godly nation, but his legacy crumbles: After a civil war, Israel is divided into the northern kingdom of Israel, usually the more powerful and more idolatrous, and the southern kingdom of Judah, which also has its share of wicked rulers and pagan shrines. The work ends with the horrific downfall of Ahab, despised by the editor as the most godless of Israel's kings.

Probably writing and editing his materials between 586 and 576 B.C., the editor praises those few monarchs who return to the law as laid down in the book of Deuteronomy. He roundly condemns the majority for misleading their subjects into sin while making it clear that the people are responsible for their own punishment. His source materials include several lost historical and prophetic works, such as archives in Solomon's temple, secular histories of the various dynasties on the thrones of Israel and Judah, and wonder tales written in the northern kingdom.

David choosing Solomon as his successor (top) and being comforted by Abishag; two scenes within an initial letter in a 12th-century Bible

King David was old and advanced in years; and although they covered him with clothes, he could not get warm.
1 KGS 1:1

David, Israel's aging warrior-king, is about 70 years old, and his apparent impotence has caused a national crisis. Like their pagan neighbors, the Israelites still harbor many primitive superstitions: If the king cannot reproduce, the land may become infertile and the people will not prosper.

Piling up blankets on the old man does not provide enough heat to restore his sexual powers. A frantic search for the country's most beautiful and alluring young woman produces Abishag the Shunammite. Her hometown of Shunem lies at the western edge of the Jezreel valley. Abishag is brought into the royal harem, but David cannot respond as a lover.

For some time, his oldest surviving son, Adonijah, has been preparing to follow him on the throne. Supported by Joab, commander of the national militia and David's nephew, and also Abiathar, a high priest, the prince has acquired chariots and cavalry as well as a personal bodyguard 50-men strong. Whether approving or too senile to understand, David does not object. But the situation is dangerously uncertain. Although the oldest son normally succeeds, a dying king can choose another heir from among his sons.

The decision will affect not just the fate of one ambitious son. Once anointed as king, Adonijah will be expected to eliminate anyone who can be considered an opponent—and the list is growing long. The prince has not sought the support of several very powerful men at court, including the forceful prophet Nathan, the other high priest Zadok, and Benaiah, who is in charge of David's small standing army of mercenaries. Inevitably, this mistake alarms the excluded leaders into forming a conspiracy in support of Solomon, whom Nathan has watched closely since his birth to the beautiful Bathsheba.

The rival faction decides to move quickly when Adonijah confidently offers a great public sacrifice at En-rogel, the traditional boundary between the lands of Judah and Benjamin. Neither Solomon nor any of his supporters is invited to this ritual event, whose political meaning is perfectly plain.

Nathan rushes to Bathsheba with a plan to save the lives of everyone in Solomon's party. She is to remind her diminished husband that he once promised the succession to Solomon; then Nathan will appear to back up her story. Is it true, or is this tale a desperately creative ruse? Either interpretation is possible, based solely on the biblical account, which seems to be taken from annals of the royal court. It is worth noting, perhaps, that young Solomon himself does

This page from a 13th-century teaching Bible links Old and New Testament scenes: Solomon dedicating his temple and welcoming the queen of Sheba (top register) are paired with Jesus creating his church and welcoming souls to it (second register); Solomon's throne and false wives (third register) with Jesus in Mary's lap and sinners (fourth register).

"As I swore to you by the Lord, the God of Israel, `Your son Solomon shall succeed me as king, and he shall sit on my throne in my place.'" 1 KGS 1:30

David sets in motion the ceremonies to anoint Solomon as both his coregent and the next king of Israel. The court faction supporting the young heir, whose age has been estimated at 18 to 20 at this time, follows the king's directions precisely.

Solomon is set on a mule, the traditional mount of kings and princes. Commoners in ancient Israel rode asses, while the horse, brought from Egypt, would not be used for riding until later in Solomon's reign. The victorious courtiers, protected by the Cherethite and Pelethite mercenaries from the palace, and many ordinary citizens make a procession to the Gihon spring east of Jerusalem.

There, Zadok anoints Solomon, an act that shows he is God's representative and his person is to be considered sacred. The ceremony is a profoundly holy event. To celebrate, the sacred shofar, a ram's horn fashioned into a curved trumpet, is given a mighty blast, and the crowd sings loudly, accompanied by pipes, one of the most popular instruments of the ancient Near East.

Within hearing distance just to the south, Adonijah and his faction at En-rogel are startled. Apparently, they have failed to keep their eyes on events at court. A young man named Jonathan races up to explain the details of the disaster.

In short order, Adonijah's terrified supporters, now themselves in danger of being "counted offenders," fade away. The forsaken prince loses no time seeking divine protection by going to the altar of sacrifice and grasping the horns at its four corners. As in other ancient Near Eastern cultures, bulls' horns were originally used on Hebrew altars to symbolize the strength of the national deity. The most sacred part of the altar, they provide sanctuary only to those who accidentally commit a crime.

Solomon sends word that Adonijah has nothing to fear as long as "he proves to be a worthy man" (1 Kgs 1:52). When his older brother and rival comes to the palace and bows down before him, the new king tells him to go home. This deceptively simple statement is a clear warning: From now on, Adonijah is to stay out of public life.

When David's time to die drew near, he charged his son Solomon, saying: ". . . . Be strong, be courageous, and keep the charge of the Lord your God, walking in his ways and keeping his statutes." 1 KGS 2:1-3

Like many other farewell addresses in the Old Testament, David's last words signal an important transition in the history of God's people. The first part, probably written by the editor of Deuteronomy, warns that Solomon and his lineage will prosper only if they honor the Law of Moses. The second part, verses 5 through 9, may date back to the original court records of the tenth century, for it contains a veteran

not seem to be involved in this backstairs maneuvering by his mother and the prophet—curiously, Bathsheba's adversary in 2 Samuel 12.

In any event, Bathsheba enthusiastically accepts the suggestion. She warns her husband that when "the king sleeps with his ancestors"—an image of the Israelite concept of death in the tenth century B.C.— she and Solomon "will be counted offenders" (1 Kgs 1:21). In other words, Adonijah will kill them for her son's threat to the throne. Nathan sweeps in to confirm Bathsheba's account, and the old king summarily changes the nation's history.

ruler's step-by-step advice about dealing with potential dangers to the continued rule of the house of David. It is also about obtaining revenge for acts of betrayal. Solomon, for all his youth, will follow his father's blueprint with diligence in the weeks to come.

After 40 years of rule, warfare, and court intrigue, the great King David dies, and Solomon's resolve is immediately tested.

The outfoxed Adonijah pretends to visit his adversary Bathsheba in peace, but she is wary, perhaps especially when he implies that the kingdom has been taken from him. He slyly asks only for Abishag the Shunammite as his wife, a request naturally made to the queen mother as head of the royal harem.

This seemingly harmless appeal in fact reveals the prince's arrogance and possible disloyalty. According to custom among ancient Semitic peoples, only a successor can inherit a dead ruler's wife or concubine.

For that reason, Solomon erupts in fury when his mother relays the request—a result this experienced woman may well have expected and even encouraged. The new king recognizes that any such breach of decorum will encourage the great numbers of people who cast their lot with his brother, and he sees that Adonijah has provided a pretext for summary execution. Benaiah is sent to kill the rash prince.

Now Solomon can move against Abiathar, the high priest who supported Adonijah. He is banished to his hereditary farm in the village of Anathoth, about three miles to the north of the capital. A king in Israel has no authority to execute a priest.

Now Joab, the third important member of Adonijah's faction, senses danger and runs to grasp the horns of the altar. "I will die here" (1 Kgs 2:30), he says. Solomon takes him at his word, ordering Benaiah to strike him dead. This execution not only removes a potential adversary, it also avenges David, who felt that Joab had unjustly killed two loyal Israelite leaders, Abner and Amasa, as part of a blood feud. Benaiah is given Joab's position as national military commander and Zadok replaces Abiathar.

Still, Solomon's rule is not yet firmly consolidated. An Israelite called Shimei once cursed David for killing some of Saul's relatives, but the king took a sacred oath not to kill him. It was David's dying wish that Solomon clear the family name by using his intelligence to get around this moral obstacle.

Solomon decides to confine Shimei to the Jerusalem area, warning that crossing the Kidron valley east of the city will be punished by death. Shimei agrees, but three years later, when two of his slaves run away, he saddles up his donkey and rides off to Philistine Gath to retrieve his property. Solomon's trap slams shut. Benaiah executes the foolish Shimei. Thus, the major threats to the continued power and honorable name of the house of David are all swept away.

Before long, the young king is playing a role on the international stage, marrying for diplomatic reasons a daughter of powerful Egypt's Pharaoh. Early in his reign, Solomon is careful to follow the Lord, making sacrifices and offering "incense at high places" (1 Kgs 3:3), open-air shrines in sites sacred

Demonstrating his wisdom, Solomon decrees that the live baby claimed by two women be cut in two and the parts given to both; the real mother halts the slaying and is rewarded with the child; a painting by Bonifacio di Pitati (1487-1553).

to other religions as well, since there is as yet no temple in Jerusalem. Because incense was not used in Israel until after the Babylonian exile, the phrase here may refer to smoke rising from burnt offerings.

At one of these ancient holy sites, Gibeon, Solomon is supposed to have offered as many as a thousand sacrifices at a time. As he sleeps there one night, the Lord appears to him in a dream. The Israelites, like their neighbors, believed that dreams could reveal messages from the divine. The new king makes clear that he wants to have the same relationship with God that his father enjoyed and hopes God will continue his covenant with Israel. Solomon calls himself "a little child" (1 Kgs 3:7), but he is speaking symbolically of his inexperience as a ruler and his humility before the great spiritual tasks that face him.

"Give your servant therefore an understanding mind to govern your people, able to discern between good and evil."
1 KGS 3:9

*W*hen the Lord offers Solomon anything he wants, the young man's wisdom and virtue are clearly evident in his reply. God rewards him as he desires, but adds to the gift of understanding what he does not ask for, the promise of wealth and honor—so long as Solomon observes Mosaic Law.

The editor follows the dream with a famous story intended to illustrate the kind of wisdom the ancient Hebrews respected: Solomon's decision rests on a practical understanding of human nature. When two prostitutes lay claim to a newborn boy, the king asks for a sword to divide the infant in half. One woman cries out, "Please, my lord, give her the living boy; certainly do not kill him!" (1 Kgs 3:26). Obviously, she is the child's true mother. Many such tales about Solomon became popular with the Hebrews in succeeding generations. Each demonstrated that he was the ideal judge for the humble but complex business of daily life.

Solomon is also the sovereign of a sizable kingdom, due to the extensive conquests of his father. The first six verses of chapter 4 suggest his power by listing important officials who serve him. The term "king's friend" in verse 5 was often used in biblical times, but the exact nature of the position is unknown. One official, Adoniram (Adoram), continues in the job he held under David: chief of forced labor.

A clue to Solomon's skill in political maneuvering comes in the list of 12 districts given in verses 7 through 19: They do not match the boundaries of the 12 tribes given in the book of Joshua. In other words, Solomon may be trying to strengthen the throne by weakening tribal ties. It is also possible that Judah was exempt from taxes imposed on the other tribes.

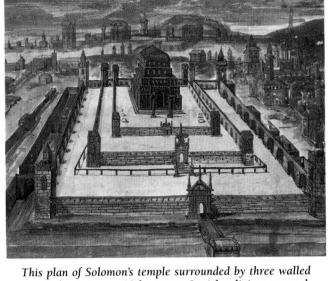

This plan of Solomon's temple surrounded by three walled courts decorates an 18th-century Jewish religious manual.

Solomon was sovereign over all the kingdoms from the Euphrates to the land of the Philistines, even to the border of Egypt. 1 KGS 4:21

*S*olomon's reign was prosperous, as archaeological evidence has shown, but the editor overstates the case. In verse 21, the king's power extends south to "the border of Egypt," or about halfway between the Isthmus of Suez and Gaza, and north and east into Mesopotamia as far as the Euphrates River. Syria was in this area but remained independent from Israel, as did the Philistine and the Phoenician enclaves along the Mediterranean coast.

Still, the editor paints a persuasive portrait of a wealthy, powerful king famed far and wide for his unusual wisdom, surpassing that "of all the people of the east, and all the wisdom of Egypt." God is praised for granting his royal servant this gift, "breadth of understanding as vast as the sand on the seashore" (1 Kgs 4:29-30). His wisdom is complemented by creativity—Solomon is credited with composing 3,000 proverbs and 1,005 songs—and by knowledge, for he speaks learnedly about the plants and animals of the Near East.

Now that he is established so well in the secular world of his day, Solomon turns his attention toward the great work of building a house of worship in Jerusalem. His father had not been able to accomplish this essential task—either because he was too busy building a nation or, as a number of scholars have interpreted the biblical account, because his success in war made him too much a man of blood to be considered fit to build a house of worship for the Lord.

Solomon placed two gold cherubim in his temple's inner sanctuary. Such winged figures, like this one of ivory, supported a king's throne.

"Now the Lord my God has given me rest on every side . . . . So I intend to build a house for the name of the Lord my God." 1 KGS 5:4-5

In a time of peace, Solomon turns to his father's old treaty partner, the Phoenician king Hiram of Tyre, for the ancient Near East's finest building materials. Cedar and cypress will be cut down and delivered to the Lebanese shore in return for food for the Phoenician loggers and the royal household.

The legendary cedars of Lebanon were prized all over the ancient world. They were unusually fragrant, hard enough to repel insects and dry rot, and appropriately close-grained for intricate decorative carving. To bring the precious logs home, and also to quarry and finish huge stones for the temple foundations, Solomon imposes a labor tax on his people, forcing thousands of men to work under some 3,300 supervisors.

The description of the temple and its furnishings in 1 Kings is not entirely clear and makes all attempts to reconstruct the building speculative. Some elements may have been added later by editors who had never seen the original and did not fully understand the technical terms. Experts do agree, however, that Solomon's temple was basically a rectangular building, much like pagan temples in the immediate area, and like them was set atop a hill facing the rising sun. The project was apparently started between 961 and 956 B.C. It was a powerful symbolic statement that the nomadic Israelites were now a permanent nation in the land of Canaan.

Since the cubit is roughly equivalent to a foot and a half, the temple's interior dimensions were about 30 feet wide by 90 feet long, with a ceiling at 45 feet. In front of the entrance was a vestibule as wide as the temple. Inside, the nave was 60 feet long, with windows cut in the stone near the roof to admit daylight and release the smoke of sacrifice. At the western end was the shrine, a room that was a 30-foot cube. Known as the Holy of Holies, it was kept in perpetual darkness.

The walls and floors were covered in the precious cedar, which was skillfully carved with fruits and flowers. Gold was used to overlay the inside and outside of the temple, according to the writer, but this was most certainly a kind of gilding rather than plates of the precious metal.

Within the inner sanctuary stood two 15-foot-high cherubim, made of olive wood and covered with gold, spreading out their wings to guard the divine

Solomon holding a model of his temple is depicted in this stained glass window by Edward Burne-Jones (1833-1898).

presence. They resembled twin spirits of the thunderstorm, thus recalling early ideas of the Lord as a storm god. Additional decorations in the interior were typical of temples of the time. Carved images of the palm tree, for example, were widely employed as symbols of fertility.

After seven and a half years of concentrated effort, the temple was completed in August, just too late to coincide with the great harvest feast of ingathering. Construction continued for another 13 years on the royal compound south of the temple courtyard; it included three great public buildings, the king's palace, and the house of his Egyptian wife. Also lavishly decorated and paneled with cedar, they rested on foundations of large, smoothly finished stones.

Finally, a skilled artisan known as Hiram of Tyre (not the king) produced fabulous decorations and temple furniture in bronze. This craftsman is identified as the son of a Hebrew mother, since a pagan could not appropriately work on the temple.

His work included a pair of 30-foot-tall freestanding bronze pillars at the entrance and a large bronze basin, known as "the molten sea" (1 Kgs 7:23), that was about 7½ feet deep and 15 feet in diameter. It stood on 12 bulls or oxen. Probably, the "sea" symbolized the formless ocean of ancient Near Eastern creation stories. The male cattle were associated with other Semitic cults.

Many gold pieces, including an altar and highly decorated lamp stands, are listed, but several probably were used only in the second temple, built four centuries later.

Then the priests brought the ark of the covenant of the Lord to its place, in the inner sanctuary of the house, in the most holy place, underneath the wings of the cherubim. 1 KGS 8:6

More important to the editor than the description of the temple, however, is the meaning of the solemn dedication. In Ethanim, the month of the harvest moon, Solomon brings his people together at the beginning of the seven-day harvest feast of Succoth, or Booths, one of three pilgrimage feasts in his day. After a huge sacrifice of sheep and oxen, the priests carry the ark of the covenant into the Holy of Holies. The Lord takes up residence there as his permanent home, the only place where he can be worshiped forever after.

Solomon reminds the assembled nation that the completion of the temple is the fulfillment of God's plan, which included bringing the Israelites out of Egypt and choosing David as king. Then he assumes the ancient attitude of worship, spreading his hands out toward the heavens, and gives many specific examples of prayer. The intent here is to remind the people of the nature of their covenant with God and to teach them how to repent of their sins. Even people from other lands are taught how to pray to the God of Israel in the temple (1 Kgs 8:41).

Solomon blesses the congregation, then consecrates the temple with the first daily sacrifice. It is huge, in part because the great crowd of worshipers needs to eat. The harvest festival is observed for the rest of the week, after which the people return home.

"If you will walk before me, as David your father walked, with integrity of heart and uprightness, doing according to all that I have commanded you . . . then I will establish your royal throne over Israel forever." 1 KGS 9:4-5

Immediately after the festival, the Lord appears to Solomon for the second time in a dream, affirming everything promised in the first vision at Gibeon. But he warns the king that worship of any other gods will bring destruction; even the gleaming temple "will become a heap of ruins" (1 Kgs 9:8).

Thereafter, Solomon continues his successful reign as an ambitious, sophisticated monarch, confident of his role in the world. He goes on with his building projects, relying again and again on forced labor from the pagans still living among the Israelites, and he builds Israel's first fleet of ships, thus setting up a seagoing commercial enterprise. Three times each year, he leads the sacrifice in his great temple.

When the queen of Sheba heard of the fame of Solomon . . . she came to test him with hard questions. 1 KGS 10:1

Somewhere in southwest Arabia, possibly modern-day Yemen, the land of Sheba had grown rich by controlling trade routes through the desert. Like other Arabian tribes, the Shebans had a reputation for great wisdom. Their queen, hearing so much of the unusually astute monarch to the north, decides to travel to the court of Jerusalem and assess Solomon for herself.

In the time-honored tradition of the ancient Near East, she challenges him with difficult questions, probably in the form of riddles. Solomon astonishes her with his answers, a clear fulfillment of God's promise in the vision at Gibeon. Her official gifts include gold, spices, jewels, and a wood called almug, which is perhaps red sandalwood. It is particularly useful for making musical instruments because it is close-grained.

The rest of chapter 10 is a catalog of Solomon's various forms of wealth, yet another demonstration that God has been generous to him beyond his expectations—but only because the king has obeyed the law. The palace is lavishly appointed with ornaments and utensils of gold and ivory, the national commercial fleet brings exotic imports home every three years from as far away as Spain and India, and fine horses are bought and bred to build Israel's first chariot troops. Solomon seems to be the richest and most powerful of kings.

Solomon did what was evil in the sight of the Lord, and did not completely follow the Lord, as his father David had done. 1 KGS 11:6

The king has one flaw that will bring disaster on the nation. Like other monarchs of his time, Solomon has a well-populated harem, including many foreign wives. By the day's standards, there was no sin in keeping 700 wives and 300 concubines, no matter where they came from. But in his old age, Solomon allows the women to lead him into idola-

The queen of Sheba kneels to present gifts to King Solomon; the scene was painted by Frans Franken the elder (1542-1616).

try. Near the very heart of the national religion, he has several pagan altars built atop the Mount of Olives just east of Jerusalem.

Furious, the Lord warns Solomon he will be punished: For David's sake, he can retain the throne until he dies, but there will be many problems and the kingdom will collapse at his death. The chronicler thus names two rebels who begin the work of weakening the nation. Hadad the Edomite, an ally of the Egyptian Pharaoh, reclaims Edom. Rezon, an adventurer not unlike the ambitious young David, leads some raiders into Damascus and takes the city and surrounding area of Syria for his own kingdom, a major development. This enemy state will bedevil the monarchs of Israel throughout the next two centuries.

Jeroboam son of Nebat, an Ephraimite of Zeredah . . . rebelled against the king.
1 KGS 11:26

King Solomon is shown sacrificing to an idol in this fanciful 17th-century painting. The goddess Astarte, whom he worshiped, was more likely represented by a clay figure such as the one at left.

Most devastating of all is the rebellion led by Jeroboam, a highly competent young man whom Solomon places in charge of the forced labor contingent from the tribe of Joseph. One day, a prophet known as Ahijah the Shilonite seeks out Jeroboam and dramatically illustrates God's judgment: Tearing his own new garment into 12 strips, the holy man urges Jeroboam to take 10 of them, symbolizing the northern tribes of Israel. Because Solomon has been worshiping idols, only Judah is to be left in the hands of the heirs of David, along with Simeon, which has already been absorbed by the larger tribe.

Evidently, Jeroboam begins to take action, because Solomon tries to have him killed. The young man seeks asylum with King Shishak of Egypt, where he remains until Solomon's death.

Thus, Solomon's 40-year reign ends with approaching chaos as punishment for his idolatries. Historically, the defections of Edom and Damascus may have occurred much earlier, but the editor wants to stress the idea that God punishes his people, even the greatest of kings, whenever they dishonor their covenant with him.

Solomon's son Rehoboam takes the throne with a wise symbolic move. By traveling from Jerusalem some 40 miles north to Shechem, which was revered by the northern tribes as a religious center, the new king appears to be making a gesture of peace.

On a practical level, however, he commits a serious political error. When Jeroboam returns from Egypt and joins the people of the northern tribes in asking that the heavy taxes Solomon imposed be eased, Rehoboam asks for three days to seek counsel. The old men who advised his father suggest that he give the people some relief, but the hotheaded young men he associates with urge him to be even harsher than Solomon had been.

"My father made your yoke heavy, but I will add to your yoke; my father disciplined you with whips, but I will discipline you with scorpions." 1 KGS 12:14

Foolishly, Rehoboam oratorically warns that he will replace the whips of his father with scorpions, probably a kind of leather scourge filled with sand and studded with metal spikes.

This idle bombast sparks rebellion. The northern tribes return to their tents. When the supervisor of the forced labor levy is sent to round up workers for Judah, he is stoned to death. Quickly, the people of the northern tribes elect Jeroboam as their king; he is the founder of the first dynasty of the northern kingdom of Israel. Rehoboam, losing control of these ten tribes, rules only the depleted kingdom of Judah in the south. The former will survive until the fall of its capital, Samaria, in 722 B.C. and the deportation and eventual disappearance of its people; the latter will end with the destruction of Jerusalem and the exile of its people to Babylon in 586 B.C.

Unable to accept reality, proud Rehoboam rashly gathers together his national militia in order to force Israel back under his rule. The army, given as 180,000 men, is drawn from the border tribe of Benjamin as well as Judah. Once again, a prophet appears to explain that the division is an act of God. Shemaiah quotes the Lord: "Let everyone go home, for this thing is from me" (1 Kgs 12:24). The people of Judah accept this judgment and disperse.

The king took counsel, and made two calves of gold. . . . He set one in Bethel, and the other he put in Dan.
1 KGS 12:28, 29

Jeroboam hastily establishes his capital in historic Shechem, but makes the puzzling decision to set up idol worship in Bethel, on the southern border of his new kingdom, and in Dan, on the northern frontier. From the political point of view, he is trying to keep his subjects from returning to Jerusalem to make sacrifices. Possibly, he is also trying to return to an earlier form of the Hebrew religion involving bulls to represent fertility and power. He institutes a harvest festival, makes the first ritual sacrifices, and installs a priesthood. But his attempts to consolidate power by establishing religious practices is anathema to the Lord, and the two cultic centers poison the religious life of Israel for generations.

Immediately, two prophets make divine displeasure clear. One of them travels from Judah and approaches Jeroboam as the king is about to offer incense and prophesies that the offending altar will one day be desecrated by a king named Josiah. Human bones will be burnt there, an act that makes any site unfit for worship. The prophecy comes true about three centuries later, but the unnamed man of God offers a sign in the present. When the annoyed Jeroboam orders him arrested, the hand he uses to issue the command instantly withers, the altar falls down, and the ashes of the sacrificial fire pour on the ground. The king begs the prophet to intercede for him with God, and the withered hand is restored.

But the prophet refuses Jeroboam's invitation to dine, as the Lord has commanded. Any two people who ate and drank together in those times entered into a kind of covenant, in this case suggesting ap-

Ignoring the elders' wise counsel, Rehoboam promises a reign of terror after succeeding his father, Solomon, on the throne.

proval of the wrongful cult worship at Bethel. Having delivered his warning and proved that the Lord stands behind him, the unnamed prophet leaves the royal presence and heads homeward.

But an old prophet in Bethel sends for him. Again, the first prophet says that the Lord has ordered him not to eat or drink with anyone, but the older man lies, claiming that an angel has countermanded this order. In fact, as the two men are eating, the Lord tells the Bethel prophet that his guest will be punished severely for disobedience: He will be buried away from his family tomb. It was the custom of the day to be interred alongside the remains of one's ancestors.

Indeed, this prophecy is fulfilled in short order. When the guest heads back to Judah on a donkey, a lion kills him, then stands beside the body and the donkey, making no move to eat either. Lions were often seen in Judah during this period, but no one had ever observed such uncharacteristic behavior. The older prophet, hearing of it, realizes that this is the work of God. He has the body brought to his own tomb for honorable burial. Both incidents—the withering of the hand and the peculiar death—show that predictions of prophets come true.

Still, Jeroboam ignores the laws of Moses, even appointing non-Levites as priests of the high altars in his kingdom. His sins demand punishment.

The king moves his royal residence to Tirzah, perhaps a site about seven miles northeast of Shechem. This will be the capital of Israel until Omri, a later king, builds a spectacularly beautiful palace compound at Samaria to the west of the two cities.

When Jeroboam's young son falls ill, he sends his wife in disguise to Ahijah, the prophet who told him to lead the ten tribes away from Judah. Perhaps the ruse is to prevent Ahijah from raising the issue of Jeroboam's improper rites. Warned by the Lord, however, the old man recognizes the royal consort despite his failing eyes.

"You have done evil above all those who were before you and have gone and made for yourself other gods . . . ; therefore, I will bring evil upon the house of Jeroboam." 1 KGS 14:9-10

Ahijah sends an ominous message back to Jeroboam: Because of his evil ways, including the worship of graven images, his family's rule of Israel will immediately end. That very day, his son will die. Eventually, the kingdom itself will be destroyed because the people followed Jeroboam into the sinful practice of idolatry. The Lord "will root up Israel out of this good land that he gave to their ancestors, and scatter them beyond the Euphrates" (1 Kgs 14:15).

Within 50 years of Solomon's death, the divided kingdoms were at war with one another. In this 15th-century illustration the forces of Judah's King Asa clash with those of King Baasha of Israel.

The princeling dies the instant his mother returns to Tirzah, and the people mourn. Jeroboam himself dies after reigning 22 years, to be succeeded by his son Nadab. For more of the royal history, the reader is referred to the Book of the Annals of the Kings of Israel, a lost collection of writings that perhaps provided some of the information in 1 and 2 Kings. Then the editor turns back in time to pick up the story of Solomon's son Rehoboam, king of Judah.

In Jerusalem, too, the Judahites have turned to pagan customs, including the employment of male prostitutes in temples modeled on Canaanite cults. Divine retribution is swift. Five years into Rehoboam's reign, Egypt's King Shishak invades many towns in both kingdoms. Among his booty is the legendary treasure of Solomon's temple and palace. The date is perhaps 923 B.C., though genealogies like those at right are disputed by scholars.

Rehoboam's reign of 17 years and his son Abijam's rule of 3 years are times of continuing conflict between Judah and Israel, probably over the territory of Benjamin. The bloody details of these wars, according to Kings, are in another lost manuscript, the Book of the Annals of the Kings of Judah.

The heart of Asa was true to the Lord all his days.
1 KGS 15:14

*T*hen, even as Jeroboam still rules in Israel, a God-fearing king ascends the throne of Judah. Asa, who will rule for 41 years, destroys the idols set up by his predecessors and evicts the male temple prostitutes from the country. He removes his own mother Maacah as queen mother, the most powerful female position at court, because she worships idols. He replaces the stolen temple furniture and utensils.

Still, he neglects to tear down the altars in the high places that have become illegitimate for worshiping God ever since the installation of the ark in the temple. He also finds himself in continual conflict with Israel's King Baasha. This particularly unattractive schemer gains the throne early in Asa's reign by killing Jeroboam's son Nadab.

At one point, Baasha feels confident enough to begin constructing a fort at Ramah, a site in Benjaminite territory only five miles to the north of Jerusalem. Evidently, Judah is much weaker than its adversary at this time. Asa gathers up whatever gold and silver remains in the treasuries of the temple and the royal compound to buy help from the king of Aram, the Syrian kingdom with its capital at Damascus. In return, the Syrian monarch begins moving toward Ramah, conquering cities along the eastern border of Israel, including the Chinneroth plain northeast of Galilee. Baasha wisely withdraws to Tirzah, and Asa makes certain that the enemy fortress is forthwith torn down.

Asa dies peacefully in old age, but he is described as suffering from some unnamed disease of the feet. Possibly, the reference is to the same impotence that afflicted David in his last years or merely to gout.

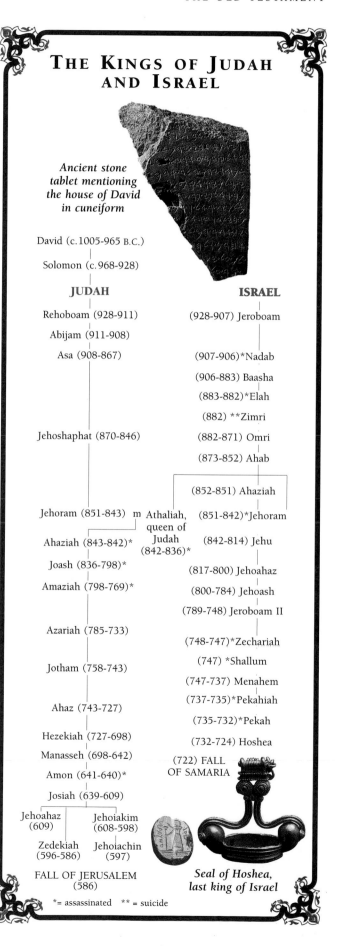

THE KINGS OF JUDAH AND ISRAEL

Ancient stone tablet mentioning the house of David in cuneiform

David (c.1005-965 B.C.)

Solomon (c.968-928)

JUDAH	ISRAEL
Rehoboam (928-911)	(928-907) Jeroboam
Abijam (911-908)	
Asa (908-867)	(907-906)*Nadab
	(906-883) Baasha
	(883-882)*Elah
	(882) **Zimri
Jehoshaphat (870-846)	(882-871) Omri
	(873-852) Ahab
	(852-851) Ahaziah
Jehoram (851-843) m Athaliah, queen of Judah (842-836)*	(851-842)*Jehoram
Ahaziah (843-842)*	(842-814) Jehu
Joash (836-798)*	(817-800) Jehoahaz
Amaziah (798-769)*	(800-784) Jehoash
	(789-748) Jeroboam II
Azariah (785-733)	(748-747)*Zechariah
	(747) *Shallum
Jotham (758-743)	(747-737) Menahem
	(737-735)*Pekahiah
Ahaz (743-727)	(735-732)*Pekah
Hezekiah (727-698)	(732-724) Hoshea
Manasseh (698-642)	(722) FALL OF SAMARIA
Amon (641-640)*	
Josiah (639-609)	
Jehoahaz (609) Jehoiakim (608-598)	
Zedekiah (596-586) Jehoiachin (597)	
FALL OF JERUSALEM (586)	

Seal of Hoshea, last king of Israel

* = assassinated   ** = suicide

Baasha killed Nadab . . . and succeeded him. As soon as he was king, he killed all the house of Jeroboam.
1 KGS 15:28, 29

To establish the second dynasty in the northern kingdom, Baasha massacres every possible heir in Jeroboam's line, just as aging Ahijah had prophesied. This was a practical course of action in a time when blood revenge was accepted. Baasha makes certain that no male lives who has the right as a family member to avenge Nadab's death and reclaim the throne for Jeroboam's dynasty.

The new royal house is as corrupt as the former. Baasha does not neglect to commit the sins of Jeroboam and encourages his people to practice idolatry. The cycle of retribution continues, for the prophet Jehu is sent by God to warn Baasha that his dynasty, too, will be destroyed. Jehu uses some of the very words of Ahijah's earlier prophetic oracle.

When Baasha dies, his son Elah begins a reign that will be cut short in two years. The chariot comman-der Zimri kills the king, while he is drinking himself into a stupor at an underling's house. Again, all of the king's male relatives are executed.

But the third dynasty of the northern kingdom lasts only seven days. The army of Israel, outraged by the sordid coup, encourages their commander Omri to move against Zimri in Tirzah. When the assassin sees that all is lost, he commits suicide by torching the palace and burning himself to death.

Omri becomes one of Israel's most effective rulers, reigning from about 882 to 871 B.C. Other countries of the period mention him by name in their national chronicles, and Israel was still known as "the land of Omri" to the Assyrians even after he died. To establish his rule, however, he had to fight a civil war with a rival named Tibni for about four years.

He bought the hill of Samaria from Shemer for two talents of silver; he fortified the hill, and called the city that he built, Samaria. 1 KGS 16:24

Omri is primarily remembered in the scriptures for two reasons, his establishment of a new capital and his memorably sinful son and successor, Ahab.

The new king chooses a site for his capital on a hill and names the place Samaria, for its original owner, Shemer. After fortifying the site, he builds a city soon famous for the luxury of its royal buildings. Described as "more evil than all who were before him" (1 Kgs 16:25), he dies, it seems peacefully, in about 871 B.C. Ahab, who reigns for about 22 years, including an apparent coregency, surpasses his father in evil. He has the temerity to introduce the worship of the Canaanite storm god Baal to Israel, undoubtedly under the influence of his clever, headstrong Phoenician wife Jezebel, whose father is the priest-king of Tyre.

In fact, Ahab sets up an official temple to Baal in Samaria and openly worships the god. The editor mentions another horror under his rule: When Jericho is rebuilt, defying Joshua's curse upon the site, the builder's firstborn son is sacrificed and buried in the foundation, apparently in a pagan rite meant to establish a kind of guardian spirit over the city. Israel is not at all the covenant kingdom envisioned by God in his conversations with Solomon.

Elijah the Tishbite . . . . did according to the word of the Lord; he went and lived by the Wadi Cherith, which is east of the Jordan. 1 KGS 17:1, 5

The famous prophet Elijah abruptly enters the story, the first of many men of God to speak out against Ahab's worship of Baal. According to pagan priests, the storm god produced the harvest in this dry part of the world by sending the annual rainy season, during which water fell in torrents and could be collected and stored for irrigation. During years

After predicting a drought in Israel, the prophet Elijah flees east of the Jordan to the Wadi Cherith (above), where ravens feed him morning and evening; inset, the scene worked in inlaid marble for the cathedral floor in Siena, Italy.

of drought, according to the myth, this deity is locked in combat with the Phoenician death god Mot.

Elijah rejects this idea, sternly explaining that the weather is solely in the hands of the God of Israel. As proof, the Lord has decided to initiate a three-year drought, when the earth will be so dry that even the morning dew will disappear.

After this announcement, the Lord warns Elijah to run for his life toward the eastern borders of the kingdom beyond the Jordan and take refuge in the Wadi Cherith, one of the many dry streambeds where water flows only during the height of the rainy season. In this barren spot, ravens bring food to Elijah morning and evening, but the drought is bringing famine to idolatrous Ahab and his people.

Soon, however, God commands his loyal prophet to travel into pagan Phoenicia to the coastal town of Zarephath, which is south of Sidon. There, Elijah is told, a widow will feed him. But this poor woman, who probably has had to support herself by begging and scavenging since the death of her husband, tells Elijah she has only enough meal and oil to make a last meal for herself and her son. They are prepared to die of starvation, for the drought has also taken hold of Baal's homeland, despite his supposed powers.

Elijah tells her not to worry. In a second miracle of plenty in the midst of famine, the Lord will ensure that neither the jar holding the tiny bit of meal nor the jug holding the few drops of oil will be emptied until rain falls again. There will be enough food for all three of them. Elijah is installed in a room built on the roof, a so-called "upper chamber" (1 Kgs 17:19) that is reached by stairs on the outside.

Soon, however, it appears that this miraculous reprieve is hollow, for the widow's young son falls gravely ill and then stops breathing. Horrified, the woman accuses Elijah of causing her son's death as divine retribution for some long-forgotten sin. Evidently, people of the time believed that God might track down wrongdoers and punish them.

Quickly, the prophet seizes the boy and takes him upstairs, laying his lifeless form on the bed. Surprisingly, to today's believers, Elijah chides God for thus causing pain to the hospitable widow, but in the ninth century B.C. even loyal Israelites are not surprised when the Lord seems to act capriciously. The prophet stretches out his body to cover the boy three separate times, loudly begging the Lord to restore the child to life. God listens, and the boy breathes again. In this story, the editor makes clear that Elijah has the Lord's ear, an intimacy that will serve the prophet and Israel well in the trials that follow.

Elijah is a constant reminder to King Ahab of his many failings; the two appear in this 19th-century stained glass window.

Back in Israel, Ahab and Jezebel are not in the least repentant. The queen has had many men of God executed, but one true believer, a palace official named Obadiah, has saved 100 of them by hiding them in caves. In the third year of the drought, Ahab orders Obadiah to search through half the land for any hidden springs and wadis that might supply grass for feeding the palace's starving horses and mules. Ahab will scour the other half.

At this point, the Lord orders Elijah to return to Israel and announce that the rains will begin to fall again. He happens upon Obadiah, who refuses to tell the king that the prophet has returned. Because Ahab has searched everywhere for his adversary, Obadiah assumes that the Lord has spirited Elijah out of harm's way. If he were to disappear this time, Obadiah would be killed. Elijah promises not to vanish again.

When Ahab saw Elijah, Ahab said to him, "Is it you, you troubler of Israel?" 1 KGS 18:17

As soon as Ahab glimpses Elijah, he puts the blame on him for Israel's plight, but the prophet rebuts him: The drought is punishment for the idolatry of the Omride dynasty. To prove the point, Elijah suggests a contest atop Mount Carmel, a ridge bordering the Mediterranean Sea known for its forests and fertile fields. The exact site, according to tradition, was on the southeastern edge of Mount Carmel about 1,800 feet above sea level and overlooking the brook of Kishon.

There, the entire nation assembles early one morning, along with the 450 prophets serving Baal and the 400 prophets of the goddess Asherah. As the sole prophet still loyal to God, Elijah sets himself against all other religious leaders. The contest is simple. Two bulls are to be slaughtered for sacrifice on wooden altars, one for Baal and the other for the Lord. But no fire is to be used. The deity who miraculously sets his altar ablaze will be affirmed as the true God.

The pagans go first. From morning until noon, they perform ritual dances around their altar, leaping about and gashing their bodies as they call on Baal to ignite their altar fire. At noon, Elijah mocks their deity, suggesting he might be asleep, a reference to the time of year when Baal is said to be in the power of the god of death. The hundreds of priests become even more frenetic, no doubt whipping themselves into the kind of religious ecstasy that was a common ritual in many early religious cults.

These exertions do not avail. At the hour of the midafternoon oblation offering, Elijah bids the Is-

The many prophets of Baal being vanquished by Elijah in the contest atop Mount Carmel, as shown in this 3rd-century A.D. fresco from the synagogue at Dura-Europos, Syria

Here, the depressed prophet learns a great spiritual truth. The Lord produces powerful natural wonders that are traditionally associated with his divinity —a windstorm, an earthquake, a roaring fire—but he is not found in any of them. There follows "a sound of sheer silence" (1 Kgs 19:12); this is where the Lord is to be found.

"You shall anoint Jehu son of Nimshi as king over Israel; and you shall anoint Elisha son of Shaphat of Abel-meholah as prophet in your place." 1 KGS 19:16

Elijah is still weary of life, but God commands him to anoint a new king of Israel, Jehu, and a younger prophet to succeed him, Elisha. He is also to anoint a new king in Syria, thus showing God's power over neighboring lands. Jehu eventually takes the throne from the Omride kings and cleanses the kingdom of idolatry. Only about 7,000 Israelites survive the civil war; everyone else has either prostrated himself to Baal or kissed his image.

Elijah finds Elisha at work sweating behind a plow. He throws his own mantle over the younger man, a kind of symbolic investiture. This garment, which was considered the appropriate clothing for a man of God, was probably made of goat's skin with the hairy side worn outward. From that moment on, Elisha travels with Elijah as the older man's servant.

Meanwhile, Ahab comes into conflict with the king of Syria, a state that frequently warred with ancient Israel. Unusually, a prophet of the Lord appears twice to announce that the impious Israelites will be given divine help in defeating the enemy, despite a disadvantage in numbers. Throughout the rest of the Old Testament, Ahab is condemned by prophets.

The Syrians besiege Samaria, but the Israelites surprise them getting drunk in their encampment and slaughter them in great numbers. King Ben-hadad barely escapes with his life. The following spring, when wars typically began in the ancient Near East, the Syrians reappear and are again soundly defeated. Ben-hadad bargains for his life with the victorious Ahab, who agrees to a peace treaty.

This is a mistake. An unnamed prophet appears before Ahab and tells him that the Lord intends for the Syrian king to be killed as an enemy of Israel. Now, Ahab will pay with his own life for letting Ben-hadad go free.

Naboth the Jezreelite had a vineyard in Jezreel, beside the palace of King Ahab of Samaria. 1 KGS 21:1

The story moves from the public stage to the sordid domestic affairs of the king and his pagan queen, Jezebel. Obviously used to having his own way, Ahab tries to buy an un-

raelites come closer to the altar of God that has been torn down, possibly on Jezebel's orders. He rebuilds it with 12 stones symbolizing the 12 tribes, then piles on the firewood and lays out the sacrificial bull. Next he has jars of water poured three times on the altar, so much liquid that the overflow fills a trench dug around the base.

After Elijah prays to God to prove his omnipotence, fire falls from the heavens, incinerating both the offering and the altar. Such bolts of lightning, followed by a violent thunderstorm, often signal the end of a drought in semitropical areas.

The people acknowledge the truth of Elijah's message, and the priests of Baal are killed in line with the injunction that false prophets "shall be put to death for having spoken treason against the Lord your God" (Deut 13:5). Curiously, nothing is said about what happens to the prophets of Asherah.

Elijah warns Ahab to race to his secondary palace in Jezreel, about 17 miles away, before the ground becomes soggy from the torrential rain and mires the wheels of his chariot. Miraculously strengthened by the spirit of the Lord, the prophet runs in front of the royal vehicle as the heavens grow black, the wind blows, and rain falls down in sheets.

Unmoved by this dramatic evidence of God's power, Jezebel determines to avenge her cult's prophets and sends Elijah a death threat. Terrified, he flees alone into the wilderness and falls down exhausted under a broom tree, a kind of spindly desert bush that can grow to ten feet. He asks the Lord to let him die, but an angel appears twice to feed him and restore his strength and courage. The food miraculously keeps him going for 40 days and nights until he reaches a cave in the Sinai Desert near Mount Horeb, the very spot where God first appeared to Moses.

The 24-year reign of Judah's King Jehoshaphat was marked by peace and religious reform.

usually fine vineyard near his secondary royal residence in Jezreel.

Unlike other rulers of the ancient Near East, Israel's kings were supposed to obey the law and respect the rights of the individual. Therefore, Ahab cannot simply seize the land when the owner, Naboth the Jezreelite, refuses to sell. Traditionally, a landowner was encouraged not to sell inherited land and let it pass out of the family.

Ahab becomes so depressed by this failure that he cannot eat, but Jezebel comes up with a cruelly clever plan. Using her husband's royal seal, she orders city officials to proclaim a fast, which can be a sign of national emergency, and then call an assembly with the unfortunate Naboth seated in plain view among the leaders. Two reprobates stand up and charge him with blasphemy against God and the king. One witness is not sufficient for conviction under Mosaic Law, but two are deemed legal proof of guilt. The innocent Naboth and also his sons, according to the account in 2 Kings 9:26, are stoned to death.

Jezebel rushes to Ahab with the good news, and he takes possession of the vineyard. It is possible that the property of criminals came under control of the king after they were executed, or perhaps no heirs were left to prevent Ahab's action. It is this flouting of the law, not the decades of idolatry, that finally leads to Ahab's death. The Lord orders Elijah to confront the king and prophesy his doom.

"Because you have sold yourself to do what is evil in the sight of the Lord, I will bring disaster on you."
1 KGS 21:20-21

Like the dynasties of Jeroboam and Baasha, the Omride house is to be destroyed. In addition to the deaths of all males, "the dogs shall eat Jezebel within the bounds of Jezreel" (1 Kgs 21:23). Ahab immediately begins fasting and wearing sackcloth, a sign of mourning that represents the king's repentance. The Lord relents, delaying the fulfillment of the dread prophecy to the next generation.

Three years after Ahab makes peace with Syria, he urges King Jehoshaphat of Judah to join in a campaign to recapture Ramoth-gilead, a Levitical city on the east bank of the Jordan River. All 400 prophets in Israel but one agree that the Lord will support this effort. Micaiah, whom Ahab summons only reluctantly because this fiery man of God has always predicted disaster for him, is fearless at court. He reports a vision of heaven in which one of God's supernatural advisers decides to "put a lying spirit in the mouth" (1 Kgs 22:23) of the other prophets. One prophet slaps him for this insult and Ahab has him imprisoned on bread and water rations until the battle is won.

The two kings lead their forces to Ramoth-gilead, with Jehoshaphat dressed in the royal robes of Israel and Ahab disguised as a charioteer. The ruse fails.

A rough-clad Elijah confronts Ahab and Jezebel over the dead body of Naboth; the royal pair had conspired to have him killed so that they might appropriate his vineyard. The scene was depicted by Thomas Matthews Rooke (1842-1942).

One of the Syrians, not recognizing Ahab, sends a fatal arrow at the join in the king's armor. Bleeding slowly to death, Ahab watches the battle from his chariot. His death fulfills Micaiah's prophecy. The chariot is washed in a pool at Samaria, where his blood is lapped up by dogs and used as bathwater by prostitutes, also fulfilling Elijah's prophecy. His son Ahaziah assumes the tottering throne.

Jehoshaphat son of Asa began to reign over Judah . . . . He walked in all the way of his father Asa; he did not turn aside from it, doing what was right in the sight of the Lord. 1 KGS 22:41, 43

The first book of Kings ends with brief comparisons of Jehoshaphat, who ruled from about 870 to 846 B.C., and Ahaziah, who probably reigned from 852 to 851 B.C. Each follows in his father's footsteps. Like Asa, Jehoshaphat honors the Lord in Judah, banishing the last of the remaining male temple prostitutes. But he does not end traditional worship at the enduring high places. Like his father, Ahab, Ahaziah encourages idolatry in Israel, further angering the Lord.

Jehoshaphat had been a kind of vassal to Ahab, which indicates Israel's superior power, but he seems now to establish a different but peaceful relationship with Ahaziah. He refuses to let the king of Israel join him in trying to reestablish the seagoing trade originally set up by Solomon. In any event, his ships are wrecked and the enterprise abandoned. The days of Solomon's wealth, power, and influence on the international scene are a dim memory as the two kingdoms jostle against each other and larger forces from the outside world move ominously near.

Elijah uses his cloak to part the waters of the Jordan, as his disciple Elisha looks on; a stained glass window from Lincoln Cathedral in England.

*T*he second book of Kings continues the story of Israel from the idolatrous monarchy of Ahaziah to the fall of Samaria in 722 B.C., which marks the end of the troubled northern kingdom. Its people vanish from history forever. To the south, Judah manages to survive for little more than a century, though caught in the midst of tremendous political and military conflicts between vast empires. The account ends with the destruction of Jerusalem and the deportation of the Jews to Babylon in 586 B.C., thus beginning their years of exile.

As in the first book of Kings, the editor continually stresses that God actively works his will in the history of his people. Throughout both books of Kings, true men of God have warned that destruction will be the punishment for breaking the covenant. To a people wondering why they must suffer their exile in a foreign land, the editor has a stern but potentially optimistic answer: They are suffering because they have so callously disobeyed the Lord, but repentance and a return to Deuteronomic law may reverse their fortunes.

As in the first book of Kings, the editor continually stresses that God can be worshiped only at the Jerusalem temple. The Bethel and Dan shrines in the northern kingdom, originally set up so that the Israelites would not travel to Judah to worship, and all of the ancient rural shrines known as "the high places" are anathema. Israel will rise again, it can be inferred, only if worship of the Lord returns to Jerusalem.

Ahaziah had fallen through the lattice in his upper chamber in Samaria, and lay injured; so he sent messengers, telling them, "Go, inquire of Baal-zebub, the god of Ekron, whether I shall recover from this injury." 2 KGS 1:2

*T*he throne of Israel is so corrupted by idolatry that the injured monarch seeks an augury from Baal-zebub, one of the many representations of Baal. The name, meaning "lord of the flies," is probably an impudent Hebrew pun on one of the god's titles, Baal-zebul, or "Baal the prince."

Alerted by the Lord, Elijah prevents royal messengers from going to the pagan shrine in the Philistine town of Ekron and rebukes them for ignoring the true God, who has decreed that Ahaziah will die of his injuries. As in the contest at Mount Carmel, Elijah is stressing that the Lord, not Baal, is God in Israel.

When the messengers tell Ahaziah what has happened, he sends a captain and 50 soldiers to arrest the prophet and bring him to court. Elijah is sitting on a hill when the captain finds him and, addressing him properly as a man of God, asks him to come down. "If I am a man of God," the prophet replies, "let fire come down from heaven and consume you and your fifty" (2 Kgs 1:10). Instantly, the 51 men are burned to death. A second captain and his men suffer the same fate. The third time, the designated captain kneels down and begs Elijah to spare the lives of him and his 50 men. The Lord tells Elijah he has nothing to fear but he must deliver his prophecy to Ahaziah in person. He does so, and the king dies after a reign of only two years.

As for Elijah, it is time for his long, exhausting, and often dangerous work to be rewarded. One day, the aging prophet tells his chosen successor Elisha three times that he must go alone to a certain place —Bethel, Jericho, then the banks of the Jordan—but each time the young man refuses to leave his side. In the towns of Bethel and Jericho, men of God approach Elisha and ask if he knows that Elijah will be taken by the Lord on this day. He does know but orders them to keep silent.

At the Jordan, while 50 prophets watch in the distance, Elijah strikes the water with his mantle and the river parts, allowing the two men to cross on dry ground. When Elijah offers to fulfill a final request, Elisha asks for a double share—the firstborn's legacy—of the prophet's spirit. Elijah leaves the matter in the Lord's hands. If his successor is allowed to see him leave the earth, the request will be granted.

As they continued walking and talking, a chariot of fire and horses of fire separated the two of them, and Elijah ascended in a whirlwind into heaven. 2 KGS 2:11

*O*nce more, God's power is linked with fire. Elisha is revealed as Elijah's heir because he can see the fiery chariot within the swirling winds. Elijah's miraculous disappearance from earth without dying inspired folklore that has lasted over the centuries, including the custom of setting a place at the Passover table for the prophet.

After tearing his clothes as a sign of mourning, Elisha uses his predecessor's mantle to part the Jordan again. It fails the first time, but when he prays to God, the prophetic power is restored to the cloak and the waters divide. The 50 prophets observing in the distance recognize instantly that "the spirit of Elijah rests on Elisha" (2 Kgs 2:15). Yet for three days, against Elisha's advice, they search for Elijah, an indication that he has disappeared before and returned.

Then several wonder tales, unlike anything else in the Old Testament, illustrate Elisha's new powers. First, the townspeople of Jericho complain about the area's notoriously bad water. Flinging salt into the spring, the young prophet sweetens the water, much as Moses purified the waters of Marah in the Sinai. Next, there is the mystifying tale of the bears. Perhaps to prevent Elisha from visiting the illegitimate shrine at Bethel, young boys harry him by calling him "Baldhead." This was an insult in many ancient cultures, for baldness was considered contemptible. In any event, the prophet's reaction is swift and violent. At his command, two female bears lumber out of the woods and maul 42 boys.

When Ahab died the king of Moab rebelled against the king of Israel. 2 KGS 3:5

Returning to the public sphere, the editor notes that Ahaziah's brother Jehoram has ascended the throne in Samaria. Despite the confusing information about various reigns in 1 and 2 Kings, he probably ruled Israel from around 851 to 842 B.C.

The transition between rulers gives King Mesha of Moab the opportunity to revolt against Israel. Under Ahab, his desert kingdom was forced to pay a large tribute in ram's wool and live lambs. The breed involved, called naqad, was small but prized for producing fine wool in large quantities. Jehoram responds quickly, inviting the king of Judah to join in a military campaign. In turn, Judah's vassal state Edom is brought into the scheme, and the three kings lead their forces south around the Dead Sea through water-starved Edomite territory. By the time they reach a wadi on Moab's southern border, their water supplies are exhausted.

Unusually, Elisha agrees to help idolatrous Israel after the three kings send for him, recognizing him as Elijah's legitimate heir. Appearing before the kings, Elisha calls for music in order to induce a prophetic trance. He prophesies that God will miraculously fill the dry wadi without using rainfall. (Even today, water is easily dug up in such wadis because seepage from the mountains of Edom is captured by the rock formations underground.) The seer also promises victory over the rebellious Moabites. Like many oracles in ancient literature, this one proves to be only partially true.

Just at sunrise the next morning, as the Moabites prepare for battle at their frontier, water rises in the valley, glowing scarlet as blood. Whether the color comes from the area's famous red sandstone or the dawn's scarlet light, the Moabites jump to the conclusion that the invaders have quarreled and killed each other. They rush down recklessly into the ambush.

As Elisha prophesied, Israel and its allies prevail, slaughtering the enemy armies and destroying cities and fields. When only one Moabite refuge remains standing, the city of Kir-hareseth some 12 miles east of the Dead Sea, the king of Moab resorts to a desperate measure: He sacrifices his own firstborn son as a burnt offering to the national god, Chemosh. The god's wrath is aroused, and the invaders are driven from Moab in a rout. In those times, it was believed that each god had supreme power in his own domain. Evidently, not unlike the Lord, Chemosh has been punishing his people with the earlier defeats but saves them in the end. This is the part Elisha neglected to tell the three kings.

But by now the prophet is elsewhere, continuing to perform miracles.

One day, the impoverished widow of a member of the prophets' guild begs him to intercede with a creditor who plans to take her two children as slaves. This practice, perhaps quite common in ancient Israel, did not flout Mosaic Law. Elisha saves the situation by causing a jar of oil to keep pouring until it fills enough vessels to pay off the woman's debt.

Elisha's fame spreads throughout the land. A wealthy couple in the town of Shunem build him a modest roof chamber atop their house, probably a single room reached by an outside stairway, as a place of rest on his travels. In return, he offers to speak on the wife's behalf to the king or the army commander, thus revealing his influence in worldly affairs. The woman needs nothing from them, but she is unhappy that she and her elderly husband have no children. Elisha says that she will bear a son within the year, a prediction she takes to be a cruel joke. Yet the child is born exactly as the prophet foretells.

Two scenes from the Nuremberg Bible: Elijah taken to heaven in his chariot of fire; the boys who jeered Elisha being mauled by bears

As directed by Elisha, the commander of the king of Aram's army, Naaman, bathes himself in the Jordan to cure his leprosy; an early-16th-century painting.

is deadly poisonous. When they cry for help, Elisha disarms the poison by throwing flour in the stew pot. Possibly, the culprit was a vine called colocynth whose melonlike fruit resembles gourd cucumber but has a toxic pulp.

In another famine tale, Elisha miraculously causes 20 barley loaves and some ears of grain to feed 100 people at Baal-shalishah, a town to the southwest of Shechem. The food is an offering of firstfruits, for at this time prophets at local shrines can share in ritual offerings just like priests.

Naaman, commander of the army of the king of Aram . . . . though a mighty warrior, suffered from leprosy.
2 KGS 5:1

Elisha's healing powers lead to the conversion of a foreigner, the Syrian army commander Naaman. When he contracts an unknown form of skin disease (probably not the leprosy called Hansen's disease today), his Israelite servant girl, captured in war, urges him to travel to Samaria to be cured by an esteemed prophet there.

Armed with a letter from the Syrian king, whose language suggests that Israel is subject to him in this period, Naaman goes to the court of the Israelite king with costly presents, including about 750 pounds of silver and some 375 pounds of gold. He assumes that the healer, whose name he seems not to know, is employed at court. The king is horrified and rends his garments, for he suspects that the Syrian monarch is setting him up for punishment if he cannot find a cure for Naaman.

But Elisha hears the story and dispatches a message to have Naaman come to his house. When the great warrior arrives, the prophet sends word that he should bathe in the Jordan River seven times to cure the affliction. Naaman is outraged. He expects the prophet to appear in person to perform a ritual, like other healers of the day, and he knows that the Jordan is a muddy stream in comparison with the coursing clean rivers near his home in Damascus. Fortunately, one of his loyal servants speaks up, urging him to try. When Naaman immerses himself the ritual seven times in the Jordan, "his flesh was restored like the flesh of a young boy" (2 Kgs 5:14).

Overjoyed, the Syrian hero offers a reward to Elisha, but the prophet refuses to benefit from his divine gifts. Then Naaman, converted to belief in the Lord, asks for earth to be taken back to Syria so that he can worship properly. Since each god was thought to have power only in his own land, the actual soil of Israel was believed necessary for effective sacrifice.

Then greed overcomes Elisha's servant Gehazi. Secretly, he hurries after Naaman with a slick story. Some prophets have just arrived at Elisha's house, he says, and they need money and clothes. Naaman gives him 150 pounds of silver and two sets of clothing, which he hides. But Elisha's powers include a kind of extrasensory perception, for he knows what has happened. As punishment, Gehazi is struck with

When Elisha came into the house, he saw the child lying dead on his bed. 2 KGS 4:32

Some years later, this long-awaited child falls ill from sunstroke and dies on his mother's lap. Desperate, the mourning woman rushes on her donkey to find Elisha at Mount Carmel some 25 miles away. When Elisha hears her story, he gives his servant Gehazi his prophetic staff and sends him racing ahead to rouse the boy. The prophet and the mother follow more slowly. But the staff is ineffective.

When Elisha reaches the house, the boy's body has been laid on the bed in the prophet's upper chamber. Closing the door and praying to God, he lies upon the body, and the child's flesh begins to warm. Exhausted, the prophet rests a moment, then returns to the child. Suddenly, the boy sneezes seven times and opens his eyes. Like Elijah, Elisha can bring the dead to life when God so wills.

He can also take care of his followers, the prophets who come to hear his teachings. During a famine, perhaps the one predicted in 2 Kings 8:1, this company dines on a stew made from wild gourds, but it leprosy, a physical curse that will be carried down upon his descendants for the rest of time. According to tradition, the four lepers who discover the abandoned Syrian camp in 2 Kings 7:3-10 are Gehazi and his three sons.

When they came to the Jordan, they cut down trees. But as one was felling a log, his ax head fell into the water.
2 KGS 6:4-5

Sometime later, the company of prophets needs to build larger quarters. Elisha accompanies them to the Jordan, where they cut down trees to make logs. Suddenly, the head of an ax falls off its handle and plunges out of sight into the muddy river. Elisha cuts a stick, throws it upon the water, and the iron ax head floats up into view. This story affirms the prophet's continuing support from the Lord.

Even more dramatically, Elisha is able, with God's help, to overpower the Syrians. On several occasions, in the ongoing conflict between Damascus and Samaria, the prophet has warned the king of Israel to avoid a Syrian ambush. The Syrian king suspects that there is a traitor in his court, but an officer explains that Elisha is responsible. Thereupon, the king sends a great force of infantry and charioteers by nightfall to surround Dothan, the town about ten miles north of Samaria where the prophet is living.

Seeing the siege in place, Elisha's servant is terrified, but the prophet prays to the Lord to open the man's eyes spiritually: In an instant, he sees the vast heavenly army arrayed in invisible ranks with their chariots of fire ablaze in the sky. Then Elisha asks God to strike the Syrian troops blind. As the shocked enemy mills about in confusion, Elisha approaches and promises to lead them where they want to go.

In fact, he brings the Syrian army inside the walls of Samaria, where their sight is restored. Israel's king expects that, as is customary, he should slaughter them all as the property of an enemy god, but Elisha orders them fed well and sent back home. When they tell their amazing story in Damascus, the Syrians end their raids into Israel.

King Ben-hadad of Aram mustered his entire army; he marched against Samaria and laid siege to it. 2 KGS 6:24

Then, in a story that seems out of sequence because it involves a Syrian advance on Israel, Samaria suffers dearly from the effects of a siege. Unappetizing food such as a donkey's head and paltry fuel such as dove's dung fetch high prices. Even worse, a woman approaches the king, possibly Jehoahaz the son of Jehu, with a horrible story. She and another woman had agreed to eat their sons. They cooked and ate her son the day before; now, the other woman has hidden her own son, refusing to share him as a meal. The king, driven past endurance by this tale, decides to kill Elisha. As so often happens, the ruler blames the prophet for having foretold the Lord's punishment of Israel for its sins.

When the king and his chief adviser confront Elisha, the prophet predicts that barley will be available for sale in Samaria in about 24 hours. The adviser scoffs, since even "if the Lord were to make windows in the sky" (2 Kgs 7:2)—that is, cause rain to pour down from openings in heaven—grain could not grow so quickly.

But Elisha has accurately foretold the future, without explanation. The next day, four men afflicted with leprosy, and therefore banished to live outside the city, decide to take their chances with the Syrians. At twilight, they discover a camp deserted but rich with food and fine goods, some of which they steal and hide. Moments before, God had caused the Syrians to hear the noise of a great army. Terrified that Israel had made an alliance with the Hittites from the north and the powerful Egyptians from the south, the enemy has faded away.

The lepers send the news to court, but the king, fearing an ambush, sends out only five horsemen to investigate. They see that the Syrians have fled across the Jordan, abandoning their possessions. The people plunder the enemy camp, and indeed choice grain is available for sale in Samaria again.

At some time, although the sequence of events is unclear, Elisha warns the Shunammite woman whose son he brought back to life that a seven-year famine will strike Israel. She takes her family to live among the Philistines somewhere on the Mediterranean coast. When she returns, her house and land have been appropriated and she asks the prophet to help her regain them. At this point, an unnamed king honors Elisha as a man of God by restoring the woman's property because she has been involved in his miraculous work.

In the next story, it becomes clear that Elisha is also highly regarded in Syria. When the king there falls ill, he sends his trusted representative Hazael on the usual mission to seek a prophet's advice. Before Elijah vanished, the Lord had commissioned him to anoint this very Hazael as king of Syria (1 Kgs 19:15). Now Elisha gives the man an oracle: The king will recover from his illness but will die from another cause. As this message sinks in, Elisha falls into a kind of trance, then weeps. As he explains to Hazael, he has just seen a vision of the great destruction the Syrian will bring upon Israel in the years to come.

Hazael returns to Damascus and tells the king that the illness is not fatal. Then, taking his cue from the prophecy, he smothers his monarch to death, thus gaining the Syrian throne.

Jehoram son of King Jehoshaphat of Judah . . . . walked in the way of the kings of Israel . . . for the daughter of Ahab was his wife. 2 KGS 8:16,18

The story returns now to Judah. The eight-year reign there of Jehoram (also known as Joram), a man despised by the editor because he marries Ahab's daughter Athaliah and apes the idolatrous ways of her royal house, sees yet more decline in the weakened state. The Edomites break away and repel the king's attempts to reconquer them. They will never again be part of Judah. Then Libnah, an area in the western part of the country near Philistia, also gains independence.

The unfortunate Jehoram is succeeded on his death by his son Ahaziah, a 22-year-old who rules only one year. He joins his uncle Jehoram, the king of Israel, in a campaign against the Syrians to win back the city of Ramoth-gilead, but the expedition fails. Jehoram is wounded and returns to his palace in Jezreel to recuperate. Ahaziah travels there to visit him.

Ahab's palace in Samaria was renowned for its ivory inlaid furniture; in this carving, a woman peers from a window.

"I anoint you king over the people of the Lord, over Israel. You shall strike down the house of your master Ahab, so that I may avenge on Jezebel the blood of my servants the prophets."
2 KGS 9:6-7

Meanwhile, Elisha sets in motion a plot to end the idolatrous Omride dynasty. Fulfilling a command given Elijah, he sees that Jehu, the commander of the national army, is secretly anointed as the legitimate king of Israel.

He orders a young prophet to perform the ritual alone with Jehu behind closed doors and to tell him that the Lord has chosen him to destroy the lineage of Ahab. He is also to execute Jezebel in retaliation for the deaths of the true prophets she has killed. The young prophet carries out these instructions, then flees as Elisha has commanded. Jehu's fellow officers ask him what has happened. When he finally tells them, they joyously proclaim him king.

Moving quickly, since news of this action can prove fatal, Jehu speeds in his chariot toward Jezreel, where King Ahaziah is still visiting his recuperating uncle, King Jehoram. When the sentinel spots the racing

chariot, a messenger is sent to ask, "Is it peace?" (2 Kgs 9:18). Jehu wins him over, as well as the next messenger sent. By now, Jehu is close enough to the city walls to be recognized by his driving, which is legendarily frenzied.

Alarmed, the two kings leap into their separate chariots and drive out to confront Jehu at the vineyard that Ahab, with Jezebel's help, had stolen from the unfortunate Naboth. This site is perfect for the fulfillment of Elisha's prophecies.

When Jehu makes his intent clear, Jehoram tries to flee, but the newly anointed heir to the throne draws his bow and sends an arrow directly to the king's heart. Jehu orders Jehoram's driver to throw the body on Naboth's property, a just punishment for the dynasty that killed the man and his sons.

Ahaziah flees toward the southwest, but Jehu sends his men to chase him down and shoot him, too. They wound the hapless young king, who gets only as far as Megiddo before dying. His bodyguards take the corpse back to Jerusalem to be buried.

Meanwhile, Jehu bursts through the gates of Jezreel. There, proud Jezebel has dressed and made herself up to appear at a palace window, as if granting a royal audience. In the style of the ancient Near East, she has probably put black antimony-based kohl on her eyelids and below her eyes to make them appear brighter and larger. Arrogant to the end, she shouts down to Jehu, taunting him by pretending that he is Zimri, who destroyed Baasha's dynasty. At Jehu's urging, two or three of the palace eunuchs grab the queen and throw her to the ground so violently that her blood splashes against the wall.

As Elijah prophesied long before, her body is torn apart and devoured by the dogs in Jezreel. Jehu orders that she be buried, since she was of royal lineage in her own country, but nothing is left save her skull, feet, and the palms of her hands.

Jehu quickly moves to forestall any rebellion. He writes to Samaria to the guardians of Ahab's 70 sons, a total that presumably includes all male relatives rather than actual sons. He challenges them to choose a representative to defend the throne, but they dare not. To kill a king, considered sacred, is proof of great power, and Jehu has just killed two. Jehu then writes an intentionally ambiguous letter, asking the guardians to send the "heads" of the sons. The word could mean either the leaders of the group or their actual heads. The guardians choose the latter interpretation and kill all 70 of the potential rivals for the throne, sending the heads to Jezreel.

Jehu has the heads heaped up in two piles beside the city gates as a warning. Then, as he rides in triumph toward Samaria, he accidentally encounters 42 relatives of Ahaziah. He

Thrown from her palace window, Jezebel is trampled to death by horses and her body devoured by dogs; a 15th-century Bible illustration.

slays them all. Next, he meets up with a certain Jehonadab, a member of the fanatical group called Rechabites. They are so appalled by Canaanite beliefs that they refuse to participate in the ordinary life of the region, neither farming nor building houses nor drinking wine. Jehonadab pledges his loyalty to Jehu, who takes him in his chariot into Samaria. There, the new king kills the remaining followers of the line of Ahab.

Then Jehu announces a huge sacrifice to Baal, and orders all of the god's priests to participate or be killed. This is a ploy. The priests gather in the temple of Baal, and Jehu offers a sacrifice. At that moment, as planned, 80 guards interrupt the service and put the priests to the sword. The temple is demolished, and the site made a public latrine.

In this way, Jehu exterminates the idolatry of Baal in Israel, and God rewards him by promising to extend his dynasty for four generations. Indeed, his progeny will rule for the next 100 years.

Still, Jehu allows the improper worship of the Lord at Dan and Bethel to continue. His reign is troubled by incursions from Hazael, just as Elisha had foreseen in his vision, and the territory of Israel is whittled away bit by bit. After 28 years, Jehu dies and is followed to the throne by his son Jehoahaz.

Now when Athaliah, Ahaziah's mother, saw that her son was dead, she set about to destroy all the royal family.
2 KGS 11:1

*I*n Judah, when Ahaziah is brought back dead to Jerusalem, his forceful and ambitious mother Athaliah makes herself queen. She tries to eliminate all possible rivals, including her own grandson Joash, but his aunt hides him and

his nurse in a temple bedroom. The aunt, Jehosheba, is married to Jehoiada, a high priest who has always remained faithful to the true worship of God.

In the seventh year of the illegitimate queen's reign, Jehoiada decides to take action. Calling together the captains of the Carites, the foreign mercenaries who act as the royal bodyguard, he arms them with weaponry stored in the temple, perhaps captured long before by King David on the battlefield. As the soldiers take positions inside and outside the temple, the seven-year-old Joash is brought forth to be crowned and anointed king, and the people shout with joy. Hearing the noise from the royal palace nearby, Queen Athaliah strides in and cries out, "Treason! Treason!" (2 Kgs 11:14). Her day is done. Jehoiada orders her killed, but not in the house of the Lord. She is swiftly taken outside and executed.

For the moment, it looks as if Judah will be cleansed of idolatry for good. Jehoiada makes a covenant between the Lord and the new king and his people. A temple to Baal, perhaps erected under Athaliah's rule, is torn down and the priest of Baal killed. The boy-king, instructed by the priest Jehoiada, takes the throne and the nation breathes a collective sigh of relief.

In the seventh year of Jehu, Jehoash began to reign; he reigned forty years in Jerusalem. 2 KGS 12:1

*H*istorians believe that Joash, also known as Jehoash, ruled from around 836 to 798 B.C. He is praised by the editor of Kings for seeing to the restoration and continuing maintenance of the temple, which had been neglected under idolatrous monarchs in Jerusalem. Still, he is considered in error for not ending the

As Queen Athaliah of Judah is seized in the temple and taken away to be executed, her grandson Joash is enthroned; a late-17th-century French painting.

*King Jehu of Israel is forced to prostrate himself before Assyria's
Shalmaneser III, a humiliation preserved in this detail from a black basalt stele.*

*When Elisha had fallen sick with
the illness of which he was to die,
King Joash of Israel went down to
him and wept.* 2 KGS 13:14

After some 50 years of serving the Lord as the foremost prophet in Israel, Elisha is dying. Ritually touching the king's hands, Elisha orders Joash to shoot an arrow toward Syria. When he does, Elisha predicts victory over the traditional enemy. Then he tells Joash to strike the ground with the remaining bunch of arrows. The king strikes three times, then pauses. Furious, Elisha scolds him for not striking five or six times. Because of the king's hesitation, Israel will not destroy Syria, only defeat its northern enemy three times.

Unlike his mentor, Elisha dies in the manner of all other mortals, but his power stays with him in death, at least for a time. The prophet would ordinarily have been interred in a cave or tomb carved in the side of a hill and closed with a large stone. When some mourners carrying another corpse think themselves threatened by raiders, they quickly thrust it into Elisha's grave. The dead man springs back to life, resurrected by the power in the prophet's bones.

After the prophet's death, his final prophecy is fulfilled. For all of his halting uncertainty, Joash does indeed defeat the Syrians three separate times, regaining some of the Israelite cities lost to the enemy during his father's unlucky reign. In part, he is victorious because Syria has fallen under the sway of the mighty Assyrian empire in 802 B.C. and has been seriously weakened.

To the south, the throne of Judah passes to 25-year-old Amaziah, who most probably ruled from about 798 to 769 B.C. He avenges his father's murder by executing the servants involved but, justly following the Law of Moses, does not kill their children as well. In other ways, too, he is portrayed as a righteous king, though worship at the high places still flourishes in the southern kingdom.

Amaziah is shown in Kings primarily as a military leader. He defeats the Edomites in battle, slaughtering some 10,000 of them, retakes the Valley of Salt, the lowland area south of the Dead Sea, and captures Sela, perhaps the famous Nabatean city of Petra.

Yet Judah is still subservient to Israel, as it has been since at least the days of Ahab. Perhaps emboldened by his success on the battlefield, Amaziah dares to send messengers to King Joash, inviting him to a meeting as equals. Israel's king replies with a kind of parable: A thornbush, the lowest and least useful of plants, asks a lordly cedar for his daughter's hand in marriage to his son, but a wild animal tramples the impertinent little bush into the ground. In case the contemptuous meaning is not clear enough, Joash spells it out: "You have indeed defeated Edom, and

custom of worshiping at the ancient high places rather than solely at the home of God. It is possible that, once his mentor Jehoiada died, the young king had strayed from the straight and narrow path.

At first, Joash arranges for certain offerings and assessments, such as the census tax, to be given to the priests for repairing and maintaining the temple. When he is 23 years old, however, he realizes that the priests have merely hoarded the sum. Under a new arrangement, a chest is set up inside the temple to receive the money. Together, the high priest and the king's secretary count it out regularly, put it in bags, then jointly pay the craftsmen who restore the temple. The money cannot be used for any other purpose, even to make ritual vessels to be used in worship.

Meanwhile, Elisha's vision of Hazael's ferocity is affirmed again and again. The Syrians capture Gath, an inland Philistine city, then march toward Jerusalem. As has happened before and will happen again in the saga of Judah, Joash barters for peace by stripping the palace and the temple of their collection of votive gifts. As evidence of royal piety, these treasures had been donated to the temple by the king and his ancestors as far back as Jehoshaphat. Suddenly, the account leaps forward to the king's unexplained assassination at the hands of his servants.

Jehu's son Jehoahaz, last seen in the midst of a terrible famine as Samaria lay under siege, now is portrayed in more detail. Ruling Israel from about 817 to 800 B.C., he and his subjects are directly punished by the Lord for their idolatry. Both Hazael and his successor Ben-hadad scourge the land repeatedly. Finally, the beleaguered Jehoahaz returns to God, begging for forgiveness. The Lord relents and sends an unnamed savior, perhaps a gifted military leader like Gideon. But, as in the time of the judges, the Israelites fall back into sin once they are saved from the enemy. In these dark years, both Israel and Judah groan under Syria's great might.

Jehoahaz is succeeded by his son Jehoash or Joash, who will reign in Samaria from about 800 to 784 B.C.

your heart has lifted you up. Be content with your glory, and stay at home" (2 Kgs 14:10). Amaziah dismisses the warning and prepares for battle against the more powerful northern kingdom.

King Jehoash of Israel went up; he and King Amaziah of Judah faced one another in battle at Beth-shemesh.
2 KGS 14:11

At Beth-shemesh, about 15 miles west of Jerusalem, Amaziah confronts Joash; the outcome is unmitigated disaster for Judah. Amaziah is captured, part of Jerusalem's walls are torn down, and the treasuries of the temple and palace are ransacked. Finally, hostages are taken to Samaria, perhaps in return for allowing Amaziah to retain his vassal throne.

After his conqueror's death, Amaziah lives for another 15 years, but conspirators plot to assassinate him. He escapes from Jerusalem to Lachish, a city some 30 miles to the southwest, but is tracked down and killed. In death, he is honored as royalty, his body carried back to his capital and buried in state. His son, 16-year-old Azariah, is unanimously acclaimed king of Judah. Also known as Uzziah, he is able to retake and rebuild Elath, a seaport on the Gulf of Aqaba still known by that name. Possibly, he hopes to reopen the seagoing trade that thrived so richly during the reign of the illustrious Solomon.

During Azariah's rule, Jeroboam II is king the of Israel, reigning from about 789 to 748 B.C. Although the editor of Kings shows little interest in his earthly achievements, Jeroboam is known to history as the most effective of the kings of the northern kingdom. He takes back land that extends north as far as Solomon's borders and south to the Dead Sea. He even takes two Syrian cities, Damascus and Hamath.

But Jeroboam's reign is not a period unmarked by suffering. As in the days of Jehoahaz, God intervenes to aid his sinful people when their troubles become nearly unbearable. His support, which is not earned by their behavior, is explained by his promise generations before that he would not "blot out the name of Israel from under heaven" (2 Kgs 14:27).

At his death, Jeroboam II is succeeded by his son Zechariah.

Three scenes from the Nuremberg Bible: the miracle of Elisha's bones (2 Kgs 13:21); Ahaz at the Damascus altar (2 Kgs 16:10-16); the angel striking the Assyrians (2 Kgs 19:35)

The Lord struck the king, so that he was leprous to the day of his death, and lived in a separate house. 2 KGS 15:5

Although Azariah rules Judah from about 785 to 733 B.C., an unusually long time for these chaotic years, the editor of Kings does not record the specific events of his monarchy. Like several of his predecessors in Jerusalem, he is praised for following the ways of God but criticized for not ending the rites at the high places.

Midway through his reign, Azariah is struck with an unknown skin condition; perhaps the affliction was a divine punishment for trying to assume some of the duties assigned by Mosaic Law to priests alone. He lives out his days in quarantine, while his son Jotham—and possibly his grandson Ahaz as well; the evidence is unclear—acts as regent or coruler.

Shallum son of Jabesh conspired against him [King Zechariah of Israel], and struck him down in public and killed him, and reigned in place of him. 2 KGS 15:10

In about 748 B.C., Zechariah, the last of Jehu's descendants to rule in Israel, assumes the throne but is soon assassinated in public by Shallum. The end of Jehu's dynasty comes as the Lord promised, in the fourth generation of descendants. From now on, the political situation in Israel becomes increasingly confused and unpredictable. Shallum, the assassin, rules for only a month before being assassinated by Menahem. The second usurper, a particularly evil king who rules from around 747 to 737 B.C., begins to feel pressure from the Assyrians, now led by the strong and wily Tiglath-pileser III. Menahem is able to hold onto the throne only by paying a huge tribute in silver to the Assyrians, a sign of vassaldom. This money is raised by exacting a special tax of 50 shekels apiece on the wealthiest families of Israel.

At his death, Menahem is succeeded by his son Pekahiah, who is assassinated in the royal citadel in Samaria a mere two years later. His killer, Pekah, is backed by Gileadites, who come from a region across the Jordan River near the southern kingdom.

Although the editor puts the assassin's reign at 20 years, the historical record suggests that he ruled only from about 735 to 732 B.C. Whatever the duration, Pekah oversees a country that is in continual crisis. Tiglath-pileser's armies swallow major parts of the nation, seizing cities and whole regions in the Transjordan and in north central Israel. In time, the assassin is himself assassinated. Perhaps with the aid and comfort of the Assyrians, Hoshea kills Pekah to claim the throne. He is Israel's last king.

There is scarcely more stability in the kingdom of Judah to the south. Jotham, long the regent for his father Azariah, rules until about 743 B.C. His reign is but sketchily noted. Although he allows the high places to remain in operation, he is faithful to the Lord and is responsible for new construction in the temple. On the international front, he feels pressure from the kings of both Syria and Israel, who want him to join them in an alliance against the ever-increasing threat from mighty Assyria.

Ahaz . . . . walked in the way of the kings of Israel. He even made his son pass through fire, according to the abominable practices of the nations whom the Lord drove out before the people of Israel. 2 KGS 16:2,3

Jotham's son Ahaz, criticized harshly in Kings, apparently practices more than one religion. Most appalling to the editor, he sacrifices his son to the Canaanite fire god Molech in the valley of Hinnom near Jerusalem. Ahaz also becomes the first ruler of Judah since Solomon to join the rites at the high places, not to mention "on the hills, and under every green tree" (2 Kgs 16:4).

Like his father, he resists the attempts of the Syrians and Israelites to force him to collaborate with them in their conspiracy against Assyria. Instead, after the Edomites recapture Elath, Ahaz decides to seek help from the awesome Tiglath-pileser himself.

As described on the prism at right, Assyria's Sennacherib captured Judah's fortress city of Lachish in 701 B.C. The city (aerial view above) presented a formidable challenge.

He backs up his plea nicely with gold and silver from Jerusalem's palace and temple. Thus encouraged to take measures that were certainly not out of keeping with his long-range plans, the Assyrian leader captures Damascus and kills the Syrian king. Following state policy, he deports many of the Syrian people to another site, whose location is not known today.

When Ahaz visits his victorious patron in Damascus, he is for some reason captivated by the design of a large pagan altar there. He sends a precise scale model back to his capital so that it will be ready for use in the temple when he returns. Ahaz dedicates this replica himself, personally presenting the burnt offering, the grain offering, and the drink offering. Then he orders the bronze altar to the Lord removed from the front of the temple to a spot north of the new altar. From then on, the people are to worship at this latter altar, while Ahaz alone uses the bronze altar to seek oracles about the future.

At his death in about 727 B.C., Ahaz is succeeded by his remarkable son Hezekiah.

The king of Assyria captured Samaria; he carried the Israelites away to Assyria. 2 KGS 17:6

Hoshea's friendship with Assyria becomes strained when Shalmaneser V takes over the empire, beginning a brief reign from 727 to 722 B.C. Evidently, Israel's king betrays his protectors from the east and begins exploring an alliance with Egypt.

This decision turns out to be a tragic error both for Hoshea and for his people. An infuriated Shalmaneser sweeps across Israel, taking the entire land, and begins a siege at the gates of Samaria. For three long years, the city holds out but finally surrenders in 722 B.C. By this time Shalmaneser has been followed by Sargon II, who removes much of the Israelite population to the eastern reaches of Assyria.

This is the long-predicted fall of the northern kingdom, and the editor inserts an explanation in Deuteronomic style. For one thing, the collapse of Israel offers a moral to the people of Judah: Their country, too, can be destroyed if God allows a powerful invader to conquer the land. For another, despite all of the preceding tales about the idolatry and other wickedness of the northern kings, it is clear that the people themselves have earned punishment.

Israel is sentenced to eternal exile. The ten northern tribes will never return to their homeland. Assyrian policy replaces them with immigrants from cities in the east. Also, as is their administrative custom, the conquerors name the whole land Samaria for its royal capital. Immediately, God sends lions to terrorize the new inhabitants, for none of them honor his name. Sargon promptly sends a Hebrew priest back to Bethel, and the worship of the Lord continues alongside the many different pagan religions that now thrive in the promised land.

The siege and fall of Israel's capital, Samaria, and the removal of its inhabitants to Assyria is depicted in this woodcut from the 1534 Luther Bible.

He [Hezekiah] trusted in the Lord the God of Israel; so that there was no one like him among all the kings of Judah after him, or among those who were before him.
2 KGS 18:5

The story of Hezekiah, who ruled from about 727 to 698 B.C., may once have marked the conclusion of Kings, for he is praised as the first king since David to honor the Lord as a Hebrew monarch should. He makes certain that, at last, the high places are torn down. He destroys the bronze image of a serpent supposedly commissioned by Moses and used to cure snakebite. Hezekiah is also a strong political leader, rebelling against the Assyrian stranglehold on Judah and probably extending the kingdom by invading Philistia.

Still, Judah is no match for the mighty power that has arisen in Mesopotamia. Hezekiah loses many of his walled cities, including Lachish, to a new Assyrian emperor, Sennacherib, who attains the throne in 705 B.C. and is determined to punish this rebellion in Judah. Hezekiah tries to buy off the Assyrians with all the silver and gold he can gather in Jerusalem, including the gold overlay on the doors of the temple.

Still furious, the Assyrian leader sends three of his top officials—his viceroy, chief eunuch, and chief steward—at the head of a great army to confront the rebels in 701 B.C. Outside Jerusalem, near a part of the city water system, they meet with a delegation that includes Hezekiah's overseer, secretary (a high administrative position), and royal herald.

Sennacherib's chief steward, the Rabshakeh, shouts to the townspeople in their local dialect of Hebrew, urging them to turn from Hezekiah and make peace with the empire. He warns that their king is misleading them by promising that God will intervene,

for the Assyrians have defeated many other nations, despite their local gods.

The common people of Judah do not reply. Meanwhile, Hezekiah sends his representatives to seek advice from the prophet Isaiah. He has good news: The Lord plans to deceive the Assyrians. A second time, Sennacherib sends threats to Jerusalem, this time in the form of a letter. Hezekiah is so alarmed that he enters the Holy of Holies and begs the Lord for help. Again, an oracle comes from Isaiah promising that the Assyrians will be sent back home.

That very night the angel of the Lord set out and struck down one hundred eighty-five thousand in the camp of the Assyrians; when morning dawned, they were all dead bodies.
2 KGS 19:35

Indeed, great numbers of the enemy are miraculously slain, and Sennacherib returns to Nineveh, where he is assassinated in 681 B.C. For the next two years, the people of Judah eat little but wild grain, since the land is too devastated for planting crops until the third year.

Another miracle story seems to affirm Hezekiah's great piety. At some point, perhaps before the Assyrian invasion, he becomes fatally ill and cries out to God to heal him. Moved by his faithful servant's bitter weeping, the Lord sends Isaiah to tell him that he will be cured within three days and will live another 15 years. The prophet treats the physical manifestation of the illness, an unexplained skin eruption or boil that could be a symptom of anthrax, by applying a lump of figs. Still fearful, Hezekiah asks for a sign of the Lord's favor, and the shadows on the dial of Ahaz, a device that keeps time as shadows lengthen down a series of steps, retreat backward ten steps.

There follows a story about a visit from delegates of the Babylonian king known as Merodach-baladan, who has heard about Hezekiah's illness. This encounter must have occurred before the Assyrian invasion of 701 B.C., for Sennacherib dethroned this rival king in 703 B.C. In any event, Hezekiah shows off his great wealth to the Babylonian visitors, who may have come to form an alliance against Assyria.

Isaiah, who detests any foreign entanglements, confronts Hezekiah immediately after this flirtation and warns that every item he displayed will someday be looted and taken back to Babylon. The king's own sons will be taken into slavery there, the prophet continues, and made into eunuchs. Hezekiah accepts this prophecy calmly, since it implies that such calamities will not occur during his own lifetime.

This is an unattractive side of the king, but the editor ends by mentioning Hezekiah's famous and lasting triumph in Jerusalem, the cutting of a water tunnel, from the Gihon spring to the inside of the city walls, through 1,749 feet of hard rock. Thus water is available during an enemy siege.

THE BABYLONIAN CAPTIVITY OF THE JEWS

The destruction of Jerusalem in the summer of 586 B.C. was total. Archaeology reveals that the Babylonians not only put military installations to the torch but leveled the city's commercial and residential quarters as well. The once splendid city of David was uninhabitable; Solomon's magnificent temple lay in ruins. Thousands died in the vain defense of the city; countless others perished of disease or starvation. Some Judahites hid from the conquerors in nearby caves; many fled to wilderness areas east of the Jordan; a few sought refuge in Egypt.

It remained for those carried off into captivity in Babylon to preserve the worship of one God and nourish the hope of reestablishing his kingdom on earth. The ten northern tribes, taken to Assyria after the fall of Samaria in 722 B.C., vanished from history. But the exiles in Babylon maintained their identity, having been allowed to live in their own communities along the Chebar River, actually a 100-mile irrigation canal parallel to the Euphrates River southeast of Babylon.

According to the prophet Jeremiah—himself an exile at Tahpanhes on the Egyptian frontier—the largest deportation of Jews took place in 597, when 3,000 families were taken to Babylon with King Jehoiachin. The number removed to Babylon in 586 may have been 830 families, with another 745 families following in 582. The total number of exiles was likely only about 18,000 people. Many of these no doubt succumbed to the pagan religion of their captors. But others, observing the sabbath, circumcising males, and preserving the scriptures that contained the Mosaic Law, ensured that Judaism would survive.

Manasseh . . . . rebuilt the high places that his father Hezekiah had destroyed; he erected altars for Baal.
2 KGS 21:1, 3

Hezekiah, the most exemplary ruler since David, is followed by his son Manasseh, one of the most wicked. Not only does he restore the high places, he builds altars to Baal even in the temple, practices child sacrifice and other forbidden rites, and enthusiastically misleads his subjects into idolatry.

The Lord becomes so enraged with the king and with the people of Judah that he promises to "wipe Jerusalem as one wipes a dish, wiping it and turning it upside down" (2 Kgs 21:13). This threat is not immediately fulfilled, however, for Manasseh lives to kill many innocent people before his own death.

Manasseh's son Amon, a true heir in terms of worshiping idols and flouting the will of the Lord, lasts only two years in power. His own servants assassinate him in the palace. Amon's eight-year-old son Josiah is acclaimed as king of Judah in about 639 B.C. He proves to be a monarch even more godly than Hezekiah, determined to enact reforms that not only restore the temple but also bring the people back to faithful adherence to the Law of Moses.

The high priest Hilkiah said to Shaphan the secretary, "I have found the book of the law in the house of the Lord."
2 KGS 22:8

Josiah may have begun his reform movement when he was only 12 years old, but the most important moment of his reign comes six years later. He sends his secretary to the temple to initiate a program of repairs, and the high priest, Hilkiah, produces a dusty, forgotten scroll found somewhere in the neglected house of the Lord.

When it is read aloud to the king, he is mortified and breaks into weeping, humbling himself before God. Probably a version of the Old Testament book of Deuteronomy, the scroll warns that the Lord will punish his people for breaking their covenant with him. Josiah asks Hilkiah to consult God about the true meaning of the scroll, and the high priest takes the question to a prophetess named Huldah. Although she appears only this one time in the Bible, she evidently shares the prophetic gifts demonstrated previously by male prophets. She explains that God will indeed punish Judah with destruction, but Josiah will live out his life in peace as a reward for his exemplary piety and humility.

The king has the book read out to the people assembled as a congregation in the temple, then leads them in renewing their ancient covenant with the Lord. More than any other previous reformer, he ensures that the southern kingdom is entirely cleansed of pagan influence. The many altars and the high places are defiled, including the altar that Jeroboam erected at Bethel. Josiah also sees that, perhaps for the first time since the Israelites invaded Canaan, Passover is observed at the house of the Lord in accordance with Mosaic Law.

The list of his reforms is prodigiously lengthy, but God cannot be moved after the many generations of disloyalty. In 609 B.C., Josiah is killed in an unexplained encounter with Neco, the second Pharaoh of Egypt's 26th dynasty. The stage is set for the fall of Jerusalem and the destruction of Judah.

Jehoahaz follows his father Josiah to the throne, but Neco, preying on Judah, has him captured and taken away to be confined in Egypt, where he dies. Suffering Judah has to pay the Egyptians a huge tribute in gold and silver, which is collected by the Pharaoh's new puppet-king. This is Eliakim, another of Josiah's sons, renamed Jehoiakim and placed on the throne by Pharaoh in 608 B.C. Neither of Josiah's sons is considered admirable by the editor.

The Babylonians enter the picture after defeating their Egyptian rivals in 605 B.C. As the victorious armies sweep through Syria and Samaria without substantial opposition, Jehoiakim prudently agrees in 603 B.C. to have Judah become a vassal to Babylon's King Nebuchadnezzar. But about three years later, the tide turns between the ancient world's two great powers, and Egypt drives Babylon out of the area. Jehoiakim seems to have rebelled against Egypt too soon. But the tide reverses once again, and the Babylonians march back into Judah.

King Jehoiachin of Judah gave himself up to the king of Babylon. 2 KGS 24:12

Jehoiakim has been succeeded by yet another impious king, his 18-year-old son Jehoiachin. Nebuchadnezzar himself leads a siege of Jerusalem, which surrenders in March of 597 B.C.

At last, the devastating punishment predicted so often throughout 1 and 2 Kings comes to pass. The palace and temple are ransacked, and all citizens except the poorest are deported to Babylon, as Isaiah proclaimed to Hezekiah after the visit of the Babylon-ian diplomats. Two different figures are given for the total number taken away, 8,000 and 10,000. Jehoiachin is thrown into a Babylonian jail.

Still, the city of David stands; Judah has not been destroyed. To the throne comes yet another of Josiah's sons, Zedekiah, age 21.

Zedekiah rebelled against the king of Babylon. . . . [who] came with all his army against Jerusalem, and laid siege to it. 2 KGS 24:20, 25:1

Nine years into his reign, Zedekiah repeats Jehoiakim's mistake. He leans politically toward Egypt, which is regaining its influence under a new Pharaoh, but Babylon is still stronger. The irate Nebuchadnezzar returns to Jerusalem with his great army in January of 587 B.C. After a terrible siege of 18 months, the Babylonians break through the city walls in July of 586 B.C.

While his people are being attacked, the feckless Zedekiah and his courtiers slip through a gate in the city's southeastern wall, but they are captured by the invaders near ancient Jericho. The Babylonian monarch is not inclined to show mercy. Nebuchadnezzar has Zedekiah's sons killed as the broken king watches, then has the Judean's eyes put out. The great buildings of Jerusalem are burnt to the ground, and the walls of the city are toppled in rubble. Piece by piece, the remaining treasures and furniture of the temple are taken away as loot. Except for humble farmers who will maintain vineyards and gardens, the people of Jerusalem are taken off to Babylon in captivity.

Hoping to stabilize the defeated kingdom, Nebuchadnezzar appoints a prominent Judean, Gedaliah, as governor of the area. Gedaliah is happy to cooperate with the Babylonians, but his own people murder him as a traitor. Many then flee for their lives to Egypt.

In a brief postscript, the editor notes that Jehoiachin, who was imprisoned after the first deportation to Babylon, is released from prison by a new emperor, Evil-merodach, when he assumes the throne in about 560 B.C. In fact, the former king of Judah is treated more respectfully than all of the other monarchs held at court. Despite the chaos and destruction of the preceding generations, this change in Jehoiachin's fortunes may bode well for the future of the monarchy. It is a slender pretext for optimism as the Jews continue to live and work in Babylon, barred from returning to their promised land and the temple that is the sole earthly home of the Lord.

The dejected exiles of Judah dream of the return to their homeland; a painting by Eduard Bendemann (1811-1889).

1 CHRONICLES

*T*he two books of Chronicles recapitulate the story of the Jewish people—tracing their ancestry all the way back to Adam and ending with their exile in Babylon. But the narrative is usually more upbeat than the earlier, more complete versions in Samuel and Kings. For example, in telling the story of David, the writer focuses on the glory of his reign without mentioning the king's adultery with Bathsheba or troubles in the royal family after a prince rapes his half sister.

Yet the writer is not revising history. He is drawing from a painfully well-known story only the material that will help answer troubling questions that the former Jewish exiles are considering. They had shattered their sacred covenant agreement with God by rejecting him and his laws. For this they have incurred the full extent of threatened punishment, including the destruction of their nation and the scattering of their people "from one end of the earth to the other" (Deut 28:64). Now, back in Israel, a remnant of Jews wonders if they are still God's chosen people, if the covenant is still valid, and if the promised land is still their inheritance. The writer answers, "Yes." As evidence, he shows how God's plan for Israel started at creation and continues to his own time, likely the fourth century B.C., with the temple rebuilt, the priesthood intact, and David's family preserved.

Like 1 and 2 Samuel and 1 and 2 Kings, the two books of Chronicles were originally one long work that was later divided at the time the Hebrew Bible was translated into Greek. Ancient Jewish tradition says that the scribe and priest Ezra wrote Chronicles along with the books of Ezra and Nehemiah, which recount the return of the exiles to Jerusalem. There is intriguing support for Ezra's authorship. First, the book emphasizes the temple and the priestly rituals, appropriate concerns for a priest descended from Aaron, Israel's first high priest. Also, the genealogies in 1 Chronicles end at about the time Ezra lived, in the fifth century B.C. Yet, without a clear indication of who wrote the book, many commentators refer to the author only as the Chronicler. The work falls into two parts: a family tree from the time of Adam (chapters 1-9), and the story of King David's rule (10-29).

Adam tilling the soil after his expulsion from Eden; a 12th-century stained glass window from England's Canterbury Cathedral

---

These are the sons of Israel: Reuben, Simeon, Levi, Judah, Issachar, Zebulun, Dan, Joseph, Benjamin, Naphtali, Gad, and Asher. 1 CHR 2:1-2

*T*he Chronicler begins his uniquely tailored history of the Jewish people by displaying nine chapters of genealogy fused together from sources scattered throughout the Old Testament—including nearly all the genealogies from Genesis. To the modern reader, this may seem like a mind-numbing way to begin a book. But to the small and beleaguered community of Jews who have survived exile in Babylon and have returned to Israel to rebuild their nation devastated by war, these chapters likely produce startling insight and profound gratitude.

To the ancient Jews, these names represent far more than obscure, faceless individuals. They reveal the history of God at work among humankind, and especially among his chosen people, the Jews. By listing Adam and the early generations who populated the earth, the Chronicler reminds his readers that God

created all the nations, and that they play a role in his plan for Israel. Then, by showing how Abraham and the 12 tribes of Israel sprang from this lineage, it becomes wondrously clear that God's plan stretches all the way back to the first human being. Abraham descended from Shem, son of Noah and forerunner of the Semitic people of the ancient Near East. Abraham's grandson Jacob—whom God renamed Israel and from whom the Jews took the name of their nation—had 12 sons, and their extended families multiplied in time to become the 12 tribes of Israel.

The Chronicler's genealogy does not linger in the distant past, nor does it abruptly end at the fall of Jerusalem in 586 B.C. The author extends the Jewish family tree all the way up to his day, when a small but growing remnant of Jews has returned from exile and started to rebuild the nation.

In a way, this genealogy is a dramatic shorthand for narrative. Name upon name quickly and graphically shows God at work on behalf of his people from the beginning of time and even into the anxious,

tiring days of Israel's reconstruction. The cast of historical figures is staggering. There are 2,087 names in the Bible, and nearly half of them appear in 1 Chronicles—most of them in this genealogy.

The Philistines overtook Saul . . . . he and his three sons and all his house died together.   1 CHR 10:2, 6

After tracing the family tree of King Saul, the Chronicler skips the story of Saul's reign and instead jumps directly to the king's tragic demise—perhaps to contrast the disgrace of Saul with the glory of David, whose story fills the remainder of 1 Chronicles.

Saul, three of his sons, and his budding dynasty come to an abrupt end in a fierce battle with the Philistines at Mount Gilboa, deep into Israelite territory some 40 miles north of Jerusalem. The Chronicler condenses the already well-known story of 1 Samuel 31, and reports that as the Israelites are being overrun, King Saul, wounded by archers, asks his armor-bearer to kill him so that the Philistines will not take him alive. When the man is unable to obey the horrifying order, Saul falls on his own sword, killing himself. His attendant does the same.

The next day, while searching for valuables among the dead, the Philistines find Saul's corpse. They carry away his head and armor as trophies, which they then display in the temple of Dagon, their chief deity. "So Saul died for his unfaithfulness; he was unfaithful to the Lord . . . . Therefore the Lord put him to death and turned the kingdom over to David son of Jesse" (1 Chr 10:13, 14).

Saul's commander, Abner, survives the battle and tries to salvage his sovereign's dynasty by installing Saul's remaining son, Esh-baal (Ish-bosheth), as king. But Esh-baal is soon assassinated by his own men. The Chronicler omits these negative details so he can quickly get on with reporting the evidence of God at work on Israel's behalf.

All Israel gathered together to David at Hebron.   1 CHR 11:1

David had been popular with the Israelite masses ever since the day when, as a young shepherd wielding only a slingshot, he defeated the heavily armed Philistine champion, Goliath. David had become so popular, in fact, that Saul drove him away in a fit of jealousy and tried to hunt him down and kill him. But now, with Saul's dynasty ex-

hausted of princes, Israelite tribal leaders turn to their fugitive hero and proclaim him king. This fulfills the destiny foretold by the prophet Samuel when he secretly anointed David years earlier—even before David killed Goliath (1 Sam 16:13).

David rules for seven years from Hebron, a village in southern Israel, in the territory belonging to his family, Judah. But to eliminate the perception that he favors his own tribe, David wisely chooses a new capital that the Israelites have not yet captured. He lays siege to the Jebusite city of Jerusalem, about 12 fortified acres on a steep hillside. A direct, uphill assault would be disastrous. Even Joshua, who centuries earlier had conquered the nearby city of Jericho, bypassed the Jebusite stronghold. David, however, discovers a secret, dangerous passage into the city. A small cave outside the wall leads to an underground spring deep beneath the city. From a nearly vertical, 50-foot water shaft, people inside the city lower water buckets down into the spring's pool. If some of David's men can scale this shaft, they will surprise the enemy and be able to open the city gates for the rest of the invasion force.

"Whoever attacks the Jebusites first shall be chief and commander" (1 Chr 11:6), David vows. First up the shaft is Joab, son of David's sister. As promised, Joab becomes commander of David's army.

Scenes from a 12th-century English Bible: Saul watching David in combat with Goliath and the Philistines fleeing the victor with his gruesome trophy (top); Saul about to spear his lyre player, David (bottom, left); Samuel anointing David king, with only members of the young shepherd's family in attendance

Though kings of Israel were initially anointed rather than crowned, this illumination from an English psalter dated about 1225 shows David being given a crown.

The following are those who came to David . . . mighty warriors who helped him in war.   1 CHR 12:1

To show the widespread support that the new king enjoys, the Chronicler reports on the formidable size of David's army. This support actually began long before David was anointed king. As soon as he became a fugitive from Saul's court, the popular hero began attracting a following. First to join him at his hideout near Bethlehem, his native village, were his brothers, soldiers in Saul's army. Then came a motley collection of desperate people in search of hope: "Everyone who was in distress, and everyone who was in debt, and everyone who was discontented" (1 Sam 22:2). In less than a year, David commanded a private army of 400 men.

Once tribal leaders decide to ask David to succeed Saul, warriors from all over Israel and beyond begin flocking to enlist in his army. At his installation celebration David suddenly has a fighting force of an improbable 340,000 men: Israelites, mercenaries from other countries, and at least two elite forces, the Three and the Thirty. The Three is a trio of champions led by a hero who single-handedly killed 300 men in one battle. The Thirty, also led by a battlefield champion, is a squad of 30 seasoned warriors who apparently serve as part of the royal bodyguard. Among David's regular army are archers and stone slingers who can shoot with either hand, along with swift-running, fierce-looking infantrymen who are experts with spears and shields.

Surprisingly, the king's own tribe—Judah—contributes only about 6,800 soldiers. The most enthusiastic supporters of all are the far-flung tribes from Israel's perimeter, perhaps because they would be the first to face an invasion force. The small Galilean tribe of Zebulun, for example, sends 50,000 soldiers, and the two and a half tribes east of the Jordan River send 120,000. These eastern tribes are Reuben, Gad, and half of Manasseh, a tribe divided by the Jordan. The actual number of soldiers may have been many fewer than modern translations suggest. Experts in Hebrew linguistics explain that "thousand" can also mean "group." So the eastern tribes, for example, may have contributed not 120,000 men, but only 120 fighting units of unknown size.

David said to the whole assembly of Israel,
". . . . let us bring again the ark of our God to us."
1 CHR 13:2, 3

David has a profound respect for Israel's long-standing religious traditions. And he realizes how these traditions can help unite the nation. The great symbol of Israel's faith is the ark of the covenant, a gold-plated chest that once contained the stone tablets inscribed with the Ten Commandments. This ark represents the earthly throne of God and his presence among the Israelites. During the time of Moses—more than 200 years before David—the ark was kept in the most sacred room of the tabernacle, Israel's tent worship center. But throughout King Saul's reign, the ark sat neglected in a private shrine at Kiriath-jearim, to which it had been brought when the Philistines returned it after capturing it in battle.

Saul had never been able to unite the 12 Israelite tribes firmly; under his rule, Israel remained a loosely linked coalition that occasionally joined forces in times of crisis. David wants more than a coalition. He wants a strong, united nation. And he has the spiritual and political insight to realize that his army—powerful as it is—cannot accomplish this alone. David needs the continued support of the people and, more important, the unifying presence of God. So he calls a nationwide assembly. Israelites arrive from as far south as the Shihor, an eastern branch of the Nile River in Egypt, and as far north as Lebo-hamath, in Syria. As king, David can simply dictate that the ark be brought to Jerusalem. Instead, he asks the people to ratify his decision "if it seems good to you" (1 Chr 13:2). The masses embrace the idea and join in a joyful procession to unite in one city the throne of God and the throne of the king.

However, disaster strikes. While the people are transporting God's holy ark in an ox-drawn cart, one of the oxen stumbles, and a driver named Uzzah reaches out to steady the ark. Instantly God strikes Uzzah dead. David is horrified and initially angry at God. But he later realizes that the tragedy happened

because he overlooked God's instructions about handling the sacred ark. Only men from the priestly tribe of Levi could carry it. Three months will pass before David makes a second, successful attempt to bring the ark to Jerusalem.

The Chronicler likely includes both of these stories in his condensed history of Israel to show David's persistent concern for the ark and his desire to obey God's law. Furthermore, the stories subtly urge readers in the time of the Chronicler to do the same—to treat sacred objects, such as the rebuilt temple, with deep respect, and to obey God's commands.

David did as God had commanded him, and they struck down the Philistine army from Gibeon to Gezer.
1 CHR 14:16

The Philistines are Israel's main competitors for the land. A military-minded, seafaring people, the Philistines had started migrating to Canaan's Mediterranean coast about the same time the Israelites arrived from Egypt. Throughout the time of Israel's famous judges and even into Saul's reign, Philistines dominated the western coast and expanded into central Canaan. By carefully guarding their secret weapon—iron making, which allowed them to produce swords that could slice off a man's head with a single blow—they were able to terrorize and subjugate Israelites in their vicinity.

When the Philistines discover that David has united the tribal armies and is building a palace in Jerusalem, a mere 25 miles east of their border, they decide to remind the Israelites who is in charge. They assemble their troops and march toward Jerusalem. David asks for and receives God's permission to defend the land. The Philistines are routed in this and at least three other battles they fight with David's forces. After these consecutive defeats, the Philistines no longer pose a threat to Israel. When David's son Solomon becomes king, he receives tribute from subservient kingdoms, including the cities of Philistia. About 400 years later, Philistia evaporates as a nation, annihilated by the Babylonians. Its name, however, survives; the word "Palestine" comes from Greek and Latin words used to describe the descendants of the Philistines.

All the good things that happen to David in this chapter—his victories over the Philistines, his many children, and his gifts from the king of Tyre—are presented as evidence that God is with him. The Chronicler is moving toward convincing his readers, the former Jewish exiles who are back in Israel, that God is with them as well.

David assembled all Israel in Jerusalem to bring up the ark of the Lord to its place, which he had prepared.
1 CHR 15:3

David prepares for a second attempt at bringing the ark of the covenant to Jerusalem. He erects a sacred tent and furnishes it with everything necessary for sacrifices and other priestly rituals. The

A regally clad King David leads the musicians accompanying the ark of the covenant as it is brought to his new capital, Jerusalem; a scene by James J. J. Tissot (1823-1910).

centuries-old tent tabernacle that Moses had built is at Gibeon, a few miles north. Next, David orders the priestly class of Levites to "sanctify" themselves. This means they are to purge themselves of any ritual defilement. At the very least, they bathe and abstain from sexual relations. Some may also need to offer sacrifices. The king wants the Levites ritually holy because they will carry the sacred ark to Jerusalem, just as Levites once carried the ark through the wilderness.

Accompanying the ark will be a huge procession of Israelites from throughout the country—30,000, according to 2 Samuel 6. The march is led by priestly musicians singing and playing instruments: harps, lyres, and cymbals. Joining the jubilant chorus is David, "leaping and dancing" (1 Chr 15:29). David's wife Michal, Saul's daughter, becomes disgusted at his unkingly behavior. The Chronicler omits the couple's argument about this dance, in which David apparently takes off some of his outer clothes. This omission is probably not meant to suggest that the garment-tossing dance and argument never happened, for the story is already five centuries old and well known. This carefully tailored history, however, is intended to convince former Jewish exiles that God is still among them, just as he had been with their ancestors. This becomes especially clear in the song that Asaph and other Levites sing after the sacred ark arrives in Jerusalem. The song—not included in the 2 Samuel account of this story—praises God for his faithfulness and asks, "Save us, O God of our salvation, and gather and rescue us from among the nations" (1 Chr 16:35). For the book's first readers, recently returned from exile, this song produces a deep sense of gratitude for an ancient prayer answered. And it generates a spark of hope that God has not given up on Israel.

David said to the prophet Nathan, "I am living in a house of cedar, but the ark of the covenant of the Lord is under a tent."
1 CHR 17:1

David is dissatisfied with storing the sacred ark in a tent, while he lives in a palace. So he asks the prophet Nathan for permission to build a temple. After consulting the Lord, Nathan denies the request. God explains that the honor of building the temple should go to a man of peace and not to a man of war

(1 Chr 22:8-10). Solomon, David's son and successor, will later receive the commission.

In the meantime, however, God promises to build David a house, meaning a dynasty. "I will raise up your offspring after you, one of your own sons, and I will establish his kingdom," God says. "His throne shall be established forever" (1 Chr 17:11, 14). Later generations see in this an irrevocable promise that David's dynasty will never end. During Israel's most spiritually distressing centuries, some of the prophets also see in this a reason to expect a Messiah ("anointed one"), a godly king from David's family who will save Israel and restore the glory that has been lost. New Testament writers present Jesus, David's descendant, as the fulfillment of these prophecies—the Messiah who offers salvation to all the world, and who will one day return in glory, to "reign forever and ever" (Rev 11:15).

The Lord gave victory to David wherever he went.
1 CHR 18:13

Evidence that David is a man of war, and therefore an inappropriate choice for building God's temple, follows in chapters 18 through 20. David takes advantage of his unified army and the waning state of affairs in neighboring Egypt and in Assyria by securing his national borders and establishing his own regional empire, which expands into several surrounding kingdoms. He defeats Philistia in the west, Syria (Aram) in the north—all the way to the Euphrates River, Ammon and Moab in the east, and Edom in the south. He then sets up garrisons in these subjugated nations and collects from them spoils of war and tribute. This revenue helps reduce taxes in Israel and launches a golden age of peace and prosperity that will endure even throughout the lifetime of David's son and successor, Solomon. Though David is not allowed to build the temple because of the blood he has shed, much of the precious metal he gathers from his wars—gold, silver, and bronze—he devotes to God or hoards for later use in building the extraordinary worship center.

David does what his predecessor, Saul, had never come close to accomplishing. In Saul's day, Israel remained a

The prophet Nathan relaying God's message that David is not to build a house for the Lord; a French Bible illustration dated about 1480

GENEALOGIES IN THE BIBLE

*I*n Israelite society, built around extended families called tribes, heritage was a determining factor in what life would be like for people. Those who could trace their family tree to descendants of Jacob—progenitor of the 12 tribes—enjoyed full citizenship in the promised land. Only they could worship God in the inner courtyards of the temple in Jerusalem. During the earliest years, after Joshua distributed the land among the tribes, heritage determined where people lived. For instance, descendants of Jacob's fourth son, Judah, lived in southern Israel, which included the village of Bethlehem, birthplace of King David and later Jesus. Only men descended from David, a ruler to whom God promised "your house and your kingdom shall be made sure forever" (2 Sam 7:16), were candidates for king. Much the same was true for Israel's priesthood since the Law of Moses dictated that only Aaron's descendants could serve as priests.

There are about two dozen genealogies in the Old Testament, and two in the New Testament. These are incomplete family trees that usually list only the more notable members. Though the lists seem to flow unbroken from one generation to the next, "father of" can mean simply "ancestor"—such as father, grandfather, or great-grandfather—and "son of" can mean "descendant." Thus, it is often impossible to determine accurate dates and time lines based on these genealogies.

The Bible's first genealogy traces seven generations descended from Cain, the son of Adam and Eve who killed his brother, Abel (Gen 4). Other important genealogies identify key people from Adam to Noah (Gen 5), the descendants of Noah (Gen 10), and the descendants of Jacob (Gen 46). But the longest genealogy in the Bible spans the first nine chapters of 1 Chronicles, stretching from Adam to the time after the Jews returned from exile in Babylon in the second half of the sixth century B.C.

Jesus tops this 12th-century tree of Jesse, in which his ancestry is traced from David's slumbering father (bottom) upward through an array of the kings of Judah to Mary and the Holy Spirit.

small, discouraged, and only marginally united confederation of tribes surrounded by powerful enemies. The impression that the Chronicler leaves is that this is because Saul had not developed the habit of consulting and obeying God. David, on the other hand, does both. For this, God rallies Israelites to his side and crushes enemies beneath his feet. The Chronicler's echoing message is that God honors and rewards faithfulness.

Satan stood up against Israel, and incited David to count the people of Israel. 1 CHR 21:1

*A*fter securing Israel, David gives a seemingly harmless order: He calls for a census. Yet both his military commander, Joab, and the Lord judge this as sinful. The Chronicler does not explain what the sin is—nor does the writer of the original account in 2 Samuel 24. But it seems that David is swelling with pride over the size of his empire—as though the accomplishment is his doing instead of God's. Whatever the sin, David repents. But there are consequences to suffer. God gives the king a choice of three possible punishments: three years of famine, three

months of destruction by enemies, or three days of pestilence. David chooses the last, relying on God, "for his mercy is very great" (1 Chr 21:13).

A plague sweeps across the nation, killing 70,000 people. As a sword-wielding angelic being arrives in Jerusalem to continue the punishment, God abruptly orders a halt—just as the angel hovers above a threshing field that will later become the site of the temple. It is for this reason that the Chronicler includes this unflattering story about David, for the end of the plague and the forgiveness of God play a crucial role in selecting the place where generations of Jews will find forgiveness and mercy. God tells David to buy the hilltop threshing area from the farmer who owns it and to build an altar on it. David obeys, offers sacrifices to atone for his sin, and watches in awe as the Lord sends fire from heaven to consume the offerings. In response, David declares, "Here shall be the house of the Lord God and here the altar of burnt offering for Israel" (1 Chr 22:1).

Some details in the Chronicler's account differ from those in 2 Samuel 24. In Samuel, the census tally is 800,000 in the northern tribes that later become known as Israel, and 500,000 in the southern tribe of Judah, for a total of 1,300,000. But the Chronicler reports 1,100,000 in Israel and 470,000 in Judah, for a total of 1,570,000. (Both figures are exaggerated.) The difference is a mystery, perhaps caused by a copyist's error or by the fact that the census was never completed or recorded in King David's annals (1 Chr 27:24). Samuel also reports that David buys the threshing field for only about a pound and a half of silver, while Chronicles sets the price at about 15 pounds of gold. The inflated price quoted by the Chronicler may be his way of expressing how precious the temple site is. But it could also be that David paid the lesser price for the threshing area where he built the altar and an additional price for the surrounding land designated for the temple.

David said, "My son Solomon is young and inexperienced, and the house that is to be built for the Lord must be exceedingly magnificent . . . ; I will therefore make preparation for it."   1 CHR 22:5

Though David is not allowed to build the temple, he begins stockpiling vast quantities of material for the project. First, he assembles foreigners living in Israel and assigns them the tedious, backbreaking job of cutting stone blocks for the temple. In David's day, people from conquered lands were often called on to serve the victor. David also acquires iron and bronze "in quantities beyond weighing," and from the forests of Lebanon, cedar logs "without number" (1 Chr 22:3).

The Chronicler further reports that David sets aside a truly staggering amount of gold and silver: 100,000 talents of gold and a million talents of silver. The weight of a common talent was about 75 pounds; the so-called light talent weighed about half that. Calculating by common talents, David amassed 3,750 tons of gold and 37,500 tons of silver. Most biblical scholars prefer not to take these numbers literally, since the annual revenue of Solomon—famous for his matchless wealth—was only 666 talents (1 Kgs 10:14). Instead, scholars interpret the Chronicler's astounding tally as a way of again expressing the measureless supply of resources that David is able to amass for what will become Israel's most important edifice, the center of the Israelites' religious life: the house of the Lord in Jerusalem.

David assembled all the leaders of Israel and the priests and the Levites. . . . And David organized them in divisions.   1 CHR 23:2, 6

Vitally interested in the temple he cannot build, David does far more than stockpile a huge inventory of building supplies; he organizes the worship personnel. David begins by taking a census of the priestly class. Unlike his previous census of Israel, his motive here is justified: He needs to know what kind of workforce is available for the project.

David divides the priests into 24 extended family groups, perhaps so they can serve in rotating shifts. Names of several of these groups appear in one of the Dead Sea Scrolls—tattered remains of an ancient Jewish library near Jerusalem that contains manuscripts and scroll fragments as old as two centuries before Jesus. By New Testament times, each priestly group is serving for a week at a time, twice a year. Zechariah received news of John the Baptist's birth while serving his shift in the temple.

This scene of David's court musicians graced the breviary of Spain's Queen Isabella, and looks as if it is set in her own palace; the painting is dated a few years after she sponsored Columbus's voyage of discovery.

David also organizes the caste of worship attendants known as Levites, assigning them areas of specialty. Levites and priests are all descendants of Jacob's son Levi, but priests are descendants of Aaron, one of Levi's great-grandsons and the man God chose to serve as Israel's first high priest. David apparently creates the guild of temple musicians by appointing some Levites as ministers of music. Their task is to sing praises to God each morning and evening and to recite publicly God's messages to the accompaniment of instruments. Like priests, Levitical musicians are divided into 24 groups. Other Levites work in the temple, assisting priests with sacrifices and related ceremonies. Some Levites work as guards who monitor the gateway entrances into the temple courtyard, and some as treasurers who keep track of the donations. Still others are appointed to work throughout the nation, apparently serving as judges and public administrators.

This information is unique to Chronicles, omitted from the earlier account in Samuel. For Jews recently returned from exile and trying to rebuild the temple worship system, this report provides helpful guidance.

In this mosaic portrait from the renowned San Marco cathedral in Venice, David brandishes a Latin motto celebrating his deeds.

This is the list of the people of Israel . . . who served the king in all matters.   1 CHR 27:1

David also organizes his army and retinue of royal officials. As he has done with the priests, he separates the army into divisions, though this time 12 instead of 24. Each division is comprised of 24,000 men who serve one month at a time. During war, the full force of 288,000—again an unlikely number—is to be mobilized.

Though remnants of the tribal system survived into New Testament times, the bulk of the ten northern tribes disappeared after the fall of the northern kingdom in 722 B.C. But the Chronicler scrupulously reports who the tribal leaders are under David, when life in Israel is at its glorious best, with king and people serving God and prospering because of their devotion to him.

The Chronicler also identifies by name some 20 men who serve the king in various capacities. Some are close friends and advisers, one teaches the king's sons, and many serve as overseers of the king's property. For example, a man is assigned to manage each of the following: the palace treasury, regional treasuries, farmworkers, vineyards, grapes and wine from the vineyards, olive and fig groves, olive oil, cattle on the Sharon Plain, cattle in the valleys, camels, donkeys, and flocks of sheep and goats.

By the list's end, the reader realizes that David has created Israel's religious and government structures with God's approval—as evidenced by the era of peace and prosperity that follows. By implication, this is a system that the Chronicler may be presenting as divinely approved for his day as well.

"And you, my son Solomon . . . . the Lord has chosen you to build a house as the sanctuary; be strong, and act."
1 CHR 28:9, 10

David, now well advanced in years, summons all the national leaders to Jerusalem: tribal elders, government officials, and army commanders with their subordinate officers. Here, in a formal and solemn ceremony, he announces that Solomon will become both his successor and the king who will build the great temple to which he has dedicated so much of his energy and resources. In words reminiscent of an aged Moses addressing the Israelites, David urges the leaders to obey God "that you may possess this good land, and leave it for an inheritance to your children after you forever" (1 Chr 28:8).

David then turns to his son and implores him to serve God with a willing heart and to accept the daunting challenge of building the temple. David presents Solomon with a detailed set of plans for building and furnishing the temple and for managing the worship personnel. These are plans David says he received from God in much the same way that Moses received plans for the tent worship center that the Israelites used during the Exodus.

Solomon now has a temple blueprint, a rich supply of building materials, and a well-developed strategy for staffing the temple. All that is left to do is begin the work.

David blessed the Lord in the presence of all the assembly . . . . He died in a good old age, full of days, riches, and honor. 1 CHR 29:10, 28

As Moses had collected voluntary donations for the tent worship center, David does the same for the temple. After receiving a generous offering of gold, silver, and precious stones, David publicly expresses his gratitude to God in a humble and eloquent prayer. On the following day the people offer sacrifices, then joyfully eat and drink.

David dies after 40 years as ruler of Israel, ending the legendary reign of a man perceived by the Chronicler and others as the ideal king—a man after God's "own heart" (1 Sam 13:14).

P art two of this version of Israel's story begins with the grand reign of Solomon, described as the wisest and wealthiest king who ever lived. The Chronicler, who may have been the scribe and priest Ezra, devotes the first nine chapters of 2 Chronicles to Solomon—especially to his most famous building project: Israel's first temple, masterfully crafted and paneled in cedar and gold. The remaining chapters, 10 through 36, cover the centuries that follow— from Israel splitting into two rival kingdoms through the destruction of both nations by foreign invaders.

Noticeably absent are reports about the northern kingdom of Israel— stories that appear in the parallel history of 1 and 2 Kings. The Chronicler apparently believes that the northern tribes were so blatantly unfaithful to God that they can never recover from their defeat. Their kings were all sinful, and the citizens proved their own unworthiness by worshiping at pagan shrines. The southern kingdom of Judah, on the other hand, enjoys at least some godly kings and access to God through the Jerusalem temple. Even so, Judah's sins become chronic and grave enough that God allows the nation to collapse, and the survivors to be deported to Babylon.

This is the last book in the modern Hebrew Bible. But Israel's story does not end with despair. The concluding message offers a release from exile and a new beginning. Cyrus of Persia, under God's direction, decrees that the Jews can return to their homeland and rebuild their temple.

Solomon deciding an infant's fate

"Give me now wisdom and knowledge to go out and come in before this people, for who can rule this great people of yours?" 2 CHR 1:10

S olomon's first recorded act as king is to lead a pilgrimage of national leaders to a holy site in Gibeon, a village about five miles north of Jerusalem. It is here that the Israelites had set up the tabernacle, the tent of meeting used as a mobile worship center during the Exodus from Egypt. On the bronze altar outside this tent, Solomon sacrifices a thousand burnt offerings. That same night God comes to him in a dream and offers him anything he wants. Solomon asks only for the wisdom to govern Israel.

God is delighted that Solomon's deepest concern is for the people, not for himself. The king could have asked for personal wealth, fame, or the death of his enemies. Because Solomon exhibits such unselfishness, God promises to give him all he asks for—and all he could have asked for: wisdom, riches, and honor "such as none of the kings had who were before you, and none after you" (2 Chr 1:12).

The first book of Kings also reports this story, then follows it with the famous case of Solomon deciding between two prostitutes who claim a newborn boy. The outcome of this trial shows that the king's prayer for wisdom has been answered. The Chronicler, however, follows the story of Solomon's request with evidence that he becomes a wealthy ruler, renowned especially for his riches and his chariot squadrons garrisoned throughout the country. By the Chronicler's day, some 500 years after Solomon, the previously recorded trial is legendary and considered solid evidence of the king's wisdom. So the Chronicler reports the other rewards of Solomon, perhaps to show that God keeps all of his promises.

Solomon began to build the house of the Lord in Jerusalem on Mount Moriah. 2 CHR 3:1

B y the fourth year of his reign, Solomon has reorganized Israel's government and military, building on his father's foundation. Israel's national security and peace have been reinforced by the chariot corps and new fortifications throughout the country. Solomon—who will earn fame as a tireless builder—turns to his most acclaimed building project: the first of only three temples in Jewish history.

In a report condensed from 1 Kings, the Chronicler says that Solomon begins by supplementing the building supplies that his father, David, had stockpiled. Solomon trades enormous amounts of grain, wine, and olive oil for the most prized wood in the ancient Near East, cedar from the forests of Lebanon. This tight-grained, rot-resistant wood emits a fragrance pleasing to humans but repellent to insects. Like his father before him, Solomon conscripts non-Israelites living in the land and assigns them to work crews. Supervised by more than 3,000 foremen, some 80,000 workers specialize in the backbreaking tasks of quarrying and cutting white limestone blocks, while another 70,000 perform general labor.

Modeled along the lines of other Near Eastern temples of the time, Solomon's majestic edifice is shaped as a rectangle and erected on a hilltop, with the sanctuary entrance facing the rising sun. The temple measures 90 feet long, 30 feet wide, and 45 feet to the ceiling—double the size of the tent tabernacle. Inside are three rooms: a small vestibule; then the main sanctuary where priests will burn incense; and, at the back, a 30-foot cube called the Holy of Holies, in which Israel will enshrine the ark of the covenant, which holds the Ten Commandments. All three rooms are elaborately decorated with angelic beings, flowers, and fruit carved into the wood and overlaid with gold.

It takes seven years to finish the building and the artfully crafted furnishings for the sanctuary and courtyard. But once finished, Solomon's temple becomes more than a worship center. Though the Israelites never say the temple is the only dwelling place of God, they believe he is a constant presence there. When Solomon dedicates the holy structure in prayer, fire flashes down from heaven and burns up the inaugural sacrifice. In that astonishing moment, "the glory of the Lord filled the temple" (2 Chr 7:1). Remarkably, Solomon's temple survives for almost 400 years, until Babylonian invaders strip away the valuables, set fire to the timbers, and break down the stone walls into a heap of rubble.

He also built . . . fortified cities . . . in all the land of his dominion. 2 CHR 8:5, 6

After spending seven years building the temple of the Lord, Solomon spends another thirteen years on the palace complex—a detail that the Chronicler omits but that the author of 1 Kings includes, perhaps as a subtle criticism of Solomon's misplaced priorities. The Deuteronomic author of Kings reports the good and the bad to show that God rewards obedience and punishes disobedience. But the Chronicler, living in the days when the former Jewish exiles have suffered epic punishment and are trying to rebuild their nation, focuses primarily on encouraging scenes of God at work on Israel's be-

Two 15th-century scenes: Solomon overseeing the temple construction (left); the ark being taken inside

SOLOMON'S STABLES

Remains of what are thought to be Solomon's legendary stables have been uncovered at Megiddo, one of the king's six chariot cities.

To maintain the peace secured by his father, King David, Solomon built a chain of six fortified bases located throughout the land, from north of the Sea of Galilee to south of the Dead Sea. The six—Megiddo, Hazor, Gezer, Lower Beth-horon, Baalath, and Tamar—became known as Solomon's chariot cities. Along with Jerusalem, these walled cities garrisoned his chariot corps, a massive force for its time. Though Solomon's army fought no major battles, he could field 1,400 chariots, each drawn by two horses with a third held in reserve, for a total of 4,200 horses. Charioteers and cavalrymen numbered 12,000. Together, these forces provided a sobering deterrent to any ruler tempted to capture Israel's lucrative trade routes between the Persian Gulf and Egypt.

At Megiddo, an outpost guarding an important mountain pass in northern Israel, archaeologists have found the ruins of several centuries of fortifications built on top of one another, including what may be stables dating to Solomon's time. Long, narrow rooms are separated by short stone pillars with holes chiseled through them, perhaps for tethering horses. The facilities are large enough to have housed three squadrons of 50 chariots and 150 horses each.

Among the ruins, but dating to the later period of King Ahab, were pieces of a chariot modeled in clay—further evidence that Megiddo was once a military base.

The 16th-century Italian artist who depicted Solomon greeting the queen of Sheba added a dwarf (lower left) to his extravagant, very European court scene.

When the queen of Sheba heard of the fame of Solomon, she came to Jerusalem to test him with hard questions.
2 CHR 9:1

The queen of Sheba rules a land that has grown rich by controlling desert trade routes in southwestern Arabia, perhaps modern Yemen, a thousand miles from Jerusalem. She hears incredible stories about Solomon's wisdom and wealth and becomes so captivated that she decides to make the journey, taking perhaps two months each way to meet this living legend.

Sheba is astonished at what she sees: a majestic palace and temple, well-disciplined court officials dressed in the finest robes, and tables filled with delicious food. When she asks King Solomon hard questions, probably riddles that are popular among sages, he answers every one correctly. The two rulers exchange a caravan load of gifts. She gives him about four tons of gold, along with jewels and immense quantities of spices. In response, he gives her "every desire that she expressed, well beyond what she had brought" (2 Chr 9:12).

Curiosity may not be Sheba's only motivation for the trip. She might have hoped to establish a trade agreement. Her nation and its African colonies deal in precious metals, gems, and expensive spices. Solomon controls overland routes to what is now Syria, Turkey, and Iraq. He also commands a commercial fleet sailing the Red Sea and trading at Arabian ports on the east shore and African ports on the west. The two monarchs apparently reach an agreement because, after describing Sheba's visit, the Chronicler immediately reports that Solomon starts receiving gold each year from traders and Arabian rulers. Also, his ships return every three years with precious and exotic cargo: gold, silver, ivory, apes, and peacocks.

Legend says Sheba had a son by Solomon: Menelik, who became king of Ethiopia. Falashas, Ethiopian Jews, trace their ancestry to Menelik. Before Ethiopia's emperor was overthrown in 1974, the nation's constitution claimed that the imperial family descended from the son of "the queen of Sheba and King Solomon of Jerusalem."

half. In chapter 8, for example, the author says only that Solomon rebuilds cities given to him by Huram, also known as Hiram of Tyre, the king who provides Solomon with timber and carpenters. But 1 Kings tells the reverse story: Solomon cedes 20 Galilean cities to Hiram, perhaps as partial payment or for gold to fund his public projects (1 Kgs 9:10-14). Hiram, displeased with the cities, apparently returns them, and Solomon eventually renovates them. Ignoring this information, the Chronicler jumps directly to the account of King Solomon refurbishing the cities.

Solomon's building projects continue virtually to the point of obsession. Throughout his kingdom Solomon constructs defensive fortifications to garrison his infantry, cities for his mounted troops, cities for his chariot corps, cities in which to store food and weaponry, cities such as Tadmor (Palmyra in the Syrian desert) to protect trade routes, and cities to guard major passes, such as the twin cities of Upper and Lower Beth-horon along the coastal road to Jerusalem. For labor, Solomon continues his policy of drafting non-Israelites who are living in the land.

Rehoboam rejecting the elders' plea for leniency; a 14th-century French Bible illustration

---

"Your father made our yoke heavy. Now therefore lighten the hard service of your father and his heavy yoke that he placed on us, and we will serve you."
2 CHR 10:4

After Solomon dies, following a long and prosperous reign, his son Rehoboam prepares to succeed him. For his installation ceremony, he travels to the sacred site of Shechem, among the northern tribes. Here is where Abraham once built an altar to God, and where the Israelites later rededicated themselves to the Lord's covenant after returning from slavery in Egypt. Though the Chronicler has reported that Solomon did not draft Israelites into forced labor, that policy has apparently changed, for at the ceremony national leaders implore the prince to lighten the demands made on the people, using terms that invoke memories of the Egyptian king's harsh treatment of enslaved Israelites.

Senior advisers urge 41-year-old Rehoboam to comply with these requests. But his younger advisers and longtime friends disagree and suggest that he make it clear exactly who is in charge of the country. "My father made your yoke heavy," Rehoboam tells the assembled elders, "but I will add to it; my father disciplined you with whips, but I will discipline you with scorpions" (2 Chr 10:14), perhaps referring to metal-tipped scourges.

The ten northern tribes break down their tents and go home, vowing to have nothing more to do with David's dynasty. They elect as their king Jeroboam, a former supervisor of Solomon's work crews. Rehoboam, however, maintains his right to rule. He expresses this by sending to the northern tribes an official in charge of work groups. The royal representative's job is to conscript workers, but he is stoned to death. Furious, King Rehoboam musters his militia; however, he soon issues a stand-down order after a prophet tells him that the secession is God's will—punishment for Solomon's decision to worship idols late in his life. Suddenly, David's dynasty is reduced from 12 tribes to 2: Judah and the absorbed tribe of Simeon. The southern Jewish nation becomes known as Judah, after the dominant tribe; the northern nation takes the name of Israel.

When the rule of Rehoboam was established and he grew strong, he abandoned the law of the Lord. 2 CHR 12:1

Though Rehoboam rules a much smaller kingdom than his father did, he rules in obedience to God—at least in the beginning. By his fifth year on the throne, however, he has lost interest in the ancient covenant and stops worshiping the Lord. Many of the Judahites follow his lead. God decides to punish the entire nation by sending an invasion force led by Egyptian King Shishak, known also as Shoshenq I, founder of Egypt's 22nd dynasty and ruler from about 945 to 924 B.C. The Chronicler reports that Shishak captures all the fortified cities of Judah, including Jerusalem, and strips treasures from the temple and palace. On the walls of the temple of Amon at Karnak, Shishak brags that he captured more than 150 towns in Judah.

Rehoboam escapes by fleeing Jerusalem. In hiding, he admits that he has done wrong and that God has every right to punish the nation. For this show of humility and repentance, God promises not to let Shishak completely destroy Judah. Instead, God says the people of Judah will temporarily be subdued "so that they may know the difference between serving me and serving the kingdoms of other lands" (2 Chr 12:8). Rehoboam retains his throne and reigns 17 years. (See list of the kings of Judah and Israel on page 127.)

Abijah engaged in battle . . . and Jeroboam drew up his line of battle against him. 2 CHR 13:3

Skirmishes between the northern and southern kingdoms become a way of life throughout the rule of Rehoboam and into the reign of his son, Abijah (Abijam). This jockeying for regional power comes to an abrupt though temporary end during a dramatic battle in buffer territory between the nations. Possibly in an effort to reunite the nations under his control, King Jeroboam of Israel musters 800,000 troops (or perhaps 800 units, since the ancient Hebrew word for "thousand" can also mean "unit"). Abijah fields only half as many men. Though dangerously outnumbered, Abijah stands on a hilltop and shouts a speech to Jeroboam and the Israelites. He boldly criticizes them for trusting in gold idols and warns them that they are fighting against God, and will certainly lose.

Even as Abijah speaks, some of Jeroboam's forces are secretly moving behind the southern army, setting up for attacks at the front and rear. When the battle begins, priests with Abijah blow trumpets as Judah's soldiers shout a primal battle cry. This description is reminiscent of Joshua's attack on Jericho. Jeroboam loses 500,000 men (no doubt an exaggerated figure) and several important cities in a crushing defeat that renders him nearly powerless as a monarch. Sometime later, the Lord strikes him dead.

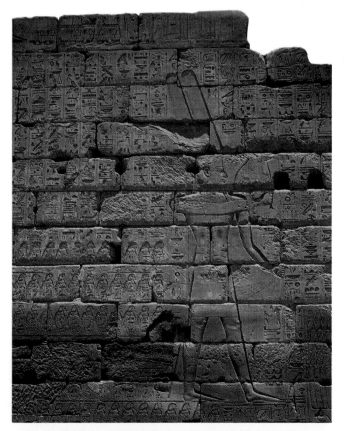

Egypt's Shoshenq I (Shishak) commemorated his victory over Judah with this inscription at the temple of Amon in Karnak.

*[Asa] took away the foreign altars . . . and
commanded Judah to seek the Lord.* 2 CHR 14:3, 4

Abijah's son and successor, Asa, is mentioned only briefly in 1 Kings. But the Chronicler spends three chapters painting a word portrait of a man who is, like David, brilliant in warfare and, like the later Hezekiah, tireless in purging the nation of idolatry. Asa, the fifth ruler of David's dynasty, begins his 41-year reign in about 908 B.C. by destroying pagan shrines throughout Judah. For this, God grants him ten peaceful years—time Asa uses to build towns and fortify them with walls, lookout towers, and gates.

Asa is eventually threatened with a massive invasion led by Zerah of Ethiopia, a warrior mentioned nowhere outside this story. Accompanying Zerah are 300 chariots and an infantry numbering a million, more literally translated "a thousand thousands," and perhaps meaning a thousand units. This is nearly double the size of Asa's army. As the invaders approach to within 25 miles of Jerusalem, Asa cries out to God: "Help us, O Lord our God, for we rely on you, and in your name we have come against this multitude" (2 Chr 14:11). God empowers the Judahites to wipe out their enemy, to the last man.

The king continues his policy of destroying pagan shrines that persistently spring up around the country. He even deposes his mother, Maacah, Judah's queen mother, for erecting an obscene image to Asherah, a Canaanite fertility goddess.

By the 36th year of Asa's reign, his fervor for God has diminished. When King Baasha of the northern nation of Israel invades and begins building a fort about five miles north of Jerusalem, Asa does not call on God for help. Instead, he sends silver and gold to the king of Syria, essentially hiring an ally who attacks Baasha's troops and forces them to withdraw. A seer condemns Asa for trusting in a human alliance instead of relying on God—and for this the seer is thrown in jail. The king later develops a serious foot disease but stubbornly persists in refusing to ask for God's help. Even when the mysterious illness becomes life-threatening, Asa turns only to physicians, who are unable to heal him.

*Jehoshaphat had great riches and honor; and he made
a marriage alliance with Ahab.* 2 CHR 18:1

Jehoshaphat, Asa's son and successor, follows the example of his father's early years: destroying pagan shrines and securing the nation's defensive capabilities with forts and a huge army. He rules at the same time as the notorious Ahab and Jezebel in Israel, yet he manages to achieve peace with them, perhaps in part by marrying his son and heir, Jehoram, to Ahab's daughter, Athaliah. When Ahab decides to fight a doomed battle east of the Jordan River and asks Jehoshaphat to join him, the king of Judah humbly replies, "I am with you, my people are your people" (2 Chr 18:3). Ahab dies in the battle, and the combined Hebrew armies are forced to retreat.

Criticized by a seer for allying himself with sinful Ahab, Jehoshaphat renews his effort to rid Judah of idolatry—a chore that becomes increasingly difficult. Despite the best efforts of godly Judean kings such as Jehoshaphat, the Hebrews find ways to break the first and most important of the Ten Commandments: "You shall have no other gods before me" (Ex 20:3).

*When Jehoram had ascended the throne of his father
and was established, he put all his brothers to the sword.*
2 CHR 21:4

When Jehoshaphat dies, leaving Judah in an era of peace, the oldest of his seven sons, 32-year-old Jehoram, becomes king. Once Jehoram solidifies his grip on the nation, he eliminates the competition by killing all six of his brothers. Had any of them killed him first, the next oldest could have claimed the throne of David.

In matters of religion, Jehoram is nothing at all like his father. Instead, the ruthless Jehoram is more like his father-in-law, Ahab. Jehoram rebuilds pagan worship centers throughout the land and woos his nation into idolatry. As punishment, God allows the previously dominated Edom to break away from Judah and gain independence. Worse, God stirs up a coalition of Philistines and Arabs to overrun and pillage Judah. These raiders carry away everything of value in Jehoram's palace, including his wives and all his sons except Ahaziah. Afterward, Jehoram is stricken with a severe intestinal disease, perhaps chronic diarrhea, dysentery, or colitis. He languishes in pain for two years before dying at age 40. At the end of his meager eight-year reign, "he departed with no one's regret" (2 Chr 21:20).

*Ahaziah was forty-two years old when he began to reign;
he reigned one year in Jerusalem.* 2 CHR 22:2

With Judah depleted of all princes but their youngest—Ahaziah—they have little choice but to crown him king. Ahaziah (22 years old, not 42 as the Chronicler writes) follows in the idolatrous footsteps of his father, and survives only one year. While visiting his uncle Jehoram, king of the northern nation of Israel, Ahaziah finds himself in the wrong place at the wrong time. Rebels overthrowing Ahab's dynasty kill his uncle and him.

Now in line for the throne of Judah are the children of Ahaziah, who are all too young to rule. Their grandmother Athaliah, queen mother of Judah, seizes the opportunity to snatch the throne for herself. She orders the immediate massacre of all her grandchildren. A single infant escapes: Joash, who is secretly raised in the temple by his aunt Jehoshabeath, wife of the priest Jehoiada. Six years later, the priest decides the time is right to present the boy-prince to the nation; perhaps he realizes that the people have had their fill of a tyrannical queen. Under the protection of armed Levitical guards, Jehoiada crowns the seven-year-old child as king. Waves of cheering and singing erupt throughout the temple courtyards, and Athaliah rushes there to investigate. Curiosity kills the queen. At the priest's command, she is seized, taken outside, and executed as ruthlessly as she had killed her grandchildren.

Joash was seven years old when he began to reign.
2 CHR 24:1

Acting in the name of the boy-king, the priest Jehoiada begins turning the nation back to God by demolishing the pagan worship centers, smashing idols, and killing priests of Baal, the dominant god among ancient Canaanites. When Joash grows up, he remains greatly influenced by this priest who had saved him from certain death and raised him as a son. Partly out of love for Jehoiada, the young king levies a tax on Judah and orders the money used for repairing the neglected, 100-year-old temple of Solomon.

Unfortunately, after the old priest dies, Judah's leaders convince Joash to abandon the Lord and revert to worshiping gods native to Canaan. Jehoiada's son, a prophet who must seem like an older brother to the king, makes a somber public announcement: "Because you have forsaken the Lord, he has also forsaken you" (2 Chr 24:20). Astonishing as it seems, royal advisers convince Joash to execute this prophetic messenger—the son of the very priest who had saved his life and crowned him king.

Joash soon pays for this callous judgment. Within a year of the prophet's death, Syrian invaders arrive. Aided by God, the Syrians defeat the much larger army of Judah, then loot the cities and kill the leaders. Joash escapes, though severely wounded. While recuperating in bed, he is murdered by his own officials as retribution for having executed the son of a priest who had shown him such love and loyalty.

[Amaziah] did what was right in the sight of the Lord, yet not with a true heart. 2 CHR 25:2

Like his father before him, Joash's son Amaziah begins his reign well but finishes in disaster. When the Chronicler says that Amaziah serves God, "yet not with a true heart," he likely means "not wholeheartedly." The king's spiritual shallowness becomes clear as the story unfolds. Initially, the king shows respect for God. First, in executing the men who assassinated his father, Amaziah stops short of killing the men's children. Ancient Near Eastern custom would have allowed this, but God's law forbids killing children for the sins of their fathers. Second, after Amaziah hires mercenaries from Israel's northern tribe of Ephraim to help reclaim Edom southeast of Judah, he obeys a prophet's order to send the mercenaries home. God will bless only the Judahites, the prophet explains, not the apostate Ephraimites.

As predicted, Amaziah conquers Edom using only his own troops. Incredibly, he brings home Edomite idols and worships them. God immediately sends a prophet to ask the king what sense it makes to worship the gods of a nation that Judah has just crushed. The king abruptly cuts short the prophet's message and sends him away.

Energized by victory, Amaziah boldly challenges the northern kingdom of Israel to meet his warriors on the battlefield. Amaziah's troops are routed in a bloody clash about 16 miles southwest of Jerusalem. Israel's king orders his victorious soldiers to loot the temple and palace, demolish 200 yards of Jerusalem's wall, and take hostages. Amaziah is allowed to retain his throne, though as a dishonored, subjugated vassal. Like his father, Amaziah is eventually assassinated by conspirators among his own people—perhaps those who hold him responsible for Judah's tragedy.

Uzziah was sixteen years old when he began to reign, and he reigned fifty-two years in Jerusalem. 2 CHR 26:3

Amaziah's son Uzziah (or Azariah) rules longer than any previous king in David's dynasty—even longer than David or Solomon, each of whom reigned 40 years. The only king to control Judah longer was the infamous Manasseh, who was 12 when he was crowned and who ruled 55 years.

Like several other kings before him, Uzziah begins his reign well but ends it tragically. In his case, it is pride—not idolatry—that gets the better of him. Initially, Uzziah seeks godly advice. "And as long as

Uzziah opened the port of Elath on the Gulf of Aqaba (above); inset, a plaque bearing the king's name.

he sought the Lord, God made him prosper" (2 Chr 26:5). The king strengthens his army and fortifications, defeats neighboring enemies, takes control of caravan routes to the south, and even manages to re-open the port of Elath on the Gulf of Aqaba.

For some unknown reason, later in his reign Uzziah decides to go into the temple sanctuary and burn incense to God. The king certainly knows that this is a sacred place and a holy rite reserved only for priests. When the high priest and 80 other priests order the king to leave the sanctuary, he refuses. Suddenly, a skin disease erupts on his forehead. Though this may not be leprosy (Hansen's disease), any serious skin disorder renders Hebrews ritually unclean and contagious; anything they touch must undergo sacred cleansing rites. Also, as long as the infected individuals remain ritually unclean, they are refused admittance to the temple area and are unable to offer sacrifices to God. Uzziah's skin ailment persists for the rest of his life, forcing him to live in isolation. His son Jotham succeeds him and earns a reputation as a righteous king throughout his 16-year reign. Learning from his father's mistake, he never dares step inside the temple sanctuary.

[Ahaz] made cast images for the Baals . . . and made his sons pass through fire. 2 CHR 28:2, 3

Jotham's son Ahaz is described as one of the worst kings in Judah's history. Not only does he reject God in favor of Canaanite idols, he even sacrifices his sons by burning them to death. As punishment,

Hezekiah's water tunnel under Jerusalem is still open; the inset inscription proclaims the engineering feat.

God allows Judah to suffer disastrous raid upon raid from the neighboring nations of Israel, Syria, Philistia, and Edom. Against the prophet Isaiah's advice, Ahaz pleads with powerful Assyria for help. This is a mistake that costs Judah its independence. Assyria helps Judah, then helps itself to Judah—taking treasures from the temple, palace, and homes of officials. Furthermore, Judah is required to start paying tribute to the Assyrian empire.

[Hezekiah] did what was right in the sight of the Lord, just as his ancestor David had done. 2 CHR 29:2

Hezekiah is nothing like his godless father, Ahaz. The Chronicler devotes four chapters to this remarkable reformer, and likens him to David, the most respected king in Hebrew history. Hezekiah's first recorded act as king is to reopen and repair the temple, which his father had closed and abandoned. Then Hezekiah sends an invitation to all Hebrews, in Judah and Israel alike, urging them to join him for a weeklong Passover celebration—a springtime event commemorating Israel's release from Egyptian slavery. Most people laugh at the messengers, since the two nations have long since stopped observing this religious holiday. But many accept the invitation. When the festival ends, the guests commit themselves to destroying pagan shrines throughout the two Hebrew kingdoms of Judah and Israel. This grassroots reform movement becomes the most extensive, and successful, in the 200 years since the Jewish nation split in two after Rehoboam instituted his reign of terror.

The king is perhaps best remembered, however, for surviving a siege led by Assyria's King Sennacherib. When the intruders arrive in the region and begin capturing one fortified city after another, Hezekiah develops a cunning strategy. He cuts off the flow of springs and streams around Jerusalem. Then, to ensure that the capital has plenty of water, he builds a 1,750-foot-long tunnel through solid rock—an engineering marvel for the time. Surviving to this day, the tunnel leads to an underground spring outside the ancient city walls. Sennacherib abandons the siege after a mysterious and fatal illness sweeps through his camp one night. Imperial records of Sennacherib boast that he captured 46 Judean cities, but they stop short of making that claim of Jerusalem. "Hezekiah," Sennacherib reports, "I made a prisoner in Jerusalem, his royal residence, like a bird in a cage."

[Manasseh] made his son pass through fire . . . , practiced soothsaying and augury and sorcery, and dealt with mediums and with wizards. 2 CHR 33:6

No king in all of David's long dynasty, which spans more than four centuries, has a worse reputation than Manasseh, son of the God-fearing Hezekiah. Crowned at the impressionable age of 12, Manasseh rebuilds pagan shrines that his father destroyed. And he practices many of the forbidden,

Sennacherib's furious assault on Jerusalem is vividly depicted in this late-15th-century Bible illustration.

mystical arts, including sorcery, witchcraft, and augury, or interpreting naturally occurring events, such as the flight pattern of birds, as omens about the future. Like his grandfather, Ahaz, Manasseh burns his infant sons to death as sacrifices to Canaanite gods. But unlike his grandfather, he does not close the temple; he does something much worse. He converts this holy symbol of God's presence among the Jewish people into a pagan shrine.

God responds by allowing the Assyrians to capture Manasseh and take him in chains to Babylon. But the Chronicler reports a dramatic turnabout in Manasseh during his captivity, one that the author of Kings omits. Citing two apparently well-known sources that are now lost—the Annals of the Kings of Israel and records of the seers—the Chronicler reports that the king repents, receives God's forgiveness, and returns to Judah, where he tears down idolatrous shrines and restores the worship of God. His lost prayer is reconstructed in the Apocrypha (see page 262). Manasseh reigns 55 years—longer than any king in David's dynasty. Assyrian inscriptions confirm that Manasseh became a loyal vassal of the empire.

Josiah kept a passover to the Lord in Jerusalem.
2 CHR 35:1

As hard as it is to envision, the Chronicler describes Manasseh's son, King Amon, as more sinful than his father. The king's own officials assassinate him after two years. His son, eight-year-old Josiah, gradually adopts the traditional Hebrew faith. By age 20 he starts ridding Judah of pagan shrines; six years later he begins renovating Solomon's 300-year-old temple. During this restoration the high priest finds a long-lost scroll of Jewish law—perhaps the book of Deuteronomy, which summarizes the laws that God gave Moses. When Josiah hears these laws read to him, and the punishment that God promises for disobedience, he suddenly understands why Judah has suffered for so long and why the northern nation of Israel was destroyed by Assyria nearly a century earlier. The king summons all Judah's leaders to Jerusalem, then personally reads the entire book to the assembly. Afterward, he convinces the people to renew the ancient Israelite covenant with God. They seal their vow by once more celebrating Passover.

Josiah dies in 609 B.C., at about age 39, in what appears to be a needless battle to prevent Egypt from peacefully crossing his land to engage the burgeoning Babylonian empire. Though the Egyptians defeat Judah, they lose to the Babylonians in 605 at Carchemish, a settlement near what is the present-day border between Syria and Turkey.

They burned the house of God, broke down the wall of Jerusalem, burned all its palaces with fire. 2 CHR 36:19

A succession of four kings follow Josiah, all of whom are evil. The nation is eventually overrun and dominated by Babylon. But the Jews repeatedly try to break free by withholding tribute and declaring independence. Babylon retaliates by sending troops, reestablishing control, and taking hostages from among the social elite. As the rebel movement persists, the Babylonian king Nebuchadnezzar runs out of patience. Once more he sweeps through the land and, in the summer of 586 B.C., his warriors loot and level Jerusalem along with the only temple the Jews have ever known. All but the poorest are exiled to Babylon. Many who remain later flee to Egypt, fearing the Babylonians will return.

God has delivered on the worst of his threats for a broken covenant: "The Lord will scatter you among all peoples, from one end of the earth to the other" (Deut 28:64). The Jewish nation ceases to exist. The Hebrews have no king, no land, and no structure but slavery and chaos.

Once more God intervenes on their behalf. For at least 700 years the Exodus from Egypt has endured in Jewish memory and tradition as the most celebrated example of God's love for them. Now comes a sequel, a new exodus out of Babylon. Cyrus of Persia overthrows the Babylonian empire, then releases the Hebrew exiles in a monumental gesture of goodwill. The Jews are free to return home with a descendant of King David to rule them, a priesthood to nurture them, and a long history to inspire them.

The pious King Josiah being laid to rest following his death in battle with the Egyptians; from the Nuremberg Bible

The rebuilding of the temple in Jerusalem is depicted in this early-15th-century French Bible illumination.

The books of Ezra and Nehemiah, which follow 1 and 2 Chronicles in Christian Bibles, continue the history of the Jewish people after their exile to Babylon. They tell the story of the Jews' return to Jerusalem and the restoration of their state under the two men for whom the books are named. But there is a gap between the fall of Jerusalem at the end of 2 Chronicles and the beginning of Ezra. By the time Ezra was compiled, great events in the ancient Near East had brought a reversal of fortune for the Jews. The shifting sands of political power had led to the decline of the Babylonian empire, climaxed by the fall of the city of Babylon in 539 B.C. to King Cyrus II of Persia. He became the Jews' savior by allowing them to return to their ancestral homeland.

The Babylonian exile lasted more than a generation, from 586 to 538 B.C., and it left a deep imprint on the Jews. Their center of culture and worship, the temple in Jerusalem, had been destroyed. The stability of their life under the monarchy in Judah had come to a disorienting halt, and they had been taken from their cherished promised land. Aside from the Exodus, no other event in Israelite history had such a profound effect on the religion and culture of the Jews. For the exiles who returned to Jerusalem and its neighboring territory, the big question was how to reconstitute the Jewish community. Several things became important: rebuilding the temple and reestablishing regular sacrifices, festivals, and worship; recognizing the authority of the Law of Moses, as preserved in the Pentateuch; and keeping separate from the other people who lived in the area surrounding Jerusalem, some of whom claimed to be legitimate descendants of the Israelites.

Like modern historians, the authors of Ezra and Nehemiah drew on a number of different written sources: the first-person memoirs of the two men, genealogies, lists of participants in building projects, Persian royal decrees and correspondence, and third-person accounts of historical events. These sources were edited and sewn together to form a narrative of the Jews' first century after the return from Babylon. Some of the seams left by the authors can be detected. Many scholars think that Nehemiah 8-10, concerning Ezra's activities, was spliced into the Nehemiah memoir. And Ezra 4:7-6:18 is in Aramaic; the rest of the two books are in Hebrew.

Ezra 1-6 recounts the return of two early groups of exiles to Jerusalem, in 538 and 520 B.C., and their ultimately successful attempts in the face of opposition from the local population to rebuild the temple. Ezra 7-10 describes Ezra's return to Jerusalem in 458 B.C. and the work of his first year with the Jewish community there.

In order that the word of the Lord by the mouth of Jeremiah might be accomplished, the Lord stirred up the spirit of King Cyrus of Persia. EZRA 1:1

The book of Ezra begins on a positive note. Cyrus has decreed that he is planning to rebuild the temple in Jerusalem. As part of the plan, he will repatriate the Jewish exiles in Babylon, one of the lands he has conquered. The wording of the edict in the first chapter reflects the perspective of the Jews. It is doubtful that Cyrus, who reigned from 559 to 530 B.C., gave credit to Israel's God for his many victo-

ries over foreign kingdoms. Another version of the edict, probably closer to the actual wording, appears in Ezra 6:3-5. The edict is cause for great celebration among the exiles, who will finally be allowed to return to their homeland. Cyrus urges the people who remain behind in Babylon to provide financial support to the Jews for their long trip to Jerusalem and to cover the considerable expenses they will face once they have arrived.

Jeremiah had foretold that the exiles would not return to Jerusalem for 70 years (Jer 29:10). The actual period of the exile, from the time of the destruction of the temple in 586 to the Jews' restoration under Cyrus in 538, was only 48 years. If the year the temple reconstruction was completed, 515 B.C., is used, the prediction is more accurate.

The heads of the families of Judah and Benjamin, and the priests and the Levites—everyone whose spirit God had stirred—got ready to go up and rebuild the house of the Lord in Jerusalem. EZRA 1:5

The exiles were members of the southern tribe of Judah and of Benjamin, which had become a protectorate of Judah. The ten (actually nine and a half) tribes of the northern kingdom of Israel had been dispersed at the time of the Assyrian conquest in 722 B.C. The priests and Levites belonged to the tribe of Levi, which had never been given a tribal allotment of land in Israel like the other tribes. Instead of living off the land, the priests and the Levites had responsibility for special duties of worship. The priests, who made the sacrificial offerings, could trace their ancestry directly to Aaron, Moses' brother. The Levites were not allowed to perform sacrifices, but played a special role in teaching and providing music at worship services.

Leading the return of the first group of exiles is Sheshbazzar, who is called the "prince of Judah" (Ezra 1:8). His paramount mission is to rebuild the temple. Before the exile, daily sacrifices had been offered to God continuously in Jerusalem since King Solomon built the first temple in the tenth century B.C. The temple's destruction by the Babylonian king Nebuchadnezzar had put an end to that crucial link to God.

As the new Persian ruler of Babylon, Cyrus has at his disposal all the treasures and booty that Nebuchadnezzar had brought back from his many foreign campaigns. In a gracious act, Cyrus gives the Jews back the temple vessels that Nebuchadnezzar had taken when he captured Jerusalem.

Now these were the people of the province who came from those captive exiles whom King Nebuchadnezzar of Babylon had carried captive to Babylonia; they returned to Jerusalem and Judah, all to their own towns. EZRA 2:1

Family lineage and descent prove very important to the postexilic Jewish community under the leadership of Ezra and Nehemiah. The second chapter purportedly contains a list of all those who returned

with the first wave of exiles. The total number of people included in the list is fairly large (49,897 plus animals), and many scholars have suggested it does not actually represent those people who traveled with Sheshbazzar. Indeed, Sheshbazzar is not mentioned in the list and soon disappears from the narrative.

There are several indications that the list was compiled some time after the arrival of the first group in Jerusalem. For instance, it is written as if the people were already settled in their towns. The returnees are listed according to family units in verses 3-20, but according to towns, all in the vicinity of Jerusalem, in verses 21-35. Another clue that this chapter comes from a later period is that verse 69 mentions that the newcomers offered 61,000 darics as a voluntary tribute when they returned. The daric coin was named for Darius I, the Persian king who reigned from 521 to 486, after Cyrus.

When the seventh month came, and the Israelites were in the towns, the people gathered together in Jerusalem. EZRA 3:1

A climactic moment occurs during the seventh month (Tishri or September/October) of 520 B.C., after a second group of exiles has reached Jerusalem. The time has arrived to rebuild the altar in order to offer proper sacrifices. The returnees believe that the essential way of restoring their correct relationship with God is reconstituting the daily and seasonal sacrificial worship at their ancestral religious

Their years of exile ended by Cyrus's decree, joyful Jews set out for the return to Jerusalem; a color engraving by Julius Schnorr von Carolsfeld (1794-1872).

ANCIENT EMPIRES

*An enthroned Darius I
is depicted in this bas-relief
from Persepolis, Iran.*

When the Israelites *marched out of Egypt as a free people, they left behind their enslaving masters. But ahead lay a gauntlet of new overlords with grandiose schemes of world domination: the Assyrians, the Babylonians, and the Persians.*

As early as 1100 B.C., nearly a century before Israel crowned Saul its first king, Assyrian ruler Tiglath-pileser I had described himself as "king of the world." His successors pushed westward to the Mediterranean, demanding tributes from conquered lands. Among their victims was the northern kingdom of Israel. Trying to break free of vassalage, Israel was crushed by Assyria in 722 B.C., its deported people disappearing from history.

Seething under Assyrian tyranny, Babylonian nomads in southern Mesopotamia joined forces with Medes from the north to capture the Assyrian capital of Nineveh in 612 B.C. Within a few years, Babylon commanded an empire nearly as expansive as Assyria's and proved to be equally demanding and brutal. Judah made the same mistake with Babylon that Israel had with Assyria some 150 years earlier—and paid for its folly with the conquest and destruction of the kingdom in 586 B.C. But Judah's story had a happier ending. Two generations later, its exiles were permitted to return to Jerusalem and rebuild their unifying worship center, the temple. Their savior was Cyrus II of Persia, who overthrew the Babylonians in 539 B.C.

*The royal seal
shows Darius I as
a warrior.*

center. Constructing the altar is the first step toward the long-desired goal of rebuilding the temple.

The task is completed under the leadership of Jeshua, the high priest, and Zerubbabel, whom the Persians had appointed governor. Jeshua and Zerubbabel were good men for the job because they both had ties to Israel's preexilic days. Jeshua's grandfather was Seraiah, the high priest in Jerusalem at the time it fell to Babylon in 586 B.C. Zerubbabel was the grandson of the exiled king of Judah, Jehoiachin, which meant he was part of David's exalted royal line. The men and their assistants are eager to set up the altar on its old foundation and to build it according to the instructions found in the Law of Moses, that is, with "unhewn stones" (Deut 27:6).

After the altar has been reconstructed, the returnees can offer the daily burnt offerings and special sacrifices for new moons. Equally important is the observance of the regular festivals, with their own sacrifices, during which the male population of Israel is supposed to travel to Jerusalem for worship. By resuming sacrifices and celebrating the ancient festivals, the Jews are establishing a crucial line of continuity with the past. Yet this is only the beginning.

In the second year after their arrival at the house of God at Jerusalem, in the second month, Zerubbabel son of Shealtiel and Jeshua son of Jozadak made a beginning. EZRA 3:8

With the altar restored, the momentum to rebuild the temple itself increases. Jeshua and Zerubbabel give preliminary payment to the specially trained masons and woodworkers who will be needed for the architectural work. They provide food to the Sidonians and Tyrians, the workers from Phoenicia, who will fashion the long, straight beams of the famous cedars of Lebanon, like those used for Solomon's temple. And so in the second year after their return, Zerubbabel and Jeshua are able to organize the labor to begin rebuilding the temple. The Levites will oversee the construction work.

The laying of the foundation is cause for celebration. To mark the event, the sons of Asaph, a guild of the Levites responsible for music, lead the people in singing. But even though the event is filled with joy, there is a bittersweet note. Those who had seen the first temple in its original glory have to ponder its demise, and the divine punishment brought about by the exile. Thus the beginning of a new era in the life of the community evokes both shouts of joy and tears among the onlookers.

Then the people of the land discouraged the people of Judah, and made them afraid to build. EZRA 4:4

The rebuilding also arouses the curiosity of some of the longtime residents of the area, the Samaritans. According to their own history, they were descendants of the people who had been forcibly relocated to the northern section of Israel by the Assyrian king Esarhaddon in the seventh century B.C. They claimed to have worshiped Israel's God ever since that time. Zerubbabel is approached by these "people of the land," who ask if they can be part of the rebuilding effort. But Zerubbabel, Jeshua, and the rest of the leaders of the community rebuff them. They contend that Cyrus gave them the exclusive responsibility to rebuild the temple. Excluded from the building project, the Samaritans mount a campaign of intimidation against the returnees that puts a stop to the rebuilding efforts.

At Ezra 4:7, the tale of the opposition to the temple building is interrupted by the story of a much later opposition to the rebuilding of Jerusalem's wall during the era of King Artaxerxes I, who reigned from 465 to 425 B.C. The second account of opposition may have been included to show how much resistance the settlers had to endure in order to make their dream come to fruition, not only during the early years of the resettlement, but also much later.

Fragrant and ideal for decorative carving, cedars of Lebanon were used in the temple rebuilding.

Now the prophets, Haggai and Zechariah son of Iddo, prophesied to the Jews who were in Judah and Jerusalem, in the name of the God of Israel who was over them.
EZRA 5:1

The temple rebuilding is finally resumed during the second year of King Darius I. This time, the prophets Haggai and Zechariah are on hand to provide divine approval of the project. The urgency that the prophets feel about the temple rebuilding is not entirely clear from these verses, but is quite explicit in the prophetic books of Haggai and Zechariah, which are also preserved in the Bible. Yet not even the two prophets of God are able to squelch suspicions on the part of the provincial officials Tattenai and Shethar-bozenai. The two men send a letter to Darius asking him to search his records to make sure that the Jews have indeed been issued the necessary building permit from the royal authorities.

They searched the archives where the documents were stored in Babylon. But it was in Ecbatana, the capital in the province of Media, that a scroll was found. EZRA 6:1-2

Darius conducts a search of the royal archives in Babylon for the edict of his predecessor Cyrus authorizing the rebuilding of the Israelites' temple. It is found at the summer palace in Ecbatana. The version in this chapter, written in Aramaic, is different from the one that appears in Ezra 1:2-4. There is no mention of the repatriation of the Jews. Instead, the decree pledges financial help for the project from the royal Persian treasury.

Zerubbabel, the rebuilder of the temple; a 16th-century stained glass window

Darius returns a letter to Tattenai and Shetharbozenai, assuring them that the Jews have indeed been given permission to rebuild the temple. Moreover, Darius now specifies that funding for the rebuilding shall come out of the taxes that are gathered in Tattenai's own province, Beyond the River, and not out of the central Persian treasury.

They finished their building by command of the God of Israel and by decree of Cyrus, Darius, and King Artaxerxes of Persia. EZRA 6:14

With the support of successive Persian rulers and God working through the prophets Haggai and Zechariah, the second temple in Jerusalem is finally completed in the spring of 515 B.C. The inclusion in Ezra 6:14 of the name of King Artaxerxes is an anachronism because he did not begin his reign until 50 years later, in 465 B.C. His name may have been included by a scribe who knew of Artaxerxes's later support for the temple (Ezra 7:11-20) and who wanted to swell the list of royal supporters for the Jews' all-important temple project.

Given the relatively impoverished circumstances of the postexilic Jewish community, the dedication of the second temple could scarcely match that for Solomon's temple centuries earlier (1 Kgs 8). Nonetheless, the priests, the Levites, and the returned exiles all participate joyfully in the ceremonies. The priests and the Levites are installed in their proper places in order to fulfill their roles in worship, "as it is written in the book of Moses" (Ezra 6:18).

On the fourteenth day of the first month the returned exiles kept the passover.   EZRA 6:19

During the period of the monarchy, the temple served as the central worship site for festivals. The second temple does the same. Just six weeks after its dedication, the priests and Levites preside over the observance of Passover, the commemoration of the deliverance from slavery in Egypt. For seven days the Jews joyfully keep their all-important feast, eating roasted lamb to remind them of the lambs killed to ward off the plague of the firstborn sons and unleavened bread to remind them of the bread baked hastily before their flight. In 515 B.C., for the first time in nearly two generations, the Jews celebrate the festival as the Law of Moses required.

After this, in the reign of King Artaxerxes of Persia, Ezra son of Seraiah, son of Azariah, son of Hilkiah . . . went up from Babylonia.   EZRA 7:1, 6

There is a more than 50-year time lapse between the account of the Passover festival in the previous chapter and the introduction of Ezra. Several important facts about Ezra are given. He is a priest by birth, with a lineage stretching back to Aaron. He is a learned man, "skilled in the law of Moses," and a scribe who probably held an elevated position in the royal court, for "the king granted him all that he asked" (Ezra 7:6). Scribes filled an essential role in the ancient Near East as conservators and transmitters of culture. They were often sent on important diplomatic missions and acted as advisers to kings. No doubt Ezra knew Hebrew, the tongue of his ancestors and the language in which their scriptures were written; Aramaic, the international language of the Persian empire; and probably Persian and Akkadian as well. As a priest-scribe who has influence with Artaxerxes, Ezra holds an indispensible leadership position in the renewed Jewish community in Jerusalem. The king commissions him to establish a court system in Judah according to Jewish law, a charge Ezra takes very seriously.

Blessed be the Lord, the God of our ancestors, who put such a thing as this into the heart of the king to glorify the house of the Lord in Jerusalem.   EZRA 7:27

The narrative resumes with a first-person memoir, which opens with a short prayer in which Ezra blesses God for disposing Artaxerxes to beautify the temple. Knowing that he is in the good graces of God strengthens him to undertake the long journey to Jerusalem. The list of people who accompany Ezra is organized according to ancestral lineage. It begins with the priestly and Davidic lines, the most important from the standpoint of the continuation of the Jewish community. According to this account, those who return with Ezra number about 1,500 men. If wives and children are included, roughly 5,000 people make the trek to Jerusalem.

The effort of rebuilding the temple is shown in this print, one of 230 Bible scenes by Gustave Doré (1832-1883).

Ezra coordinates the move of this crowd of people, first by gathering them by a canal near Ahava. The exact location of this canal is unknown, but it was undoubtedly not far from Babylon. Ezra notices the conspicuous absence of Levites, so he sends off a small delegation to the town of Casiphia, again a place whose exact location in Mesopotamia remains unknown. Iddo, a leader of the people at Casiphia, not only chooses 38 Levites for the return mission to Jerusalem, but also appoints 220 temple servants to be attached to the Levites for special service.

As additional preparation for the trip, Ezra proclaims a fast, which is a ritualized way for the Jews to humble themselves before God to gain divine protection for their journey. So sure is Ezra that God will protect the band of returning Jews that he refuses to ask the king for a mounted escort. After the fast is completed, the Levites and temple servants are given the task of transporting the silver, gold, and sacred vessels that are bound for the temple storerooms in Jerusalem. The king, his attendants, and the Jews who remain in Babylon have all given generously for the temple's support. The amounts, however, are greatly exaggerated. For example, 650 talents of silver would have been more than 21 tons. Ezra's careful preparations ultimately pay off: "The hand of our God was upon us, and he delivered us from the hand of the enemy and from ambushes along the way" (Ezra 8:31). After nearly four months of hazardous travel, the intrepid band of returnees arrives safely in Jerusalem in August of 458 B.C.

"The people of Israel, the priests, and the Levites have not separated themselves from the peoples of the lands with their abominations." EZRA 9:1

Ezra soon learns that his role as interpreter and enforcer of the Jewish law is about to begin in earnest. Some of the local leaders inform him that many of those Jews now living in Jerusalem have intermarried with various members of the "peoples of the lands." The names included are from a fairly standard list found in slightly different combinations elsewhere in the Bible. Deuteronomy 7:1-5 specifically prohibits intermarriage with such people. The threat posed by intermarriage is the temptation to worship foreign gods, described as "abominations," brought to the marriage by foreign wives. The marriages are all between Jewish men, including some of the leading members of the community, and non-Jewish women. Perhaps because women were viewed as joining the family into which they married, Jewish women who intermarried were considered lost to their community and their religion.

Ezra's response to this crisis is one of shock and mourning. He has been sent by Artaxerxes to make sure that Jewish law is being properly observed, only to find this breakdown in the community. He immediately tears his clothes in a gesture of mourning, pulls out his hair, and begins a fast.

Ezra finally rouses himself in time for the evening sacrifice and offers a long prayer of public penitence on behalf of the misdeeds of his countrymen. The prayer occurs mostly in the third-person plural as a communal confession. Ezra acknowledges Israel's past history of sinfulness, which resulted in its subjection "to the sword, to captivity, to plundering, and to utter shame" (Ezra 9:7). But he also remembers God's graciousness in allowing the exiles to return to Jerusalem under the patronage of Persia's powerful rulers. Newly charged with ensuring fidelity to the law, Ezra is spurred not only to acknowledge the guilt of the community, but to take penitential action.

"So now let us make a covenant with our God to send away all these wives and their children." EZRA 10:3

Ezra's sincere demonstration of penitence attracts a crowd. One man, Shecaniah, speaks up and tells Ezra that the communi- ty has indeed broken the law against intermarriage with foreign women. On behalf of the community, Shecaniah pledges that they will commit themselves to a covenant whose stipulations seem harsh: to divorce their foreign wives and banish them and their children. Ezra acts decisively to issue a proclamation throughout Israel, calling for a mandatory assembly to take place within three days, under penalty of expulsion from the community. All the men duly gather in front of the temple after three days. There they shiver, both because of the cold December rain drenching them and in trepidation at the fate of their fledgling community. Ezra orders them to divorce their wives and separate themselves from the local population of non-Jews.

The reaction to Ezra's decree is overwhelmingly favorable, with only four voices raised in dissent. A commission is established to determine on a case-by-case basis who has actually violated the ban on intermarriage. The work takes roughly three months. Out of a total population of about 30,000, 111 cases of intermarriage, including 27 members of the clergy, are found.

By modern standards, Ezra's solution may seem extreme and even callous in disregarding the wives and children. But it was born of Ezra's sincere concern for maintaining the integrity of the Jewish people and their adherence to the Mosaic Law during this difficult period of transition. What had bound them together in exile was the belief that such adherence would eventually bring them home.

Jews of Ezra's time were hoping to recapture the glory of Solomon's Jerusalem, with fortified walls and a magnificent temple as depicted in this German woodcut dated 1493.

The historical account begun in the book of Ezra continues with the memoirs of Nehemiah, an intelligent, spirited man who, like Ezra, has risen to a position of prominence in the court of the Persian king during the Jews' exile in Babylon. Also like Ezra, Nehemiah is determined to return to his ancestral land and to do good works in order to secure the well-being of the Jewish people in the restored community in Jerusalem. He is granted permission to do so by King Artaxerxes I, who names him governor of Judah in 445 B.C. He holds the position for at least 12 years. One of Nehemiah's principal preoccupations on first reaching the city is rebuilding the walls and gates of Jerusalem, a project that he oversees successfully to its completion. He also supports Ezra's religious reforms, helping the Jews to adhere to the Law of Moses, as preserved in the first five books of the Bible, apparently brought back with them from Babylon. However, Nehemiah is not as stridently ideological as Ezra, and his position on intermarriage is more moderate.

The book of Nehemiah is composed primarily of Nehemiah's first-person memoir. But it also includes three chapters, Nehemiah 8-10, that describe more of Ezra's activities in Jerusalem and that may originally have appeared in the earlier of the two books.

As royal cupbearer, Nehemiah might have offered a drinking vessel like this Persian one dating to the 5th-century B.C.

I asked them about the Jews that survived, those who had escaped the captivity, and about Jerusalem. NEH 1:2

As the book opens, Nehemiah is living comfortably in Susa, the capital of the Persian empire. He is cupbearer to the king, a position of some influence and prestige. During the month of Chislev (November/December) of the 20th year of Artaxerxes's reign (445 B.C.), Nehemiah encounters one of his brothers, Hanani, who has brought disheartening news from the region of Judah. The situation in Jerusalem is dire because its walls and gates are still in ruins after the destruction of 586 B.C.

Nehemiah is devastated. Moved to tears, he begins a period of mourning. Moreover, he offers a prayer of penitence and petition, asking God to forgive his sins and those of the people of Israel. The prayer recalls the divine warning in Deuteronomy 30:1-5. If the Israelites are disobedient they will be exiled, but if they follow the divine law, God will gather them to Jerusalem. At the end of the prayer, Nehemiah asks God to let him find favor in the king's eyes.

In the month of Nisan, in the twentieth year of King Artaxerxes . . . I carried the wine and gave it to the king. NEH 2:1

The king had to have a high level of trust in the persons who brought his food and drink because of the possibility of poisoning by assassins. Such a close relationship is indicated by the king's dialogue with Nehemiah. Artaxerxes notices that Nehemiah is crestfallen. When Nehemiah tells him it is because of the sorry state of his ancestral city,

Jerusalem, the king authorizes Nehemiah's trip back to Judah, apparently with a commission as governor. He provides Nehemiah with letters of safe passage, one to give to the governors of the region "Beyond the River" (Neh 2:7), which encompasses the smaller provinces of Judah and Samaria, and another to give to the person in charge of the king's forest, so that Nehemiah can procure wood for his building plans in Jerusalem.

When Nehemiah arrives in the province, the officials Sanballat and Tobiah the Ammonite express their displeasure at the king's preferential treatment of Nehemiah and the Jews. Archaeological evidence confirms Sanballat's status as governor of the neighboring province of Samaria at that time. Tobiah was likely the governor of Ammon, a province to the east of Judah in what is modern Jordan. No doubt the two men feel a strong twinge of jealousy and insecurity at the arrival of Nehemiah, who clearly has lived in the good graces of the king of Persia.

I went out by night . . . and I inspected the walls of Jerusalem that had been broken down and its gates that had been destroyed by fire. NEH 2:13

The opposition of Sanballat and Tobiah does not, however, deter Nehemiah. After he has been in Jerusalem several days, he makes a nocturnal inspection of the city's walls and gates. His surreptitious mission confirms what his brother has told him. At one point Nehemiah's mule simply can go no farther; the way is impassable.

The next day, Nehemiah approaches the local Jewish officials and priests to say that the need for repairs is urgent. When they learn that Nehemiah has found favor in the eyes of God and also has the Persian king's endorsement, they pledge their support.

Yet others are ready to impede the reconstruction. Sanballat and Tobiah, who have already demonstrated their mistrust of the Jews, again take issue with Nehemiah. They are joined in opposition by a third official, Geshem the Arab. Their response to Nehemiah's plan implies that they believe that the Jews, in fortifying the walls, are preparing for an act of sedition, perhaps an assertion of Jewish independence. Nehemiah's reply reflects his own staunch faith: "The God of heaven is the one who will give us success, and we his servants are going to start building" (Neh 2:20).

Then the high priest Eliashib set to work with his fellow priests and rebuilt the Sheep Gate. NEH 3:1

Nehemiah acts as a catalyst to start the work of reconstructing the city's walls and gates. The labor force actually employed for the job is large and varied. The names and descriptions of the workers reveal a great deal about the political and social life of Judah in the fifth century B.C. Set to work on the northern, western, southern, and eastern sides of the walls, which altogether include nine gates, are 41 work crews. There are priests and Levites, goldsmiths and perfumers, temple servants, merchants, and governors of Judah's administrative districts. Some of the participants are mentioned according to their occupations, others, according to their hometown. Yet

some of the "nobles" (Neh 3:5) of Tekoa refuse to participate. Their opposition suggests that Geshem the Arab held sway over the southern region where Tekoa was located and was able to persuade Jews there to oppose the project.

Now when Sanballat heard that we were building the wall, he was angry . . . and he mocked the Jews. NEH 4:1

Learning that reconstruction has begun, Sanballat intensifies his opposition. His first reaction is to make fun of the Jews, belittling their efforts. His crony Tobiah joins in by questioning the strength of the wall: "Any fox going up on it would break it down!" (Neh 4:3).

The Jews are encircled by a coalition of opponents: Sanballat of Samaria stands to the north, the Arabs to the south, the Ammonites to the east, and the Ashdodites to the west. The response of Nehemiah to this threat reflects both his faith and his pragmatism. He offers prayers that express his abiding trust in God's protection and concern. But he also organizes the people so they will be armed and protected in the face of enemy assault.

Animosity has grown so great that work continues in a virtual state of siege. Those workers who haul the heavy loads are forced to carry a weapon in one

Nehemiah's inspection of Jerusalem's ruins is depicted in the print at left by Gustave Doré (1832-1883). The portion of the rebuilt walls above that survived the later Roman destruction have sealed arches—the Golden Gate that will open for the Messiah.

hand for protection. Each builder straps a sword to his side. Nehemiah dictates that instead of returning to their homes in the outskirts, all the workers should sleep within the walls of Jerusalem so that they can be on guard against enemy attack.

Now there was a great outcry of the people and of their wives against their Jewish kin.   NEH 5:1

Nehemiah's leadership is tested not only by external threats, but by internal divisions among the Jews as well. The lot of the Jewish workers is becoming increasingly difficult, especially because of a famine. Some are selling their children into slavery to fellow Jews in order to pay their debts. Others are forced to mortgage their houses and land just to procure food. Still others are borrowing money to pay the royal levy.

Nehemiah becomes enraged at this situation and calls a conference to deal with the problem. He chastises his fellow Jews, the nobles, and the officials who are exacting exorbitant interest on the property of the poorer workers. He accuses them of a crime, for charging fellow Jews interest on loans contravenes the Law of Moses (Lev 25:36-37; Deut 23:19-20). After Nehemiah points out their wrongdoing, the nobles and officials agree to restore interest payments to their fellow Jews and the crisis abates.

Moreover from the time that I was appointed to be their governor in the land of Judah . . . neither I nor my brothers ate the food allowance of the governor.   NEH 5:14

Nehemiah also shows his own willingness to sacrifice for the good of the community. As the Persian-appointed governor of Judah, he is authorized by King Artaxerxes to tax the people in the form of a food allowance. Nehemiah points out that prior provincial governors had taken not only food and wine from the people, but payments of silver as well. Nehemiah refuses such payments for 12 years and does not allow his brothers to enrich themselves at the expense of the people. So single-minded is he that he does not even acquire land, and uses his "servants" (Neh 5:16)—that is, the official cadre of laborers at the disposal of the governor—to work on the construction of the walls.

Nehemiah's largesse also includes providing food, indeed, a banquet, daily for more than 150 people, serving oxen, mutton, and chicken as well as wine for the assembly. A certain self-congratulatory tone of this passage notwithstanding, Nehemiah clearly is more generous than previous governors, and he asks the Lord to remember him for his good works on behalf of his fellow Jews.

This 3rd-century A.D. fresco from a Syrian synagogue may be Ezra reading the Law.

It was reported to Sanballat and Tobiah and to Geshem the Arab and to the rest of our enemies that I had built the wall and that there was no gap left in it.   NEH 6:1

Having treated some of the internal social and economic problems that beset his community and concluded with a summary of his own legacy as governor, Nehemiah in his memoir turns once again to a discussion of the external threat that presses on him. His opponents learn that the entire circuit of the wall has been repaired and they hatch a plot in an attempt to dispose of Nehemiah once and for all. Sanballat and Geshem ask Nehemiah to meet with them in one of the villages in the plain of Ono, some 25 miles to the northwest of Jerusalem. Nehemiah, certain of their evil intentions toward him, refuses. They persist in asking for a rendezvous. Finally, on the fifth invitation, Sanballat resorts to the same kind of threat he used in his earlier attempt to halt construction. Sanballat suggests that a rumor is circulating that Nehemiah has been building the wall to prepare for open rebellion against Persia and that Nehemiah wants to proclaim himself king of the Jews. But Nehemiah ignores Sanballat and the plot is defused.

A second scheme to snare Nehemiah also fizzles. Shemaiah the prophet, in league with Sanballat, tries to convince Nehemiah to hide in the temple as a safe haven from an assassination plot. But as a layman, Nehemiah is strictly forbidden from entering the temple proper, and he angrily refuses to commit such an act of desecration.

So the wall was finished on the twenty-fifth day of the month Elul, in fifty-two days.   NEH 6:15

The organization and industriousness of the Jews pays off, and the work is completed in less than two months. Their achievement is impressive because they have worked during the hottest months of the year, July and August, and carried arms to protect themselves against attack. The work impresses their neighbors as well, who see the completion of the wall as a sign that God has been involved in the project. Even so, Nehemiah notes that Tobiah continues his attempts to intimidate the Jews. Tobiah has close ties to members of Jerusalem society, some of whom try bringing the two men together. Yet Nehemiah remains unconvinced that Tobiah has good intentions.

Once the wall is completed, Nehemiah needs to consolidate his control over the city itself. He appoints his brother Hanani, who is already commander of the citadel, to be the mayor of the city as well. Because of Tobiah's network of allies in Jerusalem, there is a need for continued vigilance. Nehemiah's memoir states that the newly enclosed city is big, but is still not fully populated, an observation that reflects Nehemiah's concern about security.

With the situation in the city stabilized, Nehemiah decides it is time for a census of the population. In doing some preliminary research, he finds the list of the first returnees to Jerusalem. The list in Nehemiah 7:6-73 is the same as that found in Ezra 2; it is likely a compilation of the first succeeding waves of people who returned, rather than just those who returned with Sheshbazzar in 538 B.C.

When the seventh month came . . . all the people gathered together into the square before the Water Gate.
NEH 7:73, 8:1

Because Ezra plays such a prominent role in Nehemiah 8-10, most scholars believe that these chapters were originally a part of Ezra's memoir. The reference to Nehemiah and Ezra in 8:9 is the first place in the book where the two are depicted as contemporaries. Nehemiah's name may have been inserted later, just as Ezra's name was probably added to Nehemiah 12:26, 33, and 36 to link the two men. There is no reason, however, to doubt that the two were contemporaries.

The events portrayed in these chapters are important in the history of the religious practice of Judaism and Christianity because they depict a public reading from and interpretation of a book that was the forerunner of today's Bible. Ezra summons all the people to gather at a square outside the walls of Jerusalem in order to hear a reading from "the book of the law" (Ezra 8:23)—that is, some version of the Pentateuch, or first five books of the Old Testament. It is the first day of the month of Tishri (September/October), a day that is celebrated by Jews as Rosh Hashanah, or New Year's Day.

As Ezra reads from the book during the morning, the assigned Levites circulate among the people to make sure they understand what is being read. The Levites may have been translating from Hebrew, the language in which the Bible was written, into Aramaic, the language that was commonly spoken. But no doubt, the Levites also helped to interpret the meaning. Parts of the Bible were written roughly 500 years before the time of Ezra. Just as modern English speakers often need help in understanding the language and meaning of Shakespeare, so too, the Jews of the fifth century B.C. needed some assistance in understanding their spiritual and cultural heritage.

The heads of ancestral houses of all the people, with the priests and the Levites, came together to the scribe Ezra in order to study the words of the law. NEH 8:13

The day after the long public reading and worship assembly, Ezra calls together lay leaders along with priests and Levites for a special study session. In examining the scriptures, they realize

FESTIVAL OF SUCCOTH

For the harvest festival of Succoth Jews bring grain offerings to the wall supporting Jerusalem's temple mount.

A weeklong thanksgiving celebration at the close of harvest, in late September or early October, Succoth marks the gathering of the season's final crops: grapes, figs, and olives. Though similar to agricultural festivals in Canaan and other Near Eastern lands, the Israelite observance had one distinction: The celebrants lived outside in temporary huts made of tree branches. Succoth is Hebrew for "booths," which is why the festival is also called Booths. The practice served not as a reminder of the Israelites' hardships en route to the promised land but as an acknowledgment of the Lord's provision.

Once the refugee nation arrived in Canaan, the people were expected to make three trips to the worship center: Passover, at the outset of the springtime harvest; Shavuot, or Pentecost, at the close of the grain harvest 50 days later; and Succoth. Each time, they were required to bring harvest offerings in proportion to the blessings they had received: "No man should appear before the Lord empty-handed" (Deut 16:16).

In and around Jerusalem, happy Succoth pilgrims filled the fields and lined the streets with huts. For a week they worshiped and celebrated, waving clusters of branches as symbols of God's bounty. Each day, men gathered with priests at the temple altar to request rain for the next season and circle the sacred site seven times.

Ezra praised the Lord for separating earth from water and creating birds and fish; the two acts of creation are depicted in 16th-century stained glass windows.

that according to divine commandment (Lev 23:39-43; Num 29:12-38) the Jews are required to observe the Feast of Booths, also called Tabernacles, or in Hebrew, Succoth, during the month of Tishri. The feast commemorates the time of wandering in the wilderness of Sinai after the Exodus from Egypt, when the Israelites had lived in makeshift tents as they slowly made their way to the promised land. Once the Israelites settled in the land, the Feast of Booths became a harvest festival as well.

Now Ezra, the priests, and the Levites observe the festival strictly according to the instructions provided in the scriptures. The people gather olive, myrtle, and palm branches to make huts for themselves in the open squares at the Water Gate to the east of Jerusalem and the Gate of Ephraim to the north. They sleep in the huts for a week, while during the day, they listen to Ezra read from their sacred scriptures. The brief note, "And there was very great rejoicing" (Neh 8:17), suggests that this was no somber observance, but a week of joyful celebration.

The people of Israel were assembled with fasting and in sackcloth, and with earth on their heads.   NEH 9:1

Another ceremony two weeks after the Feast of Booths is a more serious affair. On the 24th day of Tishri, the people gather for a rite of penitence. They are garbed in sackcloth with earth sprinkled on their heads, both of which are traditional signs of mourning. Then "those of Israelite descent" (Neh 9:2)—that is, the Jews—separate themselves from the foreigners who are present at the gathering. Just as it is only the Israelites and their descendants who are expected to dwell in booths during the joyous Feast of Booths, so too, only the Israelites and their postexilic descendants are expected to partici-

pate in this rite of penitence. The Jews are confessing the sins of their ancestors, no doubt chief among them the sin of idolatry. One-quarter of the day is devoted to listening to additional readings from the Bible; the second quarter of the day is devoted to a communal confession and worship service.

"You are the Lord, you alone; you have made heaven, . . . the earth and all that is on it, the seas and all that is in them."   NEH 9:6

Although some translations of the Bible suggest that Ezra offered the long prayer in Nehemiah 9:6-37, the original Hebrew does not contain the introduction "And Ezra said." It is safest to assume, then, that the long confessional prayer is a continuation of the prayer of the Levites begun in verse 5.

The prayer contains a long recital of the entire history of Israel, from the creation of the world to the present. The prayer presents a strong contrast between the graciousness and mercy of God and the sinfulness of the Israelites during their long relationship. It is similar to some of the psalms that rehearse Israelite history (Psalms 78, 105, 106, 135), though this prayer is unique in beginning with creation. Throughout the entire prayer, God's gracious activity toward the Israelites is recounted. Even though the Israelites repeatedly rebelled against God by worshiping idols, God repeatedly forgave them. The prayer mentions the exile only briefly in verse 30 and then treats the present situation. The descendants of the Israelites lament their current status in the promised land, where they are now at the mercy of a foreign power.

Because of all this we make a firm agreement in writing, and on that sealed document are inscribed the names of our officials, our Levites, and our priests.   NEH 9:38

The penitential ceremony concludes with a covenant, a written document signed by priests, Levites, and the lay leaders. They and all the people commit themselves to "observe and fulfill all the commandments of the Lord" (Neh 10:29). The covenant marks a fitting conclusion to a day of public confession, during which the Jews have acknowledged their corporate guilt in straying from the law.

Some scholars have suggested that the list of specifics included in Nehemiah 10:30-39 may well have been added later. The list makes more sense coming after the measures prescribed by Nehemiah in chapter 13. It includes such stipulations as not intermarrying with non-Jews, observing the sabbath and important festivals, and bringing proper sacrificial offerings. Last but not least is the pledge to maintain the temple, the central locus of worship for the returnees. The Law of Moses remains the standard by which the community's behavior and legal codes are judged legitimate.

The rest of the people cast lots to bring one out of ten to live in the holy city Jerusalem, while nine-tenths remained in the other towns. NEH 11:1

In spite of all the work done to restore the city, Jerusalem is underpopulated. The community leaders, like Nehemiah's brother Hanani, live in the city itself, but most of the people dwell in the small villages surrounding Jerusalem, where they can easily maintain their farms in the countryside. In order to increase the population in the holy city, lots are drawn to determine which tenth of the population should live in Jerusalem itself. The effort is successful and the nine-tenths of the population who remain in their towns applaud the goodwill of those who move to Jerusalem.

Now at the dedication of the wall of Jerusalem they sought out the Levites in all their places, to bring them to Jerusalem to celebrate the dedication with rejoicing. NEH 12:27

Like other sections of Ezra and Nehemiah, the story of the dedication of the city wall seems to belong in another section of the book, perhaps after the note of its completion in Nehemiah 6. Its placement nonetheless serves a good purpose because it emphasizes near the end of the book the dual contributions of Ezra and Nehemiah to the rebuilding of Jerusalem. The celebration is marked by festive music made with a variety of instruments: cymbals, harps, lyres, and the sound of human voices. Professional singers have gathered from many villages around Jerusalem. Nehemiah divides the great crowd into two groups. Starting out at the same place on the wall, each group marches in the opposite direction around the wall. When the two companies meet up with each other, they proceed to the temple to give thanks and offer sacrifices. The happiness felt by the restored community and the exuberance of their celebration is apparent: "The joy of Jerusalem was heard far away" (Neh 12:43).

On the same day that the dedication takes place, Nehemiah also charges the people with overseeing the collections for temple personnel, who are reliant on the generosity of the community. The special duties of the priests, Levites, singers, and gatekeepers are said to have dated back to the time of King David and King Solomon. In this, as in all of the reforms that he

launches, Nehemiah is careful to maintain continuity with the past. The celebration connected with the wall's dedication concludes with more reading from the book of Moses.

Nehemiah is recalled to Persia in about 433 B.C. Upon his return, he discovers that his nemesis Tobiah the Ammonite has presumptuously installed himself in a room in the temple with the help of his relative, the priest Eliashib. Nehemiah promptly evicts him and ritually cleanses the room. Chapter 13 reports other reform measures instituted by Nehemiah that correspond to the specific pledges of the covenant document of chapter 10.

Thus I cleansed them from everything foreign, and I established the duties of the priests and Levites, each in his work. NEH 13:30

The final verses of Nehemiah summarize in his own words what he tried to do for the restoration community. Painfully aware of the errors of Israel's past, Nehemiah felt acutely the need to reform the behavior of his fellow Jews in Jerusalem and Judah. Making a clear distinction between what was distinctively Jewish and what was foreign, maintaining the temple and its priesthood, and ensuring fidelity to the sacrificial system and community festivals were Nehemiah's priorities. But clearly it had been and would continue to be an uphill battle, for the book ends with Nehemiah's plaintive prayer to God: "Remember me, O my God, for good" (Neh 13:31).

Jerusalem's temple continued to fascinate artists long after its ultimate destruction; a 14th-century French artist imagined it as a turreted fortress.

A young Jewish woman marries the king of Persia and saves her people from a devastating massacre. That is the dramatic tale told in the book of Esther. The main purpose of the book is to supply an "historical" origin for the festival of Purim, which celebrates the deliverance of the Jews from persecution. The book appears in the Hebrew Bible as the last of the Five Scrolls, or Megilloth, read each year to commemorate certain Jewish festivals.

Although the story of Esther offers some historical detail, most scholars believe it to be primarily fiction, perhaps a folktale. The intrigues of a foreign court are woven into a suspenseful and ironic narrative in which good triumphs over evil. The emphasis is on the action rather than the characters, which are largely two-dimensional. Yet Esther's role as the deliverer of the Jews is striking, since in postexilic Jewish life, women's roles were mainly limited to the household.

Interestingly, God is never mentioned in the book, the only book in the Bible other than the Song of Solomon in which this is the case. This may be because it was not considered appropriate to include God in a book intended to be read at a raucous festival of merrymaking. God and piety are featured prominently, however, in the Greek version of the book (see page 177).

Esther is thought to have been written between the fourth and late second centuries B.C., but its author is unknown. Although the story has been popular among Jews since antiquity, its inclusion in the Jewish and Christian canons was controversial, largely because religion plays such a negligible role in the book and vengeance on the part of the Jews is featured so prominently. Some scholars, however, have held a high opinion of the book. Maimonides, the great medieval Jewish philosopher, believed Esther ranked second in importance only to the Torah.

Esther kneels before King Ahasuerus; a scene from a French book about famous women, dated 1505.

This happened in the days of Ahasuerus, the same Ahasuerus who ruled over one hundred twenty-seven provinces from India to Ethiopia. ESTH 1:1

A description of life in the Persian court sets the scene for the story. In his third year as king, Ahasuerus displays his kingdom's fabulous wealth by giving a sumptuous banquet for government officials and ministers, which lasts for 180 days. This is followed by a weeklong banquet for the people of the citadel of Susa. This was the fortified acropolis, or royal compound, within the city—300 miles northwest of the capital Persepolis—where the Persian kings had their winter residence. The guests drink wine with abandon from golden goblets and recline on couches of gold and silver. At the same time, Queen Vashti holds a separate banquet for the women.

King Ahasuerus was probably meant to be Xerxes I, who ruled the Persian Empire from 486 to 465 B.C. (The Greek translators of the Septuagint, however, believed him to be Artaxerxes II, who ruled from 404 to 359 B.C.) According to the fifth-century B.C. Greek historian Herodotus, Xerxes ruled over 20 satrapies, or territories, each of which contained several provinces—a considerably smaller domain than that

which the author attributes to Ahasuerus. The Persian empire did, however, stretch from the Indus valley in India to Nubia (southern Egypt). Moreover, the Persians were well known for their lavish feasts.

On the seventh day, when the king was merry with wine, he commanded . . . the seven eunuchs who attended him, to bring Queen Vashti before the king. ESTH 1:10-11

But the queen refuses to come. This act of disobedience so outrages the king that he asks his council of advisers if the queen deserves punishment for ignoring the command. Ahasuerus never considers why the queen refuses him, typifying the rashness that he displays time after time in the story.

The advisers are as outraged as the king by Vashti's behavior. They fear that when the women of the kingdom—including their own wives—learn of Vashti's refusal to honor her husband's order, they will follow her example. They recommend that the king issue a decree deposing Vashti and choose a new queen in her place. Ahasuerus assents, sending letters to every corner of the kingdom by his famed courier service. A search is begun for beautiful virgins from whom the king will select a new consort.

Now there was a Jew in the citadel of Susa whose name was Mordecai. ESTH 2:5

During Xerxes's reign, the eastern Persian empire was home to a sizable community of Jews taken into exile by the Babylonians in 586 B.C. After King Cyrus II of Persia defeated the Babylonians in 539 B.C., he allowed the Jews to return to Jerusalem, but many have chosen to remain. Among them is Mordecai, a Benjaminite who has adopted and raised his orphaned cousin Esther, also called Hadassah. The name Esther is from Ishtar, the Babylonian goddess of love; Hadassah is the Hebrew word for myrtle. The name Mordecai comes from Marduk, the Babylonian god of creation.

The beautiful Esther is taken into the palace with the other young women. She becomes a favorite of Hegai, the eunuch in charge of the virgins, who lavishes her with cosmetics, food, and seven maids from the palace. Presumably, the food referred to is not kosher. But Mordecai has instructed Esther not to reveal that she is Jewish, so it follows that she would not have called attention to her religion by adhering to Jewish dietary practices.

Esther is given the standard beauty treatment, "six months with oil of myrrh and six months with per-

With a tap of his regal wand, Ahasuerus selects the beauteous Esther as his new consort; a late-16th-century Italian painting.

fumes and cosmetics" (Esth 2:12). At last, it is Esther's turn to go in to the king. Ahasuerus, like everyone who sees her, is captivated by Esther's beauty and charm, and he chooses her as his queen. This ends a four-year search.

Apparently there are no objections to the marriage between Ahasuerus and Esther, although their union ignores the strictures on marriage at the time. The Persian king was supposed to choose a wife from one of the seven noble families, but Ahasuerus is presumably so smitten that he does not ask about Esther's background. And Esther expresses no qualms about marrying a Gentile, even though Mosaic Law forbids marriages between Jews and foreigners.

In those days, while Mordecai was sitting at the king's gate, Bigthan and Teresh, two of the king's eunuchs, who guarded the threshold, became angry and conspired to assassinate King Ahasuerus. ESTH 2:21

From his position at the king's gate—an indication that he was a palace official—Mordecai hears of the assassination plot. He reports it to Queen Esther, and she relays it to the king. The two eunuchs are hanged for their crime, and the events are duly noted in the annals, the official record of the king's actions. But Mordecai is not rewarded for his loyalty, an oversight that later proves important.

After these things King Ahasuerus promoted Haman son of Hammedatha the Agagite, and advanced him and set his seat above all the officials who were with him. ESTH 3:1

Haman is an Agagite, which designates him as an enemy of the Jews. Agag, king of the Amalek tribe, inadvertently caused the downfall of Saul when Saul disobeyed God's command and killed all the Amalekites but Agag (1 Sam 15:2-26). The Amalekites had earlier earned Israel's enmity by attacking the Hebrews fleeing Egypt (Ex 17:14-16).

The king commands that everyone bow to Haman, the new prime minister, but Mordecai refuses. Although it might be assumed that he does this because he is a Jew, there are a number of examples in the Old Testament of Jews bowing to kings and other figures of authority (2 Sam 14:4; 1 Kgs 1:16). When word of this blatant disrespect reaches Haman, his rage is so great that he schemes to destroy not just Mordecai, but all Jews in Ahasuerus's kingdom.

Haman is superstitious, and he casts a lot, called a Pur, to determine an auspicious day for the massacre. The lot falls on a date nearly a year away: the thirteenth day of the month of Adar (February/March). This may be a bad omen for Haman's chances of success, since the Persians considered 13 an unlucky number. Then Haman tells Ahasuerus that an unnamed group of people in the kingdom is breaking the king's laws, and asks for a royal decree for their destruction, promising to pay 10,000 talents of silver into the king's treasury if it is issued.

At the second banquet Esther traps her foe Haman, telling the king of the vizier's plan to destroy her people; a late-18th-century French artist painted this version of the scene.

On Haman's word alone, Ahasuerus agrees to the request. A decree is issued calling for the massacre of all the Jewish men, women, and children in the kingdom, and the plunder of their property. The king may have been influenced by the bribe, although Haman offered such an outlandish sum of money—equal to millions of dollars—that he could never have paid it. Instead, it may have been understood that the largest share of the plunder would go to the king. Ahasuerus seems to decline the bribe, replying, "The money is given to you, and the people as well, to do with them as it seems good to you" (Esth 3:11). This could be interpreted as court etiquette, with both men understanding the statement means exactly the opposite. Or the king may actually be consigning the spoils to Haman, a plot device that would leave Haman the only one to benefit from the slaughter.

When Mordecai learned all that had been done, Mordecai tore his clothes and put on sackcloth and ashes, and went through the city, wailing with a loud and bitter cry. ESTH 4:1

The Jews of the kingdom echo Mordecai's response to this devastating decree: They put on sackcloth and ashes, which were traditional signs of grief, and mourn, fast, and lament. Although praying is never mentioned, the fasting may have had a religious intent. Esther sends one of her eunuchs to Mordecai to find out what has happened, and Mordecai tells him about the decree for the destruction of the Jews and the bribe that Haman has promised the king. He charges the eunuch to show a copy of the decree to Esther and to urge her to go to the king and beg for the lives of her people.

But Esther shrinks from the task. She replies that it is common knowledge that the penalty for appearing before the king without being summoned is death. Esther has apparently lost the king's favor, for she has not been called to him for 30 days. Mordecai reminds her that her regal position will not protect her from the massacre. Indeed, he says, "If you keep silence at such a time as this, relief and deliverance will rise for the Jews from another quarter, but you and your father's family will perish" (Esth 4:14). Many scholars interpret the reference to another quarter as a prediction of divine intervention. Mordecai adds that perhaps destiny brought Esther to her royal position for just this set of circumstances.

Now a change comes over Esther. She is no longer the passive young woman who follows the instructions of Mordecai and the eunuchs, but the one in charge. She commands Mordecai to lead the Jews of Susa in a fast for her for three days, after which she will approach the king. Her fear seems to have vanished when she says, "If I perish, I perish" (Esth 4:16).

On the third day Esther put on her royal robes and stood in the inner court of the king's palace, opposite the king's hall. ESTH 5:1

In spite of Esther's misgivings, the king extends the golden scepter to her, allowing her to enter. He asks, "What is your request? It shall be given you, even to the half of my kingdom" (Esth 5:3). But Esther does not state her request right away, perhaps not believing that the king will grant it as easily as his statement promises. Instead, she invites the king and Haman to a banquet that she has prepared. While they feast and drink wine, she invites the two of them to a second banquet the following day, where she promises to reveal her petition. The second delay in relaying her request to the king is likely a literary device intended to heighten suspense.

Haman leaves the first banquet in buoyant spirits because of this special treatment by the queen. Then he encounters Mordecai, who, even though he has a death sentence hanging over him, will not so much as rise in Haman's presence. Haman is outraged, feeling that all his wealth and honors are meaningless in the face of this kind of disrespect. When he expresses his fury to his wife, Zeresh, and friends, they urge Haman to build a gallows and ask the king to hang Mordecai. He has a gallows built that is 50 cubits—some 75 feet—high, a height as extravagantly inflated as Haman's hatred of Mordecai.

On that night the king could not sleep, and he gave orders to bring the book of records, the annals, and they were read to the king. ESTH 6:1

Fortune intervenes to save Mordecai. Listening to a reading of the annals, the king learns that Mordecai was never rewarded for saving his life. At that very moment Haman comes into the outer court to ask the king to hang Mordecai. The king calls Haman in and asks, "What shall be done for the man whom the king wishes to honor?" (Esth 6:6). Haman is so self-confident that he assumes the king can only be referring to him, so he proposes his own greatest desire: that the honoree be clothed in royal robes, seated on one of the king's horses, and led in glory through the town square by a high official. To Haman's great chagrin, the king instructs him to do all this for Mordecai. The humiliated Haman is forced to obey: He leads a berobed Mordecai on horseback through the city square, proclaiming his enemy's honor.

After this indignity, Haman's wife and friends see the handwriting on the wall. Zeresh predicts that Haman will not win against Mordecai, and if Mordecai is a Jew, he will be Haman's downfall. This seems to refer to the centuries-old feud between their respective ancestors. Haman is called to the queen's second banquet, his last hope for redemption.

On the second day, as they were drinking wine, the king again said to Esther, "What is your petition, Queen Esther? It shall be granted you." ESTH 7:2

Esther replies that she and her people have been sold into destruction, and pleads for their lives. The king is taken aback and asks who has done this terrible deed. Esther says, "A foe and enemy, this wicked Haman!" (Esth 7:6). The king is so angry that he storms from the room, leaving the terrified Haman to throw himself on the couch where Esther is reclining. When the king returns, he mistakes Haman's position near the queen for an assault on her. Ironically, he orders Haman hanged on the very gallows that Haman had intended for Mordecai.

Esther tells the king about Mordecai's relationship to her, and the king bestows his signet ring on Mordecai, making him Haman's successor. The king also gives Esther Haman's estate, which she transfers to Mordecai. Haman's ruin is complete.

A mortified Haman is forced to lead his enemy Mordecai in triumph through the streets of Susa; an 1865 engraving by Gustave Doré.

In this German scroll of the book of Esther, dated 1806, blessings given before and after the reading are framed within two flags and two hearts (right).

Then Esther spoke again to the king; she fell at his feet, weeping and pleading with him to avert the evil design of Haman the Agagite and the plot that he had devised against the Jews. ESTH 8:3

But the Jews are still in grave danger, for the king replies that he is powerless to revoke an edict that has been issued in his name. (This appears to be literary license and not actually true of royal decrees in the Persian empire.) Ahasuerus will, however, allow Esther and Mordecai to issue another edict in the king's name and will leave it to them to write whatever they like. So Mordecai has an edict written that allows the Jews, on the very day that has been set for their own destruction, "to assemble and defend their lives, to destroy, to kill, and to annihilate any armed force of any people or province that might attack them" (Esth 8:11). This is an exact reversal of Haman's edict, and the stage is set for a great and bloody battle.

Mordecai appears in royal robes and a gold crown, and the Jews of Susa rejoice at the change of their fortune. Indeed, "many of the peoples of the country professed to be Jews" (Esth 8:17), which could mean that they so feared the outcome of the coming battle that they pretended to be Jews. Some theologians, however, see this as a sign of solidarity between Jews and Gentiles, with the Persians siding with the Jews or even converting to Judaism.

Now in the twelfth month . . . on the thirteenth day . . . the Jews gathered in their cities throughout all the provinces of King Ahasuerus to lay hands on those who had sought their ruin. ESTH 9:1-2

The Jews slaughter their enemies, 500 people in the citadel of Susa alone, including the ten sons of Haman. In the provinces they kill an astonishing number—75,000 people, apparently without a single Jewish casualty. "What further is your request?" (Esth 9:12), Ahasuerus queries Queen Esther. She asks that the Jews of Susa be allowed another day to destroy their enemies, and that the bodies of Haman's

sons be hanged from the gallows. The ever pliable Ahasuerus assents, and the next day the Jews of Susa kill an additional 300 people. They do not take plunder, even though they are allowed to, perhaps to signal that greed was not a motivating factor in the slaughter of their enemies.

Many biblical scholars are troubled by this massacre. Some find it repugnant that Jews would sink to the depths of their persecutors. But others consider that a people that had been so persecuted would naturally take advantage of an opportunity for revenge, especially at a time when prejudice against the Jews is apparently on the rise and their very survival is in question.

In any event, the story focuses more on the celebration afterward than on the killing itself. Because the Jews in the provinces fought only on the thirteenth day of Adar, they celebrated the victory over their persecutors on the fourteenth day. But the Jews in Susa fought on the thirteenth and fourteenth and celebrated on the fifteenth of Adar, making it "a day of feasting and gladness. . . . a holiday on which they send gifts of food to one another" (Esth 9:18-19). This discrepancy seems designed to explain why Purim, a relatively minor holiday on the Jewish calendar, is still celebrated for two days.

Scenes from the book of Esther on a late-19th-century embroidery (top to bottom): Haman leading Mordecai in triumph, and Esther before the king; horsemen spreading news of the Jews' reprieve; Haman and his sons hanged

ADDITIONS TO ESTHER

The book of Esther found in the Septuagint, the Greek version of the Old Testament, contains six major additions to the book of Esther of the Hebrew Bible and also a number of minor changes in the text. Altogether there are 107 additional verses in the Greek text.

Scholars agree that the Hebrew book was written first and the additions came later, probably intended to turn the secular tale of Esther into a religious story and inject the traditions of Judaism that are left out of the original version. Here, the characters of Esther and Mordecai have been transformed from brave and quick-thinking saviors of their people to pious individuals who rely on God for salvation. The additions contain more than 50 references to God.

Addition A, which takes place before chapter 1, recounts Mordecai's dream, in which two dragons prepare to do battle and every nation prepares to fight "the righteous nation" (Add Esth 11:7). But God answers his people's plea and, as a river springs up, the lowly are exalted. In the second part of Addition A, Mordecai overhears a plot to kill the king, here and throughout named Artaxerxes. (This is separate from the plot in Esther 2:21-23.) He warns the king, who rewards him, but in so doing, Mordecai earns the enmity of Haman.

Addition B is the text of the king's decree authorizing the destruction of all the Jews in his realm.

Addition C follows Esther's request that Mordecai lead a three-day fast for her. Mordecai prays, beseeching God to spare his people. He justifies not bowing down to Haman by saying that he will give obeisance only to God. Next, Esther prays to God for assistance before she faces the king: "Put eloquent speech in my mouth before the lion, and turn his heart to hate the man who is fighting against us"

(Add Esth 14:13). Unlike the Esther in the Hebrew book, this Esther expresses loathing for her royal position and marriage to a Gentile.

Addition D is a more dramatic representation of Esther going in to the king unsummoned. The king is so furious that the terrified Esther faints. But "God changed the spirit of the king to gentleness" (Add Esth 15:8), and Artaxerxes tenderly gathers Esther in his arms and comforts her.

Addition E is the text of the king's second decree, which vilifies Haman and annuls the first decree. It also instructs the king's subjects to aid the Jews on the day of battle, and to "permit the Jews to live under their own laws" (Add Esth 16:19).

Addition F contains Mordecai's recollection and interpretation of his dream. The two dragons were Haman and himself, the river was Esther, and the nations were all the foreign peoples that wanted to destroy Israel. A postscript attests that the book is authentic and that it was brought to Egypt in "the fourth year of the reign of Ptolemy and Cleopatra" (Add Esth 11:1), thought to be about 114 B.C.

The additions were probably completed around that time, although written in different periods and by different authors. Their inclusion in the scriptural canon has long been debated. They never appear in Hebrew Bibles. In Protestant Bibles, Additions to Esther is a separate book placed in the Apocrypha with other noncanonical texts. Roman Catholics, however, consider the additions to be deuterocanonical and therefore authoritative. In his translation of the Bible into Latin, the so-called Vulgate of A.D. 405, the church father Jerome placed the six major additions directly after the Hebrew text of Esther, a practice that Roman Catholic Bibles usually follow. In the Greek Bible they appear in sequence, integrated into the original version.

Mordecai . . . sent letters to all the Jews who were in all the provinces of King Ahasuerus, both near and far, enjoining them that they should keep the fourteenth day of the month Adar and also the fifteenth day of the same month, year by year. ESTH 9:20-21

The feast of Purim is thus introduced, probably having originated in Persian New Year's festivities in which lots (Pur) were cast to determine people's fortunes for the year to come. Mordecai, who is now prime minister, tells the Jews to celebrate these days with feasts, giving gifts of food and being charitable to the poor. They are instructed that "these days of Purim should never fall into disuse among the Jews, nor should the commemoration of these days cease among their descendants" (Esth 9:28). These explicit instructions may be designed to give legitimacy to a Jewish holiday that is not mentioned in the Torah.

The book's final chapter is a reminder of the great power of the king that was described in the opening chapter. But now, Mordecai and the Jews share that power. Jews and Gentiles are linked in a victory over persecution—a message of hope for oppressed people everywhere. The book of Esther is still read aloud in synagogues at Purim, with the congregation stomping and booing whenever Haman's name is mentioned.

Haman hanged; a 19th-century Russian silver noisemaker

The book of Job is, for several reasons, among the most challenging of the texts preserved in the Hebrew Bible. Its date of composition (perhaps the sixth century B.C.) is difficult to determine; its beautifully crafted language poses innumerable problems, even for those well versed in Hebrew; and its theology openly challenges more common forms of piety. Yet, despite the difficulties in understanding Job, the book's unwavering honesty about human suffering has won it a well-deserved place among the classics of world literature. Perhaps it is more accurate to talk about the books of Job since for some time scholars have recognized that Job can be divided into two main parts. One part includes what are called the prologue (Job 1:1-2:10) and the epilogue (Job 42:7-17). In the prologue Job is tested by God at the instigation of Satan and proves righteous. Job's faith is rewarded in the epilogue by the restitution of all he has lost. In the long, poetic central part of the book (Job 3:1-42:6), Job presents overwhelming evidence of the injustice he has suffered despite his righteousness. Here, Job seeks some answer to the problem of human suffering and, in the end, learns from God himself that it is not his place to raise such questions. It is Job's courage and integrity in probing the mystery of why God permits suffering to exist that make the book simultaneously so problematic and profound.

As Satan hovers above, the afflicted Job is berated by his wife in this 1540 woodcut.

There was once a man in the land of Uz whose name was Job. JOB 1:1

The prologue gives brief, tantalizing biographical information about Job. He lives in Uz, possibly Edom, a land east of the Dead Sea. There are subtle hints that he is a contemporary of the patriarchs (c. 2000-1800 B.C.). This time frame lends Job's experience a universal tone that may account for the book's enduring popularity. Job is "a blameless and upright man who fears God and turns away from evil" (Job 1:8), a description that supports Job's own protestations of righteousness. Finally, he is wealthy, a statement that upholds the biblical tradition of a direct correlation between human deeds and destiny. In other words, Job's good fortune is a direct result of his righteousness. What follows, however, presents a much more complicated vision of the relationship between piety and reward.

"But stretch out your hand now, and touch all that he has, and he will curse you to your face." JOB 1:11

In a scene set in the heavenly court, Satan questions Job's motivation for serving God. The name Satan is merely a transliteration of a Hebrew word meaning "the adversary." Satan is depicted as one of many members of God's divine assembly. Satan's role in that assembly resembles that of a special prosecutor whose duty it is to make sure public figures measure up to their reputations. Satan as an active evil antagonist is a later development that emerges from his relatively benign role in the Hebrew Bible. Indeed, it is God who instigates the events that lead to Job's ruin when

he addresses Satan: "Have you considered my servant Job?" (Job 1:8, 2:3). Through two cycles of disasters that he brings on Job, Satan tests whether Job's fear of God is motivated by true piety or is merely the result of having been consistently blessed.

"Shall we receive the good at the hand of God and not receive the bad?" JOB 2:10

Having lost all his possessions, his entire family other than his wife, and now afflicted with sores from head to toe, Job is challenged by his wife: "Do you still persist in your integrity? Curse God, and die" (Job 2:9). His response in the following verse raises the main issue in the book of Job. Simply put, does one love and serve God only in periods of well-being? Is such service required without any hope of reward and even in the midst of despair and disaster? Satan's wager is that Job, having been too comfortable, will abandon God once he is out of his watchful eye.

Following Job's rejection of his wife's plea to curse God, three friends of Job are introduced: Eliphaz, Bildad, and Zophar. Their appearance marks the transition from the prologue to the main poetic section of the book; their dialogues with Job form chapters 3-27. After a moving lament about the day of his birth, Job is challenged in turn by each of his friends to consider the possibility that he deserves his fate. To each friend, Job has a pointed response. Through three rounds of successive questioning by his friends (the third discourse of Zophar is missing) and replies by Job, traditional attitudes about righteousness and reward are severely put to the test and found wanting.

"Let the day perish in which I was born, and the night that said, 'A man-child is conceived.'" JOB 3:3

The first round of dialogues with his friends actually begins with Job's poignant cursing of the day on which he was born. Containing one vivid metaphor after another, Job's language is reminiscent of the account of creation in Genesis, but he seems not only to curse the day of his birth but even to call for the reversal of creation itself. At the very least, says Job, he might have been "buried like a stillborn child" (Job 3:16). Job's curse is in striking contrast to the joy usually expressed at the birth of a child, a contrast that draws attention to just how desperate Job's situation is. Yet, and most important, Job refuses to curse God. He is playing a dangerous game with his language, moving close to the blasphemy that he ultimately cannot bring himself to utter. It is ironic, of course, that Job has no knowledge that his situation is the result of a wager between God and the adversary, Satan. One of the troubling theological realities of the book of Job is that human suffering can occur as the result of God's willingness to bet that humans will love him no matter what.

"If one ventures a word with you, will you be offended? But who can keep from speaking?" JOB 4:2

The first of the three friends to speak to Job is Eliphaz. He points out to Job that, when others suffered, he always had words of comfort and encouragement. However, now that fate has brought calamity on Job, his courage fails him. Eliphaz's speech is typical of human response to what is perceived as the inconsistency of others' behavior. But it entirely misses the depth of Job's current suffering.

Eliphaz shifts his argument in a way that questions Job's innocence: "Think now, who that was innocent ever perished?" (Job 4:7). For Job, and most thoughtful readers, the answer to Eliphaz's question would be a resounding, "The innocent perish all the time." The text subtly challenges conventional wisdom and common piety by suggesting that Job's suffering, rather than being atypical, is all too common. What is at issue in the book of Job is how to cope with suffering and to love God even when life is at a low point. This has led many to presume that Job was written during or shortly after the exile in Babylon (586-538 B.C.), when the Jews were at the nadir of their existence. That likely historical situation does not obscure Job's profoundly timeless and penetrating theological insights.

"For the arrows of the Almighty are in me; my spirit drinks their poison; the terrors of God are arrayed against me." JOB 6:4

Job's response to Eliphaz's first speech draws attention to the extreme nature of his suffering. Job contends that his outcry is justified and that he is not able to take much more of the torture he now

THE DEVIL IN THE OLD TESTAMENT

Satan is one of the most mysterious characters in the Hebrew Bible, where his name is a word meaning "adversary." The seer Balaam was stopped en route to Moab by an angel standing in the road as his adversary (Num 22:22). David was described as the adversary of the Philistines (1 Sam 29:4). Perhaps most surprising are references to God and Satan used interchangeably in two parallel stories. In 2 Samuel 24:1, God provokes David into ordering a census, but in 1 Chronicles 21:1, Satan does the provoking. Apparently, the Chronicler saw no problem in assigning God the role of adversary.

Even in Job, Satan is not portrayed as a diabolical figure personifying evil in opposition to God. Instead, he appears as a cynical member of the heavenly court, probing to see if Job lives up to his reputation for righteousness. In yet another story that recalls the Satan of Job's story, the prophet Zechariah has a vision of the high priest Joshua standing trial "before the angel of the Lord, and Satan standing at his right hand to accuse him" (Zech 3:1). Here, however, the Lord rebukes Satan. It is apparently only after the return from their exile in Babylon that the Jews began to portray Satan as the leader of wicked spiritual forces pitted against all that was good. The Persians, who released the Jews from captivity, held similar beliefs of a demonic ruler.

Though Satan is not identified as the serpent that tempts Eve in the Garden of Eden, the New Testament book of Revelation seems to make the connection in referring to "that ancient serpent, who is called the Devil and Satan, the deceiver of the whole world" (Rev 12:9).

Satan destroying the sheep and all but one of Job's shepherds—one of the many trials Job endured as a test of his piety; a scene from a medieval Latin Bible

endures. Moreover, he argues that his friends are simply fickle and unable to respond in a meaningful way to his suffering and, in fact, run from him rather than provide sufficient answers to his questions. Job presses Eliphaz by asking if his words of reproof are any more valid than Job's. Turning to reproach God himself, Job questions why is it that—if God watches over him at all times—he is not moved to compassion. If he has sinned, God should let him know how: "Why have you made me your target?" (Job 7:20). Job, in essence, is demanding that there be some redeeming value to his suffering, although in all that he says he acknowledges that he sees none.

"Does God pervert justice? Or does the Almighty pervert the right?" JOB 8:3

Bildad enters the discussion in response to Job's most recent complaint and to his friend's situation in general. Bildad's question again strikes at the heart of the matter and, like Eliphaz's question in Job 4:7, requires the rather embarrassing answer, "Yes." The question assumes a perspective common to the Hebrew Bible: the notion that God's vigilance is not constant and is often provisional. There are times when the innocent do suffer and God does not instantly respond to their distress. Job's experience has much in common with the psalmist's sentiments: "Rouse yourself! Why do you sleep, O Lord? Awake, do not cast us off forever!" (Ps 44:23).

"How can a mortal be just before God?" JOB 9:2

In his reply to Bildad, Job raises another important issue, which is posed in language that, like much of what he says, has a stunning countercurrent. Should a person attempt to argue with God, Job says, he could win no more than one in a thousand times. While this supports traditional notions about God's authority, it does not sound a ringing endorsement of God's justice. In fact, it implies that whatever is just to a mortal has little to do with God's sense of justice. On the one hand, this may represent the notion that humans have no right to contend with God, since they cannot comprehend his justice. On the other hand, it could suggest that God is incapable even of living up to the imperfect human standard of justice. As Job puts it, "He destroys both the blameless and the wicked" (Job 9:22).

"Should a multitude of words go unanswered, and should one full of talk be vindicated?" JOB 11:2

Taking up Job's challenge for the first time, the third friend, Zophar, implies that verbosity is no substitute for righteousness. To him, Job seems merely to want to cover his culpability with endless words in his own defense. Zophar stresses that it is not Job's place to question God or to discover his deepest mysteries, but to remove any iniquity that still resides in him. Again, a friend fails to address

  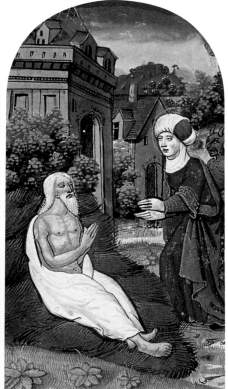

Three scenes from a French illuminated manuscript dated about 1500: raiders drive off Job's livestock (left); Job's sons and daughters are killed while dining (center); Job sits among the ashes as his wife urges him to curse God.

Job's situation adequately. To Zophar, it is not Job's place to probe God's justice but to accept it and to discover what he has done to bring on his suffering. No one seems to be able to interpret Job's anguish outside of traditional notions of piety.

"Those at ease have contempt for misfortune, but it is ready for those whose feet are unstable." JOB 12:5

Job finishes the first round of dialogues with his friends by noting that it is easy to dismiss misfortune or those who suffer it when things are going well. His words summarize just why the book of Job is so difficult: It asks us to understand truly what it means to have suffered like Job.

The sufferer next addresses Zophar with a question that has equal relevance for readers: "Will you speak falsely for God, and speak deceitfully for him?" (Job 13:7). Here Job comes directly to the problem with his friends' discourses. Are they willing to ignore his plight simply to defend and support their timeworn and inadequate theology? Job is implying that even God would not pretend to be as just as Job's friends insist that he is. For Job, the truth about God is more important than the preservation of simplistic doctrines. Remarkably, God himself later suggests that Job's accusations about his friends are true: "My wrath is kindled against you [Eliphaz] and against your two friends; for you have not spoken of me what is right, as my servant Job has" (Job 42:7).

"For your iniquity teaches your mouth, and you choose the tongue of the crafty." JOB 15:5

The second round of dialogues between Job and his three friends is about half as long as the first This may be for at least two good reasons. For one thing, the first round of dialogues lets each of the interlocutors make his points at some length. The other possible reason that the second round is shorter than the first may be seen in light of all three rounds. While the second round is about half the length of the first, the third round is only half as long as the second. This may well represent the way in which the editors responsible for the text preserved in the Bible signaled that the three friends are slowly running out of responses to Job.

At any rate, Eliphaz begins his second discourse by suggesting that Job is engaging in arguments so empty that he weakens piety. No longer able to mount a cogent defense against his suffering friend's discomforting observations, Eliphaz falls back on an age-old strategy: impugning the character of those with whom you disagree. But the question remains, if Job speaks the truth about God's justice, should it not weaken piety? What kind of piety is it that accepts such simple answers to the problem of human suffering and God's inability or unwillingness to respond? Eliphaz, unable to address this issue directly and adequately, returns to his standard line: "I will show you; listen to me; what I have seen I will de-

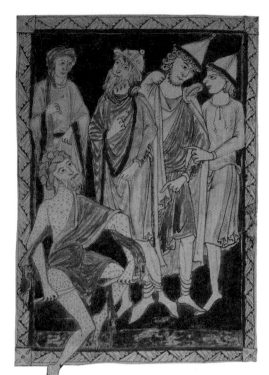

As he tries to scrape off his sores, Job is approached by his three friends: Eliphaz, Bildad, and Zophar. To the left rear, the young Elihu awaits his turn to address Job.

clare—what sages have told, and their ancestors have not hidden" (Job 15:17-18).

The sequence of alternating responses continues in the second round with Job's reply to Eliphaz (chapters 16-17), Bildad's second discourse (chapter 18), Job's response thereto (chapter 19), and finally Zophar's second questioning of Job (chapter 20), followed by Job's answer (chapter 21). Despite their great effort to get Job to accept traditional solutions to the problem of reconciling human suffering with God's divine justice, Job holds fast to what he knows. Job's most remarkable characteristic is the courage to hold to his convictions regardless of the pressure of his friends and the traditions that they espouse. His integrity is noteworthy, but it includes not only his faithfulness to a God who seems to have abandoned him but also his tenacity in maintaining the validity of his observations about his experience.

The third round of discourses and responses (chapters 22-27) is substantially abbreviated, so much so that Bildad's third response is reduced to the meager six verses that comprise chapter 25 and Zophar's third response is missing entirely. Actually, some scholars think that Job 27:7-23 represents Zophar's third and final speech. They point out that the first six verses of chapter 27 are consistent with the argument that Job has made in all his previous speeches, but starting with verse 7, and continuing to the end of the chapter, there is something much closer to the traditional platitudes that have consistently come from the mouths of Job's friends.

"Surely there is a mine for silver, and a place for gold to be refined." JOB 28:1

Chapter 28 represents a substantial shift in the book of Job. The sufferer's dialogue with his three friends is broken off by a hymn, closer to traditional speculation on the nature and, in particular, the source of wisdom. A dramatic shift from what has come before, the hymn may represent an attempt to make Job's perspective more acceptable to traditional religious sensibilities. Whatever the reason for the placement of chapter 28, it suggests that wisdom is as hidden and inaccessible as the justice of Job's God. The last verse serves to reinforce much of what Job has said all along, that concrete moral actions motivated by the love of God are what count most: "Truly the fear of the Lord, that is wisdom; and to depart from evil is understanding" (Job 28:28).

But when Elihu saw that there was no answer in the mouths of these three men, he became angry. JOB 32:5

After a sustained soliloquy (chapters 29-31) in which Job recalls his former happiness and how things went wrong, a fourth interlocutor enters the dispute. Much of what the young man Elihu has to say repeats the charges of the three friends who have fallen silent. How or why Elihu's speech came to reside in the text is difficult to determine, but it does serve as a response to Job's preceding speech in much the same way that Job's friends previously responded to him. Moreover, Elihu's speech leads up to the answer for which Job has long been waiting: the word of God.

"Where were you when I laid the earth's foundations? Tell me, if you have understanding." JOB 38:4

In what many consider the central scene of Job, and the encounter that he has sought all along, God finally responds to Job's stinging observations about injustice in the world. With one moving metaphor after another, God overwhelms Job with the majesty of his creation and Job's small place in his schemes. After this humbling speech, Job is able to muster little more than an acknowl-

edgment that he has nothing to say for himself: "What shall I answer you? I lay my hand on my mouth" (Job 40:4). God continues his response to Job in remarkable rhetorical flourishes that evoke his dominance of the world. Again, Job manages to utter a feeble defense: "I have uttered what I did not understand, things too wonderful for me, which I did not know" (Job 42:3). It is an acknowledgment of God's power and authority but, remarkably, no answer to the more troubling of Job's accusations about the lack of divine justice. One of the more deeply disturbing problems in reading Job is to decide how God's words represent an answer to Job's suffering.

The Lord said to Eliphaz the Temanite: "My wrath is kindled against you and against your two friends; for you have not spoken of me what is right, as my servant Job has." JOB 42:7

The epilogue to the book of Job is as perplexing as the rest of the work. Curiously, God reproaches Job's three friends for not speaking the truth about him and endorses what have appeared to be rather scandalous observations about him. The thrust of Job's claim is that God is not just and does not respond to human suffering. In the ultimate irony, having just endorsed Job's honesty, God turns around and restores to Job nearly all that he has lost. As true as Job's observations were, God still can be moved to respond to his suffering. But a simplistic happy reading of Job misses the point that the new children that he receives are indeed new and not those who died in the prologue. In other words, to whatever degree God has restored Job to his former state, his first children will never come back to life.

This is a fittingly complex ending to a remarkable book. Job is not only theologically challenging and courageously forthright in its exposition, but also beautifully written, with some of the most well-crafted poetry in the Hebrew Bible. Much of its enduring value comes from this combination of exquisite artistry put to the service of such stunning observations about the darker side of human experience and God's reaction to it.

Job's friends come to comfort him (top) but soon start rebuking him for not accepting blame for his misfortunes; two scenes by William Blake (1757-1827).

In this German psalter portrait dated about 980, an enthroned David plays the lyre.

One of the most beloved of all biblical books, Psalms is a diverse collection of 150 prayers, praises, and meditations that present the direct human response to God. Many of the psalms have an intimate character, revealing the author's personal relationship with God. Other psalmlike compositions, such as the song of Hannah (1 Sam 2:1-10) and Jonah's prayer from the belly of the fish (Jon 2:2-9), contain clues as to how psalms were used in biblical times.

The book is organized into five collections, or "books," of psalms (Psalms 1-41, 42-72, 73-89, 90-106, 107-150). Aside from these five basic divisions, the psalms can be classified into numerous thematic types. The largest category is laments, perhaps because it is human nature to complain. Bitter laments contain such themes as grievances about illness or enemies or a communal request for help when the nation is under siege. Joyous songs of praise laud God for his work in creation or in saving or sustaining the people of Israel. Thanksgiving psalms offer thanks for particular events in the life of an individual or in the history of the nation. Hymns offer unqualified praise to God; wisdom, or didactic, psalms teach about God's creation. Zion psalms honor the holy city of Jerusalem, and royal psalms were written to glorify the monarchy founded by King David. The superscriptions (words above the first verse) of Psalms 120-134 include the title "Song of Ascents," indicating that these psalms were used by pilgrims on their way up to Jerusalem, perhaps for major festivals.

Tradition ascribed authorship of the book of Psalms to David; the Hebrew phrase "leDavid" appears in the title of 73 psalms. But the preposition "le" can mean "to," "from," or "about," as well as "by" David. A gifted musician who calmed King Saul's bouts of madness (1 Sam 16:23), David was named as author because many of the psalms contain musical notations in their superscriptions. Scribes who worked in King David's court likely composed some of the psalms for the king's collection, but many clearly date from a much later period. The theme of Psalm 137, for instance, is the Babylonian exile, which occurred 400 years after David's death.

Just as there were various authors of the psalms, the psalms were likely used in a number of settings in ancient Israel. Psalms that mention God's eternal covenant of kingship with David, such as Psalm 89, may have been used at coronation ceremonies in Jerusalem. Other psalms, laments written in the first person, for instance, were probably used by individuals either at home or at the temple. Still others like the wisdom psalms may have been most conducive to private study. Whatever their origins or intended use, the psalms have continued to shape the worship life of generations of religious people, Christians as well as Jews.

Happy are those who do not follow the advice of the wicked, or take the path that sinners tread, or sit in the seat of scoffers. PS 1:1

The first psalm in the book is only six verses long, and with Psalm 2 serves as a kind of introduction to the entire work. Psalm 1 is categorized by scholars as a wisdom or teaching psalm because it offers a strong contrast between two approaches to life: the way of the righteous, which is governed by wisdom, and the way of the wicked, which is marked

by foolishness. It is not addressed directly to God but rather to those who are reading the book as a kind of instruction.

The righteous are those whose "delight is in the law of the Lord, and on his law they meditate day and night" (Ps 1:2). The reference to law should not be understood narrowly in a legal sense to mean a collection of prohibitions and ordinances. Rather, the Hebrew word "torah" that lies behind the English translation "law" has a much broader meaning. Torah can mean the first five books of the Bible, but in its broadest sense can also mean the study of the Bible and a life lived according to the divine norms embodied in scriptures. Psalm 119, with 176 verses the longest of the psalms, offers an even more extended reflection on the virtues of the torah.

O Lord, our Sovereign, how majestic is your name in all the earth! You have set your glory above the heavens.
PS 8:1

Psalm 8 is a hymn of praise to God for his role in crafting the heavens and earth. The psalmist is awed by the grandeur of the universe and humbly asks, "What are human beings that you are mindful of them, mortals that you care for them?" (Ps 8:4). Yet God has placed humanity in a position of honor and given them dominion over all other creatures—an echo of Genesis 1:26.

The author of the letter to the Hebrews quotes Psalm 8:4-6 and applies the words to Jesus. In his suffering and death, Jesus is understood to be for a time "lower than the angels," but he is ultimately "crowned with glory and honor" (Heb 2:9) as the ruler of all creation. Only nine verses long, Psalm 8 is direct and focused, expressing the psalmist's awe in God's presence.

According to Matthew and Mark, Jesus died with the words of Psalm 22:1 on his lips. This Italian crucifixion scene dates to the second half of the 13th century.

I love you, O Lord, my strength. The Lord is my rock, my fortress, and my deliverer. PS 18:1-2

The superscription of this psalm of thanks suggests it was offered by King David on the day the Lord delivered him from his enemies, including Saul. A slightly different version is found in 2 Samuel 22 after an account of David's struggles with the Philistines. But it is unlikely that David actually offered the psalm in those circumstances. There is no specific mention of Saul in the psalm and the only reference to David appears in the last verse. Like other psalms that provide historical superscriptions, it contains generalized language of thanksgiving that could be reused by anyone in need.

The first five verses praise God and elaborate on the distress of the psalmist before God's rescue. In verses 6-19, God is described as a cosmic warrior in metaphors that mesh both natural phenomena and war: "And he sent out his arrows, and scattered them; he flashed forth lightnings and routed them" (Ps 18:14). The Israelite poet borrowed this vivid imagery from the epic literature of the neighboring Canaanites

in which the storm god Baal fights for his people. Verses 20-30 provide the reasons why God has helped the psalmist, who "was blameless before him [God]" (Ps 18:23). In the biblical context, the warrior God of Israel fights for those who are righteous and who observe the commandments of the divine covenant. Verses 31-45 describe how God enabled the king's conquest of his foes. God "made my feet like the feet of a deer" and "girded me with strength for the battle" (Ps 18:33, 39). The final five verses detail the psalmist's conquest of his enemies, made possible only by the Lord's dramatic help, and extol the Lord for his steadfast love and deliverance.

My God, my God, why have you forsaken me? Why are you so far from helping me, from the words of my groaning? PS 22:1

An individual lament, Psalm 22 contains deeply moving phrases in which the psalmist mourns his abandonment by God. He reminds God of his deliverance of the Israelite people and then laments his own fate. He has been humiliated and calls himself "a worm, and not human" (Ps 22:6). He describes his enemies as animals: "encircling bulls," a "roaring lion," "dogs . . . all around me," and "wild oxen" (Ps 22:12, 13, 16, 21). Yet, even though the psalm begins on an anguished note, the last half contains a marked change in tone, when the psalmist realizes God has rescued him after all. The lament turns to a pledge to praise God and offer thanksgiving.

There are important echoes of this psalm in the New Testament. In all four gospels (Mt 27:35; Mk 15:24; Lk 23:34; Jn 19:23-24), Jesus' tormentors are described as casting lots for his clothing, a fulfillment of "they divide my clothes among themselves, and for my clothing they cast lots" (Ps 22:18). Another echo is sounded in Matthew and Mark, where Jesus cries out the first words of this psalm shortly before his death on the cross. Did he use these words intending to summon up the entire psalm, which ends in praise and thanksgiving, or did he use only the first words because of his own feeling of abandonment? It cannot be known. The question posed to God in the first verse of the psalm may have been rhetorical to the author, but it is made vividly clear in Jesus' agonizing and humiliating death.

The Lord is my shepherd, I shall not want.   PS 23:1

Justly famous, Psalm 23 is a comforting song of trust and confidence in God, who is described as a shepherd and a gracious host. He guides the psalmist to food, "green pastures," and to drink, "still waters." But more than that, there is a spiritual and moral dimension to God who "restores my soul" and "leads me in right paths for his name's sake" (Ps 23:2-3). Verse 4 contains the central theme of the psalm: God, equipped with the shepherd's rod and staff, protects the psalmist from his enemies and all evil and provides comfort and consolation.

The last two verses describe God as the divine host who provides sustenance for the psalmist and anoints his head with oil. Anointing the head with oil was a common Near Eastern practice in a time when hair washing was unknown, and a gracious Israelite host would welcome a guest by pouring scented oil over his head. The concluding verse reflects the psalmist's deep-seated trust in God, who will protect him in the temple at Jerusalem.

Have mercy on me, O God, according to your steadfast love; according to your abundant mercy blot out my transgressions.   PS 51:1

According to the superscription, this prayer of healing—one of seven penitential psalms in the book—was composed by King David himself after the prophet Nathan had accused him of having an adulterous affair with Bathsheba (2 Sam 11-12). Since the words of the psalm do not specify the exact circumstances of the sin, it seems unlikely that David actually wrote the psalm. Like many of the other psalms, Psalm 51 was intended to be used and reused by people in a variety of circumstances requiring repentance.

The psalm focuses on the guilt of the sinner and his need for divine forgiveness. He calls on God's "steadfast love" and

"abundant mercy," two of God's chief attributes as revealed to Moses at Mount Sinai (Ex 34:6-7). The psalmist also recognizes something essential about the nature of sin when he states, "Against you, you alone, have I sinned" (Ps 51:4), for any sin is ultimately a transgression against God. Upon acknowledging the depth of his own sinfulness, the psalmist asks God to purify and forgive him and, finally, to restore his soul. Above all, the psalmist wants to remain close to God: "Do not cast me away from your presence" (Ps 51:11). Like some of the prophets, the psalmist affirms that God prefers a sincere, contrite heart to such displays of religion as sacrifices. Because it so eloquently expresses a repentant sinner's proper attitude toward God, Christians recite this psalm during the penitential season of Lent preceding Easter.

Give ear, O my people, to my teaching; incline your ears to the words of my mouth.   PS 78:1

One of a special category of psalms that recount God's gracious acts in Israel's history, Psalm 78 is not addressed to God but to the people, who were meant to learn from it. The introduction exhorts the listeners to hear about "the glorious deeds of the Lord, and his might, and the wonders that he has done" (Ps 78:4).

The history of the Israelites recounted in the psalm stretches from the Exodus to the conquest of Canaan and the establishment of David's kingship, not told in exact chronological sequence. The greatest emphasis is on the wandering in the wilderness en route to the promised land. Despite God's care and guidance, the people repeatedly rebelled against the Lord and were punished for their faithlessness. The final part of the psalm explains that God rejected the original northern worship site at Shiloh because of idolatry practiced there, and instead chose Jerusalem as the site of the central sanctuary at the time he chose David to "be the shepherd of his people" (Ps 78:70).

Jesus as the good shepherd surrounded by his flock is depicted in this mosaic from the 5th-century tomb of Galla Placidia in Ravenna, Italy.

Surrounded by court musicians, King David recites one of the many psalms attributed to him; a marble floor mosaic from the cathedral of Siena, Italy.

The psalm was composed to teach the people of Israel that they must remember the nation's faithless past in order to learn from their ancestors' behavior. Only memory provides escape from repeating the mistakes of the past.

I will sing of your steadfast love, O Lord, forever; with my mouth I will proclaim your faithfulness to all generations.
PS 89:1

A royal psalm, Psalm 89 falls into four parts. The first four verses announce the psalmist's intention to offer a hymn of praise to God for his faithfulness to Israel and recall the divine promise to create an eternal dynasty for the house of King David. Verses 5-18 praise God for his role in creating the heavens and earth, described in language borrowed from ancient Near Eastern myths: "You crushed Rahab like a carcass; you scattered your enemies with your mighty arm" (Ps 89:10). Rahab is the mythic sea monster that the Canaanite storm god Baal slew before creating the earth. In this psalm, Israel's God has taken the role of Baal.

The third part of the psalm details God's eternal covenant with David. Their relationship is described in father-son terms: "He [David] shall cry to me, 'You are my Father, my God, and the Rock of my salvation!'" (Ps 89:26). God promises to uphold his covenant faithfulness with all David's descendants, imposing only one condition: The Davidic king must obey the divine commandments delivered to Moses at Mount Sinai.

With verse 38, the tone changes drastically to one of lament. The psalmist asks tormented questions: "How long, O Lord? Will you hide yourself forever? How long will your wrath burn like fire?" (Ps 89:46). The psalm was probably written during a period of crisis in Israel, for it contains the description of a grave situation confronting the king: "All who pass by plunder him; he has become the scorn of his neighbors" (Ps 89:41). But despite the desperation expressed in the final verses, the psalm closes with a blessing expressing the psalmist's ultimate faith in the benevolence of God: "Blessed be the Lord forever. Amen and Amen" (Ps 89:52).

Hear my prayer, O Lord; let my cry come to you. Do not hide your face from me in the day of my distress.
PS 102:1-2

The superscription to Psalm 102 reads "a prayer of one afflicted" and verses 3-11 specify the nature of the psalmist's ills. He suffers from physical ailments: "My bones burn like a furnace. . . . I am too wasted to eat my bread" (Ps 102:3-4). But that is not all. He is also tormented emotionally by his enemies, who mock him. Because of his wretched state, he feels that God has forgotten him.

Verses 12-22 are an expression of faith and confidence in God who reigns in Zion, one of the names for the city of Jerusalem. The psalm was most likely written during the Israelites' exile to Babylon. But the psalmist firmly believes that God will "hear the groans of the prisoners, to set free those who were doomed to die" (Ps 102:20). Thus liberated from captivity, the people once more will offer praise to God in his holy city, Jerusalem.

Though the psalm begins as a lament, at the end it returns to a tone of confidence as the psalmist affirms the unchangeable nature of God: "You are the same, and your years have no end" (Ps 102:27).

O give thanks to the Lord, for he is good; his steadfast love endures forever! PS 118:1

The purpose of Psalm 118 is given in the first verse: thanksgiving to God. The reason is provided in the body of the psalm: God showed his steadfast love by saving the psalmist from his enemies. Although written in the first person singular, the psalm reflects the perspective of the king who is thanking God on behalf of the entire nation for some crisis that Israel has survived. Verse 14 cites the Song of Moses (Ex 15:2), the Israelites' hymn of praise after God saved them from the Egyptians at the Red Sea. For this reason, the psalmist owes his very life to God and pledges to offer thanks and praise in "the house of the Lord" (Ps 118:26).

Many of the first Christians were born Jews and were thus familiar with the Old Testament. This psalm, which combines an individual's lament at persecution and thanksgiving to God for salvation, was clearly important for early Christians. Verse 22, "The

MUSIC IN THE BIBLE

Music was an important part *of life in the ancient Near East. Soldiers prepared for battle by singing ballads of heroic victories in the past, and womenfolk welcomed warriors home with "songs of joy, and with musical instruments" (1 Sam 18:6). To pass the time, laborers sang as they worked and pilgrims as they traveled. Lovers expressed their desires in song. And, at least occasionally, prophets were lulled into a trance by the humming strains of instruments: "While the musician was playing, the power of the Lord came on him [Elisha]" (2 Kgs 3:15).*

Jubal, a descendant of Cain, is identified as "ancestor of all who play the lyre and pipe" (Gen 4:21). But it was the lyre-playing David who propelled music to the forefront of the Israelites' religion. Although the building of the temple was left to his son Solomon, David organized the temple staff, establishing Levite choirs accompanied by musicians playing cymbals, harps, lyres, and trumpets. A professional music director led these choirs and instrumentalists, who each day filled the temple courtyards with songs of praise and repentance, and welcomed pilgrims arriving for annual festivals. During worship, the choirs sometimes sang antiphonally, with one group answering another, or with the entire choir responding to a soloist or the congregation. Some hymns were arranged for specific instruments: Psalm 5, a plea for deliverance from personal enemies, was to be accompanied by the plaintive notes of flutes; Psalm 6, an urgent prayer for recovery from illness, by the soothing strum of strings.

The Bible names about 20 instruments, but the precise translation is often a guess based on related words in other languages. The instruments seem to fall into three categories: strings, winds, and percussion. Strings included harp, lyre, and lute; winds were pipes, flute, a metal trumpet that sounded four or five notes, and the ram's horn that sounded two or three notes; percussion or rhythm instruments were tambourines, bells, and cymbals. No musical notations survive from biblical times, but the scales familiar today were available then.

stone that the builders rejected has become the chief cornerstone," is quoted not only in three of the gospels (Mt 21:42; Mk 12:10; Lk 20:17), but in Acts 4:11 and 1 Peter 2:7. In the New Testament, the verse is understood to refer to Jesus, who was rejected by many in his own community.

I was glad when they said to me, "Let us go to the house of the Lord!" PS 122:1

Psalm 122 falls into a category known as Zion psalms because its theme is the sacred city of Jerusalem and its temple on Mount Zion. The superscription reads "A Song of Ascents," the heading for each in the group of Psalms 120-134. The exact meaning of the superscription is uncertain, but it may well have been sung by pilgrims who were "ascending" to Jerusalem. All of the male Israelites were supposed to make a pilgrimage to the holy city three times a year: during Passover, the Feast of Weeks, and the Feast of Booths. Indeed, verse 4 refers specifically to the requirement that "the tribes of the Lord," that is, the 12 tribes of Israel, were required to "go up." King David had selected the centrally located city, then held by the hostile Jebusites, as a capital independent of all the tribes. There, his son and successor, Solomon, had built a magnificent temple, thus making Jerusalem the religious as well as the political center of the kingdom. The well-being of the city was important for all people and could result in the well-being of those who cared for it. "May they prosper who love you" (Ps 122:6) was the fervent wish of the psalmist.

By the rivers of Babylon—there we sat down and there we wept when we remembered Zion. PS 137:1

This bitter communal lament was written by someone who seems to have experienced the destruction of the city of Jerusalem in 586 B.C. by King Nebuchadnezzar of Babylon and the exile of

In this 14th-century French tapestry, the Lord reveals to David the vision of a heavenly Jerusalem. From David's time, pilgrims made the city on earth their goal.

its leading citizens. The first three verses of the psalm depict a scene by "the rivers of Babylon," the Tigris and the Euphrates or their tributaries. The Israelites' captors taunt them by asking them to sing "songs of Zion" (Ps 137:3), perhaps psalms that praise the former beauty and supposed impregnability of their devastated capital, Jerusalem.

The daughters of Judah mourn their exile in Babylon as their royal captors approach; an elegant but fanciful scene by Herbert Gustave Schmalz (1856-1935).

Just as Psalm 122 glorifies Jerusalem and speaks of its magnificence, so, too, this lament almost personifies the city: "If I forget you, O Jerusalem, let my right hand wither!" (Ps 137:5). The intense passion the psalmist feels for Jerusalem is also expressed in the final verses, with the call for vengeance against those who destroyed the city—even to the merciless killing of the children of Babylon.

I will extol you, my God and King, and bless your name forever and ever.   PS 145:1

Psalm 145 is known as a wisdom, or teaching, psalm. It is also an alphabetic acrostic psalm because each verse begins with a successive letter of the Hebrew alphabet, from *aleph* to the last letter, *taw* (others are Psalms 9-10, 25, 34, 37, 111, 112, 119, and 145). The alphabetic structure was, no doubt, an aid to memorizing the psalms.

The theme of the psalm is one of blessing, thanking, and praising God. The first two verses state the psalmist's intent to praise God and God's "name" forever and ever. The ineffable personal name of God, "Yahweh," rendered in English translations as "Lord," was thought to have an independent status and inherent power. Thus blessing the divine name was an important activity. The rest of the psalm elaborates on why God is worthy of praise and adoration. The personal character of God, known from Exodus 34:6 and Numbers 14:18, is cited in verse 8. Additional qualities of God, among them goodness and compassion, are mentioned in verse 9. Verses 10-14 discuss the nature of God's kingship: He is ruler over all creation and his "dominion endures through all generations" (Ps 145:12).

Praise the Lord! Praise the Lord from the heavens; praise him in the heights!   PS 148:1

Each verse in this hymn of praise to God calls on some different element in creation to praise the Lord. Unlike such psalms as 146, which cites God's care of the poor and oppressed, Psalm 148 gives no reason why God should be praised, except the brief statement, "for he commanded and they were created" (Ps 148:5). The simple fact that God created the cosmos and all its contents demands this response of praise from everything in the created order. All things in the heavens—sun, moon, stars, and angels—and all things on earth—fire, hail, snow, wind, mountains, trees, wild animals, cattle, serpents, and birds—are commanded to join the people— kings, princes, and other rulers as well as young men and women and the elderly—in a joyful chorus of praise to the Lord.

Although the largest category of psalms in the book are laments, the work concludes on an upbeat note. Psalms 146 to 150 all begin and end with the exuberant cry, "Praise the Lord!" or in Hebrew, "Hallelujah!" The exclamation is a fitting conclusion to this treasured book of prayers and praise.

Wisdom personified, King Solomon sits enthroned in this late-14th-century French manuscript illumination.

A collection of instructions and pithy sayings that present insights about the workings of nature and human behavior, the book of Proverbs is the most conservative of the Bible's so-called wisdom literature: Job, Proverbs, and Ecclesiastes. Many of the proverbs seem to be interested in maintaining the status quo, in which the king possesses unquestioned power: "The dread anger of a king is like the growling of a lion; anyone who provokes him to anger forfeits life itself" (Prov 20:2). Wealth and poverty seem foreordained: "A slack hand causes poverty, but the hand of the diligent makes rich" (Prov 10:4). Yet other proverbs show a concern for the poor: "If a king judges the poor with equity, his throne will be established forever" (Prov 29:14). Some of the proverbs still ring true: "A cheerful heart is a good medicine, but a downcast spirit dries up the bones" (Prov 17:22). Others chafe against modern sensibilities: "Do not withhold discipline from your children; if you beat them with a rod, they will not die" (Prov 23:13).

King Solomon is traditionally credited as the author of Proverbs, along with Ecclesiastes and the Song of Solomon. The reason for the association can be traced to 1 Kings 4:29-34, in which God bestows on the king wisdom that "surpassed the wisdom of all the people of the east, and all the wisdom of Egypt. . . . He composed three thousand proverbs." But like David's supposed authorship of the book of Psalms, this attribution is considered doubtful by modern scholars. If Solomon did not write all of the proverbs, then who did? Experts have several suggestions. One is that family clans in Israel were the source of these sayings, formulated, then collected and passed down orally from parent to child. Another, more popular suggestion is that the proverbs originated with the scribes of the royal court. A striking aspect of the book is that it is written from a male perspective; nowhere is this more clear than in the personification of wisdom as a woman, in contrast to the seductions of the "loose woman" (Prov 2:16).

There are two main literary genres found in Proverbs. One is the "instruction," a form borrowed from Egyptian wisdom literature. This is a longer, unified composition on a single theme that may contain any number of verses. Its form is a speech, from an older person to a youth, containing teaching about the ways of wisdom. A number of instructions as well as some wisdom poems are found in chapters 1-9. The other principle genre is the actual proverb, or in Hebrew, mashal. It consists of a two-part saying in a single verse. The first part is usually contrasted by the second part, but the two parts can be related in a number of ways—for example, "Better an X, than a Y." Such individual proverbs, some gathered in larger collections, make up most of chapters 10-30.

The proverbs of Solomon son of David, king of Israel: For learning about wisdom and instruction, for understanding words of insight. PROV 1:1-2

*T*he first seven verses of the book announce not only King Solomon's association, but the general purpose of the collection: to teach "righteousness, justice, and equity" (Prov 1:3). The "simple," another way of saying the ignorant, and the young are especially in need of learning the ways of wisdom. But those who are already wise can increase their wisdom by contemplating "the words of the wise and their riddles" (Prov 1:6). One category of individuals, the "fools," is beyond hope of ever gaining wisdom, predestined to remain as they are, scornful of insight and wise instruction.

The author has added a particularly Israelite dimension to the concept: "The fear of the Lord is the beginning of knowledge" (Prov 1:7). The phrase, "fear of the Lord," is another way of saying Israelite worship, which must be based on the proper attitude toward God.

My child, if you accept my words and treasure up my commandments within you . . . then you will understand the fear of the Lord. PROV 2:1, 5

One of the typical ways in which wisdom literature is formulated is as a parent's, or perhaps an older teacher's, instruction to a child on how to behave in order to gain wisdom. Unlike contemporary Western culture that glorifies youth, old people commanded respect in the ancient Near East. The perspective gained from a long life was greatly valued, for wisdom, once acquired, was an inoculation against evil and sinful ways.

"My child, do not forget my teaching, but let your heart keep my commandments" (Prov 3:1), admonishes the teacher. Adherence to this advice will result in a long, fruitful life. Reverence for Israel's God is essential to all wisdom. The author's advice ranges from the general, "Trust in the Lord with all your heart," to the specific such as "Honor the Lord with your substance and with the first fruits of all your produce" (Prov 3:5, 9). In this chapter, as later, wisdom is referred to as a woman (Prov 3:14-18).

Listen, children, to a father's instruction, and be attentive, that you may gain insight. PROV 4:1

Recalling his own parents' advice, a father shows how wisdom is passed down from generation to generation. He employs an extended metaphor to tell the child that "the path of the righteous is like the light of dawn," whereas "the way of the wicked is like deep darkness" (Prov 4:18, 19).

In the next chapter, he warns his son that "the lips of a loose woman drip honey . . . but in the end she is bitter as wormwood" (Prov 5:3-4). The threat posed by such a woman is spelled out in greater detail later in the book. In contrast, the father admonishes his son to be happy with his wife, "a lovely deer, a graceful doe" (Prov 5:18). Self-discipline, here understood as marital fidelity and sexual continence, is an important part of wisdom teaching.

My child, if you have given your pledge to your neighbor, if you have bound yourself to another, you are snared by the utterance of your lips, caught by the words of your mouth. PROV 6:1-2

Practical advice for the student on how to walk the path of wisdom is offered in Proverb 6. Fools have loose lips; they are prone to talk too much without saying a great deal and do not think beforehand. By contrast, wise people are reserved in their speech, considering everything before speaking.

This chapter also contains two representative forms of wisdom discourse. One collects observations from the natural world that shed light on how humans should behave. A model for hard work can be found in one of the tiniest of earth's creatures: "Go to the ant, you lazybones; consider its ways, and be wise" (Prov 6:6). The other form is the numerical proverb,

in which X number, then X plus one are listed: "There are six things that the Lord hates, seven that are an abomination to him: haughty eyes, a lying tongue, and hands that shed innocent blood, a heart that devises wicked plans, feet that hurry to run to evil, a lying witness who testifies falsely, and one who sows discord in a family." (Prov 6:16-19). As in other numerical proverbs, the final two things listed offer a contrast with the first two. In this carefully crafted proverb, the false witness and the sower of discord disrupt the social fabric of Israel by corrupting the courts and the family.

Say to wisdom, "You are my sister," and call insight your intimate friend, that they may keep you from the loose woman, from the adulteress with her smooth words. PROV 7:4-5

In Proverb 7, the author creates an imaginative scenario that contrasts the worthy companionship of the wise woman with the dangers of associating with a temptress. A youth is lured from the path of wisdom by a seductress. She is dressed provocatively, like a prostitute, ready to prey on youthful innocence. She titillates him by kissing him and describing the perfumed bed in her home. Her husband is away on a trip, she says, and so she invites him to her lair.

Using a typical wisdom device, the author compares the follies of the young man to predicaments of animals. The youth follows the adulteress, "like an ox to the slaughter," "a stag toward the trap," or "a bird rushing into a snare" (Prov 7:22-23). Each image vividly depicts the fate of the young man who is headed for death and destruction.

Does not wisdom call, and does not understanding raise her voice? PROV 8:1

In striking contrast with the image of the loose woman, wisdom in this chapter is personified as a virtuous woman. The use of a female is apparently intended to attract the attention of the largely male audience for which the book was compiled. Dame Wisdom stands speaking by the gates in front of the city, the place where Israel's judicial decisions are made. Her voice is the voice of fairness, justice, and truth, all virtues associated with wisdom. To listen to her teaching is to gain wisdom, which is to be prized because "wisdom is better than jewels" and "better than gold, even fine gold" (Prov 8:11, 19).

Wisdom also reveals that she is the first of God's creations. The account of creation in this passage varies substantially from the creation story in Genesis 1-2. Here, once created, wisdom is the guiding principle by which God fashions the sea and the foundations of the earth: "Then I was beside him, like a master worker" (Prov 8:30). The idea of personified wisdom present at creation influenced the author of the Gospel of John, in which the "Word," understood as Jesus, the source of all wisdom, coexisted with God from the beginning

Attentive scribes take down some of the 3,000 proverbs Solomon is said to have composed;
this mid-14th-century Bible illustration seems to be set in a tiled court within the palace garden.

The proverbs of Solomon. A wise child makes a glad
father, but a foolish child is a mother's grief. PROV 10:1

This verse marks the beginning of a long collection called the proverbs of Solomon (Prov 10:10-22:16). The proverbs contain antithetical sayings in which the first half of the proverb is contrasted with the second. Usually one half presents the way of the wise, the other half the way of the foolish. Two opposite words are used as catchwords. In these sayings, the "righteous" or the "prudent" are used synonymously with the "wise"; the "wicked" or the "treacherous" are substitutes for the "foolish." Many of the sayings illustrate the same principle in a slightly different way. For instance, guarded speech marks the wise: "When words are many, transgression is not lacking, but the prudent are restrained in speech" (Prov 10:19).

Some of the proverbs do not illustrate a principle, but rather fall into the category of wishful thinking about the consequences of moral and immoral behavior: "The righteous are delivered from trouble, and the wicked get into it instead" (Prov 11:8), or "The wicked earn no real gain, but those who sow righteousness get a true reward" (Prov 11:18). Such orthodoxy was challenged by the author of the book of Job—also a wisdom book, but one that calls into question the view that righteousness is always rewarded in this life.

A wise child loves discipline, but a scoffer does not
listen to rebuke. PROV 13:1

The first verse of Proverbs 13 suggests that a wise child accepts scolding when he has done something wrong; a "scoffer" ignores such reproof. This same principle is stated somewhat differently for adults. Wise adults receive advice gladly; fools do not recognize it when they hear it: "Those who ignore instruction despise themselves, but those who heed admonition gain understanding" (Prov 15:32).

Wisdom also involves control over the emotions. Fools are hot tempered and quick to reveal feelings; the wise are calm and restrained: "One who is quick tempered acts foolishly, and the schemer is hated" (Prov 14:17). Other contrasts, such as that between the lazy and the hard-working, also illustrate the difference between the two paths. Scattered among the proverbs about the way of the wise versus the way of the foolish are proverbs of a more general nature that contain insights into the human condition: "Hope deferred makes the heart sick, but a desire fulfilled is a tree of life" (Prov 13:12). The tree of life is an image used frequently in the ancient Near East to symbolize abundance of life.

The plans of the mind belong to mortals, but the answer
of the tongue is from the Lord. PROV 16:1

In keeping with the royal superscription of this collection, many of these proverbs are concerned with the king, particularly his behavior or his values: "A king's wrath is a messenger of death, and whoever is wise will appease it" (Prov 16:14).

The form of the proverbs in 16:1-22:16 is called synonymous parallelism, in which the second part of the verse repeats or somehow amplifies the meaning of the first part. The section contains such familiar sayings as "Pride goes before destruction, and a haughty spirit before a fall" (Prov 16:18). The message of some of the proverbs is immediately obvious: "Pleasant words are like a honeycomb, sweetness to the soul and health to the body" (Prov 16:24). But some of the proverbs require some meditation to dis-

WISDOM LITERATURE

From their lifetimes of experience and learning, sages throughout the ancient Near East offered their advice on living. They frequently condemned laziness, praised honesty, and promised a fuller and richer life to those who heeded their words. These words sometimes wrapped themselves in dramatic stories, such as the saga of Job, a man searching for the reason behind his suffering. More often, they appeared as short, descriptive sayings, written with a cadence and flair for imagery that made them easy to remember: "It is better to live in a corner of the housetop than in a house shared with a contentious wife" (Prov 25:24). Stories and sayings such as these were compiled in books that became known as wisdom literature. That literary genre is represented in the Bible by the books of Job, Proverbs, and Ecclesiastes.

The identity of the wise men behind these words remains a mystery. Sages of Israel possibly emerged in the early years of the monarchy, when kings such as David sought counsel from the greatest minds in the nation. Tradition holds that Solomon composed Proverbs and Ecclesiastes, and, in fact, 1 Kings 4:32 confirms that he wrote 3,000 proverbs. But each of these two books is more likely a collection of sayings by many sages, spanning several centuries. Proverbs acknowledges as much, attributing some of its teachings to otherwise unknown people such as Agur (Prov 30:1) and King Lemuel (Prov 31:1). Parts of Proverbs also bear a striking resemblance to excerpts from a collection known as the "Instruction of Amenemope," a sage who taught in Egypt between 1200 and 1000 B.C. For instance, Proverbs advises, "Do not rob the poor because they are poor, or crush the afflicted at the gate" (Prov 22:22). Amenemope says, "Do not steal from the poor, nor cheat the cripple." Both sources agree that it is best to help one's enemies: "If your enemies are hungry, give them food to eat. . . . the Lord will reward you" (Prov 25:21-22). "Give the fool your hand. Leave the punishment of the fool to the gods" (Amenemope).

Wisdom writings tend to stress the virtues of common sense, practical experience, and moral integrity. What sets biblical wisdom literature apart from similar writings of Egypt and Babylon is that scripture recognizes God as the source of wisdom. Even the pessimistic author of Ecclesiastes, who searches for meaning in life and finds none, ends his thoughtful intellectual odyssey by concluding that the most important thing in life is to "fear God, and keep his commandments; for that is the whole duty of everyone" (Eccl 12:13).

cern their truth. They are like short riddles. "The human spirit is the lamp of the Lord, searching every inmost part" (Prov 20:27). The human spirit, put into each being by God, provides each person's moral sense. It thus searches and illuminates each part of the mind to determine proper behavior.

Other proverbs present concrete metaphors to illustrate the truth: "The wealth of the rich is their strong city; in their imagination it is like a high wall" (Prov 18:11). Wealthy people think that their money will protect them from misfortune like a high wall protects a city from attackers. The author uses the phrase "in their imagination" to suggest that this is not necessarily so. The rich are far more vulnerable than they think.

The words of the wise: Incline your ear and hear my words, and apply your mind to my teaching. PROV 22:17

This verse begins a collection called the "sayings of the wise," which addresses the reader directly. The subsequent verses ask the reader to pay attention and learn the following sayings "so that you may give a true answer to those who sent you" (Prov 22:21). Proverbs 22:17-24:22 show striking similarities with an Egyptian composition, the "Instruction of Amenemope," which contains advice, perhaps from Pharaoh's adviser to his son, on how to behave in order to be a success at court. Both treat some of the same topics, such as rules dealing with pledges of money (Prov 22:26-27) and boundary disputes (Prov 23:10-11). There are instructions about how to behave in the company of a king, including the following tip on dining etiquette: "Do not desire the ruler's delicacies, for they are deceptive food" (Prov 23:3). In this collection, advice against associating with fools is transformed into an admonition against associating with gluttons and drunkards. There is also a long cautionary passage about the perils of drinking too much: "At the last it bites like a serpent and stings like an adder" (Prov 23:32).

These are other proverbs of Solomon that the officials of King Hezekiah of Judah copied. PROV 25:1

The superscription of the collection beginning with chapter 25 hints at how the book was transmitted. Hezekiah, who began his reign late in the eighth century B.C., was an esteemed king of Judah, remembered for his piety and righteousness. For that reason, this collection is associated with his court. It begins with a series of proverbs that concern the king and how to behave in his presence at court. Following those are a number of proverbs on the topic of the proper use of speech, which from the wisdom perspective means with forethought and appropriate timing. Apt similes help to drive the point of the proverbs home: "A word fitly spoken is like apples of gold in a setting of silver" (Prov 25:11). The impropriety of cheerfulness in the face of someone's sadness is expressed with a striking image: "Like vinegar on a wound is one who sings songs to a heavy heart" (Prov 25:20).

The author of a proverb had to have a keen eye and a lively imagination. Often, there was something else. Some of the proverbs make their point with delightful humor: "As a door turns on its hinges, so does a lazy person in bed" (Prov 26:14). Busybodies are skewered in another amusing proverb: "Like somebody who takes a passing dog by the ears is one who meddles in the quarrel of another" (Prov 26:17).

The words of Agur son of Jakeh. An oracle. Thus says the man: I am weary, O God, I am weary, O God. How can I prevail? PROV 30:1

Agur's identity is unknown; he is mentioned nowhere else in the Bible. The composition is labeled "an oracle," the term that normally introduces a divine message in the prophetic books. The first verse also includes the phrase "Thus says the man," which is like the formula at the beginning of a prophetic oracle. The irony in this case is that the direction of the address is reversed. Here the oracle comes from a man and not God. A man addresses God, saying "I am weary," and goes on to lament his lot in life. This reversal of direction is in keeping with the nature of wisdom, which emerges from human reflection on the natural order as opposed to divinely given revelation.

The most distinctive form of wisdom literature in this passage is the numerical saying. Drawing on his observations of the world around him, the author finds something unexpected in four of earth's creatures. "Four things on earth are small, yet they are exceedingly wise: The ants are a people without strength, yet they provide their food in the summer; the badgers are a people without power, yet they make their homes in the rocks; the locusts have no kings, yet all of them march in rank; the lizard can be grasped in the hand, yet it is found in kings' palaces" (Prov 30:24-28).

The words of King Lemuel. An oracle that his mother taught him: No, my son! No, son of my womb! No, son of my vows! PROV 31:1-2

The instruction given in Proverbs 31 is unusual because the queen mother is the one who is tutoring her son in the ways of being a king. Like Agur, King Lemuel is otherwise unknown in the Bible or in Israelite history. Lemuel's mother instructs him on three topics: wine, women, and the vulnerable members of society. Her advice on wine is simple: A king should not drink because it will impair his thinking. She suggests instead that drink be given to those who need to forget their sorry state, such as the poor or the dying. Her advice on the king's responsibility toward the vulnerable is also clear-cut: "Speak out for those who cannot speak, for the rights of all the destitute. Speak out, judge righteously, defend the rights of the poor and needy" (Prov 31:8-9).

A capable wife who can find? She is far more precious than jewels. PROV 31:10

The final passage in the book of Proverbs is an alphabetic acrostic, that is, each verse begins with a successive letter of the Hebrew alphabet. The "Ode to a Capable Wife," in which the queen mother offers advice about the characteristics of a future spouse for her son, was likely an independent composition originally. Like the figure of Dame Wisdom in Proverbs 8, the capable wife is described as "far more precious than jewels." The woman evidently comes from the upper reaches of society. "Her clothing is fine linen and purple" (Prov 31:22), which indicates that she can afford expensive clothes. Her husband takes "his seat among the elders of the land" (Prov 31:23), obviously a man with enough stature to take part in legal decisions made at the city gate. The woman's activities, like those of most proper Israelite women (Deborah the judge is a notable exception), are confined largely to the home and the marketplace. She raises children and makes sure her family is well-fed and clothed. The virtues of this good woman include strength, dignity, and kindness. No superficial values are to be found: "Charm is deceitful, and beauty is vain, but a woman who fears the Lord is to be praised" (Prov 31:30).

At the beginning of the book, wisdom is said to begin with "the fear of the Lord." Having come full circle, the reader here meets the wise, praiseworthy woman who in her values and activities already epitomizes deep respect for Israel's God.

Solomon's Greek contemporaries attributed great wisdom to women oracles such as the one at Delphi; a 17th-century stained glass window.

ECCLESIASTES

One of the most puzzling books in the Bible, Ecclesiastes is a sober reflection on human existence. The writer begins with the gloomy declaration that everything about life is meaningless and unfulfilling, and that all pursuits are like "chasing after wind" (Eccl 1:14). Human attempts at wisdom, he laments, are invariably sidetracked by foolishness. Joy is tempered by injustice and tragedy. And a lifetime of hard work ends only in death. Yet, despite his pessimism, the writer advises people to enjoy all the goodness of life: work, food, and play. These, he says, are mysterious gifts from God. Further, he calls for obedience to all of God's commands.

This contradiction between the writer's reflections and his conclusions perplexes many scholars. Some argue that the conclusions were added by another, more optimistic writer. Others insist that clashing philosophies are the point of the book—that the writer is warning people not to trust in their own accomplishments and insights, but to rely on God.

Like Job and Proverbs, Ecclesiastes belongs to a genre known as Hebrew wisdom literature—poetry that preserves deep insights about life, usually written by prophets, priests, or professional sages. The title comes from the Greek translation of a word the writer uses to describe himself: teacher. This author further identifies himself as a son of David and a king, which has led many to conclude he was David's son and successor: Solomon, a king with legendary wisdom, and author of three thousand proverbs and a thousand songs (1 Kgs 4:32). The writing style and use of words borrowed from Persian, however, suggest that the book was perhaps compiled in the fourth century B.C., six centuries after Solomon. Fragments of Ecclesiastes dating to about 150 B.C. were found among the Dead Sea Scrolls, the remains of a library belonging to a Jewish desert community 14 miles east of Jerusalem.

Solomon was once thought to have written Ecclesiastes; a woodcut of the king from the 1530 Luther Bible.

I saw all the deeds that are done under the sun; and see, all is vanity and a chasing after wind. ECCL 1:14

When the teacher says he has seen "all the deeds that are under the sun," he means such human endeavors as hard work and the pursuit of wisdom, wealth, and pleasure. He has a unique vantage point—the pinnacle of success—for he presents himself as a Hebrew king renowned for wealth and wisdom. Yet, after surveying the human condition, he offers the grim report that all is vanity, using a Hebrew metaphor that literally means a fleeting breath. Human effort is meaningless and accomplishes nothing that endures. The sun, wind, and streams all continue on their courses, the teacher says, unabated by humans. Because the teacher observes that human beings do not make a difference, he concludes that "there is nothing new under the sun" (Eccl 1:9).

Some scholars suggest that "under the sun," a favorite phrase of the teacher and one that appears in the Bible only in Ecclesiastes, refers to all human endeavors. If so, the teacher may be using this phrase—which appears 29 times—to help build a bridge to his concluding piece of advice: "Fear God, and keep his commandments" (Eccl 12:13). If the teacher's pessimistic observations are linked to this closing advice, as many scholars believe, then his lesson does not end where it begins: "Vanity of vanities! All is vanity" (Eccl 1:2). Instead, it eventually reveals that people find meaning and fulfillment in life only through a relationship with God.

There is nothing better for mortals than to eat and drink, and find enjoyment in their toil. ECCL 2:24

The teacher conducts a pair of experiments during his search for meaning in life. First, he explores pleasure. He builds houses, plants vineyards, and buys massive herds. He amasses gold and silver, hires singers, and expands his harem. "Whatever my eyes desired I did not keep from them" (Eccl 2:10). Yet he remains unsatisfied.

Next, he studies wisdom. This is considered an honorable endeavor in the more civilized cultures, for professional sages and philosophers traditionally draw great respect. Though the teacher concludes that wisdom is better than foolishness, he sees no special value in it because the wise and the foolish both end in the same place: "The wise die just like fools" (Eccl 2:16). And all the accomplishments that the wise person struggles to achieve—knowledge, skills, possessions—are left behind "to be enjoyed by another who did not toil for it" (Eccl 2:21).

In an abrupt and surprising conclusion to these experiments, the teacher encourages people to enjoy godly pleasures and hard work, declaring that both are "from the hand of God" (Eccl 2:24). Though neither pleasure nor toil is satisfying apart from God, the teacher says that each can be enjoyed when understood as a gift from God.

For everything there is a season, and a time for every matter under heaven.   ECCL 3:1

In the eight verses that make up the most famous poem in Ecclesiastes—and one of the most beautiful and often quoted in the Bible—the teacher explains that everything in the human experience has its appointed time.

To illustrate the breadth of life's events, all of which are orchestrated by God, the teacher unveils a masterfully crafted series of opposites, beginning with birth and death: "a time to be born, and a time to die" (Eccl 3:2). He employs the poetic technique known as antithesis to show that both extremes—and everything in between—are subject to God's timing. He also uses parallelism to double the strength of his point. For example, birth and death are linked to and probably symbolized by "a time to plant, and a time to pluck up what is planted" (Eccl 3:2). Even the routine seasonal activities of planting and harvesting are beyond human control. There is a divinely ordained moment for every human experience, from the mundane chore of sewing to the intimidating responsibility of declaring war.

I saw all the oppressions that are practiced under the sun. Look, the tears of the oppressed—with no one to comfort them!   ECCL 4:1

The teacher has seen merciless oppression. With images of tyranny and suffering seared into his memory, he grimly concludes that dead people are better off than the oppressed living. Best off are those who have never been born.

These words echo the moans of a tormented Job, who lost his riches, his children, and his health: "Let the day perish in which I was born" (Job 3:3). The teacher's words also express the lament of Jeremiah after the prophet has been publicly humiliated by being locked in stocks at a gateway to Jerusalem: "Cursed be the day on which I was born! . . . Why did I come forth from the womb to see toil and sorrow, and spend my days in shame?" (Jer 20:14, 18).

A time to plant, from Ecclesiastes's most famous poem; a 13th-century stained glass window from Canterbury Cathedral

Guard your steps when you go to the house of God; to draw near to listen is better than the sacrifice offered by fools.   ECCL 5:1

Though the teacher fails to understand why God allows oppression, he nonetheless calls on people to worship the Lord respectfully and sincerely. "Guard your steps" means behave. And "listen" means obey; the prophet Samuel used the same Hebrew verb when he chastised King Saul for sparing the enemy's cattle after a battle: "Surely, to obey is better than sacrifice" (1 Sam 15:22).

The teacher also advises people not to make rash promises to God that they have no intention of keeping. If people fail to fulfill their vow, says the teacher, they can expect punishment.

The lover of money will not be satisfied with money; nor the lover of wealth, with gain.   ECCL 5:10

There is good news and bad news about wealth, says the teacher, but far more bad news than good. He says that wealth can produce greed, which is insatiable. Furthermore, the rich lose sleep over worrying about their wealth, their investments, and the people who depend on them for a living. This is a legitimate concern, the teacher acknowledges; the rich can instantly lose everything they have accumulated because of a single decision or unfortunate timing. The comparatively poor worker, on the other hand, enjoys a sweet and restful sleep from the day's hard labor.

Perhaps the ultimate bad news about wealth is that rich people—like all others—die poor: "As they came from their mother's womb, so they shall go again, naked as they came; they shall take nothing for their toil" (Eccl 5:15).

The good news, says the teacher, is that wealth—like food and work—is a gift from God. People who enjoy it as such and use it responsibly "will scarcely brood over the days of their lives, because God keeps them occupied with the joy of their hearts" (Eccl 5:20). "Joy" is not in the money, or the food, or the work. The teacher more likely means that joy is the human response to God's love; it is whatever people take pleasure in doing to show their gratitude to God for the gifts he has given them.

Go, eat your bread with enjoyment, and drink your wine with a merry heart.   ECCL 9:7

Again the teacher laments that death is the fate awaiting everyone: the good and the bad, the religiously observant and the pagan. And again he complains that in life, righteous people are often treated in the way that evil people deserve. Still, the teacher concludes that life is better than death because the living have hope of finding enjoyment, while the dead are unable to enjoy the pleasures "under the sun."

The teacher's advice, then, is to live life to the fullest; and he assures his readers that God wants them to do this. They should enjoy food, merriment, festive clothes, sweet-scented oils, a loving wife, a satisfying job. They should embrace every good object in life as a gift from God.

Dead flies make the perfumer's ointment give off a foul odor; so a little folly outweighs wisdom and honor. ECCL 10:1

Sages take immense pride in their wisdom and often make a show of pursuing wisdom by publicly debating lofty and abstract ideas. But the teacher warns that even a little foolishness can neutralize a stockpile of human wisdom. He illustrates this with a pithy saying about a fly ruining a vat of perfume.

With these words, and others like them throughout this short book, the teacher attacks the ancient and honored endeavor of seeking wisdom. He portrays wisdom as elusive and unstable—hard to find and easy to undo. Yet the teacher admits that despite its limitations, wisdom is better than foolishness.

The Last Judgment; from the early-13th-century psalter of Queen Ingeburg of Denmark

Send out your bread upon the waters, for after many days you will get it back. ECCL 11:1

Speaking like a financial consultant, the teacher advises people to take risks, yet to hedge those risks by diversifying their holdings. "Send out your bread upon the waters" is probably an allusion to exporting grain and other products across the sea—a risky but often lucrative business. Adventurous people willing to take those risks will reap the benefits.

Immediately after saying this, however, the teacher recommends financial protection through diversification: "Divide your means seven ways, or even eight, for you do not know what disaster may happen on earth" (Eccl 11:2).

There are alternate ways of interpreting these two verses. Some see them as a call to charitable giving: Throw your bread on the water, for you do not know who needs it or where it will go; and give in many different ways. Others see the verses as a metaphor: Do something good even if it makes no sense, for you will be rewarded; and do not count on being able to protect yourself from disaster.

Remember your creator in the days of your youth, before the days of trouble come, and the years draw near when you will say, "I have no pleasure in them." ECCL 12:1

This verse begins a famous description of the inevitable woes of aging. Graphic, figurative word pictures present the gloomy process of growing old. "Strong men" (possibly legs) are bent. "Women who grind" (teeth) stop because they are few. The "almond tree" (white hair) blossoms. "Windows" (eyes) see dimly. "Daughters of song" (sounds) are low. "The silver cord is snapped and the golden bowl is broken" (perhaps the chain holding a lamp, representing life). "Dust" (the body) returns to the earth. And "breath" (life) returns to God (Eccl 12:3-7). None of this makes sense to the teacher. Life on this side of heaven remains a troubling mystery.

The end of the matter; all has been heard. Fear God, and keep his commandments; for that is the whole duty of everyone. ECCL 12:13

The teacher's conclusion—both grand and surprising—is that there is meaning to life after all. The meaning, unfortunately, is one that humans cannot grasp. So the teacher advises humanity to trust God—to give him the respect he deserves, and to obey his commandments.

This conclusion seems so out of character for the supposedly cynical teacher that some scholars say a tradition-minded editor added it to make the book more palatable for God-fearing readers. Yet the conclusion reflects the high regard that the teacher expresses for God elsewhere. It is God, the teacher says, who is the source of those things worth enjoying in life (Eccl 3:13; 5:19). And it is God who will judge both the righteous and the wicked (Eccl 3:17).

Radically different from any other book in the Bible, the Song of Solomon is an intimate and erotic love poem, with no mention of God or religion. Throughout this literary masterpiece, portions of which may have been sung at weddings in ancient Israel, a young man and woman boldly and unashamedly declare their love and passionate yearning for each other. Most of the song is dominated by the woman, who praises the physical features of the man she loves and expresses her need to be with him. The man replies by complimenting the woman's beauty and sensuously though not crudely revealing his fervent longing to make love to her.

Though the poem emphasizes the important roles of fidelity and sexual desire in the love between a man and a woman, this is not likely why the Song of Solomon was included in the scriptural canon. Jews saw it as a song that symbolizes God's love for Israel. Christians later interpreted it as a song that portrays Jesus' love for the church.

The Song has long been attributed to Solomon, who is mentioned on occasion throughout the book and who is reported to have written a thousand songs and had a thousand wives and concubines (1 Kgs 4:32, 11:3). But the introductory description "The Song of Songs, which is Solomon's" (Song 1:1) can mean that the Song was written by him, about him, or for him. Thus, it is possible that the Song was composed in his honor at a later date. Similar love songs from Egypt date from the 13th to the 12th century B.C., at least 200 years before the king ruled in Jerusalem.

French artist Gustave Moreau (1826-1898) imagined the woman in Song of Solomon as a seductive courtesan.

Let him kiss me with the kisses of his mouth! For your love is better than wine. SONG 1:2

The love song begins with a young woman's fantasy about being kissed by the man she loves— a fantasy she boldly declares. She explains that her skin is darkened from working in the vineyards, but she insists that she is beautiful nonetheless. The young woman also offers to meet the man, a shepherd, asking where he plans to rest his flock at noon.

It is unclear who the man is. Some scholars suggest he is Solomon, since the woman describes him as "the king" (Song 1:4). More likely, the woman is comparing her beloved shepherd to a glorious king—a kind of knight in shining armor. Others, however, see in the story the possibility of a romantic triangle: King Solomon seeks a beautiful country woman as his wife, but the woman refuses the king and remains loyal to the shepherd whom she eventually marries.

Ah, you are beautiful, my love; ah, you are beautiful; your eyes are doves. SONG 1:15

The man responds, assuring his beloved that she is truly beautiful. It may not seem like much of a compliment when he compares her to a "mare among Pharaoh's chariots" (Song 1:9), but this is flattering praise—perhaps commending the woman's graceful movements or regal stature. Theocritus, a Greek poet in the third century B.C., used similar words to describe the legendary Helen of Troy.

It is sometimes impossible to know who is doing the talking, the man or the woman. Gender clues are not always given, and both the man and the woman share equally intense passion for each other. Neither feels the least bit inhibited about expressing the most intimate feelings and desires. In the exchange of compliments that complete chapter 1, however, it is clearly the woman expressing delight in the presence of her beloved, whom she describes as "a bag of myrrh that lies between my breasts" (Song 1:13). Myrrh, like the nard that she also mentions, is a fragrant and expensive spice used as an enticing perfume. Extracted from balsam trees grown in Arabia and India, it was used to scent the wedding robes of Israelite kings (Ps 45:8).

I am a rose of Sharon, a lily of the valleys. SONG 2:1

The woman appears to be humbly describing herself as just one flower in a sea of flowers, much like the crocuses that fill the fertile plain of Sharon near the Mediterranean coast. Immediately the man refutes this with high praise; his beloved is "a lily among brambles" (Song 2:2).

The voice of my beloved! Look, he comes, leaping upon the mountains, bounding over the hills. SONG 2:8

Later, when the woman and her young love are apart, she reminisces about a springtime morning when she looked out of her bedroom window and saw the man running over the hills toward her.

A woman caught in the reverie of a daydream is Dante Gabriel Rossetti's chaste 1880 vision of the love celebrated in Song of Solomon.

"Arise, my love, my fair one," he called, inviting her to come with him to enjoy the splendor of the countryside—and the pleasure of each other's company. In a brazen and seductive refrain, the woman beckons the man to remain until the morning shadows flee, to pasture "among the lilies" and linger like a young deer "on the cleft mountains" (Song 2:10, 16, 17).

Upon my bed at night I sought him whom my soul loves; I sought him, but found him not. SONG 3:1

The woman tells her friends about what appears to be a nightmare she had about the man. Waking to find him gone, she called out for him, but he did not respond. She even rose from bed, got dressed, and searched the city until she finally found him and brought him back. Many ancient poems contain sections like this, revealing the pain that lovers experience when separated from one another.

Look, it is the litter of Solomon! Around it are sixty mighty men of the mighty men of Israel. SONG 3:7

A dust cloud rolling in from the desert announces that the groom and his procession are coming for the bride. This may be Solomon coming for the woman. But it is more likely that the woman is so much in love with her shepherd that she envisions their humble wedding as the majestic nuptial ceremony of a king and queen.

Your lips are like a crimson thread, and your mouth is lovely. Your cheeks are like halves of a pomegranate behind your veil. SONG 4:3

When the two are alone, perhaps after their wedding, the man immerses his beloved in praise, comparing her body to some of the most lovely things in nature he has ever seen: her eyes behind her veil are like doves; her wavy black locks flow gracefully down her shoulders like a flock of black goats dancing rhythmically down the slopes of a hillside, and her teeth glimmer like the shorn and freshly washed wool of ewes.

I am my beloved's and my beloved is mine. SONG 6:3

In this, the poem's most famous line, the woman defines true love: she and her shepherd belong entirely and exclusively to each other. They hold back no part of themselves; each yields completely to the desires of the other. God uses a similar expression to describe his relationship with Israel: "I will take you as my people, and I will be your God. You shall know that I am the Lord your God" (Ex 6:7).

Let us go out early to the vineyards . . . . There I will give you my love. SONG 7:12

The sensuous exchange of compliments continues, as each lover extols the body of the other and the desires they share. The intensity of their passion heats up, bursting into a flame of eroticism that is neither obscene nor ashamed. The shepherd compares his beloved to a stately palm tree that he longs to climb and cling to. She invites him to join her on what sounds like a romantic and adventurous honeymoon—the two will stroll through the fields, sleep in the villages, and make love in the vineyards.

Set me as a seal upon your heart. SONG 8:6

The woman asks her shepherd to pledge his love forever; a seal is an engraved sign that functions as a signature, identifying the owner of what bears the mark. She follows this request with a profound insight about the nature and power of love. Her words, scholars agree, provide the most enriching moment in the entire poem: "Love is strong as death, passion fierce as the grave. Its flashes are flashes of fire, a raging flame. Many waters cannot quench love, neither can floods drown it" (Song 8:6-7). There is no force on earth—not even death—that is more powerful than the love a man and a woman share for each other.

The rose of Sharon is actually a crocus, like these in a field of wildflowers near Israel's Mediterranean coast.

In this medieval Bible illumination, the Lord appears to Isaiah, calling him to a prophetic mission.

First of the major prophetic books, Isaiah expresses the divine message of judgment and future salvation of the Jews in some of the most eloquent language found in the Hebrew Bible. The refined poetry in the book indicates that Isaiah was probably highly educated; he most certainly possessed a creative spirit in the service of God. Other biographical facts about Isaiah emerge from scattered information in the early chapters. His official activity as a prophet in Judah and Jerusalem commenced about 733 B.C., the year King Uzziah (Azariah) died, and continued through the reigns of Jotham, Ahaz, and Hezekiah. Isaiah and his wife, a prophetess, had two children, each of whom was named to designate a particular aspect of his prophetic teaching. Like Jeremiah and Hosea, Isaiah dramatized parts of his message by symbolic actions, such as walking barefoot and naked through Jerusalem (Isa 20:2). He gave good counsel to Hezekiah during the siege of Jerusalem by Sennacherib in 701 B.C. Isaiah 36-39 provides a close account of the prophet's relationship to the throne during that highly charged period, yet he was not held in favor by all Judah's kings. According to legend, Isaiah met a martyr's death when the wicked King Manasseh, who followed Hezekiah, had him sawed in two.

As interesting as the prophet's personal life may have been, it is overshadowed by Isaiah's message. Indeed, in the book's 66 chapters, there is relatively little prose narrative. The bulk of the work comprises collections of prophetic oracles of judgment and promise. Frequently introduced by the phrase, "Thus says the Lord," a prophetic oracle delivers divine speech. Isaiah also includes prophetic "lawsuits" against the people, laments, and prayers. A number of themes thread their way throughout the book. The most prominent are the portrayal of God as king over all creation and the Lord's eternal commitment to the descendants of King David who reign in his holy city, Jerusalem.

The book of Isaiah was important to early Christians. The New Testament most frequently quotes Isaiah, Psalms, and the books of the Pentateuch. The birth of Immanuel, scion of the Davidic throne, prophesied in Isaiah 7:14, was understood to be a reference to the birth of Jesus. So too, the passages found in Isaiah 44-52 referring to God's "servant" were thought by New Testament authors to shed light on Jesus' mission.

The vision of Isaiah son of Amoz, which he saw concerning Judah and Jerusalem in the days of Uzziah, Jotham, Ahaz, and Hezekiah, kings of Judah. ISA 1:1

The first chapter of Isaiah contains a major theme of the book. Judah and Israel have sinned terribly, for which they will undergo severe punishment. But Jerusalem and a band of its inhabitants will ultimately be redeemed by the "Holy One of Israel" (Isa 1:4), Isaiah's frequent expression for God. A sense of the devastation wrought by Assyrian military invasions of Judah in the eighth century B.C. permeates the beginning of the book.

After the initial statement, the chapter takes the form of an Israelite lawsuit. God charges his "children," the people of Israel, with their sins. Chief among them are their sacrificial practices; all of their offerings and sacrifices are offensive to the Lord because Israel's hands are "full of blood" (Isa 1:2, 15). God desires moral behavior toward society's most vulnerable members, but Israel has ignored its obligations. In staccato rhythm Isaiah commands that the people "cease to do evil, learn to do good; seek justice, rescue the oppressed, defend the orphan, plead for the widow" (Isa 1:16-17). The chapter ends with a change of tone, promising future restoration for a remnant from Judah in the holy city. Jerusalem shall yet be redeemed, says God, but only by justice.

An oracle addressed to Judah and Jerusalem in the second chapter introduces another theme that appears throughout Isaiah: Israel's God as the Lord of all the nations. In the future, not just the Israelites, but many nations will be reconciled and go to the temple in Jerusalem to be instructed in the word of the Lord. Weapons of war and destruction will be set aside for farm implements to till the earth. Instead of blood soaking the fields, farmers will once again be able to grow crops. Isaiah describes this future time of peace in memorable words: "They shall beat their swords into plowshares, and their spears into pruning hooks" (Isa 2:4).

For now the Sovereign, the Lord of hosts, is taking away from Jerusalem and from Judah support and staff. ISA 3:1

Oracles of judgment against Judah and the holy city appear in the third and fourth chapters. The precise historical context of these passages is difficult to discern, but it appears that Judah's society is in turmoil. Divine punishment will result in an overturning of the leadership in the southern kingdom. Isaiah mentions 11 types of leaders, from warriors to judges to magicians, and warns that their power is about to end as a result of their oppression of the poor. Instead, the Lord of hosts "will make boys their princes, and babes shall rule over them" (Isa 3:4).

Isaiah also singles out the pampered women of Jerusalem, "the daughters of Zion" (Isa 3:16), for condemnation. Women who live in Jerusalem have more money for clothing and jewelry than those who lead a farming life in the countryside of Judah. These urban women have been spoiled by luxuries that come along with wealth. They walk seductively around town, "mincing along as they go, tinkling with their feet." But God promises to punish them. He will take away their finery; "instead of perfume, there will be a stench . . . and instead of a rich robe, a binding of sackcloth" (Isa 3:16, 24).

Let me sing for my beloved my love-song concerning his vineyard. ISA 5:1

The prophet uses an allegory or parable to drive home a certain point about the Israelites' sins. Isaiah sings a "love-song" about a vineyard. His "beloved" has found a fertile hill, cleared it of stones, and planted the finest vines. But after all the careful preparations made by the gardener, the vineyard yields sour grapes. Isaiah then calls on the people of Judah to judge between God and the vineyard. There is nothing left to do but to dig up the vines, tear up the walls, and let the vineyard be overrun with briers and weeds. For anyone missing the point of the parable, the identities of the vineyard and its caretaker are made explicit: "For the vineyard of the Lord of hosts is the house of Israel . . . ; he expected justice, but saw bloodshed" (Isa 5:7). In other words, although God has chosen the Israelites as his people and provided for them, they are wildly immoral, disregarding the divine laws handed down to Moses on Mount Sinai centuries ago.

The allegory is followed by a series of oracles that denounce the social injustice found in the southern kingdom of Judah. Various sins are deemed reprehensible: greedy materialism in accumulating land in Israel and drinking to excess at the expense of knowledge of God's works. Because the Judahites remain unrepentant, God will "whistle for a people at the ends of the earth" (Isa 5:26), a thinly veiled reference to the Assyrians, to punish Judah.

In the year that King Uzziah died, I saw the Lord sitting on a throne, high and lofty. ISA 6:1

Isaiah's dramatic call to be a prophet occurs in a vision that comes to him in Jerusalem's temple during the year King Uzziah dies, according to some authorities 733 B.C., though earlier dates are proposed. The call is full of visual imagery. God sits grandly on a throne as the holy king over all. The mere hem of his robe is sufficient to fill the temple. The divine retinue of angels, here called "seraphs," are by God's side, poised to serve him. They call to one another and proclaim the essence of God's character: "Holy, holy, holy is the Lord of hosts; the whole earth is full of his glory" (Isa 6:3). The voice of the angels itself is enough to make the thresholds of the temple shake as billows of incense fill the sanctuary.

Isaiah is awestruck and humbled by the grandeur of this sight. He immediately recognizes his own inadequacy. "Woe is me! I am lost, for I am a man of unclean lips; and I live among a people of unclean lips" (Isa 6:5). Not only Isaiah, but all his fellow Judahites are sinners. After Isaiah admits his guilt, one of the seraphs purifies him by touching a red-hot coal to his mouth. God calls out asking who is willing to deliver the divine message of judgment. Knowing he has been cleansed of his sin by the angel's touch, Isaiah accepts the monumental task with alacrity: "Here I am! Send me!" (Isa 6:8).

In the days of Ahaz son of Jotham son of Uzziah, king of Judah, King Rezin of Aram and King Pekah son of Remaliah of Israel went up to attack Jerusalem. ISA 7:1

The threat of an unfriendly foreign alliance animates the seventh chapter of Isaiah. Word of the alliance shakes the hearts of the Judahites "as the trees of the forest shake before the wind" (Isa 7:2). The first half of the chapter describes what is known as the Syro-Ephraimite war, which lasted from 735 to 732 B.C. Syria, here called Aram, under the leadership of King Rezin, and Ephraim, the northern kingdom of Israel, under King Pekah, decide to band together in order to form a stronger front against the encroaching power of Assyria.

The two kings want Judah to join them in their resistance to Assyria. Because King Ahaz is reluctant, Rezin and Pekah conspire to attack Judah in order to unseat Ahaz and install their own puppet king on the throne in Jerusalem. Ahaz is fraught with fear, but Isaiah's prophetic counsel remains: Trust in God and resist such foreign entanglements. As a prophetic sign, Isaiah has named his son Shear-jashub, Hebrew for "a remnant shall return," to indicate that the fate of the northern kingdom is already sealed. Shear-jashub's prophetic name will prove true in little more than ten years. In 722 B.C. the kingdom of Israel will fall to the Assyrian empire and, as most of its residents are deported, a small band of survivors will flee south for safety to the kingdom of Judah.

Again the Lord spoke to Ahaz, saying, "Ask a sign of the Lord your God." ISA 7:10-11

Despite Isaiah's best efforts, Ahaz needs more convincing. The Lord offers the king another sign concerning the future of Judah. The prophet delivers a message to the house of David predicting the birth of another son to "the young woman," presumably a person well known to Ahaz. The child's name shall be Immanuel, which means "God is with us." The import of this symbolic name is to reassure Ahaz once again that Judah will be safeguarded against evil by God's presence. Unfortunately, Ahaz continues to balk at Isaiah's counsel. The chapter closes with a series of four oracles that are full of foreboding for the future. The lands of Israel and Syria will become deserted and Judah, too, will ultimately be punished for its infidelity.

The identity of the mother and child described in Isaiah 7:14 has been a major test for interpreters. Early Christians understood the oracle as referring to events in their own day rather than to a child's birth in eighth-century Judah. In the Septuagint, the Greek translation of the Hebrew Bible used by early Christians, "the young woman" (Hebrew *'almah*) was translated as *parthenos*, or virgin. Matthew thus wrote that the birth of Jesus to the virgin Mary was the fulfillment of Isaiah's prophecy (Mt 1:22-23).

Then the Lord said to me, Take a large tablet and write on it in common characters, "Belonging to Maher-shalal-hash-baz." ISA 8:1

Isaiah 8 provides more details about the prophet's life. The prophet is commanded by God to write a name on a tablet of stone, "Maher-shalal-hash-baz," meaning "the spoil speeds, the prey hastens." The reason for using this enigmatic phrase is soon revealed. Not only is Maher-shalal-hash-baz the name of Isaiah's son by his wife the prophetess, it is also a symbolic name that predicts the fate of Judah's northern neighbors. Before the child can say "father" or "mother," the king of Assyria will have snatched away the spoils from Damascus and Samaria, the capitals of Syria and Israel.

The fall of Samaria should serve as a warning to Judah and its inhabitants. Isaiah's message is this: Do not trust in human promises or the defense of a foreign alliance to save you; trust in the Lord God of Israel. In the final part of the chapter, Isaiah instructs his followers to "bind up the testimony" (Isa 8:16)—a possible reference to the previous oracles. Since his message has largely fallen on deaf ears, Isaiah wants to leave a record of it for future generations to heed. Nonetheless, the prophet continues his work for the good of his people.

The people who walked in darkness have seen a great light; those who lived in a land of deep darkness—on them light has shined. ISA 9:2

A changed historical circumstance lies behind the optimistic tone of chapter 9. The people of Judah and Israel have "walked in darkness," that is, they have been threatened by the terrible might of Assyria. The "great light" is the hope promised by the accession of a new king to the throne of Judah, one who may be able to break the yoke of Assyrian oppression. In a passage that may have been used as part of a coronation ceremony, Isaiah speaks of a child who has been born to the nation. He is given four different throne names, reflecting his different roles as king. As "Prince of Peace," the heir to the throne of David will usher in a reign of endless peace. The promised son most likely refers to Hezekiah, who took over the throne from his father, Ahaz, in 727 B.C. Like the figure of Immanuel mentioned in Isaiah 7, this "great light" of the Davidic dynasty was also understood by early Christians to predict the messiahship of Jesus (Mt 4:13-16).

The fate of Israel described in the last half of chapter 9 stands in contrast to this vision of peace and prosperity secured by a Davidic monarch in Judah.

In paired scenes from the 1546 Farnese Book of Hours, the angel Gabriel appears to Mary (left) and Isaiah tells Ahaz of the birth of a son to a virgin.

QUOTING ISAIAH

Apart from Psalms, Isaiah is the most quoted book in the New Testament—cited about 50 times. Scholars often call it the fifth gospel because, as the early biblical translator Jerome put it, Isaiah narrates the life of the Messiah so vividly that he seems to be "telling the story of what has already happened rather than what is still to come."

All four Evangelists quote Isaiah 40:3 in referring to John the Baptist as a voice crying in the wilderness, "prepare the way of the Lord." Matthew clearly sees a reference to Jesus' birth in Isaiah 7:14: "Look, the virgin shall conceive and bear a son, and they shall call him Emmanuel" (Mt 1:23). An even more stark revelation of Jesus—quoted throughout the gospels—is in Isaiah's "suffering servant" passages, written as though the prophet had witnessed the crucifixion.

Jesus, too, saw himself in the book of Isaiah. Once, standing in the Nazareth synagogue, he read aloud a passage from Isaiah 61:1-2 about a spirit-anointed deliverer who would bring good news to the poor, heal the blind, and free the oppressed. "Today this scripture has been fulfilled in your hearing" (Lk 4:21), he told an amazed audience.

Israel's leaders have led the people astray by relying on foreign powers to save them. Because of this infidelity, Isaiah makes clear that God has not completed the punishment. Peppered throughout the oracles of divine judgment is the ominous warning, "For all this his anger has not turned away; his hand is stretched out still" (Isa 9:12, 17, 21; 10:4).

Ah, Assyria, the rod of my anger—the club in their hands is my fury!   ISA 10:5

God's punishment of the godless nation Israel will arrive by the instrument of Assyria, "the rod of my anger." In a phrase echoing the symbolic name of Isaiah's son, Maher-shalal-hash-baz, Assyria will "take spoil and seize plunder" (Isa 10:6). Yet God will not allow Assyria to remain the triumphant victor. The king of Assyria is misguided in thinking he has conquered Israel by his own strength and wisdom; rather, he unknowingly serves the Lord's purpose. The God of Israel will judge the king of Assyria for his arrogance; the oracle thus also predicts the punishment of Assyria. The "light of Israel" (Isa 10:17), the Lord, will defeat Assyria by devastating its army and by consuming its forests with fire. Like the small remnant of Jacob who escape from the northern kingdom, so few trees will remain in Assyria that even a child will be able to count them.

A shoot shall come out from the stump of Jesse, and a branch shall grow out of his roots.   ISA 11:1

A bright picture of hope for the future is painted in chapter 11. An heir to the throne of David, a shoot from the "stump of Jesse," will usher in a new era in the life of Israel. Jesse was the father of King David; the reference to his "stump" gives the impression of a family tree cut off prematurely. God had promised David an eternal dynasty (2 Sam 7:13); thus the "shoot of Jesse" is an indication that there is life left in the old tree stump. The spirit of the Lord will ensure that the promised heir will be an ideal king: wise, strong, righteous, and faithful to God. The new era over which he will hold sway will see a reversal of the natural order: "The wolf shall live with the lamb, the leopard shall lie down with the kid" (Isa 11:6). In that glorious time, God will gather up all those from Ephraim (Israel) and Judah who have been deported by the Assyrians to far-off lands. In words reminiscent of the account in Exodus, God will part the Nile "and make a way to cross on foot" (Isa 11:15). After this new exodus, there will come a time of shalom, a Hebrew word meaning reconciliation, wholeness, or, more generally, peace.

The oracle concerning Babylon that Isaiah son of Amoz saw.   ISA 13:1

As in many of the other prophetic books, a large section of Isaiah (Isa 13:1-23:18) contains oracles against foreign nations. Indeed, one of the themes of Isaiah is the relationship of those foreign nations to Israel's God. The first of the nations marked for condemnation is Babylon. The Babylonian empire did not gain strength enough to threaten Israel until the late seventh century B.C., but this oracle anticipates Babylon's eventual fall to the Persians in the sixth century. In a sardonic lament, the prophet sarcastically mourns the demise of the Babylonian king: "How are you fallen from heaven, O Day Star, son of Dawn" (Isa 14:12). The king of Babylon aspires to be as high and mighty as the astral gods the Babylonians worshiped, but the God of Israel will cast him down to Sheol, the underworld.

The Assyrians are singled out for condemnation in Isaiah 14:25. The verse appears in a longer passage that indicates the larger scope of God's plan for the whole world in punishing wayward nations. The inevitability of the divine plan is underscored in words that recall and transform an earlier refrain in Isaiah. The prophet asks a pointed question: "His hand is stretched out, and who will turn it back?" (Isa 14:27).

In an oracle dated to 727 B.C., the year King Ahaz died, the prophet berates Philistia. The Philistines, who lived in close proximity to the Israelites in the land of Canaan, constituted a persistent threat to Israel throughout its history. Philistine revolts were crushed three times by Assyria in the eighth century. The smoke coming out of the north to scorch Philistia mentioned in Isaiah 14:31 likely refers to one of those punitive missions.

Because Ar is laid waste in a night, Moab is undone.
ISA 15:1

Moab, Israel's neighbor to the east of the Dead Sea, is next on the list of wicked nations. The Moabites will wail in mourning over the devastation of their principal cities by Israel's God. The next oracle, which is titled "concerning Damascus," in fact concerns not only Syria, but also its ally during the eighth century, the northern kingdom of Israel. Their fates cannot be separated because, from the perspective of the prophet, the two nations were complicit in crimes against God during the Syro-Ephraimite war. The prophet holds Israel's idolatry in particular disdain. Israel has not "remembered the Rock [God] of your refuge" (Isa 17:10), but instead has turned to worship idols made by hand.

Isaiah moves from Israel's northeast to the southwest to describe the land of Ethiopia, located on the upper Nile south of Egypt. Scholars have suggested that the "ambassadors" from Ethiopia mentioned in Isaiah 18:2 had come to convince King Hezekiah to join them in a coalition against Assyria. Trusting in foreign alliances is a clear violation of trust in God. The "people tall and smooth" (Isa 18:7) thus also merit punishment.

See, the Lord is riding on a swift cloud and comes to Egypt. ISA 19:1

The oracle against Egypt in chapter 19 depicts the Lord in majestic terms riding on the clouds to deliver that land to its mournful fate. The punishment of Egypt will entail a civil war and the coming to power of a "fierce king" (Isa 19:4) who will make life harsh for the Egyptians. Adding to the political instability will be a disruption of Egypt's source of water and economic mainstay, the Nile. God will dry up the the river on which all life in Egypt depends.

A most unusual event in the life of the prophet is recounted in chapter 20 in connection with an oracle against Egypt and Ethiopia. Following a divine dictate, Isaiah removes the rough clothes he is wearing and for three years walks the streets of Jerusalem naked and barefoot. His shocking action is a visual symbol of what will befall the Ethiopian and Egyptian soldiers. After their conquest by Assyria, the captives will be stripped and taken away. But God's righteous judgment will extend to other countries as well. The fall of Babylon is foretold in Isaiah 21:1-10; warnings are issued to the

Arabian provinces of Dumah, Tema, and Kedar in the following verses. The seafaring nation of Phoenicia, with its capital city Tyre, is told of its dread fate in chapter 23, the last of the oracles against wicked nations, some of which may be by Isaiah's disciples.

Now the Lord is about to lay waste the earth and make it desolate, and he will twist its surface and scatter its inhabitants. ISA 24:1

The tone of Isaiah changes markedly in chapter 24, the first of four chapters many scholars refer to as the "Isaiah Apocalypse," a vision of the culmination of history. In most of the oracles early in the book, Isaiah's prophecies isolate particular nations for judgment. In chapters 24 to 27, divine anger reaches fever pitch. Not just individual nations with their armies, but the entire world and even the heavens will suffer the scourging divine punishment. Two cities that await very different futures are described in the Apocalypse. An unnamed city, variously termed "the city of chaos" (Isa 24:10), "the palace of aliens" (Isa 25:2), or "the fortified city" (Isa 27:10), will be the target of divine wrath. The devastation that the doomed city will experience is set in contrast with the future restoration of the city of Jerusalem. Interwoven throughout the description of woe for the wicked are short passages containing hope for a future redemption that will emanate from Jerusalem. God will prepare a rich feast for all people on Mount Zion. On that day, "the Lord God will wipe away the tears from all faces" (Isa 25:8). The exiled from Judah and Israel will be gathered up and once again worship God on Mount Zion.

Ah, the proud garland of the drunkards of Ephraim, and the fading flower of its glorious beauty. ISA 28:1

Isaiah 28 and 29 contain oracles of judgment against the northern and southern kingdoms of Israel and Judah. The north is the first to come in for the prophet's scathing indictment. The kingdom used to be proud and mighty, but now it is past its prime, a "fading flower." Its leaders, priests, and prophets are "bloated with rich food" and "stagger with strong drink" (Isa 28:1, 7). They are unable to think straight to render proper judgments. A righteous remnant of the people will survive, but the Lord

An early-15th-century tree of Jesse, worked in alabaster, traces the ancestry of Jesus (at top, on the lap of Mary) through a lyre-playing King David (center) to a slumbering Jesse (bottom); angels hover above the scene.

will confound the rest by speaking to the people in "stammering lip and with alien tongue" (Isa 28:11).

Judah will also come under God's judgment. He pledges to remain true to his chosen city Jerusalem: "I am laying in Zion a foundation stone" (Isa 28:16). Yet Zion, too, will be besieged before it is ultimately rescued. The prophet tries to convey his message in another way, by using the language of farming. Just as a farmer must carefully decide when to plow the ground and must sow the seeds, harvest, and thresh in due season, so God will judge, punish, and renew the people in due course.

Oh, rebellious children, says the Lord, who carry out a plan, but not mine; who make an alliance, but against my will, adding sin to sin. ISA 30:1

God condemns Judah specifically for making a foreign alliance with Egypt. In the late eighth century B.C., the "rebellious children" under Hezekiah seek protection from Assyria by linking up with the stronger power of Egypt. The alliance is unequal. Judah is required to pay tribute to Egypt, sending "their treasures on the humps of camels" (Isa 30:6), in return for military protection. Isaiah expresses God's rage at the people for ignoring the righteous prophet's counsel to trust in the Lord. Instead, they have paid attention only to false prophets, to those who speak "smooth things" (Isa 30:10), telling the people only what they want to hear.

Even though the prophet expresses divine anger at the rebellious Judahites, God will ultimately protect the people of Jerusalem. He will deliver the city by

destroying the power of Assyria. There are comforting words for the future: "No longer will you see the insolent people, the people of an obscure speech that you cannot comprehend, stammering in a language that you cannot comprehend" (Isa 33:19). But first the inhabitants of Jerusalem must eat "the bread of adversity" and drink "the water of affliction" before God "binds up the injuries of his people, and heals the wounds inflicted by his blow" (Isa 30:20, 26).

Draw near, O nations, to hear; O peoples, give heed! Let the earth hear, and all that fills it; the world, and all that comes from it. ISA 34:1

God the divine judge and warrior animates Isaiah 34 and 35, a poem about judgment and redemption. The passage begins in the form of an Israelite lawsuit, calling all people and even the earth itself to listen to God's case, "for the Lord is enraged against all the nations" (Isa 34:2). God will punish them for their treatment of his holy city, Zion. Divine wrath will affect even the elements so that "the skies roll up like a scroll" (Isa 34:4). The fate of the nation of Edom, located to the southeast of Israel, is described. God will unsheathe the divine sword to wreak vengeance on the Edomites until "their land shall be soaked with blood" (Isa 34:7). When God has completed the devastation of the nation, it will be depopulated; only such wild beasts as jackals, buzzards, hedgehogs, and hyenas will live on the barren land.

Isaiah 35 offers the reverse of the judgment by reiterating God's commitment to Jerusalem. He will gloriously restore the embattled city of Zion and comfort a righteous remnant of redeemed Israelites. In language similar to what scholars call Second Isaiah (see box, page 206), the prophet describes an ideal future when "the eyes of the blind shall be opened, and . . . the lame shall leap like a deer" (Isa 35:5-6) as the exiles return to Zion with rejoicing.

In the fourteenth year of King Hezekiah, King Sennacherib of Assyria came up against all the fortified cities of Judah and captured them. ISA 36:1

The historical prose narrative in chapters 36 to 39 differs from the oracles that precede and follow it. In an account that closely parallels 2 Kings 18:13-20:19, the chapters tell the story of the Assyrian siege of Jerusalem in 701 B.C. under the ruler Sennacherib. At the time of the siege, Hezekiah reigns as king of Judah. The narrative is interesting from a historical standpoint because it is one of the few stories in the Bible for which there is ample archaeological evidence, not only from the Israelite side, but from the Assyrian side as well.

In this detail from bas-reliefs found at Sennacherib's palace at Nineveh, Assyrian soldiers carry off booty and prisoners from the captured city of Lachish.

The siege of the Judean town of Lachish, mentioned in Isaiah 36:2, is also described in the Annals of Sennacherib and illustrated in an Assyrian relief that was found in Sennacherib's palace at Nineveh.

But the narrative is even more significant from a theological standpoint. Hezekiah's behavior provides an example of the way a pious Israelite should conduct himself in a time of trouble. When the Assyrian king's chief steward and emissary, the Rabshakeh, threatens the Jerusalemites, Hezekiah's first reaction is to go to the temple to worship. Throughout the ordeal, he consults his court prophet Isaiah. And the king prays. Not one, but two of Hezekiah's prayers are included in the narrative (Isa 37:16-20; 38:3) as well as a song of thanksgiving (Isa 38:9-20). Hezekiah's piety is ultimately rewarded because the Lord saves Jerusalem from the Assyrians and heals Hezekiah of a life-threatening illness.

Comfort, O comfort my people, says your God.
ISA 40:1

A marked change in tone characterizes Isaiah 40, the first chapter of what is often referred to as Second Isaiah, most likely shaped during the Babylonian exile. The promise of redemption anticipated in the first part of the book becomes a major theme. The divine command to "comfort my people" is a plural imperative in the original Hebrew, for God is telling the angelic host to console the exiles in Babylon. Jerusalem has now received more than a full measure of punishment, "double for all her sins" (Isa 40:2).

Who will enable the exiles to return? The subsequent oracle describes Israel's God as the creator of the world, who patterned the universe according to his own unique plan. The divine power and majesty are conveyed in a number of rhetorical questions, such as "Who has measured the waters in the hollow of his hand?" (Isa 40:12). But might is not the only characteristic of God; he also shows compassion to his faithful servants. With inspiring language, Isaiah promises that those who are faithful "shall mount up with wings like eagles, they shall run and not be weary, they shall walk and not faint" (Isa 40:31).

Listen to me in silence, O coastlands; let the peoples renew their strength; . . . let us together draw near for judgment. ISA 41:1

The tone of hope and consolation continues in chapter 41. The passage takes the form of a lawsuit in which God is judging the nations and calls on the coastlands to act as witnesses. Isaiah poses rhetorical questions to illustrate how the Lord has shown concern for Israel. Implicit in the first question is the bold and surprising assertion that God employed "a

Hezekiah, a stained glass portrait by Edward Burne-Jones (1833-1898)

victor from the east" (Isa 41:2) as the divine instrument of salvation. It was King Cyrus of Persia who defeated the Babylonians in 539 B.C. and issued an edict permitting the Jews to return to their homeland.

Isaiah reassures Israel that it has no reason to fear. God and Israel have a unique relationship. Long ago in its early history, God had chosen Israel's ancestor Abraham and made a covenant with him and his descendants. As his continuing part of the covenant, the Lord pledges to help Israel through his abiding presence. "Do not fear, for I am with you" (Isa 41:10) come the comforting words of the Lord. God, who created all and who has control over even the rulers of the foreign nations, will remain with Israel through its trials.

Here is my servant, whom I uphold, my chosen, in whom my soul delights; I have put my spirit upon him; he will bring forth justice to the nations. ISA 42:1

Chapter 42 contains the first of four passages that scholars call the "servant songs." The figure of a servant of the Lord emerges in the first four verses. God has chosen him for a special mission: to "bring forth justice to the nations." The role of the servant is an expansive one. He must be "a covenant to the people, a light to the nations" (Isa 42:6). The prophet, who can be called Second Isaiah, thus envisions a world in which everyone will recognize and worship Israel's God. The servant will play an indispensable role in achieving this goal by spreading God's teaching.

The identity of the servant has been much debated. Some interpreters view the servant in a collective sense as the entire people of Israel. Others regard the servant as an actual historical figure from the sixth century. Many Christian interpreters identify the servant as a prophetic depiction of Jesus.

The special bond between God and Israel is reflected in the language of redemption God uses: "Do not fear, for I have redeemed you" (Isa 43:1). A "redeemer" in ancient Israel was a person who would buy back a relative from indentured servitude or repurchase a kinsman's land that had been sold to escape debt. Thus God's redemption of Israel expresses the close family relationship that binds them to one another. The Lord drew together his sons and daughters from the north and the south, even from the ends of the earth, because of their family ties.

All who make idols are nothing, and the things they delight in do not profit. ISA 44:9

Isaiah 44:9-20 contains a satirical polemic against idols. It is one of many passages in Isaiah that rant against wooden or metal images (see Isa 45:16-17; 46:1-7). During the exile in Babylon, the Israelites

MORE THAN ONE ISAIAH?

*I*saiah, often called Judah's greatest prophet, may not have written all of the book bearing his name—the longest in the Bible. Striking differences between the first 39 chapters and the last 27 have led many scholars to conclude that two or even three writers—each from different eras—contributed to the work.

The most obvious differences relate to the setting. The first 39 chapters portray the turbulent years of Isaiah's own time in the late 700s B.C., when the northern kingdom of Israel fell to Assyria and the southern kingdom of Judah was beset by a variety of enemies. Chapters 40-55, often referred to as Second Isaiah, report Babylon's destruction of Jerusalem more than a century later, in 586 B.C. This section also describes the subsequent exile of the Jews, followed by their release under King Cyrus of Persia, who conquered Babylon in 539 B.C., and seems to read more like history than prophecy.

Isaiah, as painted about 1510 by Michelangelo for the ceiling of the Vatican's Sistine Chapel

Chapters 56-66, called Third Isaiah, address the Jews who have returned from exile.

There are also marked differences in words and tone between the sections. Isaiah's earlier chapters are stern and condemning, while the later chapters are tender and consoling. Some of the prophet's favorite words and ideas, such as references to a messianic king from the house of David, disappear after chapter 39. Likewise, pivotal ideas in the closing chapters, such as references to God the creator, appear nowhere in the early section. Despite such differences, Jews in ancient times considered Isaiah to be the sole author. The famous Isaiah scroll of about 100 B.C., found among the Dead Sea Scrolls, presents the book as a single unit—though the copyist had a chance to make a break after chapter 39. Instead, he put the first line of chapter 40 at the bottom of the column, indicating a continuance.

---

were exposed to foreign religious practices, including those in which statues of gods were worshiped. Israelite religion strictly prohibited any visual depiction of its own God. Verbal portraits that outlined the character and activities of God were enshrined in Israel's sacred texts and traditions, but statues of God were forbidden. Isaiah points out the delusion involved in deifying an inanimate object by describing the making of idols. An ironsmith forges the ax that a carpenter uses to cut down the cedar tree for the idol. Half of the tree is used as fuel for a fire. With the other half of the same tree, the carpenter carves an idol. Dripping with sarcasm, Isaiah imagines the thoughts of the carpenter, who says of the burning wood: "Ah, I am warm, I can feel the fire!" Then he prays to the other piece of wood that he has carved: "Save me, for you are my god!" (Isa 44:16, 17).

Thus says the Lord to his anointed, to Cyrus, whose right hand I have grasped to subdue nations before him.
ISA 45:1

*T*he oracle proclaimed in Isaiah 45 is startling in its implications. Cyrus, the founder and first king of the Persian empire, is here called the Lord's "anointed." The Hebrew word for "anointed" is *mashiah*, the basis for the English word "messiah." All kings of Judah in the Davidic dynasty were anointed by God because God had made a unique covenant with David (2 Sam 7). But according to this

oracle, God has anointed a foreign king. The meaning of this unusual event is that God works through individuals outside Israel in order to fulfill the divine plan for all the world. With his great military might, Cyrus was elected to "subdue nations before him." Even though Cyrus did not recognize the God of Israel, the Lord chose him as the divine instrument with one ultimate purpose: "So that they may know, from the rising of the sun and from the west, that there is no one besides me; I am the Lord, and there is no other" (Isa 45:6). Second Isaiah contains the clearest statement of absolute monotheism to be found in the Old Testament. The God of Israel has, in effect, become the God of all nations, one universal God available for all to worship.

Come down and sit in the dust, virgin daughter Babylon! . . . For you shall no more be called tender and delicate.
ISA 47:1

*I*saiah, like other Israelite prophets, used metaphorical language to portray a nation in female terms. Here, Babylon is described as a "virgin daughter" who must sit in the dust. Sitting in the dust was a form of ritual mourning in the ancient Near East. Babylon is mourning the fact that, though once "tender and delicate," she now has been crushed for the harm she has done Israel in exile. Daughter Babylon will become a widow and lose her children as punishment because she treated Israel without mercy.

The good news of God's redemption is repeated in chapter 48. Throughout Second Isaiah, there is mention of "former things" as contrasted with "new things" (Isa 42:9). God, who had made himself known to Israel in such "former things" as the Exodus from Egypt, now reveals himself through "new things, hidden things that you have not known" (Isa 48:6). The God of Israel will redeem the chosen people from their exile in Babylon and return them in joy to the promised land. Isaiah thereby equates this new act of deliverance with the original Exodus from Egypt. In this new exodus, God will provide Israel with water through the desert just as God did in the first Exodus, in order to sustain the Israelites on their journey homeward: "They did not thirst when he led them through the deserts; he made water flow for them from the rock" (Isa 48:21).

Listen to me, O coastlands, pay attention, you peoples from far away! The Lord called me before I was born, while I was in my mother's womb he named me. ISA 49:1

*I*n the second of the so-called "servant songs" (Isa 49:1-6), Isaiah includes more details of the mission of the servant of God. All the nations will witness the activity of the servant, who was chosen even before birth. The servant's task is not only to usher Israel back to God and restore the exiles. The Lord also requires the servant to accomplish a far greater task. The universal scope of the servant's mission, first mentioned in Isaiah 42, is articulated

again: "I will give you as a light to the nations, that my salvation may reach to the end of the earth" (Isa 49:6). The foreign nations will not be the only witnesses to these divine acts of salvation. The prophet also summons the earth itself to respond to God's gracious and noble work: "Break forth, O mountains, into singing!" (Isa 49:13).

Israel's past history with God is never far from the prophet's mind. After the third of the "servant songs" (Isa 50:4-11), Isaiah reminds the people of the Lord's past beneficence. God chose Abraham and Sarah to be the progenitors of a blessed host of descendants: "Look to Abraham your father and to Sarah who bore you" (Isa 51:2). The prophet again hearkens back to the first Exodus when God dried up the Red Sea in order for the Israelites to cross on foot. And just as he has cared for Israel in the past, in the future God will provide care and comfort by restoring his people from exile to a secure existence in Zion.

Awake, awake, put on your strength, O Zion! Put on your beautiful garments, O Jerusalem, the holy city. ISA 52:1

*B*abylon is portrayed in Isaiah 47 first as a young woman and then as a widow bereft of her children. In Isaiah 52, the city of Jerusalem is described as a captive woman who is about to be given her freedom. She can shake off her dust, the sign of mourning, and put on beautiful clothing fit for rejoicing. Isaiah describes the exultant activity that will take place as Jerusalem is restored. The messenger who

The exiled Jews in Babylon mourn the destruction of Jerusalem and its temple and the loss of their homeland; a highly romanticized scene by Ferdinand Olivier (1785-1841).

comes to proclaim peace will run swiftly on the mountaintops in bearing the good news and Jerusalem's sentinels will join with him to "sing for joy" (Isa 52:8).

The fourth and most striking "servant song" appears in Isaiah 52:13-53:12; it provides a sobering sense of the price that must be paid for redemption. The divine servant "shall be exalted and lifted up" (Isa 52:13), but only after surviving affliction and oppression. This passage contains a portrait of a "suffering servant" who bears the punishment for the sins of others: "He was wounded for our transgressions, and crushed for our iniquities" (Isa 53:5). Early Christians understood the mission of Isaiah's suffering servant to refer to the role of Jesus in redeeming the sins of all people. The author of Acts of the Apostles echoed the language of Isaiah 53:7 to describe Jesus' suffering and death: "Like a sheep he was led to the slaughter, and like a lamb silent before its shearer, so he does not open his mouth" (Acts 8:32).

God, the commanding presence throughout the book of Isaiah, appears in all his majesty in this powerful portrait by Spanish artist Francisco de Zurbaran (1598-1664).

habitants enjoy this great prosperity.

Another theme of Isaiah is also prominent in this passage. Israel can never understand the divine plan fully: "For my thoughts are not your thoughts" (Isa 55:8). Rather Israel, although blessed and glorified by its redemption, must still remain humbled by its distance from the Holy One of Israel.

Thus says the Lord: Maintain justice, and do what is right, for soon my salvation will come, and my deliverance be revealed.
ISA 56:1

The divine blessings as promised for the future, however, do not come unmerited. God expects the Israelites to be righteous, repent of their sins, and return to the worship of the Lord. The final chapters of Isaiah reflect diminishing optimism that everyone will be included in this salvation. They contain apocalyptic oracles in which Israel reaches a complete end before God restores the sanctified few.

Some scholars believe Isaiah 56 to be the beginning of a third section of Isaiah that was written in the late sixth century B.C., after the exiles had returned to Jerusalem and the temple had been rebuilt. These last chapters of Isaiah reflect a new emphasis on observing the sabbath (Isa 56:2, 4, 6). Sabbath observance became particularly important during the exile when the people of Israel were trying to preserve their traditions and distinctiveness while dwelling among foreigners. This chapter also depicts a changed role for the temple in Jerusalem. All foreigners are now seen as welcome to worship God in his house; the temple will no longer be simply a place of sacrifice. Prayer will also become an essential element of worship: "For my house shall be called a house of prayer for all peoples" (Isa 56:7).

Sing, O barren one who did not bear; burst into song and shout, you who have not been in labor! . . . says the Lord.
ISA 54:1

The motif of the barren wife whose womb is suddenly opened by God is common in the Old Testament. Abraham's wife Sarah, for example, was barren until God intervened and she produced the long promised heir, Isaac (Gen 16-17). In Isaiah 54, Jerusalem is cast as a barren wife. Although she has not borne children, she is promised that soon she will be blessed with numerous offspring. In other words, Jerusalem, a city that was deserted during the period of the Israelites' exile, will once again be inhabited. God's punishment of Israel is portrayed as only a brief interlude in an everlasting covenant of love. God recalls his compact with Noah, described in Genesis 9, in which God promises never again to flood the earth. Likewise, God will never again be angry with Jerusalem, but preserve his covenant of peace forever. The walls and buildings of Jerusalem, the beloved of God, will be adorned with sapphires, rubies, and all manner of precious stones, as its in-

Shout out, do not hold back! Lift up your voice like a trumpet! Announce to my people their rebellion, to the house of Jacob their sins. ISA 58:1

Third Isaiah foresees imminent salvation for the righteous of Israel as well as a place for righteous Gentiles in the divine plan of restoration. But wickedness, both that of the nations and of Israel, will be punished. In an oracle that may suggest tense conditions among those newly returned to Jerusalem, the prophet calls people to account for their hypocrisy. On the one hand, they piously observe fast days, yet even on those fast days they oppress their workers or quarrel angrily with one another. Such behavior is unacceptable to God, proclaims Isaiah. Addressing all the Israelites, the prophet commands: "Share your bread with the hungry, and bring the homeless poor into your house" (Isa 58:7). Such compassionate actions toward the needy will guarantee divine favor. So, too, if the people of Israel will faithfully keep the sabbath holy instead of pursuing their own interests, the Lord "will make you ride upon the heights of the earth" (Isa 58:14). God is distressed by the manifold sins of Israel, however. Like the wicked fools in the book of Proverbs, "Their feet run to evil, and they rush to shed innocent blood" (Isa 59:7; Prov 1:16, 6:17-18). The Lord's displeasure at this wickedness will be expressed in a vengeful fury.

Arise, shine; for your light has come, and the glory of the Lord has risen upon you. ISA 60:1

Chapters 60 to 62 play out the theme of the future restoration and glorification of Jerusalem. As God's chosen holy city, Jerusalem will be redeemed. Even though the rest of the earth will be shrouded in the thick darkness brought by punishment, Jerusalem will be fully restored and resplendent in wealth. Not only will the city's exiles return, but the wealth of the nations will find its way there; camels from the distant Arabian lands of Midian and Sheba will transport luxuries like gold and frankincense. Fine wood from Lebanon—cypress, plane, and pine—will be brought to refurbish the temple, "to beautify the place of my sanctuary" (Isa 60:13).

The restoration will result in a reversal of Israel's servile status while in exile: "The descendants of those who oppressed you shall come bending low to you" (Isa 60:14). Instead of violence and destruction, peace and justice shall reign supreme within the borders of Israel. God reassures the Israelites that their days will be filled with light as if the sun were never to set and the moon never to wane, "for the Lord will be your everlasting light" (Isa 60:20). The brightness of God's glory will surpass even the great lights of the heavens so that Zion's restoration can be seen by all the nations of the earth.

"Who is this that comes from Edom, from Bozrah in garments stained crimson?". . . "It is I, announcing vindication, mighty to save." ISA 63:1

The beginning of Isaiah 63 again reveals the frightening mien of the Divine Warrior. God comes dressed in crimson robes, having punished the neighboring nation of Edom, which in this case symbolizes all of Israel's surrounding enemies. The juice of grapes from the winepress, metaphorical language for blood, has stained the warrior's battle clothes red. God has judged the nations and their behavior has greatly angered him, so the Holy One of Israel has implemented a fierce punishment.

The people of Israel, too, realize that they have been judged and found wanting. Isaiah 63:7-64:12 contains a long communal lament and confession. The first part of the prayer recounts the gracious acts that God has performed on their behalf and asks forgiveness. The prayer asks for a divine manifestation, no matter how terrifying the sight, in order to prove to one and all that the Lord still fights for Israel's sake: "O that you would tear open the heavens and come down, so that the mountains would quake at your presence—as when fire kindles brushwood and the fire causes water to boil" (Isa 64:1-2).

God responds to this petition by sternly reminding the people of all their sins, a people "who walk in a way that is not good . . . who provoke me to my face continually . . . [and] who eat swine's flesh" (Isa 65:2-4). Nonetheless, God offers the promise of a joyous future for a righteous remnant. For these deserving few, God will create "new heavens and a new earth" (Isa 65:17) in which all human infirmities will disappear and there will be continual rejoicing.

Thus says the Lord: Heaven is my throne and the earth is my footstool; what is the house that you would build for me, and what is my resting place? ISA 66:1

The final chapter of Isaiah presents the scale of Israel's God in cosmic terms. God, in his enormity, is the ruler of the universe and uses the heavens for a throne; the earth serves humbly as his footstool. God's glory cannot be contained in such a small space as the temple in Jerusalem. In contrast to the grand majesty of God, Isaiah reveals who will be granted a place in the ideal future: "This is the one to whom I will look, to the humble and contrite in spirit, who trembles at my word" (Isa 66:2).

The first 39 chapters of Isaiah reflect concrete historical events from the eighth century B.C. And although Second Isaiah describes the return from the Babylonian exile in mythic terms as a new exodus and a new creation, his vision is also realized in history. But the last chapters of Isaiah depict a future reality, one in which God will fashion an entirely new heaven and a new earth. The vision of a gloriously rebuilt, heavenly Jerusalem is tempered by the sobering depiction of divine wrath: "By fire will the Lord execute judgment, and by his sword, on all flesh; and those slain by the Lord shall be many" (Isa 66:16). Hope for the righteous remains unquenchable, although the divine plan will achieve full realization only when "from new moon to new moon, from sabbath to sabbath, all flesh shall come to worship before [God]" (Isa 66:23). Spanning a time period from eighth-century Judah to the unrealized future, Isaiah's vision addresses the morbid fears of judgment and fervent hopes for consolation of countless generations past, present, and yet to come.

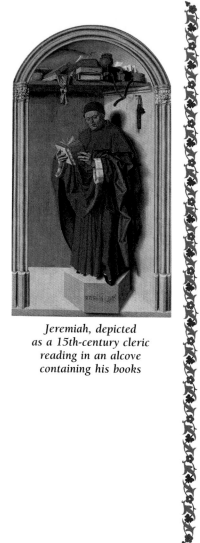

*Jeremiah, depicted
as a 15th-century cleric
reading in an alcove
containing his books*

The prophet Jeremiah lived through a pivotal and defining period in the history of the Israelites. The heightened expectations for Jewish self-rule and the accompanying optimism about the central role of Jerusalem's temple in the nation's worship were merely two of the elements that contributed to the significance of the era. A subject of Assyria, Judah began to exercise more independence with the rise of numerous pressures on its old nemesis to the northeast. With Assyria preoccupied by both internal dissent and external attack and, as it turned out, on the verge of collapse, Judah experienced a renewal that shaped its identity in indelible ways. The reforms of King Josiah (639-609 B.C.) appear to have raised hopes in Jerusalem, or perhaps heightened aspirations and Josiah's reforms were simply the happy result of a distracted and weakened enemy. At any rate, Josiah's reforms sought to make Jerusalem and its temple on Mount Zion the sole place for worshiping God. To the degree that Josiah succeeded, he inadvertently set the stage for the great tragedy of ancient Israel: the loss of its capital and its temple. The Babylonians overthrew and replaced the Assyrian empire in 612 B.C. and conquered and destroyed Jerusalem in 586, taking its inhabitants into exile in Babylon.

Jeremiah's preoccupation with the temple can be understood as the consequences of the general concerns of his historical period as well as his lineage as a "son of Hilkiah, of the priests" (Jer 1:1). The prophet probably delivered his messages beginning around 627 B.C., during Josiah's reign, and continued through the reigns of four subsequent kings, Jehoahaz, Jehoiakim, Jehoiachin, and Zedekiah, lasting until three to five years after the destruction of Jerusalem. The book bearing Jeremiah's name represents a number of difficulties for interpreters. First, the Greek translation of Jeremiah preserved in the Septuagint follows a different order and is roughly an eighth shorter than the standard Hebrew text, suggesting that later editors expanded the original book. Second, Jeremiah contains what scholars have identified as three main components: oracles from the prophet himself; biographical narratives composed by Jeremiah's scribe Baruch or later disciples; and prose discourses that echo Jeremiah's words but also may come from later writers. The disjointed and somewhat incoherent text contains four major blocks of material: mostly poetry (chapters 1-25); mostly prose (26-46); oracles against the nations (47-51); and an appendix (52).

"Before I formed you in the womb . . . I appointed you a prophet to the nations." JER 1:5

Jeremiah's call to be a prophet suggests that, by his words, he will affect world events. His summons can be compared with the call of Moses in Exodus 3:1-4:17. Like Moses, Jeremiah hears the call, denies his worthiness, and is ultimately compelled to enter the Lord's service. Also like Moses, Jeremiah's career lasts 40 years, a number that likely reflects an editor's attempt to depict Jeremiah as the final successor to Moses. Indeed, in the years of despair immediately following the destruction of Jerusalem, Jeremiah may well have seemed to be the last in the line of prophets that began with Moses. Echoing the call of other prophets, Jeremiah recounts that "the

Lord put out his hand and touched my mouth; and the Lord said to me, 'Now I have put my words in your mouth'" (Jer 1:9). Ezekiel takes the image even further when he records, "[The Lord] said to me, O mortal, eat what is offered to you; eat this scroll, and go, speak to the house of Israel. So I opened my mouth, and . . . . I ate it, and in my mouth it was as sweet as honey" (Ezek 3:1-3). This similarity can be explained, in part, by the fact that there was a growing recognition of the importance of God's word in defining the religious life of ancient Israel. This word, as Ezekiel attests, is increasingly being identified with a written tradition as well.

The remainder of Jeremiah's call is presented as a vision in which the prophet sees the image of a boiling pot tilted away from the north. Because Israel was on the trade route between Mesopotamia and Egypt, it was always subject to invasion, typically from the north. The reason for this impending doom, declares the Lord, is that Judah and Jerusalem (names used interchangeably by most prophets) have failed to maintain loyalty to God: "They have made offerings to other gods, and worshiped the works of their own hands" (Jer 1:16).

I remember the devotion of your youth, your love as a bride. JER 2:2

In chapters two and three, Jeremiah takes up another favorite prophetic theme: the metaphor of human love for the love of God and his people. Jeremiah views the period following the Exodus as a honeymoon between Israel and the Lord. Now, the nation has turned its back on its lover and sought others. As Jeremiah so graphically puts it, "On every high hill and under every green tree you sprawled and played the whore" (Jer 2:20). He continues his accusations by declaring that Israel's passion has been un-

In scenes paired with events of Jeremiah's life, Jesus is shown suffering persecutions similar to those endured by the prophet; an illustration from a 13th-century teaching Bible.

bridled; the people have sought out and been defiled by Baal, a rival Canaanite god. In his most startling language, Jeremiah records the Lord's question, "Look up to the bare heights, and see! Where have you not been lain with?" (Jer 3:2). This translation, while adequate, misses the blunt, startling quality of the original Hebrew. The prophet's goal is clearly to shock his audience into action. Beyond the compelling language in which he frames his accusations, Jeremiah is dependent on a long-standing prophetic idiom. Hosea (chapters 1-3) and Ezekiel (chapters 16 and 23) rely on similar imagery to depict the apostasy of Israel as adultery. This metaphor dramatically captures the change in a people who have ignored their holy bonds to God. Curiously, this metaphor does not deny the existence of other gods, but merely reminds Israel to remain loyal to its God and to him alone.

A lion has gone up from its thicket, a destroyer of nations has set out. JER 4:7

As a consequence of Israel's "adultery" and unwillingness to return to the worship of the Lord, the nation will be prey to an enemy from the north. God's patience has worn thin and now the Israelites will hear the charges that he brings against them. "Your ways and your doings have brought this upon you," says the Lord. "This is your doom; how bitter it is! It has reached your very heart" (Jer 4:18). So shattering is the break between God and Israel that Jeremiah must resort to language that, though dependent on the account of creation in Genesis, depicts the reversal of creation until the Lord "looked on the earth, and lo, it was waste and void" (Jer 4:23). Jeremiah claims that justice and truth are absent from the streets of Jerusalem and, as a result, the city deserves no pardon. Moreover, the people of Judah have been so bold as to think, "No evil will come upon us, and we shall not see sword or famine. The prophets are nothing but wind, for the word is not in them" (Jer 5:12-13). In response, the Lord declares that he is bringing an enemy from far away. Because Judah has refused to heed God's instruction and rejected his teaching, the nation now must pay the ultimate price.

Amend your ways and your doings, and let me dwell with you in this place. JER 7:3

Jeremiah 7:1-15, known as the "temple sermon," gives an indication of the prophet's understanding of the central role played by Solomon's house of the Lord in Israel's worship. For Jeremiah, and most of his contemporaries, the temple is the sole place where God makes contact with the world. Most of Josiah's reforms are directed at centralizing the sacrificial cult in Jerusalem. Jeremiah and many of his scholarly colleagues support the king's reforms. Josiah's religious revival seems to have been spurred by the discovery in the temple precincts of what scholars believe was an early version of the book of

Deuteronomy, around the year 620 B.C. The book, with its call for the centralization of the religious cult (Deut 12:2-7), had a profound effect on late-seventh-century Judah. But what seems to bother Jeremiah is that many of his contemporaries feel that merely observing the proper sacrificial rites allows them to behave in any manner they wish. Like many other prophets, Jeremiah reminds the people that their religious obligations are not only cultic but also social. He tells them that they are obliged to care for strangers, orphans, and widows.

Many students of the Bible have presumed that the prophet's call for ethical behavior is the essence of his message. While that call is essential to Jeremiah's goals, it is a mistake to dismiss the importance of the temple and its ritual life. Jeremiah, speaking for God, threatens to destroy the temple in Jerusalem just as he has destroyed a previous cultic shrine in Shiloh. Were the temple unimportant, such a threat would have had little effect. But the temple is crucial for maintaining the people's connection with God. Furthermore, God also takes issue with those who "pour out drink offerings to other gods" (Jer 7:18).

To Christian readers, the most familiar words in the temple sermon are the Lord's anguished question, "Has this house . . . become a den of robbers?" (Jer 7:11). Jesus uses the phrase as justification for driving out the money changers from the temple after his triumphal entry into Jerusalem (Mt 21:12-13).

How can you say, "We are wise, and the law of the Lord is with us"? JER 8:8

Jeremiah next moves from attacking the false security of worshiping in the temple to the false comfort that the people take from their covenant with the Lord. Jeremiah seems to suggest that the people are confident in merely possessing the law rather than in following it. "My people do not know the ordinance of the Lord" (Jer 8:7), he observes. Even though they have the Lord's instruction, they pay no heed. It is not only the people in general who behave badly; "from prophet to priest everyone deals falsely" (Jer 8:10). For Jeremiah, the end truly is near. Even brothers cannot be trusted in this age of utter corruption and disregard of the law. This, according to the Lord, is "because they have forsaken my law that I set before them, and have not obeyed my voice, or walked in accordance with it" (Jer 9:13). Rather, the people have followed other gods who are not gods at all: "Their idols are like scarecrows in a cucumber field, and they cannot speak; they have to be carried, for they cannot walk" (Jer 10:5). For Jeremiah, to follow the Lord is to uphold his teaching and laws; anything less is unacceptable. The Lord's law comprises instruction in both ethical behavior and proper ritual. If either of these is out of balance, Judah will suffer. This accounts for what seems so odd to the modern ear: the critique of unethical behavior that is inseparable from the issue of cultic loyalty. As a last reminder of the people's obligations to God, Jeremiah says, "Cursed be anyone who does not heed the words of this covenant" (Jer 11:3).

You will be in the right, O Lord, when I lay charges against you; but let me put my case to you.
JER 12:1

As remarkable as this challenge to the Lord seems, the original Hebrew has an even harsher tone. It can perhaps be understood to say something closer to, "You always get your way anyway, O Lord, but I have to speak my mind." In this, and six other passages, are the so-called laments of Jeremiah (Jer 11:18-23, 12:1-6, 15:10-21, 17:14-18, 18:18-23, 20:7-13, and 20:14-18). In these poems, the prophet laments that he has been called to his mission. Jeremiah's distress is so great that he, like Job, actually regrets that he was even born: "Woe is me, my mother, that you ever bore me, a man of strife and contention to the whole land!" (Jer 15:10). The prophet complains that the rejection of the people is more than he can bear. In perhaps the most striking lament, Jeremiah uses language reminiscent of seduction to convey what he sees as his present position: "O Lord, you have enticed me, and I was enticed; you have overpowered me, and you have prevailed" (Jer 20:7). Underlying these laments is Jeremiah's growing awareness of the problem of false prophecy and the people's perception that perhaps his words too are unreliable.

Quoting Jeremiah, Jesus drove the money changers from Jerusalem's temple; at left, a 12th-century mural from a Swiss church. A bronze container and shekels from the time of Jesus appear in the photograph at right.

RELUCTANT PROPHETS

Not everyone God chose to become a prophet wanted the job. Delivering the Lord's messages—often of judgment—was a frightening and dangerous responsibility. Moses, the most revered Old Testament prophet, rejected God's call no less than five times, making excuses that he was a nobody, did not know God's name, and was a poor speaker to whom the people would not listen. Jeremiah tried a similar ploy with the Lord: "I do not know how to speak, for I am only a boy" (Jer 1:6). Perhaps the most reluctant prophet of all was Jonah. When God ordered him into the heart of the evil Assyrian empire to warn the city of Nineveh that it was about to be destroyed for its wickedness, Jonah did more than voice his objections: He took ship in the opposite direction.

The lifelong task of delivering God's word at times proved overwhelming. All three of these prophets—and others such as Elijah—asked God to strike them dead. Moses said he could carry the burden no more and wanted to die. Jeremiah cursed the day he was born. And, after God spared the repentant Ninevites, a humiliated Jonah insisted on dying. Yet, to each of these tormented prophets, the Lord instead gave assurance and strength.

"Go and buy yourself a linen loincloth, and put it on your loins, but do not dip it in water." JER 13:1

In what seems a rather bizarre command, the Lord instructs Jeremiah to perform a symbolic act. He is to take the loincloth to the Euphrates River, hide it in the cleft of a rock, and later return to retrieve it. It is unlikely, of course, that Jeremiah actually made what would have been an 800-mile round-trip journey. Rather, Jeremiah's symbolic act is meant to signal that, just as the loincloth ceases to function in the absence of its owner—indeed it falls to ruin—so, too, will the nation of Judah crumble in the absence of its God. All of this leads to the warning of exile: "I will scatter you like chaff driven by the wind from the desert" (Jer 13:24). Once again, the severing of the relationship between God and Israel is depicted in terms of adultery: For their "shameless prostitutions," the Lord tells the people, "I myself will lift up your skirts over your face, and your shame will be seen" (Jer 13:26-27)—thus maintaining the metaphor of Judah as a woman. At a more subtle level, Jeremiah continues to rely on a sexual metaphor by speaking of the loss of fertility, represented by empty cisterns.

A major cause of the apostasy and subsequent infertility of Judah is that the people have believed the words of false prophets (Jer 14:13-14). Apparently, there were those who spoke reassuringly that all was going to be well in Jerusalem. Jeremiah's frustration with them is twofold. In the first place, they are contradicting his own message of doom. This, in turn, leads to the humiliation he suffers from those who consider him a doomsayer. The second reason for Jeremiah's frustration is that the reassurances of other prophets prevent the people from perceiving their predicament. The consequence of listening to these optimistic pronouncements will be utter destruction.

You shall not take a wife, nor shall you have sons or daughters in this place. JER 16:2

As another symbolic act, Jeremiah is told not to marry or have children. The prophet is to act out the notion that fertility will be markedly affected by the severance of God's relationship with his people. The command to Jeremiah is in direct contrast to that given the prophet Hosea, who is told to marry a promiscuous woman (Hos 1:2). To reinforce, one more time, the notion that God's "marriage" to Israel has been broken, Jeremiah ends this section with an answer to the people's question of why so much evil has been predicted for them: "Because your ancestors have forsaken me, says the Lord, and have gone after other gods and have served and worshiped them, and have forsaken me and have not kept my law; and because you have behaved worse than your ancestors" (Jer 16:11-12).

In typical prophetic fashion, after his prediction of utter destruction and subsequent exile, Jeremiah tells the people that there will be a new exodus out of the land of their exile. While many scholars associate such promises, especially following on prophecies of doom, with editorial additions, it is possible to see in such encouraging words the confidence of the prophet in the continuity of God's kind acts and his dependence on the ongoing validity of fundamental motifs such as the Exodus.

For the sake of your lives, take care that you do not bear a burden on the sabbath or bring it in by the gates of Jerusalem. JER 17:21

Once again, Jeremiah stresses the importance of obeying the laws set forth in Exodus and Deuteronomy. Jeremiah seems to be struggling to define the exact meaning of sabbath observance. According to both Exodus 20:8-11 and Deuteronomy 5:12-15, no work is to be done on the sabbath. Apparently, by Jeremiah's day, the definition of "work" is becoming a problem. Moreover, the commandments to observe the sabbath in the two books do not make entirely clear that the restrictions against work are to be applied in all locations. At any rate, it appears that Jeremiah attempts to add clarification to this dilemma by specifying that carrying burdens, out of the house or through city gates, constitutes work. Whatever the reason for Jeremiah's raising of the issue of the sabbath, it is clear that he perceives its proper observance as crucial to the survival of Judah.

Can I not do with you, O house of Israel, just as this potter has done?
JER 18:6

In likening God's relationship to his people to that of a potter to his clay, Jeremiah draws on an important image used by Isaiah (Isa 29:16, 45:9, 64:8), one later employed by the apostle Paul (Rom 9:20-24). The point of Jeremiah's use of this image is to insist that it is not too late for Judah to change its ways. Just as the potter can change the outcome of his work, so, too, can the Lord. But even given this opportunity, Judah refuses to reform.

Continuing with, but altering substantially, the metaphor of the potter, Jeremiah is instructed in chapter 19 to take a jug and break it in order to symbolize the irreparable damage that will take place in the relationship between God and Judah. The cause for the rupture on this occasion is connected with the practice of child sacrifice at a place called Topheth. The language of Jeremiah's critique, it has been pointed out by scholars, suggests the complexity of the issue of child sacrifice in the Hebrew Bible. The text records that this shattering of Judah is "because the people have . . . gone on building the high places of Baal to burn their children in the fire as burnt offerings to Baal, which I did not command or decree, nor did it enter my mind" (Jer 19:4-5). By criticizing the people of Judah for sacrificing their children to Baal, Jeremiah objects both to the practice of child sacrifice and to the false devotion to Baal. When he goes on to claim that child sacrifice is a practice Judah's own God "did not command or decree," Jeremiah counters the belief some in Judah may have held that such offerings were an acceptable way to honor the Lord.

I will give King Zedekiah of Judah, and his servants and the people in this city . . . into the hands of King Nebuchadnezzar of Babylon. JER 21:7

Zedekiah, the third of Josiah's sons to rule Judah, comes to the throne just after Nebuchadnezzar first conquers Jerusalem, in 597 B.C. A decade later Zedekiah rebels against his Babylonian overlord—and asks Jeremiah to petition God's help. The response is devastating. The Lord will bring Zedekiah's enemies into the heart of the city and will himself fight against the king. Moreover, Zedekiah and his court will be handed over to Nebuchadnezzar. The news for the

As Jerusalem's temple goes up in flames, Nebuchadnezzar orders the Jews deported.

populace is only slightly better; at least they get a choice. To them the Lord says, "See, I am setting before you the way of life and the way of death. . . . those who go out and surrender to the Chaldeans [Babylonians] . . . shall live" (Jer 21:8-9). Then, in what looks like a reversal of the dire prediction, the house of David is instructed to "act with justice and righteousness" (Jer 22:3). It is unclear whether this suggests that there is still a chance to avert disaster if the royal household mends its ways. Following this obscure demand is a list of the failings of the sons of Josiah that essentially reviews the reasons that the house of David finds itself in such bleak circumstances. Jeremiah concludes his catalog of wrongdoing by promising to "raise up for David a righteous Branch, and he shall reign as king and deal wisely." (Jer 23:5). Early Christians understood this passage to be a reference to Jesus. In Jeremiah, it appears to mean only that a legitimate descendant of David will rule in the future.

The Lord showed me two baskets of figs placed before the temple of the Lord. JER 24:1

In this image Jeremiah makes reference to the two-stage conquest of Jerusalem by Babylon. The good figs represent those who are carried off to Babylon in the first wave of deportations, in 597 B.C. The bad figs are those who remain during the intervening 11 years before the final conquest and deportations of 586. They will become "a disgrace, a byword, a taunt, and a curse in all the places where I [the Lord] shall drive them" (Jer 24:9).

This whole land shall become a ruin and a waste, and these nations shall serve the king of Babylon seventy years. JER 25:11

Chapter 25, which concludes the first major section of the book, offers a summary of Jeremiah's prophecies for the 23 years ending about 605 B.C. But since the people of Judah have not heeded the Lord's call for repentance, Jeremiah pronounces an awful judgment: conquest by Babylon, destruction of the kingdom, and exile for 70 years. Scholars have puzzled over the 70 years. Either Jeremiah was wrong (the exile lasted from 586 to 538, 48 years) or he was referring to the rebuilding of the temple in 515.

Then the priests and the prophets and all the people laid hold of him, saying, "You shall die!"   JER 26:8

In response to the challenge posed by Jeremiah in his temple sermon (Jer 7:1-15), the people threaten his life. The priests and other prophets are apparently most offended by Jeremiah's prediction of doom. Royal officials and the general populace, however, defend Jeremiah's right to make such predictions by citing another prophet. They argue that, in the days of King Hezekiah (727-698 B.C.), Micah warned that "Zion shall be plowed as a field; Jerusalem shall become a heap of ruins, and the mountain of the house a wooded height" (Jer 26:18; Mic 3:12). Hezekiah, they note, heeded the words of Micah, suggesting that they do the same with Jeremiah's warning. The threat posed to Jeremiah is reinforced with the following account of the fate of Uriah, who, after prophesying much the same message as that of Jeremiah, is hunted down and killed.

Make yourself a yoke of straps and bars, and put them on your neck.   JER 27:2

The Lord instructs Jeremiah to act out the submission to Nebuchadnezzar that is essential to the kingdom's survival. Jeremiah is challenged by the false prophet Hananiah, who claims that the Lord promises that he has "broken the yoke of the king of Babylon" (Jer 28:2) and within two years will bring back the exiles and return the treasures plundered from the temple in 597 B.C. Jeremiah suggests that the true test of prophecy is in the past: "Prophets who preceded you and me from ancient times prophesied war, famine, and pestilence against many countries and great kingdoms. As for the prophet who prophesies peace, when the word of that prophet comes true, then it will be known that the Lord has truly sent the prophet" (Jer 28:8-9). Jeremiah comes close to claiming that true prophecy is negative. For Jeremiah, the anguish of dealing with the doubt of his audience, not to mention his own self-doubt, is overwhelming, as his laments readily attest.

These are the words of the letter that the prophet Jeremiah sent from Jerusalem to the remaining elders among the exiles.   JER 29:1

Sometime during the decade following 597 B.C., Jeremiah writes to the first wave of exiles in Babylon to confront false assurances of a speedy return. His message from the Lord is to "build houses and live in them; plant gardens and eat what they produce. Take wives and have sons and daughters; take wives for your sons, and give your daughters in marriage" (Jer 29:5-6). All of this is to warn that the stay in Babylon will be long; the exiles are not to view their sojourn as temporary. Part of the significance of Jeremiah's letter is that the word of the Lord is becoming progressively associated with the written as much as the spoken word.

For the days are surely coming, says the Lord, when I will restore the fortunes of my people, Israel and Judah.   JER 30:3

As another sign of the increasing importance of the written word, Jeremiah is instructed to write down the promises of restoration that are contained in chapters 30-31, what scholars call the Book of Consolation. This section comprises a mixture of prose and poetry and provides the people of Judah with the promise that their exile will not be interminable. Indeed, to express this release, the Lord says, "I will break the yoke from off his [Jacob's, or Israel's] neck and I will burst his bonds" (Jer 30:8). Here, the promise that the Jews' exile will come to an end relies on the same imagery in which Hananiah cast his false promise of a short exile. In fact, lest Judah get the wrong idea, Jeremiah records, "I will make an end of all the nations among which I scattered you, but of you I will not make an end. I will chastise you in just measure, and I will by no means leave you unpunished" (Jer 30:11). God is nonetheless moved by the suffering of his people and promises to restore their fortunes. Relying on another important idiom of the covenant, Jeremiah records, "And you shall be my people, and I will be your God" (Jer 30:22, an echo of Ex 6:7). The Lord is so moved to compassion that he extends the promise of restoration not only to Judah but also to the northern kingdom of Israel, which had been destroyed by Assyria in 722 B.C., its population scattered and forever lost among peoples of the far-flung empire. All of chapter 31 is devoted to the imagery of a reunified and reconstituted nation in which the Lord makes "a new covenant with the house of Israel and the house of Judah" (Jer 31:31).

Take a scroll and write on it all the words that I have spoken to you against Israel and Judah and all the nations, from the day I spoke to you, from the days of Josiah until today.   JER 36:2

This quote provides an explanation, in part, of why so much biographical information about Jeremiah is preserved in the Bible. Given the rather sweeping nature of the instructions, it might be presumed that the entire book of Jeremiah is the outcome of these instructions. Whatever the extent of the document produced, however, it is soon revealed that Jeremiah dictates his words to the scribe Baruch. Earlier, Baruch is identified as the bearer of the deed of purchase by which the prophet acquires a plot of land from his cousin—another symbolic act by which Jeremiah proves that property ownership in Judah still has validity (Jer 32:9-15).

The purpose of the writing exercise becomes evident when Jeremiah sends Baruch to the temple to read aloud the words he has dictated. Alarmed, the temple officials tell Baruch to go into hiding with Jeremiah while they bring the prophet's unwelcome words to King Jehoiakim (609-598 B.C.). Calmly, yet deliberately, the king shows what he thinks about Jeremiah's warnings: As each section is read, the king cuts off a piece of the scroll and throws it into the fire that is warming his winter quarters. He then orders the arrest of Jeremiah and Baruch, but they cannot be found. At the Lord's request, Jeremiah dictates a second scroll to Baruch, this time adding "many similar words" (Jer 36:32) to his prophecies.

King Zedekiah sent . . . to the prophet Jeremiah saying, "Please pray for us to the Lord our God." JER 37:3

In this 10th-century Bible illustration, Jeremiah consoles Jerusalem's people as Nebuchadnezzar looms overhead.

During the brief reign of Jehoiakim's son, Jehoiachin, Nebuchadnezzar captures Jerusalem, takes the young king and a number of his subjects into exile, and appoints Jehoiachin's uncle Zedekiah as ruler of Judah. The new king's petition to Jeremiah is part of a dangerous political game that was forced on the rulers of Judah in the last decades of the kingdom's existence. Having been placed on the throne by Nebuchadnezzar, Zedekiah is suspect in the eyes of many of his subjects. He, like others before him, has to balance the prospects of remaining loyal to Babylon with the possibility that Egypt might gain control of his territory. With a strong pro-Egyptian faction in Jerusalem, Zedekiah apparently seeks from Jeremiah advice on his politically precarious position. The prophet's reply is not promising: The Babylonian conquest of Jerusalem is inevitable. Following the delivery of this message of gloom, Jeremiah is arrested and placed in prison. Zedekiah sends for Jeremiah and is again informed that his fate is sealed. Chapter 38 presents a detailed account of Jeremiah's imprisonment and the repeated efforts of Zedekiah to avert his fate.

When Jerusalem was taken, all the officials of the king of Babylon came and sat in the middle gate. JER 39:3

Nebuchadnezzar lays siege to Jerusalem in January of 587 B.C. After the city walls are breached in July of 586, Zedekiah and his soldiers flee under cover of night. The Babylonian troops catch up with them at Jericho. After Zedekiah's sons are slaughtered in his sight, the king is blinded by order of Nebuchadnezzar, who takes his captive in chains to Babylon as Jerusalem is put to the torch. The account of the city's destruction is so abbreviated that it may reflect the great despair that the event instilled in the survivors of the disaster.

In the aftermath of the destruction, Jeremiah is freed from prison and given the choice of going to Babylon or remaining in Jerusalem with Gedaliah, the man appointed governor of the remnant of Judah. The prophet chooses to remain.

Ishmael son of Nethaniah and the ten men with him got up and struck down Gedaliah. JER 41:2

At first, Gedaliah receives the support of many of those remaining behind after the second deportation of Judah's leading citizens. His rule, however, is short. Gedaliah ignores the warnings of a plot to kill him—and pays with his life. Sharing a meal with the governor, Ishmael, a member of the deposed royal family, and his men murder Gedaliah. Because the Babylonians had placed Gedaliah in power, many in Judah fear reprisals from their conqueror. A natural response is to turn to Egypt for protection.

If you will only remain in this land, then I will build you up and not pull you down; I will plant you, and not pluck you up; for I am sorry for the disaster that I have brought upon you. JER 42:10

In response to the crisis, Jeremiah declares that the remnant of Judah should stay in their homeland. At length and in no uncertain terms, the prophet warns his contemporaries not to go to Egypt. He promises that the king of Babylon will not punish them if they remain. Moreover, Jeremiah warns of the dangers of sojourning in Egypt: "All the people who have determined to go to Egypt . . . shall die by the sword, by famine, and by pestilence" (Jer 42:17). It is possible that his warnings reflect a traditional antipathy toward Egypt as the land of Israel's original bondage. Indeed, the new bondage in Babylon is often depicted in the idiom of the original.

Like most prophetic utterances, Jeremiah's is ignored. "You are telling a lie," the people charge. "The Lord our God did not send you to say, 'Do not go to Egypt to settle there'" (Jer 43:2). As a result of their disbelief in the prophet's warnings, a group of the people go to Egypt, taking Jeremiah and Baruch with them. And there, despite repeated warnings, they not only refuse to return to their homeland and their God, they actually begin to make offerings to the "queen of heaven" (Jer 44:17), the Mesopotamian goddess Ishtar, associated with the planet Venus. Like their ancestors in the wilderness who refused to obey Moses, the remnant of Judah fails to heed Jeremiah.

The word that the prophet Jeremiah spoke to Baruch son of Neriah, when he wrote these words in a scroll at the dictation of Jeremiah. JER 45:1

In the short chapter that ends the second major section of the book of Jeremiah, the Lord promises Baruch that his life will be spared. But more significant is the further identification of Baruch as Jeremiah's scribe. This apparently represents an attempt to explain how the words of Jeremiah were preserved and why so much is known about the prophet's life. If, as the text implies, Jeremiah was often accompanied by Baruch, the scribe would have had the firsthand knowledge needed to write the biographical narratives that are included in the book of Jeremiah. Moreover, the scribe's activity is a herald of the coming age in which, in the absence of their temple and capital city, the people of Judah become the people of the book—that is, the Bible.

Harness the horses; mount the steeds! JER 46:4

The third major section of Jeremiah, the oracles against the nations, begins with a pronouncement against Egypt. By starting with Egypt, the prophet appears to be continuing his warnings about flight to that land at the end of chapter 44. Jeremiah warns Egypt of an attack by Nebuchadnezzar—one that actually took place in 568 B.C., though the Babylonian ruler failed to conquer Egypt. The prophet goes on to offer the exiles—either those in Egypt or those deported to Babylon—the promise of salvation: "But as for you, have no fear, my servant Jacob, and do not be dismayed, O Israel; for I am going to save you from far away, and your offspring from the land of their captivity" (Jer 46:27). The promise, attached to an oracle against Egypt, serves to link the impending deliverance from bondage with the Exodus under Moses that gave birth to the nation of Israel.

See, waters are rising out of the north and shall become an overflowing torrent. JER 47:2

Next on Jeremiah's list are Israel's immediate neighbors and longtime enemies. This list is rather standard for prophetic oracles against the nations and includes, in order, Philistia to the west, Moab to the east, Ammon to the northeast, Edom to the southeast, Damascus to the far north, and, final-

His slain sons at his feet, the blinded Zedekiah is taken in chains to his exile in Babylon; a scene from an early-15th-century Spanish Bible.

ly, Kedar and Hazor, most likely nomadic peoples rather than geographic locations. The language in Jeremiah 47:2 is significant because the enemy from the north, usually associated with peril to Jerusalem, is now threatening Philistia. Moab and Ammon, two more historical enemies of the Israelites, are also, according to Genesis 19:30-38, distant relations. Another distant relation is Edom (Esau), whose people are descendants of the twin brother of Jacob (Israel). In the postexilic period, Edom was viewed especially harshly because it was seen as having turned on its own brother during Nebuchadnezzar's final attack on Jerusalem. The last three oracles against Judah's neighbors are directed toward the north and may have been placed at the end in order to lead to the final nation on the list, Babylon.

Babylon is taken, Bel is put to shame, Merodach is dismayed. JER 50:2

Appropriately, Babylon is saved for last in Jeremiah's oracles against the nations. By placing Egypt first and Babylon last, Jeremiah brackets his list, just as Israel itself was bracketed by these two bullying nations. Moreover, the juxtaposition suggests that, just as Israel once exited triumphantly out of Egypt, so it will some day leave Babylon. That Babylon comes last also signals that it most deserves its fate. Indeed, the length of Jeremiah's harangue reinforces the belief that Babylon's acts have been the most egregious perpetrated by Israel's enemies.

Jerusalem and Judah so angered the Lord that he expelled them from his presence. JER 52:3

The historical epilogue to the book of Jeremiah includes details, omitted from chapter 39, of events surrounding the final days of Jerusalem. Drawing on 2 Kings 24:18-25:30, the epilogue deals first with the years between the first and second rounds of deportation, 597 to 586 B.C. Zedekiah's 11-year reign is blamed for the disaster that eventually overtakes Judah. The account of Jerusalem's destruction includes a detailed list of the articles taken from the temple and gives the exact number of inhabitants taken into captivity: 4,600 in the two major deportations and a third in 582.

The rather matter-of-fact description in this section is awkward, following as it does on the impassioned oracles against the nations. It is perhaps due in some degree to the author's resignation to these tragic events. The things he records are now history, part of the course of events that led to Israel's demise. But as with most of history, the seeds of something new have been sown. It was the loss of the Israelites' temple and land that gave impetus to the process by which Judaism became the religion it is today. The great irony, of course, is that by becoming the people of the book, the Jews were able to survive the final and total destruction of Herod's magnificent temple by the Romans in A.D. 70.

LAMENTATIONS

Raising his hands in despair, Jeremiah laments the fall of Jerusalem in this early-19th-century miniature.

*T*he saddest book in the Bible, Lamentations is made up entirely of five mournful songs. Jerusalem has fallen, the kingdom of Judah has dissolved, and the survivors are exiled and suffering. The poet who composed these songs masterfully expresses the extent of his people's grief by beginning each verse with a letter of the Hebrew alphabet, starting with aleph, followed by beth, and working through the entire 22 letters. He does this in each of the first four chapters—three times in chapter 3, which has 66 verses. Chapter five is the exception; though it follows the 22-verse format, it is not an acrostic. This thoughtful, tireless approach seems to cry out that the Jews have suffered grief from A to Z. Order has vanished, and chaos rules.

The poet is unnamed, but ancient Jewish tradition from before the time of Jesus attributes the work to Jeremiah, an eyewitness to Babylon's sack of Jerusalem in 586 B.C. The Chronicler says Jeremiah delivered a lament over the death of King Josiah (2 Chr 35:25). In addition, the prophet wrote in this genre, and the throbbing emotion of the book suggests that it was crafted by an observer deeply moved by what he has seen. Many scholars, however, believe the songs were written by someone other than Jeremiah, since the writing style and thought processes are in many ways different from those in the book bearing Jeremiah's name.

Lamentations was likely penned shortly after Jerusalem fell, since the songs say nothing about the Jews returning to Judah some 50 years later. In fact, the last words of the final song ask God to restore the people, "unless you have utterly rejected us, and are angry with us beyond measure" (Lam 5:22).

How lonely sits the city that once was full of people!
LAM 1:1

*L*amentations is not the name of the book in the Hebrew Bible. The name is *'ekah,* from the first word, "How." Used as an exclamation, this word introduces the sharp and shocking contrast of a thriving, 400-year-old Jerusalem with the abandoned heap of ruins that Babylonian invaders leave in their wake. To personalize and intensify the imagery, the poet compares Jerusalem, Judah's capital, to a princess who has become a lowly servant and to a maiden daughter who has become a widow. She weeps as one with no friends to comfort her, for her neighbors—former allies—have abandoned her. Some even turn on her, joining Babylon's savage attack.

"Foes have become the masters . . . for the multitude of her transgressions" (Lam 1:5). This alludes to Judah's breach of the covenant with God. Moses had warned that if the Israelites fail to honor their agreement, "the Lord will cause you to be defeated before your enemies" (Deut 28:25). This, in fact, has become Jerusalem's fate. The poet laments that all who had once respected Judah's capital now mock her because they have seen her "nakedness" and that "uncleanness was in her skirts" (Lam 1:8, 9). These embarrassing images continue the metaphor of Jerusalem as a young woman dragged into captivity.

Ancient etchings in stone show chained and naked prisoners marching alongside armed captors. The reference to Jerusalem's uncleanness means that there is nothing she can do about the ritual defilement caused by her menstrual cycle (Lev 15:19). Just as this would utterly humiliate a young princess, exiled survivors of Jerusalem feel thoroughly disgraced.

The Lord is in the right, for I have rebelled against his word. LAM 1:18

*J*erusalem, also known as Mount Zion for the height on which the city is built, confesses that it got what it deserves. This is not just Jerusalem talking. It is the entire southern nation of Judah, symbolized by its capital, seat of the government and the only authorized place at which to offer sacrifices to God. But now the temple is gone, along with the priests, rulers, and leading citizens. There is no nation, no worship center. There is nothing left of the once proud nation that had dominated the region, and no allies willing to fight for release of the captives. Judah has only one hope of escaping the tragic fate of the northern kingdom of Israel, conquered some 150 years earlier by Assyria and its people scattered across the Near East. The maiden Jerusalem points to her enemies and pleads with God: "Deal with them as you have dealt with me" (Lam 1:22).

How the Lord in his anger has humiliated daughter Zion! He has thrown down from heaven to earth the splendor of Israel. LAM 2:1

In his second dirge, the poet describes the people's suffering, starting with the shocking devastation of their cherished capital. The second line essentially repeats the first. One of the main characteristics of ancient Hebrew poetry is not that it rhymes, but that it repeats itself, using different words to say much the same thing, or to expand the message. The people of Judah have arrogantly assumed that God will never let Jerusalem fall—no matter how much they sin—because they believe that the Jerusalem temple is God's earthly dwelling place, or "footstool" (Lam 2:1). They also know that if a nation destroys Jerusalem and the temple, the invaders will conclude that their gods are stronger than the Lord—a false boast that the people incorrectly assume God will never allow. Yet, to fulfill the punishment he has promised in his covenant with Israel, God breaks apart the temple as if it is nothing more than a temporary hut hastily erected in a harvest field.

In streets throughout the city, bodies of young and old lay motionless on the ground. This macabre scene is much like that of an ancient dirge lamenting the destruction of Ur, the home of Abraham: "In its palaces, where the festivities of the land took place, the people lay in heaps. . . . Its dead bodies like fat placed in the sun, of themselves melted away."

I am the one who has seen affliction under the rod of God's wrath . . . . He has made my flesh and my skin waste away, and broken my bones. LAM 3:1, 4

In words and tone reminiscent of the Bible's most notable sufferer, Job, the poet declares that he has personally endured the punishing rod of God's anger. Job, too, wishes that God will "take his rod away" (Job 9:34). And like the poet, "driven . . . into darkness" (Lam 3:2), Job complains that God "has set darkness upon my paths" (Job 19:8). The poet further complains that God "bent his bow and set me as a mark for his arrow" (Lam 3:12). Job expresses the same complaint: "He set me up as his target; his archers surround me" (Job 16:12, 13).

This mournful song is an unusual triple acrostic built on the Hebrew alphabet. The poet writes three verses for each letter, producing a 66-verse poem. Acrostics like these helped people memorize songs and poems—an important skill in the days when written documents were rare and few could read.

The steadfast love of the Lord never ceases, his mercies never come to an end; they are new every morning; great is your faithfulness. LAM 3:22-23

The poet complains that thoughts of his torment and homelessness are like wormwood, a bitter-tasting plant that the prophet Jeremiah used to symbolize Judah's catastrophic fall and the deportation of Hebrew survivors. Surprisingly, in an expression of faith that seems to contradict Judah's reality, the poet declares that the God who is tormenting him and his people is the God of persistent love, endless mercy, and measureless devotion toward the Israelites.

"The Lord will not reject forever," the poet explains. "Although he causes grief, he will have compassion according to the abundance of his steadfast love; for he does not willingly afflict or grieve anyone" (Lam 3:31-33). This statement reflects the poet's apparent belief that Judah is suffering because the vast majority of the people have, for centuries, failed to honor their covenant with God. They have worshiped idols, sold justice to the highest bidder, and treated the Ten Commandments as though they were ten suggestions. For this, they are reaping the consequences foretold by Moses: "The Lord will scatter you among all peoples, from one end of the earth to another" (Deut 28:64).

Those who feasted on delicacies perish in the streets; those who were brought up in purple cling to ash heaps. LAM 4:5

The fourth song in the book is the most gruesome, for it reports in graphic detail the horrors of Babylon's 18-month-long siege of Jerusalem, beginning in January of 587 B.C. Starving and surrounded by attacking Babylonian troops, citizens of Jerusalem have become lower than jackals, the poet laments, for even jackals feed their young. Worse, they have become cannibals: "The hands of compassionate women have boiled their own children" (Lam 4:10). The horrors of this siege know no class distinction. Even the wealthy, accustomed to eating exotic delicacies, search for food in trash heaps.

In the heat of July of 586, Nebuchadnezzar's invasion forces breach the walls and begin a month of slaughter, looting, burning, and razing the entire city. By August, the survivors are on their way in chains to Babylon, nearly a thousand-mile march from their beloved city, which lies in ruins.

Restore us to yourself, O Lord, that we may be restored; renew our days as of old—unless you have utterly rejected us, and are angry with us beyond measure. LAM 5:21-22

The last song is a stark and pitiful cry for God to end Judah's suffering. The poet pleads with God to remember all the tragedy Judah's people have endured because of their own sins and the sins of their ancestors. Israel's inheritance—the land God promised to Abraham and his descendants—has been turned over to foreigners. Judah is a slave nation. What remains uncertain for the poet, however, is whether God has given up on the Israelites. Earlier, the poet had confidently declared that God would not reject them forever (Lam 3:31), but now the poet's faith seems to waver. This uncertainty produces the timid and pathetic plea that closes Lamentations—a plea for God to give the Israelites a fresh start, unless he has abandoned them for all time.

The prophet Ezekiel, as depicted on a 15th-century German stained glass window

A priest as well as a prophet, Ezekiel was a member of Jerusalem's temple elite and was among the first wave of exiles deported from Jerusalem to Babylon with King Jehoiachin in 597 B.C. He lived in a colony of his fellow Jews who had settled in Tel-abib by the river Chebar, actually an irrigation canal that was connected with the Euphrates River near the Babylonian city of Nippur. Ezekiel's call to be a prophet came in 593, the fifth year of his exile; his active prophetic career lasted 22 years, until 571. Though after his call he continued to live in Babylon, Ezekiel was transported back to Jerusalem through a series of visions. The fantastic imagery of his many visions conveys the prophet's distinctive message. After being struck dumb by God for a period of time, Ezekiel also uses a kind of street theater to communicate his message through often bizarre symbolic actions.

The most prominent theme in Ezekiel's highly charged preaching is his dual emphasis on the holiness of God and the temple in Jerusalem. The Lord exiled the Israelites and will return them to Jerusalem for the sake of his own glory and to preserve the sanctity of the divine name. The purpose of all of God's actions is that Israel and the other nations might know that the Lord alone is God, sovereign over all. Ezekiel's message also places a premium on maintaining the integrity of the temple. When the people of Judah desecrated the house of the Lord with their idolatrous behavior, God's glorious presence departed. Ezekiel's final vision depicts God's glory returning only after the temple has been purified. Because of the book's daring portrayal of the divine presence, some Jews in ancient times considered Ezekiel too dangerous for anyone under the age of 30 to study.

The first 24 chapters of Ezekiel are oracles of judgment against Judah and Jerusalem. Oracles against foreign nations comprise chapters 25 to 32 while oracles of salvation are contained in chapters 33 to 48. Although his career spanned the destruction of Jerusalem in 586, Ezekiel apparently did not live to see the return of the exiles to their homeland in 538. Nonetheless, his vision of the resplendently reconstructed and reconsecrated temple in chapters 40 to 48 provided his fellow exiles with hope for the future.

In the thirtieth year, in the fourth month, on the fifth day of the month, as I was among the exiles by the river Chebar, the heavens were opened, and I saw visions of God.
EZEK 1:1

*B*efore he is officially called to be a prophet, Ezekiel receives a fantastic vision of the Lord. Though he expresses no fear, Ezekiel must have been struck by the remarkable appearance of the sight that greets him. In the middle of a great cloud flashing with fire, four living creatures emerge. They appear to be part calf and part human, but each creature also has four wings. Each head has four faces: that of a human, a lion, an ox, and an eagle. Early Christians interpreted these four symbols as references to the four gospel writers.

Although Ezekiel's description of his vision and the creatures is sometimes sketchy and seems to contradict itself, he apparently sees a chariot-throne, a ve-hicle with four wheels that is propelled by the strange winged creatures who move simultaneously, "for the spirit of the living creatures was in the wheels" (Ezek 1:21). The creatures are transporting a magnificent throne that is supported by a crystal dome. The startling vision of the divine glory is enough to knock him down: "When I saw it, I fell on my face, and I heard the voice of someone speaking" (Ezek 1:28). The commanding voice belongs to no less than the king himself, the God of Israel.

He said to me: O mortal, stand up on your feet, and I will speak with you. EZEK 2:1

*I*n the first oracle and throughout the book, God addresses Ezekiel as "mortal," translated from the Hebrew *ben adam*, literally "son of Adam" or "son of man." "Adam" is related to another Hebrew word, *adamah*, the reddish clay from which God fashioned the first human (Gen 2:7). The address "son of Adam" or "mortal" thus serves to emphasize Ezekiel's created nature and his great distance from the Holy God of Israel. In the gospels, Jesus uses the term "Son of Man" to refer to himself, but that designation derives primarily from Daniel's use of the term (Dan 7:13-14) rather than Ezekiel's.

Ezekiel is faced with a difficult mission. His commission is to deliver the message of the scrolls to the Israelites even though he must expect to meet considerable resistance to the message. God warns Ezekiel not to be like those rebellious people, and commands him to open his mouth and eat what is offered to him: a scroll. Unrolled, the scroll reveals its grim contents, for on both the front and the back it is filled with "words of lamentation and mourning and woe" (Ezek 2:10).

He said to me, O mortal, eat what is offered to you; eat this scroll, and go, speak to the house of Israel.   EZEK 3:1

A second time God commands Ezekiel to open his mouth and swallow the scroll. Ezekiel savors the scroll because it tastes as sweet as honey. The image of the prophet swallowing a scroll is striking and seems to reflect a development in how Israelite prophecy is delivered to its audience. Ezekiel's earlier colleague, Jeremiah, delivers his prophecy orally. Only after the oracles are delivered does Jeremiah dictate their contents to his scribe Baruch (Jer 36:4). Here, Ezekiel swallows the scroll; in his case, the written word of God precedes the spoken word. A third stage of prophecy can be seen in the postexilic book of Zechariah, in which the prophet sees a flying scroll that delivers its own message of judgment directly to the people (Zech 5:1-4).

After receiving the divine commission, Ezekiel is transported back to Tel-abib by the river Chebar. Charged by God to be a "sentinel for the house of Israel" (Ezek 3:17), Ezekiel must warn the people about the consequences of their sins. If he fails to

warn them, Ezekiel is complicit in unfairly sealing their fate. God then does a very peculiar thing: He strikes Ezekiel dumb. It is hard to accept Ezekiel's dumbness literally because of the many oracles and discourses that follow in the first part of the prophet's work. Some scholars suggest understanding the silence of Ezekiel metaphorically: By silencing Ezekiel, God has sealed off the divine word of judgment in order to isolate and punish the rebellious Israelites.

And you, O mortal, take a brick and set it before you. On it portray a city, Jerusalem.   EZEK 4:1

Instead of delivering the prophetic word orally, God tells Ezekiel to present his message through a series of symbolic actions relating to the fate of the city of Jerusalem. The first requires artistry. He must take a mud brick and draw a picture of Jerusalem with siegeworks set against it. The drawing is to represent the Babylonian siege against Jerusalem that will begin in January of 587 B.C. Ezekiel then undergoes a vicarious punishment for the sins of the two Israelite kingdoms. He first lies on his left side for 390 days to represent the number of years of the punishment of the northern kingdom of Israel, conquered by Assyria in 722; he then turns to lie on his right side for 40 days to signify the years of Judah's punishment. The significance of these numbers has eluded interpreters, for Israel never returned from its exile, while the length of Judah's exile was 48 years.

Ezekiel is then commanded to eat a measured amount of grain and water. The strict dietary regimen symbolizes the scarce amounts of food that will be available to the inhabitants of Jerusalem during the siege. The grain is to be baked in the form of a barley cake, using human dung as fuel for the fire. Ezekiel protests to God that he has never defiled himself in such a way. Quite the contrary, as a priest, he is especially careful about keeping himself ritually pure by strictly observing Israel's dietary laws. So God relents and permits him to use cow manure as fuel instead of offensive human waste. Harsh as it is, God's command is intended to emphasize the terrible deprivations the besieged Judahites will undergo.

And you, O mortal, take a sharp sword; use it as a barber's razor and run it over your head and your beard; then take balances for weighing, and divide the hair.
EZEK 5:1

The second symbolic act is equally bizarre and relates to the end of the siege and the sacking of Jerusalem. Ezekiel is commanded to shave off the hair of his head and beard using a sword. After weighing the hair he

Exiled in Babylon, the people of Judah bemoan the loss of Jerusalem and their temple; a romanticized view by Evelyn de Morgan (1855-1919).

has collected, he should divide it into thirds. One-third of the hair Ezekiel is told to burn within the city walls; one-third he must slash with a sword in the city; and one-third he must cast into the wind. The oracle then elaborates on the meaning of these odd commands. The sword used to cut his hair represents the devastating weapons brought by the invading army of Babylon. The weighing of the hair signifies God's judgment of the people. The three parts represent the respective fates of the population of Jerusalem: One-third will die of pestilence or famine, one-third will be killed by the invading army, and one-third will be cast into the winds, exiled. Not only will Israel's punishment be severe, but it will serve as a warning to everyone about the risks involved in transgressing the Lord's commandments: "You shall be a mockery and a taunt, a warning and a horror, to the nations around you" (Ezek 5:15).

O mortal, set your face toward the mountains of Israel, and prophesy against them. EZEK 6:2

The next oracle expands on the judgment just announced. The mountains of Israel themselves are called upon to hear the divine word. Throughout their history, the Israelites built altars on the tops of hills, sacrificed to Canaanite gods, and burned incense before idols—in direct disobedience to their covenant with the Lord.

Condemning the mountains is, of course, simply a metaphor for condemning the idolatrous Israelites. The proof comes in the next oracle: "Clap your hands and stamp your foot, and say, Alas for all the vile abominations of the house of Israel!" (Ezek 6:11). Divine judgment for these abominations is imminent. "An end! The end has come upon the four corners of the land" (Ezek 7:2). God has pronounced judgment, first on Jerusalem, then on the mountains of Israel, and now on the entire earth. The "day of the Lord," a day of destruction following God's final judgment, is described in other prophetic books as well, for example, Amos 5:18-20. In this oracle, God's punishment is depicted as merciless, affecting the entire earth and causing the land itself to tremble. The end result of this punishment will be universal recognition of the omnipotent God of Israel: "Then they shall know that I am the Lord" (Ezek 6:14).

A figure that looked like a human being . . . . took me by a lock of my head . . . and brought me in visions of God to Jerusalem. EZEK 8:2, 3

A second vision reveals the situation in Jerusalem during the years preceding the fall to Babylon in 586 B.C. As Ezekiel is sitting in his house in the company of some of the exiled elders of Judah, he is summoned by a messenger of God, who lifts him by his hair and takes him to Jerusalem. The messenger guides him through the temple to witness the abominations. Ezekiel sees a forbidden idol, the image of a foreign god, at the entrance. In a sec-

Receiving his oracles from the hand of God (top), Ezekiel reveals how the righteous will be separated from the unrighteous; from the 12th-century Lambeth Bible.

ond scene, 70 elders of Judah are worshiping in a secret room on whose walls are depicted "all kinds of creeping things, and loathsome animals, and all the idols of the house of Israel" (Ezek 8:10). Taken back to the entrance, Ezekiel sees women weeping for the Mesopotamian fertility god Tammuz. The worst abomination occurs at the very holy site where sacrifices take place. There, 25 men, their backs to the temple, worship the Babylonian sun god Shamesh by prostrating themselves to the rising sun.

Ezekiel then watches as his guide summons six executioners to the doomed city. A seventh man, clothed in linen, is a scribe. He is ordered to put an x-shaped tau, the last letter of the Hebrew alphabet, on the forehead of those who lament the worship of idols in order for them to be spared punishment. Young and old, male and female, no one who has committed idolatry will escape. Despite Ezekiel's fervent intercession for them, God has sealed their fate.

Then I looked, and above the dome that was over the heads of the cherubim there appeared above them something like a sapphire, in form resembling a throne. EZEK 10:1

As a result of the Israelites' desecration of the temple, a sobering event occurs. The "glory of the Lord" (Ezek 10:4), symbolic of God's immanent presence, departs from the temple. The Israelites experienced God's presence in different ways. To Moses, divinity was present in the fiery bush that was not consumed (Ex 3:2). Job experienced God through a whirlwind (Job 38:1). As a priest who serves God in the temple, Ezekiel experiences the glorious divine presence in worship. Thenceforth, priests and worshipers will no longer have access to the Lord's presence. Ezekiel describes the dazzling glory of the Lord enveloped in a cloud that illuminates the court of the temple with its brightness. The glory with its surrounding cloud billows up and out of the temple, enthroned above a chariot propelled by the same four cherubim that had appeared in Ezekiel's first vision.

In the final part of Ezekiel's second vision, he sees 25 elders who have been making political decisions about the fate of Jerusalem. The historical background of this situation remains obscure, but they, too, are slated for death because of the wicked counsel they have provided. When Pelatiah, one of the elders, suddenly dies, Ezekiel utters a plaintive cry: "Ah Lord God! will you make a full end of the remnant of Israel?" (Ezek 11:13). God responds with reassuring words. One day God will gather the exiles and return them to their land. Moreover, in words reminiscent of the new covenant described in Jeremiah 31:31-34, the Lord promises to transform their very natures: "I will give them one heart, and put a new spirit within them . . . . Then they shall be my people, and I will be their God" (Ezek 11:19-20).

Mortal, prophesy against the prophets of Israel who are prophesying; say to those who prophesy out of their own imagination: "Hear the word of the Lord!" EZEK 13:2

In contrast to the dreamlike visions he experiences, Ezekiel is confronted with the challenge of those Israelite prophets who are masters of deception. Though this oracle is not dated, it seems to come from a time before the fall of Jerusalem in 586 B.C. The false prophets pretend to speak for the Lord, yet their prophecy is illegitimate. They proclaim that there will be peace when, in fact, Israel is destined for war. "When the people build a wall," Ezekiel says, "these prophets smear whitewash on it" (Ezek 13:10). The wall gives a false sense of security to the Israelites because God will break it down and allow the Babylonians to conquer Jerusalem.

Using another metaphor to convey the fate of Jerusalem and its inhabitants, the oracle in chapter 15 likens Jerusalem to the wood of a vine found in the forest. Wood from trees is used to make useful objects, but vine wood is not good for anything except fuel for the fire.

Mortal, make known to Jerusalem her abominations, and say . . . to Jerusalem: Your origin and your birth were in the land of the Canaanites; your father was an Amorite, and your mother a Hittite. EZEK 16:2-3

In chapter 16, Ezekiel uses an extended metaphor to portray Jerusalem as the faithless wife of the Lord. Like Hosea and Jeremiah, Ezekiel uses graphic sexual imagery as a way of inveighing against the city's apostate citizenry (Hos 2:2; Jer 2:20, 3:1-2).

The horrifying image of Jerusalem as an adulterous wife and nymphomaniac is intended to shock members of Ezekiel's audience out of their complacency and into an awareness of their sins.

In this judgment oracle, God reminds Jerusalem of her humble origins and recounts her rise through history. She was born of a "mixed marriage" of two different peoples. After her birth, the city was neglected: "Your navel cord was not cut, nor were you washed with water to cleanse you, nor rubbed with salt, nor wrapped in cloths" (Ezek 16:4). This accords with the insignificant position of Jerusalem during the ancestral period compared with the greater cities of Egypt and Mesopotamia. But by making a covenant with Israel, God adopts Jerusalem as his own and clothes her "with embroidered cloth and with sandals of fine leather" (Ezek 16:9).

The "woman" Israel grows up to be a beauty admired by all, just as the nation Israel grows wealthy and gains renown in the international sphere under King Solomon. But Israel wickedly uses her beauty to seduce passersby, that is, she becomes involved at various times in foreign alliances with Egypt, Assyria, and Chaldea, or Babylon. Jerusalem's "sisters," Samaria, the capital of the northern kingdom, and Sodom to the south are not as lascivious as she is. At the end of the long invective against Jerusalem comes a word of hope and promise. God ultimately promises to forgive Jerusalem her sins and establish an eternal covenant: "And you shall know that I am the Lord" (Ezek 16:62).

O mortal, propound a riddle, and speak an allegory to the house of Israel. EZEK 17:2

Ezekiel employs a variety of figures of speech in order to communicate the divine word. The allegory of the two eagles and the vine in chapter 17 refers to historical events occurring in the final fateful decade before the second deportation in 586 B.C. A great eagle with multicolored plumage, King Nebuchadnezzar of Babylon, plucks off the top of the cedar, King Jehoiachin, and the elite of Jerusalem, and exiles them to Babylon. The eagle then plants a seed from the land in fertile soil by establishing the puppet king Zedekiah on the throne of Judah. But the vine that grows from the seed reaches out toward a second eagle, Pharaoh Psammetichus II of Egypt. During his reign, Zedekiah turns from Babylon and seeks military protection from Egypt. Just as a transplanted vine is easily plucked up, so, too, Judah is vulnerable to siege. The end result will be punishment by God; Zedekiah, too, will be exiled.

The chapter ends, however, with an oracle promising restoration of the house of David, again using an allegory. In the future, God will pluck off the top of the cedar and replant it on Mount Zion. As with all of God's acts in Ezekiel, the divine restoration will in time result in universal recognition of Israel's Lord: "All the trees of the field shall know that I am the Lord. . . . I the Lord have spoken" (Ezek 17:24).

What do you mean by repeating this proverb concerning the land of Israel, "The parents have eaten sour grapes, and the children's teeth are set on edge"? EZEK 18:2

In chapter 18, God uses yet another literary device to convey his divine word. The Lord asks Ezekiel a pointed question, repeating a well-known proverb that means the failures of parents hold consequences for their children. God tells Ezekiel that this proverb will no longer have currency in Israel. The Lord will hold everyone responsible for his or her own sins. This same proverb is quoted in Jeremiah 31:29 to make precisely the same point: Despite conventional wisdom, the Lord judges each person according to his deeds alone. The lesson, plain and simple, is "a child shall not suffer for the iniquity of a parent, nor a parent suffer for the iniquity of a child" (Ezek 18:20). The oracle adds that repentance will inevitably bring about reconciliation with God.

The long sermon on individual accountability contained in this chapter might seem obvious to today's society, but the culture of ancient Israel was different. The extended family was a unit of mutual responsibility and accountability. Kin were supposed to look out for each other and could be blamed for each other's faults.

As for you, raise up a lamentation for the princes of Israel, and say: What a lioness was your mother among lions! EZEK 19:1-2

Ezekiel is instructed to sing a lamentation for the princes of Israel. A Hebrew lamentation, composed to bemoan a grievous loss or a drastic change of status, carried a particular limping rhythm intended to convey the loss or change. The lament in Ezekiel 19 has two parts. The first is an allegory about a lioness and her cubs; the second is an allegory about a vine and the fate of its various offshoots. It is hard to discern the precise historical reality lying behind the first allegory. The lioness may refer to the house of Judah. One of its kings, Jehoahaz, was deported to Egypt by Pharaoh Neco in 609 B.C. Two of his successors, Jehoiachin and Zedekiah, were deported to Babylon in, respectively, 597 and 586.

The ambiguity in the allegories is their very strength, because they can be interpreted in various ways, retaining the interest of the audience. The second allegory contained in the lament, that of the vine, seems to refer generally to the monarchy in Judah. Yet the grim fate the oracle forecasts for the Davidic dynasty, a future with "no scepter for ruling" (Ezek 19:14), seems to contradict Ezekiel's oracles predicting a full restoration of the house of David.

NOT FOR CHILDREN

Not only were parts of the Bible once deemed too horrifying or erotic for children, some rabbis in ancient times ordered that no one under the age of 30 could read them. Prohibited were Ezekiel's nightmarish vision in chapter 1, along with the entire Song of Solomon, a sensual discussion between a young man and a young woman in love.

When it came time to discuss which revered Jewish writings belonged in the Hebrew Bible, many rabbis argued against both Ezekiel and Song of Solomon, fearing the damage these books might cause if read aloud in synagogues. Other books and passages were also considered inappropriate for children or even for inclusion in the Bible. The book of Esther met resistance not only because it fails to mention God, but because it presents as good news the story of threatened Jews in Persia descending to the barbarity of their enemies, slaughtering 75,000 of them.

As centuries passed, church leaders grew to believe that none of the Bible could be entrusted to the uneducated masses, who might misinterpret it. Scripture was confined to Latin, a language few could read and that many of the clergy could memorize but not understand. When the theologian and reformer John Wycliffe translated the Bible into English in the 1300s, he was condemned by the church. In reply, Wycliffe said, "Englishmen learn Christ's law best in English. Moses heard God's law in his own tongue, so did Christ's apostles."

In the seventh year, in the fifth month . . . certain elders of Israel came to consult the Lord, and sat down before me. EZEK 20:1

The exiled elders of Israel seek Ezekiel's prophetic counsel in a passage dated to 591 B.C., two years after Ezekiel is called to his prophetic office. God at first balks at providing guidance to the elders, but then asks Ezekiel to deliver a message after all, to "let them know the abominations of their ancestors" (Ezek 20:4). The oracle recounts the history of Israel from the Exodus until the Israelites' entry into the promised land. The Israelites' past is riddled with idolatry. Peppered throughout the account is the reason that God does not scorch them entirely: "I acted for the sake of my name, that it should not be profaned in the sight of the nations" (Ezek 20:9, 14, 22).

But God gives hope for the future. As does Second Isaiah, Ezekiel portrays the future return from exile as a new exodus. Using the same phrase associated with God's work in Exodus, Ezekiel predicts that "with a mighty hand and an outstretched arm" (Ezek 20:33), God will gather the dispersed exiles. But before they can return to the promised land, God must judge them for their sins in the wilderness—that is, among the nations. Only then will he bring them to his holy mountain, the site of the temple in Jerusalem.

*Mortal, set your face toward Jerusalem
and preach against the sanctuaries;
prophesy against the land of Israel.*
EZEK 21:2

Although the previous oracle provides hope for the future, the present and immediate future is another matter. Chapters 21 and 22 contain a series of oracles depicting a grim fate for Jerusalem. The unifying theme of these oracles is the use of a sword, recalling Ezekiel's earlier symbolic shaving of his head. The first is most terrifying because God is ready to unsheathe the divine sword to begin a fierce punishment for Jerusalem's idolatry. The prospect of such divine vengeance is horrifying indeed: "Let the sword fall twice, thrice; it is a sword for killing. A sword for great slaughter—it surrounds them" (Ezek 21:14).

God will also punish Judah and Jerusalem through the king of Babylon, Nebuchadnezzar. He is depicted using the superstitious rites of divining: shaking arrows, consulting his household gods, inspecting an animal's liver to decide whether to attack Rabbah, the capital of the Ammonites, or Jerusalem. The lot falls to Jerusalem. In an oracle addressed to Zedekiah, Ezekiel informs the king his time has run out: "As for you, vile, wicked prince of Israel, you whose day has come, . . . take off the crown" (Ezek 21:25-26).

Mortal, there were two women, the daughters of one mother.
EZEK 23:2

Ezekiel uses yet another allegory in chapter 23 to condemn not only the southern kingdom of Judah but also the northern kingdom of Israel, the daughters of "one mother," the united kingdom of Israel under David and Solomon. The two daughters are named Oholah, Hebrew for "her tent," and Oholibah, "my tent is in her." The reference to the tent is symbolic of the tent shrine the Israelites used for worship in the wilderness after the Exodus. Ezekiel identifies Oholah as Samaria, the capital of the northern kingdom, and her sister Oholibah as Jerusalem, the capital of Judah. Oholah is condemned for lusting after the Assyrians, a reference perhaps to treaties Israel made with the Assyrian empire in the late ninth century.

Oholibah is even more corrupt than her sister. She takes up with men from different nations: Assyria, Babylon, and Egypt. But God will punish Oholibah for her lewd behavior by rousing her former lovers against her. They will come "with chariots and wagons and a host of people" to slaughter her children and mutilate and strip Oholibah, leaving the city "naked and bare" (Ezek 23:24, 29)—all this, the Lord says, because Jerusalem has forgotten him.

*Heeding the Lord's messenger (left),
Ezekiel rises to deliver an oracle to
Judah, personified as a woman (right).*

*Mortal, write down the name of this
day, this very day. The king of
Babylon has laid siege to Jerusalem
this very day.* EZEK 24:2

On January 15, 587 B.C., Nebuchadnezzar began his siege of Jerusalem in order to complete his capture of the southern kingdom. Delivering an oracle in connection with the siege, the prophet uses the image of a pot filled with boiling water to symbolize the tension created in Jerusalem by the attack. The pot is filled with choice bones, representing all the inhabitants of Jerusalem who are suffering from the effects of the siege. To make matters worse, the pot is contaminated with rust, symbolic of the blood shed within Jerusalem. According to ancient Israel's laws of purity, touching blood renders a person impure and in need of ritual cleansing. Contamination requires purification through fire and so, once the bones are cooked, Ezekiel is instructed to turn the pot over the fire.

The subsequent oracle contains another unusual dictate from God. The Lord tells Ezekiel that the prophet's wife, the "delight of your eyes" (Ezek 24:15), will die, but he is not permitted to mourn her death. As yet another symbolic act, Ezekiel has to deny his emotions in order to show the Judahites that they will not have a chance to mourn after the destruction of the temple. There will be one positive result from Jerusalem's capture: At long last, God will put an end to Ezekiel's dumbness.

*Mortal, set your face toward the Ammonites and prophesy
against them.* EZEK 25:2

Israel was not the only target of God's wrath. Chapters 25 to 32 are filled with oracles against foreign nations. Egypt, Assyria, Babylon, and Persia were successive superpowers during Old Testament times, but there were many smaller countries that intermittently threatened Israel as well. Ammon, located to the east of the Jordan River, is the first to come under God's judgment. For their joy at Israel's downfall—"Because you have clapped your hands and stamped your feet and rejoiced with all the malice within you against the land of Israel" (Ezek 25:6)—the Ammonites, too, will be exiled to Babylon. Moab, Edom, and Philistia, smaller nations bordering Judah to the southeast and southwest, are also condemned. A crucial result of the nations' punishment will be their recognition of the Lord's omnipotence. The refrain repeated throughout is, "Then they shall know that I am the Lord" (Ezek 25:11).

The great city-state of Tyre, located on the Phoenician coast to the north of Israel, is singled out for divine punishment in an extended oracle. Tyre is famed for its seafaring traders who bring great wealth to the city. But Ezekiel predicts that a lament will be raised over Tyre: "How you have vanished from the seas, O city renowned . . . . the coastlands tremble on the day of your fall" (Ezek 26:17-18). Tyre's proud king will be cast down from his throne, and the inhabitants of Tyre and the neighboring city of Sidon "shall know that I am the Lord" (Ezek 28:23).

Mortal, set your face against Pharaoh king of Egypt, and prophesy against him and against all Egypt.   EZEK 29:2

From the countries immediately surrounding Israel, Ezekiel shifts his reproach to the mighty nation of Egypt, to rail against its treachery. Pharaoh is described in mythic terms as "the great dragon sprawling in the midst of its channels" (Ezek 29:3). The dragon mentioned here is the Nile River crocodile, whose strength and ferocity were associated with Pharaoh in ancient Egyptian crocodile cults. In the Old Testament, Egypt usually figures as a great enemy because of its role in enslaving Israel's ancestors. In Ezekiel's own time, Egypt, under Psammetichus II, enlists Judah as an ally against Babylon and thus ensures Nebuchadnezzar's wrath against his former tributary, Judah.

Egypt will be punished as will its allies to the south—Ethiopia, Put, Lud, Arabia, and Libya. Like Tyre's king, Egypt's Pharaoh is reproached for his arrogance. God declares that he "will put hooks in your jaws and make the fish of your channels stick to your scales" (Ezek 29:4). The agent for the divine punishment will be Nebuchadnezzar. In an oracle dated to April of 587 comes the divine pronouncement: "I have broken the arm of Pharaoh king of Egypt" (Ezek 30:20). This is most probably a reference to the defeat of Pharaoh Hophra by Nebuchadnezzar, when Egypt goes to the aid of Judah during the Babylonians' final siege of Jerusalem.

If any who hear the sound of the trumpet do not take warning, and the sword comes and takes them away, their blood shall be upon their own heads.   EZEK 33:4

The book of Ezekiel reaches a climax in chapter 33, which reports the culmination of the long-awaited punishment of Jerusalem. The Lord repeats his appointment of Ezekiel as "a sentinel for the house of Israel" (Ezek 3:17, 33:7), charged with making known to the righteous and the wicked their respective fates. The righteous will receive their due reward but the wicked, unless they "turn from their ways" (Ezek 33:9), are condemned to die. The key to divine forgiveness is repentance for sins. The merciful God of Israel demonstrates his infinite compassion at the first signs of contrition.

Ezekiel receives word of the fall of Jerusalem from a fugitive who has managed to escape the Babylonian net. His speech newly restored, the prophet proclaims oracles of salvation to the crestfallen exiles. In chapter 34 he uses the comforting image of God as

watchful shepherd over his flock, Israel. The Lord will search for his lost sheep scattered among the nations and return them to "good grazing land, and they shall feed on rich pasture on the mountains of Israel" (Ezek 34:14).

Mortal, set your face against Mount Seir, and prophesy against it.   EZEK 35:2

All of the oracles directed toward Israel at the end of Ezekiel are oracles of consolation and hope, but there is one of judgment against Mount Seir, another way of referring to the nation of Edom, located to the southeast of Judah. The Edomites were considered close kin to the Israelites, for the Bible traces their lineage back to Esau, Jacob's twin brother (Gen 36). As punishment for its venomous glee at seeing the destruction of Israel and Judah, the Lord promises to make Mount Seir a "perpetual desolation" (Ezek 35:9).

An oracle uttered to the mountains of Israel is set in opposition to the prophesy against Mount Seir. After God condemns the rest of the nations, including Edom, that have plundered Israel's land, he speaks to the mountains and promises them that they shall soon see the return of the people of Israel and that their slopes shall be tilled and sown as before. Israel had polluted the land with bloodshed and idolatry before the exile, but they have paid the price for this sinfulness with their exile.

The hand of the Lord came upon me, and he brought me out by the spirit of the Lord and set me down in the middle of a valley; it was full of bones.   EZEK 37:1

Propelled by the spirit of God, Ezekiel experiences a third fantastic vision. The prophet is transported to an unidentified valley that is full of dry human bones. After conducting a tour of this peculiar site, God asks Ezekiel a rhetorical question: "Mortal, can these bones live?" Ezekiel's response is both cagey and tactful: "O Lord God, you know" (Ezek 37:3). The true answer, which Ezekiel is asked

God reaches out to destroy Jerusalem's sinners; from the 3rd-century A.D. synagogue at Dura-Europos, Syria.

to prophesy, is that the bones can live, but only through the intervention of the Lord.

No sooner has Ezekiel delivered this divine word than he hears a queer rattling, the sound of the bones knitting themselves together into skeletons. As he watches, sinews grow upon the skeletons, then flesh upon the sinews, and finally skin on the resuscitated human beings. God then identifies the bones as the Israelite nation. Israel has been dried up in the exile, but God has revived it. The word then comes: "I am going to open your graves . . . and I will bring you back to the land of Israel" (Ezek 37:12). Although the opening of graves can be interpreted in a figurative sense to mean that God will revive and restore an exiled people, later Jews and Christians saw it as a reference to bodily resurrection.

Mortal, set your face toward Gog, of the land of Magog, the chief prince of Meshech and Tubal. Prophesy against him.   EZEK 38:2

Chapters 38 and 39 contain a number of oracles against Gog from Magog, a fictional character meant to represent Israel's universal enemy. Although the oracles are undated, they are set in the period after the exiles have returned to their homeland and are just beginning to acquire the trappings of settled agricultural life again. The chief prince Gog will concoct a wicked scheme to attack the Israelites and plunder their villages. Massing the combined might of Gog's army and the armies of Persia, Ethiopia, and Put, he will mount an attack against the defenseless people of Israel.

But Ezekiel prophesies that the zeal and wrath of Israel's God will counter the enemy in an apocalyptic battle. On that terrible day, the very elements of nature will be disrupted: "The mountains shall be thrown down, and the cliffs shall fall." God in his wrath will "pour down torrential rains and hailstones, fire and sulfur" (Ezek 38:20, 22) upon Gog, his troops, and all those with him. In this way, God's holy name will become known among all people. The display of God's glory and holiness entails judgment and

Another Dura-Europos fresco depicts Ezekiel's vision of dried bones miraculously restored to life.

vengeance upon all the nations. They will learn that, although the Lord punished the sins of Israel by sending them into exile, such punishment is past. God will "restore the fortunes of Jacob, and have mercy on the whole house of Israel" (Ezek 39:25).

In the twenty-fifth year of our exile . . . in the fourteenth year after the city was struck down, on that very day, the hand of the Lord was upon me, and he brought me there.   EZEK 40:1

Ezekiel has been in exile for 25 years when he is again brought in a vision to the land of Israel. The last section of the book is a record of his visionary journey in 573 B.C., which he is commanded to report in full to the house of Israel. Ezekiel is transported to a high mountain that, it soon becomes clear, is Mount Zion. There, the prophet is given a tour of the newly restored temple. His tour guide, a humanlike creature, is engaged in measuring all the dimensions of the temple: its courtyards, vestibules, gates, pilasters, and the carved cherubs and palm trees throughout. When the measurements are complete, the guide brings the prophet to the eastern gate of the temple. As Ezekiel is looking eastward, he sees in the distance the glory of the Lord approaching. The divine glory enters through the gate and fills the temple. Comforting words are heard: "Mortal, this is the place of my throne and the place for the soles of my feet, where I will reside among the people of Israel forever" (Ezek 43:7). Reversing the departure of his glory described in chapter 10, Israel's God again reigns supreme in his temple.

Then he brought me back to the entrance of the temple; there, water was flowing from below the threshold of the temple toward the east.   EZEK 47:1

In an earlier oracle of promise concerning Israel's restoration to its homeland, the once desolate land is described as being "like the garden of Eden" (Ezek 36:35). This mythic view of the land of Israel reappears in the idealized description of the restored temple. The creation story of Genesis 2:10-14 mentions a river flowing out of Eden that provides water for the garden. Now the temple is depicted as the heart of Eden, a pristine place from whose center flows life-giving water. The restoration of the temple with its reconsecrated priests and its sacrificial system for daily use and festivals will, in a sense, recreate the perfection of Eden, where the first humans lived in an undefiled state, free from sin.

Ezekiel closes with an idyllic picture of the future: All of Israel's original 12 tribes will be reestablished in the land and each will receive a special allotment of land on which to dwell. Hope for the future is sealed in the new name for Jerusalem: *Yahweh shammah;* in English, "The Lord is There" (Ezek 48:35). God, who had once departed from his sacred city because it was polluted with sin, will return in full holiness to dwell among his people forever.

A faithful Jew named Daniel, who was taken captive to Babylon as a youth and served as an influential court sage there for more than 60 years, is the protagonist of the biblical book that bears his name. The name Daniel was probably borrowed from the legendary hero Daniel, or Danel, cited by Ezekiel for the righteousness he shared with Noah and Job (Ezek 14:14, 20). Daniel is also the name of the upright ruler in the 14th-century B.C. epic of Aqhat from the Ugarit kingdom in what is now Syria.

The book of Daniel is the only example in the Old Testament of apocalyptic literature (see page 427), in which the triumph of the righteous at the end of time is revealed. The book has two parts: a group of stories in chapters 1-6 about Daniel and his companions, and four dream-visions of Daniel in chapters 7-12. For unknown reasons, the book is preserved in two languages, Hebrew (Dan 1:1-2:4a, 8:1-12:13) and Aramaic (Dan 2:4b-7:28).

The story is set in the sixth century B.C., but it is generally agreed that it actually depicts events during the reign of the Syrian tyrant Antiochus IV Epiphanes (175-164 B.C.), when observant Jews were persecuted and martyred. Some scholars hold that the book was written in the sixth century B.C., and therefore predicts the future. Most, however, believe that it was completed between 167 and 164 B.C., after the events that Daniel's visions "prophesy." The author is thought to have been a sage who supported Jewish laws and traditions during Antiochus's reign.

The Hebrew Bible places Daniel among the Writings (11 books, including Psalms and Proverbs), but Christian Bibles follow the Greek Septuagint in placing it between the prophets Ezekiel and Hosea. The Greek version supplements the Hebrew text with additional material (see page 286).

Protected by angels, Daniel survives his night in the lions' den; a 14th-century stained glass window from Mulhouse, France.

In the third year of the reign of King Jehoiakim of Judah, King Nebuchadnezzar of Babylon came to Jerusalem and besieged it. DAN 1:1

In the first of several historical inaccuracies in the book, the author dates the capture of Jerusalem by the Babylonians to the third year of Jehoiakim's reign (606 B.C.). It actually took place in 597 B.C., during the reign of Jehoiakim's son, Jehoiachin. In that year, Nebuchadnezzar took Jewish captives and treasures from the temple back to Babylon. In the biblical account the king commands that "young men without physical defect and handsome, versed in every branch of wisdom" (Dan 1:4) be brought from Judah so they can learn the ways of the Chaldeans (a term for wise men). After three years of training, they will be ready to serve in Nebuchadnezzar's court.

Among this group is Daniel, who is given the Babylonian name Belteshazzar, and his three friends, renamed Shadrach, Meshach, and Abednego. The king provides them with food and wine from his royal table, but Daniel refuses to defile himself with nonkosher food. The palace master fears the king's wrath if Daniel looks less healthy than the others, but a guard agrees to let Daniel and his friends eat vegetables and water for a ten-day trial. After this, they appear in better condition than the others, and so are allowed to eat as they like. To reward them for their loyalty, God gives them "knowledge and skill in every aspect of literature and wisdom; Daniel also has insight into all visions and dreams" (Dan 1:17).

At the end of their education, the four youths are brought before the king, who is delighted with their abilities and admits them to his court. Daniel serves until King Cyrus's first year at Babylon (539-538 B.C.), nearly 60 years after he is taken from Judah.

Nebuchadnezzar dreamed such dreams that his spirit was troubled and his sleep left him. DAN 2:1

Nebuchadnezzar summons all his wise men to interpret a dream for him, but to test them he says, "If you do not tell me both the dream and its interpretation, you shall be torn limb from limb, and your houses shall be laid in ruins" (Dan 2:5). Whoever can tell the dream, however, will be showered with riches and honor.

Wise men commonly consulted dream books for interpretations of dreams, but being required to tell the dream itself was unheard of. They reply that no one can do such a thing, which so enrages the king that he decrees the execution of all the wise men.

Daniel asks Shadrach, Meshach, and Abednego to pray to God for enlightenment so their lives will be spared, and God reveals the answer to Daniel in a vision. Daniel hurries to the king and tells him that it is beyond the power of soothsayers to do as the king asks, "but there is a God in heaven who reveals mysteries" (Dan 2:28). The dream is this: The king saw a massive statue, with a head of gold, a chest and arms of silver, torso and thighs of bronze, lower legs of iron, and feet made partly of iron and partly of clay. As the king watched, a stone plucked by otherworldly hands was thrown at the statue's feet, which shattered. The statue itself was broken into bits, and the stone became a mountain covering the earth.

Daniel then interprets the dream. Nebuchadnezzar is the statue's head. After his dynasty will come another, less powerful kingdom, followed by a third, and a fourth. This last kingdom will be divided; the attempt to reunite through intermarriage will fail. Indeed, Babylon was followed by three empires: the Medes, the Persians, and the Greeks. After the death of the Greek king Alexander the Great, Judea was dominated by the Ptolemies of Egypt and the Seleucids of Syria, who tried unsuccessfully to unite their two kingdoms through intermarriage.

Having stumped his wise men, Nebuchadnezzar turns to Daniel for the discovery and interpretation of his dream; a late-15th-century painting.

The stone that destroyed the statue represents the kingdom that God will establish, which will supplant all others and last forever. The awed Nebuchadnezzar praises Daniel's God as the "God of gods and Lord of kings" (Dan 2:47) and makes Daniel the ruler over the province of Babylon and leader of the wise men.

King Nebuchadnezzar made a golden statue whose height was sixty cubits and whose width was six cubits; he set it up on the plain of Dura in the province of Babylon. DAN 3:1

The king orders all his subjects to fall down and worship the statue. Those who fail to do so will be thrown into a fiery furnace—an uncommon but documented form of execution in Babylon. Envious of Shadrach, Meshach, and Abednego, some wise men tell the king that the three ignore his command (as Hebrew law forbids the worship of idols).

The king interrogates the three, who say that they would prefer death to worshiping a false god. The enraged king orders the furnace heated to seven times its normal level and commands his strongest guards to tie up the trio and throw them into the inferno. As they do, the guards are killed by the white-hot flames, but the king reports in wonder, "I see four men unbound, walking in the middle of the fire, and they are not hurt; and the fourth has the appearance of a god" (Dan 3:25). When they emerge from the inferno, the three companions do not even smell of smoke. At this miracle, the king decrees the destruction of any people who blaspheme this God, and rewards the trio with higher positions.

I, Nebuchadnezzar, . . . saw a dream that frightened me. DAN 4:4-5

Nebuchadnezzar tells Daniel of a dream in which a tree grew from the center of the earth all the way to heaven. It provided food and shelter for all living things. (This world tree was a well-known image in ancient mythology.) But a heavenly being appeared and ordered that the tree be chopped down, leaving only the stump and roots in the ground. The tree turned into a man whose mind became that of an animal.

Daniel recognizes the dream as such a bad omen that he proclaims, "My lord, may the dream be for those who hate you, and its interpretation for your enemies!" (Dan 4:19). He says that the tree is the king, and the decree made by the celestial watcher is the king's terrible fate: He will go mad and be driven out and live like an animal "until seven times pass over him" (Dan 4:23). Only when he accepts God's sovereignty will he be returned to his kingdom. Daniel advises Nebuchadnezzar to follow a righteous path so that he may continue to prosper.

But a year later the arrogant king says, "Is this not magnificent Babylon, which I have built as a royal capital by my mighty power and for my glorious majesty?" (Dan 4:30). Daniel's predictions come true, however, and the king is driven away in madness. After the seven years pass, Nebuchadnezzar's mind is restored and he praises Daniel's God as all-powerful in heaven and on earth. While there is no record of such a fate befalling Nebuchadnezzar, there is a tradition that Nabonidus, a later king, went mad and was banished for seven years.

King Belshazzar made a great festival for a thousand of his lords, and he was drinking wine in the presence of the thousand. DAN 5:1

Although Belshazzar is called the son of Nebuchadnezzar in this chapter, he was actually the son of Nabonidus, and not a king himself but merely regent during his father's absences. "Under the influence of the wine" (Dan 5:2), Belshazzar calls for the temple treasure that Nebuchadnezzar had stolen from Jerusalem, and then he and his guests insolently drink wine from the sacred gold and silver vessels as they toast heathen gods.

In response to this terrible sacrilege, a human hand appears and writes a cryptic message on the wall. The terrified king cries out for the court enchanters, but they cannot read the writing. The queen mother urges the king to summon Daniel, who had served Nebuchadnezzar so well.

Daniel reads the message as "MENE, MENE, TEKEL, and PARSIN" (Dan 5:25)—terms for monetary weight. The words, Daniel points out, can also be read as verbs. The king's days are numbered (mene), for he has been weighed (tekel) and found wanting. His kingdom will be divided (parsin) between the Medes and Persians. That very night, Belshazzar is killed and Darius the Mede becomes king. (Darius the Mede is unknown. Although there were three Persian kings named Darius, it was Cyrus II of Persia who overthrew Babylon's Nabonidus in 539 B.C.)

It pleased Darius to set over the kingdom one hundred twenty satraps . . . and over them three presidents, including Daniel. DAN 6:1-2

What follows is the well-known story of Daniel in the lions' den. Darius the Mede is so impressed by Daniel that he decides to put him in charge of the entire kingdom. This arouses the jealousy of the other officials, who try to discover some irregularity in Daniel's administration. Eventually, though, they are forced to concede: "We shall not find any ground for complaint against this Daniel unless we find it in connection with the law of his God" (Dan 6:5). So they approach the king and request an edict stating that anyone who begs favor from a person or god except the king for 30 days will be thrown into a den of lions. The king agrees.

Daniel continues to pray to God three times a day. When the plotters report this to the king, he is disturbed and tries to save Daniel. But he is reminded that "it is a law of the Medes and Persians that no interdict or ordinance that the king establishes can be changed" (Dan 6:15). Darius is powerless. Daniel is thrown into the lions' den. In the morning, Daniel is miraculously unharmed because, he says, "My God sent his angel and shut the lions' mouths so that they would not hurt me" (Dan 6:22). The king then orders Daniel's accusers, along with their wives and children, thrown to the lions, and decrees that all his subjects revere the God who saved Daniel.

In the first year of King Belshazzar of Babylon, Daniel had a dream and visions of his head as he lay in bed. DAN 7:1

In the first of two visions dating back to Belshazzar's reign, Daniel sees four terrifying beasts rise from the sea: a lion, a bear, a leopard, and an even more horrifying creature with iron teeth that destroy everything. This beast has ten horns; yet another horn pushes its way through them, with eyes "and a mouth speaking arrogantly" (Dan 7:8).

God appears on a fiery chariot, surrounded by a multitude of attendants, and judges the four beasts. The beast with the great horn is slain and the others are stripped of their power. Then a human figure comes through the clouds. "To him was given dominion and glory and kingship" (Dan 7:14), a kingship that shall last forever.

Uncharacteristically, Daniel cannot interpret the dream, so an angel does so instead. The beasts represent succeeding empires: the lion is Babylon, the bear is Media, and the leopard is Persia. The fourth beast represents a kingdom that "shall devour the whole earth" (Dan 7:23)—the Greeks under Alexander the Great. The ten horns represent ten kings who will rule this kingdom, and the horn that comes later represents a king whose reign shall be more disastrous than the others—Antiochus IV Epiphanes. He will blaspheme God and try to change the laws, which, indeed, Antiochus did by defiling the sanctuary and prohibiting the observance of feasts.

The Jews will suffer at his hands "for a time, two times, and half a time" (Dan 7:25)—three and a half years—after which his kingdom will be destroyed. Then the kingdom of God will be established and he will be sovereign forever.

In the third year of the reign of King Belshazzar a vision appeared to me, Daniel, after the one that had appeared to me at first. DAN 8:1

In Daniel's second vision, a ram appears, with one horn longer than the other. It charges to the west, north, and south, and nothing can withstand it. A male goat with a single horn charges from the west and destroys the ram, then grows even stronger. The horn breaks, to be replaced by four horns pointing toward the four winds of heaven. From one of them sprouts a little horn that grows up to heaven, with which it throws some of the heavenly creatures to earth. The horn becomes so arrogant that it takes the offerings from the altar for itself.

Daniel is puzzled by the vision, but a voice says, "Gabriel, help this man understand" (Dan 8:16). This reference to the archangel Gabriel is the first time in the Bible that an angel is named. Gabriel says the two horns of the ram are the kings of Media and Persia, with the mighty Persia being the longer. The goat is the kingdom of Greece, and its horn is Alexander the Great. This kingdom is replaced by four other kingdoms, and the little horn that grows powerful is the most evil king of all—Antiochus. "He shall destroy the powerful and the people of the holy ones," meaning the faithful Jews, and even challenge God. But, the Jews are assured, "he shall be broken, and not by human hands" (Dan 8:24, 25).

I, Daniel, perceived in the books the number of years that . . . must be fulfilled for the devastation of Jerusalem, namely, seventy years. DAN 9:2

Daniel prays to God, acknowledging that the Jews are being punished because "we have sinned and done wrong, acted wickedly and rebelled, turning aside from your commandments and ordinances" (Dan 9:5). He begs God to show his mercy to his undeserving people.

The angel Gabriel reappears and announces, "Seventy weeks are decreed for your people and your holy city" (Dan 9:24), which Daniel understands to mean 70 weeks of years, or 490 years. Gabriel says that from the time Daniel began his prayer until the time that a prince will be anointed is seven weeks (49 years), the length of the Babylonian exile (586-538 B.C.). This is followed by 62 weeks (434 years) in which Jerusalem will be rebuilt during a troubled time, perhaps referring to the fighting between the Ptolemies and the Seleucids. "After the sixty-two weeks, an anointed one shall be cut off" (Dan 9:26). This is just what happened when Antiochus deposed the legitimate high priest Onias III in favor of his brother Jason. Then a prince—Antiochus—will desecrate the sanctuary, accompanied by flood and war. For half a week (three and half years) this desecrator will halt sacrificial offerings, but in the second half, he will be destroyed.

In the third year of King Cyrus of Persia a word was revealed to Daniel. DAN 10:1

In the year 536-535 B.C., Daniel sees a heavenly being, probably Gabriel. The personage says that he was delayed in coming because he and Michael, the patron angel of the Jews, were battling the angels of other nations. This celestial vision leaves Daniel weak with fear, but the angel touches him and his strength returns. Gabriel asks, "Do you know why I have come to you?" (Dan 10:20). The angel proceeds to "predict" Jewish history from the time of the Persian conquest to the coming of a "con-temptible person" (Dan 11:21): Antiochus. The author lists Antiochus's crimes against the Jews, including the most heinous of all, "the abomination that makes desolate" (Dan 11:31)—the establishment of a heathen altar in the temple. The Jews who remain faithful "shall receive a little help" (Dan 11:34), perhaps referring to the Maccabees and their armed resistance to Antiochus.

Unlike the rest of this chapter, the predictions made in Daniel 11:40-45 never actually happen. It is said that Antiochus will defeat Egypt, "yet he shall come to his end, with no one to help him" (Dan 11:45) on the road home. In fact, Antiochus died in 164 B.C. while campaigning in Persia. This indicates that the author completed the book sometime before Antiochus's death.

At that time Michael, the great prince, the protector of our people, shall arise. DAN 12:1

In a period of unprecedented tribulation, Daniel's people will be saved. "Many of those who sleep in the dust of the earth shall awake, some to everlasting life, and some to shame and everlasting contempt" (Dan 12:2). This is the first time in the Bible that resurrection has been so clearly spoken of; it may have been introduced to hold out hope to those facing martyrdom at Antiochus's hands.

The question is asked, "How long shall it be until the end of these wonders?" (Dan 12:6). An angel says that it will be three and a half years, but another calculation is 1,290 days, and still another is 1,335 days. The end time may be uncertain, but Daniel is reassured that on the last day, he will be rewarded. Like Daniel, the author implies, those who remain true to their faith in spite of extreme hardship will one day reap the reward of a place in God's kingdom.

Belshazzar's feast is interrupted by mysterious handwriting on the wall. This scene decorated a 1630 edition of Martin Luther's Bible.

Carrying a scroll of his oracles, the prophet Hosea appears within an initial letter in a 12th-century German illuminated Bible.

Although Hosea followed the southern prophet Amos by a decade or so, he appears first in the Book of the Twelve. Joel, placed second and thus between Hosea and Amos, is usually dated several centuries later. Hosea and the prophetic books that follow are also known as the Minor Prophets because of their relative shortness compared with Isaiah, Jeremiah, and Ezekiel. The book of Hosea is unique in the Bible as the only written record of a native northern prophet. The opening verse states that Hosea prophesied during the reigns of four kings of Judah, Uzziah, Jotham, Ahaz, and Hezekiah (785-698 B.C.) and King Jeroboam II of Israel (789-748 B.C.), perhaps beginning around 750. Hosea bears close witness to the traumatic dissolution of the northern kingdom of Israel in the final decades before it fell to Assyria in 722. Israel is frequently referred to in the book as "Ephraim," the favored younger son of Joseph, whom the northerners regarded as their ancestor.

Charged with passionate language about a wife's betrayal and a parent's love, fierce judgments against kingship, and animated indictments of idolatry, Hosea is perhaps the most emotional of all the prophets. The book is divided into two uneven parts, chapters 1-3, which contain events from the life of Hosea, and chapters 4-14, a collection of oracles, or divine sayings, containing messages of judgment and salvation. The oracles most likely were speeches given by Hosea over his long career, probably collected by Hosea's followers after his death. Most of the oracles have no clear beginning or ending and shift frequently from first- to second- to third-person speech. For these reasons, the book is sometimes difficult to follow.

Two features of eighth-century Israelite life form the backdrop of Hosea's prophecy. One is the temptation for Israelites to worship the Canaanite storm god Baal and to participate in the Canaanite fertility cult. The second is the political corruption of the northern kingdom and the destabilizing effect of foreign alliances. Throughout the book, Hosea's message is clear: faithfulness to the demands of the Sinai covenant and worship of the Lord alone are essential to a healthy relationship between God and Israel.

The Lord said to Hosea, "Go, take for yourself a wife of whoredom and have children of whoredom." HOS 1:2

The first three chapters of Hosea contain dramatic biographical information about the prophet's unhappy marriage. God's command that Hosea marry a prostitute and have children by her is at first as puzzling as it is startling. Only in the second chapter does its full significance become clear. But Hosea obediently follows God's bidding and marries Gomer, daughter of Diblaim.

The exact nature of Gomer's prostitution is unclear. A popular view is that Gomer served as a temple prostitute, one whose fees provided a questionable source of income for Israelite houses of worship. Many scholars suggest that there were also prostitutes, especially at northern Israelite shrines, who participated in sexual fertility rites borrowed from Canaanite religion. A prostitute and her partner would reenact the consummation of a "sacred marriage" between the Canaanite god Baal and his consort Asherah. The ritual was intended to ensure the fertility of Israel's land as well as its women. The existence of such temple prostitutes, though widely accepted by biblical scholars, is supported by remarkably little evidence. Another possibility is that the description of Gomer as a "wife of whoredom" refers generally to her promiscuity, either before or after marrying the prophet. Or Gomer may simply have belonged to what is often called the world's oldest profession.

Obedient to the Lord, Hosea marries Gomer to father her children.

Gomer produces three children, each of whom is given a highly symbolic name by God. Like the names of the sons of Isaiah (Isa 7:3, 8:3), each name represents a dimension of Hosea's prophetic message. The first son is named Jezreel, meaning "God sows," but Jezreel is also the place where Jehu seized the throne after a bloody coup against King Jehoram in the ninth century B.C. (2 Kgs 9:14-26). In addition, the Jezreel valley is one of the first areas captured by Assyria en route to destroying Israel. The second child is named Lo-ruhamah, Hebrew for "not pitied," because God has decided that the fate of Israel is sealed. The third child is named Lo-ammi, or "not my people," because the Lord recognizes that the covenant bond linking him with his chosen people is threatened by Israel's apostasy.

In spite of these ominous names, God also predicts the restoration of the people and the future unification of the kingdoms of Israel and Judah under one king in the land of Israel. Some scholars think that verse 11 and others in the book favoring Judah and King David's dynasty were added by a southern editor working in Jerusalem after the fall of the northern kingdom in 722 B.C.

Plead with your mother, plead—for she is not my wife, and I am not her husband. HOS 2:2

The meaning of Hosea's painful marriage is clarified in the second chapter. The prophet's suffering love for the prostitute Gomer mirrors God's own tortured love for faithless Israel. The prophets Jeremiah and Ezekiel, likely influenced by Hosea, later use a similar allegory to depict the city of Jerusalem as an unfaithful wife of God (Jer 2-3; Ezek 16). God is in a heart-wrenching position as he watches Israel pursue other "lovers," the Canaanite gods. But he stays fervently committed to the nation by the strength of their "marriage bond." He is torn between wanting to punish Israel for its behavior and wanting to "speak tenderly to her" (Hos 2:13, 14).

At the end of the passage, God's tone softens. He looks forward to a happy future when Israel will stop confusing the worship of Baal with worship of him. In a verse that plays on the two Hebrew words for husband, *ish* and *baal*, God says, "On that day, you will call me, 'My husband [*ish*],' and no longer will you call me, 'My Baal [the name of the Canaanite god].'" (Hos 2:16). If Israel repents, God promises to renew their marriage vows. On a final note of hope, the Lord promises to reverse the fate implied in the baleful names of Gomer's children.

The Lord said to me again, "Go, love a woman who has a lover and is an adulteress." HOS 3:1

Another episode from the sad story of Hosea's marriage is recounted in chapter three, this time told in the first person. Although she is never identified by name, most scholars understand the woman to be Gomer but are unable to determine if

MINOR PROPHETS

The 12 books that conclude the Old Testament are called the Minor Prophets, not because they are any less important than the works of "major prophets"—Isaiah, Jeremiah, and Ezekiel—but because they are shorter. Jews in ancient times referred to the prophecies from Hosea to Malachi as the Book of the Twelve. These concise works were gathered into a single collection because, according to early rabbinical teaching, "as they are small, they might be lost." Christian scholars have described this section as the Minor Prophets since at least the time of Augustine in the fourth century.

Together, the ministries of these 12 prophets spanned some 300 years—from Amos and Hosea in the mid-700s B.C. to Joel, perhaps in the early decades of the 300s. The writing styles vary greatly, from the soaring poetry of Habakkuk to the dramatic prose of Jonah, and from intimate discussions with God in Hosea to urgent warnings to the nation of Israel in Amos. In the probable order in which they ministered, the Minor Prophets and their distinguishing messages are as follows:

Amos left his native Judah to condemn Israel in the mid-eighth century B.C.

Hosea also prophesied to the northern kingdom in the mid-eighth century; his promiscuous wife is a living parable of Israel's unfaithfulness.

Micah, late in the eighth century, predicted God's punishment of Samaria and Jerusalem.

Nahum, shortly before the event occurred, warned of the destruction of Nineveh in 612 B.C.

Zephaniah delivered his oracles of a dreadful day of the Lord, when God will punish the wicked, late in the seventh century.

Habakkuk asked God why he will punish Judah by sending Babylon; his ministry is dated to the late seventh and early sixth centuries.

Obadiah, most likely in the mid-sixth century, condemned Edom, Judah's hostile neighbor.

Haggai, after the Jews returned from their exile in Babylon in the second half of the sixth century, urged rebuilding of the temple.

Zechariah preached the same message as his contemporary Haggai.

Jonah preached repentance to Nineveh; his book dates between the sixth and fourth centuries.

Malachi reminded Jews to remain faithful to God and stop withholding temple offerings; his ministry dated perhaps to the mid-fifth century.

Joel, perhaps early in the fourth century, spoke of a massive invasion of locusts.

234.

◆

HOSEA

To resist Assyrian king Tiglath-pileser III,
shown in this bas-relief from his capital Nimrud,
Israel formed an alliance with Syria and invaded
Judah for not joining the coalition.

and adultery. Even nature itself is affected by the apostasy of Israel: "The land mourns . . . together with the wild animals and the birds of the air, even the fish of the sea are perishing" (Hos 4:3).

God's reproach is not restricted to the laity. The priests and prophets themselves are held responsible for false worship and for leading the people astray. The charge of "whoredom" is again made against both the priests and the people. "Whoredom" can be understood both literally and figuratively. "Play the whore" (Hos 4:10) is the prophet's expression for abandoning the covenant with the Lord and worshiping the Canaanite gods. But Hosea also accuses Israelite women of being prostitutes and Israelite men of patronizing such women.

The theme of the oracles changes in Hosea 5:8 as the prophet addresses the problem of Israel's foreign entanglements. From 735 to 732 B.C., during the reign of King Pekah, Israel tries to meet the threat of the Assyrian army under Tiglath-pileser III by allying itself with other small nations in the region, including Syria to the north. Israel and Syria want Judah to join the alliance but Judah refuses, so they invade the southern kingdom. Hosea faults both Judah and Israel for their war.

For I desire steadfast love and not sacrifice, the knowledge of God rather than burnt offerings. HOS 6:6

*A*t the end of this long passage of judgment oracles, Hosea summarizes God's expectations of Israel. In a verse containing the central theme of the book, he uses two crucial terms in poetic parallelism, "steadfast love," *chesed* in Hebrew, and "knowledge of God," *daat 'elohim.* Both of the terms suggest that a personal relationship with God is more important than the external rituals that accompany Israelite worship. A precise translation of *chesed* is difficult. In part it means an internal faithfulness or loyalty that is put into action. Hosea's own loving treatment of Gomer is one example of *chesed.* For Hosea, "knowledge of God" is not simply an intellectual exercise such as reading a book of theology; it is the experience of and faithful response to the divine presence through heart and will. True knowledge of God means a commitment to the covenant bond between God and Israel made at Mount Sinai, a bond broken by those who worship other gods. Hosea's emphasis on a personal relationship with God contrasts with that of the earlier prophet Amos, who stresses social concerns such as justice for the poor and the oppressed in his oracles.

The message embedded in this verse clearly had an impact on early Christians. According to the Gospel of Matthew, Jesus quoted Hosea 6:6 on two different occasions. He used the verse to explain his unorthodox behavior, once when he was criticized by the Pharisees for eating with tax collectors and sinners (Mt 9:10-13) and later after he and his disciples were rebuked, again by the hypocritical Pharisees, for plucking grain on the sabbath (Mt 12:1-8).

this refers to an incident separate from Hosea's experience described in the first chapter. In a sense, Gomer's adultery is worse than prostitution because an adulteress accepts no payment for her favors. But Hosea must buy her back, presumably from her lover, for "fifteen shekels of silver, and a homer of barley, and a measure of wine" (Hos 3:2). Hosea's benevolent treatment of Gomer is like God's treatment of Israel. The Lord will punish but ultimately redeem the people of Israel "though they turn to other gods and love raisin cakes" (Hos 3:1). The deeper meaning of the allegory becomes clear: Gomer's unfaithfulness is merely one example among an entire nation of faithless idolaters. Pagan worship, according to Isaiah, included eating raisin cakes.

Hear the word of the Lord, O people of Israel; for the Lord has an indictment against the inhabitants of the land. HOS 4:1

*T*here is an abrupt change in the book at the beginning of the fourth chapter, a shift from the biographical section to the collection of divine oracles delivered by Hosea. Many of the oracles repeat the same themes. In the first oracle, God uses legal language to address the Israelites. The Hebrew word used for "indictment" is *rib,* the equivalent of a lawsuit in ancient Israel. God is bringing a legal case against the Israelites, playing all three roles of plaintiff, witness, and judge. The charges boil down to the fact that Israel has disobeyed the laws contained in the covenant at Sinai. God charges the Israelites generally with having "no faithfulness or loyalty, and no knowledge of God" (Hos 4:1). For Hosea, those are the chief requirements of the covenant. But five breaches of the Ten Commandments are mentioned specifically: swearing, lying, murder, theft,

When Israel was a child, I loved him, and out of Egypt I called my son. HOS 11:1

Hosea was the first prophet to portray the covenant relationship of God and Israel in terms of a faithful husband and an adulterous wife. In the later part of the book he uses another metaphor grounded in family relationships: the image of God as the loving but agonized parent of a wayward child. Hosea 11:1 recalls Exodus 4:22-23, in which God refers to Israel as his "firstborn son." God remembers Israel's "youth," the period beginning with his rescue of Israel from slavery in Egypt and continuing in the time of their wandering in the Sinai wilderness. But already in their youth, the Israelites began to rebel and worship other gods. Yet God in his compassion taught "Ephraim to walk" (Hos 11:3), tenderly picked him up after a fall, and fed and nurtured him. Like a parent who is torn between anger at willful disobedience and deep, compassionate love, God wavers between knowing he must punish the Israelites and an inclination to forgive them. In a series of anguished questions, God asks: "How can I give you up, Ephraim? How can I hand you over, O Israel?" (Hos 11:8). God claims he will not "destroy Ephraim" (Hos 11:9), but in subsequent oracles, the balance shifts and God again mentions punishment.

The Evangelist Matthew cited Hosea 11:1 as an Old Testament prophecy that Jesus would be taken as a child to Egypt and summoned back to his native land after the threat posed by Herod had ended. The flight to Egypt was painted by Michael Pacher (1435-1498).

This verse is also used by Matthew, who understands it as a prophecy that is fulfilled when Jesus' parents flee into Egypt shortly after the child's birth, returning after Herod's death (Mt 2:15).

I gave you a king in my anger and took him away in my wrath. HOS 13:11

As the power and influence of the Assyrian empire expands during the second half of the eighth century, the political situation in the northern kingdom becomes increasingly precarious. The stable dynastic monarchy of the southern kingdom of Judah has always been ruled by a descendant of King David. By contrast, the throne in the north is unsteady. Hosea begins his work toward the end of the prosperous four-decade reign of Jeroboam II (789-748 B.C.), but in the 20 years after Jeroboam's death, six different kings reign, four of whom are assassinated in a series of palace coups.

Hosea's final years of work are difficult. His preaching about the dangers of worshiping Canaanite gods and relying on fickle foreign allies falls largely on deaf ears. He is mocked by his compatriots: "Israel cries, 'The prophet is a fool, the man of the spirit is mad!'" (Hos 9:7). Yet he continues to deliver the divine word warning of imminent disaster: "Because of your great wickedness, at dawn the king of Israel shall be utterly cut off" (Hos 10:15). Israel's last king, Hoshea (in Hebrew his name is spelled the same as the prophet's, but in English they are different to avoid confusion), thinks he can get support from Egypt and rebels against Assyria. This turns out to be a tragic mistake that ultimately leads to the end of the northern kingdom. After a three-year siege, the Assyrian king Sargon II completes the conquest begun by his predecessor, Shalmaneser V, finally taking the Israelite capital, Samaria, toward the end of 722 B.C. and early the next year deporting 30,000 of the nation's residents to Mesopotamia.

They shall again live beneath my shadow, they shall flourish as a garden. HOS 14:7

The last chapter of the book begins with a call for Israel to repent. Hosea even provides a short prayer of penitence that people can offer to God: "Take away all guilt; accept that which is good, and we will offer the fruit of our lips. . . . In you the orphan finds mercy" (Hos 14:2-3). Nonetheless, the divine scales of justice demand reckoning for sin, and it comes in the form of the destruction of the northern kingdom. Yet from Hosea's perspective, God does not want to destroy, but to heal and restore Israel. That hope is woven like a golden thread from the beginning to the end of the book. Whether Hosea lived to see the final calamity is unknown. But he left an indelible model of faithfulness and obedience to the Lord for future generations. Just as Hosea is able to love Gomer despite her infidelity, God's love for Israel knows no bounds.

The prophet Joel as portrayed in a ceiling painting from the Vatican's Borgia apartments

*J*oel is the second of the 12 Minor Prophets, placed in the Bible after Hosea, who prophesied in the eighth century B.C. Little is known about Joel aside from the fact that he was the son of Pethuel, who is mentioned nowhere else in the Bible. Joel is a common name in the Old Testament, meaning "Yah[weh] is God," the inverse of the name Elijah. The prophet Joel is thought to have lived in or near Jerusalem because of his intimate knowledge of the rituals of the temple.

The book of Joel is one of the shortest in the Old Testament, composed of only three chapters in English translations (four in the Hebrew text), yet it rings with powerful oracles of destruction and divine might. The book is in two parts. The first (Joel 1:1-2:27) is a poetic narrative of great devastation caused by a plague of locusts, and a call to sinners to repent. The second (Joel 2:28-3:21) tells of an apocalyptic war between God and Israel's enemies, followed by the restoration of Judah and Jerusalem. Most scholars view the book as a whole, with the locust plague as a metaphor of the coming apocalypse; others believe that the book's two parts are so distinct that more than one author was involved.

The date of the book is controversial as well. Some theologians place it in the seventh or eighth century B.C., based on its position in the Hebrew Bible between Hosea and Amos. But there are many arguments in favor of a postexilic date, about 400 to 350 B.C. No kings are mentioned, and priests play a leading role—as they did in the postexilic theocracy. Joel also refers to the scattering of the Israelites (Joel 3:2), which would place the book after the exile. And there are a number of phrases that echo the writing of other prophets, notably Obadiah and Malachi, who wrote in the sixth and fifth centuries B.C.

The word of the Lord that came to Joel son of Pethuel. JOEL 1:1

*J*oel identifies himself as a prophet by announcing that he brings a message from God. But unlike many of the writing prophets, Joel does not mention a reigning king in his salutation, which could indicate that the monarchy had already ended. He summons people to listen, as was customary when proclaiming a prophetic message, and tells them to pass along to future generations the words that he is about to utter. Then he draws in his audience by asking, "Has such a thing happened in your days, or in the days of your ancestors?" (Joel 1:2).

What the cutting locust left, the swarming locust has eaten. What the swarming locust left, the hopping locust has eaten, and what the hopping locust left, the destroying locust has eaten. JOEL 1:4

*T*he prophet tells of the horror of wave after wave of locust swarms sweeping through the land, devouring everything in their path. Some early biblical commentators interpreted the locust plagues to represent four invading foreign armies. Most modern scholars, however, believe that Joel wrote about an actual invasion of locusts.

Infestations of this insect have plagued North Africa and the Near East since ancient times. For reasons that are not well understood, desert locusts periodi-

cally multiply swiftly, congregating in vast swarms that migrate in search of food. As they go, they strip crops, trees, and every other form of vegetation utterly bare. Palestine lies along the migration route of locusts originating in the African and Arabian deserts.

The book uses terrifying metaphors to illustrate the threat that locust swarms present to the Israelites. They are a massive and powerful invading army, and are compared to lions with fearful fangs. Joel's descriptions of the effects of the locust infestation are equally alarming. The crops are destroyed, the vineyards and trees are stripped of their bark, and fruit withers on the vine. There is no wine to be drunk, nothing is left for farmers to harvest, and the priests have no offerings for the altar.

Joel interprets this crisis as God's judgment on the sinning inhabitants of Judah, for which all of creation—animals, plants, and trees as well as people—are punished. He calls the entire community to lament—to cry to God to have mercy and save them from starvation and death—and urges priests to put on sackcloth and lead the people in prayer and fasting.

Alas for the day! For the day of the Lord is near, and as destruction from the Almighty it comes. JOEL 1:15

*T*he locust plague symbolizes and heralds the day of the Lord, which is an important theme throughout the book of Joel. In the Old Testament, the day of the Lord, or judgment day, was tradition-

ally interpreted as a day when God would triumph over Israel's enemies and reward his chosen people. But Joel, as do Amos and Zephaniah, reverses this understanding. Joel warns, "Let all the inhabitants of the land tremble" (Joel 2:1), meaning that the people of Israel, too, will face God's vengeance if they continue to live corrupt lives.

Joel laments the terrible destruction. He describes a land where fire has consumed pasture and wilderness alike. Herds of sheep and cattle roam in a futile search for grazing land, and wild animals moan with thirst because all the streams have dried up.

In striking poetic language, he paints an even more dreadful picture of the locust plague and relates it to the coming day of the Lord. Dark clouds blacken the sky, an image also used by other prophets for the day of the Lord (Am 5:18-20; Zeph 1:14-16). The locusts are "like the crackling of a flame of fire" (Joel 2:5), which is how their noise has been described by people who have witnessed locust swarms. Houses provide no refuge, for the locusts sneak in through windows like thieves. Most disturbing of all, at their head is a wrathful God.

Yet even now, says the Lord, return to me with all your heart. JOEL 2:12

*I*t is not too late to repent. Joel renews the call to lament, not with a ritual show of rending of garments, but with repentance that comes from the heart. Sinners must return to the path of God, who is described as "gracious and merciful, slow to anger, and abounding in steadfast love" (Joel 2:13).

The entire community is called to an assembly, even those normally free from public obligations such as the elderly, infants, and newlyweds. There they must repent their sins and beg God for mercy.

"I will no more make you a mockery among the nations" (Joel 2:19), God assures the Israelites, and promises that the terrible destruction will be re-

versed. The locusts, here called the army from the north—the direction from which Israel's enemies usually invaded—will be driven into a wasteland and the sea. A horrible stench will remain from the dead locusts left behind by the plague. Crops will grow again, the trees will flower and bear fruit, and the animals will have pasture. The drought will end, and rain will fall. As the people once again praise him, God makes a promise that the invasions will end.

Then afterward I will pour out my spirit on all flesh. JOEL 2:28

*B*ecause his wayward people have returned to God, a startling oracle is made. Sometime in the future, prophetic powers will be given to both men and women, of all ages and all classes—even slaves. In the past, this gift was reserved for a select group of prophets, but now everyone will possess it. The author of Acts of the Apostles believed that this prophecy is fulfilled at Pentecost, when Peter quotes Joel to explain that the Holy Spirit has filled all who are assembled (Acts 2:16-21).

But this blessing is reserved for "everyone who calls on the name of the Lord" (Joel 2:32) from Mount Zion and Jerusalem. Joel excludes foreigners from this gift of the Spirit, which probably reflects Judah's bitterness after decades of invasion and occupation by other nations.

I will gather all the nations and bring them down to the valley of Jehoshaphat, and I will enter into judgment with them there, on account of my people and my heritage Israel, because they have scattered them among the nations. JOEL 3:2

*S*o begins the apocalypse, a great and decisive war in which God will defeat all of Israel's enemies and Israel will be restored. God vows that Phoenicia, Philistia, and all the nations that invaded and persecuted Israel will be judged in the valley of Jehoshaphat, a name that means "the Lord judges." Because these nations looted Israel's treasures and carried its people into slavery, the same fate will befall them as punishment.

Joel says to the Israelites, "Beat your plowshares into swords, and your pruning hooks into spears" (Joel 3:10), an exact reversal of Isaiah 2:4 and Micah 4:3, which are calls to abandon warfare. The peaceful negotiation that those prophets anticipated has no part in Joel's oracle of a final cosmic battle. Egypt and Edom are singled out for destruction because they have been Judah's traditional enemies.

Judah will be restored and will overflow with abundance and fertility. The Israelites are assured that "the Lord dwells in Zion" (Joel 3:21), and that he will remain in their midst. God's presence is intended to urge the people of Judah to renew their faith in him, and to inspire hope for their own salvation.

A swarm of locusts nearly obliterates a field under attack. Joel used the threat of the insatiable insects (left) to call for repentance.

Considered the first of the writing prophets, Amos is best known for his passionate call for social justice in an Israel that had reached the apogee of its wealth and influence. Amos came from the town of Tekoa, about ten miles south of Jerusalem in neighboring Judah, to declare his message to the northern kingdom of Israel. The period of his activity seems to have been relatively short, perhaps all within a year around 760 B.C. The first verse of Amos reads, "The words of Amos, who was among the shepherds of Tekoa, which he saw concerning Israel in the days of King Uzziah of Judah [also known as Azariah, 785-733] and in the days of King Jeroboam [Jeroboam II, 789-748] son of Joash of Israel, two years before the earthquake." The reigns of the two kings and the earthquake, possibly mentioned in Zechariah 14:5, are the only means of determining the period of Amos's mission. His message, or perhaps it would be more accurate to say messages, lacks cohesion to the degree that it is difficult to outline the book. Most scholars accept a threefold division: chapters 1-2, oracles against the nations; chapters 3-6, oracles against Israel; chapters 7-9, visions of things to come. While Amos's message is overwhelmingly pessimistic, there are sporadic signs of hope in his book. The preservation of Amos's words is likely due to the fact that they seem to have come true not long after he spoke them. The northern kingdom was destroyed by Assyria in 722 B.C., some 40 years after Amos's proclamation.

A shepherd in Judah, Amos is summoned to his prophetic mission; a 16th-century stained glass window.

The Lord roars from Zion, and utters his voice from Jerusalem; the pastures of the shepherds wither, and the top of Carmel dries up. AM 1:2

Amos begins his oracles against the nations with the roar of the Lord from Mount Zion, site of the temple in Jerusalem. By so doing, and by including the reference to Carmel in central Israel, he asserts God's authority over both the southern and northern kingdoms. Indeed, for Amos, the term "Israel" can refer to both the northern kingdom and the combination of the two, formerly united, kingdoms. Significantly, he forms an envelope construction (beginning and ending with similar references) for each of his oracles in the first two chapters.

For three transgressions of Damascus, and for four, I will not revoke the punishment. AM 1:3

The oracles against the seven neighbors of Israel, namely Damascus, Gaza, Tyre, Edom, Ammon, Moab, and Judah, all begin with these phrases. The total of the "transgressions" is seven, the same number as the neighbors of Israel. With this literary device Amos would appear to establish the expectation that the seventh nation to receive his attention would be the last. In contrast to this expectation, Amos reserves the longest of his harangues for Israel, the eighth on his list. The structure of these oracles contains another reversal of expectations. Amos begins his list with Damascus, to the northeast of Israel, then moves to Gaza, to the southwest. The next two on his list are Tyre, to the northwest, and Edom, to the

southeast. The third set that he indicts are Ammon, to the east, and Moab to the southeast. With this sequence Amos slowly draws in the geographical references, in north-south oppositions, just as he draws in the focus of his accusations. At the center of both is Israel writ large. His final pair of nations reverses the order of the previous indictments by beginning with the southern kingdom of Judah and then moving north to Israel. While references to Israel and the authority of its God begin and end this section, it is Israel that is surrounded by the other indicted nations. By this means, Amos, even within the intricate literary structure of his book, draws tighter his noose of accusation against the northern kingdom.

They have rejected the law of the Lord, and have not kept his statutes. AM 2:4

Amos's complaint against Judah sets the tone for the extended harangue of Israel, which he accuses of unfair, unjust, or improper treatment of the poor and the afflicted as well as indecent cult worship. This indictment is crucial for understanding Amos's message. While he seeks social justice, that justice derives its significance through Israel's dedication to its God and the observance of his laws. Many of the actions for which he indicts Israel seem to be in violation of specific rules from Exodus 21-23. This is all the more intriguing considering that Amos makes a point of reminding Israel of the Exodus and its subsequent conquest of the land now inhabited.

This section comprises a first-person reminder of God's kindness in bringing the Israelites to their land

and of their obligation to live by his commandments given during their wilderness wanderings after the Exodus. Equally significant is the suggestion that just as God removed nations from the land to facilitate the Israelite invasion (a typical number is seven), he is now about to reverse the conquest by removing seven nations (Israel, as a united kingdom, makes the seventh) from the land. Amos finishes the first division of the book by emphasizing the inexorable nature of the impending punishment: "I will press you down in your place, just as a cart presses down when it is full of sheaves" (Am 2:13).

You only have I known of all the families of the earth; therefore I will punish you for all your iniquities. AM 3:2

The second division of Amos, the oracles against Israel in chapters 3-6, displays the complexity of the interlacing themes of the book. After another mention of the Exodus, Amos continues the indictment of Israel. References to the roaring of a lion echo the earlier roar of the Lord. Nonetheless, it is useful to consider these chapters as a new division of the book. Amos asks a number of rhetorical questions, each containing imagery of impending peril and each requiring the answer "no"—for example, "Does a lion roar in the forest when it has no prey?" (Am 3:4). The section is concluded when Amos declares, "The lion has roared; who will not fear? The Lord God has spoken; who can but prophesy?" (Am 3:8). This declaration subtly implies a number of important points: God's "roar" is not to be taken lightly, any more than the roar of the lion; like the inevitable peril facing the prey that hears the lion roar, Israel had better stand forewarned.

Amos continues his indictment of Israel for its "oppressions" and declares that it will be surrounded by adversaries. Again, this seems to repeat the geography of the oracles against the nations that surround Israel. But Amos appears to soften his message of doom. Picking up again on the lion imagery, he says that some of Israel shall be saved just as a shepherd saves a leg or piece of ear from the mouth of a lion. The hopeful tone of this declaration has to be balanced against the realization that a lamb does not survive if only its leg and ear are redeemed.

Continuing with his list of Israel's offenses, Amos proclaims that the signs of Israel's affluence shall be torn down. These include the altars of Bethel, the summer and winter houses, as well as the houses of ivory—especially the palace at Samaria, famous for its ivory furnishings. Amos apparently puts a finer edge on his indictment when he announces to the Israelites "who oppress the poor, who crush the needy" (Am 4:1) that they are about to meet their end. Amos seems most concerned with the hypocrisy of those who go through the motions of daily cultic life but fail to treat their fellow citizens by covenant standards. Amos concludes chapter 4 with a number of sayings that remind Israel of God's warning signs that have gone unheeded. Each saying ends with the phrase "yet you did not return to me, says the Lord" (Am 4:6). Because they have utterly failed to live up to their obligations and have failed even to recognize God's warnings, Amos makes a grim announcement: "Prepare to meet your God, O Israel" (Am 4:12).

Fallen, no more to rise, is maiden Israel; forsaken on her land, with no one to raise her up. AM 5:2

This verse sets the nearly unrelentingly dire tone for the second half of Amos's oracles against Israel. The rabbinical authors of the Babylonian Talmud, an interpretation of the scriptures, found this verse so distressing that they insisted on reading in these words the opposite of their plain sense: "Fallen, but not again; Arise, O maiden Israel!" As fanciful as this reading may seem, it merely extends the faint voices of hope in the rest of Amos to a verse that shows none. Indeed, chapter 5, standing in the middle of the book, contains several hints that not all is lost. Interspersed within the negative and hopeless tone of much of the chapter are vague suggestions that Israel may still redeem itself. The refrain "seek me and live" (Am 5:4) is followed by warnings to reform. In a passage reminiscent of Job 38, God next asks, in essence, who created all that you know "and turns deep darkness into the morning, and darkens the day into night?" (Am 5:8). By employing language reminiscent of the creation of the world and words that resound with the Israelite legal codes, the text implies that Israel's transgressions go against God and the very nature of his creation.

In what is the heart of the book lies another passage that seems to hold out hope, at least for some in Israel: "Seek good and not evil, that you may live" (Am 4:14). Of significance, however, is the notice that only a "remnant of Joseph" (Am 4:15) will survive. As if to emphasize the fluctuating fortunes of Israel, Amos follows this slightly optimistic message with an ominous passage: "Alas for you who desire

Prophets were often depicted holding scrolls of their oracles, as in this portrait of Amos by Juan de Borgona (1470-1535).

the day of the Lord." Those who expected triumph over their enemies on that day, Amos reveals, are in for a surprise: "Is not the day of the Lord darkness, not light, and gloom with no brightness in it?" (Am 5:18, 20). Again, the prophet emphasizes the serious consequences of Israel's transgressions in language that echoes his earlier reminder of creation. The implication is that Israel should not doubt for a minute that God can reverse his creation and, in effect, decree, "Let there be darkness." The chapter concludes with the Lord's declaration that Israel's festivals, assemblies, and offerings are not enough; rather, in the justly famous words of Amos 5:24, God would prefer that Israel "let justice roll down like waters, and righteousness like an ever-flowing stream." In language full of the imagery of fertility, God declares that Israel's cultic life is meaningless without the justice that should accompany it.

The inhabitants of Israel, Amos says, consider themselves "at ease in Zion . . . secure on Mount Samaria" (Am 6:1)—that is, immune from the punishment of God. Yet they will soon see that they are no better than those neighboring peoples who have suffered God's wrath. "The Lord, the God of hosts" will bring a nation, Assyria, to oppress them "from Lebo-hamath to the Wadi Arabah" (Am 6:14). The description of Israel's territory—from as far north as Solomon's empire once stretched to the Dead Sea—matches that given in 2 Kings 14:25 for the extent of the kingdom under Jeroboam II.

This is what the Lord God showed me: he was forming locusts at the time the latter growth began to sprout. AM 7:1

The third section of Amos (chapters 7-9) comprises a series of five visions and a brief biographical narrative. Amos's first vision is of locusts consuming all vegetation. "How can Jacob stand?" (Am 5:2), the prophet asks, using the original name of the progenitor of the 12 tribes (Gen 25:26) to plead for mercy from God. Amos's effort is rewarded with the declaration of God, "It shall not be" (Am 7:3); the plague of locusts, which Amos correctly interprets as the destruction of Israel, is to be stayed. Amos's second vision, of a consuming fire, again elicits a call for mercy that likewise is answered in the affirmative. The third vision contains a variation on the pattern established by the first two. After this vision, Amos does not even get the chance to ask for clemency. Here, the Lord simply shows Amos a plumb line and announces that since the

Ruins of the shrine at Bethel, from which the priest Amaziah expelled Amos

Israelites are not a "straight" people, they shall suffer the consequences of their inequities.

Amos's visions are interrupted by a biographical narrative in which Amaziah, the priest at the shrine of Bethel, informs Jeroboam that Amos has conspired against him and tells Amos to go home to Judah. Amos's response begins with the famous "I am no prophet, nor a prophet's son" (Am 7:14) and ends with a prediction of doom for Jeroboam and Israel. This represents the only extended biographical information about Amos, and it seems to contain an echo of 1 Kings 13:1-10, in which another Jeroboam, the first ruler of the northern kingdom of Israel (928-907 B.C.), while standing at the altar at Bethel, is confronted by a nameless "man of God" from Judah. The brief biographical narrative in Amos may have been included to emphasize that the northern kingdom was doomed from the start.

This is what the Lord showed me—a basket of summer fruit. AM 8:1

More elaborate than the first three, this vision relies on an intricate pun: *qayits*, the Hebrew word for "fruit," calls to mind and signifies *qets* ("end") —that is, the end of Israel. The sinful nation is once more indicted for its social injustice, a people who "trample on the needy, and bring to ruin the poor" (Am 8:4) by using false weights and selling inferior goods. Their punishment will be in kind: The Lord will send a famine, not a famine of bread and water but one "of hearing the words of the Lord" (Am 8:11).

The fifth vision is of the Lord standing by the altar and declaring, "Strike the capitals until the thresholds quake" (Am 9:1)—that is, bring down the edifice of the nation on the heads of the people. Yet another litany of doom concludes with an awful pronouncement: the Lord will wipe the nation "from the face of the earth . . . . all the sinners of my people shall die by the sword" (Am 9:8, 10). The last five verses of the book (Am 9:11-15) are universally considered a later addition because their positive tone contrasts so sharply with what has preceded them. Whatever the source, the conclusion of Amos draws on the vague and faint signs of hope that are spread throughout the rest of the book. Nonetheless, the overwhelmingly negative message of the book serves to emphasize the irony of prophecy. Very likely, nothing would be known of Amos had his warnings not tragically come true within a generation or two of his mission.

Obadiah, the shortest book in the Old Testament, was written during the tragic and bitter days after Babylon defeated Judah in 586 B.C., then leveled the Jewish capital of Jerusalem and destroyed the sacred temple. The writer identifies himself only as Obadiah, a common name shared by a dozen people in the Old Testament. The name means "servant of the Lord" and could have been a pen name for a prophet wishing to remain anonymous. Nothing more is known about Obadiah, although tradition once linked the prophet to Obadiah the steward of Ahab, the apostate king of Israel. That individual remained faithful to the Lord, even defying his monarch by hiding 100 prophets in a cave to avoid a massacre ordered by Ahab's queen, Jezebel. But the 300-year discrepancy between Ahab's reign (873-852 B.C.) and the destruction of Jerusalem makes such an identification implausible.

In his brief prophecy of only 21 verses, Obadiah promises that God will punish the nation of Edom—Judah's neighbor to the south—for gloating over Judah's defeat, looting the ruins, and turning Judah's fugitives over to Babylon. The prophet also assures the surviving Jews, exiled to Babylon, that God will restore them to the promised land, and that Israel will one day rule over Edom and other neighboring lands as well.

Obadiah as painted by the 15th-century Italian artist Melozzo da Forli for a church in Loreto

---

Thus says the Lord God concerning Edom. OB 1

Obadiah begins his oracle by declaring that he speaks the words of God as received in a vision. These words indict the people of Edom and encourage the people of Judah. Edom and Judah are both neighbors and relatives, though hostile toward one another. The Edomites live on Judah's southern doorstep, in the arid and mountainous region southeast of the Dead Sea. Both nations claim descent from Abraham and Isaac. Isaac's son Jacob became father of the 12 tribes of Israel, while Jacob's twin brother, Esau, produced the Edomites.

In Obadiah's day, the tense relationship between these two nations could be traced back more than a thousand years, to the animosity that erupted between their ancestors. Jacob, through opportunism and trickery, managed to secure for himself the inheritance rights and deathbed blessing of his father, both of which were intended for Esau, the oldest son. Though Esau vowed to kill his brother, forcing Jacob to flee the land, Jacob eventually returned and the brothers reconciled. By then, Esau had settled in Edom, which means "red" and likely refers to the region's cinnamon-colored sandstone cliffs.

Several centuries later, when Moses led the Israelites out of Egypt and back toward Canaan, the Edomites adamantly refused to grant them peaceful passage through the land. Because Moses wanted to enter the promised land from east of the Jordan River and God ordered him not to attack the sons of Esau, Moses was forced to lead the Israelites on a long and dangerous detour back into the barren deserts of the south. It was there that many complaining Hebrews died of snakebite. King David later defeated Edom;

his nephew Abishai was responsible for the slaughter of 18,000 Edomites.

Like Judah, Edom was forced to live in subjugation, first to Assyria, then to Babylon. Hatred between the neighboring relatives was so intense that it kept them from uniting against their common enemies. When Judah finally rebels against Babylon, Edom sides with Babylon—even providing the foreign army with resources and a staging area for attacks against the Judahites. This, however, is not what angers God; Judah should not have rebelled in the first place. The prophet Jeremiah had told the king of Judah to accept Babylon's domination as punishment for sin, but the king refused. Edom's sins are revealed in the eight-count indictment of Obadiah 12-14. The writing style uses repetition to emphasize the seriousness of the charges. The Edomites should not have gloated and boasted over Judah's misfortune. Nor should they have entered Jerusalem, rejoiced with others, looted the city, and arrested and turned over fugitives to the victorious Babylonians.

Though you soar aloft like the eagle, though your nest is set among the stars, from there I will bring you down, says the Lord. OB 4

For its sin against Judah, Edom will endure similar destruction and dishonor. Obadiah says the people will be driven from their mountain fortresses "in the clefts of the rock" (Ob 3). This phrase may refer to any of several highland fortresses—the ruins of which are still preserved—or to a major Edomite city known as Sela and later identified by some as Petra ("rock") in modern Jordan. Petra, about 50 miles south of the Dead Sea, was a valley community in which an ancient people chiseled masterfully crafted homes and temples into the solid cliff walls. This city, located beneath high rock formations and accessible only through a narrow and sheer vertical canyon, seemed impenetrable.

The first-century B.C. Greek historian Diodorus Siculus said the Edomites stockpiled their great wealth—accumulated from trade—in vaults chiseled into the rocks. But Obadiah sees in his vision that "Esau has been pillaged, his treasures searched out!" (Ob 6). Obadiah's comparison of the Edomites to their forefather is ironic: Esau was pillaged of his inheritance, and the Edomites will lose theirs as well.

Not only are the Edomites famous for their mountaintop fortresses and wealth from trade, both of which they will lose, they are also renowned for their professional sages. One of Job's comforters, Eliphaz, was from the Edomite city of Teman. "I will destroy the wise out of Edom," the Lord warns, "and understanding out of Mount Esau" (Ob 8).

During the same century that Judah fell, many Edomites began moving westward into the land vacated by Jews exiled to Babylon. In turn, Arabian desert invaders started taking over Edomite territory, which they secured in the 300s B.C. By the time of Jesus, Edom had disappeared as a nation. King Herod, however, was recognized as a descendant of the Edomites—which is one reason the Jews despised him.

The day of the Lord is near against all the nations. As you have done, it shall be done to you. OB 15

Obadiah now expands his prophecy beyond Edom; he warns all nations that have harmed Judah that they will face the wrath of God. "The day of the Lord" is a popular phrase among Old Testament prophets. Though the prophets often minister in times of crisis, when the nation teeters on the brink of moral or military disaster, they foresee a day when God will somehow intervene in human history and set everything right. The day of the Lord is most often portrayed as a terrifying judgment in which God unleashes his fierce anger on sinfulness. Some prophets go so far as to describe the world being consumed and humanity destroyed. Others, such as Obadiah, speak of the wicked receiving punishment to fit their crimes.

After this time of judgment and punishment, say many prophets, injustice and wickedness will be displaced by compassion and kindness. Warfare will end, and peace will prevail. The prophets depict what appears to be the divine reversal and redoing of creation. God's creation, which came from chaos, is returned to chaos. Then God makes creation anew. As the prophet Isaiah says on behalf of the Lord, "I am about to create new heavens and a new earth; the former things shall not be remembered or come to mind. But be glad and rejoice forever in what I am creating; for I am about to create Jerusalem as a joy, and its people as a delight" (Isa 65:17-18).

Details of this new creation remain an intriguing mystery. Some today interpret the prophecies as describing a new physical world. Others see in them a glimpse of spirit life in the heavenly realm. But for the prophets of old, the day of the Lord certainly means the end of sadness and evil, followed by the new beginning of joy and goodness—however and wherever God chooses to accomplish it.

Those who have been saved shall go up to Mount Zion to rule Mount Esau; and the kingdom shall be the Lord's. OB 21

Obadiah delivered his fierce oracles against Edom, a long-forgotten nation now best remembered for the fabled ruins of the city of Petra in modern Jordan.

Mount Zion is another name for the hilltop city of Jerusalem, established by King David as the Israelite capital. Obadiah uses this name in a poetic parallel to contrast the kingdom of Judah with the Edomite nation of mountaineers founded by Esau. In the final three verses of his short prophecy, Obadiah assures the Jewish exiles that not only will they return to their homeland, they will capture and rule many surrounding territories as well, including Edom in the south. The Jewish nation will again stretch west to the Mediterranean coast, where the Philistines once lived. It will also expand north into what is now Lebanon, and then east across the Jordan River.

All of this kingdom, says Obadiah, "shall be the Lord's." No longer will the Jews worship the Lord as just one god among the many revered at that time; they will worship him as the one and only authentic God.

It was not unusual for prophets to resist God's call, but none was as reluctant as Jonah. Sent by the Lord to the Assyrian capital of Nineveh to warn the residents of that notoriously corrupt city to repent, Jonah instead tries to run away. When he finally delivers his terse oracle— only eight words long—and is instantly successful, he is furious that the Ninevites are spared God's wrath.

Jonah is fifth among the 12 Minor Prophets, though the book—a story about the prophet himself—is strikingly different from the other prophetic books, which are mostly collections of oracles. The character of Jonah is believed to be loosely based on an eighth-century B.C. Galilean prophet named Jonah son of Amittai. The historical Jonah accurately prophesied that Jeroboam II (789-748 B.C.) would reclaim the original territory of the northern kingdom of Israel through victories over Assyria (2 Kgs 14:25).

The book is thought to have been written in the postexilic period, probably between the sixth and fourth centuries B.C. This is partly based on an inference in Jonah 3:3 that Nineveh no longer existed at the time of the writing. (The city was destroyed in 612 B.C.) Although Jonah was once believed to be historical, today the short book is generally considered to be a parable. With its message of God's love for all humanity, many scholars think that Jonah was written to protest the ultranationalism of Ezra after the Israelites returned from exile in Babylon.

The book does not preach, but instead poses a number of questions for readers to consider. For Jews scattered throughout the Persian empire in the postexilic period, is it necessary to be intolerant of other religions to keep their own cultural and religious identity intact? Is justice more important than mercy? And if, as the Jews believed, the exile was divine punishment for turning away from God, why were their heathen neighbors spared?

The book of Jonah is read in temple by Jews on Yom Kippur, the Day of Atonement, as a symbol of repentance.

Cast into the sea, Jonah is swallowed by a large fish; a mid-14th-century German Bible illustration.

Now the word of the Lord came to Jonah son of Amittai, saying, "Go at once to Nineveh, that great city, and cry out against it; for their wickedness has come up before me." JON 1:1

With dramatic economy, the scene is set for Jonah's prophetic mission: He is to visit Assyria's capital and pronounce an oracle against its wickedness. Instead, the reluctant messenger of the Lord's warning boards a ship at the Mediterranean port of Joppa bound for Tarshish—possibly the Phoenician colony Tartessus in southwestern Spain. Tarshish is also mentioned in Isaiah, Jeremiah, and Ezekiel, where it is named as the source of silver, iron, tin, and lead (Ezek 27:12). It is at the outer limits of the known world. Clearly, Jonah hopes to put as much distance as possible between himself and the destination God has in mind for him.

But Jonah cannot escape the Lord, who sends a storm that threatens to capsize the vessel. After jettisoning cargo to keep the ship afloat, the crew casts lots to see who is responsible for their predicament. Jonah is revealed as the one to blame.

Then they said to him, "What shall we do to you, that the sea may quiet down for us?" JON 1:11

Jonah tells them to cast him into the sea, since the fierce storm is due to his disobedience to God. But the sailors are loath to throw a man to his death, and instead try to row back to shore. As the sea becomes even stormier, they beseech Jonah's God to spare their lives, and finally throw Jonah into the raging water. The storm ceases immediately—a miracle that makes the heathen sailors convert to believers and offer God a sacrifice.

But God still has plans for Jonah. He both punishes him and rescues him by sending a large fish to swallow him whole. Jonah stays in the belly of the fish for three days and three nights. In spite of popular belief, a whale is never mentioned in the book of Jonah. Yet some interpreters, believing that the book is an historical narrative, have argued that there are sperm whales in the Mediterranean with throats large enough to swallow a man whole, and possibly even keep him alive for a brief period. But Jonah's survival is clearly meant to be miraculous.

JONAH: A PROPHET WITHOUT A PROPHECY?

*J*onah is a peculiar book of prophecy because it contains only a one-sentence oracle—which does not come true: "Forty days more, and Nineveh shall be overthrown!" (Jon 3:4). The remainder of the book tells the well-known tale of the prophet being swallowed by a large fish as he flees from God, then sulking after Nineveh repents of its evil ways and is spared by the Lord.

As a prophet, Jonah was among a unique group who received God's messages, usually through visions or dreams, and then delivered them by speech or in writing. Elijah and Elisha were prophets who apparently never wrote down the messages God gave them, but who performed astonishing miracles to prove that their words came from heaven. Other prophets, such as Isaiah and Jeremiah, preserved their messages in writing.

Moses anticipated that the Israelites would encounter fraudulent prophets and told the people how to identify real ones—advice that seems to portray Jonah as a fake. Moses said, "If a prophet speaks in the name of the Lord but the thing does not take place or prove true, it is a word that the Lord has not spoken" (Deut 18:22). The story of Jonah, however, reveals that prophets do not always fit a neat mold—especially when there is an opportunity for God to show his mercy.

Then Jonah prayed to the Lord his God from the belly of the fish. JON 2:1

*R*ather than the expected plea for release from his perilous situation, Jonah's prayer is a psalm of thanksgiving, perhaps interpreting the fish as a vehicle of deliverance. (Some scholars believe that the prayer existed independently and was added later.) "Out of the belly of Sheol I cried, and you heard my voice" (Jon 2:2), Jonah prays. Sheol is the most common word used in the Hebrew Bible for the underworld—a walled city beneath the sea where the spirits of the dead go.

Jonah compares himself favorably to those who worship false gods, though he has not repented his own disobedience. He ends his prayer with the cry, "Deliverance belongs to the Lord!" (Jon 2:9), and God demonstrates his mercy by causing the great fish to vomit Jonah out unharmed onto dry land.

Jesus later speaks of Jonah's three days in the belly of the fish as a harbinger of the three days between his own death on the cross and his resurrection: "For just as Jonah was three days and three nights in the belly of the sea monster, so for three days and three nights the Son of Man will be in the heart of the earth" (Mt 12:40). Jesus also compared his mission to that of Jonah: "Just as Jonah became a sign to the people of Nineveh, so the Son of Man will be to this generation" (Lk 11:30).

The word of the Lord came to Jonah a second time, saying, "Get up, go to Nineveh, that great city, and proclaim to it the message that I tell you." JON 3:1-2

*T*his time Jonah does as he is told, setting out for Nineveh. The author describes the city as so vast that it takes three days to walk across. However, excavations of Nineveh show this to be an exaggeration: The circumference of the walls was about eight miles. Jonah walks for a day across the city, then grudgingly proclaims his oracle: "Forty days more, and Nineveh shall be overthrown!" (Jon 3:4).

Unexpectedly, the sinful Ninevites do not reject his message or even question it, but immediately don sackcloth and begin a fast—traditional acts of mourning and repentance. Jonah's halfhearted effort has achieved astonishing success.

When the news reached the king of Nineveh, he rose from his throne, removed his robe, covered himself with sackcloth, and sat in ashes. JON 3:6

*T*he Assyrian king takes Jonah's message as seriously as Nineveh's residents do. He decrees that neither person nor animal shall eat or drink anything, and that both people and animals shall put on sackcloth and lament. He also orders all his subjects to stop their wrongdoing immediately. Even though Jonah's message offers no hope of mercy, the king says, "Who knows? God may relent and change his

Dating to the early centuries of Christianity, this stone sarcophagus includes scenes showing Jonah swallowed and disgorged by a sea monster (top) and Daniel in the lions' den (bottom right), framing events from the life of Jesus (center).

Jonah vomited up by a sea monster (below left) and seeking protection from the sun under a booth he erected outside Nineveh (right); two mosaic scenes from the basilica at Aquileia in northeastern Italy

mind; he may turn from his fierce anger, so that we do not perish" (Jon 3:9). Jonah's success with the king is unequaled in the history of the Israelite prophets. In contrast, when the prophet Jeremiah delivered an oracle to the king of Judah, the king not only burned the scroll on which it was written, but ordered the prophet arrested (Jer 36). God sees that the Ninevites have stopped their evil ways and repented, and he does change his mind. He spares the city from the devastation he had planned for it.

But this was very displeasing to Jonah, and he became angry. JON 4:1

Once again, Jonah is unpredictable. While he might be expected to rejoice that the Ninevites have responded so completely to his oracle, he does just the opposite. He is furious that the Assyrians have been spared the judgment they deserve, and tells God, "That is why I fled to Tarshish at the beginning; for I knew that you are a gracious God and merciful . . . and ready to relent from punishing" (Jon 4:2). He is so angry, he says, that he wants to die— a fate preferable to life with a God who shows mercy even to non-Israelites. Ironically, Jonah fails to perceive that God also spared him from the judgment that he deserved when he was in the belly of the fish. God asks him, "Is it right for you to be angry?" (Jon 4:4). In response, Jonah goes to the outskirts of the city, where he makes a flimsy shelter and sits in it,

convinced that it is only a matter of time before Nineveh returns to its corrupt ways.

God sends a bush to provide some protection for Jonah, which greatly pleases the disgruntled prophet. But the next day, the Lord sends a worm to make the bush wither, so Jonah is again blasted by the sun and wind. To him, this is just another example of God's fickle behavior, and he again cries out that he wants to die. God asks him, "Is it right for you to be angry about the bush?" (Jon 4:9), and Jonah asserts that it is. But God points out that Jonah took pity on a bush that he had no hand in growing, and that existed for only one day. Should not God, therefore, show concern for a city like Nineveh, "in which there are more than a hundred and twenty thousand persons who do not know their right hand from their left, and also many animals?" (Jon 4:11). Some scholars interpret this to refer to 120,000 children—again, an exaggeration, since the entire population of the city has been estimated at 175,000 people.

The moral of the book of Jonah is that God's compassion is not restricted to the Israelites, but extends to Gentiles as well, as should Jonah's. It also demonstrates that God loves all creation, even animals. The story carries another message for the Israelites: If God can spare even the immoral Ninevites when they reject their evil ways and repent, so can he show compassion to his disobedient chosen people if they do the same. In this sense, Jonah is in the company of the other Hebrew prophets.

icah was a rural prophet from a small village in the Judean foothills, 20 miles southwest of Jerusalem. He did not have the political savvy or international insights of the aristocratic Isaiah, who ministered at the same time and who had access to the palace in Jerusalem. But Micah was intimately acquainted with the torment of the common people, who were losing what little they had to corrupt and greedy rulers and nobles. In graphic, gruesome imagery, Micah accuses the wealthy of slaughtering and cannibalizing the poor. His attack is directed primarily toward leaders of Samaria and Jerusalem, the capital cities of the two Hebrew kingdoms: Israel in the north and Judah in the south.

The prophet's ministry spans the reign of three kings of Judah: Jotham, Ahaz, and Hezekiah, who rule between 758 and 698 B.C. Micah warns that God will punish both nations, and the prophet lives to see this happen. Assyria destroys Israel in 722 B.C. and subjugates Judah as a vassal nation, forcing the people to pay heavy taxes.

Like other Old Testament prophets, Micah does not end his message on a note of doom. He promises that, after the punishment, God will forgive and restore the Jewish people. Furthermore, says Micah, God will raise up from Bethlehem a majestic leader who will restore justice and peace and who "shall be great to the ends of the earth" (Mic 5:4). Jewish scholars saw in this a foreshadowing of the Messiah, a new temporal ruler for a restored Israel; New Testament writers saw it as a portrait of Jesus.

Micah appears among other prophets in a 15th-century ceiling fresco adorning the Vatican's Borgia apartments.

Disaster has come down from the Lord to the gate of Jerusalem.   MIC 1:12

Samaria and Jerusalem are destined for tragedy, warns the prophet Micah. These capital cities symbolize the two kingdoms of Israel and Judah, and especially their corrupt political and religious leaders. In the first three chapters of his short oracle, Micah employs provocative eloquence and piercing poetic bite to describe the sins of these leaders and the divine judgment they will face.

Micah charges that the rulers hate justice and twist the truth. They accept bribes in return for dishonest decisions and make cruelty and murder a way of life. They ruthlessly confiscate what little property the poor own, and in so doing consume the citizens like cannibals: "You . . . tear the skin off my people, and the flesh off their bones . . . and chop them up like meat in a kettle, like flesh in a caldron" (Mic 3:2, 3). Priests and prophets are no better, prostituting themselves by accepting money to tell the people what they want to hear: "Priests teach for a price . . . prophets give oracles for money; yet they lean upon the Lord and say, 'Surely the Lord is with us! No harm shall come upon us.'" (Mic 3:11).

The Lord is not with them, Micah declares. The Lord is against them, and will prove it by turning Samaria and Jerusalem into ruins and plowed fields (Mic 1:6, 3:12). Though this sounds like a final, irreversible judgment, it is actually a stern warning of what will happen if the leaders refuse to repent. As other prophets, such as Jeremiah, make clear, the Jewish people still have the option of confessing their sins and receiving God's pardon and blessing.

They shall beat their swords into plowshares, and their spears into pruning hooks.   MIC 4:3

God intends for there to be peace on earth. Micah declares this in prophecies of hope preserved in chapters 4 and 5. Nothing will stop God, says Micah, not even self-serving political servants and profiteering prophets. Though the Jewish people will be conquered, first by Assyria, then by Babylon, the Lord mercifully vows to rescue the scattered survivors and reunite them in a glorious restoration of King David's earthly dynasty.

Jerusalem will become an international center of worship during a new age of peace. Micah's promise that nations will meet for worship in Jerusalem and melt their weapons into peacetime tools is repeated in (or possibly echoes) Isaiah 2:4. The two prophets ministered at about the same time and delivered messages that occasionally overlapped, suggesting that the men discussed their prophecies with one another. Yet neither mentions the other by name in oracles recorded in the Bible.

Some scholars believe that the genuine prophecies of Micah end with chapter 3 and that the remaining four chapters were added later, since they often reflect the period of exile and restoration. But without those closing chapters, Micah would be missing the promises of restoration and comfort that typically follow warnings of judgment in other prophetic books.

You, O Bethlehem of Ephrathah, who are one of the little clans of Judah, from you shall come forth for me one who is to rule in Israel, whose origin is from of old, from ancient days. MIC 5:2

The king who will inaugurate this new era of peace and who will reign over a restored Israel will not be born in the capital, Jerusalem, but in the village of Bethlehem, birthplace of Israel's most notable ruler, King David. The origin of this king will be "of old, from ancient days." This points to a time long before the future ruler's birth—perhaps to the very beginning of time or to the centuries-old promise of the Lord regarding David: "I will establish the throne of his kingdom forever" (2 Sam 7:13).

When the Jews later find themselves oppressed by nations and empires, prophecies such as Micah's provide them with hope for a Messiah, or anointed one, from among King David's descendants. Micah describes this mysterious ruler as a person who is exactly the opposite of most Jewish kings of the day. Instead of feeding off the people, "he shall stand and feed his flock in the strength of the Lord" (Mic 5:4). He will be like a good shepherd, who gives the nation a lasting peace and a sense of security.

Eight centuries after Micah delivers this oracle, sages from somewhere east of Judea pay a surprise visit to King Herod. The men explain that they have been following a star that they believe is a sign that Israel's future king has been born. Herod is shocked because he has no newborn son. In fact, he has already killed some of his sons to secure the throne for himself. Wondering if the strangers might be talking about the promised Messiah, Herod convenes an emergency session of the chief priests and scholars and asks where the Messiah will be born. They quote Micah, and identify Bethlehem as the birthplace (Mt 2:5-6). Herod sends the sages there, five miles south of Jerusalem, where they find the infant Jesus with Mary and Joseph. By this time in Jewish history, there is a general agreement that the Messiah will come from this Judean village. For when many people later witness the miracles and teachings of Jesus, and wonder if he is the Messiah, some skeptics who think

The Evangelist Matthew interpreted Jesus' birth in Bethlehem (left) as the fulfillment of Micah's prophecy; the Nativity scene above is dated 1515.

PROPHETIC ECHOES IN THE BIBLE

Beating swords into plowshares, a sculpture given to the United Nations in 1959 by the U.S.S.R.

Prophets sometimes quoted from each other, just as New Testament writers referred to supportive excerpts from the Old Testament. For example, Micah and Isaiah, both ministering in the last decades of the eighth century B.C., looked beyond their own troubled times to an age of peace, in which nations would "beat their swords into plowshares, and their spears into pruning hooks" (Mic 4:3; Isa 2:4). Joel, writing several hundred years later, foresaw imminent war and reversed the imagery, calling on people to "beat your plowshares into swords" (Joel 3:10).

Scholars debate whether echoes such as these might be the work of editors who compiled the Hebrew scriptures and perhaps decided to emphasize converging themes with duplicate language. It is possible, however, that the imagery of beating swords into plowshares was a common expression for peace used by prophets who knew it would strike a responsive chord in their listeners.

In another prophetic echo, Obadiah 1-4 is so similar to Jeremiah 49:14-16 that it is obvious one prophet was drawing on the other or that both used a third, unknown source. Today such blatant borrowing would be called plagiarism. But as prophets, both men spoke for the Lord and credited him alone as the source of their timely and timeless messages.

he was born far to the north, in Galilee, reply, "Has not the scripture said that the Messiah is descended from David and comes from Bethlehem, the village where David lived?" (Jn 7:42).

Rise, plead your case before the mountains . . . . for the Lord has a controversy with his people, and he will contend with Israel. MIC 6:1, 2

In the style of an ancient covenant lawsuit, God lodges a formal complaint against all classes of Israelites. He challenges the people to defend themselves against charges that they have forgotten the miracles he has performed for them and have neglected their contractual obligations: "to do justice, and to love kindness, and to walk humbly with your God" (Mic 6:8).

"Woe is me!" laments the prophet, with a stark and painful sense of abandonment. "The faithful have disappeared from the land, and there is no one left who is upright" (Mic 7:1, 2). Jews from all walks of life—apparently even the abused lower classes—have learned too well from the example set by their wicked leaders. The people worship idols, cheat one another, and lie incessantly. For this, Micah says, God has already started the process of transforming the promised land flowing with milk and honey into a wasteland. But Micah places his complete trust in God, as did the prophet Habakkuk, who ministered about a century later and who also foresaw the inevitable destruction. "As for me," Micah says, "I will look to the Lord, I will wait for the God of my salvation" (Mic 7:7; compare with Hab 3:18).

Who is a God like you, pardoning iniquity? . . . You will cast all our sins into the depths of the sea. MIC 7:18, 19

As is common among books of prophecy in the Old Testament, Micah concludes with a majestic song of comfort for the Jewish people. Though the Jews will suffer tragic consequences for their sinful choices, Micah declares that God still loves them and will restore their nation in due time. Jews later agonizing through the exile in Babylon will find solace in his words: "Do not rejoice over me, O my enemy; when I fall, I shall rise" (Mic 7:8).

Many ancient civilizations believed that when they went to war, it was not the stronger army that won, but the stronger god, who empowered the army. For this reason, Babylonians would likely taunt the Israelites with questions such as, "Where is the Lord your God?" (Mic 7:10). The prophet looks ahead to this dark day, and encourages the Jewish exiles to wait patiently for God to halt these insults and to humble the arrogant people who speak them.

Micah's song ends with verses 18-20, an expressive tribute to the seemingly endless compassion God shows his chosen people. The Lord will pardon the Israelites, forgive them, and preserve them as a nation, just as he promised their ancestor Abraham. Though the people of Israel may forsake God, Micah insists that God will not forsake them.

For Assyria, the prophet Nahum declares, the end is near. Using explicit word pictures, Nahum prophesies that the wrath of God, which no one can resist, is about to destroy the monstrous empire to the north of Judah.

For centuries the brutal Assyrians had terrorized nearly all of the ancient Near East—from the Persian Gulf to Egypt. They pillaged smaller nations, then bragged about their vicious conquests; on public display in the king's palace were massive, stone-chiseled murals of realistic battle scenes with heaps of decapitated corpses and row upon row of captives impaled on wooden stakes. By the prophet Nahum's day, in the late seventh century B.C., Assyria had already destroyed the northern Hebrew kingdom of Israel and sent the survivors of its brutal siege warfare into an exile from which they never returned. The southern kingdom of Judah, like most other small nations of the area, lived in constant fear of the Assyrians and paid oppressive taxes to appease their overlords.

Almost nothing is known about the prophet Nahum. He says he is from Elkosh, but the location of this village is uncertain. Nahum likely delivered his brief prophecy sometime after the Assyrians captured the Egyptian capital of Thebes in 663 B.C. but before the fall of Nineveh—Assyria's capital—in 612 B.C. This time frame is probable because Nahum mentions the fall of Thebes and predicts the destruction of Nineveh. This means that Nahum lived at about the time the young Jeremiah began his ministry.

The prophet Nahum, framed within an initial letter from a 13th- or 14th-century Italian Bible

---

The Lord is slow to anger but great in power, and the Lord will by no means clear the guilty. NAH 1:3

Before beginning his message, the prophet describes what he is about to say as an "oracle" and a "book of the vision." Oracle is a technical term that literally means "burden," but ancient peoples understood an oracle as a divine message. Like nearly all Old Testament prophets, Nahum receives this divine insight during a visionary state. As God once explained to Aaron and Miriam, brother and sister of Moses, "When there are prophets among you, I the Lord make myself known to them in visions; I speak to them in dreams" (Num 12:6). Moses was an exception—with him, God spoke face-to-face, or directly, and without an intermediary.

Nahum begins his oracle not by citing the sins of the Assyrians or the fierce punishment that awaits them, but by explaining what God is like. This lays a theological foundation to help people understand why God is going to destroy Assyria—and why he has waited so long. By Nahum's day, the Assyrians have been plundering the region for some 200 years. They are now savoring their golden age—a half-century of immense wealth and power.

The prophet explains that God is patient and good, but that he is also jealous, avenging, and immeasurably powerful: "The mountains quake before him, and the hills melt . . . . He will make a full end of his adversaries" (Nah 1:5, 8). Though the Assyrians are "at full strength and many, they will be cut off and pass away" (Nah 1:12).

Look! On the mountains the feet of one who brings good tidings, who proclaims peace! NAH 1:15

Nahum paints the picture of a military courier racing home from the now silent battlefront, on his way to deliver good news to the king: The battle is won; Judah is finally free. The people can celebrate their annual religious festivals in peace, without fear of Assyrian disruption. And they can now honor the vows they made to God during their time of suffering.

Assyria has not yet fallen, but Nahum is so confident this will happen that he speaks as though it is history and as though God is already "restoring the majesty of Jacob, as well as the majesty of Israel" (Nah 2:2). "Jacob" refers to the former kingdom of Israel in the north, while "Israel" refers to the remnant of God's chosen people, the kingdom of Judah. Though each country has been stripped, much like a vineyard robbed of its grapes, Nahum anticipates the day when both will be restored.

Nineveh is like a pool whose waters run away. "Halt! Halt!"—but no one turns back. NAH 2:8

The prophet abruptly shifts to stark and graphic scenes from Nineveh's fall. His words are written as a fast-paced poem designed to be sung joyfully by people celebrating the destruction of the capital and collapse of the cruel empire. Nahum captures the sights and sounds of Nineveh's frantic but futile attempts to survive, telling of well-armed invaders appearing from out of nowhere. They are clothed in crimson uniforms and stand astride gleaming and lethal chariots that race madly through Nineveh's streets. Assyrian commanders order their troops and the citizens to stay and fight, but everyone flees in terror, and the city is drained like a pool.

Nineveh was built on the east bank of the Tigris River, with the tributary river Husur running through it. Babylonian and Greek accounts of the battle reveal that coalition forces of Medes from the north and Chaldeans (Babylonians) from the south surrounded Nineveh. While the Assyrians hastily assembled their forces, the enemy opened the nearby floodgates, inundating the city and causing a section of the wall to collapse. Nahum confirms that "the river gates are opened, the palace trembles" (Nah 2:6). Invading charioteers and infantry burst into Nineveh and quickly dispatch the thriving population into "heaps of corpses, dead bodies without end" (Nah 3:3). Assyrians who manage to survive are exiled and enslaved—suffering the same fate that the empire had imposed on so many other kingdoms throughout the centuries. Medes and Babylonians then begin their systematic pillaging for anything of value: "Plunder the silver, plunder the gold! There is no end of treasure! An abundance of every precious thing!" (Nah 2:9). What the Assyrians stole from conquered peoples is stolen from them. Nineveh, once as formidable as a "lions' den," is now as impotent as "young lions" slain by the sword (Nah 2:11, 13).

Ah! City of bloodshed, utterly deceitful, full of booty.
NAH 3:1

Nineveh's sins are well known in Nahum's day. This capital city is both headquarters and source of Assyrian terror and bloodshed, as well as beneficiary of the plunder that imperial soldiers steal from weaker nations.

Nahum compares the city to a deceitful prostitute who tricks others into trusting her, then robs them. For this, Nineveh will be treated like a prostitute: humiliated in a public spectacle. Nahum describes this with shocking, taunting flair that vividly reveals how ancient communities punished prostitutes. God will lift Nineveh's skirt, exposing her nakedness to the nations. Then he will throw filth at her to show that she is no better than trash. For all that Nineveh will suffer, no one will pity such a vile and contemptible people: "Where shall I seek comforters for you?" (Nah 3:7).

In case the Assyrians think this prophecy is no more than a Judean's fantasy, Nahum reminds them of what happened to the great and seemingly indestructible city of Thebes in southern Egypt. The Assyrians know the story well, for it was their soldiers, in 663 B.C., who overran the legendary and sprawling metropolis best known for its massive monuments and its royal burial ground, the Valley of the Kings. Even today, the impressive ruins cover about 18 square miles and astonish visitors. Yet, despite the grandeur of Thebes and Egypt's powerful allies of Ethiopia, Libya, and Put (a location unknown), the city fell and the captives were enslaved. Mighty Nineveh is just as vulnerable, assures the prophet, and will just as certainly endure the same destiny.

When Nineveh collapses, Nahum adds, so will the empire. As Assyria's far-flung forts are attacked, they will become "like fig trees with first-ripe figs—if shaken they fall into the mouth of the eater" (Nah 3:12).

Your shepherds are asleep, O king of Assyria; your nobles slumber. Your people are scattered on the mountains with no one to gather them.　NAH 3:18

Shepherd is a word that, in ancient times, often symbolized a national leader. The king of Assyria learns that his appointed officials are "asleep," probably dead, or at least incapacitated. Citizens fortunate enough to escape the massacre become like a flock of sheep unprotected by shepherds and scattered helplessly throughout the mountains.

Nahum promises that because every nation in the region has suffered from Assyria's unrelenting brutality, there will be one unified reaction to the empire's demise: "All who hear the news about you clap their hands" (Nah 3:19).

Warning the Assyrians of their fate, Nahum reminds Judah's enemy of their destruction of Thebes; the ruins of the Egyptian capital as depicted by a 19th-century French artist.

Habakkuk is a prophet of Judah who boldly and without apology asks the Lord to explain what appears to be his distorted sense of justice: "Why do you look on the treacherous, and are silent when the wicked swallow those more righteous than they?" (Hab 1:13).

The first two chapters of this three-chapter book read like a frank conversation between the prophet and the Lord. The third chapter is the prophet's prayer of response after the discussion. In the first chapter, Habakkuk learns that the Lord is about to punish the sinful Hebrew kingdom of Judah by allowing the emerging Babylonian empire to crush the nation. Habakkuk understands why a holy and just God needs to chastise a sinful people, but the prophet complains that it is unfair to punish Judah by sending invaders from an even more wicked nation.

Nowhere in the book does God explain his actions. But he does, however, give assurance that he will punish the Babylonians in his own time. In the meantime, God says, the righteous are to trust him and obey his commandments, even though they cannot understand his reasoning or see any sign that he is alive and at work among his chosen people. The prophet responds with a majestic prayer of trust in God—a prayer so beautiful that it was later set to music and sung in worship.

Habakkuk's reference to the "fierce and impetuous nation" of "Chaldeans," or Babylonians (Hab 1:6), places him in Judah after Babylon overthrew Assyria in 612 B.C. and before Babylon's first capture of Jerusalem in 597. Nothing more is known about the prophet. According to the apocryphal book Bel and the Dragon, an angel miraculously transported Habakkuk to Babylon, where he fed stew and bread to Daniel in the lions' den.

A youthful Habakkuk appears in this fresco from a Yugoslavian church; it is dated about 1415.

O Lord, how long shall I cry for help, and you will not listen? HAB 1:2

The prophet's dialogue with God begins with Habakkuk complaining that for a long time he has been praying for God to stop the violence and injustice in Judah, but God has not been listening. On the contrary, replies the Lord, perhaps in a vision or dream, he knows exactly what is happening. Furthermore, he is going to deal with the problem while Habakkuk is alive to witness the divine intervention: "A work is being done in your days that you would not believe if you were told" (Hab 1:5).

"I am rousing the Chaldeans," God says. ". . . they gather captives like sand. . . . They laugh at every fortress and heap up earth to take it" (Hab 1:6, 9, 10). The Chaldeans were Babylonians from southern Mesopotamia. After defeating Assyria, they established a ruthless empire of their own, continuing the Assyrian tradition of terrorizing, looting, and oppressively taxing weaker kingdoms of the ancient Near East, including Judah. Fortified cities that resisted were quickly cut off, surrounded, and besieged by the formidable Babylonian army, which then built earthen ramps outside the city walls. Once captured, a city was often leveled and its inhabitants slaugh-

tered or deported as slaves. This is the fate in store for Jerusalem, which first fell to Babylon in 597 B.C., after which thousands of its leading citizens were taken captive to the imperial homeland between the Tigris and Euphrates rivers.

Why do you look on the treacherous, and are silent when the wicked swallow those more righteous than they? HAB 1:13

God's shocking reply to this question draws a stern protest from Habakkuk. Judah is certainly sinful; the prophet has already acknowledged this. But Babylon is the epitome of evil. In Habakkuk's day, there was no earthly power that was stronger or more hated and feared. The prophet cannot understand why God is allying himself with such a wicked and idol-worshiping people. To Habakkuk, this divine action seems inconsistent with both the nature of God and the nature of humanity. The Lord is holy, "too pure to behold evil" (Hab 1:13). Yet he has decided to stand with the Babylonians against Judah. The Lord is turning his nation over to a fierce enemy that treats people like a ravenous fisherman treats fish: "The enemy brings all of them up with a hook; he drags them out with his net" (Hab 1:15).

In Habakkuk's first complaint, he had asked how long God will refuse to listen to prayers about violence in Judah. Now the prophet concludes his second and final complaint by asking how long God will allow Babylon to fish for human beings: "Is he then to keep on emptying his net, and destroying nations without mercy?" (Hab 1:17).

The righteous live by their faith. HAB 2:4

God does not explain why he has chosen wicked Babylon to punish the less sinful Judah. Nor does he explain why he will allow Babylon to treat human beings like animals. His unwillingness to explain his actions is reminiscent of his dealings with Job. It was not fair of God, Job complained, to make him suffer the loss of his health, children, and riches. To this challenge, God frankly replied that mortals cannot fully understand the divine plan. "Where were you when I laid the foundations of the earth?" God asks the suffering Job. "Tell me, if you have understanding" (Job 38:4).

God acknowledges that Habakkuk is right; the Babylonian empire is wicked. Arrogant and insatiably greedy, the Babylonians gobble up people from all nations: "They open their throats wide as Sheol [the place of the dead]; like Death they never have enough" (Hab 2:5). But God assures his prophet that Babylon's feast will end. This proud empire, like Judah, will one day answer for its sins. Meanwhile, God says, "the righteous live by their faith" (Hab 2:4). This is the most famous line in the book of Habakkuk, one that will later have a profound effect on the Christian church. God is telling Habakkuk that righteous people should continue to trust the Lord and obey his commandments, no matter how long he chooses to let the Babylonians plague the region. The apostle Paul later reinterprets this phrase,

broadening it to show that belief in Jesus is more important than Jewish rituals. Quoting this passage, Paul declares that "no one is justified before God by the law; for 'The one who is righteous will live by faith'" (Gal 3:11; see also Rom 1:17). To Paul, "the law" means Jewish regulations such as those concerning diet, circumcision, and religious holidays. These do not save, Paul insists; faith saves. The Protestant reformer Martin Luther was deeply influenced by Paul's theology. Luther criticized what he considered the overemphasis in the 16th-century Roman Catholic church on salvation through obedience to rules and rituals established by church leaders.

Alas for you who heap up what is not your own! HAB 2:6

Habakkuk responds with five "woes," describing the reversal of fortune in store for Babylon and other wicked nations. Robbers will be plundered. Exploiters who profit from evil will lose their lives. Tyrants who build on crime and violence will see their work go up in flames. Immoral people who get their neighbors drunk to degrade them will be shamed. And idol worshipers who trust in speechless images will be struck mute in the presence of God.

These woes represent sinful forces in opposition to God. Though these forces seem to rage out of control, causing some to wonder if God is still master of his creation, Habakkuk declares that God's holiness is greater than humanity's wickedness, and that in the end evil will fall silent and goodness will prevail.

Though the fig tree does not blossom, and no fruit is on the vines . . . yet I will rejoice in the Lord; I will exult in the God of my salvation. HAB 3:17, 18

Chapter three is an extraordinary prayer of confidence in God—one of the most inspiring in all of scripture. The passage reads like a psalm sung in temple rituals; in fact, this prayer's opening and closing instructions to the temple music leader show that the Jews read or sang Habakkuk's hymn to the accompaniment of stringed instruments.

Visually compelling, Habakkuk's prayer depicts God as a warrior, heavily armed and racing to the rescue of his people. Yet in a poignant statement of resignation, Habakkuk reveals that God will not arrive until after Judah has suffered the consequences of its sinful choices. Invaders or natural disasters may destroy Judah's orchards, vineyards, and grain fields. They may even take all the livestock—sheep as well as cattle. Nevertheless, Habakkuk is determined to do what God has told him the righteous should do in grim times like these: live by their faith. Habakkuk says he will wait patiently for God to act on behalf of the righteous and against the wicked. In the meantime—even in the face of imminent and inevitable national disaster—the prophet rejoices in the persevering strength he receives from God and in the confidence that, when the time is right, God will defeat the wicked and save the righteous.

Borne by an angel, Habakkuk brings food to Daniel in the lions' den; from Schnorr von Carolsfeld's 1860 book of Bible pictures.

*T*he book of Zephaniah, ninth of the 12 Minor Prophets, contains oracles apparently delivered during the reign of King Josiah of Judah (639-609 B.C.). The period is best known for Josiah's reform, an attempt to remove foreign influence from Israelite religion. After being under the dominance of Assyria from around 700 to 640 B.C., Judah experienced during Josiah's reign a period of independence that ended when Egypt asserted hegemony over Judah and Josiah was killed in battle with Pharaoh Neco at Megiddo in 609. According to the prophet's genealogy in the first verse, Zephaniah is a fourth-generation descendant of Hezekiah, perhaps the king who was famous for his religious reforms in the late eighth century (2 Kgs 18-19). In Zephaniah, the nation of Judah and its capital city, Jerusalem, are indistinguishable; in nearly all instances, one stands for the other.

Zephaniah's diction and imagery bear a similarity to a number of other biblical books. He shares much in vocabulary with his contemporaries who produced the book of Deuteronomy and the Deuteronomic history in Joshua through Kings. With other prophets he shares the notion of the ominous nature of "the day of the Lord." The book of Zephaniah can be divided into two parts; the first, likely from just after 640 B.C., contains oracles of doom (Zeph 1:1-2:15); the second, likely from around 610, offers promises of deliverance despite Judah's failures (Zeph 3:1-20).

The prophet Zephaniah; a detail from the ceiling frescoes of the Vatican's Borgia apartments

---

I will stretch out my hand against Judah, and against all the inhabitants of Jerusalem. ZEPH 1:4

*Z*ephaniah begins with his oracles of doom for Judah and its capital, Jerusalem. In language that suggests the reversal of creation, he declares that Judah is about to suffer for its apostasy: "I will sweep away humans and animals; I will sweep away the birds of the air and the fish of the sea" (Zeph 1:3). The target of Zephaniah's harangue is the worship of the god Baal. This Canaanite god is the one that Elijah put to the test in 1 Kings 18:20-40 and the one who apparently continued to attract the worship of Israelites over an extended period of time. Indeed, much of Josiah's reforms were directed at eliminating the worship of Baal and other forms of idolatry from Jerusalem.

Next on Zephaniah's list of wrongdoers are court officials and merchants whom he accuses of inappropriate behavior, violence, and fraud. Following this, Zephaniah warns that his people have become complacent and presume that "the Lord will not do good, nor will he do harm" (Zeph 1:12). Comparing them to wine that has settled, Zephaniah suggests that the inhabitants of Jerusalem shall pay the price for their inaction; "though they plant vineyards, they shall not drink wine from them" (Zeph 1:13). By applying the metaphor of wine to the residents of Jerusalem, and then suggesting that they shall not enjoy the fruits of their labor in the vineyard, Zephaniah nicely alludes to the tit-for-tat nature of their impending punishment.

The great day of the Lord is near, near and hastening fast. ZEPH 1:14

*W*ith his reference to "the great day of the Lord," Zephaniah joins a number of other prophets in warning of the awesome consequences of the people's sinfulness—for example, Isaiah 13:9, Jeremiah 46:10, Ezekiel 30:3, Amos 5:18, and Joel 2:1-3. The day of the Lord will bring utter devastation to Jerusalem and people of every walk of life. According to Zephaniah, the Lord is so disgusted by the behavior of his chosen people that the entire world will suffer the consequences: "In the fire of his passion the whole earth shall be consumed; for a full, a terrible end he will make of all the inhabitants of the earth" (Zeph 1:18).

With the first three verses of chapter 2, Zephaniah changes tone and commands his "shameless nation" to gather together and begin to follow the Lord's commands before he takes out his anger on them. The most that this newfound obedience can gain, however, is the chance to be hidden on the day of the Lord's vengeance. It is important to recognize in Zephaniah's words the hyperbole born of frustration with the inattentiveness of his people. Indeed, much of his rhetoric is designed to induce people to proper action rather than to predict the future. By employing the metaphor of "the day of the Lord," the prophet joins in a traditional and familiar prophetic rhetorical device. It is likely meant to drive home the seriousness of the situation in which Zephaniah and his audience in Judah find themselves.

For Gaza shall be deserted, and Ashkelon shall become a desolation. ZEPH 2:4

Employing another standard prophetic rhetorical device, Zephaniah next launches into his oracles against the nations. Not only have Jerusalem and Judah drawn the Lord's anger, but so have their surrounding neighbors. Whereas Amos begins his oracles against the nations with those farthest from Israel and slowly draws in his references to zero in on the northern kingdom, Zephaniah, having already delivered his warning to Judah, starts with its nearest neighbors and works outward. Gaza, Ashkelon, Ashdod, and Ekron represent the Philistines on the southwestern Mediterranean coast. Their enmity toward the Israelites is documented in Judges and 1 Samuel. With hints of the restoration that is elaborated on in Zephaniah 3:8-20, the prophet says that the Philistine lands will become the possession of those who shall remain in Judah. Moving to the east and south, Zephaniah next addresses Moab and Ammon, which he compares to Sodom and Gomorrah, cities destroyed for their wickedness. This comparison is likely based on traditions such as those in Genesis 19:30-38, where the ancestors who gave their names to Moab and Ammon are born of the union of Lot with his daughters. The prophet, no doubt, is making the point that the loss of their lands relates to the immorality of their incestuous origins. Finally, Zephaniah moves to more remote enemies of Judah, the Egyptians and Assyrians. For nearly a century beginning around 687 B.C., Judah experienced the devastation of being a political pawn manipulated by these two giant rivals in their continuing struggles to dominate the entire Near East. Shifting sides led to only worse consequences for tiny Judah.

Ah, soiled, defiled, oppressing city! ZEPH 3:1

The first eight verses of chapter 3 display the difficulty in establishing clear boundaries in Zephaniah's message. This segment has associations with the oracles of doom that precede it but also serves as a transition to the reassuring words that follow. Here, Zephaniah does not warn of impending doom but, rather, laments Judah's unwillingness to accept correction. He cites the failure of judges, prophets, and priests in maintaining a lawful and ordered city. Next, Zephaniah cites the ruined nations and other signs that the Lord has given to Judah to no avail. Now, says the Lord, all there is to do is wait for his indignation.

At that time I will change the speech of the peoples to a pure speech, that all of them may call on the name of the Lord and serve him with one accord. ZEPH 3:9

It turns out that the day of the Lord's indignation is not as dire as it sounds. In fact, on this day, those who have been scattered will bring offerings to his mountain. Moreover, the remnant of Judah shall have security; laughter and singing will echo in Jerusalem. At this time, Zephaniah says, the Lord will remove his curse and make Jerusalem "renowned and praised among all the peoples of the earth" (Zeph 3:20).

Zephaniah delivered oracles against Moab and Ammon, nations descended from Lot's incestuous relations with his daughters; a painting by Jan Massys (1508-1575).

Haggai and Zechariah, contemporaries in postexilic Judah, appear with an anachronistic king in this 1230 Bible illustration.

*T*he first verse of Haggai gives a wealth of information about the prophet's audience and historical period. His ministry began in late August or early September of 520 B.C., the second year of the reign of Persia's Darius I. Indeed, all of Haggai's message seems to have come within a brief span of three to four months during that year. His audience is clearly identified as well and reveals much about the social and political situation in Judah as it began to reconstitute itself after returning from exile in Babylon. According to a Persian mandate, Judah was to have a governor and a high priest who would share in the effort to restore the nation. Zerubbabel was a descendant of King David and, therefore, could claim legitimacy as a political ruler. Joshua was of priestly lineage and had equal legitimacy as a religious leader.

Haggai is the tenth of the 12 Minor Prophets; his book immediately precedes that of his contemporary Zechariah. This is significant because some scholars view the two chapters of Haggai as the first half of an envelope construction that is closed by chapters seven and eight of Zechariah. In fact, there are a number of common issues that arise in the two books. Both prophets are mentioned in the book of Ezra, where they are associated with the rebuilding of the temple (Ezra 5:1, 6:14), an undertaking that occupied much of the energy of the returnees in the last decades of the sixth century B.C. In the opinion of many, Judah's existence as a renewed nation was dependent on the building of the second temple, which would, in turn, induce the return of God to Jerusalem. This deeply felt need for a temple is central to the motives of Haggai and is the guiding principle of much of the literature of the period, in particular the books of Ezra, Nehemiah, and Zechariah as well as Haggai.

Is it a time for you yourselves to live in paneled houses, while this house lies in ruins? HAG 1:4

*A*ccording to this verse, it is Haggai who inaugurates the rebuilding of the temple. Persian king Cyrus II had mandated the release of the Jews from their captivity in Babylon in 539 B.C. and authorized the temple's reconstruction. But the first returnees had apparently made little progress. Haggai's bold declaration seems to have reenergized the building effort. Important to an understanding of Haggai's address is the echo of 2 Samuel 7:2, in which King David first proposes to build a temple for God. David says, in essence, "Should I dwell in a house of cedar while the Lord has only a tent?" God responds through the prophet Nathan that it is not David's place to build him a house but rather his to build David a house—that is, a dynasty to rule Israel forever.

There is a contrast as well as a parallel between the words of Nathan and Haggai. Whereas Nathan's message to David is to delay the building of the temple, Haggai's message is to begin immediately. And at the end of Nathan's address, the Lord promises to establish David's house forever. That Haggai's message sounds so much like Nathan's is likely meant to signal that this new temple is a legitimate replacement of the first. Moreover, by making the association with the eternal promise to David, Haggai may be signaling that the governor Zerubbabel, a descendant of Judah's last king, Zedekiah, is to be understood as the legitimate heir of David. Whatever the reasons for this resonance, it places the origins of the second temple in the idiom of the delayed start of the first. Haggai's listeners would have understood the prophet's deliberate echo of the scriptures.

Who is left among you that saw this house in its former glory? HAG 2:3

*I*n chapter 2:1-9, Haggai delivers reassurance that the Lord will be present with Zerubbabel, the high priest Joshua, and all of the people in their efforts to rebuild the temple. "Take courage," the prophet pronounces, ". . . for I am with you, says the Lord of hosts, according to the promise that I made you when you came out of Egypt" (Hag 2:4-5). Of particular interest in this declaration is the reference to the Exodus, the release of the Hebrews from slavery in Egypt, the pivotal event through which all of Israel's subsequent history must be viewed. The reference is clearly meant to suggest that the return from captivity is the Jews' new exodus. During their years of wandering in the wilderness, the Lord's presence was in the ark of the covenant, a portable precursor to the temple. Haggai seems to be reminding the Jews that the Lord is awaiting his permanent house now just as he did after Israel escaped from the Egyptians. "The latter splendor of this house shall be greater than the former," the Lord promises; ". . . in this place I will give you prosperity" (Hag 2:9).

Ask the priests for a ruling.   HAG 2:11

In this, the third section of Haggai, the prophet takes aim at a people who have attempted to make offerings that are unclean. Scholars are unsure about to whom Haggai is referring, but it seems likely it is the Samaritans. They were a mixture of peoples that included those left behind after Assyria conquered the northern kingdom of Israel in 722 B.C. Other scholars think Haggai is referring to the people of Judah themselves, whose offerings are unclean because they have been made before the temple is rebuilt and its altar reconsecrated. More important, the ruling that Haggai seeks has to do with what comprises a clean or pure offering. He implies, especially with the discussion that follows in verses 15-19, that keeping separate from the local population is

Haggai urged the rebuilding of Jerusalem's walls and temple in the period following the Jews' return from their exile in Babylon; a fanciful version of the construction effort.

crucial to the maintenance of the new temple and its purity. In his association of the purity of the temple with the homogeneity of the returning Jews, Haggai shares much with Ezra 4:1-5 and Nehemiah 10:30 and 13:1. While a complicated matter, this association stems, in part, from a consistent use throughout the Hebrew Bible of sexual metaphors to describe relations between Israel and the Lord. Those relations require unwavering fidelity to God and, by association, to one's own people. As that fidelity to God came to be understood, personal fidelity within the Jewish community ensured sanctity.

Before a stone was placed upon a stone in the Lord's house, how did you fare?   HAG 2:15-16

Haggai next turns to another ancient theme: God's relationship to the people of Israel as dependent on their worship in the temple. In point of fact, this relationship, when it is proper, is defined by the fertility that Israel experiences. Haggai suggests that it is only with the laying of the foundation stone that the Lord's blessing can be reactivated. God's relation to his people, conceived in terms of fertility, is ancient and ongoing. One of the most explicit accounts of this relationship is found in the book of Hosea, where Hosea's wife, the prostitute Gomer, represents the wayward people of Israel. More significantly, chapter 2 of Hosea contains an extended description of the proper relations between God and Israel in terms of the fertility of the land. Once again, Haggai asserts that things can only go well with the returnees once the temple is rebuilt and the fertility of their land is reestablished.

I am about to shake the heavens and the earth.   HAG 2:21

In a great rhetorical flourish, Haggai ends his book by associating the impending new age with the grandeur of Israel's past. This new age will literally comprise ground-shaking events. Moreover, when the prophet quotes the Lord, saying, "I am about to destroy the strength of the kingdoms of the nations, and overthrow the chariots and their riders; and the horses and their riders shall fall" (Hag 2:22), Haggai once again makes a close connection between the building of the new temple and the events of the Exodus. The new era is messianic and is marked by the renewal of God's promises to Zerubbabel, the descendant of David. It is important to note that in Haggai this divine promise is merely the assurance that the long and ancient line of Judah's kings will be reestablished and maintained forever. The word "messiah" simply means one who is anointed. Anointing was the means by which Israel had designated its rulers since Samuel anointed Saul to show that he was God's choice to rule Israel. Haggai's message is striking for its attempt at associating current events with stories of Israel's past. In so doing, the prophet reassures his audience that what has happened before is about to occur again.

*T*he words of Zechariah, 11th of the 12 Minor Prophets, date from the years 520 to 518 B.C. His ministry overlaps with that of the prophet Haggai, who was active during the second half of 520. Indeed, given similarities in their time frames and structure, the two books bearing their names are believed by many to be a composite literary work. It is clear that the two are from the same period and share the same concerns over the rebuilding of the temple, its purity, and what they believed to be the dawning messianic era.

The book of Zechariah, as it is preserved in the Bible, can be divided into two parts. The first (chapters 1-8) comprises a set of eight visions interspersed with a few oracles. The second section (chapters 9-14) contains two additional oracles and is sometimes referred to as Second Zechariah. It is generally agreed to be independent of and later in origin than the first section. In fact, it is also generally accepted that the second part of Zechariah represents two separate works: chapters 9-11 and 12-14. Neither of these two additions to Zechariah makes any claim to stem from the prophet. Moreover, because they share with the beginning of Malachi the phrase "An oracle. The word of the Lord . . ." (Zech 9:1, 12:1; Mal 1:1), some think that all three sections were originally anonymous works that only later became associated with their respective prophets.

It is difficult to interpret just how Zechariah relates to the book of Haggai, which precedes it, or to the book of Malachi, which follows. More important than identifying their exact relationship is the fact that they have been shaped by a final editor of the Hebrew Bible to represent the prophetic response to the situation in which Judah found itself after returning from exile in Babylon. All three books share the central ideal of a newly constructed temple and a pure nation in which it can be built. As Zechariah puts it in the introduction to his work, "Return to me, says the Lord of hosts, and I will return to you" (Zech 1:3). By this, God apparently means that if Judah will observe his commandments, including rebuilding his dwelling, the temple, he will live up to his covenant with the people.

The prophet Zechariah, depicted by Netherlandish artist Jan Provost (c. 1462-1529) as a man of his own times

---

In the night I saw a man riding on a red horse! ZECH 1:8

*T*his sentence introduces the first of Zechariah's eight visions. The man—later revealed to be an angel of the Lord—is in the midst of a myrtle grove; nearby are three other horses. In answer to the prophet's question, the man says that the Lord has sent the horses "to patrol the earth" (Zech 1:10). After the patrol reports to the angel that the world is at peace, God declares that he has returned to Jerusalem, that his house will be rebuilt there, and that the nation will prosper. The 70 years of God's anger approximates the period from the destruction of Jerusalem in 586 B.C.

Zechariah's second vision is of four horns. Four blacksmiths appear who are to punish the four horns, now understood to be nations responsible for the dispersion of the Jews. Zechariah's third vision is of "a man with a measuring line in his hand" (Zech 2:1). This image is meant to suggest that the Lord is about

to take a measure of Jerusalem's worthiness. But no sooner has the man left than the divine messenger is told to chase after him and tell him the Lord has promised to protect and dwell within the city. This vision is followed by an oracular passage in which the Lord promises that any nation that harmed Judah shall pay the price. Moreover, the Lord promises that on his return to Zion, his temple mount in Jerusalem, other nations will join themselves to Judah, which is called "the holy land" (Zech 2:12). In this oracle, as in the last ten chapters of Isaiah, is the notion of an expanded perspective of God's rule. These texts attest to the emergence in the second temple period of a conception of the God of Israel as a universal rather than a national deity.

In his fourth vision Zechariah sees the high priest Joshua with Satan standing at his side. Here, as in the rest of the Old Testament, Satan (a Hebrew word meaning "the adversary") is not the embodiment of evil as in the New Testament. Rather, he is the accuser or special prosecutor of the divine assembly (see Job 1-2). An angel of the Lord rebukes Satan and has Joshua remove his filthy clothes and put on fresh festal attire. This vision symbolizes the purification of the priesthood and its acceptance by the Lord.

"I see a lampstand all of gold, with a bowl on the top of it; there are seven lamps on it, with seven lips on each of the lamps." ZECH 4:2

Zechariah's fifth vision, taking up all of chapter 4, is an elaborate metaphor for the authority vested in Joshua and the governor Zerubbabel. In short, the vision signals that it is through Zerubbabel that the temple will be rebuilt. In his sixth vision Zechariah sees an immense flying scroll for which dimensions are given (30 by 15 feet). Of interest here is the resonance this passage has with others in the Hebrew Bible. Jeremiah says "Your words were found, and I ate them, and your words became to me a joy" (Jer 15:16). Ezekiel has an even more elaborate report of his encounter with God's word. He says that he was given a scroll and that, when he ate it, "in my mouth it was as sweet as honey" (Ezek 3:3). Each of these texts attests to the growing importance of God's word and the emergence of a recognition of scripture as a guide to life.

Zechariah's seventh vision is of a woman, who represents wickedness, in a basket. This elaborate imagery is apparently meant to suggest that Judah will deport all the wickedness it had absorbed during its stay in Babylon back to the country of its origin. In the eighth and final vision, Zechariah sees four chariots that represent the four winds of the heavens. Like the horses of the first vision, these teams go out to patrol the earth and report back to God. This vision ends with the team that went north putting the "spirit at rest in the north country" (Zech 6:8). Just what it means for the spirit to be at rest in the north country has always puzzled readers. It may suggest that the "north," from which so many of Israel's enemies came (Jer 1:13-15), will no longer be a threat.

The word of the Lord came to me. ZECH 6:9

Having completed the account of his eight visions, Zechariah next delivers a series of oracles that take up the rest of the original book. Each of the ensuing sections begins with the same, or a similar, oracular formula: "The word of the Lord came to me." The first dictates the crowning of Joshua the high priest, calls him "Branch" (a standard messianic designation; see Jer 23:5, 33:15), and says that he shall build the temple. Since being crowned, being called "branch," and building the temple would

Zechariah's eighth vision was of four chariots pulled by horses of different colors.

normally be associated with a king rather than a priest, many suspect that Joshua's name has been substituted for that of Zerubbabel, the heir of David. It is hard to know what to make of this crucial change, but it attests to the rising fortunes of the high priest and the relative weakening of his royal counterpart during the postexilic period in what was originally conceived as an authority shared by the two.

Although chapter 7 contains three separate oracular formulas, the entire chapter can be understood as a coherent whole. The first seven verses deal with whether it is still necessary to mourn the loss of the first temple after 70 years. This corresponds roughly to the time that has elapsed since the temple was destroyed in 586 B.C. and corresponds exactly to predictions of how long Judah would be under the control of Babylon (Jer 25:11). There is no clear answer to this query, but Zechariah 7:8-14 may be understood as a rather loose response. Zechariah, in traditional prophetic language, reminds the people that God desires justice, mercy, and care for the widow and orphan. Next, Zechariah says that because God's chosen people failed to follow these rules in the past, the Lord "scattered them with a whirlwind among all the nations" (Zech 7:14).

Jerusalem shall be called the faithful city, and the mountain of the Lord of hosts shall be called the holy mountain. ZECH 8:3

Chapter 8 contains the last of the material that can be ascribed to the prophet himself. Like other prophets, Zechariah ends on a note of encouragement and promise. The good news in this chapter is repeatedly introduced by the phrase "Thus says the Lord of hosts." God promises to return to his mountain and bring health and happiness to the streets of Jerusalem. Using traditional language for articulating this renewed bond, Zechariah records, "Thus says the Lord . . . . They shall be my people and I will be their God" (Zech 8:7-8). The promising language continues in verses 9-13, where images of renewed fertility dominate. Zechariah assures that all will be well with Judah so long as the people abide by traditional moral standards. Finally, Zechariah notes that the fasts of mourning for the first temple and other previous disasters "shall be seasons of joy and gladness, and cheerful festivals for the house of Judah" (Zech 8:19). Moreover, the Lord's appeal, and that of his temple and city, will lure peoples of other nations. With this universal promise, Zechariah ends his message to the Jews about the coming age in which the temple will ensure God's presence and the well-being of his people.

Lo, your king comes to you; triumphant and victorious is he, humble and riding on a donkey, on a colt, the foal of a donkey. ZECH 9:9

Scholars call chapters 9-14 Second Zechariah. They place this material as early as the end of the sixth century, soon after Zechariah's career, and as late as the end of the fourth century, during the Hellenistic period. Much of the material in Second Zechariah is messianic in tone. In the context of the early second temple period, this means that there was substantial hope for the reemergence of King David's dynasty. "Messiah" is the Hebrew word for one who is anointed—according to Israelite tradition, the king. The messianic nature of Second Zechariah made it fertile ground for early Christian interpretation. Chapter 9 begins, like Amos, with oracles against the nations. Targeted are Aram (Syria) to the north and Philistia to the southwest. Both nations, as bordering neighbors, had long histories of animosity with Israel and Judah.

Zechariah 9:9 contains a messianic passage that was to have considerable import for early Christian understanding of Jesus, speaking as it does of the entrance of Judah's new king into Jerusalem in strikingly hyperbolic language. Several things about this verse are of interest. In typical Hebrew poetic form, the king's donkey is referred to twice. This double reference is what scholars call parallelism: for emphasis, a term is repeated. An English equivalent would be something like responding to the question "How are you?" with, "Well, very well." When early Christians came to understand this passage in Zechariah as referring to Jesus' triumphal entry into Jerusalem, some took the double reference to mean that he would ride on both a donkey and a colt (Mt 21:1-7). Others, however, understood the Hebrew idiom for what it was, recording that Jesus rode into Jerusalem on only one animal, a donkey (Jn 12:12-15).

The reference in Zechariah 9:13 to the Lord arousing the sons of Zion against the sons of Greece indicates to some that Second Zechariah contains relatively late texts. The remainder of chapters 9 and 10 describe the restoration of the land of Israel and the humiliation of Israel's traditional enemies.

Zechariah 11:1-3 uses arboreal imagery, reserved in much of the Hebrew Bible for royal descriptions, to suggest the failure of Judah's shepherds. The shepherd is another metaphor for royal office in the rest of the Hebrew Bible. This passage is difficult, but it does seem to introduce the last topic of the first section of Second Zechariah: an autobiographical account of a shepherd whose flock "is doomed to slaughter"

(Zech 11:4). The 30 shekels of silver mentioned in Zechariah 11:12-13 is the same fee paid to Judas for his betrayal of Jesus (Mt 26:14-15). It is also the penalty for causing a slave's death (Ex 21:32).

See, I am about to make Jerusalem a cup of reeling for all the surrounding peoples. ZECH 12:2

The last half of Second Zechariah, chapters 12-14, is marked by a rather disjointed style, with a number of themes being addressed. In chapter 12 is an oracle that promises that Jerusalem will be restored. Included in these encouraging words is an assertion that the house of David "shall be like God, like the angel of the Lord, at their head" (Zech 12:8). New Testament writers interpreted the following verses as referring to Jesus as God's only son (Jn 1:14, 18), as Mary's firstborn (Lk 2:7), and as one pierced at his death (Jn 19:37; Rev 1:7). Chapter 13 begins with the notice that prophecy will end and then, in verses 7-9, returns to a messianic message that many think belongs with chapters 9-11. Again, the messianic implications of the stricken shepherd in Zechariah 13:7 were seen by the New Testament authors as referring to Jesus (Mt 26:31; Mk 14:27).

Chapter 14 represents a final message about Jerusalem. After initial defeat, the city will be defended by the Lord and he will become "king over all the earth" (Zech 14:9). Furthermore, Jerusalem will be secure forever and its enemies will suffer great hardship, pay tribute to it, and worship its God.

Enacting Zechariah's prophecy of the coming of the messianic king, Jesus rides a donkey into Jerusalem; one of Giotto's famed frescoes in the Arena chapel at Padova, Italy, painted in 1305-1306.

*T*he Hebrew word malachi *means "my messenger." There is considerable doubt among biblical experts whether this Malachi is the name of an historical person or simply a title: "I am sending my messenger to prepare the way before me" (Mal 3:1). Like the additions to Zechariah beginning at Zechariah 9:1 and 12:1, Malachi opens with the phrase, "An oracle. The word of the Lord." Some think that the short book of Malachi is simply the third of three related works, each of which was originally anonymous. As such, Malachi may represent a continuation of the book of Zechariah rather than an independent book. This possibility has to be weighed against the fact that the contents and literary form of Malachi do not seem to be a continuance of the last six chapters of Zechariah, or what scholars call Second Zechariah. Although it is difficult to determine just why the word Malachi appears in the first verse of the book, it came to be understood as the name of the author. Whatever the reason for its use, the name takes on considerable significance for Christians, given that Malachi is the last of the 12 Minor Prophets and thus the final book of the Old Testament, immediately followed by the New Testament.*

The book of Malachi is representative of those biblical books produced in the period following the return of the exiled Jews to their homeland beginning in 538 B.C. It concerns itself with the temple, cultic purity, and intermarriage, as do Ezra and Nehemiah. Malachi, however, represents a time when the high hopes evinced in such other biblical books as Haggai and Zechariah have faded and the harsh realities of reformulating religious and cultural identity have made themselves known. Most scholars agree that Malachi dates to the middle of the fifth century B.C. Written in a disputational style, Malachi repeatedly presents the people with their failings only to have them debate his claim with a question which, in turn, allows Malachi to get to the heart of the problem.

The prophet Malachi, as portrayed by Frederick James Shields (1833-1911)

Is not Esau Jacob's brother? says the Lord. Yet I have loved Jacob but I have hated Esau. MAL 1:2

*M*alachi begins with the assertion that the Lord, indeed, has loved Israel. To drive his point home, he uses the ancient story of Jacob (Israel) and Esau, rival twins from birth (Gen 25:22-26). The Lord tells Israel that he loved their ancestor Jacob and hated his brother Esau. The reference reminds Israel that God's love for them is ancient and they have survived because of his concern and compassion for them. Moreover, it serves to raise an issue that was crucial to the emerging identity of the returnees. It was Esau's descendants, the Edomites, who were understood to have been key to the defeat and exile of the people of Judah. The reference to these hostile neighbors also serves to remind the Israelites of their history, both as the beloved of God and as a people who must be wary of other nations, even those that, according to tradition, are closely related. All of this likely is directed at discouraging intermarriage with the Samaritans, those who were once part of the Israelite fold but who now, for various complicated reasons, are considered suspect.

A son honors his father, and servants their master. If then I am a father, where is the honor due me? MAL 1:6

*I*n the next section of his book, Malachi 1:6-14, the prophet addresses what he sees as disrespect for the Lord. Using conventional wisdom, he notes that the Lord fails to receive the respect due him. In response, the people say to the Lord, "How have we despised your name?" (Mal 1:6). Again, in the book's characteristic disputational style, Malachi makes the point that even when confronted with their failings, the people resist acknowledging them. What is at stake for Malachi is the offering of impure sacrifices as defined by such scriptural texts as Leviticus 22:17-25. In addition to the insult of making entirely unacceptable offerings, the people apparently believe that God's requirements can be ignored with impunity, their assumption being that God is powerless to hold them to their obligations under the covenant with him. All of this suggests that the great hopes for national renewal that surrounded the rebuilding of the temple late in the sixth century have faded by Malachi's time—even though only a few decades have passed.

And now, O priests, this command is for you. MAL 2:1

In the next section, Malachi takes on those he holds responsible for the sorry state of the temple and its ritual life, the priests. Malachi tells his audience of the Lord's covenant with the Levites (Num 3:6-13). He harkens back to those original promises to remind the current priestly officiants that theirs is a high calling. All of this comes to a head when the Lord declares, "And so I make you despised and abased before all the people, inasmuch as you have not kept my ways but have shown partiality in your instruction" (Mal 2:9). It is difficult to know what Malachi means by this, but it has been suggested that perhaps another part of the Levite tribe, pushed aside by the Zadokite branch of the family at the time of Solomon, may be trying to reassert its claim of pre-eminence. Whatever the intentions of this section of Malachi, it is clear whom he holds responsible for the state of impurity of the temple.

Chapter 2 concludes with a brief discussion of what the Lord considers proper marital relations, including the strongest condemnation of divorce in the Hebrew Bible. Like most of the biblical texts produced from the late sixth through the middle fifth centuries, the issue of temple purity and marriage is linked in these verses. There seems to be a growing sense of cultural identity that turns on notions of purity that surround the temple and marriage bonds.

The Evangelists interpreted John the Baptist's ministry as fulfilling Malachi's prophecies; a painting by Paolo Veronese (1528-1588).

Underlying these parallel trends appears to be the conception that right relations between God and Israel depend equally on correct temple ritual and proper relations between individuals.

See, I am sending my messenger to prepare the way before me. MAL 3:1

In a passage that came to be understood as a prophecy concerning John the Baptist (Mt 11:10; Mk 1:2; Lk 7:27), Malachi relays the warning of the Lord. The gospel writers merely recorded what was the general early Christian understanding of this verse. Their interpretation was, in part, dependent on the two closing verses of the fourth and last chapter of Malachi as well. In what seemed to early Christians to be a second reference to John the Baptist, the promise to send "the prophet Elijah before the great and terrible day of the Lord" (Mal 4:5) repeated the pledge of a messenger in Malachi 3:1. The early Christian reading of these verses assumed an analogy between the Old and New Testaments that saw in the pair Elijah/Elisha a precursor to the pair John the Baptist/Jesus. Other examples of this so-called typological analogy are the stories of Jesus' miracles, which are modeled closely on those of Elijah and Elisha (1 Kgs 17-2 Kgs 8). Like most Jewish biblical interpreters of the second temple period, early Christians read their scripture with an uncanny ability to make insightful associations among its constituent parts. As the last prophetic book in the Hebrew Bible, Malachi was understood to be the final word on the promises to a disheartened Israel. It is no wonder that this final chapter of the Hebrew Bible came to be understood in Christian circles as the prediction of the lives of John the Baptist and Jesus.

Malachi clarifies the problem of a priesthood "despised and abased" (Mal 2:9) by claiming that one of the Lord's first acts on his return to the temple will be to purify the descendants of Levi. This process will reinstitute the purity, and therefore the legitimacy, of the temple ritual. In Malachi's mind, the return of the Lord will not negate but rather make whole again the temple cult and its officiants. In the section comprising Malachi 3:6-4:3, the Lord reassures the Israelites that he has not wavered in his affection for them. All they have to do to regain this constant affection is to return to those practices that are required by their religious tradition as it is recorded in Leviticus and Numbers. Failure to observe those traditions will result in dire consequences, indeed.

Remember the teaching of my servant Moses. MAL 4:4

The last three verses of Malachi are considered to be editorial additions. In them, Malachi is placed in the line of the great teachers of the Hebrew Bible. Viewed as continuing the mission of Israel's first and greatest prophet, Malachi is shown to be in full support of those traditions that stress the importance of obeying Mosaic Law.

THE APOCRYPHA

The heroine Judith by Andrea Mantegna (1431-1506)

During the several centuries between the Old and New Testament periods—from about 300 B.C. until Rome destroyed Jerusalem in A.D. 70—Jews wrote many books considered helpful and even inspired. These ancient texts were filled with dramatic Israelite history, romance, mysteries, miracles, wise sayings, prayers, and songs. Though the Jews eventually decided to exclude these books from the Hebrew Bible, Christians retained most of them with confidence for more than a millennium, until Protestants broke with the Roman Catholic church and began eliminating the texts from new editions of their Bible.

This collection of writings is called the Apocrypha (Greek for "hidden"), a name coined by Jerome, a fourth-century Christian scholar who translated Jewish and Christian scriptures into the language of his day, Latin. Jerome was among a minority of church leaders with a low regard for the Apocrypha. He said that many of its books read like "the crazy wanderings of a man whose senses have taken leave of him," and that they deserved to be "hidden" or separated from the canon of

sacred scriptures. Most early Christians and many Jews disagreed. Three centuries before Jerome disparagingly classified the writings as "hidden," a Jewish writer suggested that they contained hidden secrets for discerning readers: "In them is the spring of understanding, the fountain of wisdom, and the river of knowledge."

These additional writings became popular among early Christians because the Apocrypha was part of the only written Bible they knew: the Septuagint, a second-century B.C. translation of the first five books of the Bible into Greek. In the centuries that followed, other Jewish works were translated and added to the Septuagint, including the remaining books of the Old Testament, as well as the Apocrypha. By about A.D. 100, the Jews sifted through this ever growing library of revered texts and established their canon of scripture, which included only the oldest and most sacred writings. The Apocrypha was excluded. Christians felt no compulsion to follow the Jewish lead.

Inspired or Tainted?

During the first few centuries of the church, influential Christian leaders quoted the apocryphal books of the Greek Septuagint, describing them as "divine scripture" and "inspired." Few church leaders knew any of the Hebrew on which the Septuagint was based or made any effort to compare the 24 books of the newly established Jewish Bible to the more inclusive Septuagint. For instance, church fathers seemed unaware—or at least unconcerned—that the Hebrew version of Daniel did not include the story of Susanna, which is found in the Septuagint's Daniel. By the early second century, the Septuagint had become so popular among Christians and so associated with the Christian movement that Jews banned it as tainted.

Exactly how many apocryphal works the early Christians used is unknown, since there is no widely agreed upon list of books in the Apocrypha. The book of 2 Esdras, probably written late in the first century A.D., mentions 70 works. But many modern scholars set the number much lower, at 13, since that is the number of texts that appear in the oldest surviving Greek codices (bound books) of the Septuagint. These 13 are Tobit, Judith, additions to Esther, Wisdom of Solomon, Sirach, Baruch, Letter of Jeremiah, three additions to Daniel, 1 and 2 Maccabees, and 1 Esdras.

By the fourth century, church leaders recognized the difference between apocryphal books and those in the Hebrew Bible, yet maintained a generally high regard for the Apocrypha. The scholar Jerome disagreed, arguing in favor of dropping the Apocrypha from the list of sacred texts. He made this recommendation after moving to Palestine, learning Hebrew, and undertaking the commission of Pope Damasus to translate into Latin the entire Bible—Jewish and Christian writings combined. Jerome grudgingly included a few apocryphal works: Tobit and Judith, along with the Greek additions to Esther and the three Greek additions to Daniel (the Prayer of Azariah and the Song of the Three Jews, Susanna, and Bel and the Dragon). But Jerome carefully separated the supplemental materials, noting they were not in the Hebrew originals. Later copyists, however, did not always retain Jerome's notes or his distinction between the two classes of Jewish writings. Furthermore, the church later added more apocryphal books to Jerome's celebrated translation, the Vulgate ("common," so called because it was written in the common language of the day, Latin).

For another millennium the Apocrypha continued to influence people in ways small and large. William Shakespeare named two of his daughters after apocryphal heroines: Susanna and Judith. More notably, Christopher Columbus quoted a passage of the Apocrypha when pleading with the queen of Spain to finance his sailing expedition. According to 2 Esdras 6:42, God created a world that was six parts land and one part water. Columbus reasoned that since only a seventh of the earth is covered in water (actually, it is almost three-quarters), the ocean between the west coast of Europe and Asia would be no more than about 3,000 miles, which he could sail in just a few weeks.

Protestants Versus Catholics

By the time of the Protestant Reformation, beginning in 1517, many Christian scholars were raising serious questions about the reliability of the Apocrypha. Three years later, in the first detailed Protestant opinion on the matter, the prominent scholar Andreas Bodenstein (commonly known as Carlstadt, after his birthplace) not only distinguished between the Hebrew canon and the Apocrypha, he also divided the Apocrypha into two categories: helpful books and dangerous books. Among the helpful were Wisdom of Solomon, Sirach, Judith, Tobit, and 1 and 2 Maccabees. The second group—namely 1 and 2 Esdras, Baruch, Prayer of Manasseh, and the additions to Daniel—Carlstadt ridiculed as thoroughly unreliable and worthy of a censor's ban.

Protestant doubts about the Apocrypha continued to grow because it was in these books that the Roman Catholic church found support for several passionately disputed teachings: belief in purgatory, praying for the dead, and the widely abused practice of doing penance for sin. Various Protestant movements—especially the Lutheran and Anglican—began publishing Bibles with the Apocrypha set apart from "the best books." Protestants generally believed that the apocryphal books offered helpful advice on how to live, but were not reliable enough to dictate doctrinal beliefs.

Roman Catholics responded sternly and decisively at the Council of Trent in 1546 by formally adding 12 contested apocryphal books to the canon, then vowing to excommunicate anyone who "does not accept as sacred and canonical the aforesaid books in their entirety." This collection became known among Catholics as deuterocanonical, meaning "added to the canon." The 12 are Tobit, Judith, additions to Esther, Wisdom of Solomon, Sirach, Baruch, Letter of Jeremiah, three additions to Daniel, and 1 and 2 Maccabees. In 1592 three other books denied canonical status—the Prayer of Manasseh along with 1 and 2 Esdras—were added to the Vulgate, not as a further expansion of the canon, but "lest they should perish altogether."

Included and Excluded

Protestants began debating what to do with the apocryphal books, sequestered and reduced to a low status in their Bibles. Beginning in 1549, the Church of England tried to find a use for them by developing lessons from selected chapters of the Apocrypha and publishing them in the lectionary that accompanied the Book of Common Prayer. On the other hand, Puritans did not want the Apocrypha in the Bible at all. In fact, the first English Bible that excluded the Apocrypha was a 1599 edition of the Geneva Bible—which quickly became the favored translation among Puritans.

When the now acclaimed King James Version of the Bible was completed in 1611, it included the Apocrypha. But within four years, printers began dropping the disputed section, perhaps to save money. The archbishop of Canterbury—one of the version's translators—was furious. In 1615 he issued public notices that anyone caught binding and selling Bibles without the Apocrypha risked a year's imprisonment. Yet the practice continued. During the centuries that followed, Bibles without the Apocrypha came to outnumber by far Bibles with it.

Today, Bibles produced for Roman Catholics weave the deuterocanonical writings among other books of the Old Testament (see page 434). The Eastern Orthodox church, which broke with the Roman church during the Crusades, in A.D. 1054, accepts all books in the Catholic Bible and adds more. Some Bible editions try to attract readers from diverse Christian traditions—Protestant, Catholic, and Orthodox—by publishing all these apocryphal books between the Old and New Testaments.

Though Christians still debate the value of the Apocrypha—and cannot even agree on which books make up the collection—these fascinating texts help trace Jewish history and the blossoming of new beliefs in the era between the Old and New Testaments. For instance, 2 Maccabees introduces the idea of a bodily resurrection—a teaching not found in the Old Testament, but central to the New Testament. For reasons such as these, the Apocrypha has a prominent role in helping people better understand some of the important traditions shared by Jews and Christians.

The book of Tobit is a romance—a tale of a successful quest for money and a bride. The unjust tribulations and ultimate triumph of Tobit, a pious and generous Jew, and his beautiful cousin Sarah demonstrate that, though the innocent may suffer, they will be blessed with an even greater reward by God. The book has entertained readers since ancient times, but it is also valued as a glimpse into the social and religious customs of the ordinary Israelites of the Diaspora—the dispersion of the Jews to areas outside Palestine.

Tobit is based on popular folk legends, skillfully interwoven with stories and themes from the Old Testament. Notable among the latter are the betrothal stories of Isaac and Jacob (Gen 24, 29), Job's suffering in the book that bears his name, and the idea of retribution found throughout Deuteronomy. Although the story incorporates well-known places and people, many of these details are inaccurate, indicating that it was probably written long after its setting in the late eighth and early seventh centuries B.C. Indeed, most scholars believe it was composed between 225 and 175 B.C., probably by a Jew in the eastern Diaspora. The original text is thought to have been written in Aramaic, although fragments in Hebrew have been found along with the Aramaic text among the Dead Sea Scrolls.

Tobit is not in the Hebrew Bible. Protestants place the book in the Apocrypha, while Roman Catholics consider it deuterocanonical.

The angel Raphael takes young Tobias by the hand; a sculpture by Veit Stoss (c. 1440-1533).

I, Tobit, walked in the ways of truth and righteousness all the days of my life. TOB 1:3

Tobit hails from Thisbe in Galilee and belongs to the tribe of Naphtali. His kinsmen have rebelled against both the house of David and the divinely ordained temple in Jerusalem; instead, they worship the golden calf that King Jeroboam had erected in Dan (1 Kgs 12:25-33). Tobit alone makes pilgrimages to Jerusalem for festivals, giving the temple priests "the first fruits of the crops and the firstlings of the flock, the tithes of the cattle, and the first shearings of the sheep" (Tob 1:6). When he is grown, he marries a kinswoman named Anna and has a son, Tobias (meaning "Yahweh [God] is my good").

After Assyria conquers the northern kingdom of Israel in 722 B.C., Tobit and his relatives are among the Hebrews deported to Nineveh, the Assyrian capital. There he continues his virtuous lifestyle, refusing to eat forbidden food, giving alms to the poor, feeding the hungry, and clothing the naked. He also provides a proper burial for any Jews who are left unburied, a charitable act that will soon be his undoing. Because of his piety and generosity, God sees that Tobit is promoted to the court of King Shalmaneser. (In reality, Shalmaneser V died in 722 B.C.—before the Israelites were exiled to Assyria. The narrator also errs in naming Sennacherib as Shalmaneser's successor; Shalmaneser was succeeded by Sargon II, who was followed by Sennacherib.)

Once, on a trip to Media to buy supplies for the court, Tobit leaves ten talents of silver—a substantial sum of money—with a man named Gabael for safekeeping. But after Sennacherib assumes the throne, travel becomes too dangerous for Tobit to return to reclaim his money.

Sennacherib's rule brings other dangers, too. The king murders many Israelites and contemptuously leaves them unburied. When Tobit secretly takes them away for burial, Sennacherib quickly learns of it. In a fury, he hunts for Tobit to kill him for his defiance, but Tobit flees. So Sennacherib confiscates all of Tobit's property and possessions, leaving his once prosperous family penniless.

The author says that 40 days after returning from a campaign in Judea, Sennacherib is murdered and succeeded by his son Esarhaddon. (In fact, Sennacherib reigned 20 years after besieging Jerusalem.) Now Tobit's fortunes change, for his nephew Ahikar is appointed to a high position in Esarhaddon's court and intercedes for his uncle. (The character Ahikar comes from the ancient legend of Ahiqar, which tells of a wise man who is falsely accused of treason by his adopted son—called Nadab in Tobit 14:10—but later exonerated.) Tobit can now return home.

During the reign of Esarhaddon I returned home, and my wife Anna and my son Tobias were restored to me. TOB 2:1

In spite of what has befallen him, Tobit continues to be pious. On the festival of Pentecost, he tells his son, Tobias, to go out and bring any poor, God-fearing Jews to share their meal. But Tobias returns saying, "One of our own people has been murdered and thrown into the market place, and now he lies there strangled" (Tob 2:3). Tobit brings the body to his house and buries it after sunset, even though his neighbors mock him for doing the very thing for which Sennacherib had wanted to kill him.

Tobit sleeps in his courtyard that night because contact with a corpse makes one ritually unclean. As he slumbers, sparrow droppings fall into his eyes, creating a white film. Although he consults doctor after doctor, he is soon completely blind. (Tobit's charitable act and misfortune are apparently based on the folktale of the Grateful Dead, about a man who faces danger because of burying a corpse but is later rewarded by the dead man's spirit.)

Tobit is supported by Ahikar until the latter moves to Elymais, and by Anna, who takes on domestic work—a great humiliation for the former courtier's wife. One day, Tobit accuses Anna of stealing a goat that she has brought home. She protests that it is a gift from someone she works for, but Tobit does not believe her. Anna angrily says to him, "Where are your acts of charity? Where are your righteous deeds?" (Tob 2:14), implying that all his generosity has only led them to this pitiful state.

His wife's reproach and the derision of his neighbors so aggrieves Tobit that he begs God for death. In prayer, he acknowledges that Israel has willfully disobeyed God's commands and has been justly punished with exile. But, he protests, any sins he has committed were unintentional and he prefers death to a life of unfair punishment: "It is better for me to die than to see so much distress in my life" (Tob 3:6).

Sarah, the daughter of Raguel . . . . had been married to seven husbands, and the wicked demon Asmodeus had killed each of them. TOB 3:7-8

Now the author turns to the tragic plight of Sarah, Tobit's kinswoman in the distant city of Ecbatana, who is also unjustly tormented. Sarah's seven husbands have all been killed before the marriages could be consummated. (Her story comes from the folk legend "The Bride of the Monster," in which a demon who cannot have the woman he desires kills his rivals on their wedding nights.) When one of her father's maids says to her, "You are the one who kills your husbands!" (Tob 3:8), Sarah decides to hang herself. She reconsiders when she thinks of the anguish and shame this will cause her father, and instead prays to God that she may die and be spared her suffering, in part because she believes there is no other "close relative or other kindred for whom I should keep myself as wife" (Tob 3:15).

God hears the prayers of both Sarah and Tobit, and sends the angel Raphael (meaning "God heals" or "Heal, O God!") to help them. The author reveals that Tobit will regain his vision and Sarah will be freed from the evil embrace of the demon Asmodeus. The reader also learns that there is one eligible kinsman left to marry Sarah: Tobit's son, Tobias.

ANGELS OF THE LORD

Delivering messages, punishing the wicked, helping the afflicted, angels are celestial beings who serve God in various ways. The Bible's first mention of an angel is the one who comforts the maid Hagar after she flees the wrath of Sarah (Gen 16:7). Often, the angel of the Lord appears to be none other than God himself; Exodus uses the terms interchangeably to describe the divine presence traveling before the Israelites (Ex 13:21, 14:19).

Though angels appear throughout the Bible, only five are named: Gabriel and Michael in the Old Testament; Raphael, Uriel, and Jeremiel in the Apocrypha. Gabriel, the angel who interpreted Daniel's visions, also appears in the New Testament, announcing the births of John the Baptist and Jesus in the Gospel of Luke. Michael also appears in both testaments: He is the guardian of Israel in Daniel, a warrior fighting with the devil for Moses' body in the letter of Jude, and the leader of righteous angels in a battle with Satan in Revelation. Raphael, at first in disguise, appears in Tobit; Uriel and Jeremiel are archangels who interpret Ezra's vision in 2 Esdras.

References to cherubim, seraphim, and archangels led many early Christians to conclude there was a celestial hierarchy. Raphael describes himself as "one of the seven angels who stand ready and enter before the glory of God" (Tob 12:15). The Bible does not speak of guardian angels, but the idea may have emerged from Jesus' words about children: "Their angels continually see the face of my Father in heaven" (Mt 18:10).

The Italian artist Verrocchio (1435-1488) gave Raphael and Tobias two angelic companions: Michael (in armor at left) and Gabriel (with lily at right).

*As instructed by his traveling companion, Raphael posing as Azariah, Tobias hauls in a huge fish
from the Tigris River; a painting by Rembrandt's teacher, the Dutch artist Pieter Lastman (1583-1633).*

*That same day Tobit remembered the money that he had
left in trust with Gabael at Rages in Media.*   TOB 4:1

Since Tobit believes he is about to die, he calls Tobias to tell him about the money, which would solve the family's financial problems. He also delivers his last testament, a series of instructions—reminiscent of wisdom literature—on how to live a righteous life. These include giving his father a proper burial, honoring his mother, following the commandments, paying wages promptly, and drinking wine only in moderation. Tobit particularly emphasizes giving alms to the poor, saying, "Do not turn your face away from anyone who is poor, and the face of God will not be turned away from you" (Tob 4:7). This is ironic, since Tobit's generous almsgiving has not prevented his poverty and blindness.

He counsels Tobias to take a wife from his father's tribe, and reminds him that their ancestors—Noah, Abraham, Isaac, and Jacob—married kinswomen. This practice, known as endogamy, was intended to preserve the religious and cultural identity of the Israelites, even in exile.

In the earliest appearance of the Golden Rule in scripture, Tobit advises: "And what you hate, do not do to anyone" (Tob 4:15). This is essentially the formula stated by the great first-century B.C. Jewish teacher Hillel: "Do not do to another what you would not wish done to yourself." Jesus turned it into a positive statement (Mt 7:12; Lk 6:31).

Tobit again emphasizes that Tobias should feed and clothe the needy, but if they are sinners, it is better to leave food on the graves of the righteous (an obscure practice). Lastly, Tobit tells Tobias about the money that had been left with Gabael.

*Then Tobias answered his father Tobit, "I will do
everything that you have commanded me, father; but how
can I obtain the money from him?"*   TOB 5:1-2

Tobit responds that Gabael had given him his written pledge, and that he had divided it in two, keeping half and leaving the other half with the money. But Tobias does not know the way to Media, so his father sends him out to hire a guide. He quickly encounters the angel Raphael. Tobias and his family, however, do not know who Raphael is, which leads to humorous double meanings. Raphael claims to be one of Tobit's kinsmen, saying that he can take Tobias to Media and indeed even to the house of Gabael, since he has stayed there many times.

When Tobias tells his father about Raphael, Tobit insists on meeting him to make sure he is trustworthy. He asks Raphael what family he comes from, and the angel responds, "I am Azariah, the son of the great Hananiah, one of your relatives" (Tob 5:13). Tobit is delighted that a kinsman will be guiding Tobias, and asks God's blessing on them for a safe journey.

But Tobias's mother weeps, afraid that, in their quest for money, they will lose their son forever. Tobit tries to reassure her, saying, "Do not fear for them, my sister. For a good angel will accompany him" (Tob 5:21-22). Little does he know that Tobias is indeed in the care of "a good angel."

The young man went out and the angel went with him.
TOB 6:1

On the first night of their journey, Tobias and Raphael camp on the banks of the Tigris River. (This is another inaccuracy, since the Tigris is west of Nineveh, the opposite of the direction in which they were traveling.) Tobias is washing his travel-weary feet in the river when a huge fish jumps out of the water and attacks him. Raphael says, "Catch hold of the fish and hang on to it!" (Tob 6:4). Tobias is able to drag the fish onto land. The angel tells him to cut the fish open and remove its gall, heart, and liver, which can be used as medicine. When they resume their travels, the angel explains: "As for the fish's heart and liver, you must burn them to make a smoke in the presence of a man or woman afflicted by a demon or evil spirit, and every affliction will flee away" (Tob 6:8). The gall, he says, can be used to remove white film from a person's eyes.

As they approach Ecbatana, the capital of Media, Raphael says that they will spend the night at the home of Tobias's kinsman Raguel. He tells Tobias of Raguel's beautiful and virtuous daughter Sarah, saying that Tobias has the right to claim her in marriage and that Raphael will arrange it. But Tobias has heard about Sarah's seven previous husbands, and is understandably afraid of sharing their fate. Raphael reminds him of his father's instruction to marry a kinswoman. Besides, he knows of some magic that will protect Tobias: When he enters the bridal chamber, he should put some of the fish's liver and heart on the incense ashes; the foul odor will chase the demon from Sarah's presence forever. But magic alone will not save the young couple; Tobias and Sarah must also pray to God, begging for his mercy and safekeeping. The angel adds, "Do not be afraid, for she was set apart for you before the world was made" (Tob 6:18).

Raguel and his wife, Edna, welcome Tobias with great joy when they learn that he is the son of Tobit. They prepare a welcoming meal, but Tobias is anxious to have the marriage arranged first. Raguel agrees to give Sarah to Tobias in marriage, but, being an honest man, he offers Tobias a way out by telling him of the tragedy that befell her other husbands. Still, Tobias is determined, so Raguel summons Sarah and says, "Take her to be your wife in accordance with the law and decree written in the book of Moses" (Tob 7:12). He then writes out a marriage contract. (According to rabbinic tradition, it was the bridegroom who wrote out the marriage contract.)

Edna prepares the bridal chamber, weeping because she fears that Tobias's destiny is the same as that of Sarah's other seven husbands. Parting from her daughter, she urges Sarah to be courageous.

When they had finished eating and drinking they wanted to retire; so they took the young man and brought him into the bedroom. TOB 8:1

Following the angel's instructions, Tobias takes the liver and heart of the fish and burns them in the incense ashes. The smell is so repellent that it drives the demon "to the remotest parts of Egypt" (Tob 8:3). But Raphael follows him there and catches and binds him—a traditional technique for incapacitating a demon in folklore.

Tobias and Sarah pray, blessing the institution of marriage and begging God for a long life together. Meanwhile, Raguel has so little faith in Tobias's survival that he has his servants dig a grave so the groom can be buried before the neighbors find out about the latest nuptials. Then he sends a maid into the couple's bedroom to see what has happened to Tobias. She announces the miraculous news that both are alive and well. After Raguel blesses God for his compassion, he has his servants fill in the grave before anyone notices it.

The happy parents set about to prepare the wedding feast. Raguel summons Tobias and insists that he stay and celebrate the wedding for 14 days. This was double the traditional length of a wedding feast, an indication of Raguel's great relief and joy. He then gives half his property and possessions to his new son-in-law, with the promise of the other half when he and Edna die.

A pet curled at their feet, Tobias and Sarah fall asleep on their wedding night; an intimate scene worked in stained glass by a 16th-century German artisan.

Then Tobias called Raphael and said to him ". . . . Go to the home of Gabael, give him the bond, get the money, and then bring him with you to the wedding celebration."   TOB 9:1-2

Tobias knows that his delay will worry his father, so he sends Raphael with four servants and two camels to Gabael's house for the money. Like all the story's characters except the demon Asmodeus, Gabael is honest. He unhesitatingly counts out the money for Raphael and helps him load it on the camels. The next morning he goes with the angel to the wedding feast, where he blesses Tobias's marriage: "Good and noble son of a father good and noble, upright and generous! . . . I see in Tobias the very image of my cousin Tobit" (Tob 9:6).

Happily married, Tobias and Sarah set out for Nineveh; a 14th-century Italian artist put them on horseback and dressed them in typical Renaissance costumes.

But Anna is convinced that he is dead, and she mourns him, saying, "Woe to me, my child, the light of my eyes, that I let you make the journey" (Tob 10:5). In her distraught state, she spends her days watching by the side of the road and her nights weeping and mourning.

When the 14 days of the wedding feast have ended, Tobias begs his father-in-law to send him home to his parents. But Raguel is reluctant to part with his daughter and his new son-in-law, and asks him to stay longer, offering to send messengers to Tobit so he knows of his son's whereabouts. But Tobias again begs to be sent home. So Raguel loads up half his property, including slaves, livestock, money, and household items. In a moving farewell to a daughter they may never see again, Raguel and Edna instruct Sarah to honor her father- and mother-in-law, since they are now her parents. Likewise, they call Tobias their son, and he vows always to honor them.

Now, day by day, Tobit kept counting how many days Tobias would need for going and for returning.   TOB 10:1

The mood is far from festive in Tobit's home, since he and Anna have no knowledge of what is keeping their son. Tobit grows increasingly anxious, although he consoles himself with the thought that some unexpected problem has delayed Tobias.

A kneeling Tobias and his father, Tobit, are amazed at Raphael's rejection of their gift and the revelation of his true identity.

When they came near to Kaserin, which is opposite Nineveh, Raphael said, ". . . . Let us run ahead of your wife and prepare the house while they are still on the way."   TOB 11:1, 3

From her station by the road, Anna sees Tobias and Raphael approaching and calls out the news to her husband. As they draw near to Tobit, Raphael tells Tobias, "Smear the gall of the fish on his eyes; the medicine will make the white films shrink and peel off from his eyes, and your father will regain his sight" (Tob 11:8). Tobias follows his instructions, and Tobit—his sight indeed restored—praises God, saying, "Though he afflicted me, he has had mercy upon me" (Tob 11:15).

Tobias gives his father the happy news of his marriage to Raguel's daughter, Sarah. The overjoyed Tobit goes to the gate of Nineveh to welcome his new daughter-in-law. Passersby are amazed at his miraculous transformation and learn that it was God who cured his blindness. Tobit welcomes Sarah as a daughter, and a wedding feast is held for seven days.

When the wedding celebration was ended, Tobit called his son Tobias and said to him, "My child, see to paying the wages of the man who went with you, and give him a bonus as well."   TOB 12:1

Tobias intends to give Raphael much more than the one drachma a day originally agreed upon, offering him half of the possessions he brought back with him in payment for all he has done. But Raphael calls Tobias and Tobit aside and reveals his identity: "I

*Having secured a wife for Tobias and cured Tobit's blindness, the angel Raphael
extends a blessing to the two men he has served so well and bids them farewell as he
ascends to heaven; the dramatic scene was painted by Pieter Lastman.*

am Raphael, one of the seven angels who stand ready
and enter before the glory of the Lord" (Tob 12:15).

Father and son fall to the ground with fear.
Raphael tells them to bless God forever, as he is carrying out God's will. He adds that everything they
see him do is an illusion—including eating and
drinking. (As spiritual beings, angels had no need of
food.) He directs Tobit to write down all that has
happened, then ascends into the air and disappears.

Tobit sings a hymn of praise to God, and calls on
the Israelites to do the same, for their situation parallels his. They have sinned and have been punished,
but if they wholeheartedly repent, God will show
them mercy.

*[Tobit] was sixty-two years old when he lost his
eyesight, and after regaining it he lived in prosperity,
giving alms and continually blessing God.* TOB 14:2

Tobit lives an exemplary life until his death at
the venerable age of 112. On his deathbed, he
summons Tobias and his seven grandsons and instructs them to leave Nineveh for Media. Israel's de-

liverance is at hand, he says, beginning with the destruction of Nineveh and fall of the Assyrian empire,
as foretold by the prophet Nahum. (The capture of
Nineveh by the Babylonians and Medes in 612 B.C.
was the death knell of Assyria.) Tobit predicts that
the Israelites will again be exiled and the temple will
be destroyed, but that God will once again have
mercy and restore his chosen people to Jerusalem.
The temple will be rebuilt, and "the nations in the
whole world will all be converted and worship God
in truth" (Tob 14:6). In the postexilic period in which
Tobit was most likely written, the end of the Diaspora, as foretold by prophets such as Isaiah, and the
universal acceptance of Judaism were widely held
beliefs among pious Jews.

When Tobit and Anna die, Tobias gives them an
honorable burial, then moves his family to Ecbatana,
settling with his father-in-law. Upon Raguel's death,
Tobias inherits the rest of his property, adding to his
substantial wealth. Tobias himself dies at the age of
117, but not before witnessing the fall of Nineveh
and the taking of its people into captivity, the first
step on the long road to the salvation of Israel.

A beautiful and pious widow risks her life to save the Israelites from destruction—that is the gripping folktale contained in the book of Judith. The story is the most ironic of those found in the Bible, beginning with the premise, in a patriarchal era, that God would destroy Israel's enemy by the hand of a woman. Yet, the story has a precedent. In the book of Judges, it is a woman, the prophetess Deborah, who rouses Israel to throw off the Canaanite yoke. And it is a woman, Jael, who slays the enemy commander Sisera.

Most scholars believe that Judith was written by a Palestinian Jew in the late second or early first century B.C. Although it was likely written in Hebrew, it has been found only in its Greek translation, in the Septuagint. The backdrop is thought to have been a period of national crisis: the tyranny over the Jews by the Seleucid tyrant Antiochus IV Epiphanes (175-164 B.C.), and the defeat of his general, Nicanor, by Judas Maccabeus.

Judith was excluded from the Hebrew canon, probably because the book presents several problems, especially concerning the character of its protagonist. Although Judith is described as God-fearing, virtuous, and observant, in her quest to save her people she lies, becomes a skilled seductress, and finally brutally assassinates the enemy leader. To the author, however, Judith is a heroine (her name is the feminine of Jew or Judean), and her objectionable tactics are more than justified by her courageous accomplishment.

The book also has historical problems. The story covers a period of about two months, but includes events that span five centuries. It is equally confused geographically, jumbling real cities and topographical features together with fictional ones. This may have been done intentionally by the author as a clear signal that the story is not historical.

Judith's 16 chapters have a chiastic, or crisscross, pattern. Certain events in the first part (chapters 1:1-7:32) are repeated internally in reverse order, as are some events in the second part (chapters 8:1-16:25).

Judith gives her maid the head of Holofernes; a painting by Lucas Cranach the Elder (1472-1553).

Nebuchadnezzar, king of the Assyrians, called Holofernes, the chief general of his army, second only to himself, and said to him, ". . . . March out against all the land to the west, because they disobeyed my orders." JDT 2:4, 6

*N*ebuchadnezzar has ordered Persia and the nations to the west to help him wage war on King Arphaxad of Media, but they refuse, "for they were not afraid of him, but regarded him as only one man" (Jdt 1:11). (In reality, Nebuchadnezzar was the king of Babylonia, not of Assyria, and Arphaxad is unknown.) After he defeats Arphaxad without any help, Nebuchadnezzar and his vast armies celebrate their victory for 120 days. Then he turns his attention to exacting revenge on the disobedient lands.

The king assigns Holofernes an army of 120,000 troops on foot and 12,000 on horseback, and commissions him to besiege every land that refuses him and hold it for the king. Should any people resist, they are to be slaughtered and their country plundered. "Tell them to prepare earth and water" (Jdt 2:7), Nebuchadnezzar says, referring to tokens of submission traditionally demanded by Persian kings.

From Nineveh to Damascus, Holofernes and his troops cut a swath of destruction and death, burning crops and destroying herds, plundering towns, and killing all who resist. Holofernes's fierce reputation convinces the people of the Phoenician coast to surrender, and they welcome him with dancing and garlands. And, as commissioned by the king, the general destroys their shrines "so that all nations should worship Nebuchadnezzar alone" (Jdt 3:8). Then the army moves to the great plain of Esdraelon, within striking distance of Judea, where it rests for a month and is resupplied.

When the Israelites living in Judea heard of everything that Holofernes . . . had done to the nations, and how he had plundered and destroyed all their temples, they were therefore greatly terrified at his approach. JDT 4:1-2

*T*o the Jews, Holofernes is both a military and a religious threat. According to the author's inaccurate history, they are newly returned from exile and their temple is recently restored. Although the Jews are a small and weak group faced by a powerful enemy, they are determined to defend themselves. So they prepare for war, spreading the alarm to all the regions of Samaria, fortifying strategic hilltop villages, and storing food from the recent harvest.

The high priest in Jerusalem, Joakim, writes to the residents of Bethulia, a town opposite the plain on which Holofernes is encamped, instructing them to seize the narrow mountain passes so the invading army cannot advance. Then all the men, women, and children fast and put ashes on their heads and sackcloth around their waists—and on their animals. They also cover the altar in sackcloth and pray for help to God, who hears their pleas.

It was reported to Holofernes . . . that the people of Israel had prepared for war. JDT 5:1

The general is outraged, and calls together his commanders to ask who these defiant people are. Achior, the Ammonite leader, steps forward and recites a basically factual history of the Israelites, from Abraham through the Exodus from Egypt to the return from exile in Babylon. He cautions Holofernes that "the God who hates iniquity is with them" (Jdt 5:17); as long as they do not sin against their God, he reports, they cannot be defeated.

Holofernes roars in response, "What god is there except Nebuchadnezzar? He will send his forces and destroy them from the face of the earth" (Jdt 6:2). In his anger at Achior's message, Holofernes orders the Ammonite bound and handed over to the Jews of Bethulia, where he will share their fate.

The Bethulians untie the Ammonite and lead him before a town council led by Uzziah, where he truthfully tells them of Holofernes's boast to destroy them. The Bethulians praise Achior and Uzziah fetes him with a banquet. But the townspeople spend an uneasy night praying for God's help.

The next day Holofernes ordered his whole army . . . to break camp and move against Bethulia . . . and make war on the Israelites. JDT 7:1

When the Israelites see the vast army swarm across the plain and camp near their spring, terror seizes them. Nevertheless, they arm themselves and remain on guard throughout the night. The next day, Holofernes's commanders announce that they have a plan for overcoming the Israelites without the loss of a single one of their own soldiers: "Let your servants take possession of the spring of water that flows from the foot of the mountain, for this is where all the people of Bethulia get their water" (Jdt 7:12-13). They also propose that troops guard the mountain passes to make sure that none of the Israelites can flee. Before long, the people of Bethulia will succumb to thirst and starvation. Holofernes follows this advice and orders his men to seize the springs and block any escape routes for the Bethulians. Encamped before the town, the Assyrian army "spread out in great number, and they formed a multitude" (Jdt 7:18).

The Israelites then cried out to the Lord their God, for their courage failed, because all their enemies had surrounded them, and there was no way of escape from them. JDT 7:19

For 34 days Bethulia is besieged, until the cisterns are running dry and people are collapsing from thirst. The townspeople confront their leaders, saying, "You have done us a great injury in not making peace with the Assyrians. For now we have no one to help us; God has sold us into their hands" (Jdt 7:24-25). They believe that the Lord has forsaken them in punishment for their sins or the sins of their ancestors. They demand that the leaders surrender the town to Holofernes, reasoning that slavery and apostasy are preferable to death.

But Uzziah pleads with them to hold out for five more days, for by then God will surely help them. He promises, however, that if nothing has happened in that time, he will surrender.

THE WRONG KING

Judith begins with a bold historical error. In the first verse, the author calls Nebuchadnezzar the ruler of Assyria; in fact, he was the king of Babylon, the empire that defeated Assyria. Jews knew him well as the despot behind the greatest tragedy in their nation's history: In 586 B.C., Nebuchadnezzar destroyed Jerusalem and razed Solomon's temple, then exiled the survivors to Babylon. This blatant mistake, followed by others that compress historical facts from several centuries and refer to unknown geographical locations, may have been intentional—to give Jews a compelling, if fictional, model for resisting foreign oppressors in the second century B.C.

There are other questionable historical details in both the Old and New Testaments. For example, Ezra 2 and Nehemiah 7 both report the number of Jews returning from their Babylonian exile as 42,360—but their numbers do not add up. The discrepancies can perhaps be attributed to careless scribes. Scholars also ponder the reliability of the report in the Gospel of Luke that Mary and Joseph went to Bethlehem in response to a census ordered by Quirinius, governor of Syria. Roman records indicate that Quirinius did not become governor until A.D. 6, a decade or so after Jesus was born. Herod, the Judean king who tried to find and kill Jesus, died in 4 B.C.

The Bible is not primarily a historical work, but an account of God's dealings with humanity. Yet it does contain a wealth of accurate history—often to the surprise of skeptics who have written off biblical material as myth.

Now in those days Judith heard about these things.
JDT 8:1

Nearly halfway into the book, the heroine is introduced. The author lists her genealogy and states that her husband, Manasseh, died of sunstroke. For three years and four months Judith has been a widow. Although she is beautiful and wealthy, she lives an ascetic life, dressing in widow's clothing and sackcloth, fasting rigorously, praying, and observing all of God's commandments.

Judith summons the leaders of Bethulia and rebukes them for the promise they made to the townspeople: "Who are you to put God to the test today, and to set yourselves up in the place of God in human affairs?" (Jdt 8:12). She says that instead they should beg the Lord for mercy; it is up to him to protect them or destroy them.

She denies that God has forsaken them, for they have been loyal to him. Furthermore, she reminds them that, if Bethulia capitulates, there will be nothing to block the destruction of Jerusalem's temple.

"Therefore, my brothers, let us set an example for our kindred, for their lives depend upon us." JDT 8:24

She says they should thank God, for he is testing them, as he tested Abraham and Isaac. Uzziah praises her for her wisdom, but points out that the promise they made the townspeople cannot be broken. He urges her to pray for them; perhaps, then, God will send rain to fill their cisterns. Uzziah is clearly hoping for a miracle.

But Judith has another plan—something so dramatic that word of it will be passed on for generations. "Stand at the town gate tonight so that I may go out with my maid; and within the days after which you have promised to surrender the town to our enemies, the Lord will deliver Israel by my hand" (Jdt 8:33). That is all she will tell them.

Then Judith prostrated herself, put ashes on her head, and uncovered the sackcloth she was wearing. JDT 9:1

Judith begins to pray, invoking her ancestor Simeon, the son of Jacob, who, with his brother, Levi, avenged the rape of their sister Dinah (Gen 34:25-26). She asks God for the same support in her quest to prevent the violation of the Israelites and the temple. She acknowledges that God controls history, and asks that he give her the strength to carry out her plan, calling him the God of the lowly and hopeless. Indeed, the very fact that a weak woman will cause the downfall of the powerful Assyrians is considered especially disgraceful for them. "Make my deceitful words bring wound and bruise on those who have planned cruel things against your covenant, and against your house" (Jdt 9:13), Judith prays. Some biblical commentators have criticized this prayer—asking for God's help in deceit—as morally wrong.

When Judith had stopped crying out to the God of Israel . . . . she made herself very beautiful, to entice the eyes of all the men who might see her. JDT 10:1, 4

Judith bathes, puts on perfumed ointment, and ornaments herself with rings, earrings, bracelets, and a tiara. Then she and her maid gather up food and dishes (in order to follow Jewish dietary laws even among the Assyrians) and go to the town gate. When Uzziah and the town elders see her approach, they are astonished at her beauty. They bless her efforts and let her pass through the gates.

Judith and her maid are soon stopped by an Assyrian patrol; she tells them she is fleeing from the Israelites because they are soon to be destroyed. Judith asks to see Holofernes, "to give him a true report" (Jdt 10:13). The soldiers are so mesmerized by her appearance that they personally escort her to Holofernes's tent. As news of her arrival travels ahead, soldiers gather to admire her beauty.

Dressed in her finest, the disingenuous Judith beguiles the unsuspecting Assyrian commander, Holofernes; a painting by Jan van den Hoecke (1611-1651).

When Judith came into the presence of Holofernes and his servants, they all marveled at the beauty of her face.
JDT 10:23

Holofernes seeks to put her at ease by saying that he has never hurt anyone who was willing to worship Nebuchadnezzar as god. This, of course, is a lie, and Judith lies in return, promising, "I will say nothing false to my lord this night" (Jdt 11:5). She goes on to flatter Holofernes, calling him the wisest and most skilled warrior in the whole world.

She tells Holofernes that Achior's words were true—the Israelites cannot be harmed unless they sin against their God. But, she says, they are about to do just that. Since they are succumbing to thirst and starvation, they have decided to eat food forbidden to them: "the first fruits of the grain and the tithes of the wine and oil, which they had consecrated and set aside for the priests who minister in the presence of our God in Jerusalem" (Jdt 11:13). They are simply awaiting permission from the council of elders in Jerusalem, which will arrive soon. On the day that they commit this sin, she says, the Assyrians will be able to destroy them with ease.

Judith assures the general, "God has sent me to accomplish with you things that will astonish the whole world" (Jdt 11:16), which surely means something different to the smitten general than to Judith. She establishes that she will stay in Holofernes's camp, but every night she will go into the valley to pray to God, who will tell her when the Israelites commit their sin. Then she will inform Holofernes, and he and his army can launch their attack.

I will lead you through Judea, until you come to Jerusalem; there I will set your throne. JDT 11:19

Holofernes is delighted with what she tells him, and he and his advisers marvel that one so beautiful can also possess such great wisdom. Ironically, Holofernes did not believe Achior, who spoke the truth, but he does believe Judith, who is lying. Holofernes promises her, "If you do as you have said, your God shall be my God, and you shall live in the palace of King Nebuchadnezzar" (Jdt 11:23). Holofernes can also lie: Given that he has already proclaimed the king to be the only god, it seems unlikely that he would ever worship the Hebrew God.

The general invites Judith to dine with him, but she declines, saying that she must eat the food she brought with her. That night, she rises at midnight and asks to be allowed to go out and pray. Holofernes orders the guards to let her go. She walks into the

Judith's gruesome dispatch of Holofernes is shown in this scene by Michelangelo da Caravaggio (1573-1610).

valley, purifies herself in the spring, and prays to the Lord for his help. Each night for three nights she follows the same pattern.

On the fourth day Holofernes . . . said to Bagoas, the eunuch who had charge of his personal affairs, "Go and persuade the Hebrew woman who is in your care to join us and to eat and drink with us."
JDT 12:10-11

Holofernes thinks that this will give him the opportunity to seduce Judith. Bagoas delivers the message to Judith, who pretends that the invitation gives her great pleasure. She dresses herself in her finest clothes and is admitted to Holofernes's tent. The general's passion is aroused when he sees her, and he urges her to drink and be merry. She says that she will be delighted to do so, and eats and drinks what her maid has prepared. In his excitement, Holofernes drinks a great deal, "much more than he had ever drunk in any one day since he was born" (Jdt 12:20).

At the end of the long evening, everyone withdraws from the tent, leaving Judith alone with the now drunk and comatose Holofernes. Judith's maid waits outside. Seizing her opportunity, the brave widow takes Holofernes's sword, prays, "Give me strength today, O Lord God of Israel!" (Jdt 13:7), and with two strokes, cuts off the general's head. Holofernes had intended to overcome Judith, but just the opposite has happened. She takes the bed canopy as proof, and gives the severed head to her maid to put in the food bag. Then the two of them go out of the camp, as if to pray.

But instead of going to the valley, they go up the mountain to Bethulia. Judith calls to the sentries to open the gates, and all the townspeople and elders come running at the sound of her voice, for they have long since given her up for dead. Before their unbelieving eyes, Judith pulls Holofernes's head from the bag, and says, "The Lord has struck him down by the hand of a woman" (Jdt 13:15). She swears that her honor is intact, that she seduced him with her face alone. The people all immediately bow down and praise God, and Uzziah praises Judith for her courage and piety.

Then Judith said to them, "Listen to me, my friends. Take this head and hang it upon the parapet of your wall."
JDT 14:1

When the sun comes up, Judith tells the people that the men must arm themselves and go out as if to do battle with the Assyrians. The Assyrians will try to awaken Holofernes and find him dead. In their panic, they will flee. "Then you and all who live within the borders of Israel will pursue them and cut them down in their tracks" (Jdt 14:4).

But Judith asks first for Achior, so that he may see the man who threatened him with death. When Achior beholds Holofernes's head, he is so overcome that he faints. After he is revived, he falls at Judith's feet and blesses her. Then he asks her how this came about. She tells him—and all the people assembled—about her exploits. After hearing this, Achior believes in the greatness of Israel's God and converts to Judaism. (In fact, the Ammonites were enemies of Israel from their years of wilderness wandering, and Deuteronomy 23:3 forbids their conversion to Judaism. This may have been a factor in excluding the book of Judith from the Hebrew canon.)

The Israelites hang the head on the town wall, then take their weapons and advance on the Assyrian camp. The Assyrian sentries notify the generals, who tell Bagoas to waken Holofernes, "for the slaves have been so bold as to come down against us to give battle, to their utter destruction" (Jdt 14:13). Bagoas discovers the headless body; weeping and tearing his clothes, he rushes to Judith's tent and finds her gone. Then he realizes her treachery. When the leaders find out, there is a great cry of dismay in the camp, and the soldiers flee in fear.

When the Israelites heard it, with one accord they fell upon the enemy, and cut them down as far as Choba.
JDT 15:5

The Bethulians and Israelites from the whole region plunder the Assyrian camp for 30 days, giving Judith all the treasure from Holofernes's tent. The high priest Joakim and the elders come from Jerusalem to see Judith and bless her heroic deed, saying, "You have done all this with your own hand; you have done great good to Israel, and God is well pleased with it" (Jdt 15:10).

Then the women of Israel celebrate, dancing in Judith's honor and crowning each other with olive wreaths (a Greek custom). The men follow, singing and wearing garlands, and they all set off in a procession to Jerusalem.

Judith began this thanksgiving before all Israel, and all the people loudly sang this song of praise. JDT 15:14

In her psalm, Judith calls on the Israelites to worship God and praises him as their deliverer. She retells the story of the threat by the Assyrian army and its downfall at the "hand of a woman" and concludes with a warning, "Woe to the nations that rise up against my people! The Lord Almighty will take vengeance on them in the day of judgment" (Jdt 16:17).

Upon reaching Jerusalem, the Bethulians make offerings at the altar, and Judith gives Holofernes's possessions to the temple priests. After three months of feasting and praying, the residents of Bethulia return home.

For the rest of her life, Judith is regarded with great honor. Many men seek to marry her, but she remains a widow and resumes her solitary life. Before her death at 105, she frees her maid and distributes her husband's property to his kindred and to her own, in accordance with Mosaic Law. The book ends with a note of great hope for the Israelites: "No one ever again spread terror among the Israelites during the lifetime of Judith, or for a long time after her death" (Jdt 16:25). By following Judith's example of complete trust in God coupled with active resistance to oppressors, the Israelites will be free.

Returning home to Bethulia, a triumphant Judith proudly displays her grisly trophy to her fellow Jews; a painting by Francesco Solimena (1657-1717).

*D*espite its name, the Wisdom of Solomon was not written by the renowned king who ruled Israel in the tenth century B.C. Rather, an anonymous learned Jew, well-versed in Old Testament traditions yet schooled in Greek literary styles, wrote the book some ten centuries after Solomon's reign, perhaps about the time of Jesus. The pretense of Solomon's authorship bestowed on the book a special kind of legitimacy and authority in the Jewish community. As its title also suggests, the book is a compilation of wisdom literature in its various forms: proverbs, instructions, and exhortations of the kind found in such other biblical wisdom books as Proverbs and Ecclesiastes. The book contains many ideas shared with nonbiblical wisdom literature, which emphasizes the importance of careful speech, righteous conduct, emotional restraint, and sexual continence. The author's passion is channeled into a platonic desire for Dame Wisdom, the personification who first appears in chapter 6 and whose virtues are enumerated in chapter 10.

Although there is no clear indication of where the book was written, scholars suppose that its author lived in Alexandria, Egypt, a major center of Diaspora Judaism during the second temple period (538 B.C.-A.D. 70). The argument is supported by the fact that the second half of the book contains a strong polemic against Egypt as Israel's cruel oppressor before the Exodus, possibly a veiled way of condemning the Egyptians' mistreatment of Jews during the Hellenistic era. The book is addressed primarily to fellow Jews in order that they might appreciate their traditional faith and resist total assimilation by Greco-Egyptian culture, always a threat where Jews lived as a minority. The most important avenue for maintaining Jewish identity in second temple times was through learning the sacred texts that constituted the Jewish heritage. The author of the Wisdom of Solomon thus larded his work with allusions to the Hebrew Bible and Jewish scriptural traditions.

Purported author of Wisdom of Solomon, Israel's great monarch studies the Torah in this portrait from a 13th-century French Bible.

Love righteousness, you rulers of the earth, think of the Lord in goodness and seek him with sincerity of heart.
WIS 1:1

The prologue to the Wisdom of Solomon in verses 1-15 introduces one of the recurring themes in wisdom literature: Righteousness earns the gift of wisdom from God, while wickedness results in death and destruction. The first verse does not actually call for righteous acts, however, but exhorts the "rulers of the earth" to love, think, and seek, all verbs involving the heart and will. Right desire is the starting point on the path to wisdom, "for perverse thoughts separate people from God" (Wis 1:3), and God is the source of all wisdom. Separation from God is equated with death, and God "does not delight in the death of the living" (Wis 1:13). God made creation good and does not want to see souls forfeit life by disregarding their relationship with him.

Using a diatribe, a Hellenistic literary form that projects an imaginary discourse with a feigned opponent, the author then concocts the thoughts of the ungodly. They think of life as swift, fleeting, and without purpose. They see no larger meaning in life other than to indulge their senses: "Come, therefore, let us enjoy the good things that exist . . . . Let us take our fill of costly wine and perfumes" (Wis 2:6-7). Their cynical attitude leads them to disregard the ethical dictates of the Torah. The ungodly oppress the poor and ignore the needs of the widow. Moreover, the wicked will bait a trap for the righteous man, "because he is inconvenient to us and . . . reproaches us for sins against the law" (Wis 2:12).

But the souls of the righteous are in the hand of God, and no torment will ever touch them. WIS 3:1

The author assures his readers that, no matter what devious plans the wicked may have, the souls of the righteous are protected by God. He goes on to say that even though it may appear to the foolish that the righteous suffer scourges and die, this is not the case. Rather, God is merely testing their mettle, "like gold in the furnace he tried them" (Wis 3:6).

From the more general theme contrasting the righteous with the wicked, the author moves on to discuss various cases that might test people and thereby indicate the degree of their rectitude. Sexual behavior is one arena. The woman who knows she is barren, for example, yet does not succumb to illicit sex, has proved her righteousness. Contrary to the teaching of Ezekiel and Jeremiah, who affirm only individual retribution for sin, the author of Wisdom of Solomon states that the second generation, the "illegitimate seedlings" (Wis 4:3) born of adulterous unions, will be punished for their parents' sins.

They will come with dread when their sins are reckoned up, and their lawless deeds will convict them to their face.
WIS 4:20

*A*final judgment scene vividly contrasts the fate of the wicked with that of the righteous. Like a ship that leaves "no track of its keel in the waves" (Wis 5:10), the wicked will make no imprint on history. Their lives and deeds will come to nothing.

By contrast, the exemplary lives of the righteous will be vindicated. God will reward them for their good deeds. One verse in this passage may anticipate the Christian church's understanding of Jesus' victory over death and the hope of immortality for believers: "The righteous live forever and their reward is with the Lord" (Wis 5:15). The final battle against the chaotic forces of evil will be waged not by humans but by the divine warrior himself. The language and imagery is similar to that of Isaiah, for God is described in military imagery: "The Lord will take his zeal as his whole armor" (Wis 5:17; Isa 59:16-17).

Listen therefore, O kings, and understand; learn, O judges of the ends of the earth.   WIS 6:1

*H*aving established his case that righteousness results in eternal rewards and wickedness in death, the author, "King Solomon," addresses other rulers of the world. He argues that because their power and dominion derive ultimately from the Lord, they, too, must seek out God's wisdom. The beginning of wisdom for Solomon is not the fear of the Lord as it is in Proverbs and Sirach, but "the most sincere desire for instruction" (Wis 6:17).

Solomon then provides the world's rulers with the instruction that they need to learn the ways of wisdom from his words. The author exhibits his knowledge of the scriptures by referring to the story of Solomon's prayer for wisdom in 1 Kings 3:6-9. God grants his request and gives the king "unerring knowledge of what exists" (Wis 7:17).

"O God of my ancestors and Lord of mercy, . . . give me the wisdom that sits by your throne, and do not reject me from among your servants." WIS 9:1, 4

*A*t the center of Wisdom of Solomon is an expanded, interpretive version of King Solomon's original prayer. The author does not simply ask for the abstract gift of wisdom as in 1 Kings 3. Instead,

he asks God, the divine king, to give him "the wisdom that sits by your throne" (Wis 9:4). This personified wisdom is the same Dame Wisdom mentioned in Proverbs 8, who was present at the beginning of creation. Solomon hopes that she might guide him to be as good a king as his father, David.

Although Solomon was one of Israel's greatest kings, here he is humble, calling himself "weak and short-lived, with little understanding of judgment and laws" (Wis 9:5). He acknowledges that he can govern only with wisdom obtained from God.

Wisdom protected the first-formed father of the world, when he alone had been created; she delivered him from his transgression.   WIS 10:1

*C*hapters 10 and 11 describe how Wisdom, still personified as a wise woman, intervened in the lives of Israel's ancestors. No figure is actually named because the book's readers were familiar with all the scriptural examples. The first referred to is Adam, whom Wisdom saved from his sin of eating the forbidden fruit to give him dominion over all living things. Cain, by contrast, disdained Wisdom's restraint and killed his brother in a rage. His sin is cited as the cause of the great Flood. Wisdom then rescued Noah, "steering the righteous man by a paltry piece of wood" (Wis 10:4). Abraham, Lot, Jacob, and Joseph are alluded to as men guided by Wisdom.

"A holy people and blameless race," that is, the Israelites, were also delivered by Wisdom from the Egyptians, "a nation of oppressors" (Wis 10:15). "She brought them over the Red Sea" (Wis 10:18) and vanquished the ungodly enemy by drowning them. The author takes pains to point out that the Egyptians' punishment by drowning illustrates a general principle of divine justice: The wicked are punished by the very instrument through which they sinned. According to Jewish tradition, the Egyptians had tried to drown the firstborn of the Israelites in the Nile.

Wisdom prospered their works by the hand of a holy prophet.   WIS 11:1

*T*he historical review continues with a reference to Moses. Chapter 11 contains the first of seven antitheses that contrast the different ways in which God treated Israel and Egypt. God's chosen leader Moses led the Israelites through the perilous wilderness en route to the promised land. On the way, God provided for the people. When they were thirsty, they prayed to him and "water was given them out of flinty rock" (Wis 11:4). The author sees a special divine purpose at work in Israel's thirsting in the desert. God wanted to give the Israelites a sense of how their own tormenters, the Egyptians, had been punished. But whereas the Israelites were "disciplined in mercy" because their thirst was finally quenched by God, the Egyptians were "tormented when judged in wrath" (Wis 11:9). The author then turns from discussing Israel's history to condemning idolatry.

Miserable, with their hopes set on dead things, are those who give the name "gods" to the works of human hands.
WIS 13:10

The satirical passage about idols in chapter 13:10-19 is similar to that in Isaiah 44:9-20. Both passages describe the process by which an artisan makes an idol. Wisdom of Solomon focuses on a woodcutter who chops down a tree, strips its bark, and uses the wood to make a bowl and fuel a fire for cooking. But with "a stick crooked and full of knots" (Wis 13:13), the woodcutter fashions a statue, places it in a niche, and prays to it. The woodcutter's folly is described ironically: "For life he prays to a thing that is dead; . . . for a prosperous journey, a thing that cannot take a step; . . . he asks strength of a thing whose hands have no strength" (Wis 13:18).

For even in the beginning, when arrogant giants were perishing, the hope of the world took refuge on a raft.
WIS 14: 6

Though not named, Noah is easy to recognize in this passage. Chapter 14 contains traditional Jewish interpretation of events leading up to the Flood. The "arrogant giants" is a reference to the Nephilim,

Dame Wisdom protected Adam after his expulsion from Eden; in this 17th-century Flemish painting, the first man tills the earth as Eve tends their sons in a crude shelter.

the offspring of the "sons of God" and "daughters of humans" (Gen 6:1-3), who are blamed for introducing wickedness on earth that resulted in the ultimate punishment of the Flood.

The account of Noah's ark is mentioned here to contrast true divine guidance with the false protection offered by idol worship. But the Flood story also held special significance for early Christians. Church fathers viewed the story of the Flood and Noah's ultimate rescue as a foreshadowing of the crucifixion. "Blessed is the wood by which righteousness comes" (Wis 14:7) refers, according to them, not just to the wood from which Noah's ark was built, but also to the cross through which salvation from sin comes.

But you, our God, are kind and true, patient, and ruling all things in mercy. WIS 15:1

God's merciful treatment of his chosen people is first contrasted with the dreadful punishment he meted out to their Egyptian enemies in chapter 11:1-14. The antitheses continue in chapters 16:1-19:22. In the second antithesis, God provided delicate quail for the Israelites to eat in the wilderness, but the Egyptians were tormented by "odious creatures" (Wis 16:3, a reference to the plague of frogs). The third antithesis mentions that God healed the Israelites after they were bitten by snakes, whereas the Egyptians were "killed by the bites of locusts and flies" (Wis 16:9). The fourth antithesis contrasts God's provision of manna, "the food of angels," to the Israelites with the Lord's destruction of the Egyptians' crops through natural disasters.

But for your holy ones there was very great light.
WIS 18:1

The fifth antithesis also offers a strong contrast between the wicked Egyptians and the righteous Israelites. As punishment for trying to conceal their sins in the dark, measure for measure, the Egyptians were punished by God with a plague of darkness. But the Israelites, God's "holy ones," were provided with a pillar of fire to illuminate their way at night in the wilderness. The sixth antithesis contrasts the death of the Egyptians' firstborn with the Israelites being acknowledged as the children of God "through whom the imperishable light of the law was to be given to the world" (Wis 18:4). According to rabbinic tradition, which is enshrined here in the Wisdom of Solomon, the Israelites' responsibility for their part in accepting the law was to make its contents known to non-Jews.

The seventh antithesis, and the climax of the book, is the description of the destruction of the Egyptians in the Red Sea. Wisdom portrays the event in hyperbolic terms, in which "the whole creation in its nature was fashioned anew" (Wis 19:6). God's salvation of Israel at the Red Sea serves as an example of the Lord's abiding providence, his protection of his people "at all times and in all places" (Wis 19:22).

THE WISDOM OF JESUS SON OF SIRACH

*S*irach belongs to the wisdom literature of ancient Israel along with the books of Proverbs, Ecclesiastes, and Job; yet the book also represents a new development in that literary genre. The earlier books portray wisdom primarily as insights to be gained through human observation of and reflection on the natural world and social behavior. While this dimension of wisdom is still attested in Sirach, the book expands the notion of wisdom by depicting the law revealed on Mount Sinai, or scripture itself, as the preeminent source of all wisdom.

Also known as Ecclesiasticus, the book of Sirach is named after its author, Jesus son of Sirach, or in Hebrew, "Joshua ben Sira." Ben Sira wrote early in the second century B.C., a time of Hellenistic domination in the ancient Near East. The attribution of the book to a man who was neither a prophet nor a priest, king, or judge, represented a departure from ancient Israelite practice. Ben Sira represents the ascendancy in postexilic Judaism of the "sage," the wise man who gained stature in his community by virtue of his study of sacred texts and knowledge of Jewish traditions.

Much of the book contains pithy adages of the kind known from Proverbs and Ecclesiastes. Ben Sira also uses the instruction form of a teacher or parent giving advice to a student or son. The influence of Greek literary style can be seen in chapters 44-50, the so-called Hymn in Honor of our Ancestors, which extol the contributions of Israel's greatest heroes.

Though Sirach was originally written in Hebrew, many Jews, especially those living in lands far from Jerusalem, were not fluent in their ancestral language. Ben Sira's grandson thus took it upon himself to translate the book into Greek in order to gain a wider readership. The brief prologue to the book of Sirach was written by the grandson, who began translating the book after 132 B.C. The prologue contains the earliest reference to the threefold division of the Old Testament into "the Law" (the Pentateuch), "the Prophets" (Deuteronomic history and the classical prophets), and the "other books," later called "the Writings" (including such works as the Song of Solomon, Psalms, and Job). The prologue calls attention to the nature of the work as a Greek translation by apologizing for any inexactitude in the wording. While reading the book in English, one should remember the grandson's advice. Not only Sirach, he cautions, but also the rest of the books of the Bible, "differ not a little when read in the original."

God sets the sun and moon in the heavens; an early-14th-century English Bible illumination of creation.

All wisdom is from the Lord, and with him it remains forever. SIR 1:1

*T*he book in Hebrew begins with an alphabetic acrostic poem, a composition of 22 lines in which each verse starts with a successive letter of the alphabet. The wisdom poem contains two major themes of the book. The Lord is the source of all wisdom in the world, and wisdom, which God created first of all things, permeates the cosmos. Sirach emphasizes the importance of cultivating "fear of the Lord," a deep and abiding faithfulness in Israel's God. Like other wisdom authors before him, Ben Sira affirms that "to fear the Lord is the beginning of wisdom" (Sir 1:14; Job 28:28; Prov 1:7). He uses a metaphor of a tree to illuminate the idea: "To fear the

Lord is the root of wisdom, and her branches are long life" (Sir 1:20).

More than earlier wisdom books, such as Proverbs and Ecclesiastes, Sirach ties wisdom to the revealed truth found in the Torah. "Fearing the Lord," therefore, also entails obedience to the divine law. Chapter 3 contains an extended discourse on one specific law, the commandment to honor one's father and mother. Ben Sira offers reasons for honoring parents, stating, for example, that such kindness "will be credited to you against your sins; in the days of your distress it will be remembered in your favor; like frost in fair weather, your sins will melt away" (Sir 3:14-15). So, too, he says in Sirach 4:1-10, generosity in supporting the poor is mandated by the Torah and observing this law is evidence of one's wisdom.

Wisdom teaches her children and gives help to those who seek her. SIR 4:11

Wisdom is personified as a teacher who tutors students in her own ways. The rewards of seeking wisdom are many: joy, glory, security, and even the ability to judge the nations. Wisdom tests her students "with her ordinances" (Sir 4:17). In other words, along with wisdom goes the requirement to obey the laws of the Torah. How does Wisdom "teach" her children? One way is by studying the writings of wise men, such as Ben Sira. Following the advice of the author, heeding his admonitions, and studying rules pertaining to social behavior advances an individual on the path to wisdom.

Ben Sira takes up the subject of friendship and the importance of finding true friends in chapter 6. Be friendly with everyone, suggests Ben Sira, "but let your advisers be one in a thousand" (Sir 6:6). There are many kinds of false friends, he warns. Some turn into enemies "and tell of the quarrel to your disgrace" (Sir 6:9). And fair-weather friends "who will not stand by you in time of trouble" are to be avoided: "When you are prosperous, they become your second self . . . but if you are brought low, they turn against you" (Sir 6:10-12). Faithful friends, on the other hand, are described as "a sturdy shelter," "a treasure," and "life-saving medicine" (Sir 6:14, 16).

WHO WAS BEN SIRA?

The author of Sirach, the longest and one of the earliest books of the Apocrypha, was a sage and teacher called Jesus son of Sirach (Ben Sira). He lived in Jerusalem early in the second century B.C. During this time, Palestine was dominated by the Seleucid dynasty of Syria, which tried to impose Greek culture and religion on the Jews. Ben Sira resisted these intrusions by devoting his life to studying scriptures and traditions and teaching others how to live according to Jewish law. He apparently operated his own school, calling prospective students to "draw near . . . and lodge in the house of instruction" (Sir 51:23).

Based on his advice in Sirach, scholars have concluded that Ben Sira was an affluent and respected Jewish elder, well-traveled, well-read, and a man who enjoyed pleasant company, sumptuous food, and fine music. Yet Ben Sira was a religious man who wanted nothing more than to teach others how to serve God in everyday life. His advice reflects the practical counsel of prophets and sages throughout Jewish scripture: Help the poor and oppressed, visit the sick, forgive erring neighbors, shun pride, and stay away from prostitutes and other men's wives.

Do not contend with the powerful, or you may fall into their hands. SIR 8:1

Chapter 8 continues in the same vein, providing a long list of admonitions for the aspiring sage. Ben Sira starts with advice about dealing with various types of people: the rich, the powerful, the wise, the aged, and women. Fighting with powerful people is sure to cause grief because they can use their influence to cause your downfall. Caution and restraint are the watchwords in all relationships.

More advice on friendship appears in chapter 9: "A new friend is like new wine; when it has aged, you can drink it with pleasure" (Sir 9:10). Like new wine, one cannot know at first how a friendship will develop. A new friend may act charming, but the relationship has not yet been seasoned. The process of getting to know how a friend will react to disagreements or adverse circumstances cannot be known overnight. To gain such insight and to discover whether a friend will be trustworthy, loyal, and honest requires the test of time. The noble qualities that make a true friend are not immediately apparent, just as a wine reveals its many dimensions to the palate only after it has been allowed to age. Chapter 11 elaborates on a related theme: Appearances can be deceiving. Humble or homely looks are not evidence of unworthiness. Ben Sira points to the bee, which, though one of the smallest of creatures, produces the sweetest of substances.

If you do good, know to whom you do it, and you will be thanked for your good deeds. SIR 12:1

Beneficence toward the poor is essential, says Ben Sira, but you must know to whom you are giving your charity. Alms are wasted on an unworthy, dishonest recipient. On the other hand, a faithful, humble person will deeply appreciate the needed help. While wealth is clearly preferable to poverty in Ben Sira's view, his advice is also tinged with cynicism about the social advantages unfairly held by the wealthy. The rich can get away with more abuses than the poor: "A rich person does wrong, and even adds insults; a poor person suffers wrong, and must add apologies" (Sir 13:3). This is not to say that all the wealthy are undeserving, but those who become rich through small-minded miserliness do not deserve to have their wealth.

Ben Sira also provides plentiful advice on the topic of choosing one's associates. Like the contemporary saying, "A gentleman is known by the company he keeps," Ben Sira believes that a person can become like the unworthy individuals he associates with, be they dishonest, arrogant, or hypocritical. Added to the difficulty in choosing proper companions is the fact that some apparent friends can, in fact, be enemies: "An enemy speaks sweetly with his lips, but in his heart he plans to throw you into a pit; . . . if he finds an opportunity he will never have enough of your blood" (Sir 12:16).

When the Lord created his works from the beginning . . . he arranged the works in an eternal order. SIR 16:26-27

Ben Sira includes a long poem (Sir 16:24-18:14) about God's work in creation and the place of human beings and the nation of Israel in the divine scheme. Throughout the composition, the author reveals his thorough knowledge of the scriptures. He alludes to the creation account at the beginning of Genesis in saying, for example, that God "created human beings out of earth, and makes them return to it again" (Sir 17:1; Gen 2:7, 3:19). He refers to Israel, with whom God established an eternal covenant at Sinai, as "the Lord's own portion" (Sir 17:17), a phrase that derives from Deuteronomy 32:9. Ben Sira also displays his familiarity with the psalms. In a passage similar to Psalm 8:4, the author poses rhetorical questions, including: "What are human beings, and of what use are they?" (Sir 18:8). This is an idea central to much wisdom literature: Ultimately, the ways of the Lord are unfathomable to finite human minds. The proper response to God, asserts Ben Sira, is humility and acceptance of the yoke of studying the ways of wisdom.

Among Israel's ancestors praised by Ben Sira is Moses, shown receiving the law in this 12th-century gilt enamel plaque.

Wisdom praises herself, and tells of her glory in the midst of her people. SIR 24:1

Chapter 24, a poem in praise of wisdom, is a significant passage for understanding how the wisdom tradition developed in the centuries after the Jews returned to Israel from their exile in Babylon. The poem was probably patterned after the composition in praise of wisdom contained in Proverbs 8. Following a two-verse introduction, Wisdom, personified as a woman, utters a speech that exalts her role in creation and in the history of Israel. Wisdom "came forth from the mouth of the Most High" (Sir 24:3) at the time of creation. Not only was she present at creation, but Wisdom specifically identifies herself as "the book of the covenant of the Most High God, the law that Moses commanded us as an inheritance for the congregation of Jacob" (Sir 24:23). Whereas wisdom in ancient Israel was discerned by human observation of the order of nature and social behavior, by the time Sirach was written in the second century B.C., the true source of wisdom was understood as scripture, in particular the law that was revealed by God to Moses on Mount Sinai. The sage had to be a student of scripture to gain a thorough knowledge of the written traditions of Israel. Thus, the author, Ben Sira himself, was a figure of wisdom to be revered by his community. The characterization of wisdom in this passage may have influenced the Evangelist John, who in his prologue identified the divine "Logos" or "Word" existing at creation as Jesus.

There is a rebuke that is untimely, and there is the person who is wise enough to keep silent. SIR 20:1

There are different facets to the fine art of wise discourse. One of the cardinal virtues associated with the way of wisdom is carefully guarded speech. First, as in great comedy, timing is everything: "A proverb from a fool's lips will be rejected, for he does not tell it at the proper time" (Sir 20:20). Sometimes it is best simply to say nothing. Yet, Ben Sira points out that there is some irony in the commonly held notion in ancient Israel that "silence is golden." In fact, sometimes fools are silent simply because their heads are empty! The wise person is silent until the moment is ripe for speech. Above all, empty speech is deplored in the wisdom view: "The lips of babblers speak of what is not their concern, but the words of the prudent are weighed in the balance" (Sir 21:25). So, too, careless speech, such as boasting, gossiping, cursing, and lying, results from loose lips and signals a lack of restraint.

The author is a pious man, it is clear, because he also includes prayers in his wisdom reflections. In Sirach 23:1-6, he petitions God to "remove evil desire from me" and otherwise spare him from the tribulations brought about by both his own weaknesses and the assaults of his enemies. Ben Sira's prayer is another indication of his view that wisdom derives ultimately from the God of Israel.

The vengeful will face the Lord's vengeance, for he keeps a strict account of their sins. SIR 28:1

Another cardinal virtue of the sage is the self-control that is manifest in all his behavior. An individual who can restrain his most powerful emotions is likely to be able to exert self-discipline in other parts of his life as well. Vengeance and anger are emotions that are particularly dangerous, to the extent that they are bound up with forgiveness of sin. How can a person who stays angry at a neighbor who has wronged him expect forgiveness from God for his own sins? Another reason Ben Sira gives for keeping a lid on anger is that heated arguments can easily escalate to violence: "A hasty quarrel kindles a fire, and a hasty dispute sheds blood" (Sir 28:11).

Ben Sira also offers advice on financial issues. At times, he seems to hold conflicting opinions. On the one hand, he counts it a virtue to lend to one's needy neighbors; on the other, he considers taking out a loan to be an unsound practice. Ben Sira sounds at times like nothing more than a good banker: "Lay up your treasure according to the commandments of the Most High, and it will profit you more than gold" (Sir 29:11).

He who loves his son will whip him often, so that he may rejoice at the way he turns out. SIR 30:1

Ben Sira offers a second-century B.C. version of "tough love" in this passage, which discusses essential strategies for rearing children. Physical punishment is but one way to keep an errant son in line. Much danger lies in spoiling a child, according to the author: "Pamper a child, and he will terrorize you; play with him, and he will grieve you" (Sir 30:9). But while much of Ben Sira's advice on children seems hopelessly draconian to late-20th-century sensibilities, one principle has a timeless truth: A parent's responsibility is to teach.

Another piece of wisdom that resonates well with a health-conscious era is the importance of physical well-being: "Health and fitness are better than any gold" (Sir 30:15). So, too, is the insight that a joyful disposition can cause someone to live longer. Bitter or stressful emotions—excess sorrow, jealousy, anger, and anxiety—all serve to make a person old before his time.

If they make you master of the feast, do not exalt yourself. SIR 32:1

Not only regulating one's emotions, but also learning proper etiquette for eating and drinking are essential for the would-be sage. As in all things, the wise path is marked by moderation. Gluttony and overimbibing are frowned upon. The advice outlined in chapter 30 presumes the social setting of wealthy court life. If you should be so honored as to be chosen the master of ceremonies at a banquet, remain humble, urges Ben Sira. And above all, make your speech short. Nobody likes a speaker who is a blabbermouth, especially if he disrupts the fun: "Speak . . . for it is your right, but . . . do not interrupt the music" (Sir 32:3).

Ben Sira lived in an era in which slavery was an accepted fact of the social landscape and his conservative tendencies did not allow him to see beyond the mores of his day. He nonetheless advocates a certain humanitarian, if self-interested, treatment of slaves: "If you have but one slave, treat him like yourself, because you have bought him with blood" (Sir 33:31).

The senseless have vain and false hopes, and dreams give wings to fools. SIR 34:1

Ben Sira pointedly calls into question the practice of interpreting dreams. During the Hellenistic era in which he lived, professional diviners made their living by discern-

ing the supposed meaning of dreams. Ben Sira, certainly aware of such biblical figures as Joseph and Daniel, who successfully interpreted dreams, had to qualify his remarks. The only dreams that are worth paying attention to are those "from the Most High" (Sir 34:6). Ben Sira does not, however, provide his readers with criteria for deciding which are which.

As someone who held the priesthood and temple in high regard, Ben Sira also offers advice on sacrifices. The best sacrifices are offered by the righteous. But the author sounds like the prophet Amos when he emphasizes the ethical dimension of the law. Righteous behavior and charitable actions are as pleasing to God as sacrificial offerings. Using very strong language, Ben Sira also condemns the practice of defrauding the poor: "Like one who kills a son before his father's eyes is the person who offers a sacrifice from the property of the poor" (Sir 34:24).

Honor physicians for their services, for the Lord created them. SIR 38:1

Although Ben Sira for the most part holds traditional views, he offers some decidedly progressive advice on the issue of physicians. In ancient Israel, sickness was commonly viewed as punishment for one's sins. Only prayer, repentance, and offering sacrifices could restore health. But Ben Sira accepts

Abraham, another celebrated ancestor, is spared the sacrifice of his son Isaac in this painting by Domenico Zampieri (1581-1641).

Ben Sira called Noah "perfect and righteous"; this Bible illustration, dated about 1250, shows him releasing the dove that brings news of the Flood's end.

and once married, whether they will be well taken care of. Headstrong daughters cause particular concern because they can be the source of gossip among townsfolk. Ben Sira's perspective on women is certain to raise some objections in the present day and age: "Better is the wickedness of a man than a woman who does good; it is woman who brings shame and disgrace" (Sir 42:14).

While Ben Sira's attitude toward women may not be in accord with contemporary views on gender, his reflections on the wonders of nature certainly are: "The glory of the stars is the beauty of heaven, a glittering array in the heights of the Lord" (Sir 43:9). The splendor of rainbows sparks in Ben Sira the desire to praise God. So, too, are snow, thunder, hail, and dew all marvels of nature that God has made. The Lord's awesome works deserve human praise and ceaseless exaltation of their creator.

Let us now sing the praises of famous men, our ancestors in their generations. SIR 44:1

Chapters 44-50 contain the most unified piece in the book. These chapters were written according to the Greek rhetorical style, the encomium, a hymn of praise of certain individuals, lauding their contributions to society. Although in most ways Ben Sira is a traditional Jew, he is also a product of his age. By using a formal Greek literary style, he shows that he had a Greek education. He lived in an era during which Greek culture permeated the Near East, just as American culture and norms have influenced many parts of the world today.

The poem announces its purpose from the first verse: to "sing the praises of famous men," some named and some anonymous, who all contributed in some way to Jewish tradition. Kings, soldiers, prophets, sages, musicians, and poets are among the renowned ancestors from Israel's history included in the roster of heroes. The first figures Ben Sira mentions (with the exception of Enoch, who is thought to have been a later addition to the poem) all entered into covenants with God. Noah, "perfect and righteous" (Sir 44:17), was promised by God that the earth would never again be destroyed by flood. Israel's patriarchs, Abraham, Isaac, and Jacob, were also parties to a divine covenant that promised three things. Their offspring would multiply and be a blessing to the nations, and the land stretching from "the Euphrates to the ends of the earth" (Sir 44:21) would become their inheritance forever.

The Lord brought forth a godly man, who found favor in the sight of all and was beloved by God. SIR 44:23-45:1

Moses, of course, is counted among Israel's great men. In the covenant made at Mount Sinai, God gave Moses the law, "commandments for his people" (Sir 45:3). Not only was Moses "beloved by God," but he also "found favor in the sight of all." As he does in all his descriptions of heroes, Ben Sira

the skills of a physician as worthy, "for their gift of healing comes from the Most High." So, too, God created "medicines out of the earth" (Sir 38:2, 4). Ben Sira cites an example from scripture to prove his point. Moses used a tree to make bitter water sweet (Ex 15:23-25); therefore, reliance on physicians is perfectly fine as long as one does not neglect prayer in seeking healing as well.

Ben Sira offers disheartening news for the would-be sage who comes from the wrong social class. Wisdom can come only when one has sufficient leisure to pursue it. "How can one become wise who handles the plow . . . and whose talk is about bulls?" (Sir 38:25). Not only farmers, but artisans and blacksmiths, potters, and generally all those who rely on their hands for their living, do not have enough time for the reflection required to become wise. Ben Sira readily acknowledges that their work is indispensable, even though their role in society does not involve decision making or the rendering of fair judgments as does that of the sage.

O death, how bitter is the thought of you to the one at peace among possessions. SIR 41:1

A hodgepodge of observations on various themes is contained in chapters 41-43. A dismal perspective on death is articulated in chapter 41. Those who are well-off and secure in life do not look forward to death, whereas for the poor and ailing, death comes as a welcome relief from life's misery. Daughters provoke special anxieties for their fathers. First, there is the worry over whether they will be married, makes many allusions to biblical literature in his depiction of Moses. This provides even more evidence that the author was thoroughly knowledgeable in Jewish tradition.

Next mentioned of the honored heroes is Aaron, the brother of Moses, who initiated the hereditary priesthood in Israel. The section praising Aaron is 17 verses long, the second longest of all the passages in the encomium. Only Simon, the high priest in Ben Sira's day, was allotted more verses of praise. God made "an everlasting covenant" (Sir 45:7) with Aaron to give him charge of the priesthood of the people. Clothed in splendid garments and adorned with precious jewels, he was anointed by Moses as a priest so that both Aaron and his descendants might perform the daily temple sacrifices in perpetuity. The amount of space devoted to two priests is understandable. In the second century B.C., when the book was most likely written, the temple in Jerusalem stood as the religious and political center of the Jewish community. The high priest was in charge not only of the sacrificial system in Israel, but was also a highly regarded and prominent figure in Jewish life—in fact, the leading provincial official.

As the fat is set apart from the offering of well-being, so David was set apart from the Israelites. SIR 47:2

King David is accorded an especially honored place in the list of heroes. Events both from David's youth, such as his slaying of Goliath, and from the time of his reign are recalled. David is remembered for establishing the guild of temple singers and fixed times for observing festivals, although this contribution is recorded only in the book of Chronicles. David's son Solomon is also included in the catalog. As is fitting for a book of wisdom such as Sirach, King Solomon is extolled for his sagacity: "Your songs, proverbs, and parables, and the answers you gave astounded the nations" (Sir 47:17). But the darker side of his reign, his many marriages to foreign wives and his worship of their gods, is also mentioned. Solomon's practices weakened the kingship. His foolish son Rehoboam led the country into civil strife that resulted in the division of the kingdom into the nations of Israel and Judah.

In contrast to the mixed appraisal of most of Israel's kings, the prophets Elijah and Elisha

elicit only unvarnished praise from Ben Sira. Isaiah, too, "who comforted the mourners in Zion" (Sir 48:24), Jeremiah, Ezekiel, and the 12 minor prophets are all mentioned in turn, as are the two righteous kings of Judah, Hezekiah and Josiah. The final figure mentioned in the catalog is Simon, son of Onias, the high priest. In a passage that stretches 21 verses, Ben Sira paints a glorious picture of Simon, "the morning star among the clouds . . . the full moon at the festal season" (Sir 50:6). Simon provided daily sacrifices at the altar of the temple and blessed the people, very likely using the ancient priestly blessing recorded in Numbers 6:24-26.

I give you thanks, O Lord and King, and praise you, O God my Savior. SIR 51:1

The book of Sirach ends not with proverbs or wisdom sayings, but with a prayer of thanks and praise to the Lord. Ben Sira addresses God as "King," a common epithet for the Lord in Jewish and Christian prayers, but he also addresses God as "Father" (Sir 51:1, 10), a term rarely used for God in the Old Testament but one that Jesus later employs at the beginning of the Lord's Prayer. In form and theme, it is very much like a number of the psalms, for example, Psalms 9, 18, and 30. The prayer provides the reasons for Ben Sira's feelings of gratitude. He recounts an experience of distress. Though the exact circumstances surrounding the event are hazy, he is near death. The perils he faces are described in metaphorical terms. The many troubles he endures range from "grinding teeth about to devour me" and "choking fire on every side" to "the slander of an unrighteous tongue to the king" (Sir 51:3, 4, 6). Like anyone in a period of distress, multiple troubles seem close to overwhelming him. Ben Sira feels besieged and alone, without any human help in view. He then remembers God's kindness and mercy, which has been abundant in the past toward all those who remained faithful: "And I sent up my prayer from the earth, and begged for rescue from death" (Sir 51:9). God hears his prayer and saves him from destruction.

By ending his work with a prayer, Ben Sira puts into practice his own advice on how best to gain wisdom. Through a sincere expression of the "fear of the Lord," namely worship, he manifests his deep trust in the source of all wisdom.

Extolled by Ben Sira, King David is shown praying to God; the 15th-century French artist included David's lyre and a book of psalms.

aruch and the Letter of Jeremiah purport to have been written early in the Jews' exile to Babylon—either in 597 B.C., or possibly in 586, after the Babylonians (Chaldeans) burned Jerusalem. It is more likely, however, that Baruch was composed sometime between 200 and 60 B.C. and the Letter of Jeremiah earlier, perhaps around 300 B.C. In some early manuscripts the Letter of Jeremiah is appended to Baruch as chapter 6. The two were most likely combined because of their claims to be from the hands of a pair of famous historical personages who were indeed associates. Baruch was the scribe to whom the prophet Jeremiah dictated much of his message and to whom credit is given for recording Jeremiah's words (Jer 36:4, 45:1). Yet, the prophet and his scribe were taken to Egypt (Jer 43:1-7), not Babylon, from which Baruch is written. The Letter of Jeremiah is no doubt dependent on the report in Jeremiah 29 of a letter that the prophet sent to the first group of exiles sometime after 597. Baruch was apparently written in Hebrew; the Letter, in Hebrew or Aramaic. Both survive mainly in Greek.

Rather than a single cohesive composition, Baruch is a collection of materials divided as follows: prose introduction (chapter 1:1-14); prose confession (1:15-3:8); wisdom poem (3:9-4:4); and poetic prophetic address (4:5-5:9). Because Baruch represents a collection of diverse materials, the addition of the Letter of Jeremiah would not necessarily have occasioned suspicion. While both books claim to address the concerns of the exilic community, each is better understood as providing comfort to Jews struggling to maintain their faith during the Hellenistic period, 330 to 60 B.C.

Jeremiah; a fresco from a Cypriot monastery

Baruch

Then they wept, and fasted, and prayed before the Lord. BAR 1:5

When Baruch reads his book to the captive King Jeconiah (Jehoiachin) and his fellow exiles, they weep, fast, pray—and gather money for offerings to send back with the looted temple vessels. This reveals the willingness of the exiles to support the temple cult in Jerusalem; by implying that worship is still being conducted there, it suggests the text was written between the initial capture of Jerusalem by the Babylonians in 597 B.C. and the destruction of 586. Addressed to a people subject to a ruling power but with their temple still intact, the text would appeal equally well to the restored Jewish community in the Hellenistic period. The introduction is reminiscent of the books of Ezra and Nehemiah, on which the book of Baruch, at least in part, depends. In particular, concern with the temple and a call for sustaining it are shared with the earlier books. Furthermore, the reading aloud of a text with the hope of motivating reform has much in common with Ezra and Nehemiah. By drawing attention to the temple, the author hopes to use the confession and prayer that follow to remind Jews that the worship center in Jerusalem is still the focus of their religious life.

The Lord our God is in the right, but there is open shame on us today. BAR 1:15

Baruch next offers a confession of the sins that led to the exile. This confession seems to be addressed by the exiles in Babylon to their fellow Jews in Jerusalem. Scholars have noted that the confessions that comprise this unit are a pastiche of biblical or near biblical quotes. In particular, parts of Ezra 9, Nehemiah 1 and 9, and Daniel 9 seem to have inspired the composition; indeed, Baruch 1:15-2:19 is basically a rewrite of Daniel 9:4-19. Baruch notes that the shortcomings of his people began with the Exodus and include, most grievously, the failure to heed the words of the prophets. As a result, the Lord carried out the threat contained in the Law of Moses. This reference to Moses and the Exodus from enslavement in Egypt would have been particularly significant to a people under subjugation, whether to Babylonians or Greeks. Their hope is for a new exodus and renewed independence, but such liberation is clearly dependent on reversing their pattern of sin and escaping the consequences of transgressions. Baruch 2:6-10, which begins with a virtual repeat of Baruch 1:15, seems to represent a summary of the first half of the confession.

The second half of the confession comprises a prayer addressed directly to the Lord. Baruch pleads for the welfare of the people by confessing the sins that brought their calamity upon them. Of most interest, Baruch identifies the unwillingness of the Jews to submit to the king of Babylon as their crucial failure. It was this error that seems to have been the final and most significant event that led to their exile. Next, Baruch reminds God of his promise to Moses that, even after their failures, his chosen people will experience redemption. Baruch ends with an impassioned plea that the Lord will act on his previous promises of salvation: "Remember your power and your name" (Bar 3:5).

Hear the commandments of life, O Israel; give ear, and learn wisdom! BAR 3:9

Baruch 3:9-4:4 is a wisdom poem. Its placement after the previous confession is apparently motivated by the notion that the remedy to the sins just enumerated is a rededication to the Law of Moses—associated in this poem as in Sirach 24:23 with God's wisdom. In making this association, Baruch joins a tradition that emerged in the second temple period that viewed the Torah as the written form of God's wisdom mentioned in Proverbs and Ecclesiastes. By making this association, Baruch suggests that the solution to the present tribulations is a renewed dedication to textual traditions of the past. In this, Baruch is very much part of emergent Judaism.

The poem, like the confession that precedes it, is apparently dependent on various biblical books. Job 28 and Sirach 24 stand out as especially significant for the concepts embedded in the poem. Of most importance in this poem is Baruch 4:1: "She [Wisdom] is the book of the commandments of God, the law that endures forever." The transition from a people whose religious life is centered on temple worship to a people of the Book (scripture) is well under way; in the author's mind, the solution to current difficulties is found in focusing on the textual traditions at hand.

Take courage, my people, who perpetuate Israel's name! BAR 4:5

The next section of Baruch is an address, apparently from the scribe himself, meant to edify and sustain the people. The author suggests that the Jews are not in danger of imminent destruction but are merely experiencing punishment for having ignored the Lord. The text records the voice of Jerusalem, the bereaved mother, lamenting the loss of her children and encouraging them to turn to God, who will deliver them. Next, Jerusalem is encouraged to wait for God to return her children and punish those who destroyed her:

"Take courage, O Jerusalem, for the one who named you will comfort you" (Bar 4:30). Associating Jerusalem with a woman is in keeping with much of biblical tradition, but of most interest is the way this section relates to Lamentations. In that book, the laments come from a third party and bewail the loss of "daughter Zion" or "daughter Jerusalem" (Lam 1:6, 2:13). By putting the lament in Jerusalem's own mouth, Baruch makes even more poignant the destruction of Jerusalem and the loss of her people.

Letter of Jeremiah

Because of the sins that you have committed before God, you will be taken to Babylon as exiles by Nebuchadnezzar, king of the Babylonians. BAR 6:2

The sixth chapter of Baruch is more properly considered an independent text and, as such, is called the Letter of Jeremiah. This "letter" seems to have been influenced to a great degree by the letter of Jeremiah in Jeremiah 29:1-28. In that missive, the prophet writes to the exiles taken to Babylon in 597 after the initial defeat of Jerusalem. Jeremiah's goal is to convince his readers that their stay in Babylon will be an extended one and that, while they will return some day to Jerusalem, they should not count on returning in the near future.

This new "letter" of Jeremiah may be inspired by the form of the first but its content has much more to do with Jeremiah 10, in which the prophet ridicules idol worship. For the author of the Letter of Jeremiah, there seems to be no greater threat to the Jews in exile than idol worship. Picking up on the concerns of Jeremiah and other prophets, the author of this "letter" engages in traditional arguments against the worship of idols. First, he points out that idols are nothing but the work of craftsmen. They are merely polished gold and silver and have no effect on the world: "They cannot take pity on a widow or do good to an orphan" (Bar 6:38). While the issue of idol worship plagued the Israelites throughout their long history, the author here reflects about the anxiety over Greek influence on Jewish religious practices during the Hellenistic era in which he lived.

The books of Baruch and the Letter of Jeremiah attest not only to the increasing status of scripture, or at least the traditions that are now preserved in the Hebrew Bible, but also suggest the ways in which those traditions became central to interpreting historical events in later times. That these two books are attributed to Baruch and Jeremiah is evidence of the importance in the second temple period of understanding events of that era in light of defining persons and moments in the long history of Israel.

Jeremiah, depicted in Michelangelo's famed ceiling fresco for the Vatican's Sistine Chapel

ADDITIONS TO DANIEL

*T*he pious and shrewd prophet Daniel inspired many more stories than those found in the biblical book that bears his name. The Greek translations of the Hebrew Bible contain three major additions: the Prayer of Azariah and the Song of the Three Jews, Susanna, and Bel and the Dragon. All are believed to have circulated independently before being added to the book of Daniel by about 100 B.C.

The Prayer of Azariah and the Song of the Three Jews is placed between Daniel 3:23, when Shadrach, Meshach, and Abednego are bound and thrown into a fiery furnace for refusing to worship King Nebuchadnezzar's idol, and 3:24, when the astonished king arrives to see the three walking unharmed inside the inferno. The addition reports the prayers of the brave youths and God's benevolence in delivering them from the flames.

Susanna is an engaging short story that uses a theme popular in folk literature, that of a falsely accused young woman who is rescued by a wise child, in this case the boy Daniel. The story is placed before Daniel 1 in the Greek translation by Theodotion, but after Daniel 12 in the Septuagint. Bel and the Dragon—placed at the end of the book of Daniel—tells of Daniel risking his life to prove the Babylonian gods to be false idols. In Protestant Bibles, the additions to Daniel are placed in the Apocrypha, while Roman Catholic Bibles incorporate them into the book of Daniel.

An angel protects the three Jews in the furnace; a painting by Solomon Simeon (1840-1905).

The Prayer of Azariah and the Song of the Three Jews

They walked around in the midst of the flames, singing hymns to God and blessing the Lord. Then Azariah stood still in the fire and prayed aloud. SONG OF THR 1-2

*H*ere, only the Hebrew names of Daniel's three companions are used: Hananiah (Shadrach), Mishael (Meshach), and Azariah (Abednego). Azariah's prayer combines a communal lament with an admission of national sin, echoing the prayer of supplication in Daniel 9:3-19. Azariah confesses that the Israelites have broken God's commandments, and acknowledges, "So all that you have brought upon us, and all that you have done to us, you have done by a true judgment" (Song of Thr 8).

Azariah laments that God has delivered the Jews into the hands of the most evil ruler of all. This refers to Nebuchadnezzar, although for the story's original audience, it would have called to mind Antiochus IV Epiphanes, who desecrated the temple in 167 B.C. Azariah pleads for mercy based on God's promise to Abraham of numerous descendants (Gen 22:17). Instead, says Azariah, the Jews "have become fewer than any other nation, and are brought low this day in all the world because of our sins" (Song of Thr 14). By lifting up his penitent people, God can demonstrate his power to their enemies and bring glory to himself.

The flames of the furnace burn hotter and hotter, spitting out jets of fire that sear the men who are near. All the more miraculous, then, that the three Jews inside the furnace are unharmed. They are protected by an angel who descended "and made the in-side of the furnace as though a moist wind were whistling through it" (Song of Thr 27). This is presumably the same heavenly creature Nebuchadnezzar sees walking with the youths in Daniel 3:25.

Then the three with one voice praised and glorified and blessed God in the furnace. SONG OF THR 28

*W*hat follows are beautifully poetic hymns of praise for God. In the first song, verses 29-34 (called the Benedictus es Domine in the Roman Catholic liturgy), God is praised directly as the king on his heavenly throne. Each verse is followed by a slightly different refrain glorifying God.

In the second song, verses 35-68 (or the Benedicite), all of creation is called on to praise God, beginning with the heavens and angels, and descending through the sun and moon, the elements, the earth and all its creatures, mankind, and finally Israel. Every verse has the same refrain: "Sing praise to him and highly exalt him forever" (Song of Thr 35). Hananiah, Azariah, and Mishael are called on to praise God for mercifully rescuing them from the fire.

Susanna

When the people left at noon, Susanna would go into her husband's garden to walk. Every day the two elders used to see her . . . and they began to lust for her. SUS 7-8

*W*ithin a few verses, an intriguing plot is set in motion. Susanna is a beautiful and virtuous woman married to Joakim, a wealthy and respected Jew living in Babylon during the exile. The two elders are esteemed judges who hold court in the garden of Joakim's house, but of them God had said, "Wickedness came forth from Babylon, from elders who were judges, who were supposed to govern the people" (Sus 5). Although they both long to seduce Susanna, they are too ashamed to admit it to each other. One day, they each announce that they are going home, only to sneak back and catch the other doing the same thing. They confess their passion for Susanna to each other, and together plot her seduction, hoping for a time when they can find her alone.

One hot day, Susanna goes into the garden to bathe and sends her two maids for perfumed oils, instructing them to shut the garden doors behind them. The lecherous elders are hiding, waiting for just this moment, and they rush up to her and demand that she submit to them. If she refuses, they will claim that they found her with a young man. Susanna is trapped, since she is well aware that Mosaic Law decrees death as the punishment for adultery (Lev 20:10). Nonetheless she says, "I will fall into your hands, rather than sin in the sight of the Lord" (Sus 23). Susanna screams and the servants come running, only to hear the elders make their wicked accusation. They are astonished, believing their mistress to be above approach.

The next day, the elders come to Joakim's house to pass judgment on Susanna. She is brought in, accompanied by her family, and in a further affront,

the two judges order her veil lifted "so that they might feast their eyes on her beauty" (Sus 32). The accusers testify that they witnessed her liaison with a young man, who got away. The people assembled believe the elders because of their respected positions, and Susanna is sentenced to death by stoning. But the innocent heroine appeals to a higher judge, crying out to God that the two old men have borne false witness against her.

Just as she was being led off to execution, God stirred up the holy spirit of a young lad named Daniel.
SUS 45

Daniel dramatically shifts the action by shouting, "I want no part in shedding this woman's blood!" (Sus 46). The people are dumbfounded, and Daniel demands that they return to the court to learn the facts, for the so-called witnesses have not been cross-examined. They hurry back, and the other judges invite the youth to join them, "for God has given you the standing of an elder" (Sus 50).

The young prophet has a plan for uncovering the truth: He will question the elders separately. He accuses the first one of prosecuting the innocent and freeing the guilty, then asks him, "Under what tree did you see them being intimate with each other?" The elder answers, "Under a mastic tree" (Sus 54). Daniel calls him a liar, and sentences him to being

A voluptuous and vulnerable Susanna attracts the unwanted attentions of the lustful elders in this painting by Joseph-Marie Vien (1716-1809).

The young Daniel arrives to defend Susanna (left) against the accusations
of the lecherous elders; Italian artist Francesco Vanni (1563-1609) placed the scene in a
Renaissance palace opening to a formal garden in the rear.

cut in two. This is a pun, since the Greek words for mastic tree and cut are similar.

Daniel denounces the second elder for assaulting the "daughters of Israel" (Sus 57). When Daniel asks him under what tree he saw Susanna committing adultery, he says, "Under an evergreen oak" (Sus 58). For this lie, says Daniel, the elder will be split in two by the sword of an angel—another pun, as the words for evergreen oak and split are similar in Greek.

In an ironic reversal, the people execute the elders just as the elders were planning to execute Susanna. (Deuteronomy 19:18-19 states that whatever a false witness intended to do to his victim shall be done to him.) The virtue of youth triumphs over the evil of the elders. The author ends the story with, "And from that day onward Daniel had a great reputation among the people" (Sus 64).

Bel and the Dragon

Now the Babylonians had an idol called Bel, and every day they provided for it twelve bushels of choice flour and forty sheep and six measures of wine. BEL 3

Cyrus, the Persian king who captured Babylon in 539 B.C., worships the god Bel, also called Marduk—the chief god of the Babylonians. (According to the ancient historian Herodotus, an 18-foot-tall golden idol of Bel stood in Babylon.) Cyrus asks

Daniel, his confidant, why he does not worship Bel, and Daniel replies, "Because I do not revere idols made with hands, but the living God" (Bel 5). Cyrus protests that only a living god could eat and drink as much as Bel does every day, but Daniel laughingly says that this statue of clay and bronze could not possibly eat or drink anything.

This angers the king, who summons the priests of Bel and says that if they do not tell him who is eating Bel's offerings, they will die. If, however, they can prove that Bel is eating the food, it is Daniel who will die, for blasphemy. The priests tell the king to set out the idol's food and wine himself, then seal the door with his signet. "When you return in the morning, if you do not find that Bel has eaten it all, we will die" (Bel 12), they say. Unknown to the king, the priests have made a secret entrance into the temple, through which they pass nightly with their wives and children to eat all the food placed before the idol. But Daniel has a trick up his sleeve, too. When he and the king are the only ones left in the temple, he has ashes scattered over the floor.

That night, the priests and their families come and eat all of Bel's offerings, as usual. In the morning, King Cyrus and Daniel come to the temple and open the sealed door. When the king sees all the offerings gone, he foolishly proclaims, "You are great, O Bel, and in you there is no deceit at all!" (Bel 18). But

Daniel points to the floor, which is covered with footprints. The priests and their families are arrested and admit their deceit to the king, who orders them executed. Then he turns Bel over to Daniel, and Daniel destroys the idol and his temple.

Now in that place there was a great dragon, which the Babylonians revered. BEL 23

The "dragon" is actually a large living snake. The king orders Daniel to worship the snake, since it is undeniably a living god. But Daniel says he worships his own God, and he can prove the snake is not a god by slaying it "without sword or club" (Bel 26). The king gives him permission to try, and Daniel makes cakes of pitch, fat, and hair and feeds them to the dragon. They swell up and make his stomach burst open. "See what you have been worshiping!" (Bel 27), Daniel says.

The Babylonians are outraged when they hear of this. The king has allowed the destruction of their gods and has killed the priests. They accuse him of becoming a Jew and threaten him with death unless he hands Daniel over to them. The king has no choice but to comply.

The Babylonians throw Daniel into a den of lions, the same fate he suffered in chapter 6 of the book of Daniel. For six days, he sits in the midst of seven lions made ravenous by having their usual food withheld. To make the story even more fabulous, the prophet Habakkuk is suddenly introduced. He is in Judea, on his way to take food to harvesters in the field, but an angel tells him to take it to Daniel instead, in the lions' den in Babylon. A mystified Habakkuk responds, "Sir, I have never seen Babylon,

To expose the great snake worshiped by the Babylonians, Daniel feeds it poisoned cakes; a 14th-century Flemish manuscript illustration.

BIBLICAL DRAGONS

The dragon the Babylonians believe to be a living god in Bel and the Dragon was most likely a huge snake that represented the sea serpent in Mesopotamian creation myths. The creature is also alluded to in the Old and New Testaments. According to Babylonian legends, the universe was created after the chief god—called Bel or Marduk—defeated the powers of chaos, symbolized by a sea creature known as Leviathan. Similar tales appear in the literature of Egypt and Canaan. For instance, tablets from the Canaanite city of Ugarit in Syria describe a powerful struggle in which the storm god Baal defeats the seven-headed sea monster Lothan. A cylinder seal dated about 2500 B.C., found near Baghdad, Iraq, shows two men trying to kill a seven-headed serpent.

Several biblical writers draw on their readers' familiarity with these legends to help explain the nature and might of God. The Psalmist praises God's power to create the world, singing, "You broke the heads of the dragons in the waters. You crushed the heads of Leviathan" (Ps 74:13-14). Job, in contrast, laments his suffering by asking why God is treating him like an enemy: "Am I the sea, or the Dragon, that you set a guard over me?" (Job 7:12). And the prophet Isaiah foresees an era of peace and renewal when the Lord "will punish Leviathan" (Isa 27:1).

In his vision of the end of time, John of Patmos witnesses a cosmic battle between good and evil in which the angels of heaven defeat Satan, described as "a great red dragon, with seven heads" (Rev 12:3). Ultimately, this monstrous being, the epitome of spiritual chaos, is cast out of heaven into eternal torment.

and I know nothing about the den" (Bel 35). And so, in a scene based on Ezekiel 8:3, the angel lifts him by his hair and takes him to the lions' den in Babylon. Habakkuk shouts that he has brought food from God, and a grateful Daniel praises the Lord for remembering him. The angel returns Habakkuk to Judea, presumably the same way he brought him.

On the seventh day, the king comes to the lions' den in mourning and finds that, miraculously, Daniel is unharmed. He cries, "You are great, O Lord, the God of Daniel, and there is no other besides you!" (Bel 41). The king takes Daniel out of the den and throws in those who wanted him dead; they are instantly devoured. Thus, foreign idols are ridiculed and the God of the Jews is shown to be superior—an important message in a time when some Jews were eager to abandon the purity of their worship and assimilate the popular culture of the Greeks in their midst into their religion.

1 MACCABEES

The rise of the Maccabees, though presented in the Bible as testimony to God's love for his people when they remain faithful, is essentially a complex tale of political intrigue, internal dissension within the Jewish community of Judea, and the canny, courageous strategies of an intrepid band of rebels determined to gain political and religious independence for their beleaguered nation. By taking advantage of their familiarity with the hidden valleys and rocky hills of their homeland, these guerrillas were able to defeat a better armed foe that could not maneuver its cavalry and other forces in the wilderness.

Not a continuous narrative, as are the two books of Samuel or Kings, 1 and 2 Maccabees independently cover much the same historical period— that is, from the beginnings of the Jewish revolt in 167 B.C. through the reclamation of the temple and the death of the rebellion's greatest hero, Judas Maccabeus, to the murder in 134 of the high priest Simon, whose wealth and power show that Israel had achieved most of the Maccabean aims. In short, after three decades of strife during which the great powers of Egypt and Syria contended with each other and the latter plagued tiny Judea, "the yoke of the Gentiles was removed from Israel" (1 Macc 13:41).

Although 1 Maccabees survives today only in a Greek version, its stylistic resemblances to the Old Testament books of Samuel and Kings suggest that it was composed in Hebrew. Evidently, the writer was familiar with public historical documents, including state archives, for several official letters are quoted. From time to time, he refers to the Greek calendar—that is, the years of the Seleucid kingdom, which was established in 312 B.C. Although much of the history described is affirmed by secular writers, the exact sequence and timing of the events in 1 Maccabees, probably written about 104 B.C., do not always agree with the version given in 2 Maccabees.

Alexander the Great introduced Greek culture to Judea; a mosaic portrait from the ruins of Pompeii.

After Alexander son of Philip, the Macedonian, who came from the land of Kittim, had defeated King Darius of the Persians and the Medes, he succeeded him as king.
1 MACC 1:1

The death of one of history's most famous conquerors, Alexander the Great, opens the story. In building an empire that stretched from Egypt to India, this ambitious leader hoped to bring Greek ideas and ways of living to the entire known world. That culture, known as Hellenic, became a powerful influence, even in the land of Israel.

But when Alexander died in Babylon in 323 B.C., his empire and his ideals fell into the hands of weaker, lesser men. Eventually, his legacy was divided into three kingdoms, which often struggled with each other. The family known as the Seleucids was given Syria and won Palestine from the Egyptian rulers, known as the Ptolemies. The third dynasty, the Antigonids of Macedonia in northern Greece, did not figure directly in the conflicts of the Near East.

In 175 B.C., Antiochus IV Epiphanes succeeds his father on the Seleucid throne. This arrogant, possibly insane young man is convinced that Greek religion, as well as culture, is superior to the ancient laws and religious beliefs of the Jews, who are now in his power. In return for a sizable bribe, he appoints Jason, an admirer of everything Greek, to replace his brother Onias III as high priest. Called renegades by the author of 1 Maccabees because they defy Mosaic Law, Jason and his followers enthusiastically build a Greek gymnasium in Jerusalem. Because athletes exercise and compete in the nude, some young Jews even undergo an operation to reverse circumcision, which the Greeks consider a mutilation. The actions of the renegades cause serious internal strife among God's chosen people.

[Antiochus] invaded Egypt with a strong force, with chariots and elephants and cavalry and with a large fleet.
1 MACC 1:17

Secure in his power, Antiochus decides to take Egypt from the Ptolemies. Partly because of his formidable elephant troops, which have been forbidden by Rome, he conquers his enemies and plunders their famous riches. The Romans order him out of Egypt, however, and there are rumors of a possible revolt among the Jews. Passing through Judea on his way back to his Syrian capital, Antioch, in 169

B.C., he loots Jerusalem's temple of its treasures. To pay for gifts to his Greek cities, the king steals from the temples of other subject states as well.

This cruel abuse of state power is movingly recalled in a fragment from a memorial poem written at the time (1 Macc 1:25-28). "All the house of Jacob was clothed with shame," it concludes, perhaps explaining the psychological basis for events that follow.

Only two years later, in 167 B.C., the Seleucid king's chief tax collector brings a large force to Jerusalem. Easing the fears of the people with smooth words, he suddenly turns on them, killing many and razing much of God's city. Making slaves of the women and children of the faithful, he installs Jews loyal to Antiochus in a strong new citadel, thus setting up "an evil adversary of Israel at all times" (1 Macc 1:36).

The victory for Hellenic culture could hardly have seemed more complete and lasting. Antiochus sends letters establishing Greek worship as the state religion throughout his kingdom. Every citizen from Palestine to Persia is to dress in the same way and speak the same language. Jewish sanctuaries are to be abandoned, circumcision is made illegal, and the sabbath is to be profaned. Death is the punishment for anyone who resists this program of assimilation.

Antiochus makes certain his decree is enforced. In the month of Chislev (November/December), he erects "a desolating sacrilege" (1 Macc 1:54), possibly a statue to Zeus, king of the Greek gods and goddesses, on the altar of burnt offerings at the temple in Jerusalem. His pagan predecessors, interestingly, had preferred the worship of Apollo, the god of music and poetry. Judaism's sacred scriptures are seized and burned; entire families are slaughtered if it is discovered that an infant boy has been circumcised. As told in the books 2 and 4 Maccabees, many Jews choose to become martyrs to the faith during this bloody repression.

Competing in the nude, Greek athletes like these runners on a 6th-century B.C. vase scorned circumcised Jews.

In those days Mattathias son of John son of Simeon, a priest of the family of Joarib, moved from Jerusalem and settled in Modein. 1 MACC 2:1

When Mattathias and his five brave sons leave Jerusalem for the mountain town of Modein some 17 miles to the northwest, they take the first step in founding a Jewish dynasty to rule Israel. Known as the Hasmoneans for an ancestor named Heshmon or Hashmonah, or possibly the place from which he came, the family decides to revolt against Antiochus because Judea "has become a slave" (1 Macc 2:11). The movement to free Jerusalem combines the Jews' nationalism with their enduring outrage at the desecration of the temple.

When Seleucid officials go to Modein to force the Jews to sacrifice to Greek deities, Mattathias defies them in ringing tones: "I and my sons and my brothers will continue to live by the covenant of our ancestors" (1 Macc 2:20).

Deed swiftly follows word. When an unnamed Jew moves to perform the rite, Mattathias kills him as well as a Seleucid officer, then destroys the pagan altar. The author compares Mattathias with Phinehas, the grandson of Aaron who killed an Israelite and his pagan wife for their sinful union (Num 25:6-15). Withdrawing to the nearby Gophna hills, Mattathias and his sons launch a full-scale rebellion against the Hellenic tyranny of the Seleucids.

Mattathias cried out in the town with a loud voice, saying: "Let every one who is zealous for the law and supports the covenant come out with me!" 1 MACC 2:27

A great many other Jews flee the increasing persecution, most bringing their families with them. One group is pursued to their wilderness retreat by Seleucid forces from Jerusalem. On the sacred sabbath, the enemy orders these fugitives to obey the will of Antiochus, but the faithful Jews refuse. Because of Mosaic Law, they decline to lift up their arms in self-defense on God's holy day. About 1,000 men, women, and children are slaughtered as the soldiers rampage unopposed among them.

This savage massacre leads to a practical revision of ancient law, expressed for the first time in a surviving text in 1 Maccabees 2:41: "Let us fight against anyone who comes to attack us on the sabbath day; let us not all die as our kindred died in their hiding places." Indeed, this change is accepted even by the Hasideans, an ultrareligious group that joins with Mattathias solely to restore the faith though they have no interest in his nationalistic aims.

Once passivity is replaced by retaliation, the rebellion thrives. Guerrilla forces roam through the Judean countryside, punishing the idolatrous with death and destroying Greek altars and shrines. Under Mattathias's leadership, many people are forcibly brought back to their ancestors' faith and Mosaic Law is again upheld. As in ancient days, decisions are reached by discussions that involve the whole community.

Now the days drew near for Mattathias to die, and he said to his sons: ". . . . show zeal for the law, and give your lives for the covenant of our ancestors."
1 MACC 2:49-50

Like a patriarch of old, the dying Mattathias delivers his final words as both warning and inspiration to his offspring. Citing the examples of Abraham, Joseph, Phinehas, Joshua, Caleb, David, Elijah, Daniel, and others, he reminds them that both worldly and spiritual rewards come to those who obey God's law.

Mattathias appoints his son Simon as his successor but gives command of the army to another son, Judas Maccabeus, whose surname probably meant "hammer" in ancient Hebrew (see the Maccabees' genealogy on page 301). Mattathias gives explicit orders: "Pay back the Gentiles in full, and obey the commands of the law" (1 Macc 2:68).

In 1 Maccabees 3:3-9, the battlefield successes and reconquests of Judas Maccabeus are celebrated in a poem written at the time. Like a heroic warrior-judge in the Old Testament, he saves people from the wrath of God by performing deeds that uphold the law.

Apollonius now gathered together Gentiles and a large force from Samaria to fight against Israel.　1 MACC 3:10

Annoyed by this rebellion in the south, Apollonius, the Seleucid governor of Samaria, leads an army against Judas Maccabeus. The Samaritans are routed and their leader killed. For the rest of his career, Judas carries Apollonius's sword into battle.

Then an even stronger and more ambitious foe storms into Judah. Seron, who is commander of the army of all Syria, meets Judas on the dangerous, winding highland road to Beth-horon, a town some 12 miles northwest of Jerusalem. Judas has only a small band of men who are weak from not eating that day, but he knows that God will enter the battle and defeat the overconfident Seleucids. "It is not on the size of the army that victory depends," he says in predicting success, "but strength comes from Heaven" (1 Macc 3:19).

Indeed, the determined Judeans swiftly overpower Seron's troops, driving them down to the coastal plain and killing some 800 of them. Then the Judeans are able to slip back into hiding in the Gophna hills. These first two major victories, which are immediately reported to Antiochus, make Judas famous throughout the Seleucid kingdom as a skilled and powerful adversary.

Antiochus's first enraged response is to muster all of the troops scattered throughout his kingdom into one vast army. But after giving them a healthy year's salary in advance, he realizes that there are not enough resources in the royal treasury to sustain a campaign against the rebels. Probably, the tyrant is beginning to lose his grip on the kingdom. Desperate for money, he decides in 165 B.C. to travel to Persia and collect taxes from his subjects there. He takes half his soldiers and elephants along.

The Seleucid regions from the borders of Egypt northeast to the Euphrates River are left in the hands of Lysias, an older royal relative acting as regent for the king's nine-year-old son, Antiochus V, at the capital city of Antioch. Lysias is specifically ordered to destroy Jerusalem and Judea, then resettle the area with alien peoples, just as the Assyrians had done centuries before in capturing Samaria. He is to remove the Israelites and bring in strangers.

A force of 40,000 foot soldiers and 7,000 horsemen under the generals Nicanor and Gorgias set out immediately and make camp some 20 miles west of Jerusalem at Emmaus, an area with plentiful supplies of water.

Now Judas and his brothers saw that misfortunes had increased and that the forces were encamped in their territory.　1 MACC 3:42

Undaunted, the rebels prepare for battle in the traditional Jewish way, by meeting in a congregation and asking the Lord for victory. The poem in verse 45 poignantly portrays the condition of occupied Jerusalem at the time. Judas is determined to reconquer the devastated Holy City.

Under cover of darkness, guided by Jews who are loyal to Antiochus, a

Nemesis of the Jews, Antiochus IV Epiphanes (on coin at left) plundered Jerusalem's temple in 169 B.C. A 15th-century French artist depicted the scene as warfare in his own times.

CAMPAIGNS OF THE MACCABEAN WARS

After the priest Mattathias raised the flag of revolt against the Seleucid oppressors of the Jews at Modein in 167 B.C., his son Judas Maccabeus gathered and trained a band of guerrilla warriors. Using their knowledge of Judea's forested valleys and rocky hills, they were able to overcome the larger and better armed forces that the Syrians mustered against them. First to feel the Maccabean sting was Apollonius, the governor of Samaria; he was ambushed at Lebonah en route to Jerusalem in response to a plea for help from Hellenized Jews.

Four more times the Syrians attempted to restore communications with their supporters in Jerusalem. Seron, commander of the army, brought his troops south along the coastal plain before turning inland through the hills. At Beth-horon, just 12 miles northwest of Jerusalem, Judas attacked, driving the invaders back toward the coast and killing 800 of them. Next to come were the generals Nicanor and Gorgias, sent by Lysias, the regent for nine-year-old Antiochus V. After making camp at Emmaus, Nicanor sent Gorgias to the rebels' base at Mizpah. But Judas outflanked Gorgias to surprise the main body of Syrians at Emmaus. Returning just in time to see his compatriots overcome, Gorgias joined the flight to the coast.

Frustrated by three successive defeats, Lysias took to the field. Looping south through friendly territory, he approached Jerusalem from the southwest. But at Beth-zur, he, too, was defeated, losing 5,000 men before withdrawing to Syria. This fourth victory encouraged the Jews to return to Jerusalem to rededicate their desecrated temple in December of 164. While the Seleucids were preoccupied with events far from Judea, Judas and his brothers liberated the Jews of Galilee and Gilead, east of the Jordan River. Continuing his offensive, Judas launched two successful attacks against Gorgias, now governor of the coastal cities. But Judas's siege of the Seleucid garrison holding the citadel of Jerusalem brought Lysias back to Judea. Mustering the strongest Syrian force yet—a reputed 100,000 infantry, 20,000 cavalry, and 32 elephants—the regent retraced his southern approach to Jerusalem. This time he got as far as Beth-zechariah. In the battle joined there, Judas's brother Eleazar attacked what he thought was the royal elephant—only to die when the injured beast fell on him. Unable to resist the Syrian juggernaut, the Jews fell back as Lysias set his siege engines before Jerusalem's walls. But a challenge to his authority at home forced Lysias to negotiate a settlement and again withdraw northward.

In 161 B.C., Demetrius I seized the Seleucid throne and killed his cousin Antiochus V and Lysias. He was determined to put an end, once and for all, to the

The ruins of Beth-zur, where Judas Maccabeus defeated the large, well-equipped army of the Seleucid regent Lysias

Maccabean menace. Twice, Judas defeated the attempts of the general Nicanor to open a route from Jerusalem to the coast. But at the approach of Demetrius's general Bacchides, Judas's supporters deserted him. Almost alone, the heroic warrior fell in battle a few miles north of Jerusalem. The torch passed to Judas's brother Jonathan, who made a strategic retreat to the Transjordanian region.

Jonathan next negotiated an agreement with Bacchides that brought seven years of peace to Judea. But further dynastic struggles among the Seleucids made it difficult for him to maintain independence. The would-be ruler Trypho lured the Jewish leader to Ptolemais, where he seized Jonathan and carried him captive on a campaign through Judea—finally putting him to death near Bascama. It was left for another Maccabean, Simon, to establish Jewish political and religious freedom in 142 B.C.

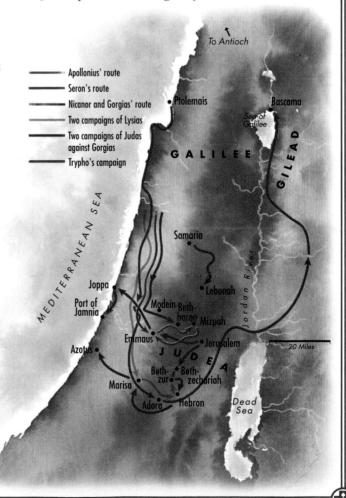

After defeating the Seleucids, Judas Maccabeus led his men to Jerusalem to cleanse and rededicate the desecrated temple; a scene by Julius Schnorr von Carolsfeld (1794-1874).

force of 1,000 cavalry and 5,000 infantry under Gorgias breaks into the rebel camp. It is deserted. Hearing of the plot, Judas has secretly led his forces toward the tents of the enemy. Meanwhile, Gorgias assumes that the Jews have fled in terror and begins looking for them in the nearby hills.

At dawn, the Jewish force of 3,000, though lacking in armor and weaponry, advances toward the well-fortified, well-armed Greek camp. Judas spurs his men onward by reminding them that God crushed the mighty chariot troops of Egypt by drowning them in the Red Sea. With a great blast of trumpets, the Jews fall upon the enemy camp, overpowering them swiftly. The surprised Greek forces lose heart and flee in every direction.

On the instant, Gorgias's night raiders appear in the distance, drawn by the smoke of their burning camp. What they see unnerves them. The well-trained, arrogant warriors turn and make for the safety of formerly Philistine territory.

News of this defeat bewilders and depresses Lysias. The following year he himself leads a greater army, including 60,000 handpicked foot soldiers and 5,000 cavalry, that meets Judas and his force of 10,000 some 20 miles south of Jerusalem at Beth-zur, a town on the way to Hebron. Again, Judas publicly puts the fate of his people in the hands of the Lord. Again, the larger, better armed enemy is quickly routed.

"See, our enemies are crushed; let us go up to cleanse the sanctuary and dedicate it." 1 MACC 4:36

At last, the triumphant Jews feel secure enough to devote time and energy to restoring the desolate temple mount. The destruction includes the ruined chambers of the priests, which may have been built around three sides of the sanctuary.

The restoration of the temple is extremely careful. The most pious priests cleanse the sanctuary, removing everything that has been defiled by Greek idols or decoration. Because the Jews do not feel that a true prophet of God is among them in these times, they completely remove the desecrated altar and store its stones until someone worthy can instruct them as to what to do with them. A new altar is built, following instructions in Exodus and Deuteronomy. The sanctuary is rebuilt, and the ritual objects and furniture used in worship are replaced.

The first sacrifice is offered in the restored temple on the 25th day of Chislev in 164 B.C., almost three years to the day after the Greeks first desecrated it. With joyful music and deep gratitude to the Lord, the Jews celebrate this rededication and cleansing for eight days. The length of the observance matches a similar reconsecration under Hezekiah 500 years earlier (2 Chr 29:17) and becomes the model for the Jewish festival of Hanukkah observed to this day by Jews around the world.

Having reclaimed holy ground for their religion, Judas and his followers turn to the work of defending the nation's capital. Strong walls and towers are built as fortifications, and troops are garrisoned in the city to protect it from Greek attack.

When the Gentiles all around heard that the altar had been rebuilt and the sanctuary dedicated as it was before, they became very angry. 1 MACC 5:1

The great Jewish victories do not initiate a time of peace. On the contrary, tensions mount as the Greeks make scattered attempts at revenge. For his part, Judas determines to take back ancient lands of the Jewish people, perhaps beginning his campaign only after Antiochus's death.

First, Judas wars against peoples who continually harass and ambush the Jews. At the town of Akrabattene, probably south of the Dead Sea on the border between Judea and Idumea, he defeats the Edomites. Somewhere to the east of the Jordan River, he slays the people of the town of Baean by setting fire to the towers in which they have sought safety. He also defeats the Transjordanian Ammonites.

Clearly, Judas has established himself as the trusted hero of Jewish people everywhere, and pleas for assistance begin to flood into Jerusalem. Jews who had fled persecution in Gilead beg for help against the vengeful Greeks, as do the Jews of Galilee, who feel threatened by the hostile people living along the Mediterranean coast.

Judas accepts the challenge. He sends his brother Simon with 3,000 soldiers north to rescue the Jews in Galilee, while he and his brother Jonathan set out for Transjordanian Gilead with an army of 8,000. He leaves Jerusalem in the care of Joseph, not a member of his family, and orders him to protect the people but avoid engaging the Gentiles until the armies return. In short order, Simon's forces rout the foe, pursuing them northwest to Ptolemais and killing as many as 3,000. They bring the Galilean Jews to Judea "with great rejoicing" (1 Macc 5:23).

Meanwhile, Judas and Jonathan lead their troops on a three-day journey through the eastern desert, where they learn from friendly Nabatean Arabs that the Gentiles are preparing to attack several Jewish towns and destroy them in a single day. Judas does not hesitate. He lays waste the enemy town of Bozrah, then races during the night to Dathema, where a great army, under the leadership of a certain Timothy, has already launched an attack on the Jews. Judas's forces intervene with such ferocity and discipline that 8,000 of the enemy are killed and the rest flee in haste. The Jews march on and take several hostile towns in the Gilead region.

Timothy has not given up in the meantime. Gathering together a large army that includes Arab mercenaries, he encamps beside a tributary of the Yarmuk River, knowing full well that Judas will be drawn to the challenge.

Now as Judas and his army drew near to the stream of water, Timothy said to the officers of his forces, "If he crosses over to us first, we will not be able to resist him."
1 MACC 5:40

Timothy feels confident of success if Judas pauses to camp on the other side of the river, but the Jews press forward, showing no fear. As Judas leads his army directly into battle, the enemy breaks ranks and runs. Now the Jews throughout Gilead are free to return to their homeland.

Unfortunately, Judas discovers that Joseph has foolishly disobeyed orders. Envious of the other leaders, he and another commander, Azariah, have marched out of Jerusalem to attack Jamnia, a town held by Gorgias. This is a serious blunder. Some 2,000 Jewish soldiers are killed in the rout that follows. To the author of 1 Maccabees, the incident affirms that God has placed the future of the nation and the religion solely in the hands of the Hasmoneans.

During these events, Antiochus has not succeeded in his Persian venture. He fails to take a town where rich treasures that once belonged to his legendary predecessor Alexander the Great are stored. Worse, news of the successful Jewish rebellion reaches him on the march. Depressed, the king falls into a fatal decline during which he begins to feel that his misfortunes stem from his desecration of the temple in Jerusalem. Antiochus dies near today's Isfahan in Iran and power passes to young Antiochus V Eupator (see the genealogy of Seleucid rulers on page 306).

The king was enraged when he heard this.
1 MACC 6:28

Meanwhile, Judas has begun a siege against the Seleucid garrison of disloyal Jews in the citadel of Jerusalem. Some of the soldiers escape to Antioch to ask for help. Furious, the new king brings together a huge engine of war made up of the entire

THE FESTIVAL OF HANUKKAH

The only major Jewish festival not mentioned in the Old Testament commemorates the dramatic rededication of the Jerusalem temple in 164 B.C. The story of Hanukkah, Hebrew for "dedication," began three years earlier with the daring Hebrew revolt against the Seleucid kingdom of Syria. King Antiochus IV Epiphanes, a successor to Alexander the Great, had decided to impose Greek culture and worship throughout his domain—including Judea. Part of his strategy was to order that sacrifices to the Greek god Zeus be offered in the temple. A defiant priest named Mattathias refused and fled to the Judean hills, where his son Judas Maccabeus and Judas's four brothers launched a successful guerrilla war against the Seleucids.

After recapturing Jerusalem, the Jews began purifying the temple by removing and replacing everything that had been used in pagan rituals. Once this was done, priests lit the temple lamps, filling the sanctuary with a warm glow and signaling that the temple was again a holy place. For eight days, the Jews celebrated by offering sacrifices, singing, and eating together. The festivities began on Chislev 25 (December 14) in 164, exactly three years after Antiochus's defilement. The story, reported in 1 Maccabees 4 and 2 Maccabees 10, suggests that the Jews decided to celebrate for eight days because Solomon and Hezekiah had previously dedicated the temple during the eight-day harvest festival of Booths.

Hanukkah is also known as the Feast of Lights, from the ritual of lighting the temple lamps. According to legend, the original lamps—though holding only enough oil to burn for a single day—miraculously burned throughout the eight-day rededication. Eventually, pious Jews began the custom of lighting eight-candle Hanukkah lamps in their homes, adding one flame for each night of the joyous festival.

Lights are lit on eight successive days to celebrate Hanukkah; this 16th-century Italian brass menorah, or lampstand, has eight receptacles for oil wicks.

forces of the Seleucid kingdom and mercenaries from abroad, as well as 32 elephants trained in battle.

First, the Greeks, under Antiochus V and the regent Lysias, attack newly fortified Beth-zur, but the courageous Jews torch the enemy's siege engines. Judas then moves his army six miles away to Beth-zechariah, where the Jews meet the Seleucids early in the morning after a forced march. Here, the author of 1 Maccabees provides a fascinating glimpse of elephants as weaponry. Given wine and mulberry juice to make them angry and perhaps to remind them of blood, the animals are each protected by 1,000 armed foot soldiers and 500 cavalry. Four armed soldiers and an Indian driver, or mahout, sit atop each elephant in a covered wooden tower attached by a specially made harness.

Daring to go against the superior enemy forces, Judas and his followers are at first successful, slaying 600 of their foes. Eleazar, another of Judas's brothers, notices that one elephant is taller than the others and decorated with royal armor. Assuming that the king is riding on it, he bravely battles his way to the animal's side and stabs its great belly, killing it. Unfortunately, Eleazar cannot withdraw quickly enough. The dying elephant falls on him, crushing him to death. It is an omen of disaster.

When the Jews saw the royal might and the fierce attack of the forces, they turned away in flight. 1 MACC 6:47

At last, with the full armed might of the Seleucid kingdom thrown against them, the Jews are forced to flee. Antiochus negotiates a peace with Beth-zur, then sets up assault engines around the city of Jerusalem. This siege begins in a sabbatical year, when the land is not farmed. For that reason and because the refugees from Gilead and Galilee have been consuming the city's store of supplies, there is little food to sustain a long siege.

The regent Lysias is having his own problems. On his deathbed, Antiochus IV had appointed a good friend to take charge of his son. This man, Philip, has returned from Persia with the crown, robe, and signet ring symbolizing royal power, and is eager to take over the regency himself.

Not wanting to become mired in a lengthy and draining siege, Lysias proposes an accord to the Jews, promising to end the campaign of enforcing Greek culture. The regent returns to Antioch and wins the capital city back from Philip.

In the one hundred fifty-first year Demetrius son of Seleucus set out from Rome, sailed with a few men to a town by the sea, and there began to reign. 1 MACC 7:1

Antiochus V is doomed to have a short reign. In 161 B.C. his cousin Demetrius escapes from captivity in Rome and makes his way to the town of Tripolis, some 170 miles south of Antioch. Determined to seize the Seleucid throne, Demetrius convinces the army to support him and has Lysias and

Antiochus V executed. "And Demetrius [I Soter] took his seat on the throne of his kingdom" (1 Macc 7:4).

Almost immediately, Jews who support Greek culture pay the new monarch a visit. Among them is Alcimus, ambitious to become high priest in Jerusalem, even though he is not a legitimate claimant by birth. The self-appointed delegation asks Demetrius to send an army to defeat Judas Maccabeus and his followers, who "have destroyed all your Friends, and have driven us out of our land" (1 Macc 7:6).

The king dispatches an army under one of his close advisers, Bacchides, who is governor of the Seleucid province lying west of the Euphrates River. He also rewards Alcimus, making him high priest.

When the troops draw near Jerusalem, a group of scribes comes out to seek peace, certain that Alcimus will not allow them to be harmed. In fact, the puppet high priest breaks a pledge to spare them and has 60 of these pious scholars slain. Worse yet, their bodies are left unburied in the open, a grievous insult.

After a further demonstration of cruelty, Bacchides withdraws, leaving Seleucid soldiers to protect the wicked Alcimus and work his will. Hellenized Jews take advantage of the situation to oppress their countrymen.

Courageously if unwisely, Judas Maccabeus's brother Eleazar stabs the royal elephant—only to be crushed as the beast falls; an 1865 engraving by Gustave Doré.

Judas saw all the wrongs that Alcimus and those
with him had done among the Israelites; it was more
than the Gentiles had done.   1 MACC 7:23

Although Alcimus holds power in the capital, Judas and his men take revenge in the surrounding countryside and keep the citizens of Seleucid Jerusalem bottled up within the walls. Alcimus races to the court of Demetrius to ask again for help in dealing with the stubborn rebels.

Charged to destroy the Jews at last, the Seleucid general Nicanor marches to Judea with a large army. He arranges a peace parley with Judas: "Let there be no fighting between you and me; I shall come with a few men to see you face to face in peace" (1 Macc 7:28). Although he meets with Nicanor, Judas discovers that there is a plot to kidnap him and declines a second conference. Instead, they battle some five miles northeast of the capital at Caphar-salama. After losing 500 men, Nicanor and his troops seek refuge within the city walls of Jerusalem.

When several priests and elders show him how offerings are being made for Demetrius's benefit in the temple, Nicanor scoffs and swears to burn the place down if Judas is not given up. The horrified priests cry out to the Lord for punishment of this blasphemous man: "Take vengeance on this man and on his army, and let them fall by the sword" (1 Macc 7:38). Their plea contains echoes of Solomon's prayer at the dedication of his temple (1 Kgs 8:22-53).

When Judas and Nicanor meet in battle sometime in March of 161 B.C., the impertinent Seleucid general is the first to be slain. His dismayed troops immediately lose heart and flee, pursued by Jewish troops blasting their trumpets. The noise brings out loyal villagers in the Judean towns. They drive the enemy back upon the swords of their pursuers. All of Nicanor's soldiers are killed.

Nicanor's head and right hand are cut off and displayed in grisly triumph. The day became known to Jews as Nicanor Day, observed every year with a festival during which mourning was not allowed. It is no longer celebrated today.

Now Judas heard of the fame of the Romans, that they
were very strong and were well-disposed toward all who
made an alliance with them.   1 MACC 8:1

Sometime later, Judas the warrior begins exploring diplomatic avenues to protect his people. For about 30 years, the Roman republic has been moving into Near Eastern politics as Seleucid power has weakened. The author of 1 Maccabees cites many of Rome's great conquests, from Gaul to Spain to Macedonia, to show that it is virtually unbeatable but has also proved itself a reliable ally.

In brief, the Romans are portrayed as preferable to the Seleucids as rulers. They have never had a king, and their republican senate is said to rule by deliberation and agreement in the manner of Jewish councils. To this very senate Judas sends two repre-

Judas Maccabeus shows a priest the field where he
defeated Nicanor; a 17th-century Dutch painting.

sentatives to set up an alliance. As if the two countries are peers in power, each agrees to refuse to help anyone who makes war against the other. In addition to the treaty, the Romans agree to tell Demetrius to cease troubling Jerusalem. However, history does not record that Rome actually took action against him.

Meanwhile, in revenge for the defeat of Nicanor, Demetrius sends a new army under Bacchides and Alcimus to suppress the continuing Jewish rebellion. En route from Antioch to Jerusalem early in 160 B.C., the troops find many Jews hiding in caves and kill them. Judas handpicks 3,000 warriors to meet the threat, but 2,200 of them are so awed by the enemy force of 20,000 infantry and 2,000 horsemen that they desert.

When Judas saw that his army had slipped away
and the battle was imminent, he was crushed in spirit.
1 MACC 9:7

Characteristically, Judas decides to die fighting. In a fierce battle that sees many casualties on both sides, Judas is able to put the right wing of the invading army to flight, but the left swiftly wheels upon him. Finally, the hero who has so many times beaten the odds with God's help is killed on the battlefield.

Buried alongside his father at Modein, Judas is mourned in a lament that echoes David's elegy for Saul and Jonathan: "How is the mighty fallen, the savior of Israel" (1 Macc 9:21; 2 Sam 1:19). Nonetheless, Judas's passing is a signal for supporters of Demetrius, including Jews, to defy Jewish traditional beliefs and practices again. When famine strikes, rebellion against the Seleucids grows faint. To the horror of true believers, many men close to Judas are arrested and harassed by the victorious Bacchides.

There was great distress in Israel, such as had not been since the time that prophets ceased to appear among them.
1 MACC 9:27

The flame of liberty lit by the Hasmonean family does not gutter out completely. Judas's remaining followers choose his brother Jonathan "to take his place as our ruler and leader, to fight our battle" (1 Macc 9:30). When Bacchides tries to have Jonathan killed, he and his brother Simon flee with their supporters into the desert southeast of Bethlehem. Bacchides leads his army after them and crosses to the east of the Jordan, hoping to catch the Jews by surprise on the sabbath.

The Maccabees take up hiding places in the marshes east of the Jordan, with the Greeks camped farther east. Thus trapped, with the river to their backs when Bacchides attacks, the Jews fight back furiously, killing some 1,000 of the enemy. After failing to strike Bacchides, Jonathan leads his men in a tactical retreat; they swim across the river, but the enemy does not press the advantage and follow.

Bacchides returns to Jerusalem and garrisons many towns in Judea as protection against Jonathan's band. The Seleucid position seems militarily secure, but then the faithless priest Alcimus makes a fatal mistake. In order to allow Greeks access to the sanctuary, he orders the inner court wall of the temple torn down. As soon as he gives the word, Alcimus is struck with paralysis and dies an agonizing death. The wall remains.

Bacchides withdraws to Antioch, and Judea is at peace for two years. Then some of the renegade Jews ask him to come back to kill Jonathan. In revenge, Jonathan's men slay about 50 of the renegades. In a wilderness town called Bethbasi, the rebels build fortifications. Bacchides attacks but makes no headway,

These rock-cut tombs at Modein, 17 miles northwest of Jerusalem, are said to hold the remains of Mattathias and his sons, leaders of the Maccabean revolt against the Greeks.

even with his siege engines. While Jonathan sneaks out and wages war against some nearby Bedouins, Simon surprises Bacchides by burning his war engines and beating back his troops. Defeated and angry, Bacchides takes revenge on some of the Jews who have asked him to come and then returns to Antioch. Frequently, the Seleucid leaders are shown acting in anger; the Jews believe that a wise leader should always control his emotions.

Jonathan and Bacchides thereafter conclude a peace agreement that lasts for seven years. Like a hero in Judges, Jonathan begins to govern the people from his home in Michmash, about eight miles northeast of Jerusalem. Then Seleucid internal affairs once again affect the Jews. Alexander I Epiphanes (also called Alexander Balas), who claims to be a son of Antiochus IV, challenges Demetrius for the throne. Demetrius hastily tries to patch up his relationship with the Jews. He gives Jonathan the authority to raise an army and releases to him Jewish hostages who have been put in the citadel by Bacchides.

Jonathan took up residence in Jerusalem and began to rebuild and restore the city.   1 MACC 10:10

Alexander is not to be outdone. He appoints Jonathan as high priest of Israel, gives him the prestigious title "King's Friend," and sends him a royal robe and crown. Thus Jonathan is transformed finally from guerrilla chieftain hiding in the marshes to spiritual and secular leader of the nation, affirmed by the power of the ruling Seleucids.

This turn of events inspires further intrigue. Perhaps hoping to alienate the Jews from Jonathan, Demetrius writes directly to them offering the welcome gift of tax relief. He also promises to free all Jewish captives living in any part of the kingdom. Moreover, Demetrius pledges to respect Jewish religious holidays and to allow Jews to join his army, yet keep their own laws. He also adds three Samaritan districts to Judea and grants 15,000 silver shekels annually to pay for expenses at the temple. Finally, Demetrius offers to pay for rebuilding all of the sanctuary structures and all of Jerusalem's fortifications.

The memory of the Jews is not so short, however, that they can bring themselves to trust the man who has so assiduously oppressed them. They choose to remain with Alexander, who also has the backing of Rome. In 150 B.C., Demetrius is killed after his army is defeated by Alexander's forces.

Alexander moves quickly to make his position secure. He seals an alliance with Egypt's King Ptolemy VI Philometor by marrying one of his daughters. At the time of the opulent state wedding, Jonathan is invited to meet both kings and is seated beside Alexander in public and given rich gifts.

It is not long before Alexander's judgment is amply rewarded. The son of Demetrius, Demetrius II Nicator, raises an army to seize the throne. Apollonius, one of his governors, is ordered to punish Jonathan and the Jews for siding with Alexander.

Though he defeated his son-in-law Alexander Balas in battle near Antioch in 145 B.C., Egypt's King Ptolemy VI Philometor sustained fatal wounds; the fallen king is shown in this German engraving dated about 1630.

Then, unexpectedly, Demetrius is won over by Jonathan when they meet at Ptolemais to discuss peace terms, and the king pledges to support him as high priest. Demetrius also affirms several of the gifts promised by his father, including tax relief and the granting of the three Samaritan districts to Judea.

Later, the Seleucid king accedes to Jonathan's request to remove his troops from the Jerusalem citadel and other Judean strongholds. Now it is Demetrius's turn to call for help. Many soldiers who have fought for other Seleucid kings despise him and revolt, hoping to put Alexander Balas's son Antiochus VI Epiphanes on the throne.

Jonathan sends 3,000 of his men to Antioch to protect his ally, who is forced to take refuge in his palace when the townspeople begin rioting. The Jews restore order after killing about 100,000 people (this figure, like most of those in 1 and 2 Maccabees is, no doubt, inflated).

But Demetrius eventually forgets these events and turns his back on Jonathan. Civil war heats up again as young Antiochus VI, backed by a certain Trypho, attracts an army of soldiers hostile to Demetrius II. As fortune favors one side or the other in the Seleucid civil war, the land of Judea is often caught in the middle. Antiochus affirms Jonathan as high priest, then Demetrius tries to have him removed. Jonathan repels a Seleucid attack even though, at one point, most of his men desert him. On this occasion, the Jewish leader mourns and prays to the Lord to secure victory against the Gentiles.

Returning to the diplomatic arena, Jonathan reaffirms his alliance with Rome in a letter to the senate and also sends a friendly letter to the Spartans in Greece. Curiously, Jonathan writes to the king there that "it has been found in writing concerning the Spartans and the Jews that they are brothers and are of the family of Abraham" (1 Macc 12:21). Apparently, this unlikely kinship between the two peoples was a popular belief of the time.

In response, Jonathan and his brother Simon, with a force of 10,000 men, attack and capture the city of Joppa, which gives the Jews access to the Mediterranean. Soon, Apollonius draws Jonathan out by marching with his large army and 2,000 cavalry toward the Philistine city of Ashdod, called Azotus by the Greeks. The Jews attack, but are suddenly rushed from behind by 1,000 horsemen Apollonius has cleverly left in hiding to the rear. The Jews stand firm until Simon appears with reinforcements and routs the enemy. Some 8,000 of Demetrius's men are put to the sword or burned alive in Azotus.

Jonathan returns in triumph to Jerusalem, and a grateful Alexander presents him with yet more gifts, honors him with the title "King's Kinsman," and awards him the Philistine city of Ekron.

Then the king of Egypt gathered great forces, like the sand by the seashore, and many ships; and he tried to get possession of Alexander's kingdom by trickery and add it to his own kingdom. 1 MACC 11:1

Alexander, however, is doomed. Ptolemy brings his army to his son-in-law's kingdom, where he meets cordially with Jonathan even though he has been shown the destruction at Azotus. Ptolemy is after a greater prize. He now offers friendship to Demetrius, along with the daughter who is already married to Alexander. In a battle near Antioch, the Egyptians defeat Alexander, who flees to Arabia but is killed there; his head is sent to Ptolemy. However, three days later the Egyptian king dies of wounds suffered in battle. Thus, Demetrius II, Jonathan's enemy, is left sole ruler in the kingdom.

Now Jonathan heard that the commanders of Demetrius had returned, with a larger force than before, to wage war against him. 1 MACC 12:24

But the Jews' allies are far away and warfare continues in Judea. Jonathan defeats one invading army sent by Demetrius, and both he and Simon move separately through the region, making sure that towns are garrisoned for defense. Jonathan also improves the fortifications at Jerusalem.

In a surprising turn of events in Antioch, meanwhile, Trypho sets himself up against young Antiochus VI.

The revolt of the Maccabees is celebrated in this cast bronze sculpture, located in modern Israel's parliamentary gardens.

Hoping to remove Jonathan as a potential adversary, the upstart marches into Judea, but decides not to risk a battle when he sees the size of the Jewish forces, a reputed 40,000 men.

Instead, Trypho welcomes Jonathan as an ally, urges him to send his troops home, and promises to give the Jews the disputed town of Ptolemais and other properties. Taking the man at his word, Jonathan dismisses most of his army and goes to Ptolemais with only 1,000 men at his side. Once they enter the city, the gates are closed and the trap sprung. Word goes out that the great Jewish hero and all of his men have been killed by the sword. Trypho hopes to crush the rest of Jonathan's followers now that they are leaderless, but they fight valiantly and return safely to Judea as the entire nation mourns Jonathan.

A true Hasmonean leader, Simon rallies a nervous nation when rumors spread that Trypho is preparing to devastate the land. His brave words convince the Jews to elect him their military leader, and he immediately begins strengthening national defenses.

When the Syrian and Jewish armies meet on the battlefield, Trypho makes an astonishing offer: In exchange for the fees that a vassal at Jonathan's level would normally pay to Antioch, he will release Jonathan himself, not dead but still alive as a hostage. Simon knows Trypho is treacherous but sends the money anyway so that he can never be blamed for his older brother's death.

Sadly, his instincts are correct. Trypho takes the money and keeps Jonathan prisoner. The two armies circle around each other aimlessly. When Trypho tries to take food to one of his garrisons, an unusual snowfall prevents him. Somewhere northeast of the Sea of Galilee, just before leaving for Antioch, he has Jonathan killed.

Simon has his brother's bones buried in the family tomb at Modein. In an echo of foreign practice, he also builds an elaborate memorial that includes seven stone pyramids. The decorations feature armor to symbolize Jewish victories and ships to warn off potential invaders by sea.

Meanwhile, Trypho kills Antiochus VI at last and seizes power. Simon sees to the defense of Judah, then sends emissaries to Demetrius II to ask for assistance after the depredations of Trypho. Demetrius provides tax relief and makes places available for Jews to serve in his personal bodyguard. Probably, the king's kindness is evidence of his decaying power.

In the one hundred seventieth year the yoke of the Gentiles was removed from Israel. 1 MACC 13:41

The Maccabean wars end about 142 B.C. The Hasmonean kingdom exists as a free, independent state. Under Simon, who may have been the first of his dynasty to mint coinage, idolatry is driven from Judea. But Simon is merciful to the idolaters, allowing them to move elsewhere whenever a defiled city is ritually cleansed, rebuilt, and settled by Jews.

Most important, the long-standing insult of the enemy citadel at Jerusalem is finally ended. The Seleucid soldiers, who may have been disloyal Jews, are allowed to leave in peace, the citadel is cleansed, and a great festival celebrates this removal of foreign domination from the city of God.

On the larger political stage, Demetrius II tries to strengthen his army against Trypho by marching into Media to gather help from the Seleucids there. But the Persian monarch has him arrested and detained.

In Judah, as explained by a joyous poem of the day (1 Macc 14:4-15), the wise and benign reign of Simon brings peace and prosperity prophesied but rarely seen in the Old Testament. Warm letters and rich gifts continue to flow from Sparta and Rome. In an unusual but ancient ceremony, Simon is elected high priest as well as Judea's ruler, embodying in his person the family's enduring concern with both religion and national independence.

"When we gain control of our kingdom, we will bestow great honor on you and your nation and the temple, so that your glory will become manifest in all the earth." 1 MACC 15:9

Confirming Simon's power, Antiochus VII Sidetes, who succeeded his elder brother, Demetrius II, on the Seleucid throne in 138 B.C., writes to Simon to extend the tax benefits and other gifts promised by his sibling. Next, he besieges Trypho in coastal

Dor, attacking by land and sea. In the meantime, letters arrive from Rome, informing various city-states of the ancient world that Simon and his people are under Rome's protection.

Antiochus VII levies a second siege against Dor, and the Jews contribute 2,000 soldiers, money, and equipment to the effort. Evidently, the Seleucid ruler rejects this help and turns against Judea, demanding control of Joppa, Gazara, and the Jerusalem citadel. Simon refuses to give them up, and Antiochus prepares for war on two fronts: He will pursue Trypho, who has escaped Dor by sea, while asking Cendebeus, the commander of Seleucid troops along the Mediterranean coast, to send raiding parties into Judea. Eventually, though not reported in 1 Maccabees, Trypho is defeated and commits suicide.

"Take my place and my brother's, and go out and fight for our nation, and may the help that comes from Heaven be with you." 1 MACC 16:3

Too old to fight by this time, Simon sends his sons Judas and John Hyrcanus into battle with 20,000 troops, including the first Judean cavalry. In the tradition of the Hasmonean family's exploits, the Jewish army routes the invaders and pursues them in their flight, killing 2,000 of the enemy.

Ironically, the great leader will not die gloriously or in the peace of his home. Ptolemy, the governor of the Jericho plain and Simon's son-in-law, plots to gain power for himself. Early in 134 B.C., he invites the aging Simon and his sons Mattathias and Judas to a banquet at the small fort of Dok that he had built about three miles northwest of Jericho. When the three guests become drunk on wine, Ptolemy and his henchmen overpower and kill them.

The ambitious Ptolemy also means to kill Simon's son John Hyrcanus, who commands the garrison at Gazara, and then seize many towns in Judea, including Jerusalem. But John gets wind of this scheme. He slays the men sent to kill him, then succeeds his beloved father as high priest.

The writer does not describe the career of John Hyrcanus I, who served as high priest from 134 to 104. According to other historians, John made peace with Antiochus VII after being defeated in battle; he eventually extended the Hasmonean kingdom to include almost all of ancient Palestine. In little more than a generation, marked by persecution and struggle, the remarkable Hasmoneans had been able to set up a viable Jewish state and reclaim their religion, helped in no small part by divisive conflicts among the more powerful, wealthier, and better armed Seleucids. As high priests and kings, the family dominated Judean politics and religion until John's great-grandson, Antigonus II, was overthrown by the infamous Herod the Great in 37 B.C. Herod still ruled the kingdom at the time of Jesus' birth.

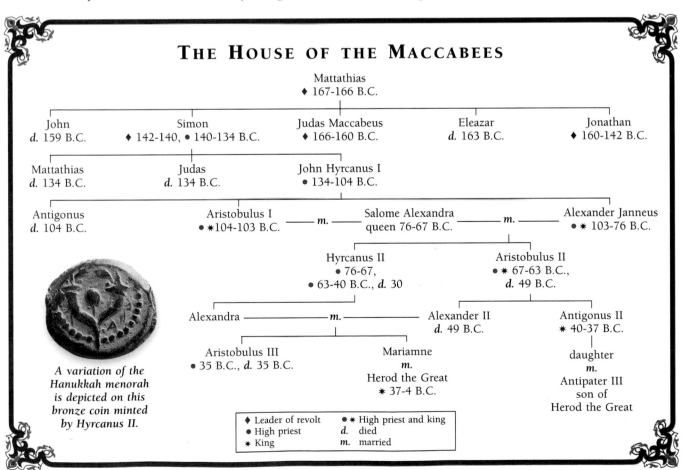

THE HOUSE OF THE MACCABEES

Mattathias
♦ 167-166 B.C.

John
d. 159 B.C.

Simon
♦ 142-140, ● 140-134 B.C.

Judas Maccabeus
♦ 166-160 B.C.

Eleazar
d. 163 B.C.

Jonathan
♦ 160-142 B.C.

Mattathias
d. 134 B.C.

Judas
d. 134 B.C.

John Hyrcanus I
● 134-104 B.C.

Antigonus
d. 104 B.C.

Aristobulus I
●✱104-103 B.C.

— m. —

Salome Alexandra
queen 76-67 B.C.

— m. —

Alexander Janneus
●✱ 103-76 B.C.

Hyrcanus II
● 76-67,
● 63-40 B.C., d. 30

Aristobulus II
●✱ 67-63 B.C.,
d. 49 B.C.

Alexandra ——— m. ——— Alexander II
d. 49 B.C.

Antigonus II
✱ 40-37 B.C.

Aristobulus III
● 35 B.C., d. 35 B.C.

Mariamne
m.
Herod the Great
✱ 37-4 B.C.

daughter
m.
Antipater III
son of
Herod the Great

A variation of the Hanukkah menorah is depicted on this bronze coin minted by Hyrcanus II.

♦ Leader of revolt	●✱ High priest and king
● High priest	d. died
✱ King	m. married

2 MACCABEES

The author of 2 Maccabees cares less about historical accuracy than about the religious and political issues that divide the Jews in the second century B.C. The Jerusalem faction that accepts the Greek culture of Judea's Seleucid overlords is shown as faithless and corrupt. But those who strive to uphold Mosaic Law and reject all foreign influence are rewarded by God. He intervenes dramatically on several occasions to punish the arrogance of pagan leaders, demonstrating the justice of divine retribution for outrages against the Jews and their traditions. By the same token, the most blessed Jews are those who suffer death for their faith, notably the mother and her seven sons in chapter 7. Their stories inspired many martyrdom narratives by later Jewish and Christian writers.

Several religious concepts that became important to both Judaism and Christianity are expressed in this book, appearing for the first time in surviving Jewish writing: the promise of bodily resurrection of the dead (2 Macc 7:23), the idea that God created the world from nothingness (2 Macc 7:28), and the effectiveness of prayers for the departed (2 Macc 12:45).

Biblical scholars believe that the writer based his account on official temple sources and records of the Seleucid court. He uses the style of Greek historians of the period, speaking directly to his readers in a distinctive voice and obviously delighting in wordplay. It appears that he completed 2 Maccabees by 124 B.C. Like 1 Maccabees, which contains a parallel account and was most likely written 20 years later, the book is accepted as canonical by Roman Catholics and Orthodox churches.

Menorahs, lampstands used at Hanukkah, often have eight receptacles for oil wicks; this German one is dated 1830.

May God do good to you, and may he remember his covenant with Abraham and Isaac and Jacob, his faithful servants. 2 MACC 1:2

Two letters by unknown writers have been prefixed to 2 Maccabees. The first, written in 124 B.C. by the Jews of Judea to their brethren living in the Egyptian community established in the days of Alexander the Great, reminds them to celebrate the new festival of Hanukkah.

The second letter is addressed to Aristobulus, a well-known sage and tutor at the Ptolemaic court in Egypt. It explains in detail why the festival is so important. The writer draws a parallel between the achievements of Judas Maccabeus and those of Nehemiah, who kept the faith even in captivity in Babylon. In a dry cistern, fire taken from the Jerusalem altar had been kept burning secretly for years. When their captors decided to allow Jews to worship, priests sent to retrieve the fire found only a thick liquid. Nehemiah sprinkled it over an altar. When the sun came out from beneath some clouds, a huge fire blazed up, consuming the sacrificial offering. The strange liquid was petroleum, called naphtha from a Persian word. But the fire inspired the Jews to offer a prayer of thanksgiving and then ask to be allowed to return to Jerusalem and restore the temple.

The letter also reminds Aristobulus that Solomon held a festival for eight days after consecrating his temple. Finally, a parallel is drawn between Nehemiah's efforts to find and protect all sacred writings and the attempts of Judas Maccabeus to do the same thing. These various examples are used to support celebration of a festival not prescribed by Mosaic Law. "Will you therefore please keep the days?" (2 Macc 2:16), the author pleads.

All this, which has been set forth by Jason of Cyrene in five volumes, we shall attempt to condense into a single book. 2 MACC 2:23

Before turning to the historical record to explain the achievements of Judas Maccabeus and the other Hasmoneans, the author explains that his account is a greatly condensed version of a five-volume work by Jason of Cyrene. This historian is unknown to today's scholars, and none of his writings have been found. The theme of 2 Maccabees is deeply religious: The outnumbered Jews can defeat huge pagan armies, liberate Jerusalem, and restore the temple only because God smiles on their exploits. For the first time in surviving literature, the religion of the Jews is called "Judaism" (2 Macc 2:21).

The narrative focuses on the ongoing conflict between religious Jews and pro-Seleucid Jews portrayed throughout 1 Maccabees. In this case, during a period of relative peace in Judea some time before 175 B.C., the high priest Onias III has a working relationship with the Syrian king Seleucus IV Philopator, who even subsidizes the temple services.

But a personal vendetta has national consequences. A certain Simon, peeved at Onias about some dispute over managing the Jerusalem marketplace, goes to Apollonius, the Seleucid governor, seeking revenge. He reports that vast sums of money in the temple treasury can be appropriated by Seleucus because they are not assigned to the sacrifices.

When Apollonius met the king, he told him of the money about which he had been informed.   2 MACC 3:7

In due course, Apollonius informs his sovereign of the supposed hoard, and the king sends his man Heliodorus to confiscate it. Onias tries to prevent him, explaining that the money includes deposits belonging to widows and orphans. Moreover, he adds, the amount is relatively small. In fact, Onias is probably not being entirely truthful. He secretly prefers Egyptian rule to that of the Seleucids and may have been hoarding tribute owed to the king.

In any event, Heliodorus is unmoved. Onias is seized by "terror and bodily trembling" (2 Macc 3:17), and the entire population of Jerusalem mourns and makes supplication to the Lord. But when Heliodorus strides up to the temple treasury, he and his armed guard are suddenly struck with abject fright by a manifestation of God's authority.

A richly decorated horse carrying a fierce-looking rider armored in gold bears down on the astonished Heliodorus, striking him with its hooves. Suddenly, two handsome, strong, and beautifully dressed young men also appear and flog the helpless Seleucid official until he loses consciousness and has to be borne away on a stretcher.

This divine intervention causes the Jews to rejoice throughout the temple precincts. Men in the Seleucid retinue beg Onias to save their friend's life by calling on "the Most High" (2 Macc 3:31), a term frequently used by Gentiles to refer to the Lord. Onias duly offers a sacrifice, fearful that Seleucus will discount any miraculous explanation for his emissary's beating and suspect the Jews of foul play.

Immediately, the two mysterious young men reappear to Heliodorus, explaining that he will live only because the Lord granted Onias's prayer and ordering him to spread the word about God's supreme power. Indeed, the recovered official meekly offers sacrifice to God and returns to Antioch, the Seleucid capital in Syria, to tell the story to his king.

When Seleucus died and Antiochus, who was called Epiphanes, succeeded to the kingdom, Jason the brother of Onias obtained the high priesthood by corruption.
2 MACC 4:7

In 175 B.C., Heliodorus assassinated Seleucus, hoping to spark a revolution, but the throne was taken by the king's brother, Antiochus IV (see the genealogy on page 306). This capable but hot-blooded ruler took the official epithet Epiphanes, or "god manifest," but his detractors changed this to Epimanes, meaning "madman." No friend of Onias, he accepts a large bribe from the high priest's brother, Jason, and appoints him to the supreme religious post.

Jason is eager to participate in the new king's national program of Hellenization, the promotion of Greek culture and religious beliefs. He sets up a gymnasium in the Greek mold at Jerusalem, an indication that the priestly class is wealthy enough to fund such an expensive enterprise. In other ways, too, he "shifted his compatriots over to the Greek way of life" (2 Macc 4:10). Young Jews begin wearing broad-brimmed hats for protection from the sun. Their characteristic shape, associated with the god Hermes, indicates a youth's enthusiasm for Greek ideas.

Since the days of the conqueror Alexander the Great, sports contests had been held every four years throughout the Seleucid kingdom. One year, when Antiochus is attending the games at Tyre, the faithless Jason sends the price of a sacrificial ox, 300 silver drachmas, to honor the local god Melkart, called Hercules by the Greeks. But even his own delegates consider this use of Jewish

In this 13th-century French illustration, the battles of the Maccabees against their Seleucid enemies are shown as clashes between contemporary European crusaders and the Saracens; upper right, the victors kill a Saracen (Seleucid) who worships an idol set up in Jerusalem's temple.

In the ancient Near East, wealthy people were buried in rock-hewn tombs such as this one in Jerusalem, said to contain the remains of the corrupt high priest Jason.

money to be highly improper. Instead, they contribute it to the construction of the sleek, swift Greek warships known as triremes because they were powered by three parallel rows of oarsmen.

When Antiochus goes on the march to strengthen the defenses of the kingdom, Jason warmly welcomes him in Jerusalem, but this show of support does not help the high priest in the long run. Only three years later, probably in 172 B.C., he makes the mistake of sending an equally duplicitous man as his emissary with tribute money to Antioch: Menelaus, brother of the very same Simon with whom he had a previous dispute. Menelaus offers a larger bribe than Jason's, and the high priesthood instantly becomes his.

After receiving the king's orders he returned, possessing no qualification for the high priesthood, but having the hot temper of a cruel tyrant and the rage of a savage wild beast. 2 MACC 4:25

Outwitted, Jason is forced to flee eastward across the Jordan River, as the high priesthood falls even further into corruption and chaos. The untrustworthy Menelaus even dares cheat his patron the king, neglecting to pay tribute. Because Antiochus has to leave Antioch to quell a minor revolt, a certain Andronicus is appointed to deal with Menelaus. The corrupt high priest tries to curry the royal emissary's favor by handing over gold vessels stolen from the temple treasury.

This sacrilegious larceny is exposed by the former high priest Onias, who has taken sanctuary in a Greek temple to Apollo and Artemis about five miles outside the Seleucid capital. Urged on by Menelaus, Andronicus tricks Onias into leaving the protection of the holy ground and slays him. This new affront outrages Greeks as well as Jews, one of the many times in the book that the two peoples show respect for one another. When Antiochus returns to his capital city, he marches Andronicus to the spot where Onias died and forthwith kills the killer. The author notes that the execution is the work of the Lord: "The Lord thus repaid him [Andronicus] with the punishment he deserved" (2 Macc 4:38).

During these events, Menelaus has remained in Antioch. His brother and partner in stealing and selling sacred temple goods, Lysimachus, is exposed by the citizens of Jerusalem, who become enraged. Lysimachus mounts an attack against the crowds, but his 3,000 men are repulsed and he is slain near the treasury. This appalling incident leads at last to charges being levied against Menelaus, who wins acquittal by bribing a governor to speak in his favor to Antiochus. Unjustly, the righteous Jews who testified against the corrupt high priest are executed. The author wryly observes that even the Scythians, people from the Russian steppes noted for their cruelty, would have freed these victims of cynical plotting.

For almost forty days, there appeared over all the city golden-clad cavalry charging through the air. 2 MACC 5:2

In 169 B.C., about three years into the unholy tenure of Menelaus, Antiochus mounts an invasion of Egypt, heralded by a miraculous vision of golden-clad cavalry displaying their battlefield skills in the skies above Jerusalem. The citizenry hopes that this is a good omen.

Then word comes that the king has died in Egypt. Jason speedily raises a force of 1,000 men to regain the high priesthood, forcing his successor, Menelaus, to flee to the citadel. But the maneuver fails. In fact, Antiochus is very much alive, and his garrison at Jerusalem evidently foils Jason's desperate gamble. He had failed to realize that "success at the cost of one's kindred is the greatest misfortune" (2 Macc 5:6). Defeated and disgraced, Jason seeks refuge in vain; no city will give safe harbor to a man infamous for killing his own countrymen and conspiring against his own brother. From the Nabatean cities of the Arabian desert to the shores of Egypt to mountainous Sparta in Greece, he is rejected. Jason dies alone, unburied and unmourned.

Unfortunately for Judea, Jason's adventure has been gravely misinterpreted by Antiochus, who thinks a Jewish rebellion is brewing against Seleucid rule. Already seething with anger because he has been turned back from Egypt by the Romans, the king brings the full force of his great war engine against Jerusalem, slaughtering 80,000 Jews within a mere three days and selling an equal number into slavery. As is customary in both 1 and 2 Maccabees, the number of casualties in this instance is without doubt greatly exaggerated.

With Menelaus's complicity, the king then violently profanes the temple, destroying many precious gifts placed there by other rulers. Antiochus's blasphemy is allowed, according to the writer, because the Lord is permitting the Jews to be punished for their sins. The powerful Seleucid ruler is an unwitting instrument of the Lord's wrath, although he feels that his earthly power is almost boundless, "thinking in his arrogance that he could sail on the land and walk on the sea" (2 Macc 5:21). He leaves oppressive governors in his stead in devastated Jerusalem, but none is as brutal as the renegade Jew Menelaus, "who lorded it over his compatriots worse than the others did" (2 Macc 5:23).

At this point, Judas Maccabeus—making his first appearance in the narrative—flees into the desert with his band of rebels. The outrages against religion and country have become intolerable.

Not long after this, the king sent an Athenian senator to compel the Jews to forsake the laws of their ancestors and no longer to live by the laws of God. 2 MACC 6:1

This book supplies details that augment the account in 1 Maccabees. The king's program of Hellenization is directed by a senator from Athens who dedicates the house of God to Zeus, while the temple on Mount Gerizim in Samaria is profaned in the same way. Imitating pagan practices in the region, men have sexual intercourse with prostitutes and other women within the temple precinct and offer pork on the sacred altar.

Even pious Jews are forced to participate in pagan rites, including various sacrifices and a procession in honor of Dionysus, the Greek god of wine. Those who refuse are tirelessly persecuted. Women caught circumcising their infant sons are flung, along with their babies, off the tops of the city walls. Faithful Jews who secretly keep the sabbath in caves are sought out and burned to death.

Has God deserted his people in these horrifying days? The author of 2 Maccabees argues otherwise: "In fact, it is a sign of great kindness not to let the impious alone for long, but to punish them immediately" (2 Macc 6:13). Chastisement of the Jews is a sign that God is continually with them.

JEWISH HISTORIAN FLAVIUS JOSEPHUS

Some of the most extensive ancient sources of Jewish history, which include otherwise unknown details about the Maccabean wars, are the works of a first-century Jewish historian descended from the Hasmonean family that led the rebellion and later ruled Judea. He is Joseph ben Mattathias, better known by his Roman name, Flavius Josephus.

Born in A.D. 37 to an affluent priestly family in Jerusalem, Josephus received a superb education. Even as a youth, he was highly esteemed by Jewish leaders. At age 27, he was sent to Rome to win the release of Jewish priests imprisoned there. Shrewdly, he appealed to the emperor Nero's mistress, a Jewish sympathizer, to win the priests' freedom. Two years later, when the Jews revolted against Rome, Josephus was entrusted with leading the Galilean militia—Israel's first line of defense against a Roman invasion. But Galilee fell to the Roman general Vespasian in A.D. 67. Surrendering, Josephus predicted that Vespasian would become emperor—a prophecy fulfilled a short time later when Nero committed suicide. Josephus became the trusted aide to Vespasian's son and eventual successor, Titus, who took command of the Roman army. As the Romans surrounded Jerusalem, Josephus pleaded with his fellow Jews to surrender.

After Jerusalem fell, Josephus returned to Rome, never again to see his homeland. He adopted Vespasian's family name, Flavius, and was granted Roman citizenship, an imperial pension, and an apartment inside the palace. Over the next 20 years, Josephus wrote two histories to help the Romans understand and accept the Jewish people. In his first work, *The Jewish War*, he explained that the recent uprising was the result of fanatics retaliating against corrupt Roman officials. He followed this with *Jewish Antiquities*, a massive 20-volume work that retraced the story of the Jews from creation until the fateful revolt against Rome. Near the end of his life, he wrote two more books: an autobiography and an apologia, *Against Apion*, which defended Judaism against a wave of anti-Semitism.

Josephus died in about A.D. 100. Much of his work has survived, though not because Jews preserved it; they considered him a traitor. Christians, however, became captivated by his histories because they chronicled so well the transition between the Old and New Testaments and because Josephus's references to Jesus, James the brother of Jesus, and John the Baptist substantiated Christian scriptures.

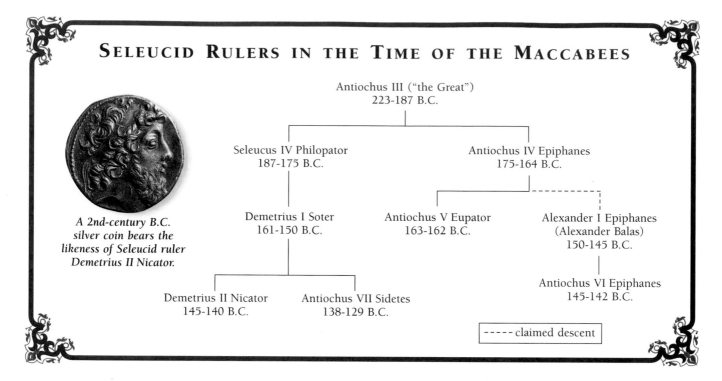

SELEUCID RULERS IN THE TIME OF THE MACCABEES

Antiochus III ("the Great")
223-187 B.C.

Seleucus IV Philopator
187-175 B.C.

Antiochus IV Epiphanes
175-164 B.C.

Demetrius I Soter
161-150 B.C.

Antiochus V Eupator
163-162 B.C.

Alexander I Epiphanes
(Alexander Balas)
150-145 B.C.

Antiochus VI Epiphanes
145-142 B.C.

Demetrius II Nicator
145-140 B.C.

Antiochus VII Sidetes
138-129 B.C.

----- claimed descent

A 2nd-century B.C. silver coin bears the likeness of Seleucid ruler Demetrius II Nicator.

Eleazar, one of the scribes in high position, a man now advanced in age and of noble presence, was being forced to open his mouth to eat swine's flesh. 2 MACC 6:18

Eleazar, a respected 90-year-old scholar, courageously defies an oppressive new law, refusing to eat pork at a sacrifice. His friends worriedly advise him to bring other meat and pretend that it came from the pagan sacrifice, but he nobly refuses, fearing that his pretense will lead younger Jews astray.

Slowly and cruelly tortured to death on the rack, the old man remains true to his faith in the Lord. "I am enduring terrible suffering in my body," he says at the last, ". . . but in my soul I am glad to suffer these things because I fear him" (2 Macc 6:30). His example becomes an inspiration to the suffering nation.

The seven sons of a pious mother are flogged mercilessly when they also refuse to eat the forbidden swine's flesh. Their determination infuriates Antiochus, who orders the torturer to seize one of the brothers, cut out his tongue, scalp him, and cut off his hands and feet before frying him, still breathing, in a large pan suspended over a fire. Thus he is dehumanized, symbolically, into the flesh of an animal.

Even as the smoke from his torment spreads throughout the room, the remaining six brothers and their mother remain steadfast. One by one each brother in turn defies the torturers and is killed in the same manner as the first. The mother bears this carnage bravely before meeting her own death, certain that God will reward the faithfulness of her offspring and "in his mercy give life and breath back to [them]" (2 Macc 7:23). Her conviction reveals that Jews of the period accepted the concept of bodily resurrection and eternal reward for the faithful, a belief hinted at in Daniel 12:2.

They implored the Lord to look upon the people who were oppressed by all; and to have pity on the temple that had been profaned by the godless. 2 MACC 8:2

Now the author turns from martyrdom to the exploits of Judas Maccabeus, essentially giving the highlights of the campaigns described at greater length in 1 Maccabees 2-7. Here, more attention is paid to the spiritual lesson embodied in the historical events. For example, Judas's victories occur because "the wrath of the Lord had turned to mercy" (2 Macc 8:5) for his people. There is also more discussion in this version of the hero's precise military skills, such as his concentration on capturing strategic positions and his deft use of nighttime assaults to overcome the enemy's superior forces.

Judas, clearly fighting for the ancient religious heritage of his people, gives them the battle motto "The help of God" (2 Macc 8:23), and the enemy under Nicanor is routed. The writer takes care to stress that plunder is delayed so that the sabbath can be observed. Moreover, the spoils are carefully shared with widows and orphans and those who have been tortured by the agents of the Seleucid oppressor. The writer repeats his theme in the mouth of the defeated Nicanor himself, who proclaims in Antioch that "the Jews were invulnerable, because they followed the laws ordained by [the Lord]" (2 Macc 8:36).

About that time, as it happened, Antiochus had retreated in disorder from the region of Persia. 2 MACC 9:1

Antiochus's death is portrayed in 1 Maccabees 6:1-16 after the purification of the temple, probably to make the point that he dies feeling guilt for his persecution of the Jews. In this account, the king dies earlier. But the author of 2 Maccabees also draws a religious moral from history: The king is struck down by the Lord because he intends to renew his assaults on holy Jerusalem. Secular writers of the period do not explain exactly how Antiochus died, but this writer provides several grisly details and gives each a moral significance. At the last, the once-proud king submits to a higher authority: "It is right to be subject to God; mortals should not think they are equal to God" (2 Macc 9:12). Before dying, he makes a vow to liberate Jerusalem and make the Jews equal to citizens of his realm.

The author takes a dim view of these last-ditch efforts at repentance, noting that they come too late to spare Antiochus God's punishment; he describes the monarch's deathbed letter to the Jews as "a supplication" (2 Macc 9:18). In fact, as the lengthy quotation from the letter shows, Antiochus writes in an attempt to maintain stability in the kingdom, informing his vassals in Jerusalem that his son Antiochus V Eupator is his legitimate heir.

They purified the sanctuary, and made another altar of sacrifice; then, striking fire out of flint, they offered sacrifices.   2 MACC 10:3

Meanwhile, as described in 1 Maccabees 4:36-61, Judas and his victorious rebels cleanse and restore Jerusalem's temple and celebrate "for eight days with rejoicing, in the manner of the festival of booths" (2 Macc 10:6). These events are shown taking place two years after the sanctuary had been profaned in December of 167 B.C. This is a year earlier than in 1 Maccabees, which places them in 164. The account, however, does agree in saying that the celebration lasted for eight days.

As Antiochus V takes over, Ptolemy, the former governor of Cyprus who had switched allegiance from Egypt to Syria, evidently tries to calm the situation in Judea. Perhaps because he had deserted the Egyptian post in Cyprus, perhaps because he sought justice for the Jews too warmly, he is discredited in Antioch and kills himself with poison.

The way lies open for his successor Gorgias on the one hand and the Idumeans (Edomites) on the other to increase their harassment of Judea. As Judas strikes back, he learns that some Jewish soldiers under his brother Simon have accepted bribes to let a number of the Idumeans slip away to freedom. The traitors are found out and execut-ed, and the Maccabees continue their relentless campaign of vengeance and preventive strikes against their oppressors.

The battle east of the Jordan against the forces of the Ammonite Timothy, described in 1 Maccabees 5:28-34, is pictured here as a conflict between those who rely on God and those who are governed by their heathen rage. Divine intervention is dramatically proved by a stunning vision of five horsemen from heaven. Two of them protect Judas from the enemy as all hurl thunderbolts and showers of arrows at the unfortunate forces under Timothy. In this version, the enemy leader flees to the fort at Gazara but is found ignobly hiding in a well and killed. (But Timothy, or another man by that name, reappears to plague the Jews in 2 Maccabees 12:17-24.)

Now, as also told in 1 Maccabees 4:26-35, the Seleucid regent Lysias marches on Jerusalem with his troops and elephants. Faced with this huge challenge, Judas prays for divine relief. This time, a single supernatural rider "clothed in white and brandishing weapons of gold" (2 Macc 11:8) joins the Jewish forces, strengthening their courage.

When Lysias is routed, the writer wryly notes that this particular Greek is "not without intelligence" (2 Macc 11:13); in other words, he is clever enough to realize that the weaker Jews won because of God's support. Not recognizing Judas as a legitimate leader, he writes directly to the Jews in a brief missive the author quotes, seeking their goodwill and promising to advance their interests. A similar letter from Antiochus V explicitly promises religious freedom to the Jews. A second letter from the new king, evidently

Judas Maccabeus's victories over Judea's enemies sparked the imaginations of countless artists over the centuries. This spirited scene of the attack on the fortified city of Caspin is by the noted Swiss engraver Matthäus Merian (1593-1650).

influenced by Menelaus, promises that all Jews can return to their ancient capital and live in freedom. Finally, a letter from the Romans affirms the promises of Lysias. Peace seems secure, but lesser officials in the Seleucid kingdom still harbor evil designs against the troublesome Jews.

The people of Joppa did so ungodly a deed as this: they invited the Jews who lived among them to embark, with their wives and children, on boats that they had provided, as though there were no ill will to the Jews.
2 MACC 12:3

In coastal Joppa, the pagan townspeople trick their Jewish neighbors into a boat trip on the Mediterranean Sea that is a murderous ruse: Some 200 are drowned. In revenge, Judas launches a nighttime attack on the harbor, burning the vessels there and killing the sailors. As a preventive measure, he also burns down the Jamnia harbor 12 miles to the south. Although he is distracted from this coastal campaign by an attack of a large force of Arabs, he defeats them as well and works out a peace agreement, then violently overthrows the Gentile town of Caspin, perhaps the same as Chaspho in Transjordanian Gilead mentioned in 1 Maccabees 5:36.

The account of attacks on northeastern towns and the search for the Ammonite leader Timothy provides some details not given in 1 Maccabees. The enemy is seen as vulnerable on many occasions as the Maccabean victories mount. When captured once, the wily Timothy earns his freedom by promising to release elderly Jewish hostages. Later, Gorgias, the Seleucid governor of Idumea, is captured by a single brave warrior but escapes when some of his troops cut the man's arm off. Throughout the campaign, the writer repeatedly stresses that Judas is doing the work of God. On one occasion, as the Maccabees prepare to bury their dead, pagan idols are found in their clothing. This hidden idolatry explains why the Lord has allowed them to be slain.

The first written statement, so far as is known today, of the belief in the efficacy of prayer for the dead appears in 2 Maccabees 12:45: "Therefore he [Judas] made atonement for the dead, so that they might be delivered from their sin."

[Antiochus] ordered them to take him [Menelaus] to Beroea and to put him to death by the method that is customary in that place. 2 MACC 13:4

Alarmed and impatient with Judas's continuing campaigns, Antiochus turns the full might of the Seleucid army at last upon nettlesome Judea. The traitorous high priest Menelaus eagerly joins the effort but, for unexplained reasons, the king has had enough of him. Menelaus is executed by a Persian method: He is thrown into the interior of a tall tower filled to the top with ashes.

Hearing of the approaching army, the Jews of Jerusalem pray to the Lord day and night. By nightfall, the pragmatic Judas races out of the city to meet the enemy on the march, attacking their encampment in the dark and killing the advance guard. In this version of events, Antiochus attacks well-defended Beth-zur twice but is repulsed each time. Because of court intrigues in Antioch, the king hastily makes peace with the Jews. The land is at rest and religion is allowed to flourish for three years.

Then Demetrius I Soter seizes power from his cousin, Antiochus V. With a new regime in place, the former high priest Alcimus plots to regain his power.

[Alcimus] found an opportunity that furthered his mad purpose when he was invited by Demetrius to a meeting of the council. 2 MACC 14:5

Alcimus warns the new ruler that the Jews will continue making trouble as long as Judas is alive. The king names Nicanor governor of Judea and sends him south with orders to kill the rebel. But Nicanor avoids battle with the crafty Judas and offers peace. Placing guards at key positions in case this is yet another case of Seleucid treachery, Judas meets with the enemy leader. In this account, the two become friends. At the urging of Nicanor, Judas marries and settles down, giving up his warrior's life for a peaceful domestic existence.

As the priest Onias prays, the prophet Jeremiah appears to hand Judas Maccabeus a golden sword; an 1860 engraving by Julius Schnorr von Carolsfeld.

ADDITIONAL BOOKS OF THE MACCABEES

The books of 3 and 4 Maccabees are generally considered to be works of only minor religious significance. In each, the writer is trying to comfort beleaguered Jews by proving that God will defend his people from oppression. Orthodox churches consider 3 Maccabees deuterocanonical but place 4 Maccabees in an appendix to their Bible.

Misnamed, 3 Maccabees is a historical novel that takes place about 50 years before the Maccabean revolt. It was probably written in Greek by an Egyptian Jew early in the first century B.C. The Egyptian king Ptolemy IV Philopator (221-204 B.C.) is prevented by divine intervention from entering the sacred holy of holies at the temple in Jerusalem. A heavenly power "shook him on this side and that as a reed is shaken by the wind, so that he lay helpless on the ground" (3 Macc 2:22). Embarrassed and infuriated, the Egyptian monarch decides to take revenge on the large colony of Jews living in Alexandria.

Like later rulers in Syria, Ptolemy tries to force his Jewish subjects to worship Dionysus, the Greek god of the grape harvest and wine. He is thwarted by miraculous interventions. When he orders the Jews to be registered before cruel torture and execution, the pens and paper necessary for the task miraculously run out. When a herd of 500 elephants, maddened by wine, is sent to trample the Jews to death, two angels appear and turn them back against their Egyptian masters. Frightened, Ptolemy reverses his policy of persecution and becomes a friend of the Jewish community, explaining that he realizes now that "the God of heaven surely defends the Jews" (3 Macc 7:6).

Essentially, 4 Maccabees is an extended interpretation of two stories of martyrdom told in 2 Maccabees: the torture-killing of Eleazar, and the protracted sufferings of a pious mother and her seven faithful sons. Written in Greek in a highly elevated style, it may have first been delivered as a speech honoring the martyrs of the Maccabean period at a festival between about 63 B.C. and A.D. 70, when Jerusalem fell. Because the writer refers to Jews as "Hebrews," as was the custom in Antioch, it seems likely that the book was composed in the Seleucid capital.

The writer of 4 Maccabees explains that he means to prove that "reason is dominant over the emotions" (4 Macc 1:7); in other words, the martyrs resist fear and excruciating pain because they know that their faith is correct. Influenced by Persian beliefs, the author of 2 Maccabees writes that the martyrs will be rewarded by the Lord with bodily resurrection. But the writer of 4 Maccabees, indebted to the Greek concept that the soul is immortal, promises that the martyrs earn "immortality in endless life" (4 Macc 17:12). At the same time, he argues, the martyrs purify Judea by their steadfastness to the faith, and their deaths under torture are accepted by God as atonement for the sins of their countrymen. "Because of them," he writes, "the nation gained peace, and by reviving observance of the law in the homeland they ravaged the enemy" (4 Macc 18:4).

Alcimus, embittered by this turn of events, reports to Demetrius that Nicanor is no longer serving the interests of the Seleucid kingdom. Greatly displeased, Demetrius writes a letter commanding his deputy to have Judas arrested and sent in custody to Antioch. Nicanor cannot refuse the royal command, of course, but his psychological turmoil over this injustice communicates itself to the sharp-witted Judas. Sensing danger, he goes into hiding.

Furious and undoubtedly terrified of the king, Nicanor threatens to raze the temple "and build there a splendid temple to Dionysus" (2 Macc 14:33) if Judas is not turned over to him. He also decides to make an example of an elder named Razis, famed for having risked his life for the faith in the past. Some 500 soldiers are sent to arrest this "father of the Jews" (2 Macc 14:37). Preferring martyrdom, Razis falls on his sword but misses the mark. Gravely wounded, he rushes to the top of a wall and leaps to the ground. Still living and inflamed with anger against the pagans, he climbs a steep rock, tears out his own entrails, and hurls them toward everyone watching the bloody scene. In this manner, he dies for the faith.

[The Jews] declared, "It is the living Lord himself, the Sovereign in heaven, who ordered us to observe the seventh day." 2 MACC 15:4

*W*hen Nicanor decides to hunt down Judas on the sabbath, Jews compelled to join him protest. But the governor brushes aside their objections, declaring that he is sovereign on earth. Then, as the just Onias prays to God to protect the Jews, the prophet Jeremiah appears and hands a golden sword to Judas. The hero interprets the vision to mean that his people are now allowed to defend themselves against annihilation even on the sabbath. In the huge battle that follows, the Seleucids are defeated and Nicanor is slain.

Concluding his narrative with the events covered in 1 Maccabees 7, the author notes that water and wine are most enjoyable when mixed together; so, too, a story is most effective and enjoyable when written in a lively style. Because the book would customarily be read aloud, even by someone reading to himself, this engaging writer hopes that his work "delights the ears" (2 Macc 15:39).

THE NEW TESTAMENT

The four Evangelists by Jacob Jordaens (1593-1678)

irst-generation Christians were in no hurry to establish a canon of sacred writings. Their faith centered on Jesus: his words and his actions. Christians did not need books about him as long as there were people, such as the apostles, who had known him. Eyewitness stories, often including astonishing miracles, were far more convincing than any written document. Besides, Jesus himself wrote none of his teachings, but spoke them instead. Likewise, his commission to the disciples was not to write about what they had seen, but to travel the world, teaching and baptizing people.

For several decades, this was enough to establish the Christian faith. But as the church continued growing and the apostles began dying, Christians decided it was time to preserve in writing the best loved stories and sayings of Jesus, previously passed along by word of mouth; these became the gospels of Matthew, Mark, Luke, and John, written from about A.D. 70 until the end of the century. Yet, these are not the oldest books in the New Testament. All of the apostle Paul's letters are probably older than the four gospels. Scholars believe that Paul wrote 1 Thessalonians, his earliest surviving letter, about A.D. 50, during his second missionary journey. He continued writing to local congregations—answering their questions and trying to resolve their problems—until his death, possibly during Nero's persecution of Christians in A.D. 64.

Neither Paul nor the other New Testament writers considered their work to be scripture, equal in status to the sacred Jewish Bible, the Old Testament. Yet they firmly believed that their message about Jesus fulfilled prophecies from the Hebrew scriptures. Paul even appealed to the authority of the Jewish Bible by insisting that his teachings were "in accordance with the scriptures" (1 Cor 15:3).

It remains a mystery exactly when and how Christian writings began to emerge as scripture in their own right, distinct yet equal in divine authority to the Jewish Bible. But it seems that before the end of the first Christian century, churches throughout the Roman Empire had started compiling and copying Paul's letters, to read aloud in worship services as a supplement to the often repeated stories of Jesus. About A.D. 95, Bishop Clement of Rome wrote to the Corinthians, urging them to read the first letter Paul addressed to their forefathers. Also about this time—possibly earlier—the author of 2 Peter equated Paul's letters with "other scriptures" (2 Pet 3:16), perhaps the Jewish Bible. Thus, by the end of the first century, a body of revered Christian writings was beginning to emerge.

Early Collections

The first mention of the gospels shows up in the writings of Papias, bishop of Hierapolis in what is now Turkey and reportedly a disciple of the apostle John. Writing in the early decades of the second century, Papias indicated that he knew and accepted the gospels, though he preferred oral traditions—the "living voice of the elders" who had been taught by the apostles.

Strangely, the earliest known collection of Christian writings deemed acceptable for the church was compiled by a man later condemned as "the firstborn of Satan." Marcion, a successful shipping entrepreneur and son of a bishop in Asia Minor, rejected the entire Old Testament—including its God, whom Marcion considered cruel. He said the New Testament God—the Father of Jesus—was a separate and loving deity. Furthermore, Marcion insisted that Jesus never actually became human, but only appeared human. In about 140, Marcion recommended that the church unite in truth by adopting as authoritive the ten letters of Paul and the Gospel of Luke—each of which Marcion freely edited, deleting references to the Old Testament and to Jesus' humanity, death, and resurrection. Marcion was excommunicated four years later. But his work seemed to serve as a wake-up call to the church, prompting leaders to consider which writings were reliable. This became a matter of serious discussion—sometimes bitter argument—throughout the next 200 years.

Even late into the second century, many in the church felt that the most revered Christian writings fell short of sacred, and could still be improved. Tatian, a

Syrian teacher, decided to combine the four gospels into one, removing the duplications and harmonizing apparent discrepancies. His work, the *Diatessaron* ("harmony of four"), was completed about 170 and remained the authorized gospel in many Syrian churches into the fifth century. But within ten years, Irenaeus, bishop of Lyons in what is now France, was vigorously resisting such harmonizing of the gospels. He insisted on preserving all four as separate but equally authoritative witnesses to the life of Jesus, calling them the four pillars of the church. Beyond the gospels, Irenaeus's list of reliable Christian writings included most of the 27 books in the modern New Testament, with the exceptions of Hebrews and the short letters of James, 2 Peter, 3 John, Jude, and Philemon.

Disputed Works

As the earliest Christian writings and stories circulated throughout the church, curious listeners wanted to know more—especially about Jesus and the apostles. Christian writers rose to the challenge, producing a bewildering assortment of pious accounts, many of which read suspiciously like fiction. The Gospel of Thomas, perhaps written late in the first century, contains dozens of Jesus' sayings that closely parallel those of Matthew, Mark, and Luke. Yet the gospel stops short of describing the all-important death and resurrection of Jesus, suggesting that the writer may have tailored his account to a growing Christian sect that believed Jesus was thoroughly divine, and not at all human. The Infancy Gospel of Thomas, written in the second century, reports miracles that Jesus supposedly performed as a child, including some that portray him as vindictive. In one episode, the young Jesus angrily curses two of his playmates, instantly killing them.

Scores of well-intentioned but fanciful writings such as these prompted church leaders to continue generating lists of dependable Christian texts. These lists remained somewhat fluid for two centuries after Marcion's controversial first list, but church leaders generally accepted the majority of what is now the New Testament: the four gospels, Acts, Paul's letters, and Revelation. The most enlightening list came from Eusebius, bishop of Caesarea and author of a multivolume church history published about 325. His list was prompted by a request from the emperor Constantine, the first Roman ruler to favor Christianity. Constantine decided that a way to unify the church, which had been divided over various theological issues, was to establish which Christian writings were trustworthy. Eusebius began by reviewing the available Christian literature and dividing it into three categories. In the first category were texts almost universally accepted as sacred: the four gospels, Acts, the letters of Paul, 1 John, and 1 Peter. In the second were seven disputed writings whose authenticity was still debated: James, 2 Peter, Jude, 2 and 3 John, Hebrews, and Revelation. In the third group were texts that Eusebius firmly rejected, such as the gospels attributed to Peter and Matthias and a letter of Barnabas.

Eusebius's reasons for approving certain writings were based on several factors: apostolic authorship (or authorship by followers such as Luke); antiquity (dating to the earliest years of the church); and public usage. In addition, the stories and teachings in approved writings had to be consistent with long-held, widely accepted beliefs. Interestingly, Eusebius did not say that inspiration by the Holy Spirit was a requirement—perhaps because all Christians were considered spirit-filled. The claim of inspiration did not distinguish one Christian text from another. In fact, the only New Testament author to claim that God played a direct role in his writing is the author of Revelation.

A pivotal moment in church history arrived about 40 years after Eusebius composed his three-tiered ranking: publication of the first known list that matches the current New Testament. It appeared in an Easter letter sent in 367 to the churches and monasteries of his diocese by Bishop Athanasius of Alexandria, Egypt. In the letter he identifies the 27 books that the church would eventually proclaim as the New Testament. Athanasius agreed with Eusebius's first and third categories—texts that should be accepted and those that should be rejected. Then he added to the approved list the disputed works from Eusebius's second category.

Agreement at Last

Most church leaders agreed with Athanasius. Clergy in the eastern region of the empire ratified his canon at North African council meetings in Hippo Regius, in 393, and again at Carthage, in 397. Some leaders, however, continued questioning the authenticity of James, Jude, and Hebrews. But a second Carthage council reaffirmed the canon in 419. Clergy of the western church, centered in Rome, concurred with these previous councils, as evidenced by the pope's statement of support in 405. Jerome, a noted scholar who accepted the pope's daunting challenge of translating Jewish and Christian scriptures into Latin—common language of the Roman Empire—included these 27 texts in his definitive work, the Vulgate. He did this even though he believed that the Letter of Barnabas should be added, since the author was one of Paul's colleagues. Jerome's willingness to set aside his best scholarly opinion in deference to the ever strengthening consensus within the church shows that by the early 400s, the New Testament had achieved a sacred and unchangeable status. Scholars throughout the centuries continued to question the wisdom of including certain disputed writings in the canon, but all 27 have endured as the nonnegotiable core of Christian belief.

THE GOSPEL ACCORDING TO MATTHEW

Matthew most likely is not the oldest of the four gospels; that distinction is generally accorded Mark. Yet there are some significant reasons why it stands first in the New Testament canon. A laudatory biography of Jesus, Matthew introduces such distinct Christian themes as a strong emphasis on Jesus as the Messiah, his birth to the virgin Mary, baptism, prayer, the rites of the Last Supper, a leading role for the apostle Peter, and the promise of Jesus' continuing presence. In addition, the first Gospel contains such Jewish elements as a poetic structure, scribal arguments, an emphasis on law, observance, and piety, the use of symbolic numbers, scriptural quotations to indicate fulfillment of prophecies, and the genealogy with which it begins.

Like the other three gospels, Matthew was written in Greek, the common language of commerce and culture in the Roman Empire. It was evidently composed in the 80s of the first century of the present era, perhaps by a Jewish member of the Christian church at Antioch in Syria. The anonymous author seems to have known of the destruction of the temple in A.D. 70 and depicts the Pharisees, a sect particularly active at that time, as Jesus' principal opponents. In the second century the name of Jesus' disciple Matthew was given to the first Gospel in order to lend it authority—though there is no evidence that he had anything to do with its composition.

The Gospel is carefully ordered around five major speeches of Jesus that punctuate the biographical narrative: the Sermon on the Mount (chapters 5-7), instructions for missionary disciples (chapter 10), a collection of Jesus' parables (chapter 13), teachings on forgiveness and reconciliation (chapter 18), and a discourse about last things (chapters 24-25). All these lead up to the powerful account of Jesus' crucifixion and resurrection.

The adoration of the wise men, as depicted in a 15th-century Bible

An account of the genealogy of Jesus the Messiah, the son of David, the son of Abraham. MT 1:1

Though modern readers often think of genealogies as especially boring parts of the scriptures, for Matthew and his readers the genealogy of Jesus was significant. It showed a pattern of order and purpose in the whole history of Israel leading to Jesus' birth, and helped early Christian readers understand how God was involved in Jesus' story. Matthew begins by asserting that Jesus is the Messiah, or Christ, a title that means "anointed one." This title refers to the cherished hope of the Jews that one day God would send an anointed king, a descendant of the great King David, to restore Israel as a nation and to make good on God's promise that David's dynasty would "be established forever" (2 Sam 7:16). The first assertion of Matthew's Gospel is that Jesus indeed fulfills that long delayed hope: He is the Messiah.

Matthew had to sacrifice some accuracy in his genealogy by omitting several generations and by counting some names twice. But for Matthew the symbolic importance of the pattern, which expressed the truth that God was involved in the events leading up to Jesus' birth, was more significant than the exact list of names, most of which anyone could derive from the genealogies in 1 Chronicles.

Though Jesus' genealogy, like all such lists of the time, was reckoned through male ancestors, Matthew also indicates the surprising character of this history by noting four women among the long list of men: Tamar, Rahab, Ruth, and the wife of Uriah (Bathsheba). Each woman was either a non-Israelite or a person whose story involved some irregularity, thereby showing that God could use people in unexpected ways to accomplish his will and that the Gentiles were represented in the ancestry of the Messiah. A young virgin named Mary was to be the fifth in this series of the Lord's highly unusual choices.

Now the birth of Jesus the Messiah took place in this way. When his mother Mary had been engaged to Joseph, but before they lived together, she was found to be with child from the Holy Spirit. MT 1:18

Both Matthew and Luke recount Jesus' birth, but the two narratives are quite different in their emphases and content. Matthew stresses Jesus' royal ancestry and portrays his birth as a confrontation between the kingdoms of this world as represented by Herod the Great and Jesus, God's new king, born of a virgin in fulfillment of prophecy.

Matthew begins with the potential scandal of an engaged young woman named Mary who is found to be pregnant. An engagement or betrothal in those days was practically as binding as a marriage, and Joseph in kindness chooses to divorce Mary rather than bring charges against her in court. Only divine intervention—an angel appearing to Joseph in the first of four dreams—changes his mind. The angel tells Joseph that Mary's child is by the Holy Spirit and names the child Jesus ("he will save") to signify his role as savior of his people.

The sentence "All this took place to fulfill what had been spoken by the Lord through the prophet" (Mt 1:22) for the first time introduces an Old Testament quotation—here Isaiah 7:14, which tells of a young woman conceiving a son whose name, Immanuel, means "God is with us." In 13 nearly identical formulas, Matthew shows how Jesus fulfills and gives new meaning to Old Testament prophecies.

An angel hovers over the dreaming Joseph in this 11th-century ivory panel.

In the time of King Herod, after Jesus was born in Bethlehem of Judea, wise men from the East came to Jerusalem, asking, "Where is the child who has been born king of the Jews?" MT 2:1

Told only in Matthew, the story of the wise men is a *haggadah*, one that draws on scriptural materials to make a theological point. The sources here are Numbers 24:17, Isaiah 60:1-7, and Jeremiah 23:5. By admitting they do not know that the Jews' messianic king is to be born in Bethlehem, the wise men reveal an unfamiliarity with the scriptures that marks them as Gentiles. Writing at the time when many Jewish Christians were opposed to sharing the good news of Jesus' mission with the Gentiles, Matthew here demonstrates that the Messiah came to redeem all people, not just Jews.

The tradition that there were three wise men is based on their three gifts: gold, frankincense (an aromatic resin), and myrrh (an anointing and embalming ointment). Since they are guided by a star, the wise men appear to have been astrologers, most likely from Persia. Magi, as they are sometimes called, is the plural of "magus," a Greek word for sorcerer or magician. Only much later were the wise men called kings and given the names Caspar, Melchior, and Balthasar—one of whom was said to be black.

About the year 1200, a French artist painted the Holy Family in flight to Egypt— giving them an angel as a guide and a servant.

An angel of the Lord appeared to Joseph in a dream and said, "Get up, take the child and his mother and flee to Egypt." MT 2:13

By escaping to and returning from Egypt, the Holy Family echoes the Israelites' sojourn in the land of the pharaohs as told in Genesis and Exodus. Herod's massacre of the innocent children of Bethlehem can be compared with Pharaoh's slaughter of Hebrew children—a fate from which Moses escaped through his mother's ingenuity just as Jesus did by his parents' timely flight. Each of the three scenes—the flight to Egypt, the slaying of the children, and the return to the land of Israel—contains one of Matthew's formula quotations of an Old Testament prophecy now fulfilled.

Warned in his fourth dream of the danger of returning to Judea, where Herod had been succeeded by his equally cruel son Archelaus, Joseph takes his wife and the child to Galilee and settles in Nazareth. Scholars have puzzled over the concluding Old Testament prophecy: "He will be called a Nazorean" (Mt 2:23). Because there is a similarity in sound between the Aramaic word "Nazareth" and a Hebrew word translated as "branch," they suggest that Matthew was referring to an oracle of the prophet Isaiah: "A shoot shall come out of the stump of Jesse, and a branch shall grow out of his roots" (Isa 11:1).

In those days John the Baptist appeared in the wilderness of Judea, proclaiming, "Repent, for the kingdom of heaven has come near." MT 3:1

Matthew skips nearly 30 years from the time Jesus' family returns from Egypt to the moment when John the Baptist begins preaching in Judea and around the Jordan River. John's message is an urgent call for people to repent—make a radical change in their values and commitments—because, he asserts, the kingdom of heaven is drawing near. John's phrase "kingdom of heaven" means God's rule in the lives of people, and he expects that rule to be manifested in a powerful way in the near future.

John's manner of preaching and strange clothing cause people to think of ancient prophets such as Elijah. As people repent and confess their sins because of his message, he plunges them in the Jordan River. Washings of purification were common in Judaism, but this sort of onetime baptism as a sign of preparation for the coming kingdom was so distinctive that it gave John his nickname, "the baptizer" or the Baptist. John also speaks mysteriously of one greater than himself who is coming and will baptize them not with water as he is doing but with "the Holy Spirit and fire" (Mt 3:11).

Jesus, now grown to manhood, joins the crowds being baptized. John recognizes Jesus as the one greater than himself, and only at Jesus' insistence does he consent to baptize him in the Jordan. That moment marks the beginning of Jesus' own ministry as he experiences a threefold revelation: He sees heaven open above him; he sees the Spirit of God descend as a dove; and he hears God's voice acknowledge him as his beloved son.

Then Jesus was led up by the Spirit into the wilderness to be tempted by the devil. MT 4:1

Immediately after the divine proclamation of Jesus as the Son of God, that identity is put to the test. Weak with hunger from 40 days and nights of fasting, Jesus is confronted by the devil, a word that means "slanderer" or "accuser," as does the Hebrew word *Satan.* The devil is also called "the tempter," or the one who puts a person to the test.

Matthew's account of this mysterious encounter is presented in a formal, stylized way, marked by repeated phrases and three explicit temptations. The temptations come in rapid succession. Jesus turns each aside by quoting the scriptures, particularly passages from Deuteronomy.

The tempter begins challenging Jesus' identity as the Son of God by urging him to prove his power by turning stones into bread to relieve his hunger. Jesus quotes Deuteronomy 8:3. Next the tempter urges Jesus to make God prove his love for him by throwing himself from the pinnacle of God's house, the temple in Jerusalem. Jesus refuses, quoting Deuteronomy 6:16. And finally, the devil brazenly asserts his claim to control all the kingdoms of the world, and he offers them to Jesus if he will forget about the kingdom of God and worship Satan. Jesus shows that he already has authority beyond that of Satan by commanding him to depart and quoting Deuteronomy 6:13: God alone is to be feared, worshiped, and served.

Following the defeat of Satan, Jesus begins his ministry in Galilee. Unlike John the Baptist, he goes out into the villages and towns. He does not wait for followers to seek him but rather with uncanny authority summons disciples to his side. He chooses ordinary people, like the fishermen Peter, Andrew, James, and John, who leave everything to follow him. And as he begins to demonstrate his power by helping the sick and afflicted, inevitably his fame spreads throughout the region.

As John baptizes Jesus, the Holy Spirit descends as a dove and God gives his blessing from heaven; a painting by Pietro Vannucci, known as Perugino (c. 1450-1523).

THE HOLY LAND IN THE TIME OF JESUS

At the death of Herod the Great in 4 B.C., his domain was divided among three of his sons. From Jerusalem Archelaus ruled as king over Judea, Idumea, and Samaria. His younger brother, Herod Antipas, was tetrarch over Galilee and Perea, territories separated by the Decapolis, a league of ten cities mainly east of the Jordan River. Their half brother Philip was tetrarch of the largely Gentile areas to the north and east of the Sea of Galilee. Herod's sister Salome received Phasaelis and several cities on the Mediterranean coast. In reality, all were vassals of the Roman emperor, represented by his procurator in Jerusalem—Pontius Pilate at the time of Jesus' arrest, trial, and execution there.

With the exception of the brief sojourn in Egypt recounted by Matthew, Jesus spent most of his childhood and adult years in Galilee. After he was scorned in his hometown of Nazareth, Jesus settled in Capernaum, a fishing village on the north shore of the Sea of Galilee. His only journeys apparently were a trip to the Jordan River valley to be baptized by John, missionary visits to Gadara and other cities of the Decapolis, Caesarea Philippi, and Tyre some 60 miles to the north, and festival pilgrimages to Jerusalem about 70 miles to the south. The full extent of the territory he covered was somewhat smaller than the state of Vermont.

When Jesus saw the crowds, he went up the mountain; and after he sat down, his disciples came to him. Then he began to speak, and taught them, saying: "Blessed are the poor in spirit, for theirs is the kingdom of heaven."
MT 5:1-3

At the very beginning of his account of the ministry, Matthew includes an extensive and challenging presentation of Jesus' teaching, traditionally called the Sermon on the Mount (Mt 5-7). Comparison with the other gospels suggests that the sermon is a collection of teachings that may have been given at various times. But Matthew brings them together so that his readers can experience the full range and impact of Jesus' proclamation. Much of the material is also found in Luke. Chapters 5 and 7, for example, have numerous parallels to the so-called Sermon on the Plain in Luke 6:20-49.

In the sermon Jesus teaches both his disciples and the crowds. He starts with what are traditionally called the Beatitudes, or blessings; these begin to define a new set of values that fit life in God's kingdom. True blessing or happiness, he says, is found where people ordinarily least expect it. Phrases like "poor in spirit," "those who mourn," "the meek," "the peacemakers," or "those who are persecuted for righteousness sake" define an understanding of deep happiness and blessing very different from the surface values of ordinary society. Jesus asserts that those who share these values are the most crucial people in the world—its salt and its light.

His message, Jesus states emphatically, does not abolish the law and the prophets of the Old Testament, but fulfills them. Yet he immediately describes six contrasts between traditional understanding of the law as regulating external behavior and his own teaching, which seeks to transform a person's heart and deepest values so that actions flow from that new core. Traditionally, one would love a neighbor but hate an enemy. Jesus wants to create a new heart that will love even an enemy.

"Beware of practicing your piety before others in order to be seen by them; for then you have no reward from your Father in heaven." MT 6:1

In the central section of the Sermon on the Mount, Jesus turns his attention to traditional practices of piety: giving alms, praying, and fasting. Jesus warns that any of these can be practiced to gain praise from people, making the acts hypocritical and meaningless for a relationship with God. Only piety that is without display or ulterior motive, that flows from a transformed heart, is important to God.

Jesus gives his disciples a very brief, focused prayer as an exemplar: "the Lord's Prayer." In it a disciple affirms God's holiness, prays that his kingdom will be realized, and then makes basic requests of God.

In addition to condemning self-serving hypocrisy, Jesus warns that money is a great danger to genuine trust in God. Money becomes an idolatrous god, he says: "You cannot serve God and wealth" (Mt 6:24). Instead, Jesus urges his disciples toward a profound trust in God as a father who knows them intimately, loves them completely, and will always care for them.

"Everyone then who hears these words of mine and acts on them will be like a wise man who built his house on rock." MT 7:24

Finally, Jesus emphasizes the seriousness of the challenge that he is making to his disciples in the sermon. He warns them about being judgmental and about the danger of self-deception. In his typically colorful manner, he asks why they can see a tiny speck in a friend's eye while missing a whole log lodged in their own eyes.

While being appropriately self-critical, the disciples must realize that they are on a quest. They must not be passive in putting God's rule first in life, but must actively ask, search, and knock at every door. Just as they as parents delight in giving gifts to their children, so God wants to give them the blessings of his kingdom, but they must ask.

As a basic guideline for action that flows from the heart, Jesus gives his followers the principle later called the Golden Rule: "In everything do to others as you would have them do to you" (Mt 7:12). Jesus was quite aware of the demanding character of his teaching. He describes it as a "narrow gate." Keeping external commandments has always been easier than the deep transformation of heart that requires one to love one's enemies, trust God in everything, and live without hypocrisy. But Jesus asserts that his narrow gate leads to life.

The sermon concludes with a vivid image to clarify for the disciples what is at stake in their response to Jesus' teaching. Hearing the teaching and acting on it creates a life that is like a house built on solid rock. Failure to turn these words into action builds a life that is like a house on shifting sand. In other words, everything is at stake.

A windstorm arose on the sea, so great that the boat was being swamped by the waves; but he was asleep. And they went and woke him up, saying, "Lord, save us! We are perishing!" MT 8:24-25

Following his powerful presentation of the words of the Messiah in the Sermon on the Mount, Matthew presents an equally striking array of the Messiah's deeds. He recounts ten miracles of Jesus, divided into three groups. Matthew has drawn these re-

ports from different parts of the Gospel of Mark and other sources and has in several cases changed the order of events from that in Mark. Matthew is not interested in presenting a sequential account but in giving an overview of the meaning of those deeds comparable to his overview of Jesus' teaching.

The three groups of miracles are divided from each other by narratives that focus on discipleship. These narratives help Matthew show that Jesus' miracles are not only deeds of raw power, but also acts with profound meanings that help define discipleship.

The first group of miracles (Mt 8:1-17) shows Jesus reaching out to people who were outside the normal religious society of his time. Lepers were untouchable outcasts who had to warn people away by crying "unclean!" However, Jesus chooses to touch an unclean leper and heal his disease. In the next miracle it is a Gentile soldier, a despised mercenary hired to enforce the authority of Herod Antipas, who recognizes the power of Jesus so forthrightly that Jesus marvels at his faith. Walls between clean and unclean, Jew and Gentile are beginning to crack.

In the first narrative on discipleship (Mt 8:18-22), Jesus' authority is translated into a challenging summons. The disciple must be willing to face deprivation to follow Jesus and absolutely nothing—not even burying a father—can be placed before the Lord's call.

The second group of miracles (Mt 8:24-9:8) elaborates on the authority of the Messiah by showing Jesus overcoming the power of nature in saving his followers from a storm, conquering demonic power to free two Gentile men, and vanquishing even the power of sin by forgiving the sins of a paralyzed man.

In the second narrative section (Mt 9:9-17), Jesus enlists as followers people who are religious outcasts. He calls Matthew, a despised tax collector, as a disciple, and pointedly shares a banquet with a group of tax collectors and sinners.

The final group of miracles (Mt 9:18-34) completes the picture of this surprising, unconventional, but authoritative Messiah. Jesus gives new hope to an otherwise hopeless woman who touches his garments. He conquers even the power of death over a young girl when others think such a possibility laughable. He gives sight to the blind and voice to the voiceless. He shows his compassion for the crowds of distressed people, "because they were harassed and helpless, like sheep without a shepherd" (Mt 9:36).

Jesus commissioning the twelve apostles is framed within the initial letter "E" in a page from a 15th-century illuminated Bible.

"See, I am sending you out like sheep into the midst of wolves; so be wise as serpents and innocent as doves." MT 10:16

After describing the powerful deeds of the Messiah, Matthew presents the second of Jesus' discourses, the one in which he commissions

Although the site of the Sermon on the Mount is unknown, this graceful basilica overlooking the Sea of Galilee is dedicated to the Beatitudes.

twelve of his most loyal disciples as apostles. The word "disciple" means learner or student; "apostle" means emissary, one sent on a special mission. The needs of the hapless crowds along with the urgency of the message of the kingdom of God motivate Jesus' selection of these men for a special but limited mission. The twelve apostles, named in Matthew 10:2-4, are sent out only to Jewish towns. Jesus explicitly instructs the twelve to take nothing with them—no money, extra clothes, or even sandals—nothing except his message that the kingdom of heaven is near and the authority over disease and the power of evil he transfers to them. They must learn not to depend on their own resources but on the power of God.

Jesus describes in some detail the conflicts and persecutions that await the twelve—partly in language that anticipates their missionary work after his death. The message of God's kingdom brings profound transformation that provokes inevitable conflict and opposition. But Jesus assures them that no one is worthy of fear except God, and God loves and cares for them. Therefore they can live without fear.

"Come to me, all you that are weary and are carrying heavy burdens, and I will give you rest." MT 11:28

Matthew portrays the period after the commissioning of the twelve as a time of questions and controversies swirling around Jesus, a time of increasingly dangerous opposition to his work. The questions begin with one from John the Baptist, imprisoned by Herod Antipas. He has heard about the deeds of the Messiah and sends his disciples to ask for assurance that Jesus is indeed the "one who is to come" (Mt 11:3). Jesus tells the questioners to report what they hear and see: Jesus heals, gives life, and brings good news to the poor.

But the issue that is becoming dangerously controversial is the observance of the sabbath. Jesus' opponents insist on rigorously avoiding any semblance of work, while Jesus insists that God intended the sabbath for good and never for harm. The controversies escalate to the point that Jesus' opponents begin plotting to kill him and argue that his amazing deeds are all from the power of Satan.

And he told them many things in parables, saying: "Listen! A sower went out to sow." MT 13:3

In the midst of such controversies Matthew describes Jesus' third discourse—teaching in parables. Jesus' story of a sower casting seeds by hand (Mt 13:3-9, 18-23) reflects how the message of the kingdom of heaven went out to the people. The fate of the seed (or message) reveals the character of the ground (or heart) into which it falls. Some ground is unyielding and unproductive; some is initially fruitful but for various reasons fails before harvest; some is good and the producer of great fruit.

For many hearers such parables remain simply interesting stories. But for those who have ears to hear their deeper meaning, they serve as a powerful revelation of the kingdom of heaven. One who comprehends the message of the kingdom, Jesus explains, finds something so valuable ("treasure hidden in a field" or a "pearl of great value"—Mt 13:44, 45) that

TEACHING IN PARABLES

Jesus' parable of laborers in the vineyard (Mt 20:1-16) is commemorated in this enamel plaque from a medieval reliquary box.

Jesus was a masterful storyteller. He put that skill to good use when he taught his disciples and the expectant crowds. Rather than make the vague observation that God is more gracious than people can grasp, he recounted the entertaining tale of a vineyard owner who paid one-hour workers a full day's wage.

In the New Testament a parable can be anything from a catchy saying to an extended story—as long as it teaches a spiritual lesson by illustrating the point with images from everyday life. For example, Jesus used a pithy saying to warn the self-righteous against hypocrisy: "Take the log out of your own eye, and then you will see clearly to take the speck out of your neighbor's eye" (Lk 6:42).

Jesus did not invent the parable; other teachers in ancient times used this compelling technique—notably the fifth-century B.C. Greek philosophers Plato and Aristotle. And a thousand years before Jesus, the prophet Nathan used a parable to confront King David about his sin with Bathsheba (2 Sam 12). Jesus, however, used parables so often that they became his hallmark; there are about 40 in the gospels. Most of them appear in Matthew and Luke, with several being duplicated. Only a handful are in Mark; there are none in the Gospel of John.

Why Jesus used so many parables is an intriguing mystery. Sometimes, clearly, he intended to help his listeners understand difficult spiritual ideas, such as the kingdom of heaven. For this he used situations familiar to shepherds, farmers, housewives, and travelers. But at other times his parables were so heavily symbolic that they had to be explained even to his disciples. Nonetheless, Jesus insisted that his parables contained spiritual messages for "anyone with ears to hear" (Mt 4:9)—meaning those seeking the truth about God's ways. To people who resisted his message, however, the parables often sounded like nothing more than perplexing riddles.

he is willing to sell every other possession with bold abandon in order to gain admittance to the kingdom. From that point on, the kingdom is the center of his very existence.

"Is not this the carpenter's son? Is not his mother called Mary?"... But Jesus said to them, "Prophets are not without honor except in their own country and in their own house." MT 13:55, 57

The question of who Jesus is and the significance of his words and deeds continue to perplex many. When he goes to his hometown of Nazareth, the people think they know who he is, a local man whose family still lives among them. Their preconceptions cause them to take offense at his prophetic message, and Jesus leaves town.

News of Jesus penetrates even into the royal court of Herod Antipas. Herod had foolishly put John the Baptist to death in order to fulfill a birthday promise, and now Herod's guilty conscience convinces him that Jesus is John raised from the dead.

But Jesus reveals who he is by his deeds. When huge crowds bring the sick to him even out in the deserted countryside, in compassion he heals them all and then feeds more than 5,000 with only a few loaves of bread and two fish—tenderly serving people's needs by the power of God.

In recounting the incident in which Jesus walks on the sea, Matthew tells how Peter wants to walk out to Jesus, and Jesus allows it. However, when Peter takes his eyes off Jesus and becomes afraid of the wind, he begins to sink, and Jesus has to save him. Jesus is one who challenges his disciples to risk everything on their trust in him but is there to help them when their human weaknesses cause distress.

Controversy flares over Jesus' refusal to practice all the rituals of purification that are so important to the Pharisees. Jesus goes so far as to insist that nothing outside a person can defile him. As always, Jesus focuses on the heart. The evils of the heart are the real danger, not unwashed hands.

He said to them, "But who do you say that I am?" Simon Peter answered, "You are the Messiah, the Son of the living God." MT 16:15-16

In the midst of all the controversies, Jesus' disciples are also struggling to understand who Jesus really is and what his identity means for their lives. Even after many experiences of Jesus' power, the disciples have difficulty in any new situation simply trusting in God's abundant love and power to provide for them through Jesus. They are beginning to understand some things about their master, but they have not yet grasped the meaning of his miraculous feeding of the 5,000.

As they travel north of Galilee to the source of the Jordan River, Jesus asks them about popular opinions of his identity. They recount the rumors that he is John the Baptist or one of the ancient prophets.

Jesus then turns the focus on themselves: "But who do you say that I am?" When Peter speaks for them all by saying that Jesus is the Messiah and "Son of the living God," Jesus blesses him for making that confession. "You are Peter [*Petros*]," Jesus says in a play on words, "and on this rock [*petra*] I will build my church" (Mt 16:18).

The disciples still have much to learn, however. When Jesus begins to tell them that he must go to Jerusalem, suffer, and be killed, Peter cannot tolerate such terrible words. His understanding of the Messiah has no place for such unimaginable events, and he rebukes Jesus. Just as Jesus had blessed Peter for his partial understanding, now he emphatically condemns him for refusing to hear the remainder of the message. Not only must he himself die, Jesus proclaims, but any who truly want to be his followers must deny themselves and take up the cross. Only by losing his temporal life can a disciple gain eternal life.

And he was transfigured before them, and his face shone like the sun, and his clothes became dazzling white.　MT 17:2

*I*f Peter was dismayed when Jesus had begun to speak of his coming suffering and death, the events a week later surely only added to the confusing mix of thoughts in his mind. Jesus takes his innermost circle of disciples—Peter, James, and John—up a mountain. There they experience what Jesus calls a vision, in which they see him transformed into a semblance of heavenly glory. The spectral figures of the revered Moses and Elijah, representing the law and the prophets, appear talking to Jesus.

Peter struggles to make sense of the moment. He believes that the vision reveals that Jesus is as great as Moses and Elijah, and he impetuously proposes building dwellings for all three. The voice of God from a bright cloud, however, strikes down such notions: Jesus alone is God's "Son, the Beloved" and they must "listen to him" (Mt 17:5).

As they descend the mountain, the three disciples ask Jesus about the traditional expectation that Elijah will come before the Messiah appears. Jesus leads them to see that John the Baptist has already fulfilled that role.

Upon returning to the crowds, however, Jesus is again confronted with a need for healing that demonstrates how far from full faith in God the crowds and even his own disciples are. He speaks to his disciples of the infinite power of faith in God, even "faith the size of a mustard seed" (Mt 17:20).

Scenes from Matthew's Gospel (from top): Jesus heals a man's withered hand, restores sight to two blind men, walks on water, defends disciples' picking grain on the sabbath, gives Peter keys to heaven.

Then Peter came and said to him, "Lord, if another . . . sins against me, how often should I forgive? As many as seven times?"　MT 18:21

*J*esus' fourth discourse in Matthew's Gospel emphasizes mutual responsibility, reconciliation, and forgiveness among his followers. The discourse originates with the disciples' misunderstanding of the kingdom of heaven. Talk of a kingdom implies for them hierarchy, rank, and power, and they argue about where they stand in that hierarchy. Jesus begins by turning such conceptions upside down. They must "change and become like children" (Mt 18:3), not act like powerful courtiers, in order even to enter God's kingdom.

Jesus warns that they must be responsible for each other and not cause even the most seemingly insignificant person to falter in his faith. As he often did, Jesus uses hyperbole to speak of cutting off one's hand or foot or plucking out an eye rather than allowing it to cause a stumble. Jesus tells the parable of the lost sheep to reemphasize God's concern for any who go astray and his desire that not one disciple be lost.

As an example, Jesus describes a procedure to follow when one disciple sins against another. Step-by-step, the disciples are to seek mutual understanding and reconciliation. Only as a last resort, when the one who has sinned refuses even the efforts of the whole church to solve the problem, must the sinner be excluded from the body of disciples.

When Peter asks if he must forgive a fellow disciple seven times, Jesus multiplies Peter's number to seventy-seven times—that is, there is no limit to the amount of forgiveness.

"Whoever wishes to be great among you must be your servant . . . just as the Son of Man came not to be served but to serve, and to give his life a ransom for many."　MT 20:26, 28

*A*t this point Jesus ends his many months of ministering in Galilee and departs for the region east of the Jordan. Large crowds follow him but few if any understand what is at stake in the move nearer to Jerusalem. In this new location, Jesus continues to instruct his disciples about a variety of issues that are difficult for them to comprehend.

Regarding divorce, Jesus urges his disciples to reject the practice of easy divorce by the husband that is common in their day and to return to God's original intent that husband and wife be permanently joined (Gen 2:24).

The example of a rich young man who comes seeking to do some good deed in order to gain eternal life serves as a warning about the dangers of wealth. Jesus urges the man to break the grip that his possessions have on him by selling them and giving to the poor. His refusal moves Jesus to warn that "it is easier for a camel to go through the eye of a needle" (Mt 19:24) than for the rich to accept God's rule.

When Jesus again foretells his suffering and even his crucifixion, his disciples still insist on expecting a glorious kingdom. The mother of James and John asks that Jesus make her sons the principal ministers in his kingdom. Jesus once again tries to reshape their values. Greatness is found only in genuinely humble service, just as he himself came to serve and give his life for humanity.

The crowds that went ahead of him and that followed were shouting, "Hosanna to the Son of David! Blessed is the one who comes in the name of the Lord!" MT 21:9

When Jesus arrives at Jerusalem, a confrontation between him and the wealthy establishment of religious authorities in the temple there is inevitable. The high priest Caiaphas and his clan work hand in glove with the Roman authorities and will not tolerate anyone who does not accept their mutually beneficial arrangements.

As he enters Jerusalem just before Passover, Jesus makes sure that he approaches the city in a way that reminds the gathering holiday throngs of Zechariah's prophecy of the king of Zion coming to the city on a humble donkey. The crowds recognize this prophetic sign and respond enthusiastically with cries of joy and celebration. Immediately on his arrival, Jesus challenges the temple authorities by driving out the money changers in order to restore the temple as a house of prayer and healing.

Every action and teaching of Jesus focuses on that challenge. When the priests question Jesus' authority, he ridicules them by showing how they had been unable to recognize the prophetic work of John the Baptist. He compares them to a son who promises to work for his father but then does nothing. With scorching words Jesus denounces them, saying that "the tax collectors and the prostitutes are going into the kingdom of God ahead of you" (Mt 21:31). But Jesus clearly knows that his attacks on the corrupt authorities will bring an inevitable response.

Then the Pharisees went and plotted to entrap him in what he said. MT 22:15

At first the authorities underestimate Jesus. They think they can entangle him in a web of sophisticated words. Some Pharisees come to him with oily flattery and ask a trick question about paying taxes to the emperor. Jesus responds with an equally challenging answer that urges them to fulfill their responsibilities to God. Next the Sadducees try an old conundrum that was supposed to make faith

Spreading their cloaks and cut branches before him, a festive throng welcomes Jesus to Jerusalem; a 19th-century Russian painting.

in the resurrection look ridiculous. Jesus blasts their aristocratic ignorance of both the scriptures and the genuine power of God.

When an individual lawyer asks a classic question concerning the greatest of the many commandments in the law, Jesus answers in a way that reflects all his teaching. The greatest command is that which flows most from the heart: love for God with all of one's heart, soul, and mind. Similarly, the second command is love for one's neighbor.

Finally, Jesus focuses his attack on the Pharisees' hypocrisy and arrogance and their desire to make their demanding interpretation of the law apply to everyone. They have created a wall of purity regulations, ritual practices, and arguments about minutiae, Jesus argues, that blocks off most people from approaching obedience to God. And yet their methods, focusing on external behavior, too often fail to transform the heart. They may appear beautiful on the outside, but are often corrupt within.

When he was sitting on the Mount of Olives, the disciples came to him privately, saying, "Tell us, when will this be, and what will be the sign of your coming and of the end of the age?" MT 24:3

Jesus' fifth and final discourse in the Gospel of Matthew follows the moment when Jesus leaves the temple for the last time. Though the sacred complex is both massive and beautiful, Jesus foretells a day when "not one stone will be left here upon another" (Mt 24:2), a prediction fulfilled in A.D. 70, when the Romans destroy the temple.

Jesus first foretells the tribulations that will befall Jerusalem and lead to the destruction of the temple. He then points beyond that day to the time when the Son of Man will return, "coming on the clouds of heaven with power and great glory" (Mt 24:30). He warns the disciples against trying to predict these events, since no one knows the day except God.

Jesus urges his disciples to be continually watchful, to live each day prepared for the joyful return of their Lord. Through a vivid series of comparisons with the time of the Great Flood or with a thief breaking in or with a servant awaiting the return of his master or with bridesmaids awaiting a wedding party, Jesus teaches them always to be prepared. Further, through the parable of servants entrusted with large sums of money, he teaches them not simply to wait for his return, but to make good use of the time and opportunities given to them.

The conclusion of the discourse and of all of Jesus' teaching in the Gospel of Matthew comes in his striking portrayal of the final judgment scene when the Son of Man as king separates all people to his right and to his left. Those on the right inherit the kingdom that God has prepared. Those on the left are banished to eternal fire. To those on his right the king says, "I was hungry and you gave me food" (Mt 25:35). Those on the left had failed in this and similar acts of charity.

But neither side can remember either serving or failing to serve the king in this manner. To each side the king reveals that as they had acted or failed to act "to one of the least of these" (Mt 25:45), so they had acted or failed to act toward him.

While they were eating, Jesus took a loaf of bread, and after blessing it he broke it, gave it to the disciples, and said, "Take, eat; this is my body." MT 26:26

As the Passover approaches, Jesus' enemies scheme to get rid of him after the festival. They do not realize that another timetable, set by God, will determine the course of events. On the Wednesday before Passover, Jesus stays in Bethany and visits the house of Simon the leper, perhaps one who had been healed by Jesus. A woman comes to him there and in an extravagant gesture pours a jar of costly ointment over his head. Some of the disciples are angered by the excess, but Jesus interprets it as anticipating his coming burial.

Judas Iscariot, possibly realizing at last that the hopes of many for a national revolution will not be fulfilled, decides to turn Jesus over to his enemies for 30 pieces of silver.

When Passover—which extended from sundown Thursday to sundown Friday—arrives, Jesus meets his disciples at a private home in Jerusalem. The atmosphere is filled with foreboding as Jesus begins by announc-

The apostles react with horror and disbelief to Jesus' announcement at the Last Supper that one of them will betray him; the dramatic moment is captured by the Venetian master Jacopo Robusti, called Tintoretto (1518-1594).

ing that one of the disciples will betray him. During the meal Jesus uses the Passover bread and wine to show the meaning of the events that are about to take place. He breaks a loaf and says that it is his body and asks the disciples to eat of it. He takes a cup of wine and asks them to drink of it, saying, "this is my blood of the covenant, which is poured out for many for the forgiveness of sins" (Mt 26:28).

Jesus knows the good intentions of his disciples, and also their weaknesses, and predicts that Peter will deny knowing him that very night. While Judas withdraws to make plans for the betrayal, the rest of the company leave Jerusalem for the Mount of Olives. There, in a place called Gethsemane, Jesus prays to God and finds strength to face the coming horror.

Then the high priest said to him, "I put you under oath before the living God, tell us if you are the Messiah, the Son of God." MT 26:63

Events move quickly. Judas arrives with a crowd armed with swords and clubs, and he quickly identifies Jesus by kissing him. Jesus forestalls violence by commanding one of his followers to put away his sword. As his disciples flee, Jesus is taken as a prisoner back to the city.

An impromptu nocturnal trial is convened in the house of the corrupt high priest Caiaphas. The equally corrupt Sanhedrin summoned by Caiaphas tries to find any witnesses, even false witnesses, to accuse Jesus of crimes. But ultimately the kangaroo court comes down to Caiaphas's demand that Jesus say whether he is the Messiah and Son of God. When Jesus refuses to deny these titles and predicts that they will see the Son of Man in power and glory,

Three scenes are depicted in this 13th-century French ivory carving: Judas accepting silver for his betrayal, identifying Jesus with a kiss, and hanging himself.

Caiaphas and his cronies condemn Jesus for blasphemy. In the morning, the midnight verdict is ratified by the high-priestly clan and the aristocratic elders, and Jesus is sent to Pilate, the Roman governor, for sentencing and execution.

While Jesus stands before his powerful accusers and is condemned, Peter is outside, faltering before a servant girl and bystanders, denying that he knows Jesus. But when he realizes his failure, he weeps bitter tears of repentance. Even Judas repents of the evil of his betrayal and returns the money he has received. But he cannot assuage his sense of guilt, and hangs himself.

And when they had crucified him, they divided his clothes among themselves by casting lots . . . . Over his head they put the charge against him, which read, "This is Jesus, the King of the Jews." MT 27:35, 37

Matthew tells of Jesus' trial before Pilate and crucifixion very much as Mark does, but with a few notable additions. For Pilate, the Roman governor, the only question that matters is that of treason: "Are you the King of the Jews?" (Mt 27:11). Jesus' ambiguous answer hardly constitutes a convincing case, however, and Pilate decides to use Jesus' popularity with the people to get the crowds to condemn the notorious prisoner Barabbas. Matthew notes that Pilate's wife had premonitions in a dream that Jesus was innocent and warned her husband. However, Pilate had already allowed the people to choose Barabbas, thus condemning Jesus.

Pilate symbolically washes his hands of guilt, while the inflamed mob welcomes responsibility for

As Jesus predicted, Peter denies his master three times before the cock crows on Friday morning; a mosaic from the 6th-century basilica of San Apollinaire Nuovo in Ravenna.

the death of a man accused of blasphemy. Only Jesus knows that these events had been decided in Gethsemane and that his death is to atone for the sins of all people, not just those involved that day.

After being flogged and mocked, Jesus is led to Golgotha for crucifixion. Like Mark, Matthew highlights those details of the events that fulfill scriptures, especially Psalms 22 and 69. For example, Jesus' final mysterious cry from the cross: "My God, my God, why have you forsaken me?" (Mt 27:46) echoes the ancient cry of Psalm 22:1.

When Jesus breathes his last, Matthew records that remarkable signs occur. The temple veil is torn; the earth shakes; many of the saints who had died are raised from the dead and appear in the city. For Matthew, such amazing events are but proof that Jesus' death is part of a great transition, the passing of one era and the beginning of a new age.

But the angel said to the women, "Do not be afraid; I know that you are looking for Jesus who was crucified. He is not here; for he has been raised." MT 28:5-6

Matthew, like the other three Evangelists, does not describe the resurrection of Jesus directly. He notes that many women disciples who had followed Jesus from Galilee observed his crucifixion and that Joseph of Arimathea, a wealthy disciple, lay Jesus in his own new tomb. With Pilate's approval, the Jewish authorities seal the tomb and set guards to prevent Jesus' disciples from stealing the body. And so the sabbath passes quietly.

On Sunday morning, when Mary Magdalene and Mary the mother of James and Joseph approach the tomb, there is a violent earthquake. An angel of the Lord descends and rolls away the stone. What the angel reveals, however, is an empty tomb. Jesus has already risen from the dead.

Matthew emphasizes that the women receive the same message from both the angel and from Jesus himself when they encounter him as they flee in terror from the empty tomb: They are to tell the disciples to meet Jesus in Galilee.

While the guards are bribed by the chief priests and the elders to hide the fact of the resurrection, the disciples hurry north to Galilee. On a mountaintop there the eleven hear the risen Jesus herald a new age in which "all authority in heaven and on earth" (Mt 28:18) belongs to him. He sends them forth to take his message to all nations, baptizing people and teaching them to follow his commands. In the last words of the Gospel, Jesus gives his disciples an assurance that echoes his designation as Emmanuel, "God is with us," at the beginning of Matthew: "I am with you always," Jesus promises them, "to the end of the age" (Mt 1:23, 28:20).

As Jesus falters under the burden of the cross he is carrying to Golgotha, Mary his mother reaches out to console him; a painting by the Renaissance master Raphael (1483-1520).

*T*he shortest of the four gospels and in all probability the first to be written, the Gospel of Mark appeared at a turning point in Christian history. Although scholars have disagreed on both its date and its place of origin, it was likely written near the time of the destruction of Jerusalem in A.D. 70 and for Gentile Christians living beyond Palestine, perhaps in Italy. Since Jesus' death, his followers had spread the message of his deeds and teachings by word of mouth. Hundreds of brief stories about Jesus were probably well known. Some Christians no doubt had compiled collections of Jesus' sayings, but Mark was evidently the first to draw both his deeds and teachings together in a single, unified narrative. One of the most important things that Mark did was to stress the events around the crucifixion of Jesus—the Passion narrative. Indeed, Mark has often been described as a Passion narrative with an extended introduction. The early chapters show how opposition to Jesus' message hardened into conspiracies to destroy him. Later chapters are structured around Jesus' three predictions of his death and resurrection. The final third of the Gospel is devoted to the last few days of Jesus' life.

Mark's narrative is vivid and fast-paced; one of his favorite words is "immediately"—*eythys* in the Greek original. But Mark always recounts events with their message in mind. He did not intend simply to record interesting information; rather, he wanted to proclaim the good news of what God had done in sending Jesus and to create or strengthen faith in his readers.

The Gospel itself gives no indication of its author. In the second century, it was attributed to John Mark, an early believer from Jerusalem and—according to Acts of the Apostles—a companion of both Peter and Paul. Tradition also held that the Gospel was really based on Peter's preaching as recorded by Mark shortly before the apostle's death in Rome. The book itself, however, gives no clear indication of such an origin.

Jesus' baptism, from Andrea Pisano's 14th-century bronze baptistery doors at the cathedral of Florence, Italy

---

The beginning of the good news of Jesus Christ, the Son of God. MK 1:1

Mark is the only one of the four Evangelists who uses the term "good news," or gospel, in his opening sentence as a designation for the book as a whole. The term conveys the excitement of early Christians that in telling Jesus' story they were sharing the announcement of a wonderful event—one that would transform human life. In addition, the term emphasizes that Mark is a book with a strong message. From the very beginning the author wants his readers to know his fundamental purpose for writing—to show that Jesus is the Christ, the Son of God.

Mark begins the story not with Jesus' birth, as Matthew and Luke later did, but with the beginning of Jesus' ministry in Galilee or, more specifically, with the work of John the Baptist, who immediately anticipated the appearance of Jesus. He quotes the Old Testament prophets Malachi and Isaiah (though naming only the latter) as having foretold the role John would play as a voice crying out in the wilderness to prepare the way for the Lord.

John's baptism was not like the many washings for ritual purification that were common in religious life of that time. Rather, it was a sign of repentance and a fundamental change of direction in life, looking forward to one who would, as John said, "baptize you with the Holy Spirit" (Mk 1:8).

Jesus first comes on the scene as a partisan of John, sharing in John's baptism along with many others. Jesus' baptism, however, is marked by visionary signs as the heavens are torn open, the Holy Spirit descends on him in the form of a dove, and God himself affirms Jesus' identity: "You are my Son, the Beloved; with you I am well pleased" (Mk 1:11).

In short order Mark sketches the 40 days of temptation in the wilderness that Jesus experiences (recounted more fully in Matthew and Luke) and sets the beginning of Jesus' ministry at the time John the Baptist is arrested and thus removed from his prophetic work. Jesus leaves Judea and the Jordan River area where John had been known and goes north to Galilee with an urgent message: "The time is fulfilled, and the kingdom of God has come near; repent, and believe in the good news" (Mk 1:15).

The authority that Jesus embodies is immediately manifested as he walks by the Sea of Galilee and calls fishermen in the midst of their work to follow him. They immediately drop their nets, leave their families and coworkers, and follow him.

They were all amazed, and they kept on asking one another, "What is this? A new teaching—with authority! He commands even the unclean spirits, and they obey him." MK 1:27

Following the call of the disciples, Mark further reveals Jesus' authority to his readers by taking them through a day in the life of the Messiah, a sabbath. He first shows Jesus in the town of Capernaum on the north shore of the sea, teaching in the local synagogue. The people recognize that his manner of teaching is different from the traditional instruction to which they are accustomed. Jesus does not cite the authority of former scribes, rabbis, or oral tradition, but speaks as though he himself bears the right to establish the truth of his teaching.

Suddenly, the synagogue seems on the verge of chaos as "a man with an unclean spirit"—who was therefore believed to have uncanny, though distorted, insight—disrupts the instruction. The possessed man seems to speak with the voice of the demonic world and to know Jesus with the same clarity that the voice of heaven had known him. In terror the voice cries, "Have you come to destroy us? I know who you are, the Holy One of God" (Mk 1:23, 24). Jesus silences the unclean spirit and commands it to leave the man.

The people at once perceive the connection between the amazing authority of Jesus' teaching and his authority over the demonic spirit. They are receiving "a new teaching—with authority!"

In these first few paragraphs of his Gospel, Mark provides his readers with a threefold assertion of Jesus' identity—from Mark's own words in the first line of his book, from the voice of God, and from the voice of the unclean spirit. Along with Mark, the readers now know clearly who Jesus is, and they begin to anticipate the moment when the ordinary people around Jesus will also recognize who he is.

The day continues as Jesus heals Simon Peter's mother-in-law of a fever. When the sabbath ends at sundown, people begin to move about more freely and crowd Jesus with their needs for healing or delivery from evil spirits.

Mark concludes his day in the life of Jesus early the next morning as Jesus seeks solitude for prayer. But Simon tries to draw him back to the crowds. Insisting that spreading his message has priority, Jesus goes on to neighboring towns in Galilee.

"Which is easier, to say to the paralytic, 'Your sins are forgiven,' or to say, 'Stand up and take your mat and walk'?" MK 2:9

Mark next describes how Jesus' ministry breaks down conventions of piety. Both the positive and negative reactions to Jesus' acts create an atmosphere in which religious leaders feel threatened and begin to seek his ruin.

People with any of a number of skin diseases that in those days were grouped under the term leprosy were required by religious law to remain separate from all other people, and they were considered unclean as long as they had the disease. (Lev 13:45-46). Such a leper comes to Jesus begging to be healed: "If you choose, you can make me clean" (Mk 1:40). In compassion, Jesus disregards the purity regulations of Judaism and reaches out to touch the untouchable man, curing him instantly with a word.

Flanked by his first two disciples, Peter and Andrew, Jesus summons to his side two other Galilean fishermen, James and John the sons of Zebedee; the painting dates to the 16th century.

The paralytic lowered through the roof to be healed by Jesus, as depicted in a 6th-century mosaic at Ravenna, Italy

Jesus seems to have more hope for sinners than for the self-proclaimed righteous. When he speaks of the Pharisees as "righteous," his words are full of irony.

Fasting was an important practice of piety, observed by both "John's disciples and the Pharisees" (Mk 2:18). Jesus avoids fasting, however, insisting that he and his disciples must be true to the particular character of his own ministry. The good news that Jesus is proclaiming—"new wine"—demands new patterns of thought and new manifestations of piety—"fresh wineskins" (Mk 2:22).

When the disciples break the conventional practice of the sabbath by plucking grain to eat on the day of rest, Jesus defends them. He makes the radical claim that there is a hierarchy of values in God's commands. Doing something for human good is more important than strictly avoiding all semblance of work on the sabbath.

Jesus sternly commands the man to tell no one except the priests, who have to certify his new status. But whereas Jesus' command could compel the obedience of an unclean spirit, Jesus assumes no such power over ordinary people. Their obedience has to be freely given, and in this case, the healed man understandably tells of his healing everywhere. As a result, the throngs streaming to Jesus become so overwhelming that he can hardly move.

When Jesus is at home in Capernaum, the place becomes so packed that no one can penetrate the mass of humanity. In that situation, Mark recounts, four men, who were determined to get their paralyzed friend to Jesus, dig through the roof of the house and let him down through the opening.

Jesus almost always responds to situations in surprising ways. Instead of simply healing the man, he first says to him, "Son, your sins are forgiven" (Mk 2:5)—words sure to spark the ire of skeptical religious teachers who think Jesus is usurping God's prerogatives. But for Jesus all the various aspects of his unique ministry are united. Just as earlier his authority over the unclean spirit had served to confirm the authority of his teaching, so now his ability to heal physical paralysis with a word confirms the far more important ministry to heal the devastation of sin with forgiveness. The people are amazed: "We have never seen anything like this!" (Mk 2:12).

As he was walking along, he saw Levi son of Alphaeus sitting at the tax booth, and he said to him, "Follow me." And he got up and followed him. MK 2:14

Jesus goes against another marker of piety by including among his followers people such as the tax collector Levi (called Matthew in the Gospel of Matthew), a person who would have been despised because of his profession. To the Pharisees, Jesus does not seem to demand sufficient repentance before sharing fellowship with these people. He eats with the sinners first and does not consider them on a different, lower plane from clearly pious people. Indeed,

VIEWING TOGETHER

All four gospels tell about the life and teachings of Jesus. But the first three—Matthew, Mark, and Luke—are so much alike in both content and order that they are called the Synoptic Gospels, from a Greek word that means "viewing together." Readers who study these books in a "synopsis," an edition in which related texts are printed side by side, soon discover striking similarities. Appearing in all three books, and in the same order, are reports of Jesus' baptism and temptation, his calling the disciples and calming the storm, the transfiguration, the teaching in the temple, the Last Supper, and his crucifixion and resurrection. Even more startling is that in passage after passage the words are exactly or nearly the same. For example, all three gospels use the same words for Jesus' instructions to feed the 5,000: "You give them something to eat" (Mt 14:16; Mk 6:37; Lk 9:13).

An explanation for these similarities came from Augustine, a fourth-century theologian. He proposed that Matthew was written first, Mark drew from Matthew, and Luke drew from both. Scholars today, however, generally agree that the shortest gospel, Mark, was written first and that Matthew and Luke independently used it as their principal source.

Mark evidently was not the only source for Matthew and Luke. The latter noted supplemental sources in the first verse of his gospel. Apparently one such source, used by both Matthew and Luke, was a collection of Jesus' sayings and teachings that unfortunately has been lost. Scholars call it the Sayings Source or "Q," from the German word *Quelle*, which means "source."

The controversy over Jesus' challenges to piety boils over one sabbath when a man with a withered hand appears in the synagogue. There is a sense of impending threat as everyone watches Jesus to see if he will heal the man and thus work on the day of rest. Jesus is not seeking persecution but wants simply to be true to the full meaning of his proclamation. Fundamental issues of how to understand God's commands are involved. Jesus could have backed down and bided his time, but he refuses to be untrue to the character and urgency of his message—and to who he is. He says to the man, "Stretch out your hand" (Mk 3:5). In the face of opposition, he heals the man, and, as Mark shows, he thereby steps onto the road to his crucifixion.

And the scribes who came down from Jerusalem said, "He has Beelzebul, and by the ruler of the demons he casts out demons." MK 3:22

Mark vividly portrays how confusing it was to be around Jesus in those days. The news of this bold teacher, who challenged traditional authorities and gave healing and hope to all sorts of people, brought throngs from distant places south, east, and north. When people possessed with demons cried out that he was God's son, speculation ran wild. Jews had never thought of God having a son, except as the king in ancient times was described metaphorically as God's son. Could the word of unclean spirits contain any truth?

To escape the hordes and wild speculation, Jesus goes up a mountain alone and then summons twelve of his closest and most loyal followers to appoint them apostles—from a Greek word meaning "to send away." They are to remain with Jesus now but later are to be sent out as his emissaries. Unlike the crowds who come out of curiosity or for miracles or the religious authorities who watch Jesus only to condemn him, these are to be the ones who come to see clearly who Jesus really is. Mark shows, however, that the twelve are only at the beginning of what will be a difficult struggle.

The opposition to Jesus hardens. His fearless stands against conventional religious authority convince even his family that he is "out of his mind" (Mk 3:21). Scribes from Jerusalem are even harsher, saying that he is an agent of Beelzebul or Satan. Such an accusation, Jesus says, is the opposite of the truth. He is engaged in a struggle in which his allies are defined not by family ties or traditional authority but by commitment to doing the will of God.

And he said to them, "To you has been given the secret of the kingdom of God, but for those outside, everything comes in parables." MK 4:11

One way that Jesus deals with the diverse reactions to himself and his message is by telling brief stories called parables. A parable involves some element of comparison or parallel between a surface meaning and a deeper meaning. The surface meaning is readily understandable, but whether a listener understands on the deeper level depends on whether he or she has, as Jesus says, "ears to hear" (Mk 4:9). Jesus tells the parable of a sower broadcasting seed onto four kinds of soil to point to the various responses to his message. Some people are like soil on a hard path where birds eat the seed. Some are like rocky soil: They respond positively to the message but cannot face the difficulties it brings. Some are like soil with thorns: Their love of money or other desires choke the message. But some are like fertile soil and the message produces an astonishing harvest. Many, he says, would "indeed listen, but not understand," but when one accepts the message, understanding multiplies, "for to those who have, more will be given" (Mk 4:12, 25).

Jesus helps his disciples to see in the parables "the secret of the kingdom of God," though he expresses surprise at their difficulty in understanding him. Through his parables Jesus exhibits total confidence that in spite of the opposition to his mission, the kingdom of God will prosper. It is like seed that grows from the nourishing earth and produces a full harvest. It is like a tiny mustard seed that produces an enormous shrub.

He woke up and rebuked the wind, and said to the sea, "Peace! Be still!" Then the wind ceased, and there was a dead calm. MK 4:39

In spite of the many astonishing events that they are witnessing and being chosen for Jesus' innermost circle, the disciples, as Mark continues to show, have difficulty in progressing from their commitment to Jesus as their teacher to faith in Jesus as someone far more than a teacher. Mark

For casting out demons, Jesus was accused of being an agent of Satan. In this detail from a 12th-century Latin Bible, Jesus drives unclean spirits into the Gerasene swine, who then plunge to their deaths in the sea.

stresses that difficulty of coming to faith in the story of Jesus stilling a storm on the Sea of Galilee.

As they cross the sea, Jesus falls asleep, and a violent windstorm arises. The disciples' panic and failure of trust are clearly captured in their shout to rouse Jesus: "Teacher, do you not care that we are perishing?" Jesus wakes and with a word turns chaos and danger into calm tranquillity. But then he turns to the deeper danger: "Why are you afraid?" he asks. "Have you still no faith?" The faith in Jesus that can destroy fear has yet to sprout. Yet this event helps transform the disciples' fear of external forces into a "great awe" before Jesus and helps them realize that the ways they had understood their master in the past were too feeble to apply to one whom "even the wind and the sea obey" (Mk 4:38, 40-41).

Across the lake, they enter the Gentile region of the Gerasenes. With vivid detail Mark recounts how Jesus meets a man who embodies the destructive force of demonic power. As before, the evil spirit recognizes Jesus as "Son of the Most High God" (Mk 5:7), and gives himself the name Legion (a large unit of the Roman army) because many spirits possess the man. Effortlessly, Jesus casts out the army of demons and sends them into a herd of swine—fittingly, unclean spirits into unclean animals. The inhabitants of the land are so afraid of Jesus' power that they beg him to leave. But the healed man becomes Jesus' first messenger among the Gentiles, telling what God has done for him through Jesus.

The death of John the Baptist—recorded in Mark 6:14-29—is the subject of this medieval Bible illustration: For her dance (top left), Herodias's daughter asks for and is given John's head on a platter, which she promptly brings to Herod's table (bottom right).

Overhearing what they said, Jesus said to the leader of the synagogue, "Do not fear, only believe." MK 5:36

Jesus returns to Jewish territory and encounters two situations of need. One is a matter of life and death, the other a kind of ritual impurity that is like a perpetual religious death. Mark narrates the events in greater detail than either Matthew or Luke.

Jairus, a leader of a synagogue, begs Jesus to come heal his daughter who is on the point of death. Jesus quickly follows Jairus, accompanied by throngs of people, but his urgent response is interrupted when a woman in the crowd touches his garment. The woman suffers from a continual hemorrhage that, according to religious law, renders her ritually unclean and bars her from all religious rites. God works so powerfully through Jesus that when she touches him, she is immediately healed. Jesus senses what has happened and insists on identifying the woman and praising her faith, which had conquered her fear and moved her to act.

The delay appears tragic, however, when messengers announce that Jairus's daughter has died. Even the power of death does not deter Jesus, however. For others death is the end of hope, but for Jesus it is no more than a sleep from which he can awaken the child with a word.

Then Jesus said to them, "Prophets are not without honor, except in their hometown, and among their own kin, and in their own house." MK 6:4

Demonic power, incurable physical suffering, even death—nothing can hinder God's power at work in Jesus. But nonbelievers are another matter. Against them, Jesus refuses to impose his will. When Jesus returns to his hometown synagogue in Nazareth (though Mark does not mention the town's name in his account), the people's familiarity with the young man makes them distrust him. To them he is no more than a local carpenter whose mother and brothers and sisters they know, and they take offense at his claim to authoritative teaching. Jesus evidently cannot perform his miraculous works in Nazareth without feeling that he is forcing himself upon his fellow townsmen, and he refuses to do that. He well understands their feelings about him, but is nonetheless amazed at their level of distrust.

After the disciples have experienced Jesus' teaching and the full range of his authority and of people's response to him, Jesus sends the twelve in pairs out into the villages of Galilee. They are to take no resources except the message and the authority to heal that Jesus gives them.

To mark the interval while the disciples are traveling, Mark recounts in detail the events that led to the beheading of John the Baptist. Herod Antipas's foolish promise to the daughter of his vengeful wife pushed him to produce "the head of John the Baptist on a platter" (Mk 6:25). Then Herod's guilty conscience makes him worry about the identity of this Jesus he has heard about and conclude that he is John raised from the dead.

As he went ashore, he saw a great crowd; and he had compassion for them, because they were like sheep without a shepherd; and he began to teach them many things. MK 6:34

When the twelve return from their mission, they have much to share with Jesus, and he tries to take them away from the continual press of the crowd so that they can rest. The needs of the people will not be denied, however, and before Jesus and his disciples can reach an isolated place, the throngs have anticipated them. Jesus responds to their demands not with frustration but with compassion, and he shares with them his message of God's love. Thousands strain to listen for hours until the day is drawing to a close.

Despite all they have experienced on their mission, the disciples can see the situation of a hungry multitude only as a looming disaster and they urge Jesus to send the multitude away. They know it will take more than half a year's wages to feed such a crowd, and they have hardly enough bread and fish to feed two or three.

But Jesus perceives the situation through the prism of God's power, unlimited by available resources. With God, the five loaves and two fish on hand become abundance for more than 5,000 people.

Finally, Jesus sends the disciples across the lake by boat, dismisses the crowd, and finds a few hours alone for prayer. At dawn he can see the disciples still out on the lake and he walks out toward them on the water. They have seen astonishing things before, but still find it impossible to accept the miraculous. Their thoughts revert to childhood fears of ghosts, and only Jesus' reassurance can overcome their terror. The struggle to believe and think and see in new patterns is profoundly difficult.

"There is nothing outside a person that by going in can defile, but the things that come out are what defile." MK 7:15

The Pharisees and other religious leaders were regrouping to challenge Jesus again. Such men took the purity regulations of the temple very seriously and tried to establish a standard of ritual purity for many situations of everyday life. To them such practices expressed a rigorous devotion to God that Jesus and his disciples seemed to flout. When they challenge Jesus on the matter, he says that they have fundamentally misunderstood what God wants and have substituted the tradition of pure hands for God's central command for purity of heart. Their rigorous devotion is more apparent than real, Jesus notes. When they seem to be devoting their resources to God, he asserts, they are actually keeping those resources from their parents and thus disobeying one of the Ten Commandments.

Jesus goes so far as to declare that nothing outside a person can ever cause impurity that has any spiritual significance. Only the evils that well up from the human heart can truly defile. This radical statement is the basis for Christianity's later rejection of the system of ritual purity.

Jesus travels north from Galilee into the Gentile regions around Tyre and Sidon. Even there his reputation has preceded him. One Syrophoenician woman refuses to be deterred by Jesus' desire for privacy with his disciples. Jesus admires her tenacity and humility and heals her suffering daughter.

Returning home, he visits the league of eastern cities known as the Decapolis, where he heals others, including a deaf man. The people are astounded, saying, "He has done everything well" (Mk 7:37).

Since his client was Holy Roman emperor Henry III, the unknown 11th-century artist who produced this Bible illumination of Jesus feeding the 5,000 was unsparing in his use of gold paint to enrich the image.

And he cautioned them, saying, "Watch out—beware of the yeast of the Pharisees and the yeast of Herod."
MK 8:15

Mark wished to show through the example of the disciples how tremendously difficult it is for human beings to learn to think in ways that truly take the power of God into account and to trust that power. Again and again he shows how the disciples' patterns of thought are mired in their preconceptions of ordinary human values and possibilities. One of the most striking examples Mark uses is the feeding of the 4,000 (Mk 8:1-10) so closely following the feeding of the 5,000 that he had earlier recounted. Though the disciples had already seen Jesus feed a large throng with meager resources, they still cannot reach beyond their own sense of weakness and limitation to imagine and to trust God's power. Jesus possesses that power, and from nearly nothing he produces what is needed.

Jesus' authority in both word and deed has been demonstrated repeatedly, and yet some of the Pharisees discount his every action and come demanding some special heavenly sign to prove his standing as a prophet. Jesus flatly refuses to play their game and leaves with his disciples to cross the lake.

The disciples fall back in awe as Jesus is transfigured into a blinding apparition flanked by Moses and Elijah. Fra Angelico (c. 1400-1455) painted the scene for the cell of a fellow monk at a monastery in Florence, Italy.

Jesus warns his disciples about the yeast of the Pharisees and Herod—that is, their insidious influence. As it happens, the disciples have forgotten to bring enough bread and think Jesus has caught them. Again, Mark emphasizes the difficulty of their transformation. "Do you have eyes, and fail to see?" (Mk 8:18) Jesus asks them. His gradual healing of a blind man immediately thereafter perhaps symbolizes the step-by-step process by which they must come to regard the world with a new vision.

Then he began to teach them that the Son of Man must undergo great suffering, and be rejected by the elders, the chief priests, and the scribes, and be killed, and after three days rise again. MK 8:31

A major step in the disciples' transformation comes when they are traveling with Jesus near the source of the Jordan River. Jesus first asks about popular speculation concerning his identity, but then turns the question directly to the disciples: "Who do you say that I am?" Peter responds simply and profoundly: "You are the Messiah" (Mk 8:29).

Here for the first time in Mark's Gospel a normal human being recognizes and confesses Jesus' identity. It is seemingly a tremendous step, and yet Jesus' response is surprisingly stern and unenthusiastic.

Rather, he begins immediately to teach the disciples something that is wholly unexpected, namely that he must suffer and be killed and rise again. Peter had just asserted his conviction that Jesus is the Messiah, a title that to most Jews meant an anointed king who would restore the nation of Israel, sit on David's throne, and overthrow Gentile rule. Jesus' statements about suffering and death seem to contradict his role as Messiah, and Peter protests.

Jesus responds to Peter in the strongest possible terms, showing that he and the other disciples have only begun to understand the astonishingly unexpected way that God has chosen to send the long-expected Messiah into the world. Indeed, Jesus asserts that the mark of his suffering must be the mark of every disciple: "Let them deny themselves and take up their cross and follow me" (Mk 8:34).

And there appeared to them Elijah with Moses, who were talking with Jesus. MK 9:4

As Peter and the others are trying to reconcile their own conceptions of the Messiah with Jesus' prediction of his coming suffering and death, he adds another ingredient to their mental and spiritual struggle. About a week after Peter's confession, Jesus takes his three closest disciples—Peter, James, and John—up an isolated mountain peak. Suddenly they see Jesus in a brilliant, supernatural glory talking to Elijah and Moses, representatives of the prophets and the law. They are filled with fear and do not know what the vision means. But Peter tries to interpret it. Jesus, their rabbi, should have a standing equal to Moses and Elijah—high praise indeed.

A switchback road leads to the 1,843-foot summit of Mount Tabor, venerated since the 6th century as the site of Jesus' transfiguration.

everything they thought they knew about how God would save his people. It is still too much for them: "They did not understand what he was saying and were afraid to ask him" (Mk 9:32).

What they can understand is the glory of the Messiah, and they argue with each other about which of them will have the greatest positions in the coming kingdom. Again Jesus tries to turn their thinking on its head. He takes a child in his arms to show that greatness is not to be found in power and position. When they welcome and serve a powerless child, they are serving Jesus and, indeed, are welcoming God who has sent him.

Jesus insists that they not think of themselves as an exclusive circle with something like a copyright on his name: "Whoever is not against us is for us." Rather, they must be very careful not to damage a fragile growing faith in "one of these little ones who believe in me" (Mk 9:40, 42). Similarly, in the strongest possible terms, Jesus warns them to remove any cause within themselves that will block or destroy their faith in God and prevent them from entering into his kingdom.

But God himself intervenes to show the inadequacy of Peter's still muddled understanding. Jesus is to stand far above Moses and Elijah: "This is my Son, the Beloved; listen to him!" As they descend the mountain, Jesus orders them to keep the vision secret until he has "risen from the dead" (Mk 9:7, 9), a statement that only adds to the questions churning within their minds.

When the four rejoin the other disciples, they find that they have been unable to cast out a spirit that is causing severe convulsions in a boy. The boy's father turns plaintively to Jesus: "If you are able to do anything, have pity on us and help us." Jesus' response expresses the trust in God that the disciples find so difficult to grasp: "If you are able!—All things can be done for the one who believes." The father's anguished cry expresses in turn the difficult human journey toward real trust: "I believe; help my unbelief!" (Mk 9:22-24).

He sat down, called the twelve, and said to them, "Whoever wants to be first must be last of all and servant of all." MK 9:35

*J*esus knows that his disciples must undergo a wholesale transformation of their thinking, and he begins to concentrate his efforts entirely on personally teaching them. The transformation has to grow out of their understanding of his suffering. And so for the second time, Jesus gives them a preview of his future betrayal, death, and resurrection. But to unite in their hearts the concept of Messiah with betrayal, suffering, and death requires them to rethink

As he was setting out on a journey, a man ran up and knelt before him, and asked him, "Good Teacher, what must I do to inherit eternal life?" MK 10:17

*J*esus' ministry in Galilee is finished, and he travels with his disciples south into the region of Judea (controlled by the Romans) and Perea east of the Jordan (controlled by Herod Antipas). Again crowds surge around Jesus as he preaches.

When Pharisees ask Jesus about divorce, he reminds them of God's original intent in marriage and insists that no marriage can be dissolved without sin being committed. When parents bring their little children for Jesus to bless, the disciples rouse Jesus' anger by keeping the children away. They had already forgotten what he had taught them and were blocking from Jesus those who were the proper inhabitants of God's kingdom.

When a man kneels and asks what he must do to inherit eternal life, Jesus begins with rather conventional instructions about obeying God's laws. Jesus soon perceives, however, the one idol that enslaves the man's life—his wealth. Jesus points him toward freedom by asking him to sell his possessions and follow him. When the man departs unchanged, Jesus tries to help his disciples to understand. Again, their values have to be turned upside down. Wealth is not

Giotto's early-14th-century fresco of Jesus driving the money changers from the temple decorates the Arena chapel in Padua, Italy. Inset is a Roman coin such as the one Jesus used to make a point about what was due the emperor (Mk 12:13-17).

young colt of a donkey that has never been ridden. Jesus wants to fan the people's anticipation by enacting the well-known prophecy found in Zechariah 9:9 that Jerusalem's messianic king will arrive triumphant and humble, riding not on a king's great warhorse but a colt.

On the Sunday before Passover, as Jesus rides the colt toward the Holy City, the people respond enthusiastically. They recognize the prophetic message and line the road, shouting blessings on the one who comes in the Lord's name and on the coming renewal of David's kingdom. Late in the day, Jesus finally reaches the eastern gate of the city, which opens directly into the great temple complex built by Herod the Great. Mark, in contrast to Matthew, indicates that Jesus waits till the next day for his dramatic challenge to the temple authorities.

Then they came to Jerusalem. And he entered the temple and began to drive out those who were selling and those who were buying in the temple, and he overturned the tables of the money changers and the seats of those who sold doves. MK 11:15

God's stamp of approval, but an almost insuperable obstacle to entering God's kingdom.

As they approach the city of Jerusalem, Jesus tells his disciples for the third time about his coming suffering and death. Again, however, the disciples can grasp only the hope of future glory. James and John boldly ask for prime positions in the coming glorious kingdom. Jesus turns aside their request by urging his disciples to imitate himself: "The Son of Man came not to be served but to serve, and to give his life a ransom for many" (Mk 10:45).

The blind man said to him, "My teacher, let me see again." Jesus said to him, "Go; your faith has made you well." Immediately he regained his sight and followed him on the way. MK 10:51-52

On the final stage of his fateful journey to Jerusalem, Jesus heals a blind beggar named Bartimaeus just outside Jericho—a healing that in some ways symbolizes the believer's journey to discipleship. Bartimaeus cries for mercy and comes to Jesus in spite of many obstacles. His faith gives him new sight, and he immediately follows Jesus.

By the time Jesus finally arrives on the outskirts of Jerusalem, the Passover feast is approaching and the people are filled with messianic expectations. Jesus sends two of his disciples into a village to obtain a

Mark frames the account of Jesus' return to the temple with an incident that helps symbolically to show the meaning of his actions in the temple. On Monday morning, Jesus comes to a fig tree that has nothing but leaves. Jesus condemns it never to bear fruit again. So also he condemns the priestly aristocracy around the corrupt high priest Caiaphas. Elaborate temple ritual conceals a lack of real devotion and service to God.

Jesus enters the temple that morning like an ancient prophet filled with righteous indignation at the corrupting commerce that has turned God's "house of prayer" into "a den of robbers" (Mk 11:17). Wrathfully, he drives out the buyers and sellers. The chief priests find his daylong interruption of temple business intolerable and immediately begin planning ways to kill him.

On Tuesday morning, the disciples find the fig tree withered—both a prophetic sign of the fate of the temple aristocracy and an object lesson for the disciples of the power of faith in God. When Jesus returns to the temple, the religious leaders demand some proof of prophetic authority for his actions. But Jesus challenges them concerning their evaluation of John the Baptist in order to show that they lack any integrity that deserves such proof. He pointedly condemns them by telling the crowds a parable about murderous tenant farmers.

One of the scribes came near and heard them disputing with one another, and seeing that he answered them well, he asked him, "Which commandment is the first of all?"
MK 12:28

*J*esus spends Tuesday in the temple teaching and answering questions. Pharisees and Herodians try to use a tricky question about paying taxes to Caesar to catch Jesus in some incriminating or unpopular statement. Jesus turns their trick on themselves and challenges them further to give "to God the things that are God's" (Mk 12:17).

Next it is the Sadducees' turn. The Sadducees were mostly aristocratic priests who did not believe in the resurrection of the dead. Thus they bring a clichéd old question about a woman who survived seven husbands, a question intended to ridicule the idea of resurrection. Jesus attacks them for knowing neither the scriptures nor God.

Finally, a teacher of the law brings a more serious question, a classic one concerning the most important commandment in the law. Without hesitation Jesus cites the command to love God with one's whole being as most important, followed by the command to love one's neighbor. The teacher agrees, and Jesus praises his perception: "You are not far from the kingdom of God" (Mk 12:34).

The wisdom of Jesus' answers silences his challengers, and when he questions them concerning the relation of King David to the Messiah, none will answer. Jesus' final word of instruction in the elaborate temple complex highlights the great generosity of a poor widow who gave all her resources to God's house—two copper coins that could buy practically nothing but were more valuable to God than the huge gifts of the wealthy.

"But when you see the desolating sacrilege set up where it ought not to be (let the reader understand), then those in Judea must flee to the mountains." MK 13:14

*A*s Jesus leaves the temple for the last time that Tuesday evening, his Galilean disciples are still agog at the magnificence of the structure Herod had built. Indeed, it was one of the largest and most opulent temple complexes in the Greco-Roman world. Jesus, however, foretells the leveling of the temple, an event that occurred in A.D. 70 when Roman armies destroyed Jerusalem. The Roman desecration of the holy place is described as "the desolating sacrilege," and it evidently was happening or had recently happened when Mark wrote his Gospel, since he adds the note, "let the reader understand."

Jesus' predictions range widely from the destruction of the temple, to the future mission of the disciples and their persecution, to the appearance of false Christs and false prophets, to the coming of the Son of Man with power and glory to gather his followers from all over the earth. The time of these events, Jesus insists, is known only to God, and thus the disciples must be ever vigilant. "What I say to you," Jesus concludes his lesson, "I say to all: Keep awake!" (Mk 13:37).

And when they had taken their places and were eating, Jesus said, "Truly I tell you, one of you will betray me, one who is eating with me." MK 14:18

*J*esus spends the next day in Bethany and joins a banquet in the home of a man called Simon the leper. The banquet becomes a significant event when a woman enters with an extravagantly expensive jar of fragrant ointment and without a word pours the entire contents over Jesus' head. This mysterious action clearly means something special, but what? Some of the diners think it is a wasteful extravagance that shows unconcern for the poor. But Jesus defends the woman, interpreting her act as anointing his body "beforehand for its burial" (Mk 14:8). For already in Jerusalem his enemies have found a way to bring about his death. Judas Iscariot has come to them offering to betray Jesus in return for money.

At dinner in the house of Simon the leper, a woman pours ointment on Jesus' head in a symbolic anointing for his burial. El Greco (c. 1541-1614) painted this version of the event.

*With a kiss Judas betrays Jesus, who turns
to heal the slave's ear cut off by an impetuous Peter.*

On Thursday, preparations are made for the Passover feast that begins at sundown. When Jesus comes with his disciples to a large upper room in Jerusalem, the company is likely exuberant. Jesus had entered Jerusalem in triumph and had met every challenge during the week. Thus it is a crushing blow when Jesus begins by announcing that one of the disciples there will betray him to his mortal enemies. However, he continues to share the meal without identifying the betrayer.

Jesus had repeatedly foretold his coming death, but now he stamps its meaning forever in their hearts. With thanks to God he gives them broken bread from the meal. "Take," he says, "this is my body." He gives them a cup of wine to drink: "This is my blood of the covenant," he says, "which is poured out for many" (Mk 14:22, 24). These symbolic gifts are given to them not because of their strength or worthiness but in the midst of their weakness. They will all become deserters, Jesus warns them; even Peter will deny him three times before daybreak.

*He said, "Abba, Father, for you all things are possible;
remove this cup from me; yet, not what I want, but
what you want."* MK 14:36

Jesus crosses the valley east of Jerusalem and climbs the Mount of Olives to a place called Gethsemane, meaning "olive press." Jesus feels overwhelming sorrow and distress at the prospect of the

spiritual pain he faces. In a soul-wrenching prayer he expresses the horror, calling on God as "Abba," a child's word similar to papa or daddy, and asking for deliverance. But no voice from heaven intervenes. Rising from the ground where he had prostrated himself, Jesus finds his disciples asleep.

In short order Judas the betrayer arrives with an armed mob. Jesus is arrested and led away to the high priest's residence. Mark describes an almost surreal nocturnal trial in which the high priest presides over a search for witnesses against Jesus, but no two can be found who agree. Finally, in frustration, the high priest directly asks Jesus, "Are you the Messiah, the Son of the Blessed One?" And Jesus answers simply, "I am" (Mk 14:61-62). Almost the exact words of confession that open the Gospel of Mark now become the indictment that condemns Jesus to death on the cross for blasphemy.

At the very time when Jesus is confessing his identity and being condemned, Peter is outside denying his identity as a follower of Jesus. He, too, stood condemned by his own conscience, and "he broke down and wept" (Mk 16:72)

*At three o'clock Jesus cried out with a loud voice, "Eloi,
Eloi, lema sabachthani?" which means, "My God, my
God, why have you forsaken me?"* MK 15:34

On Friday morning the high priest's contrived verdict is ratified and Jesus is sent to Pontius Pilate, the Roman prefect. Pilate has but one concern, whether the Jewish man before him is trying to overthrow Roman rule and make himself a king. When Jesus makes no defense of himself, Pilate apparently concludes that he is no threat to Rome but that his popularity is a threat to the temple leaders. Pilate tries to manipulate the situation by using a traditional amnesty at Passover by which the people can gain the release of one Roman prisoner. Pilate hopes the people will choose Jesus and condemn an insurrectionist named Barabbas, who is dangerous to Rome. The people, however, hate Roman rule and do not hesitate to choose Barabbas for release. The fate of Jesus is sealed.

In short order, Roman soldiers flog Jesus, mock him as a pitiful king of the Jews, and lead him to Golgotha ("the place of the skull"). By 9:00 A.M. Jesus is being nailed to a cross. Mark notes a number of details that echo the words of scripture, especially Psalms 22 and 69. Abandoned by his followers, Jesus suffers insult and abuse from every side as he hangs naked on the cross.

From noon to 3:00 P.M. a preternatural darkness covers the land. Then Jesus' cry rings forth with words so filled with anguish and mystery that Mark gives them in Aramaic before translating them for his readers: "My God, my God, why have you forsaken me?" The words come from the first line of Psalm 22, but in this context express the profound spiritual suffering and abandonment Jesus experiences on the cross, far more painful than any physical hurt. His cry causes only confusion among those standing by. When Jesus dies, however, a Roman centurion there speaks with uncanny perception: "Truly this man was God's Son!" (Mk 15:39).

They had been saying to one another, "Who will roll away the stone for us from the entrance to the tomb?" When they looked up, they saw that the stone, which was very large, had already been rolled back. MK 16:3-4

A wealthy follower named Joseph of Arimathea requests Jesus' corpse from Pilate, and, since the sabbath is approaching, he quickly wraps the body and lays it in a rock-cut tomb. This process is observed by a number of women, followers and supporters of Jesus in Galilee who had traveled with him to Jerusalem.

When the sabbath is over, Mary Magdalene, the apparent leader of this group, comes with two other women to cover Jesus' body with fragrant spices, as was the custom. When they arrive the tomb is open, and a young man in white sits beside the spot where Jesus had lain. He speaks to them with calm assurance: "You are looking for Jesus of Nazareth, who was crucified. He has been raised." The figure in white instructs the women to tell the disciples that Jesus is going ahead of them to Galilee and "there you will see him, just as he told you." Hearing these astonishing words, the women flee from the tomb, but "they said nothing to anyone, for they were afraid" (Mk 16:6, 7, 8).

With these surprising revelations, the text of Mark ends. They are so disconcerting in the way they leave the story hanging, as it were, in midsentence, that several different attempts were made in ancient times to add an appropriate ending to the Gospel. Indeed, a number of scholars have suggested that the original ending of Mark was somehow lost. The well-known long ending (Mk 16:9-20) began to be commonly added to the text of Mark only after the fourth century A.D.

If Mark originally closed his Gospel with verse 8, the ending would simply be the final example of human misunderstanding and struggle that had characterized Jesus' followers throughout the narrative. It was not their strength or courage but Jesus' authority and God's power that could bring forth a great plant from a mustard seed, that could feed thousands from little more than a family lunch, that would build God's kingdom amid the weakness of frail human messengers. Yet the existence of the Gospel of Mark itself bears witness to the fact that God's power is sufficient. "The good news of Jesus Christ, the Son of God" flourished and grew.

Serial scenes from the death of Jesus appear in this triptych by Jean Bellegambe (1470-1534): carrying his cross to Golgotha; his crucifixion between two thieves; his body taken down from the cross for burial.

The angel Gabriel telling Mary she will conceive a son; from a French book of hours, dated about 1500

*O*f the four gospels, only that of Luke is accompanied by a second volume: the Acts of the Apostles. Written by the same author, the two books unfold a great vision of how the Spirit of God worked both in the life of Jesus and in the lives of the early believers to bring the message of salvation to the world. Together, the Gospel of Luke and Acts form about a quarter of the New Testament. Though neither of these works names the author, second-century church leaders attributed both books to an early Gentile Christian whom Paul called "Luke, the beloved physician" (Col 4:14). Probably written in the 80s of the first century A.D., the works address the church at large and do not seem to reflect the specific concerns of any particular group of people or the situation in any particular geographic location.

In his prologue (Lk 1:1-4) Luke clearly describes his undertaking. First, he notes that "many" others had begun compiling the accounts handed down from the first generation of believers—"eyewitnesses" to the remarkable birth of Christianity. Comparison with the other two Synoptic Gospels indicates that Luke probably had at least a copy of Mark and shared with Matthew a written collection of Jesus' teachings, sometimes called "Q," or Quelle, German for "source." Luke also had a variety of additional oral and written traditions about Jesus, including accounts of his birth, post-resurrection appearances, and other events of his life.

Carefully researched, Luke's narrative shows how God had ordered these events from beginning to end so that a Christian believer such as his patron Theophilus—whose very name means "lover of God"—could be certain of their truth. Within this overall picture, Luke's Gospel interweaves a rich tapestry of related themes, such as the importance of prayer, the guidance of the Holy Spirit, God's concern for the poor, the dangers of wealth and greed, women disciples, the importance of Jerusalem, and the compassion of Jesus.

In the sixth month the angel Gabriel was sent by God to a town in Galilee called Nazareth, to a virgin engaged to a man whose name was Joseph, of the house of David. The virgin's name was Mary. LK 1:26-27

*L*uke prefaces his story of Jesus' miraculous birth with an account of the birth of John the Baptist. John's birth was much like those of several others in the Old Testament—namely, Isaac, Jacob, Samson, and Samuel. As with those births, God intervenes to give a son to a previously barren woman and thereby raise up a leader for his people. The angel Gabriel tells the priest Zechariah that his son will fulfill the role of Elijah, prophesied in Malachi 4:5, in returning to prepare for the coming of the Lord. Although Zechariah doubts the angel and is struck dumb in punishment, his elderly wife Elizabeth does indeed become pregnant.

Mary visiting Elizabeth; from a late-15th-century French book of hours

Six months later, Gabriel again appears to announce a birth, this time to a young woman in Galilee named Mary, who is still an unmarried virgin and thus likely in her mid-teens. Gabriel foretells that the birth of her son will mark the beginning of a new era. As a virgin, she will conceive by the power of the Holy Spirit and give birth to one who will inherit the throne of his ancestor David and be called the Son of God. Mary responds with faith and acceptance: "Here am I, the servant of the Lord; let it be with me according to your word" (Lk 1:38).

Gabriel also tells Mary of Elizabeth's pregnancy, and Mary hurries to Judea to visit her kinswoman. Elizabeth at once recognizes Mary as "the mother of my Lord"; even the baby in her womb "leaped for joy" (Lk 1:43, 44). Mary responds in poetic words traditionally called "The

Magnificat," from the first word of the Latin translation: "My soul magnifies the Lord and my spirit rejoices in God my savior" (Lk 1:47). Largely based on Hannah's prayer in 1 Samuel 2:1-10, Mary's words reveal her profound understanding of the greatness of what God is doing for her and her people.

Similarly, when John is born and given his name by his father, Zechariah—his speech restored—celebrates in poetry the son's great destiny as a prophet.

"Do not be afraid; for see—I am bringing you good news of great joy for all the people: to you is born this day in the city of David a Savior, who is the Messiah, the Lord." LK 2:10-11

Both Matthew and Luke tell of Jesus' birth, but with strikingly different emphases. Matthew reports dream revelations given to Mary's betrothed, Joseph, the coming of the wise men, Herod's slaughter of the innocent children of Bethlehem, and the family's flight into Egypt. Luke describes Gabriel's visit to Mary, the Roman census that brought Mary and Joseph to Bethlehem, the newborn infant Jesus laid in a manger because the inn was full, and the angelic announcement to shepherds.

Luke's emphasis is on the humble nature of Jesus' birth. The high and mighty appear only in the emperor's census decree that ironically brings about the fulfillment of a prophecy that the Messiah will come from David's hometown. With few words Luke hints that Jesus was born in an animal stable, since he was laid in a manger or feed trough. The announcement of the birth of the Messiah and Savior is not made to the powerful of the world but to shepherds, who go to find the Lord in the form of an infant in a stable.

Mary and Joseph spend over a month in Judea fulfilling the rites required by the law for Jesus' circumcision after eight days and Mary's purification thirty-three days after the birth of her son (Lev 12:3, 4-8). They bring Jesus to the temple in Jerusalem as the firstborn son to offer the sacrifice of redemption. Their offering of two turtledoves or pigeons indicates that they are too poor to afford a sheep. In the temple an aged man named Simeon, who had been promised by God that he would not die before seeing the Messiah, celebrates the child as the fulfillment of God's word but warns Mary that he will also cause her pain: "a sword will pierce your own soul too." Similarly, Anna, an elderly prophet who lives in the temple, praises God and speaks of Jesus as a sign of "the redemption of Jerusalem" (Lk 2:35, 38). Then, Luke records, Mary and Joseph take Jesus back to their home in Nazareth.

Summoned by angels to worship the newborn Messiah, shepherds crowd about the infant Jesus; a painting from a church in Venice by Paolo Veronese (1528-1588).

He said to them, "Why were you searching for me? Did you not know that I must be in my Father's house?" LK. 2:49

The only story about Jesus' life between his birth and his baptism by John the Baptist at about the age of 30 appears in Luke. A pious couple, Mary and Joseph were accustomed to making the journey to Jerusalem each year to celebrate Passover. At the age of 12, Jesus accepts the responsibility to obey God's law for himself, not simply to accompany his parents. The story of Jesus being missing from Mary and Joseph's company and found three days later among the teachers in the temple highlights the youth's precocious understanding of the scriptures

Mary and Joseph (left, rear) find the 12-year-old Jesus among teachers in the temple; Albrecht Dürer (1471-1528) added an unlikely monkey to his painting of the event.

and tradition and his awareness of his responsibility to God: "I must be in my Father's house." But with a child's humility, he obediently returns to Nazareth with his family to grow "in wisdom and in years, and in divine and human favor" (Lk 2:52).

The word of God came to John son of Zechariah in the wilderness. He went into all the region around the Jordan, proclaiming a baptism of repentance for the forgiveness of sins. LK 3:2-3

In anticipation of the beginning of Jesus' ministry, Luke, along with the other three Evangelists, describes the work of John the Baptist. In phrases that echo the introductions to prophetic books in the Old Testament, Luke gives the approximate date (about A.D. 26) when John receives his calling. Luke emphasizes not only John's fiery, prophetic words but also his practical instructions about compassion and honesty. By describing the end of the Baptist's ministry and his imprisonment by Herod Antipas before telling of Jesus' baptism, Luke suggests both the connection between Jesus and John and their separation.

While praying after his baptism, Jesus receives both a manifestation of the coming of the Holy Spirit as a dove and the acclamation of God calling out from heaven: "You are my Son, the Beloved; with you I am well pleased" (Lk 3:22).

Luke concludes his account of the preparations for Jesus' ministry by recording his genealogy. Like Matthew, Luke reckons Jesus' ancestry back to David and the patriarchs but, unlike Matthew, Luke records a nonroyal line of descent from David to Jesus. Luke also extends Jesus' genealogy all the way back from Abraham to "Adam, son of God" (Lk 3:38).

The scroll of the prophet Isaiah was given to him. He unrolled the scroll and found the place where it was written:

"The Spirit of the Lord is upon me, because he has anointed me to bring good news to the poor." LK 4:17-18

Luke begins his account of Jesus' ministry by emphasizing that he was "full of the Holy Spirit" (Lk 4:1) and spent 40 days of fasting in the wilderness and being tested by the devil. Like Matthew, Luke records three temptations: to fulfill physical desires, to strive for power and wealth, and to show pride and self-assertion in forcing God to prove himself. Jesus turns aside each temptation with a word of scripture.

The power of the Spirit accompanies Jesus as he emerges onto the public stage in Galilee, teaching in synagogues and being well received. At the synagogue in Nazareth that he customarily attended, Jesus reads from Isaiah 61, boldly proclaiming that the words are being fulfilled at that very moment. At first, all praise Jesus. But when he reveals that his ministry will reach out to Gentiles and foreigners, the people are outraged and try to kill him. Though Jesus fulfills scriptural prophecies, he overturns many popular expectations related to those prophecies.

Jesus shifts his work to Capernaum on the shore of the Sea of Galilee, attracting great crowds.

When he had finished speaking, he said to Simon, "Put out into the deep water and let down your nets for a catch." Simon answered, "Master, we have worked all night long but have caught nothing. Yet if you say so, I will let down the nets." LK 5:4-5

The remarkable teacher and miraculous healer was ready to gather disciples. He first calls a fisherman named Simon, whose mother-in-law he had previously cured of a fever. Now he uses Simon's boat as an offshore pulpit to preach to the crowds pressing in on him. His lesson concluded, Jesus tells Simon to put out into deep water and let down his nets for a catch. Simon is frustrated by a night of fishing without success but nevertheless obeys Jesus. When the nets swell with a huge catch, Simon realizes the power of Jesus. At first he is so afraid that he begs Jesus, "Go away from me, Lord, for I am a sinful man!" But Jesus calls Simon and his partners

James and John, the sons of Zebedee, to follow him. "From now on you will be catching people" (Lk 5:8, 10), he tells these humble men.

As he begins to gather steadfast disciples, Jesus continues to stimulate controversy by his actions. Once, when a leper begs him for healing, Jesus ignores the ban on contact with lepers. He touches the man and heals him. The crowds around Jesus become so vast that some men tear through the tiled roof of a house to let down a paralyzed friend into the room where Jesus is healing. Jesus stirs both amazement and opposition when he forgives the man's sins and then heals him as a sign that he has "authority on earth to forgive sins" (Lk 5:24).

Opposition intensifies from those who demanded rigorous obedience to the law after Jesus calls a tax collector named Levi as a disciple and banquets with tax collectors and sinners. He also refuses to follow common pious practices of fasting, and defends his disciples when they pluck grain to eat on the sabbath. When Jesus heals a man with a withered hand in front of an assembly of Pharisees and scribes in a synagogue on another sabbath, his enemies are stimulated to find a way to stop what has become a dangerously revolutionary ministry.

Then he looked up at his disciples and said:
"Blessed are you who are poor,
*   for yours is the kingdom of God.*
"Blessed are you who are
hungry now,
*   for you will be filled.*
"Blessed are you who
weep now,
*   for you will laugh."*
LK 6:20-21

Jesus found strength for his ministry through nights spent in prayer to God. After one of those nights, Jesus calls the company of his disciples to him and names twelve of them to be apostles, or emissaries for special missionary work. It is in this context that Luke recounts the so-called Sermon on the Plain, a summary of Jesus' teaching that has many similarities to the Sermon on the Mount in Matthew 5-7.

Jesus is surrounded by disciples and a vast crowd that has come from Judea and Jerusalem to the south and the region of Tyre and Sidon to the north. On this occasion, his teaching includes four blessings and four woes that show the Lord's judgment on the values built into the society around him. Those blessed by God, he says, are the poor, the hungry, those who weep, and those who are hated and excluded because of their com-

mitment to him. Those who deserve woe are the rich and those who are full, are laughing, and are well spoken of by everyone.

Jesus calls his disciples to practice a radical standard of love and service that extends to those who actively hate and abuse them and to their enemies. Love and service have power, Jesus teaches, only when they go far beyond a reasonable response to fair treatment by others: "Love your enemies, do good, and lend, expecting nothing in return. . . . and you will be children of the Most High . . . . Be merciful, just as your Father is merciful" (Lk 6:35-36).

Jesus urges his followers to avoid being judgmental and condemning, but to forgive readily and to remember how easily a person can spot "the speck in your neighbor's eye" while ignoring "the log in your own eye" (Lk 6:41). Putting these teachings into action, Jesus says, is like building a house on solid rock, so firm that it can withstand the flood of life that breaks around it but leaves it unshaken.

"Go and tell John what you have seen and heard: the blind receive their sight, the lame walk, the lepers are cleansed, the deaf hear, the dead are raised, the poor have good news brought to them. And blessed is anyone who takes no offense at me." LK 7:22-23

Jesus always provoked strong responses, negative as well as positive. A centurion in the army of Herod Antipas developed close ties to the Jewish population and learned of the power of Jesus. When one of his servants becomes ill, he enlists some Jewish leaders to ask for Jesus' help. However, as Jesus approaches, the soldier sends word that he is not worthy of a visit from Jesus. Nonetheless, he recognizes Jesus' unique authority and trusts that his word will heal his servant. Jesus is amazed and holds up this soldier's faith as an example to his followers.

The extent of Jesus' authority is demonstrated even more vividly when he encounters a burial procession for the only son of a widow at the town of Nain. Out of compassion for her, Jesus commands her son to rise, and he is restored to life. Tremendous awe floods the crowd, and the people praise Jesus as a great prophet.

Even in prison, John the Baptist hears reports of Jesus and dispatches two of his followers to ask, "Are you the one who is to come, or are we to wait for another?" (Lk 7:19). Jesus sends them back to report

To enlist Simon Peter and the sons of Zebedee as disciples, Jesus fills their nets with fish; a stained glass roundel from Canterbury Cathedral.

what they have seen and heard. Jesus speaks of John as more than a prophet, the one sent to prepare his way. He notes that, though he and John are very different from each other, the message of each is being rejected by the fickle people of the day.

Once, when Jesus is reclining at dinner with a Pharisee named Simon, a woman known as a sinner comes up behind him weeping, bathing his feet with her tears, drying them with her hair, kissing them, and anointing them with ointment. Simon sees this as proof that Jesus is not a prophet or he would not allow such a woman to touch him. Jesus challenges Simon not to judge him but to see that the woman's actions show her great love and desire for forgiveness. Jesus grants that forgiveness: "Your faith has saved you; go in peace" (Lk 7:50).

Because of such compassion, Jesus gathers around him not only his male disciples but an extensive group of women followers, evidently led by Mary Magdalene. These women provide for the disciples' needs "out of their resources" (Lk 8:3).

"No one after lighting a lamp hides it under a jar, or puts it under a bed, but puts it on a lampstand, so that those who enter may see the light." LK 8:16

In a section closely parallel to materials he found in Mark, Luke recounts how Jesus uses the parable of the sower and the soils to describe people's responses to the message of God that he proclaimed. These responses range from total rejection to fruitful acceptance. For Jesus, however, the message is like a lamp that cannot be hidden, but each person by his response renders a judgment on himself: "Then pay attention," Jesus says, "to how you listen." Even Jesus' earthly family can claim no special status; Jesus says that his true family are "those who hear the word of God and do it" (Lk 8:18, 21).

Crossing the Sea of Galilee in a boat with some disciples one day, Jesus falls asleep as a windstorm arises. For all their experience as fishermen on that extensive lake, the disciples are terrified—until Jesus wakes and instantly calms the storm. Their hearts are now raging with amazement as well as fear. "Who then is this," they ask one another,

"that he commands even the winds and the water, and they obey him?" (Lk 8:25).

When they arrive on the other side of the lake, they enter Gentile territory, land inhabited by people known as Gerasenes or Gadarenes, from the name of their principal town. There Jesus heals a man plagued with a legion of demons who at once recognizes Jesus as the Son of God and fears him intensely. When the people of that region see Jesus' power—manifested by casting the demons into a herd of swine who plunge into the lake and drown—they too are greatly afraid and ask him to leave. After sending the healed man home to tell what God has done for him, Jesus recrosses the lake to Galilee.

Luke again closely follows Mark in recounting the great miracles in which Jesus further demonstrates his authority over life and death. First, he heals a woman whose bleeding no one else can cure after she comes from behind as he is surrounded by a crowd and touches his robe. Next, he raises from the dead the 12-year-old daughter of a synagogue leader named Jairus.

Then he said to them all, "If any want to become my followers, let them deny themselves and take up their cross daily and follow me." LK 9:23

Narrating the events leading up to Jesus' departure from Galilee toward his ultimate destination of Jerusalem, Luke follows the account in Mark 6-9 fairly closely—except that he does not include any material parallel to Mark 6:45-8:26. This way of compressing the narrative helps Luke to bring several incidents that focus on Jesus' identity into close proximity with Peter's confession of Jesus as the long-awaited Messiah, a turning point.

Jesus sends the twelve out to the villages of Galilee to heal and proclaim the kingdom of God. He dispatches them on their mission with no food or extra clothing but with his message of salvation and the authority he has bestowed on them to heal the sick and drive out evil spirits from those possessed. During this time, Herod Antipas hears speculation that Jesus is John the Baptist raised from the dead or some other prophet. "John I beheaded," he says;

In this detail from a large painting by Cosimo Rosselli (1439-1507) in the Vatican's Sistine Chapel, Jesus reaches out to heal a supplicant leper.

"but who is this about whom I hear such things?" (Lk 9:9).

As the apostles return, Jesus shows his character as a compassionate provider by feeding a crowd of 5,000 with only a few loaves and fish. At this point, Luke moves directly to the moment when Jesus asks his disciples, "Who do the crowds say that I am?" (Lk 9:18), and they recount speculation much like that heard by Herod. When Peter names him as the Messiah, Jesus immediately begins to tell the disciples about his coming suffering and death and to link that suffering to the life of the disciples, who must "take up their cross daily and follow me."

About a week later Jesus allows three of his disciples to see that plans determining his future were already prepared. Jesus appears to them in glory with Moses and Elijah discussing his departure for Jerusalem and what he is about to accomplish there. As Jesus continues to show God's greatness in his works and to teach them about his coming betrayal and suffering, it is too much for the disciples. The meaning of Jesus' words "was concealed from them, so that they could not perceive it." Instead, the disciples argue about which of them is the greatest, so that Jesus uses a small child to teach them that "the least among all of you is the greatest" (Lk 9:45, 48).

When the days drew near for him to be taken up, he set his face to go to Jerusalem. LK 9:51

Here Luke comes to a great turning point in his Gospel. In a single sentence Mark told how Jesus left Galilee "and went to the region of Judea and beyond the Jordan" (Mk 10:1). Luke expands that brief account of Jesus' journey into about ten chapters, and the journey to Jerusalem becomes the organizing theme of the second half of Luke's narrative of Jesus' ministry. In Luke's structure the journey falls into two parts: the first (Lk 9:51-13:35) concludes with Jesus' lament over Jerusalem; the second (Lk 14:1-19:44) concludes with Jesus weeping over the Holy City. Most of the extensive material concerning Jesus' ministry not found in Mark is contained in this section of Luke.

Recognizing that the time for his death has almost arrived, Jesus sets out with prophetic determination. As he moves south to Samaria, he experiences immediate rejection because his destination is what the Samaritans consider the rival sanctuary at Jerusalem. On the other hand, several people volunteer to follow him as disciples, and Jesus has to warn them of the demands of discipleship.

All four Evangelists tell of a woman who anointed Jesus while he was dining. Matthew and Mark place the event in the house of one Simon the leper in Bethany; Luke, in the house of a Pharisee named Simon; John, at dinner with Lazarus.

WHO WAS MARY MAGDALENE?

Early in his ministry, Jesus healed several wealthy women who then became his devoted followers. Mary Magdalene, exorcised of seven demons, was apparently the leader of this group that supported Jesus and his twelve apostles "out of their resources" (Lk 8:3). Mary's name suggests that she came from the village of Magdala on the western shore of the Sea of Galilee, near Jesus' headquarters in Capernaum.

Some early Christian writers claimed that Mary was the unnamed sinner, presumably a prostitute, who had previously intruded on the Pharisee's dinner party to bathe Jesus' feet with her tears and dry them with her hair. But this is highly unlikely because such a woman would not have been a companion of the wife of Herod Antipas's steward, as Luke notes.

Mary Magdalene was among the brave few who stayed with Jesus to the end, standing beside his mother at the foot of the cross, lingering to see him buried, and going to his tomb on Sunday morning. Either alone (as in Mark and John) or with another woman (as in Matthew), she was the first to see the risen Jesus.

Just as he had sent out the twelve, Jesus now dispatches 70 disciples ahead of him with no resources except the power of healing and the message of the kingdom of God. When the 70 return, they are filled with joy over the defeat of demonic power, and Jesus rejoices with them. He thanks God for choosing to use such ordinary people as the disciples to carry out his will and blesses them because they are seeing the fulfillment of the hopes and aspirations of the prophets of old.

But the Lord answered her, "Martha, Martha, you are worried and distracted by many things; there is need of only one thing. Mary has chosen the better part, which will not be taken away from her." LK 10:41-42

Many topics of Jesus' teaching come up during the journey to Jerusalem. A teacher of the law asks what to do to inherit eternal life. Jesus turns the question back to him and agrees with him when the lawyer cites the great commands to love God and love one's neighbor. "Do this," Jesus says, "and you will live" (Lk 10:28). When the lawyer asks for the definition of "neighbor," Jesus responds with the parable of the Good Samaritan in order to show that there can be no artificial limits on the responsibility to be a neighbor. After a priest and a Levite ignore the plight of a man robbed and left to die by the roadside, a Samaritan takes pity on the man.

Transfixed by his teaching, Mary kneels at Jesus' feet as he turns to admonish Martha, who has come to complain that her sister has left the serving to her; a painting by Alessandro Allori (1535-1607).

Again the question of what is central to life arises—but in different form—when Jesus visits with his friends Mary and Martha. Mary spends her time learning from Jesus while Martha becomes frustrated with the responsibilities of entertaining her guest. Jesus urges Martha to concentrate, as Mary has, on his teaching of what is really necessary in life.

Another time, Jesus' disciples ask him to teach them to pray, and he gives them the brief and well-focused prayer known through the centuries as the "Lord's Prayer." He also teaches them to be persistent in prayer in the confidence that God will "give the Holy Spirit to those who ask him!" (Lk 11:13).

Jesus' opponents begin to attribute his power to demonic forces. Jesus ridicules such an inversion of reality that would have Satan "divided against himself." But since it is by God's power that he casts out demons, Jesus says, "then the kingdom of God has come to you." Those are blessed, he adds, "who hear the word of God and obey it" (Lk 11:18, 20, 28).

And he said to them, "Take care! Be on your guard against all kinds of greed; for one's life does not consist in the abundance of possessions." LK 12:15

When a Pharisee invites Jesus to a dinner with the other Pharisees and lawyers, Jesus goes but refuses to follow their rituals of purification before eating. When the host expresses amazement at this, Jesus responds with a forceful critique of the Pharisees' approach to their religion. They define their relation to God through the careful performance of precisely delineated acts of obedience, down to tithing "mint and rue and herbs of all kinds." But because the emphasis is on observable performance, the Pharisees' approach is hollow, neglecting "justice and the love of God" (Lk 11:42). Such criticism leads the Pharisees to be increasingly hostile to Jesus, who warns his disciples that the pervasive yeast of the Pharisees is their hypocrisy.

As hostility grows, Jesus teaches his disciples to fear no one except God and to realize that God loves them dearly: "Even the hairs of your head are all counted" (Lk 12:7). They must be courageous in standing for their faith in the face of opposition, trusting that the Holy Spirit will teach them what to say.

Repeatedly, Jesus warns them about the corrupting power of greed for wealth. He tells the story of a wealthy farmer who stores up such an abundance of crops that he thinks he has made himself secure for many years to come, but he dies that very night.

Jesus urges his disciples to learn to trust God for all the needs of life and not to be filled with anxiety. If God feeds the birds and clothes the lilies, "how much more will he clothe you—you of little faith!" Rather, Jesus says, "strive for his kingdom, and these things will be given to you as well" (Lk 12:28, 31).

A medieval artist depicted the parable of the Good Samaritan, told only in Luke.

laments the Holy City that killed the prophets and is yet unwilling to accept him. By the time he arrives, he predicts, the people will say, "Blessed is the one who comes in the name of the Lord" (Lk 13:35).

"But when you give a banquet, invite the poor, the crippled, the lame, and the blind. . . . for you will be repaid at the resurrection of the righteous." LK 14:13-14

On another occasion Jesus shares a sabbath banquet with a leading Pharisee and his friends, but there is tension in the air. The Pharisees watch Jesus as a man with the symptoms of dropsy suddenly appears before him. Jesus recognizes the challenge, however, and does not hesitate to heal the man on the sabbath. Jesus then turns on his hostile hosts to rebuke their love of honor at such banquets. He teaches them to act with humility and to invite those in need to their banquets, rather than those who would repay in kind.

Jesus brings his denunciation of the Pharisees into focus through a parable about a great banquet. When time for the banquet came, all of the invited guests made lame excuses and did not attend. Undeterred, the host then dispatched his servants into the streets to "bring in the poor, the crippled, the blind, and the lame" (Lk 14:21) because none of the invited guests had deigned to share his feast.

Halfhearted followers, Jesus teaches, are not acceptable for the kingdom of God. Jesus' call to discipleship must be placed absolutely first in life. All that a person defines as his own—material possessions, parents, family, even life—must be surrendered to the call to discipleship. Jesus respects all these family relationships but knows that they must never take the place of God. A disciple must count the cost: "None of you can become my disciple if you do not give up all your possessions" (Lk 14:33).

"Quickly, bring out a robe—the best one—and put it on him; put a ring on his finger and sandals on his feet. And get the fatted calf and kill it, and let us eat and celebrate; for this son of mine was dead and is alive again; he was lost and is found!" LK 15:22-24

Jesus' opponents often criticized him for refusing to separate himself from sinners. When notorious sinners such as tax collectors come to listen to him, the Pharisees charge, "This fellow welcomes sinners and eats with them" (Lk 15:2). Jesus responds by telling three parables about the lost and found.

The first concerns a shepherd who was so concerned over one lost sheep that he left 99 out in the wilderness while he searched for the missing one. When he found the lost sheep, the shepherd took it on his shoulders and rejoiced. Similarly, a woman who had lost a single coin searched her house relentlessly until she found it, and she celebrated with her friends. "Just so," Jesus says, ". . . there is joy in the presence of the angels of God over one sinner who repents" (Lk 15:10).

"Jerusalem, Jerusalem, the city that kills the prophets and stones those who are sent to it! How often have I desired to gather your children together as a hen gathers her brood under her wings, and you were not willing!" LK 13:34

Jesus instructs his disciples not to feel anxiety but to practice urgency in using the brief time they are allotted: "Be dressed for action and have your lamps lit" (Lk 12:35). Their lives will be lived with faithfulness and prudence, he teaches, if they are always ready for the end of life. Jesus realizes that his call for people to serve God's kingdom will cause division and conflict: "I came to bring fire to the earth, and how I wish it were already kindled" (Lk 12:49). Similarly, his disciples must be ready for the conflicts ahead. Their lives must be shaped by repentance to bear fruit like a good fig tree.

Conflict flares once again on a sabbath when Jesus heals a woman who had been crippled for 18 years and is rebuked by the leader of the synagogue. Jesus, in turn, rebukes his critic, causing consternation among his opponents while the crowd rejoices.

Jesus urges his disciples to realize that in spite of the apparent opposition, God's kingdom is powerful, like a tiny mustard seed that grows into a tree or a bit of yeast that leavens a large lump of dough. They must strive to follow Jesus' teachings and thereby enter the narrow door of the kingdom.

When some friendly Pharisees warn Jesus that Herod wants to kill him, Jesus responds that he must follow his own timetable. He knows that he must ultimately go to Jerusalem, because, as Jesus says with deep irony, "it is impossible for a prophet to be killed outside of Jerusalem" (Lk 13:33). As Jesus is about to set out on the second half of his journey, he

Jesus' third and most elaborate parable is about a father and his two sons. The younger son asked for his inheritance early and set out for a distant land, where he soon squandered his wealth and ended up in poverty and degradation. Realizing his wrongdoing, the young man resolved to return home, not to claim his original status as a son but to ask to be accepted as a hired hand. As he neared home, rehearsing the admission of guilt that he was going to make, his father saw him at a distance and ran to meet him. The father's joy did not permit a guilty speech, and he insisted on celebrating the return of his child with food, music, and dancing. When the elder son became angry at this welcome for his vagabond brother and refused to join in the festivities, the father tried tenderly to win him over but refused to forego his happiness: "We had to celebrate and rejoice," he insisted, "because this brother of yours was dead and has come to life; he was lost and has been found" (Lk 15:32).

Luke's parable of the prodigal son has inspired numerous artists, including English painter Edward Poynter (1836-1919), who depicted the father welcoming home the wastrel.

"There was a rich man who was dressed in purple and fine linen and who feasted sumptuously every day. And at his gate lay a poor man named Lazarus, covered with sores, who longed to satisfy his hunger with what fell from the rich man's table; even the dogs would come and lick his sores." LK 16:19-21

Questions about money, its dangers and its proper uses, were often a concern to the people Jesus taught. Jesus once told a parable about a shrewd but dishonest manager who was caught misusing the wealth of his employer. When he realized that he was about to be fired, the manager used his last hours of authority over the estates to reduce the debts of many who owed money to his master. He thus ensured that they would help him when he was dismissed. Disciples, Jesus argues, should be equally shrewd. Even though money has a corrupting influence, they should use it effectively to serve others and do good and thus "make friends" who will welcome them "into the eternal homes" (Lk 16:9). But one must not underestimate the danger of wealth, and Jesus personifies it as a demonic god. No one can serve two masters: "You cannot serve God and wealth" (Lk 16:13).

To show how God's values often reverse human values, Jesus told a parable about a rich man who feasted in luxury while a beggar by the name of Lazarus starved at his gate and dogs licked his sores. Both died. Angels carried Lazarus to be with Abraham in a realm of delight, while the rich man found himself in Hades suffering fires of torment. The rich man pleaded for Abraham to send Lazarus with a drop of water to comfort his agony and, when refused, asked that Lazarus be returned to earth to warn his brothers of the punishment awaiting them. People must learn how to act faithfully in loving service on the basis of the teaching they have already received, the sufferer was told; they must realize that their actions in this life have fixed and eternal consequences.

"The kingdom of God is not coming with things that can be observed; nor will they say, 'Look, here it is!' or 'There it is!' For, in fact, the kingdom of God is among you."
LK 17:20-21

Jesus urges his disciples to be concerned for each other. They must take great care not to cause any to stumble in their faith in God. When someone offends them, they must forgive, over and over again, and keep in mind God's greatness. With faith no larger than a mustard seed, God can empower them for great things. But they can never claim that God owes them anything. When they have done everything possible, they are still simply servants of God, saying, "We have done only what we ought to have done" (Lk 17:10).

Such a relation to God is open to anyone. Once when Jesus heals ten lepers, only one, a Samaritan, returns to express gratitude and faith. Jesus praises him: "Your faith has made you well" (Lk 17:19).

Jesus discounts all speculation about when the kingdom of God will come. Indeed, he teaches that the kingdom is already present in his own work. As for the future coming of the Son of Man, that day will be sudden and universally recognized, Jesus announces: "For as the lightning flashes and lights up the sky from one side to the other, so will the Son of Man be in his day" (Lk 17:24). The only appropriate preparation is continuous readiness.

"The tax collector, standing far off, would not even look up to heaven, but was beating his breast and saying, 'God, be merciful to me, a sinner!'" LK 18:13

Through both his teaching and his actions Jesus continually helped his disciples reshape their understanding of how they should be related to God, to other people, and to the circumstances of their lives. He tells the story of a powerless widow who so persistently pestered a corrupt judge that he finally granted her justice in her suit. How much more,

Jesus reasons, would a just and loving God give help to those who needed it.

It is important to approach God in humility, since that corresponds to the reality of the human situation before God. Jesus tells of a Pharisee who prayed to God with proud boasting while a tax collector simply asked, "God, be merciful to me, a sinner!" The second man was blessed, Jesus says, "for all who exalt themselves will be humbled" (Lk 18:14). Again, Jesus welcomes little children brought to him: "Whoever does not receive the kingdom of God as a little child," he teaches, "will never enter it" (Lk 18:17).

When a wealthy ruler who was devoutly obedient to the law comes to him, Jesus helps the man to focus on the one area that blocks genuine discipleship: "Sell all that you own and distribute the money to the poor, and you will have treasure in heaven; then come, follow me" (Lk 18:22). Jesus' command reveals that the man's allegiance to his money is greater than his desire for the rule of God in his life.

Zacchaeus stood there and said to the Lord, "Look, half of my possessions, Lord, I will give to the poor; and if I have defrauded anyone of anything, I will pay back four times as much." Then Jesus said to him, "Today salvation has come to this house." LK 19:8-9

As Jesus' journey to Jerusalem nears its conclusion, he again tells his disciples of the shame and suffering that await him, but Luke notes that they are simply unable to understand what he is talking about. In symbolic contrast to their blindness, Jesus begins the final stage of his journey by giving sight to a blind beggar in Jericho who cries out to him for mercy. When he receives sight, he immediately follows Jesus, glorifying God and causing everyone to praise God.

A second manifestation of the transforming power of the kingdom also occurs in Jericho, in the person of Zacchaeus, a chief tax collector, wealthy from his fraudulent and oppressive trade. A short man, Zacchaeus climbs a tree to see Jesus, who spies him and decides to go to his house in spite of severe criticism for associating with such a man. By the end of their conversation, Zacchaeus is transformed, devoting himself to helping the poor and restoring the money he has gained by cheating others.

As he draws near Jerusalem, Jesus tells the parable of a nobleman who left his funds in the care of his servants while he went far away to receive the right of kingship. When he returned, he required each servant to show how he had used the resources he had given him. He praised those who were bold and resourceful and condemned the timid and fearful.

In his final approach to the city, Jesus rides a colt down a road strewn with cloaks from the multitudes of disciples who shout:

"Blessed is the king who comes in the name of the Lord!" (Lk 19:38)—the very greeting Jesus had earlier foretold. As the city comes into view, Jesus' journey is at an end. He weeps over Jerusalem's coming destruction— "because you did not recognize the time of your visitation from God" (Lk 19:44).

He said to them, "Then give to the emperor the things that are the emperor's, and to God the things that are God's."
LK. 20:25

Luke follows Mark fairly closely in describing Jesus' teaching in the temple, though Luke does not emphasize the period as a single week, but says more generally that "every day he was teaching in the temple" (Lk 19:47).

On entering the temple, Jesus' first action is to drive out all who were selling there and to reestablish the temple as a house of prayer. The chief priests resolve to kill him but dare not because "all the people were spellbound by what they heard" (Lk 19:48).

As in Mark, Luke recounts a series of attempts to entrap and condemn Jesus for his teachings. First, the chief priests and other temple authorities challenge Jesus to show the authority for his actions. Jesus responds by challenging them to recognize the authority of John the Baptist. When they demur, Jesus condemns them through a parable of wicked tenants, based partly on Isaiah 5:1-7.

Next, the chief priests send spies to entrap him in a question about paying taxes to the emperor. Jesus, however, turns their trick into a trap for themselves, urging them not only to pay what is due the emperor but also to serve God.

Jesus then deals with a question from the Sadducees concerning the resurrection. Jesus answers so well that even some of the temple scribes praise his

Jesus' parable of the rich man and Lazarus, also unique to Luke, is the subject of this panel from a 16th-century German altarpiece.

According to tradition, Jesus prayed the night before his death in the olive grove to the left of the multidomed church in this aerial view of the Mount of Olives.

responses. Most of the scribes, however, come under Jesus' condemnation for their pride and their love of pretense and display. In contrast, Jesus points to a poor widow who has only two small coins but gives them to God in complete trust.

"Be alert at all times, praying that you may have the strength to escape all these things that will take place, and to stand before the Son of Man." LK 21:36

As his teaching in the temple draws to a close, Jesus announces to his disciples that the cherished religious structure will be destroyed. Luke again follows Mark in this narrative but highlights elements of Jesus' discourse indicating an extended period of time after the destruction of Jerusalem and before the return of the Son of Man.

Jesus warns that many evils "must take place first, but the end will not follow immediately" (Lk 21:9). He predicts the persecution of his disciples and cautions them, "When you see Jerusalem surrounded by armies, then know that its desolation has come near"; indeed, "Jerusalem will be trampled on by the Gentiles, until the times of the Gentiles are fulfilled." Only after many more signs, will people see "the Son of Man coming in a cloud" and know then that "redemption is drawing near" (Lk 21:20, 24, 27-28). Disciples must be alert and prayerful as they look forward to his return.

Only Luke tells of Jesus' appearance to two disciples at Emmaus; Rembrandt (1606-1669) depicted the moment he blessed their bread before vanishing.

He said to them, "But now, the one who has a purse must take it, and likewise a bag. And the one who has no sword must sell his cloak and buy one. For I tell you, this scripture must be fulfilled in me, 'And he was counted among the lawless.'" LK 22:36-37

In describing Jesus' last days, Luke builds on the foundation of Mark but considerably supplements Mark's account of the Last Supper. As the Passover approaches, Satan, who had departed from Jesus after his temptation, actively reenters the story by seizing the heart of Judas Iscariot. When the time for the feast arrives, Jesus meets with his apostles in an upper room in Jerusalem.

As the meal begins, Jesus expresses his deep desire to observe Passover with his followers, but promises that he will not eat again "until it is fulfilled in the kingdom of God" (Lk 22:16). He then gives them broken bread, saying, "This is my body, which is given for you. Do this in remembrance of me." After supper he offers the apostles a cup of wine, saying, "This cup that is poured out for you is the new covenant in my blood" (Lk 22:19-20).

Jesus then reveals that one of them who has shared this meal will betray him, but the disciples fall to arguing who among themselves is the greatest. Jesus uses his own role in serving them the meal as an example of greatness: "I am among you as one who serves" (Lk 22:27).

Jesus then begins to tell the apostles of the blessings as well as the dangers that are before them. Satan had asked to sift all of them like wheat, but Jesus had prayed for Peter's faith to be strong enough to strengthen the others; even so, he says, Peter will deny Jesus three times. Earlier they had gone forth with no resources at all; now they must be equipped for any situation.

They go out to the Mount of Olives where Jesus prays to God and yields himself to God's will. Soon Judas arrives with a crowd to arrest him. "This is your hour," Jesus tells his enemies, "and the power of darkness" (Lk 22:53).

Then he said, "Jesus, remember me when you come into your kingdom." He replied, "Truly I tell you, today you will be with me in Paradise." LK 23:42-43

Luke indicates that after his arrest, Jesus was taken to the house of the high priest. Filled with fear, Peter enters the courtyard to warm himself by a fire. Three people challenge him, and three times he denies that he knows Jesus. Then, "the Lord turned and looked at Peter" (Lk 22:61); Peter remembers and goes out weeping bitterly.

In the morning, Jesus is tried and condemned by the elders and chief priests for his supposed claims to be the Messiah and Son of God. In short order, they bring Jesus to Pilate, the Roman governor, to press charges that he forbade paying taxes and called himself a king. Pilate recognizes that the charges are trumped up, but since Herod Antipas is in Jerusalem for the Passover festivities and Herod's territory embraces Galilee, he sends this Galilean to Herod for examination. Herod is delighted to have a chance to question a famous prophet and perhaps even see one of his miracles. But when Jesus responds to him with stony silence, Herod sends him back to the Roman governor. That same day, Luke adds, the former enemies "became friends with each other" (Lk 23:12).

Though Pilate explicitly finds Jesus innocent of any crime, he perverts justice by condemning him to crucifixion, pressured by a crowd that clamors for Jesus' death. As he is crucified, Jesus recognizes the greater event of salvation that Pilate, the priests, and the throngs cannot see: "Father, forgive them," he prays, "for they do not know what they are doing" (Lk 23:34). Luke describes how a sense of calm remains with Jesus throughout the horrible hours of crucifixion. When one of the criminals crucified with him asks Jesus for mercy, Jesus replies, "Truly I tell you, today you will be with me in Paradise." Even in his last words, Jesus speaks with the certainty of the psalmist: "Father, into your hands I commend my spirit" (Lk 23:46; Ps 31:5).

When he was at the table with them, he took bread, blessed and broke it, and gave it to them. Then their eyes were opened, and they recognized him; and he vanished from their sight. LK 24:30-31

Just before the sabbath begins, Jesus is taken down from the cross and placed in a tomb by Joseph of Arimathea, while the women who had followed Jesus from Galilee look on. As dawn breaks on the first day of the new week, the women return to find the stone covering removed from the tomb and the body gone. Two men in dazzling clothes appear and remind them of Jesus' predictions that he would rise again. Mary Magdalene and the other women indeed remember but, when they report these events to the apostles, they are greeted with disbelief, as though they were telling "an idle tale" (Lk 24:11).

Later that day, Luke relates, two disciples were walking to the nearby town of Emmaus when Jesus appeared to them. Failing to recognize him, they tell the story of Jesus' crucifixion to this apparent stranger, who in turn urges them to believe all that the prophets had foretold about the Messiah. They prevail on the stranger to eat with them that evening, but when he breaks bread for them, they recognize Jesus and he disappears from view. The two disciples hurry back to Jerusalem where they learn that Jesus has also appeared to Peter.

As the disciples are excitedly discussing these things, Jesus suddenly appears among them with a greeting of "Peace." He demonstrates his reality to them by eating some of their food and allowing them to approach and touch him. As Jesus speaks to the group, he opens their minds to all the mysteries of his suffering that had earlier been hidden from them and helps them to understand how the scriptures have been fulfilled in him.

He commands them to stay in Jerusalem until they receive the "power from on high" (Lk 24:49) that God had promised. As Jesus walks out with them to the nearby village of Bethany and blesses them, he is carried up into heaven, and the disciples return to the city to worship him with joy.

Andrea Mantegna (1431-1506) painted Mary with the disciples at Bethany as Jesus ascends to heaven—though in his account Luke does not put her there.

*T*he Gospel of John takes a radically different approach to the story of Jesus than do the other gospels. Matthew, Mark, and Luke are so much alike in the way they tell the story that they are called the Synoptic Gospels, from a Greek word meaning "viewing together." John, on the other hand, is sometimes called the Spiritual Gospel because it does more than report the events in Jesus' life—it explains what those events reveal about him. The writer carefully chooses only incidents that help answer the question, "Who is Jesus?" The reason lies in the purpose stated near the conclusion: "These [words] are written so that you may come to believe that Jesus is the Messiah, the Son of God" (Jn 20:31).

Guided by this objective, John recounts only seven miracles, which he calls "signs," that prove the divinity of Jesus. The Gospel also preserves long conversations between Jesus and others about who he is and why God has sent him. The writer admits he has left out much that Jesus did; if all were set down, he says, "the world itself could not contain the books that would be written" (Jn 21:25). Events chronicled by the other Evangelists, but missing in John, include the birth of Jesus, his baptism and temptation, his casting out demons and teaching in parables, his blessing of bread and wine at the Last Supper, and the trial before the Jewish council. Yet John enriches our knowledge of Jesus by reporting events excluded from the Synoptic Gospels: the wedding at Cana, the meeting with the Samaritan woman, the raising of Lazarus from the dead, the washing of the disciples' feet, the charge to the beloved disciple to take care of his mother after his death, and the post-resurrection confrontation with a doubting Thomas.

The Gospel's well-developed theology suggests that it was written late in the first century, perhaps in the 90s. Though the author never reveals his name, a tradition dating from at least the second century attributes the work to John the son of Zebedee, one of Jesus' three closest disciples. John's conspicuous absence from the stories, along with cryptic references to the disciple "whom Jesus loved" (Jn 13:23), gives some credence to the tradition that John wrote the Gospel late in his life while living in Ephesus. If so, he may have written it to help Jewish converts to Christianity defend their beliefs against Jews who insisted that Jesus was not the Messiah.

John the Baptist,
Jesus' precursor,
as sculpted in bronze
by Donatello
(c. 1386-1466)

In the beginning was the Word, and the Word was with God, and the Word was God. JN 1:1

*T*his startling introduction to the Gospel of John, drawn from the opening words of Genesis, boldly declares Jesus' divinity. At the dawn of creation, Jesus "was with God," and yet "was God." John does not try to explain the mystery of how two distinct entities could be one. He simply states it, then spends the rest of his Gospel showing how the miracles and teachings of Jesus reveal that Jesus is God.

By describing Jesus as the Word (from the Greek word *Logos*), John is using a technical term that powerfully conveys who Jesus is in a way that both Gentiles and Jews can understand. Among Greek philosophers, Logos is cosmic reason, the divine force that structured the universe. Among Jewish scholars, "Word" represents both the message and the power

of God. Jews would understand that John is calling Jesus the embodiment of all God's revelation in scripture—the message. They would also see John intimately associating Jesus with God, who has the power to create merely by speaking: "God said, 'Let there be light'; and there was light" (Gen 1:3). In describing Jesus, John says, "All things came into being through him, and without him, not one thing came into being" (Jn 1:3).

Matthew traces Jesus' family tree to Abraham, to reveal him as the Jews' Messiah; Luke's genealogy goes back to Adam, to portray Jesus as the Savior of humanity. John takes Jesus all the way back to the beginning, to reveal him as part of God the Creator.

John, gifted as one who writes in rich symbolism and who often heaps several layers of meaning onto his words, seems to take the term Logos even further. By calling Jesus the Word, John also announces what he intends to prove in his Gospel: Jesus is the genuine expression of God. Just as a word reveals an invisible thought, Jesus reveals the invisible spiritual presence of God.

And the Word became flesh and lived among us.   JN 1:14

The Jews understood and accepted the idea of God living among them, and John draws on this understanding by using a word for "lived" that literally means "occupy a tent." Jews would have immediately realized that John was comparing Jesus to the tabernacle, a tent worship center the Israelites used during their 40 years of wandering in the wilderness. This tent, located in the center of the camp, represented God's earthly dwelling place—as did the temple in later centuries. "I will place my dwelling in your midst," God told the Israelites. ". . . I will walk among you, and will be your God" (Lev 26:11, 12). When the tabernacle was dedicated, the cloud of God's presence that had been leading the Israelites across the wilderness entered and "filled the tabernacle" (Ex 40:34). This cloud lifted only when God wanted the people to break camp and follow him on the journey to the promised land.

What neither Jewish scholars nor Greek philosophers could accept, however, was the idea of God becoming human. For Greeks, divinity was a mysterious ideal that was both invisible and eternal—not physical and temporal. For Jews, God's glory could not even be witnessed by a human, let alone be contained in one. When Moses asked to see God in all his glory, God replied, "You cannot see my face; for no one shall see me and live" (Ex 33:20). God did, however, allow Moses to hide himself in the crevice of a rock he pointed out in order to catch a fleeting glimpse of his back as he passed by. What God revealed in that moment was that he is "abounding in steadfast love and faithfulness" (Ex 34:6). The words for love and faithfulness can also be translated as grace and truth. John may have this translation in mind when he says that in Jesus "we have seen his glory, the glory as of a father's only son, full of grace and truth" (Jn 1:14).

John explains that just as God came to live among his people in the tabernacle, God has come again—this time in the flesh and blood of Jesus. "No one has ever seen God," John says, drawing attention to Moses' story. But now, this is changed. "It is God the only Son, who is close to the Father's heart, who has made him known" (Jn 1:18). Because of the incarnation— God coming to earth in the flesh—when a person looks into the face of Jesus he sees the face of God: "The Father and I are one" (Jn 10:30).

There was a wedding in Cana . . . . The mother of Jesus said to him, "They have no wine."   JN 2:1, 3

Shortly after Jesus chooses his disciples, the group attends a wedding in Cana, a village about ten miles northwest of Nazareth, Jesus' hometown. Jewish wedding celebrations usually lasted a week, and during the festivities it was the host's responsibility to provide food and drink for the guests.

Mary, the mother of Jesus, discovers that the supply of wine has run out. When she tells her son, his reply is mystifying: "Woman, what concern is that to you and to me? My hour has not yet come" (Jn 2:4). John does not explain why Jesus addresses Mary in this impersonal manner, using a word that is respectful though not typical for a son talking to his mother. "Woman," however, is how Jesus will later address Mary from the cross, when he entrusts her to the care of a new son, "the disciple whom he loved" (Jn 19:26), possibly the author of this Gospel. John also fails to explain what Jesus means by "my hour." But again, as the Gospel unfolds, the connection seems to be to the crucifixion. Moments before his arrest Jesus says, "It is for this reason that I have come to this hour" (Jn 12:27). Jesus realizes at Cana that by performing miracles, he will set in motion a chain of events that will culminate in his death.

Only John reports Jesus' miracle of turning water into wine (typically stored in a pottery vessel, right) at the wedding feast in Cana; a Flemish artist painted this scene about 1470.

To Jews of Jesus' time, Samaritans were outcasts and heretics. In his conversation with the Samaritan woman at the well, Jesus reveals that his salvation extends to non-Jews. Paolo Veronese painted the scene about 1580.

Mary may understand that her son's life must follow a divine plan, but she also knows how embarrassing it will be for the bridal couple to run out of wine. So she discreetly tells the household servants to do whatever Jesus says, thereby leaving the matter in his hands. And so Jesus turns water into wine, "the first of his signs," John says, ". . . and revealed his glory; and his disciples believed in him" (Jn 2:11).

John builds the first eleven chapters of his Gospel around seven such "signs," or miracles, which prove Jesus is God. Some readers searching for why John chooses this miracle as one of those seven find clues in the rich symbolism so prevalent in this Gospel. At the wedding in Cana, Jesus demonstrates his creative power by transforming the natural substance of water into the new creation of wine. Not only does he do this physically, he also does this spiritually. As Paul later declares, "If anyone is in Christ, there is a new creation: everything old has passed away; see, everything has become new!" (2 Cor 5:17).

God so loved the world that he gave his only Son, so that everyone who believes in him may not perish but may have eternal life. JN 3:16

This verse, perhaps the most cherished in all of the New Testament, is the one that Protestant reformer Martin Luther called "the Gospel in miniature." It actually sums up the message of all four gospels—revealing the depth of God's love for humanity, that Jesus is God's Son, and that salvation comes through belief in Jesus.

John reports Jesus speaking these words in a private conversation with Nicodemus, a Pharisee and a leader among the Jews. Nicodemus comes to Jesus at night, perhaps to avoid being seen with this apparent troublemaker who—having come to Jerusalem for Passover—has recently disrupted temple activities by chasing away merchants at work on the premises.

"Rabbi," Nicodemus says, "we know that you are a teacher who has come from God; for no one can do these signs that you do apart from the presence of God." Jesus apparently realizes that Nicodemus has come to learn, so he begins presenting the core of his message. But when Jesus says that only those "born from above" can enter God's kingdom, Nicodemus is bewildered. "Can one enter a second time into the mother's womb and be born?" (Jn 3:2, 3, 4) he asks.

Jesus is frustrated that a biblical scholar and spiritual guide like the Pharisee Nicodemus does not understand. Yet he continues the lesson, explaining that he is talking about a spiritual rebirth—perhaps the one prophesied by Ezekiel: "A new heart I will give you, and a new spirit I will put within you" (Ezek 36:26). Jesus says this spiritual rebirth will become available after he is "lifted up" (Jn 3:14), a cryptic phrase pointing to his death on the cross.

God's sacrifice of "his only Son" echoes the language of Abraham offering his son Isaac. When the time came for Abraham to fulfill his test of faith, Isaac asked where the offering was. Abraham replied, "God himself will provide the lamb" (Gen 22:8). A short time later, as Abraham raised a knife to sacrifice his son, an angel stopped him. New Testament writers saw in this story a foreshadowing of the supreme sacrifice offered by God, "who did not withhold his own Son, but gave him up for all of us" (Rom 8:32).

Those who drink of the water that I will give them will never be thirsty. JN 4:14

When Jesus leaves Jerusalem to return home to Galilee, he soon finds himself in a most unlikely place, with a most unlikely conversation partner. He is at a village well in the hill country of Samaria, speaking with a woman. According to ancient Jewish custom, rabbis are not supposed to talk in public with women because people might start gossiping. Also, Jews avoided Samaria because of a long-standing rivalry between the two groups. Jews considered the Samaritans a mixed race—Israelites who intermarried with foreigners after the Assyrian empire annexed the northern kingdom in 722 B.C. The rift deepened when the Samaritans built their own temple in about 400 B.C., and again when Jews destroyed it some 300 years later.

Jesus and the disciples arrive in the Samaritan village of Sychar at about noon. Weary, Jesus sits by the well as his disciples go to buy food. When a woman arrives with a bucket for drawing water, Jesus asks her to give him a drink. She is surprised that a Jew would ask anything of her and tells him so. Jesus replies, "If you knew the gift of God, and who it is that is saying to you, 'Give me a drink,' you would have asked him, and he would have given you living water" (Jn 4:10). Furthermore, Jesus adds, this special water quenches thirst forever—an enticing prospect for someone living in arid Samaria.

The woman mistakes what Jesus says. She takes his words literally, as Nicodemus had done earlier. "Living water" is a common expression for fresh, flowing water from a spring or a river. The woman asks Jesus for some of this magical water, "so that I may never be thirsty or have to keep coming here to draw water" (Jn 4:15).

Jesus uses his miraculous insight into the woman's personal history to help her realize he is not talking about physical water. He is describing himself as the source of spiritual life. This is similar to how Jeremiah described God: "the fountain of living water" (Jer 17:13). Jesus tells the woman she has been married five times and is now living with yet another man. This may be why she is drawing water in the midday heat—to avoid the sneering crowds. The woman rushes back into the village and brings the

people to meet Jesus. As a result, many Samaritans in the city become convinced "that this is truly the Savior of the world" (Jn 4:42).

Welcomed back to Galilee, Jesus performs his second miracle: healing the son of a Gentile official.

Jesus said to him [a lame man], "Stand up, take your mat and walk." JN 5:8

Jesus returns to Jerusalem to celebrate one of the Jewish festivals. While he is there, he notices a man who has been ill for 38 years. This man is lying on a mat beside a pool that was renowned for its five impressive porticoes—walkways with columns that support roofs. Archaeologists have found the ruins of such a pool just outside the courtyard where the temple once stood.

The crippled man is lying there with other invalids. They all apparently believe that every once in a while an angel touches the water, creating a ripple, and that the first person in the pool afterward will be healed. In a miracle reported only in John, Jesus heals the lame man and tells him to pick up his mat and walk.

When Jewish leaders hear what has happened, remarkably they express no joy for this man who has been cured. Instead, they condemn the miracle as a breach of the sabbath, the Jewish day of rest. Old Testament law teaches that Jews should refrain from work on the sabbath. Scripture provides little instruction beyond this. But Pharisees, strict observers of the law, follow a long list of sabbath prohibitions. Healing on the sabbath—except in life-threatening cases—is one of the outlawed activities.

Confronted with this charge, Jesus offers a short but astounding reply: God, his Father, works on the sabbath—and so does he. The Jews retaliate by plotting to kill him "because he was not only breaking the sabbath, but was also calling God his own Father, thereby making himself equal to God" (Jn 5:18).

Jesus said to Philip, "Where are we to buy bread for these people to eat?" JN 6:5

After finishing a preaching tour of Galilee, Jesus and the disciples need to rest. They sail across the Sea of Galilee to a hilly area in the east. But a crowd of 5,000 has become so captivated by Jesus' miracles and teachings that they follow him along the shore to this isolated area. It is here that Jesus performs a miracle so astonishing that it becomes the only one recorded in all four gospels. Using a little boy's lunch of five barley loaves and two fish, Jesus feeds all the people. After everyone eats their fill, the disciples collect 12 baskets of leftovers.

The crowd becomes electrified. Many believe that the long-awaited Messiah has finally

The only miracle recorded in all four gospels—Jesus' feeding the 5,000 with only five barley loaves and two fish—was depicted about 1590 by Hendrik de Clerck.

arrived, and they are ready to crown Jesus king of Israel. Jesus, however, slips away into the mountains. That evening, Jesus proves his mastery of nature by miraculously walking on water to reach his disciples' boat and returns with them to the western shore of the Sea of Galilee. Again the crowds track him down. Surprisingly, Jesus is upset with these people, most of whom are probably working-class farmers and fishermen struggling to survive. He accuses them of following him only to get more food. Then he tells them to look for "food that endures for eternal life" (Jn 6:27).

The people understand that Jesus is telling them to do God's work, so they ask what exactly they need to do. "This is the work of God," Jesus replies, "that you believe in him whom he has sent" (Jn 6:29). The crowd asks Jesus to perform another miracle to prove that he comes from God. Ironically, these people, who only the day before had eaten miraculously produced bread and fish, ask Jesus to repeat the miracle they attribute to Moses: bringing manna from heaven. This, they believe, will prove that Jesus is the new prophet and deliverer of the greatness of Moses.

Jesus immediately corrects their interpretation of scripture. It was God, not Moses, who sent the manna, he reminds them. Furthermore, it is God

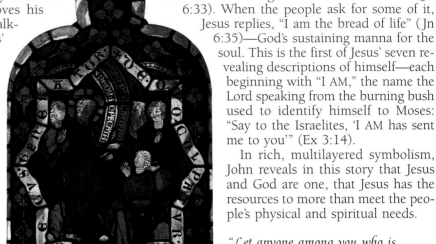

Jesus healing the man blind from birth is depicted in this 13th-century stained glass window.

who again has provided bread that "comes down from heaven and gives life to the world" (Jn 6:33). When the people ask for some of it, Jesus replies, "I am the bread of life" (Jn 6:35)—God's sustaining manna for the soul. This is the first of Jesus' seven revealing descriptions of himself—each beginning with "I AM," the name the Lord speaking from the burning bush used to identify himself to Moses: "Say to the Israelites, 'I AM has sent me to you'" (Ex 3:14).

In rich, multilayered symbolism, John reveals in this story that Jesus and God are one, that Jesus has the resources to more than meet the people's physical and spiritual needs.

"Let anyone among you who is without sin be the first to throw a stone at her." JN 8:7

The story of Jesus and the woman caught in adultery may come from a collection of stories separate from John's Gospel. The earliest Greek manuscripts of John do not include it; other ancient sources preserve it in Luke's Gospel. Wherever it belongs, the wisdom and compassion the story reveals about Jesus suggest that it is authentic.

One morning Jesus is teaching a crowd in the temple courtyard. A group of scribes and Pharisees, experts in the Jewish law, interrupt his talk by bringing him a woman who has been caught in the act of adul-

Challenging those who condemned the woman caught in adultery, Jesus stoops to write their own sins in the dirt; a painting by Giovanni Domenico Tiepolo (1727-1804).

tery. "In the law," say the antagonistic intruders, "Moses commanded us to stone such women. Now what do you say?" (Jn 8:5).

This is one of many attempts to trap Jesus. People know that he forgives sinners, so the Jewish leaders probably suspect he will favor releasing the woman. If he does, he will defy Jewish law. Yet if he agrees to the death penalty, he will defy Roman law. Roman authorities occupying and governing the region reserved the sole right to execute criminals.

Tension heightens as everyone waits for Jesus to speak. With the eyes of the crowd on him, Jesus bends down and writes with his finger in the dirt—according to some ancient sources, naming the sins of the woman's accusers. His act hints of his divine authority, for it is reminiscent of the Ten Commandments being written by "the finger of God" (Ex 31:18).

Finally Jesus speaks. He gives approval for the execution—under the condition that the person without sin cast the first stone. This is an ingenious reply, for there is no such person among the group. One by one, the experts in Jewish law walk away. Jesus turns to the woman and releases her, though without condoning her sin: "Go your way, and from now on do not sin again" (Jn 8:11).

"I am the light of the world." JN 9:5

One sabbath day, Jesus notices a beggar who has been blind from birth. "Rabbi," Jesus' disciples ask, "who sinned, this man or his parents?" Jews of the day commonly believed that such tragedy came as punishment from God. Jesus refutes this: "He was born blind so that God's works might be revealed in him" (Jn 9:2, 3).

Jesus then calls himself "the light of the world," a gripping description for a blind man to hear. Jesus immediately mixes a paste of clay and saliva, which he smooths onto the beggar's eyes. Next, Jesus directs the man to wash his eyes in the Pool of Siloam. John explains that Siloam means "sent," perhaps to symbolize that Jesus has been sent from God to bring spiritual light into the world.

The man does as Jesus instructs, and his sight is restored. Word reaches the Pharisees, who are infuriated that Jesus has once again broken the sabbath. They interrogate the man, then his parents, to confirm that he was born blind. Then they grill the man a second time, and publicly condemn Jesus as a sinner for having broken the sabbath. "I do not know whether he is a sinner," the man boldly answers the Pharisees. "One thing I do know, that though I was blind, now I see" (Jn 9:25).

Jesus as the good shepherd who lays down his life for his flock; a 5th-century marble statue

The Pharisees accuse the bewildered man of being one of Jesus' disciples, and promptly excommunicate him from the synagogue. Jesus later finds the healed man, who confesses his fervent belief in Jesus as the Son of Man, the Messiah.

"I came into this world for judgment," Jesus tells him, "so that those who do not see may see, and those who do see may become blind" (Jn 9:39). These words are perplexing, but in the context imply that belief in Jesus opens the spiritual eyes of people. Doubt, however, especially among those who think they are spiritually perceptive, proves only that they are blind and sinful.

Prophets had said that when the Messiah comes, "the eyes of the blind shall see" (Isa 29:18). By healing the blind, and performing other miracles of healing, Jesus convinces many people that he is the long-awaited deliverer sent from God.

"I am the good shepherd." JN 10:11

Jesus often described himself and the kingdom of heaven by using word pictures to which people could easily respond. When he calls himself the good shepherd, and the people of God a flock, his listeners understand that he is talking about a relationship between sheep and shepherd, one of trust and care. They also quickly pick up on other ideas he wants to teach.

"I am the gate for the sheep" (Jn 10:7), for example, means he is the only entrance into the protection of God's fold. His listeners know that a typical sheepfold is a corral of rock walls. The entrance is merely an opening through which the sheep pass. Shepherds spend the night in the entryway, serving as a human gate that keeps the sheep in and the predators out. Inside the sheepfold, the flock is safe. With this vivid metaphor, Jesus teaches that all who enter God's fold, by way of him, "will be saved" (Jn 10:9).

Jesus also reminds the people that shepherds sometimes risk their lives for the flock. David, as a shepherd in Bethlehem, fought lions and bears that tried to carry off some of the sheep. Jesus says he will not only risk his life, he will give it—a foreshadowing of the crucifixion.

As Jewish scholars listen to Jesus describing himself as a spiritual shepherd, they likely remember that several prophets had said God would one day come to lead his people as a shepherd (Isa 40:11; Jer 23:3; Ezek 34:11-12). Some Jews pick up stones to kill Jesus for the blasphemy of "making yourself God" (Jn 10:33). But Jesus escapes his tormentors and leaves Jerusalem.

The dead man [Lazarus] came out, his hands and feet bound with strips of cloth, and his face wrapped in a cloth. JN 11:44

The raising of Lazarus—reported only in the Gospel of John—is the last and most dramatic of the seven "signs," or miracles, that John uses to prove the divinity of Jesus.

When Lazarus lies dying in Bethany, his sisters, Mary and Martha, send the news to their friend Jesus. They expect him to come right away to heal their brother. But Jesus waits for two days. "This illness," he explains to his disciples, ". . . is for God's glory, so that the Son of God may be glorified through it" (Jn 11:4).

By the time Jesus arrives, Lazarus has been dead four days. Many Jews of that era believed a dead person's soul lingered near the corpse for three days, in case the body was resuscitated. By the fourth day, all hope of reuniting soul and body was gone.

Family and friends of Lazarus gathered to grieve at the home of Mary and Martha in the village on the outskirts of Jerusalem. When Jesus witnesses their heartache, he too weeps. Then he leads the mourners to the tomb.

To the astonishment of the crowd, Jesus orders the tomb opened. Martha objects immediately, arguing that the tomb will smell of decay. Jesus gently replies, "Did I not tell you that if you believed, you would see the glory of God?" When the entrance stone is removed, Jesus cries out in a loud voice, "Lazarus, come out!" (Jn 11:40, 43). To the horrified shock of the bereaved, Lazarus walks out, wrapped from head to feet in burial strips.

For many people, this dramatic miracle proves that Jesus has power over life and death, and that he is both the Messiah and the Son of God. Many Jewish leaders, however, remain unconvinced. Worse, they see Jesus as an extreme, immediate threat to Jewish national security. They fear that the nation will rally around Jesus as the Messiah, then launch a revolution for independence, which Rome will inevitably crush. "If we let him go on like this," the Jews lament, "everyone will believe in him, and the Romans will come and destroy both our holy place and our nation" (Jn 11:48).

As astonishing as it sounds, the solution they come up with is to kill both Jesus and the man he has raised from the dead. John does not report what happens to Lazarus, but he carefully documents some of the most revealing moments in Jesus' final days on earth.

Mary took a pound of costly perfume made of pure nard, anointed Jesus' feet, and wiped them with her hair. JN 12:3

On Saturday, six days before his crucifixion, Jesus returns to the home of Lazarus and his sisters, Mary and Martha. There, Jesus and his disciples enjoy a dinner served in his honor. Sometime during the meal, or perhaps immediately afterward, Mary brings out an alabaster flask of expensive, scented ointment imported from the Himalayas of India. This perfume was worth about a year's salary for a common workman of the day. Mary rubs the ointment on Jesus' feet, then wipes off the excess with her hair.

Mary no doubt intended this as an expression of her devotion to Jesus, for

By raising Lazarus from the dead, Jesus became the target of religious authorities who feared his growing popularity; a 15th-century Dutch artist gave the event a setting appropriate to his own time.

people did occasionally anoint loved ones and special guests with expensive oil. But they also used perfumed oil to anoint the dead, as a substitute for embalming—to cloak the odor of decay. Perhaps Mary saw this as a particularly fitting way to thank Jesus for resurrecting her brother. The other three gospels tell of a similar anointing, which may have taken place another time.

Judas objects to this extravagance. He argues that Mary should have sold the perfume and given the proceeds to the poor—or perhaps given the money to Jesus to distribute to the poor. John reports that Judas carried the money bag for the disciples, and that Judas occasionally stole from it. A year's salary would have been an irresistible temptation to the dishonest treasurer.

"Leave her alone," Jesus replies. "She bought it so that she might keep it for the day of my burial" (Jn 12:7). Though Mary may have intended the anointing as a celebration, Jesus knows that he will soon be killed. He interprets Mary's act as the Jewish last rite: an anointing for burial.

"Hosanna! Blessed is the one who comes in the name of the Lord—the King of Israel!" JN 12:13

Many Jews of Jesus' day were eagerly waiting for God's promised Messiah. They believed he would carry King David's royal blood, liberate the nation from Rome, and restore the glory of Israel. This nationalistic passion cycled to a climax each year during the Passover festival, a springtime celebration commemorating Israel's release from Egyptian slavery. The Roman governor of Judea was so convinced of danger that he routinely ordered extra troops into Jerusalem to control the exuberant crowds that arrived from throughout the Near East.

Throngs of Jews who have heard about Jesus, especially about his raising Lazarus, release their pent-up expectation and wondrous joy. They are certain he is the Messiah and that this year's Passover will mark a new emancipation. When the crowds learn that Jesus is on his way into Jerusalem from nearby Bethany, they assemble along the road as though awaiting a triumphal warrior returning from battle.

On the pathway the people spread a carpet of cloaks and freshly cut palm branches. Finally, they catch sight of him cresting the Mount of Olives and riding on a donkey. Jesus, who usually walks, has arranged to ride a donkey on this special occasion in order to fulfill the messianic prophecy of Zechariah: "Shout aloud, O daughter Jerusalem! Lo, your king comes to you; triumphant and victorious is he, humble and riding on a donkey" (Zech 9:9). Jesus is determined to confirm for the people that he is indeed the promised Savior—though he is not the warrior-king they are expecting.

"Hosanna!" the people shout, a Hebrew word meaning "save us." This is fully what Jesus intends to do during this fateful week, though not in the way the holiday crowds anticipate.

Jesus interrupts the Passover feast with his disciples to wash their feet—a dramatic lesson in humility. The scene appears in a 12th- or 13th-century French manuscript.

He [Jesus] poured water into a basin and began to wash the disciples' feet. JN 13:5

John reports the Last Supper in a unique way. He omits the blessing and serving of the bread and wine, commemorated by Christians as the Eucharist, or communion, service. Perhaps John leaves this out because Christians of his day were well aware of this story; many scholars believe John's Gospel was the last of the four written. Instead of retelling the story of the Last Supper, John relates a revealing incident that takes place just before the food is served—an event excluded from the other gospels, but one that dramatically shows why Jesus came to earth.

Jesus wraps himself in a towel, fills a basin with water, and begins washing the feet of his disciples. This is a startling object lesson in humility and service, for Jesus exchanges his role as master for that of household slave. "The Son of Man came not to be served but to serve," Jesus once told his disciples, "and to give his life a ransom for many" (Mk 10:45). At the Last Supper, Jesus graphically illustrates this point, then urges the disciples to follow his example by serving others.

The foot washing, however, is more than a lesson in humility, with divinity showing humanity how to behave. The external washing is a symbol of the internal cleansing from sin that Jesus' death will provide for everyone who believes in him. This is implied in Jesus' stern reply after Peter objects to the foot washing: "Unless I wash you, you have no share with me" (Jn 13:8). Later, first-generation Christians will rejoice over "sins washed away" (Acts 22:16).

During the course of the Passover feast, Jesus announces that one of the twelve will betray him and confides to Judas that he knows him to be the traitor. Quietly, Judas slips off into the night on his nefarious mission.

"If I go and prepare a place for you, I will come again and will take you to myself." JN 14:3

Jesus has just given the disciples shattering news: He is going to die. For the past several years, these men have devoted their lives to Jesus. The prospect of his imminent death devastates them.

"Do not let your hearts be troubled," Jesus reassures them. "Believe in God, believe also in me." Jesus then explains that he needs to return to his Father's house to prepare a place for them. Later, he says, he will return to take them there, too. "You know the way to the place where I am going" (Jn 14:1, 4), he adds. Thomas quickly disagrees, saying he does not know where Jesus is going or how to get there.

"I am the way, and the truth, and the life. No one comes to the Father except through me" (Jn 14:6). Because of teachings such as this, first-generation Christians would call themselves followers of The Way. For them, Jesus was the only way to eternal life.

It is unclear what Jesus meant when he said he would come again. Scholars speculate Jesus may have been referring to his post-resurrection appearances, or the arrival of the Holy Spirit at Pentecost, or his mystical presence in church rituals, or perhaps an appearance immediately after death, when he would escort the faithful into their eternal reward. Many scholars, however, believe Jesus was referring to a more literal return known as the Second Coming—after which he will take all believers to heaven.

Until this return, Jesus promises his disciples, he will personally answer any request that advances the work he started—the likely meaning of "I will do whatever you ask in my name" (Jn 14:13). Furthermore, Jesus adds, the Father will send the Holy Spirit to remind them of what he taught them, and to teach them further.

"I am the true vine." JN 15:1

Old Testament prophets repeatedly described the nation of Israel as a choice grapevine that God planted in the land of Canaan and carefully tended—yet it produced only bad fruit, like a wild vine (Isa 5:1-7; Jer 2:21; Ezek 19:10-14). This language is figurative, but incredibly clear to the Israelites who lived off a land rich in vineyards. The prophets were accusing Israel of persistently disobeying God and doing as they pleased. For this, God treated them like a vine grower treats unproductive vines, cutting and burning them (Ps 80:16). Throughout Israel's long history of apostasy, God punished the nation for its

disobedience. In the end, Israel failed to fulfill its purpose "as a light to the nations, that my salvation may reach to the end of the earth" (Isa 49:6).

Jesus, however, accomplishes this mission by being completely obedient to God's will. For this reason he describes himself as "the true vine."

Simeon, the elderly prophet who blessed the infant Jesus, had predicted his success: "My eyes have seen your salvation," Simeon said to God in prayer, ". . . a light for revelation to the Gentiles and for glory to your people Israel" (Lk 2:30, 32).

As Jesus continues to teach his disciples about who he is and why he has come, he expands the analogy of the vine. Jesus describes his followers as branches that will bear much fruit. They do this by obeying all of Jesus' commandments—one of the most important of which is to love one another. People who are not Jesus' followers, however, are like withered branches "gathered, thrown into the fire, and burned" (Jn 15:6). Jesus warns that these people, like the disobedient nation of Israel, will reap a harvest of tragedy and destruction.

The flogging of Jesus as shown in the early-15th-century book of hours of the duc de Berry

"Father, the hour has come, glorify your Son so that the Son may glorify you." JN 17:1

In his longest recorded prayer—preserved only in John's Gospel—Jesus takes a variety of requests to God the Father. Jesus prays for himself, his apostles, and those who will later find faith through the apostles.

Jesus looks up into heaven and acknowledges that the hour of his crucifixion is at hand. Because of this, the words he now utters represent his deepest desires. He asks that when his work is completed he will be restored to his heavenly position at the side of his Father—a position he has enjoyed since "before the world existed" (Jn 17:5). He asks that God will restore him in a way that will reveal God's own eternal majesty and show that Jesus was sent by him.

On behalf of the apostles, whom Jesus is sending into the world as the Father had sent him, Jesus asks God to "sanctify them in the truth; your word is truth" (Jn 17:17). "Sanctify" means consecrate or reserve for God. Jesus is asking that the disciples remain dedicated to God and to the truth about salvation, instead of reverting back to the ways of worldly people who have rejected both the Lord and the one he sent.

Jesus also prays for everyone who will believe in him through the testimony of the apostles. His prayer for what will develop into a church of believers spanning the entire world is "that they may be one, as we are one" (Jn 17:22). This is a request for unity. Jesus wants his followers to get along with each other. He wants to see them united by the same kind of love that unites the Father and the Son "so that the world may know that you have sent me and have loved them even as you have loved me" (Jn 17:23).

The Jewish police arrested Jesus and bound him. JN 18:12

After the Last Supper, along with the final instructions and prayer that Jesus offers there, Jesus leads his disciples to a garden just outside the city. There, he awaits his arrest. A joint patrol of Roman soldiers and temple police, guided by Judas, finds Jesus and arrests him. Peter tries to stop them, drawing a sword and cutting off an ear of the high priest's slave, Malchus. None of the gospels explain why Judas betrays his master. Most likely, he had become contemptuous of a Messiah who promised not

Looking down from his cross, Jesus entrusts the care of his mother Mary to the beloved disciple; a stained glass roundel from Chartres.

the glory of a new kingdom of Israel, but only suffering and death to reach the kingdom of God.

Religious leaders try Jesus in an all-night emergency session of the Sanhedrin, the 70-member Jewish council. Early the next morning they deliver him to Pilate, the Roman governor of Judea. When Pilate tells the Jews to deal with Jesus themselves, they reply, "We are not permitted to put anyone to death" (Jn 18:31). They want Pilate to pass sentence and issue the execution orders.

Pilate interrogates Jesus, asking if he is king of the Jews. Jesus replies that his kingdom is not in this world. After closing this hearing, Pilate tries repeatedly to talk the Jews out of the execution. "Shall I crucify your King?" he asks. "We have no king but the emperor" (Jn 19:15), they reply.

This powerfully symbolic moment is the climax of John's account of the trial. Spiritual leaders of the Jewish people have just rejected the kingship of God, as Israel had done before. Early in Israel's history, the people had no king but God. Then one day they demanded that the prophet Samuel choose a king for them. This left Samuel devastated, and feeling that he was a failure. God, however, consoled the elderly prophet by saying, "they have not rejected you, but they have rejected me from being king over them" (1 Sam 8:7). When the Jews reject Jesus, they are repeating history by again rejecting God as king.

Confronted by such persistent opposition to Jesus, Pilate hands Jesus over to the Jews for execution—a death sentence to be carried out immediately.

They crucified him, and with him two others, one on either side, with Jesus between them. JN 19:18

In describing the crucifixion, John leaves out much of the detail that appears in the other gospels—such as Simon of Cyrene being pressed into service to carry the cross of Jesus to Golgotha. John is more interested in pointing out facts that reveal Jesus as the Messiah.

The first such fact is that Pilate orders a sign posted on the cross: "Jesus of Nazareth, the King of the Jews" (Jn 19:19). This sign is written in three languages—Hebrew, actually Aramaic, the Jews' spoken language; Latin, the language of Rome; and Greek, the most widespread language in the empire. Jewish leaders object to the sign. They argue that Jesus only thinks he is the king. Pilate overrules them, and John reports the incident because he believes the sign to be a correct statement.

John presents other crucifixion details to show how Jesus' death fulfills prophecy. Jesus is executed between two criminals, a fact that early Christians will associate with Isaiah's suffering servant who, when he dies, is "numbered with the transgressors" (Isa 53:12). Soldiers gamble for the clothes of Jesus, a scene reminiscent of Psalm 22:18—"for my clothing they cast lots." In addition, Jesus dies before soldiers are able to break his legs, an act that expedites the execution by making it impossible for the victim to push upward and catch a breath. Instead, they pierce him with a spear to make sure he is dead. Scripture speaks of one who will be pierced, yet not suffer broken bones (Ps 34:20; Zech 12:10).

"It is finished" (Jn 19:30), Jesus says. Then he bows his head and gives up his spirit. John does not portray these last words of Jesus as a proclamation of defeat, but of victory. Jesus has finished what God sent him to do: "The good shepherd lays down his life for the sheep" (Jn 10:11).

Joseph of Arimathea, a wealthy member of the Sanhedrin but also a secret disciple of Jesus, obtains permission from Pilate to bury Jesus. Joseph, who had opposed the decision of the Jewish council, chooses an unused tomb in a nearby garden. A Pharisee helps him retrieve the body: Nicodemus, the man to whom Jesus once said, "You must be born from above" (Jn 3:7). Together,

these men wrap the body of Jesus in strips of linen laced with spices. Then they gently lay the body in the tomb, seal the entrance, and return to the city to observe a gloomy sabbath.

Early on the first day of the week, while it was still dark, Mary Magdalene came to the tomb and saw that the stone had been removed from the tomb. JN 20:1

None of Jesus' followers seem prepared for the stunning discoveries that begin on Sunday morning—even though Matthew and Luke each report that Jesus told the disciples he would die and be raised on the third day (Mt 16:21; Lk 9:22). Perhaps they thought the resurrection he spoke of was into the kingdom of heaven, since many Jews believed that the soul lingered near the corpse for three days before leaving.

The gospel accounts of the resurrection vary somewhat, possibly because the writers drew from different eyewitnesses. John implies that Mary Magdalene, a follower of Jesus, went to the tomb alone. The other three Evangelists report that she had one or more woman companions as she made her way there.

John says that when Mary Magdalene arrives at the tomb and discovers the stone covering rolled away, she immediately concludes that someone has stolen the body and runs to summon Peter and another disciple, "the one whom Jesus loved" (Jn 20:2). Back in the garden, Mary weeps before the

According to John, Joseph of Arimathea was joined by the Pharisee Nicodemus in taking Jesus' body down from the cross and preparing it for burial in an unused tomb in a nearby garden. This deposition scene was painted by Flemish religious artist Rogier van der Weyden (c. 1399-1464).

John places only Mary Magdalene at the tomb; the other Evangelists say she was joined by one or two other women disciples of Jesus.

Galilee. Seven disciples have been fishing all night, without success. As they draw near the shore, Jesus calls out from the beach, telling them to throw their nets on the right side of the boat. Though they do not recognize Jesus, they comply—and haul in an enormous catch of fish. Early Christians later saw in this miracle a symbol of the rapid growth of the church, brought on by the humble fishermen to whom Jesus once had said, "Follow me, and I will make you fish for people" (Mt 4:19).

Jesus did many other signs . . . . But these are written so that you may come to believe that Jesus is the Messiah, the Son of God, and that through believing you may have life in his name.   JN 20:30-31

This passage states the purpose that lies behind the entire Gospel. In choosing what to write and what to omit, John is guided by this single goal. He selects teachings and miracles of Jesus that will help convince people that Jesus is both the Messiah and the Son of God. John does this because he is convinced that once people begin believing in Jesus, they will enter into the kingdom of God one day and forever thereafter enjoy the company of Jesus in a place he has prepared for them.

John's Gospel concludes with a beautiful tribute to the multitude of wonders that Jesus accomplished while he lived on earth: "There are also many other things that Jesus did; if every one of them were written down, I suppose that the world itself could not contain the books that would be written" (Jn 21:25).

empty tomb. "Woman, why are you weeping?" (Jn 20:15) Jesus asks. Engulfed in tears, Mary fails to recognize him. She thinks he is a gardener, and asks where the body of her Lord has been taken. Jesus replies with one word: "Mary." Immediately the sobbing woman realizes who he is. Perhaps she reaches out to touch him, for his next words are: "Do not hold on to me, because I have not yet ascended to the Father" (Jn 20:16, 17). He may be assuring her that he has not yet returned to heaven; she will have more time with him there.

Jesus appears to the disciples later that day, though Thomas is not there. By the time Thomas returns, Jesus has gone. Only John's Gospel tells the story of Doubting Thomas. "Unless I see the mark of the nails in his hands," Thomas tells the other disciples, ". . . I will not believe" (Jn 20:25). Jesus returns the next Sunday and extends his scarred hands to Thomas, who instantly believes that this is Jesus standing before him. "Have you believed because you have seen me?" Jesus asks Thomas. "Blessed are those who have not seen and yet have come to believe" (Jn 20:29).

John does not report the ascension of Jesus into heaven, but he tells an otherwise unrecorded story of Jesus appearing again to the disciples at the Sea of

Until he touched Jesus' wounds, the apostle Thomas refused to believe he had risen; a painting by Bernardo Strozzi (1581-1644).

THE ACTS OF THE APOSTLES

A sequel to the Gospel of Luke, Acts of the Apostles tells the remarkable story of how Christianity began after Jesus ascended to heaven. The book records the first sermon by the apostles, their first miracle, their first steps at organizing the growing community of believers, the first persecution against them, the death of the first Christian martyr, the conversion of the first non-Jews, and the establishment of the first church in Europe. Acts provides a natural transition between the four gospels and the 21 letters written by Paul and others. The early half of the book begins with the ascension of Jesus, then highlights the work of the apostles, especially Peter and John. The second half focuses on Paul during his three missionary journeys. Yet, throughout the book the most important role belongs to the Holy Spirit. It is he who empowers the church to carry on the ministry of Jesus. For this reason, some scholars suggest that a more accurate title would be Acts of the Holy Spirit.

Like all four gospels, Acts is anonymous. But church leaders since the second century have attributed both the Gospel of Luke and Acts to a Gentile physician named Luke, who accompanied Paul on some of his missionary travels. In fact, the writing style is among the most sophisticated in the New Testament, suggesting the author was well educated. In some passages—always beginning and ending with a ship voyage—the writer switches from talking about "they" to talking about "we." This hints that the author is drawing from his personal travel diary. A meticulous historian, Luke also taps into a rich variety of other written and spoken sources. He covers about the first 30 years of the church's history, presumably writing about 20 years later, in the 80s of the first century.

Luke addresses this second volume to the mysterious Theophilus, as he did his gospel. Theophilus may have been a convert and patron who paid Luke to write the history of Jesus and the early church. Or perhaps he was a Roman official to whom Luke was explaining Christianity, possibly to convince Rome to let the church operate in peace. But since Theophilus means "lover of God," Luke may also have been writing to all God-loving Jews and Gentiles to help them understand that this seemingly upstart religion fulfills Old Testament prophecy about where the Jewish faith is headed: "I have set you to be a light for the Gentiles, so that you may bring salvation to the ends of the earth" (Acts 13:47, quoting Isa 49:6).

With Mary and the disciples watching, Jesus ascends to heaven; a Bible illumination dated about 1420.

You will receive power when the Holy Spirit has come upon you; and you will be my witnesses in Jerusalem, in all Judea and Samaria, and to the ends of the earth.
ACTS 1:8

Luke begins by linking this book to his earlier volume, the Gospel of Luke. "In the first book," he says, "I wrote about all that Jesus did and taught from the beginning until the day when he was taken up to heaven" (Acts 1:1-2). Now Luke picks up where he left off—with the final instructions that Jesus gives the apostles, moments before his ascension. Luke, like the other three gospel writers, reports that John the Baptist baptized with water, but said that the Messiah would baptize with the Holy Spirit. John's prediction had been captivating because throughout Jewish

history the spirit of the Lord—as the Holy Spirit is usually called in the Old Testament—was not available for everyone. God's spirit empowered heroes of Israel, especially prophets and kings. For example, when young David was anointed Israel's future king, "the spirit of the Lord came mightily upon David from that day forward" (1 Sam 16:13). But John the Baptist had predicted that the Messiah would make the Lord's spirit widely available. Hundreds of years earlier the prophet Joel, speaking on behalf of God, had also promised that the day was coming when "I will pour out my spirit on all flesh" (Joel 2:28).

With this background in mind, Luke quotes Jesus telling the apostles that the new baptism of the spirit will arrive "not many days from now" (Acts 1:5). The apostles have only to wait in Jerusalem. After the spirit comes, the men will receive all the motivation and power they need to begin telling everyone—in Jerusalem and beyond—about the astonishing miracles and teachings they witnessed.

As Jesus finishes these instructions, he ascends into the heavens. The disciples, awestruck, stand on the Mount of Olives and stare at the sky until two angels arrive and promise that Jesus will one day return in the same way he left. The disciples then descend into the Kidron valley and climb to Jerusalem, about half a mile away—the distance a Jew is permitted to travel on "a sabbath day's journey" (Acts 1:12). In Jerusalem they wait in an upstairs room, perhaps the same room where they had held the Passover seder, or Last Supper, with Jesus some 40 days earlier. While they await the spirit, they choose a man to succeed Judas Iscariot, the apostle who betrayed Jesus and then committed suicide. With the selection of Matthias, there are again twelve apostles, the number Jesus had chosen, perhaps to represent the twelve tribes of Israel. The implication behind this expressive number is that Jesus' message is for all of God's people.

Suddenly from heaven there came a sound like the rush of a violent wind . . . . All of them [the disciples] were filled with the Holy Spirit. ACTS 2:2, 4

The Holy Spirit arrives on a morning perfect for spreading the Gospel of Jesus. Jerusalem's population is swollen by thousands of Jewish visitors who have come from all over the Near East to celebrate the Festival of Weeks (Shavuoth), known also by its Greek name, Pentecost, meaning 50. Observed as an important pilgrimage holiday 50 days after Passover, Pentecost is remembered as the day God gave Moses the Ten Commandments. It is a happy time, also marking the end of the spring grain harvest.

A roaring sound of wind fills the house where the apostles are waiting. Flames that look like fiery tongues hover above each person. Throughout the Old Testament, wind and fire are symbols of God's power and presence. A strong east wind once parted the Red Sea for the Israelites. And God first spoke to Moses from a burning bush, then led the Israelites of the Exodus as a pillar of fire and smoke. Miraculously, the apostles receive the power to speak in languages they never studied—languages of the Jews now visiting from northern Africa, Egypt, Arabia, the Persian Gulf territories, Turkey, Italy, and other lands. The roar of wind is so blaring that a crowd rushes to the house to see what has happened. There, this international contin-

gent of Jews is astonished to find the Galilean apostles speaking in all languages represented. Humanity's curse at the Tower of Babel, which transformed a one-language world into a confounding cacophony of many languages, seems temporarily lifted to receive Jesus' message.

Peter, consistently the leader among the apostles, steps forward to address the bewildered masses. He cites the prophet Joel's prediction that God will some day pour out the spirit on all people. That prophecy, Peter boldly declares, is fulfilled today. Peter then tells the crowd about the recent execution, resurrection, and ascension of Jesus, and of a psalm that predicted each of these events. Jesus' "deeds of power, wonders, and signs" (Acts 2:22) verify to many in the crowd that God is behind everything being said and done. A staggering throng of about 3,000 believe Peter's message and accept his joint invitation and promise: "Repent, and be baptized every one of you in the name of Jesus Christ so that your sins may be forgiven; and you will receive the gift of the Holy Spirit" (Acts 2:38).

This emerging community of believers begins meeting frequently in the temple courtyards and eat-

As was common from the Middle Ages through the Renaissance, Mary the mother of Jesus was central in such images as this 16th-century depiction of the descent of the Holy Spirit on Pentecost.

ing together in one another's homes. Before long they develop such a bond of love for each other that the richer ones sell some of their possessions and give the proceeds to the needy among them.

Peter said, "I have no silver or gold, but what I have I give you; in the name of Jesus Christ of Nazareth, stand up and walk." ACTS 3:6

A few weeks before Pentecost, when Jesus was arrested and crucified, the apostles had gone into hiding for fear of meeting a similar fate. Now, after the resurrection of Jesus and the arrival of the Holy Spirit, they are cowering no longer. They fearlessly tell the story of Jesus, even in the temple precincts frequented by the same Jewish leaders who had arranged the execution of Jesus—and who could do the same to them. At three o'clock one afternoon, Peter and John walk to the temple to attend one of the daily services of sacrifice and prayer. They approach the main courtyard by way of the Beautiful Gate, facing east toward the Mount of Olives, the huge doors of which gleam with polished Corinthian bronze and patterns of silver and gold. Outside the gateway sits a man in his 40s, crippled since birth. Each day some friends carry him to the gate so he can beg. As Peter and John come toward him, he asks for alms. Peter replies that they have no money, but that what they do have—the power of the Holy Spirit to heal—they give freely.

Peter healing the man crippled from birth outside Jerusalem's temple; an 18th-century stained glass window from an English church

Peter takes the man by the hand, commanding him to stand up and walk. The man does more. He jumps up, then accompanies the two into the temple, "walking and leaping and praising God" (Acts 3:8). He stirs a commotion as he strides past Jews who for a generation have walked past him. As a crowd forms inside the temple courtyard, Peter recognizes another opportunity to explain the story behind a miracle. Addressing laity and leaders alike, he says they killed the long-awaited Messiah. Yet, Peter consoles them by explaining that this had to happen to fulfill prophecy and even now they can experience forgiveness and God's presence if they repent.

Peter and John are both arrested that evening, while still addressing the crowd. Temple officials hold them in custody overnight, then bring them before the Sanhedrin, the same ruling council and supreme court of Jewish law that convicted Jesus. The 70 elders on the council order them to stop teaching about Jesus, the man they had found guilty of blasphemy for claiming to be God's son. "We cannot keep from speaking about what we have seen and heard" (Acts 4:20), the defendants reply.

They are released with a stern warning—which they completely disregard. Later the Sanhedrin arrests all twelve apostles. "We gave you strict orders not to teach in this name," the high priest charges, "yet here you have filled Jerusalem with your teaching." Peter's reply is blunt: "We must obey God rather than any human authority" (Acts 5:28, 29). Enraged at this blatant disrespect for their authority, some on the council argue that the two men should be executed. Gamaliel, a respected Pharisee, replies that if this new religious movement is of human doing, it will fail without any opposition from the council. But if it is of God, he adds, it will endure no matter what the council does. The men reach a compromise by ordering the apostles beaten and released.

Ananias, with the consent of his wife Sapphira, sold a piece of property; . . . he kept back some of the proceeds, and brought only a part and laid it at the apostles' feet. ACTS 5:1-2

Believers living in Jerusalem continue to pool their resources, somewhat like the Jewish Essene sect in Qumran, the small desert community 14 miles east of Jerusalem that produced the famous Dead Sea Scrolls. Luke identifies Barnabas as a notable example of generosity. This man, who later teams up with Paul to launch the first Christian missionary expedition, sells a field and turns the money over to the apostles to distribute among the needy. A couple named Ananias and Sapphira apparently envy the attention that Barnabas and other donors receive, so they conspire to sell a piece of property and give only part of the money to the apostles—pretending to give it all. This is the first recorded sin among the emerging, impressionable community of believers.

When Ananias brings the contribution, Peter immediately accuses him of lying to God. Ananias falls

The Italian artist Vittore Carpaccio (c. 1460-1526) placed the deacon Stephen in a setting reminiscent of his native land and gave members of his audience Arab turbans.

dead and is carried away. His wife arrives three hours later and suffers the same fate. When news of this spreads among the church, the people are terrified to discover that the Holy Spirit's power is not limited to healing; it can be used in reaching such lethal judgments as those against Ananias and Sapphira.

When the disciples were increasing in number, the Hellenists complained against the Hebrews because their widows were being neglected in the daily distribution of food. ACTS 6:1

The burgeoning church begins to experience growing pains potent enough to split the community into two cultural groups. Food is the divisive issue. Each day, when provisions are given to the poor, Jewish widows native to Judea apparently get more than their fair share—at the expense of Jewish widows who have immigrated from Greek-speaking countries throughout the Near East. The twelve apostles, all native Hebrews, decide they need associates who will settle such problems; they prefer to spend as much time as possible teaching what they learned from Jesus. At the apostles' request, the church selects seven men, all with Greek names and apparently immigrants from Greek-speaking lands. They are Stephen, Philip, Prochorus, Nicanor, Timon, Parmenas, and Nicolaus. Since Nicolaus alone is identified as a proselyte, or convert to Judaism, the others were likely born into Jewish families. These seven deacons are chosen to direct the church's humanitarian efforts, but they do not limit themselves to this narrow role. Stephen and Philip soon appear performing miracles and teaching.

Stephen, full of grace and power, did great wonders and signs among the people. ACTS 6:8

Stephen becomes a leader among Greek-speaking believers and defends the church's teachings in Jerusalem synagogues. While doing this, he becomes embroiled in a heated debate. Acts does not say what he and the other Jews argue about, but clues in the text suggest that Stephen is among the first believers to realize that the teachings of Jesus will eventually change many Jewish customs inaugurated at the time of Moses, and will even erode the sacrificial system at the temple. After all, why continue offering sacrifices for sin if God's Son died for the sins of humanity and if people can find forgiveness by believing in Jesus and repenting?

The fear of Stephen's opponents can be measured by the intensity of their response. Unable to defeat him in debate, they do much the same thing that Jewish leaders did to Jesus. They persuade some men to bring false charges against him, telling the crowds that Stephen insults Moses and God. Stephen is quickly arrested and brought before the high council that had executed Jesus and ordered the apostles beaten. Witnesses testify that Stephen said Jesus will destroy the temple and change Mosaic Law.

When the high priest asks if these accusations are true, Stephen answers with a speech that traces Jewish history from its founding and that portrays the Jewish people as persistently rebellious toward God. The council agrees with most of what he says—until he challenges the belief that God lives in the temple, and then forcefully attacks the council leaders themselves for disobeying the Law of Moses.

As enraged Jews execute the deacon Stephen by stoning, the young Pharisee
Saul (lower left) sits holding their cloaks; a painting by Annibale Carracci (1560-1609).

Denying that God lives in the temple, Stephen quotes the prophet Isaiah's message from God: "Heaven is my throne, and the earth is my footstool. What kind of house will you build for me?" (Acts 7:49, quoting Isa 66:1-2). Stephen then turns on the council and, using scriptural terms charged with a long history of hostile emotion, calls them stubborn lawbreakers.

As the council's rage begins to burn out of control, Stephen sees a vision. "Look," he tells the assembly, "I see the heavens opened and the Son of Man standing at the right hand of God!" (Acts 7:56). Any semblance of a formal hearing instantly comes to an end. The men mob Stephen, drag him outside the city, and begin stoning him to death, an ancient method of execution in this land plentiful with stones. The executioners lay their cloaks at the feet of Saul, a strict Pharisee who is thus a consenting witness to the killing of the first Christian martyr.

That day a severe persecution began against the church in Jerusalem, and all except the apostles were scattered throughout the countryside of Judea and Samaria.
ACTS 8:1

Jewish leaders intent on squashing the new religious movement launch a persecution that has the opposite effect. Jesus had promised the apostles that they would become his witnesses "in Jerusalem, in all Judea and Samaria, and to the ends of the earth"

(Acts 1:8). Now, Stephen's martyrdom becomes the catalyst for extending the circle of believers beyond Jerusalem. Threatened with arrest, imprisonment, beatings, and possibly execution, most believers in Jerusalem leave town and scatter throughout the region—taking their newfound faith with them.

Philip, the late Stephen's colleague as an assistant to the apostles, travels north to Samaria. Despite long-standing rivalries between Jews and Samaritans, Philip's miracles and teachings convince many to repent of their sins and form a local community of believers. The apostles Peter and John visit Samaria and give dramatic evidence of their approval by praying for the converts to receive the Holy Spirit. Luke does not reveal why the Samaritans had not received the Holy Spirit, as was customary, at their conversion. Nor does he divulge what evidence proves that the Samaritans subsequently received the Holy Spirit. In other settings, the evidence includes the sound of wind, the sight of hovering flames, and the ability to speak in unlearned languages and to prophesy. Whatever the evidence is in Samaria, a converted magician named Simon offers to buy the power to invoke the Holy Spirit; he is firmly rebuked. The point, however, is that the Gospel has reached non-Jews.

Perhaps symbolizing the Gospel's continuing spread to the ends of the earth, Luke reports that Philip is told by an angel to travel to a southern desert road. There he meets an Ethiopian official. Various ancient writers, such as Homer in the Odyssey, describe Ethiopians as handsome people from the ends of the known world. The official is riding home in a chariot and puzzling over a prophecy he is reading from Isaiah. Philip explains that the prophecy points to Jesus. Then Philip tells the official enough of the gospel story that the man chooses to stop and be baptized. Afterward, Philip is spirited away, leaving the official to continue his journey. Luke says no more about the Ethiopian, but a second-century theologian named Irenaeus says the man started the church in his North African homeland.

"Saul, Saul, why do you persecute me?" ACTS 9:4

As Jesus' message is carried farther afield, Jewish leaders apparently realize that their attempt to suppress this threat to their ancient religion is proving counterproductive. One of the most zealous persecutors is Saul, from the Pharisee branch of Judaism, which prides itself on preserving tradition. With letters from the high priest backing his mission, Saul begins a more than 100-mile journey to the synagogues of Damascus in the hopes of arresting "any who belonged to the Way" (Acts 9:2). Believers call themselves followers of the Way, perhaps because Jesus described himself as the way to God (Jn 14:6).

As Saul and his associates approach Damascus, a blaze of light strikes him, knocking him to the ground. Suddenly, a voice from out of nowhere asks why Saul is persecuting him. When Saul asks who is talking, the voice replies, "I am Jesus, whom you are persecuting" (Acts 9:5). Jesus instructs Saul to continue into Damascus and to wait there. Because Saul has been blinded by the light, his traveling companions lead him by the hand into the city. For three days, he remains blind. During this time he eats and drinks nothing, until a follower of the Way named Ananias restores his sight and prays for him to receive the Holy Spirit. Saul is then baptized into the faith, in the most dramatic turnabout in all of Acts. He begins telling his story in the synagogues and proclaiming that Jesus is the Son of God. For this, tradition-minded Jews plot to kill him when he leaves town. They post a 24-hour guard at all the gates, but Saul's new-found friends lower him over the wall in a basket and he escapes the trap. Saul returns to Jerusalem, where he stays only briefly before fleeing to the comparative safety of his hometown Tarsus, about 400 miles north in what is now southeastern Turkey.

Thrown from his mount and blinded by a dazzling vision, Saul hears Jesus ask why he is being persecuted; an illustration from a missal dated 1448-1449.

Peter went up on the roof to pray. He became hungry and wanted something to eat; and while it was being prepared, he fell into a trance. ACTS 10:9-10

Despite continuing persecution, the apostles preach throughout their homeland—but only to Jews. Merely touching a Gentile, or even anything a Gentile has touched, renders a Jew ritually unclean. Before Jews contaminated in this way can return to the temple to worship, they have to undergo purification rites that include a waiting period. While Peter visits a tanner's home on the Mediterranean coast, he has a noontime vision that radically changes the relationship between Gentiles and Jewish followers of the Way. In this vision, Peter sees a large sheet descend from the sky. Filling the sheet are all kinds of animals, including ones that Jewish law forbids as food. Eating any prohibited animals—such as camels, rabbits, or shellfish—will render a Jew as ritually unclean as contact with a Gentile. Suddenly, a voice instructs Peter to eat. Peter instantly objects, arguing that he has never eaten anything unclean. The voice replies, "What God has made clean, you must not call profane" (Acts 10:15). The command is repeated twice more, perhaps for emphasis, then the animal-filled sheet ascends to heaven.

While Peter struggles to interpret what the vision means, messengers arrive from Cornelius, a Roman commander—and a Gentile. They ask Peter to accompany them on the 35-mile trip to their master's home in Caesarea, a predominately Gentile city that is the Roman headquarters in Judea. They explain that an angel told Cornelius to send for Peter. The next morning Peter sets out with the messengers and some Jewish associates. When Peter arrives, he explains to Cornelius that he has come because "God has shown me that I should not call anyone profane or unclean. . . . I truly understand that God shows no partiality, but in every nation anyone who fears him and does what is right is acceptable to him" (Acts 10:28, 34-35). While Peter is still speaking, the Holy Spirit fills everyone in the room—including the Gentiles, to the astonishment of Jewish observers.

When Peter returns to Jerusalem, Jewish followers of the Way criticize him for associating with Gentiles. But Peter tells the group about his vision and about the Gentiles receiving the Holy Spirit. Sometime later, believers scattered abroad by the persecution in Jerusalem start a church among Gentiles at Antioch in Syria. The apostles dispatch Barnabas

**In this dual scene by the 15th-century German artist Konrad Witz,
an angel taps a slumbering Peter (right) and leads him out of prison (left).**

to investigate. He likes what he sees, and invites Saul to join him there in ministering to the people. Both men had been raised outside of Judea, in cities where Jews were in the minority.

It is in this church that followers of the Way are first called Christians, a word derived from Christos, the Greek equivalent of the Hebrew term for Messiah. People outside the church possibly generate this term to mock those who believe Jesus is the Jews' promised Messiah.

King Herod laid violent hands upon some who belonged to the church. He had James, the brother of John, killed with the sword. ACTS 12:1-2

Herod Agrippa I, grandson of Herod the Great, who tried to kill the infant Jesus, is appointed by the Roman emperor Claudius as king over the territories of Judea and Samaria. Herod openly favors the Pharisees and joins in persecuting Christians. For reasons unstated, he orders the execution of the apostle James, one of Jesus' closest disciples and the first of the twelve to be martyred. When Herod sees how much this pleases his Jewish constituents, he arrests Peter with the intention of executing him after Passover, the same time of year in which Jesus was crucified. But the night before Peter's trial, an angel beaming with light miraculously releases him.

Luke says Herod dies, apparently a short time later, after accepting the praise of people who declare him a god. Luke's placement of this report after the execution of James and the arrest of Peter suggests that

those who oppose the church risk the judgment of God. The first-century Jewish soldier and historian Josephus, a Roman citizen who provides independent information for many events in the New Testament, confirms that Herod died of severe abdominal pain in the spring of A.D. 44.

The Holy Spirit said, "Set apart for me Barnabas and Saul for the work to which I have called them." ACTS 13:2

Luke returns to his narrative about the ministry to the Gentiles. One day, while five leaders of the church in Antioch are worshiping God and fasting, the Holy Spirit tells them to send Barnabas and Saul on what becomes the first of three missionary expeditions (see map on page 369). The pair, accompanied by Barnabas's cousin John Mark, sail to Cyprus, the island where Barnabas was raised. There, they travel from town to town, taking advantage of the Jewish custom of inviting guests to address the sabbath-day assembly. At Paphos, capital of the island, the two are summoned by the Roman governor Sergius Paulus, who wants to hear their teachings. The governor is converted after hearing the message and seeing Saul render a magician blind; the man had tried talking Sergius Paulus out of becoming a Christian. At this point in his narrative, Luke reveals that Saul's Greco-Roman name is Paul. From here on, Luke refers to him by this name, as the story turns almost exclusively to Paul's work among the Gentiles.

From Cyprus, Paul and Barnabas sail north to the mainland of what is now Turkey. John Mark leaves them to return to Jerusalem, but the two head for the inland town of Antioch of Pisidia, where they are initially well received and invited to speak again on the following sabbath. On that second sabbath, nearly the whole town packs the synagogue. But jealous elders slander and heckle the guests. Paul and Barnabas then declare that they feel obligated to bring the good news about Jesus to the Jews first, since they are God's chosen people. But because most of the Jews have rejected the message of salvation, the missionary team vows to take the Gospel to the Gentiles, in fulfillment of Isaiah's prophecy that God will save Gentiles the world over.

In Lystra, a city with a temple to Zeus, the missionaries cure a lame man and are hailed as gods: Barnabas as Zeus and Paul as Hermes, since Hermes is the messenger god and Paul does most of the talking. The missionaries put a quick stop to this, but furious Jews who have trailed them from the previous cities they have visited incite a mob to stone Paul and leave him for dead. Paul survives this attack, however, and others that follow.

Certain individuals came down from Judea and were teaching the brothers, "Unless you are circumcised according to the custom of Moses, you cannot be saved."
ACTS 15:1

*A*s more Gentiles are converted, Christians become sharply divided over what to do about the Law of Moses. Some leaders, such as Paul, preach that under the new covenant that God has established through Jesus, no one—neither Jew nor Gentile—is required to keep the ancient rules that the Jews themselves have never been able to obey fully. Others, however, insist that all of the laws still apply, and that anyone who wants to become a Christian must first convert to the Jewish faith. Some Judean proponents of the law are brazen enough to take their opinion to the heart of Paul's work among the Gentiles: the church at Antioch in Syria.

Church leaders convene a council meeting in Jerusalem to discuss the matter. Christians converted from among the Pharisees, the tradition-minded Jewish sect to which Paul had belonged, argue that everyone—Gentiles included—need to observe all the ordinances of Moses. These laws include food restrictions and the painful ritual of circumcision, which symbolizes God's covenant with Abraham.

Peter reminds the council of the vision he experienced and of Cornelius's household receiving the Holy Spirit. Paul and Barnabas report on the miracles that God has done among the Gentiles. (Paul's independent report of the council appears in Galatians 2:1-10.) At the end of the discussion, James, the brother of Jesus and apparently the recognized administrative leader of the church, decides to ask the Gentiles to observe only minimal food restrictions and to abstain from sexual immorality. This is more of a temporary compromise than a ruling, for the volatile issue will dog Paul's long ministry. Years later, Paul will abandon even the minimal food restrictions, and angrily condemn advocates of the Mosaic Law as false teachers who do not understand that "there is no longer Jew or Greek . . . for all of you are one in Christ Jesus" (Gal 3:28).

Paul said to Barnabas, "Come, let us return and visit the believers in every city where we proclaimed the word of the Lord and see how they are doing." ACTS 15:36

*T*he second missionary journey begins after Paul suggests that he and Barnabas return to the cities where they previously made converts. The two immediately become deadlocked over whether again to take John Mark, Barnabas's cousin and the man identified by a second-century church leader as the author of the Gospel of Mark. Paul absolutely rejects the idea, arguing that John Mark deserted them during the first expedition. But Barnabas is adamant about taking him. The missionaries decide to split into two teams. Barnabas and John Mark will revisit the island of Cyprus. Paul and a new associate, Silas, will return to churches on the mainland.

Throughout the remainder of the book, Luke traces only the work of Paul and his traveling companions. Barnabas and John Mark are never mentioned in Acts again. Sometime during those later years, however, Paul and John Mark settle their differences. While Paul is in jail, perhaps for the last time, he writes asking for John Mark to come, "for he is useful in my ministry" (2 Tim 4:11).

During the night Paul had a vision: there stood a man of Macedonia pleading with him and saying, "Come over to Macedonia and help us." ACTS 16:9

*P*aul and Silas travel north to Derbe and then Lystra, where they recruit Timothy, a man whose father is a Greek and whose mother is a Jew. Timothy is in fact a Jew because of his mother but he is uncircumcised. Though Paul had argued earlier against requiring Gentiles to observe Jewish customs, he has Timothy circumcised, perhaps to protect him from prejudice in Jewish communities.

Instead of turning back after visiting the cities on Paul's first itinerary, the men continue west until they arrive in Troas, near the site of ancient Troy, on the northwestern coast of what is now Turkey. There, Paul receives a nighttime vision in which a man from Macedonia—a region in northern Greece—pleads with him to come and help the people there. Paul, Silas, and Timothy sail across the northern tip of the Aegean Sea—and for the first time in recorded history, the Gospel arrives in Europe. Greeks would have understood Paul's motivation for the journey, since their religion is filled with stories of gods using visions to send people on missions.

It is possible that a fourth person joins the missionary team: the book's author, Luke. Normally, Luke describes the events as a nonparticipant. But here, and on three additional occasions describing the outset of a sea journey, the author uses the

The martyrdom of James, the first apostle to meet that fate; an illustration from a book of hours by 15th-century French court painter Jean Fouquet

Following his healing of a crippled man at Lystra, Paul was hailed as a god; this
tapestry from the ducal palace at Mantua, Italy, is based on a design by Raphael (1483-1520).

first-person plural: "We set sail from Troas" (Acts 16:11; see also 20:6, 21:1, and 27:1). The missionaries arrive on the European continent and travel inland to the large city of Philippi. There they meet Lydia, a dealer in cloth, who accepts Paul's teachings and opens her home as a meeting place for converts. The congregation develops an affectionate and enduring relationship with Paul. But when Paul and Silas exorcise a slave girl who has brought her master wealth by telling fortunes, the two are mobbed, severely beaten, shackled, and thrown into a dungeon.

At about midnight, while the two are worshiping God with songs and prayer, an earthquake breaks open the prison doors and loosens their restraints. (Philippi lies on a thousand-mile-long fault line where two tectonic plates grind past one another.) After converting the jailer and his family, the two are released and continue their travels. In Thessalonica, their preaching sparks a riot that drives them from town. And in Beroea, new believers escort Paul out of the region to protect him from angry crowds stirred up by Thessalonian Jews trailing him. Silas and Timothy remain behind to continue teaching.

While Paul was waiting for them in Athens, he was deeply distressed to see that the city was full of idols.
ACTS 17:16

The Beroeans accompany Paul all the way to Athens, traveling by ship along the coastline. While Paul waits for his associates to join him, he starts preaching in the synagogues and the public square, where philosophers debate the ongoing stream of new ideas. Paul piques the interest of several philosophers, who invite him to present his ideas at the Areopagus, perhaps a hilltop gathering place (Areopagus means "hill of Ares," god of war) or a council that meets there.

Paul begins by saying he can tell that the Athenians are very religious because they have so many objects of worship, one of which he singles out: an altar with the inscription "To an unknown god" (Acts 17:23). Paul says he is going to tell them about this God they already worship as unknown. When Paul declares that God raised Jesus from the dead to preside at the final judgment, some in the audience begin laughing out loud. Many Greeks believe in immortality of the soul, but the idea of resurrecting a decayed corpse seems foolish. Some listeners, nonetheless, believe what they hear and become converts to the new religion.

Paul left Athens and went to Corinth. . . . Every sabbath he would argue in the synagogue and would try to convince Jews and Greeks. ACTS 18:1, 4

Paul continues his missionary expedition by traveling to Corinth, a bustling trade center about 50 miles west of Athens. In a rare exception to his rule of staying only a short time in each city—just long enough to establish a small core of believers—Paul remains in Corinth for a year and a half. Initially he finds work and lodging with Priscilla and Aquila, who, like him, are skilled tent makers. They

PAUL'S FIRST AND SECOND MISSIONARY JOURNEYS

Called by the Holy Spirit to spread the Gospel of Jesus, Saul set out from Antioch in Syria on the first of what would be three missionary journeys. He sailed for Salamis on the island of Cyprus, homeland of his colleague Barnabas. The two were accompanied by Barnabas's cousin, John Mark, by later tradition the author of the Gospel of Mark. At the island's capital, Paphos, Saul (from this point called by his Greco-Roman name, Paul) blinded a magician and converted the Roman proconsul. Crossing over to the mainland, Paul and Barnabas headed inland while John Mark returned to Jerusalem. A region of rugged mountains, swift rivers, and sizable lakes, Pisidia was a haven for robbers and slave traders—which is what Paul may have had in mind when he later wrote of being "in danger from rivers, danger from bandits" (2 Cor 11:26). At Antioch of Pisidia, Paul and Barnabas were challenged by Jews after speaking in the local synagogue and so decided to take their message to Gentiles— a momentous development in the history of Christianity.

Turning east, the two missionaries went to Iconium, an important commercial center on the road between the Roman province of Asia and Syria. There, they met with the same response, converting Gentiles and some Jews but making enemies of most of the inhabitants, who forced them to flee. At Lystra, the people were almost too receptive—hailing Barnabas as the reincarnation of the god Zeus and Paul as the divine messenger Hermes. But Jews trailing the missionaries from Antioch and Iconium incited a mob to drive the two away to Derbe. Retracing their route and stopping to encourage the converts they had made, the two returned to Antioch.

This aerial view of the ruins of Caesarea shows the breakwater Herod the Great built as Judea's first seaport.

At a contentious meeting of church leaders in Jerusalem, Paul and Barnabas received confirmation of their mission to the Gentiles and decided to revisit the converts they had made on their first journey. But the pair had a falling out over John Mark: Barnabas wanted to take him along but Paul considered him a deserter and refused. And so Barnabas and John Mark sailed for Cyprus while Paul, with a new companion, Silas, set out on his second journey. Paul and Silas went through Cilicia, possibly stopping at Paul's hometown, Tarsus. At Lystra, the missionaries were joined by Timothy, who would be Paul's faithful companion for most of the rest of his life.

Not content with limiting their mission to the towns visited earlier, Paul and his colleagues continued west toward Troas, site of ancient Troy. It was there that Paul received a vision calling him to Macedonia—which meant taking Christianity to Europe. At Philippi, Paul and Silas were arrested and thrown into prison for disturbing the peace with their advocacy of a religion alien to Roman beliefs. An earthquake freed them and they moved on to Thessalonica. Hostile Jews of that city pursued the missionaries to Beroea, from which Paul fled by ship to Athens. Paul made few converts at Athens but spent 18 months in nearby Corinth, establishing a faithful band of believers there and writing his first letters, to his converts in Thessalonica. En route back to Syria, Paul stopped at Ephesus, promising Jews there that he would return. He then sailed for Caesarea and visited Jerusalem before returning to Antioch.

come from Rome but, like all other Jews living in the imperial city, they were expelled in about A.D. 49 because of riots over Christian preaching.

Eventually, Paul wins over Crispus, leader of a synagogue, and moves into a home next door to the worship center. But a group of Jews unite against Paul, taking their complaint to Gallio, the regional governor and brother of the philosopher Seneca. Gallio interprets the problem as an internal Jewish squabble and refuses to rule on "questions about words and names and your own law" (Acts 18:15).

When Paul leaves Corinth, he takes Priscilla and Aquila with him and sails to Ephesus, a major city on the west coast of the Roman province of Asia. This is a second city in which Paul stays for a long time, though not on this trip. He remains only a short while, but promises to return if God permits. Priscilla and Aquila, however, do stay and find themselves tutoring Apollos, an educated and gifted speaker who becomes an early church leader. Paul concludes his second missionary journey by sailing back to Judea to meet with church leaders at Jerusalem and at Antioch in Syria—the congregation that had launched his missionary career.

Paul . . . came to Ephesus, where he found some disciples. He said to them, "Did you receive the Holy Spirit when you became believers?" ACTS 19:1-2

From Antioch, Paul begins his third and last recorded missionary journey (see map on page 372). He works his way westward until he reaches Ephesus. When he arrives, he asks the dozen or so believers there if they have received the Holy Spirit. They reply that they have never even heard of such a being. So Paul baptizes them in the name of Jesus and lays his hands on them. Instantly, the Holy Spirit fills them and they begin speaking in other languages and prophesying.

Paul preaches in the synagogue for three months, until the Jews reject him. For the next two years he preaches each day in a lecture hall, and his teachings spread by word of mouth throughout the region. God works such miracles through Paul that even handkerchiefs or aprons he has touched are used to cure the sick and drive out evil spirits. His preaching and miracles apparently have quite an effect on the community because the silversmiths stir up a riot, charging that the Christian movement is undercutting the sale of figurines of Artemis, the city's patron goddess. Pilgrims to the temple of Artemis, one of the seven wonders of the ancient world, bring considerable wealth to the city. But the new religion, the silversmiths contend, is harming the goddess's prestige. A city leader manages to calm the crowd by urging them to take their complaint through the proper legal channels so as not to upset Roman officials.

Afterward, Paul leaves to visit his fledgling congregations throughout Macedonia and Greece before returning for one last, tearful meeting with the Christians of Ephesus. Paul is near the end of this journey and in a hurry to get back to Jerusalem in time for the Festival of Pentecost.

The main street of Ephesus, one of the ancient world's most thoroughly excavated cities, leads to the impressive theater, set into the hillside in the background, to which Paul's colleagues were dragged. Their preaching hurt sales of Artemis figurines (right).

FATE OF THE APOSTLES

Just before his death, Jesus warned his twelve disciples of the fate that awaited them: "They will arrest you and persecute you . . . . they will put some of you to death" (Lk 21:12, 16). The Bible reports the deaths of two: James the son of Zebedee and Judas Iscariot. Early Christian writers attempted to fill in the gaps, but it is impossible to know which stories are true.

Peter is said to have been executed in Rome during Nero's persecution of Christians in A.D. 64. Andrew, Peter's brother, supposedly preached in Greece before being crucified there. James, as recorded in Acts, was beheaded by order of Herod Agrippa I. His brother John, by tradition the author of the Gospel and three letters of John, is reported to have lived in Ephesus until about A.D. 100. Martyrs' deaths are claimed for Philip in Turkey; Bartholomew and Thomas in India; and Simon the Zealot, Judas the son of James, and Matthew in Persia. The fate of James the son of Alphaeus is unknown. Judas Iscariot suffered the most tragic fate. Rebuffed in his attempt to return the money he had taken to betray Jesus, Judas hanged himself in a field (Mt 27:5; Acts 1:18).

So he asks the Ephesian Christians to meet him at a nearby port town, a request they gladly honor. "I am on my way to Jerusalem," Paul tells them, "not knowing what will happen to me there, except that the Holy Spirit testifies to me in every city that imprisonment and persecutions are waiting for me." Clearly, he anticipates death, for he tells his huddled and weeping flock, "I know that none of you, among whom I have gone about proclaiming the kingdom, will ever see my face again" (Acts 20:22-23, 25).

After stopping to visit believers in Tyre and Ptolemais, Paul arrives at the Judean port city of Caesarea. During the several days he spends there in the house of the deacon Philip, Paul is visited by a prophet with an ominous message from the Holy Spirit. The prophet takes off Paul's belt, ties his own hands and feet, then declares, "This is the way the Jews in Jerusalem will bind the man who owns this belt and will hand him over to the Gentiles" (Acts 21:11).

Jews from Asia, who had seen him [Paul] in the temple, stirred up the whole crowd. ACTS 21:27

At last arriving in Jerusalem, Paul is greeted warmly by the church leaders. They warn him, however, that thousands of Jewish Christians are furious with him for teaching Gentiles that they can serve God without obeying Jewish laws. Later in the week, while Paul is worshiping at the temple, some Jews from the province of Asia recognize him and begin shouting accusations. Their most serious charge is that he brought a Gentile into the temple; they had earlier seen Paul in Jerusalem with a Gentile and wrongly concluded that he brought the man into the temple precincts. An ancient stone recovered from the Court of the Gentiles and engraved with a warning painted in red reveals that it was a capital offense to take non-Jews beyond that point.

A riot erupts, and the crowd begins beating Paul. He is rescued only by the swift action of Roman troops, who take him into custody. Surprisingly, the Roman commander Claudius Lysias allows Paul to address the crowd. Paul gives a brief account of his remarkable conversion, then reports that God has chosen him to preach to the Gentiles. The moment he speaks these inflammatory words, the riot erupts again. Soldiers take Paul back to their barracks to protect him from the enraged citizenry.

On the next day, the commander orders a special session of the Jewish high council to settle the dispute. Paul cunningly divides the council by claiming that he is on trial for his belief in life after death—which is partly true because this is a distinctive teaching of Christianity. It is also a belief among Pharisees on the council, though one bitterly opposed by Sadducees—another branch of Judaism represented on the council. In the clamor that follows, both sides begin pulling on Paul. Again, the soldiers come to his rescue and whisk him away to the safety of imprisonment. As far as the book of Acts reports, Paul is never again a free man.

In the morning the Jews joined in a conspiracy and bound themselves by an oath neither to eat nor drink until they had killed Paul. ACTS 23:12

Paul's nephew hears of a plot to assassinate his uncle and reports the news to the Roman commander Claudius Lysias. That night, Paul is escorted out of town—accompanied by an intimidating squadron of 200 infantrymen, 200 spearmen, and 70 cavalrymen. They take him to Caesarea, since it serves as Roman headquarters in Judea. The governor, Felix, apparently sees little merit in the charges against Paul. Yet he holds the apostle for two years, hoping to receive a bribe for releasing him. In A.D. 59, a new governor, Porcius Festus, suggests settling Paul's case with a trial in Jerusalem. But Paul, knowing that the hatred toward him in Jerusalem has only intensified, rejects the suggestion and appeals for a hearing in the imperial court of Rome. As a Roman citizen, this is Paul's right.

A few days later Festus is visited by King Herod Agrippa II, son of Herod Agrippa I who had martyred the apostle James. The two rulers listen to Paul's story and agree he has done nothing worthy of imprisonment, let alone death. "This man could have been set free," Herod tells Festus, "if he had not appealed to the emperor" (Acts 26:32).

Paul's Third Missionary Journey and Voyage to Rome

After an indefinite period at his base in Antioch, Paul set out on his third and final missionary journey. Paul wanted to confirm to his earlier converts that belief in Jesus alone was necessary for salvation. Apparently revisiting some of the cities where he had established churches during his first and second journeys, Paul reached Ephesus and its small band of believers. He stayed there for more than two years—preaching in the synagogue for three months until he was ejected and then using a lecture hall belonging to a local group of philosophers.

At Ephesus, Paul once more stirred controversy. This time his opponents were silversmiths who earned their living by selling images of the goddess Artemis to pilgrims visiting her renowned temple just outside the city. Two of Paul's companions were dragged into the theater, apparently to be executed, and Paul had to be restrained from coming to their rescue. The town clerk quieted the crowd and Paul left to revisit converts in Macedonia and Achaia (Greece). Little is known of Paul's activity there, except that it was apparently from Corinth that he wrote to Christians in Rome of his great desire to visit the imperial capital. En route back to Judea, Paul stopped at Troas. Although bypassing Ephesus in his anxiety to be back in Jerusalem by Pentecost, he summoned church leaders from that city to meet him at the nearby port of Miletus for a tearful farewell. At Patara, Paul found a

Paul's final approach to Rome likely was along the famed Appian Way.

Phoenician ship to take him to Tyre. After visiting disciples there and in Ptolemais, the apostle reached Caesarea and proceeded to Jerusalem.

The prediction of a man named Agabus that Paul would be handed over to the Gentiles for punishment by the Jews of Jerusalem proved all too true. Falsely accused of bringing a non-Jew into the inner temple, Paul sparked a riot from which Roman soldiers rescued him—taking him into a protective custody that seems to have lasted for the rest of his life. After a two-year confinement in Caesarea, Paul demanded, as a Roman citizen, to be judged at the imperial court in Rome.

Turned over to a centurion named Julius, Paul was placed on a ship bound for Myra in Asia Minor. There he was transferred to another vessel headed for Italy. Reaching Crete, the ship stopped at Fair Havens before heading for a winter port at Phoenix. But a sudden storm carried the vessel off course. Remaining afloat only after cargo was jettisoned, the ship survived the storm to reach Malta, where it was run aground on a reef. Only the intervention of Julius prevented the crew from killing the prisoners, including Paul.

After three months in Malta, Paul was put aboard yet another ship and, via Sicily, reached Italy. Believers from Rome came out to meet the apostle as he neared the imperial city. As far as the Bible reveals, the tireless missionary spent the rest of his life a prisoner in Rome.

When it was decided that we were to sail for Italy, they transferred Paul and some other prisoners to a centurion.
ACTS 27:1

*I*n the custody of a compassionate Roman officer named Julius, Paul boards a ship with 276 passengers and crew—apparently including Luke because another "we passage" starts here. The number of seafarers is not particularly large for the times; the Jewish historian Josephus tells of another ship with 600 aboard. The vessel sets sail from Caesarea late in the year, when winter winds churn the Mediterranean into a tempestuous sea. The voyage begins well, with the ship sailing along the coastline, making several stops along the way. Captain and crew hope to get about halfway to Rome before wintering in Phoenix, a protected harbor on the island of Crete. But as they approach the port, their ship is suddenly caught in a storm that appears to pack cyclone-force winds. For two weeks the voyagers are pummeled 600 miles farther west. They survive only by reinforcing the hull and by throwing overboard all the cargo and equipment—which allows the ship to ride higher in the water.

The vessel eventually runs aground and breaks up near the small island of Malta, directly south of Sicily. Miraculously, no one drowns—fulfilling Paul's prediction the night before. Passengers and crew stay on the island for three months, where they are hospitably treated. There, Paul astonishes the inhabitants by surviving a deadly snakebite and by healing all the sick who are brought to him, including the father of the island leader. When spring of A.D. 60 arrives, Paul and his escort board an Egyptian ship bound for Rome. Luke is apparently with them throughout the harrowing journey, since he again uses the first-person plural to tell the story: "We set sail on a ship that had wintered at the island . . . . And so we came to Rome" (Acts 28:11, 14).

[Paul] lived there two whole years at his own expense . . . teaching about the Lord Jesus Christ with all boldness and without hindrance. ACTS 28:30

*B*ecause the Romans see Paul as nonthreatening, they allow him to rent private quarters, which they guard with a single soldier. This exceptional treatment is probably the result of favorable reports submitted by both Festus and Julius. Three days after his arrival, Paul invites Jewish leaders to his residence and tells them what has happened. Then, for a full day and into the evening, he introduces them to the teachings of Jesus. Afterward, the Jews debate among themselves and most reject Paul's ideas. The apostle's last words to them are a quote from Isaiah, accusing the Jews of being hard-hearted and spiritually deaf and blind: "You will indeed listen, but never understand, and you will indeed look, but never perceive" (Acts 28:26, quoting Isa 6:9-10).

Paul remains under house arrest for two years, but is allowed to welcome and teach all who visit. It is dur-

According to tradition, both Peter and Paul were martyred in Rome: Peter by being crucified upside down (left) and Paul by being beheaded (right). The two deaths are often paired, as in this page from an Italian choir book attributed to the workshop of Pacino di Buonaguida (1303-1339).

ing this imprisonment that Paul most likely writes several letters preserved in the New Testament, including letters to churches in Colossae and Ephesus, along with the short letter to Philemon about a runaway slave, in which Paul identifies himself as a prisoner.

Luke ends the story as a cliffhanger, without reporting the outcome of the trial for which Paul has been brought to Rome. Yet near the end of the book, Luke repeatedly hints of Paul's approaching death. The apostle to the Gentiles may have been executed in A.D. 62, immediately after his trial. As a Roman citizen, Paul had the right to a quick death, and was likely beheaded. Gaius, a second-century church leader, reports that Paul's grave marker could still be seen on Vatican hill, though another tradition holds that he died and was buried outside the city walls, a site now marked by an impressive basilica.

Writing to the Corinthians about A.D. 96, the Roman bishop Clement reports that Paul "went to the limit of the West"—perhaps a reference to Spain at the edge of the Roman Empire. In his letter to the Romans, Paul expresses a desire to preach there (Rom 15:24, 28). If Clement is correct, Paul may have been released after his imperial trial, traveled to Spain, rearrested on his return to Rome, and executed during Nero's persecution of Christians in A.D. 64—when a mysterious fire wiped out much of Rome. Lending support to this theory, Paul's letter to Philemon anticipates release from his imprisonment in Rome: "Prepare a guest room for me" (Philem 22). In addition, Paul's second letter to Timothy, seemingly written during a second arrest, speaks of imminent death: "The time of my departure has come. I have fought the good fight, I have finished the race, I have kept the faith" (2 Tim 4:6-7).

Paul's letter to the Romans is probably the most influential single letter written in the history of Western civilization. Its passion, vision, and reason seek to capture and convey the heart of the message of faith in Jesus Christ. It is not the earliest of Paul's surviving letters—that honor goes to 1 Thessalonians—but it is the longest and weightiest. Romans was evidently written from Corinth about A.D. 56, at the end of Paul's intense decade of proclaiming the message of Jesus and establishing Christian communities in the region of Asia Minor (modern Turkey) and Greece. Paul had become the leader in spreading the Gospel among Gentiles, while Peter and most of the original apostles seem to have concentrated primarily on Jewish populations.

Paul had grown up in a strict Jewish household, was trained as a Pharisee, and began his adult career as a fierce opponent of any who believed that a crucified man such as Jesus could be the Messiah. His dramatic conversion, however, convinced him that the faith he opposed was indeed the true one. That realization forced him to reconsider everything he thought he knew about God and his purposes, and to search the scriptures to understand how Jesus' story was connected to the history of God's chosen people. The letter to the Romans reflects the profound insight that Paul gained through God's revelation to him and his subsequent spiritual journey.

The fact that Paul's writing takes the form of a letter reflects his situation. Paul was a man on the move. He traveled from city to city, preaching the message of Jesus the Messiah. In most places he stayed only a few weeks or months, long enough to establish a community of believers and teach them the basics of their new way of life before moving on to the next city. When questions or difficulties arose in the new communities, the converts sent inquiries to Paul, and he responded by letter in Greek, the universal language of the day, often carried by one of his coworkers. The letter substituted for the absent Paul, and the coworker added a living voice to help deal with a problem. Paul's letters became versatile instruments of communication that combined personal elements with more formal theological instruction and exhortation. Romans leans decidedly to the more formal side of the scale, though it is clearly filled with emotion as well as argument.

Paul handing a letter to a disciple; a mosaic portrait from the 12th-century cathedral at Monreale in Sicily

---

For I am not ashamed of the gospel; it is the power of God for salvation to everyone who has faith, to the Jew first and also to the Greek. ROM 1:16

Paul's letter to the Romans is powerful and dramatic. Within what is preserved as the first chapter of Romans, Paul identifies the special roles played by himself and his readers, establishes the theme he will unfold, and begins the process of revealing God's plan for human salvation.

If Romans were a typical letter of its time, it might well have begun: "Paul to the Christians in Rome, Greetings. I pray that all things are well with you as they are with me." From Paul's pen such stereotyped words turn into several paragraphs that set the stage for the letter. Many of Paul's readers do not know him well and the way he identifies himself is important. He is the union of two identities, he says, first "a servant" (literally, "slave") of Jesus Christ and sec-

ond an "apostle," or emissary, specially commissioned to proclaim God's good news, or "gospel" (Rom 1:1). His message is about Jesus, who was both a human descendant of King David and the divine Son of God, who manifested the power of life over death. More specifically, Paul is assigned to proclaim this faith among "all the Gentiles" (Rom 1:5), the entire non-Jewish population of the known world. Every element of this self-description is important for Paul and helps define his task as he writes.

His readers are Christians (Paul calls them "saints," or holy ones) living in the capital of the mighty Roman Empire and thus, symbolically, at the very center of the Gentile population of the world. As greeting, Paul wishes them "grace" and "peace," words combining the core of the Christian message and the blessing of shalom, or peace, from the Hebrew scriptures. Paul elaborates his prayer of thanksgiving for the Romans to explain his plans to visit

Rome and to set the stage for his message. He is approaching the Romans as both a fellow believer, so they can learn from each other, and as an apostle with a special obligation to go to all Gentiles.

The central theme of his letter is spelled out in Romans 1:16-17, where Paul links together several major concepts that he will develop. For Paul the Gospel is far more than an enlightening teaching or a fascinating story; it is power—God's power to save humanity. That power becomes effective to everyone, regardless of background, who has faith. The Gospel of Jesus has this power because it reveals the righteousness of God, that is, God's way of putting people right with himself, a process that is wholly centered in faith or trust in Jesus. This pattern, Paul will argue, fulfills God's purposes already revealed in the ancient scriptures.

Therefore you have no excuse, whoever you are, when you judge others; for in passing judgment on another you condemn yourself. ROM 2:1

*P*aul's assertion that the Gospel is "the power of God for salvation" implies that humans need to be saved from something. After stating his theme, Paul immediately turns to the task of demonstrating that need, described as "the wrath of God" (Rom 1:16, 18) against evil. His goal is to show that all people share the same basic predicament before God, that a fundamental corruption enmeshes human life, and that all people are caught in the web of sin and cannot break free. He focuses on three situations to represent the breadth of this corrupting power.

First, Paul describes the corruption of pagan society, using arguments similar to those often used by his fellow Jews in that period to condemn the evils of idolatry. God has revealed much of "his eternal power and divine nature" (Rom 1:20) through his creation visible to all people. But many have chosen not to honor God but to make their own gods by worshiping images. Because they destroy the possibility of a relationship with the Lord, "God gave them up" (Rom 1:24, 26, 28), Paul thrice asserts, to a debased way of life as the manifestation of his wrath. Their sexual relations became depraved, Paul says, referring evidently to the pederasty and other immoral practices that were long associated with ancient Greek society. He also cites the other evils, from envy, gossip, and slander to ruthlessness and murder, that plague their lives.

Second, Paul turns to moralists, whether Gentiles or Jews, who affirm a higher moral standard and condemn the practices of others. Actions, not attitude, make the difference, he argues, and those who judge others fall into various practices of sin.

Third, Paul turns the focus on Jews like himself who believe that because they have received God's law from Moses, they are set apart in a higher category from the rest of humanity. Their "relation to God" is long established and they are confident that they are "a guide to the blind, a light to those who are in darkness, a corrector of the foolish" (Rom 2:17, 19-20). Paul asserts, however, that the scriptures themselves show that God's people have persistently and repeatedly broken and dishonored the law. The circumcision that was a sign of the covenant for male Jews needed to be more than an outward sign: "A person is a Jew who is one inwardly, and real circumcision is a matter of the heart—it is spiritual and not literal" (Rom 2:29).

For there is no distinction, since all have sinned and fall short of the glory of God; they are now justified by his grace as a gift, through the redemption that is in Christ Jesus. ROM 3:22-24

*T*he situation he describes is not new, Paul insists, but has been clearly taught in the scriptures. He and his fellow Jews have great advantages over other peoples in that God has chosen to give

The early Christians to whom Paul addressed his letters often faced persecution; those in Rome and Naples were forced to worship in underground cemeteries called catacombs.

them his revelation in the scriptures. But they have no advantage over any other peoples in that they have fallen into the same traps of sin as others. Their unfaithfulness stands in stark contrast to the faithfulness and justice of God, as revealed so often by the prophets. Thus, in spite of God-given advantages, Jews end up no better off than Gentiles, Paul argues; "all, both Jews and Greeks, are under the power of sin" (Rom 3:9). Paul piles up a series of statements from the psalms and prophets that drive home the general verdict that all are caught by sin: "There is no one who is righteous, not even one" (Rom 3:10; Ps 14:3). People are responsible for their actions and deserve condemnation, but they are also trapped by the enslaving power of sin and cannot free themselves, not even by the revelation of God's law, which brings "the knowledge of sin" (Rom 3:20).

Into this hopeless situation that no human being can change, God has intervened to reveal a new kind of righteousness. It is a fresh way for people to stand innocent before God and enjoy a loving relationship with him based not on what they have done but on what God has done in Jesus Christ. For Paul, the word "righteousness" (Greek, *dikaiosyne*) often expresses an action rather than a condition. It is closely related to the Greek word translated "justify" (*dikaioun*). Both draw on images from the law courts to describe God's action in declaring a person "not guilty" before him.

THE CHRONOLOGY OF PAUL'S LETTERS

Modern Bibles do not print Paul's letters in the order in which he wrote them—nor did ancient collections of his works. The oldest extant copy of Paul's letters is dated about A.D. 200; they are generally arranged from longest to shortest: Romans, Hebrews (no longer attributed to Paul), 1-2 Corinthians, Ephesians, Galatians, Philippians, Colossians, 1-2 Thessalonians, Philemon.

Attempts to reconstruct the order in which Paul wrote are based largely on clues within the letters and on the book of Acts. Most scholars agree that 1 Thessalonians is the oldest, written about A.D. 50, followed in a few months by 2 Thessalonians. Galatians is likely next, written after Paul established churches in Galatia on his second missionary journey about the year 52. Philippians and 1 and 2 Corinthians were perhaps written in 53-55. Paul composed his theological masterpiece, Romans, about 56, shortly before leaving for Jerusalem, where he was arrested. Colossians, Philemon, and Ephesians may have come around A.D. 60-61. The letters to Timothy and Titus are difficult to date.

The Gospel reveals "the righteousness of God through faith in Jesus Christ for all who believe" (Rom 3:22), that is, God pronounces a verdict of "not guilty" over all those who trust in Jesus. Since "all have sinned" and are in fact guilty, Paul argues, this verdict flows from God's own loving character: "They are now justified by his grace as a gift" (Rom 3:24).

In addition to images from the law court, Paul also uses metaphors from the slave market and the temple to point to what God has done through Jesus. When Paul speaks of "the redemption that is in Christ Jesus" (Rom 3:24), he alludes to the process of buying back or redeeming someone from slavery. Human beings cannot break their own chains, but God has cut through the shackles. From the temple, Paul draws the metaphor of "a sacrifice of atonement by his blood" (Rom 3:25). Jesus' crucifixion is seen as a sacrifice offered by God himself that covers and removes the guilt of sin.

All three images—the "not guilty" verdict, the redemption of the slave, and the sacrifice of atonement—reveal that salvation is God's action, and no human being can take credit. It is also unlimited in its scope, since the Lord is the God of all people.

What then are we to say was gained by Abraham, our ancestor according to the flesh? ROM 4:1

Paul is fully aware of how profoundly his insight into the scriptures has changed since his days as a Pharisee and an opponent of faith in Jesus, and he is conscious that many charge him with overturning the whole intent of the Law of Moses. But Paul believes that faith in Jesus has simply clarified his understanding of the scriptures and helped him understand the role God intended for the law to play.

The pattern of God justifying people by faith, Paul asserts, is not new but goes all the way back to the very beginning of the story of God's people—to Abraham. Paul highlights the account in Genesis, when God promised the elderly, childless man that his descendants would be numerous like the stars: "Abraham believed God, and it was reckoned to him as righteousness" (Rom 4:3; Gen 15:6). That statement, Paul believes, captures the essence of Abraham's relationship with God and the kind of relationship that God has always wanted with people. Abraham's sins are on bold display in Genesis: He could not claim to deserve God's favor. But by trusting a God who promised seemingly impossible blessings to a person who clearly did not deserve them, Abraham became the archetype of faith for all people.

All this happened, Paul notes, before the covenant of circumcision was established with Abraham as a sign of the law later given to Moses. Through his faith Abraham was not only the ancestor of the Jews, but also, as God explicitly promised, "the father of many nations" (Rom 4:17; Gen 17:5). In both Hebrew and Greek a single word is translated as either "nations" or "Gentiles," and thus Abraham is the father of all who share his faith. The fulfillment of God's promise

*Christians decorated their underground chapels with frescoes
such as this one in Rome showing Jesus seated among his disciples.*

to Abraham depends not on the virtue of his works, or it would have long since collapsed, but on the grace of the God he trusted; therefore, it is absolutely secure. The same ancient pattern, Paul says, applies now to those who trust the God who raised Jesus from the dead.

Therefore, since we are justified by faith, we have peace with God through our Lord Jesus Christ. ROM 5:1

Humanity needs the Gospel, Paul affirms, because it offers God's power for salvation from slavery to sin; he has defined its newness in contrast to salvation by works and its ancient roots that antedate the Law of Moses. Now Paul begins to unfold its effects as they are shaped by the particular way God has revealed himself in Jesus.

"Since we are justified by faith"—God has set us right with himself, based not on our deeds but on our trust in Jesus—our relationship to God is defined by peace rather than the wrath Paul had mentioned earlier. Because of Jesus we can stand confident before God and experience the open flow of his grace. All boastfulness in our lives is gone; rather, our pride is in what God has done in sharing his glory with humans. Even the suffering that we endure takes on a positive meaning because it builds a strength of character focused on hope beyond this world and shaped by God's trustworthy love, which "has been poured into our hearts through the Holy Spirit that has been given to us" (Rom 5:5).

Though he has told the story countless times, Paul still cannot mask his amazement at God's unconditional love as shown in Jesus bearing the brunt of our punishment for sin, when we are weak, ungodly, and hostile: "God proves his love for us in that while we still were sinners Christ died for us" (Rom 5:8). Since our reconciliation is based on God's own action in Jesus Christ, it is unshakable and sure.

Paul draws a contrast of types between Adam, as described in Genesis, and Jesus. As the first man and woman established the example of sin and death that became the defining pattern of human life—"death spread to all because all have sinned" (Rom 5:12)—so Christ broke the pattern by bringing life as a free gift from God to humanity. Sin and death had held dominion over humanity, but by Jesus freely giving his life and conquering death in his resurrection, that oppression was broken. "Just as sin exercised dominion in death," Paul says, "so grace might also exercise dominion through justification leading to eternal life through Jesus Christ our Lord" (Rom 5:21).

What then are we to say? Should we continue in sin in order that grace may abound? ROM 6:1

Paul now begins to drive home to his readers what his teaching thus far means for their daily lives. In a dialogue style that orators and writers of his day often used, Paul poses an objection that some readers may raise. Since grace is good and destroys sin, does not Paul's Gospel make it reasonable for a convert to sin more so that grace can multiply? The idea is that by arguing against salvation by human good deeds, Paul has undercut the motivation for people to live a moral life. Paul emphatically rejects any such idea.

The power of the Gospel lies in its story of Jesus' selfless love, with which Christians are called to identify both in thinking and in action. Paul begins with the practice of baptism, already well known to his readers. The immersion of baptism, as practiced in the early church, is for Paul an immersion into the very death of Jesus. The new Christian experiences in his life a transformation analogous to the death and resurrection of Jesus: "We have been buried with him by baptism into death, so that, just as Christ was raised from the dead by the glory of the Father, so we too might walk in newness of life" (Rom 6:4). A new moral life begins immediately because "whoever has died is freed from sin" (Rom 6:7).

Paul speaks of "sin" in the singular, as a personified power in opposition to God, an enslaving master so strong that only death can set one free: "You also must consider yourselves dead to sin and alive to God in Christ Jesus" (Rom 6:11). But until the final resurrection, sin still battles to take back its slaves. Thus, Paul calls his readers to engage in the moral struggle to let the reality created by their baptism be fulfilled in their daily lives. Every human being is under one master or the other, either serving sin, who pays his servants with death, or serving God, who gives the free gift of "eternal life in Christ Jesus our Lord" (Rom 6:23).

Wretched man that I am! Who will rescue me from this body of death? Thanks be to God through Jesus Christ our Lord! ROM 7:24-25

Paul now turns to what is for his fellow Jews the most difficult and controversial element of his argument—the relation of the Law of Moses to sin. He has talked of death freeing the believer from slavery to sin; now he extends the analogy to freedom from the binding effects of the law, using the example of marriage responsibilities ending with the death of a spouse. Just as participation in the death of Christ has freed one from sin, Paul argues, so also "you have died to the law through the body of Christ" (Rom 7:4).

But Paul goes further to describe how sinful passions are "aroused by the law" and "work in our members to bear fruit for death." Being "discharged from the law," he says, is an essential part of breaking the slavery that "held us captive" so that we can live "the new life of the Spirit" (Rom 7:5-6). Paul immediately recognizes that many will object that he is giving the law the same role as sin. Not so, Paul responds, but the law does reveal sin's character and power and sin is able to make use of the law for its own purposes. Paul uses the last of the Ten Commandments—"You shall not covet"—to explain his meaning from personal experience. Sin's enslaving power is such that it can use the very commandment that condemns covetousness to produce "in me all kinds of covetousness" (Rom 7:7, 8).

The problem lies in the human being's fundamental susceptibility to sin's power—a weakness that Paul symbolizes by the term "flesh" in contrast to "spirit," which is life empowered by God's presence. The law can delight the mind with its holiness and beauty but it does not free a person from enslavement to sin because of the flesh. Even the most high-minded person is left with an insoluble conflict, Paul says. A new way of life, not based on the old law, so abused by sin, is needed to overcome the power of sin.

For you did not receive a spirit of slavery to fall back into fear, but you have received a spirit of adoption. When we cry, "Abba! Father!" it is that very Spirit bearing witness with our spirit that we are children of God. ROM 8:15-16

God sent his only son in human form to break the power of sin and to give human life new power by his spirit, Paul affirms. Those who live according to the spirit fulfill the requirement of the law without the vulnerability of the law to sin. Thus, the believer is set on a new and powerful course of life strengthened by the spirit. But

moral struggle never ceases in this world, as sin tries to reclaim its slave. However, as frustration and defeat were inevitable before, God now offers a new reality: "You are not in the flesh; you are in the Spirit, since the Spirit of God dwells in you" (Rom 8:9).

The believer is led by the spirit in a confident new life without the former slavery and fear of defeat. The spirit allows the believer to experience special intimacy with the Lord and to address God like a child, "Abba" (meaning something like "Papa" or "Daddy"). The spirit empowers a moral life in which sin is destroyed and even the sufferings that believers have to face anticipate the glory of God's future redemption of his entire creation. Prayer takes on new power as the spirit participates in the believers' prayers "with sighs too deep for words" (Rom 8:26).

Under sin's power everything, no matter how good, ended in evil. Now God is able to turn everything, no matter how bad, toward good. Nothing can stand against the power of God's grace: "If God is for us, who is against us?" God has shown his determination to save by giving "his own Son" (Rom 8:31, 32). For one who trusts God, Paul triumphantly concludes, nothing, absolutely nothing "in all creation, will be able to separate us from the love of God in Christ Jesus our Lord" (Rom 8:39).

They are Israelites, and to them belong the adoption, the glory, the covenants, the giving of the law, the worship, and the promises. ROM 9:4

Paul begins a distinctly new section of the letter in chapter 9, dealing with a problem that is of intense interest to himself and many other Christians of his day, especially Jewish Christians. How could it be that so many Jews, who study the same scriptures that Paul does, reject the message of Jesus as Messiah while the Gentiles flock to it? This causes Paul "great sorrow and unceasing anguish" (Rom 9:2) because he longs for all his fellow Jews to share the joy he has in his faith. In explaining the background and meaning of this reality, Paul develops several points.

First, he emphasizes that the promises God made to Abraham and the people of Israel have not failed. God's promises were never simply to physical descendants. They always involved God's sovereign right to select the recipients of his promises, just as he chose Isaac over Ishmael, Jacob over Esau. They also involved God's right to respond to the faith or faithlessness of the people and to offer his promise to "only a remnant of them" (Rom 9:27; Isa 10:22). Israel's quest for righteousness before the Lord had gone awry, Paul argues,

Jesus and the Samaritan woman at the well, an incident from the Gospel of John, decorates a Roman catacomb.

"because they did not strive for it on the basis of faith, but as if it were based on works" (Rom 9:32). They missed "the righteousness that comes from God" (Rom 10:3) and tried to create their own righteousness from the law. But Christ, the Messiah they sought, "is the end of the law," Paul asserts; "if you confess with your lips that Jesus is Lord and believe in your heart that God raised him from the dead, you will be saved" (Rom 10:4, 9). The message of Christ has gone out, and, if many in Israel who should have responded positively to it do not, that reaction is simply the repetition of a pattern found again and again in the prophets: "All day long I have held out my hands to a disobedient and contrary people" (Rom 10:21; Isa 65:2).

I ask, then, has God rejected his people? By no means! I myself am an Israelite, a descendant of Abraham, a member of the tribe of Benjamin. ROM 11:1

*I*srael's refusal to follow the Messiah does not mean that God has rejected his people. As there had been so many times in the past, "so too at the present time there is a remnant, chosen by grace" and not "on the basis of works" (Rom 11:5, 6). This remnant, within which Paul sees himself, enjoys the fulfillment of the Lord's promises. Others temporarily stumble over the unexpected character of the message of Jesus. Their opposition—such as Paul himself had formerly led—drove believers to take the message of Jesus to the Gentiles and thus opened up "riches for the world" (Rom 11:12). Paul hopes and believes that the very success of his tireless missionary work among the Gentiles will in turn stimulate many of his fellow Jews to see their error and trust in God's Messiah.

Paul warns the Gentiles to whom he is writing that they are like branches of a wild olive tree grafted into a cultivated trunk "to share the rich root of the olive tree" (Rom 11:17). Paul believes that the scriptures indicate that not only will "the full number of the Gentiles" come to faith, but that ultimately "all Israel will be saved" (Rom 11:25, 26). God's ways are rich and deep, Paul concludes; ultimately "from him and through him and to him are all things. To him be the glory forever, Amen" (Rom 11:36).

I appeal to you therefore, brothers and sisters, by the mercies of God, to present your bodies as a living sacrifice, holy and acceptable to God, which is your spiritual worship. ROM 12:1

*I*n the third major section of his letter, Paul begins to urge and exhort the Romans toward a practical way of life that is based on the message of Jesus Christ. He begins with an appeal that expresses the basic thrust of all that will follow. He appeals to believers, as recipients of so many manifestations of God's mercy, to give themselves to God as a living sacrifice, that is, to live a life of holiness before God. In this way their entire lives become acts of worship

Still vivid after 2,000 years, scenes from the life of Jesus adorn the chapel of a Roman catacomb.

flowing from heart and mind. They must resist the pressure of society all around them to form and mold their values and actions. Instead, they must allow God to transform their lives by shaping a new way of thinking within themselves so that they can begin to perceive and understand God's will and realize how right and true it is. For Paul, the Gospel remakes a person from the inside out, beginning from the deep values of heart and mind and moving outward into action that manifests the transformation.

Paul urges the Romans to take especially seriously their life as a community that forms "one body in Christ" with "many members" that have "gifts that differ according to the grace given to us" (Rom 12:4-6). In such a community they must "love one another with mutual affection; outdo one another in showing honor," share their prayers and hopes, avoid any haughty class consciousness or any tendency to take revenge—in short, "live peaceably with all" (Rom 12:10, 18). Paul urges believers to live a quiet life of obedience and honor toward the imperial Roman government, though Paul's own life ultimately led him to such conflict with that government that he was executed in Rome.

He urges the faithful to guide their actions not by detailed regulations but by central values, such as love for one's neighbor, that incorporate all other values. Fundamentally, the goal in their ethical and moral lives is following Jesus so that they "put on the Lord Jesus Christ" (Rom 13:14) as they would an all-encompassing garment.

Who are you to pass judgment on servants of another? It is before their own lord that they stand or fall. And they will be upheld, for the Lord is able to make them stand.
ROM 14:4

In the final portion of his exhortations, Paul addresses a perennial problem that vexed early Christian congregations. People came into the community from highly diverse backgrounds with different religious sensibilities. Some grew up in Jewish families; some came from traditional Roman or Greek households where many gods were worshiped. When they became believers, some rejected the eating of meat as a matter of conscience (perhaps because most meat sold in Roman markets came from animals slaughtered in the temples); for others, the observance or nonobservance of certain holidays was an important issue. How was the community to handle problems in which one person believed an issue to be a matter of right and wrong while another instead saw it as a matter of opinion and freedom?

Paul urges mutual acceptance and respect for each other's consciences. He does not demand that all agree on issues or take the point of view that he himself thinks is right: "I know and am persuaded in the Lord Jesus that nothing is unclean in itself; but it is unclean for anyone who thinks it unclean" (Rom 14:14). He urges believers to avoid two things: passing judgment on each other and doing things that will cause another person to go against his or her conscience. Each person is responsible for his own actions before God, and no one has the right to take the role of God in judging anyone else. The people must keep clear about priorities: "The kingdom of God is not food and drink but righteousness and peace and joy in the Holy Spirit" (Rom 14:17).

Each believer is responsible for the good of the others in the community—for "walking in love" and pursuing "what makes for peace and for mutual upbuilding" (Rom 14:15, 19). The righteous should follow the example of Christ's selfless love, Paul asserts, and "welcome one another . . . just as Christ has welcomed you, for the glory of God" (Rom 15:7). Christ served and united Jews and Gentiles in one community so that all people might glorify God.

I commend to you our sister Phoebe, a deacon of the church at Cenchreae, so that you may welcome her in the Lord as is fitting for the saints. ROM 16:1-2

In the final portion of his letter, Paul deals with a number of practical concerns that surround the sending of this letter to the church in Rome. He touches again on his special ministry to the Gentiles, which provides his reason for boldness in writing to a church that he does not know well. He then turns to the scope of his past missionary work and the philosophy that guided it. He has been commissioned to proclaim "the good news of Christ" among the Gentiles and has done so "from Jerusalem and as far around as Illyricum [modern Albania]" (Rom 15:19). Paul has always tried to open new geographical areas for the Gospel "so that I do not build on someone else's foundation" (Rom 15:20). That same philosophy is now calling him to Spain, a territory where the Gospel had not yet been preached. Paul plans to stop in Rome on his way to Spain and hopes "to be sent on by you, once I have enjoyed your company for a little while" (Rom 15:24).

Only one task remains for Paul to complete his work in the east. He must take to Jerusalem the gifts of money gathered in the churches in Greece for the poor believers in Judea. He is aware that danger awaits him in Jerusalem, but prays that his "ministry to Jerusalem may be acceptable to the saints" (Rom 15:31) so that he can come to Rome with joy. In fact, Paul is arrested in Jerusalem and because of corrupt officials in Judea eventually arrives in Rome as a prisoner accused of sedition.

The letter concludes with a recommendation for Phoebe, a church deacon at the Corinthian seaport of Cenchreae, "a benefactor of many and of myself as well" (Rom 16:2). Phoebe may well have been the one who carried the letter to Rome. The number of those to whom Paul sends greetings is so great that some scholars suggest that this chapter may have been intended for the church in Ephesus, where Paul knew everyone; the chapter was appended to a copy of the letter to Rome that he shared with the Ephesians. It is perhaps more likely, however, that in writing to a church such as that in Rome, Paul would try to mention every person that he knew there. The

Paul in manacles is being led to his death in this detail from a 4th-century marble sarcophagus in Rome.

list gives a vivid insight into those men and women who were the hands and feet of Paul's ministry: "Greet Mary, who has worked very hard among you. Greet Andronicus and Junia, my relatives, who were in prison with me; they are prominent among the apostles, and they were in Christ before I was" (Rom 16:6-7). At the end, Tertius, Paul's scribe, who evidently wrote the letter as the apostle dictated it, adds his greeting.

Paul's final words are praise "to God who is able to strengthen you," to "the only wise God, through Jesus Christ, to whom be the glory forever! Amen" (Rom 16:25, 27). The scroll was copied, rolled, sealed, and sent off by Phoebe to Rome. The ripples of its influence continue to surge across the world to this day.

THE FIRST LETTER OF PAUL TO THE CORINTHIANS

No church was closer to Paul's heart or caused him more anxiety than the one he founded in Corinth, the capital of the Roman province of Achaia. Corinth was an ancient city, but it had been totally destroyed by Roman armies in 146 B.C. After a century in ruins, Corinth was rebuilt in 44 as a Roman colony. Paul first preached the message of Jesus in Corinth during an 18-month sojourn there in A.D. 50-51, during which he built a principally Gentile congregation in this commercial center of southern Greece (Acts 18:1-18).

After the church was firmly established, Paul moved on to other regions, especially across the Aegean Sea to the large city of Ephesus, where he spent more than two years. During that time Paul began to hear disturbing reports about the Christian community in Corinth. Although he wrote the congregation a letter of instruction, which is now lost, he continued to hear of difficulties, especially from members of the household of a Christian woman named Chloe. There were deep problems of division and competition among the Christians, with some claiming superiority over others because of their spiritual experiences. Paul was stimulated to write a second letter— preserved in the New Testament as 1 Corinthians—when the church in Corinth sent him a letter with a series of specific questions about some of the group's most serious concerns.

No letter gives a more vivid picture of life inside a first-century Christian community than 1 Corinthians. In its pages can be seen the believers' enthusiasm, their struggles, and their attempts to understand a new religious and social order, different from either the Jewish or Greco-Roman cultures in which they had been reared. The letter also reveals Paul's attempts to guide them in building their community, based on his understanding of the fundamental values of faith in Jesus Christ. This was a time of excitement and danger for all involved, since so many of the foundation stones of Christianity were in the process of being laid and the ultimate character of the whole movement seemed to be at stake.

Paul with the instrument of his death, a sword; by Tommaso Guidi, known as Masaccio (1401-1428)

'Paul, called to be an apostle of Christ Jesus by the will of God, and our brother Sosthenes, to the church of God that is in Corinth, to those who are sanctified in Christ Jesus, called to be saints.   1 COR 1:1-2

Paul opens his letter to the Corinthians with the basic elements with which he begins each letter: the names of the senders and recipients, greeting, thanksgiving. He emphasizes his own ministry as an apostle "called . . . by the will of God" and adds the name of Sosthenes, evidently a leading Jew in Corinth, who has been converted to faith in Jesus and who has perhaps brought news of the Corinthian Christians to Paul (Acts 18:17). Paul stresses the link of the Corinthian church to all other Christian communities and emphasizes that they all have been made holy by Jesus.

Paul surely knows how many criticisms and corrections he will level at the Corinthians, but he begins the body of the letter with words of thanksgiving that express a deep sense of assurance that the Corinthians' growth in faith will end well. But Paul is careful to build his confidence not on his own effectiveness in teaching or the Corinthians' responsiveness but on the gifts and faithfulness of God.

As the Corinthians have come to faith, they have experienced many gifts of God's grace that have filled them with a sense of abundance and power in their new spirit-filled lives. Paul expresses complete confidence that God's strength and faithfulness will bring them through their difficulties "blameless on the day of our Lord Jesus Christ" (1 Cor 1:8).

Paul, however, immediately focuses on the core of their problems: a misapprehension of the central message of the Gospel, the meaning of Jesus' death and resurrection, that has allowed the whole series of troubles that are plaguing them to break out. For Paul, the presence of divisions among the Corinthians is obvious evidence of that misunderstanding. The fact that they are aligning themselves in groups according to affinities with a particular teacher—Paul, Apollos (Acts 18:24-19:1), Cephas (Peter), or even

Christ himself—demonstrates that the Corinthians have not grasped the basic tenet of the transforming power in their lives: Jesus dying on the cross for them. The status or eloquence of the one who has taught or baptized them makes no difference at all in their identity as believers.

We proclaim Christ crucified, a stumbling block to Jews and foolishness to Gentiles, but to those who are the called, both Jews and Greeks, Christ the power of God and the wisdom of God.   1 COR 1:23-24

For Paul, "the message about the cross" (1 Cor 1:18) is the defining center of Christian faith. All theology, ethics, spiritual experience, organizational structure, or other aspect of Christianity is shaped by that central reality.

In earlier days, when Paul as a Pharisee had tried to destroy the church (Acts 8:3, 9:21, 22:4; Gal 1:13), he found particularly offensive the idea that God's Messiah (anointed one) could be so weak or defeated as to be executed in a brutal, unjust, and shameful crucifixion carried out by pagan Romans. The idea of a crucified Messiah seemed an absolute contradiction in terms. But the revelation that Paul experienced on the road to Damsacus convinced him that Jesus was indeed God's Messiah (Acts 9:3-6, 17-20; Gal 1:15-16). Paul realized that everything he had formerly understood about the character of God and the way God works in the world had to be refocused through the lens of Jesus' crucifixion as the ultimate revelation. To believe that the Lord of all creation chose to reveal his self-giving love, grace, and power in an event that seemed so full of shame, injustice, suffering, and weakness turned the world and its values upside down for Paul.

But that strange and unexpected message of the cross, Paul has learned, is filled with God's own power to transform the lives of those who trust in what he has done in Jesus. It stands in stark contrast to traditional Jewish expectations of a Messiah, and thus is "a stumbling block to Jews," one that Paul himself had previously encountered. It has none of the elements of divine might or philosophical elevation that impress the Greeks, and thus seems sheer "foolishness" to many Gentiles. Such evaluations only demonstrate to Paul, however, how far the world's perceptions fall short of grasping the eternal reality of God.

To trust in "Christ crucified" is to move into a new world in which what appears scandalous and foolish is seen to be the embodiment of God's wisdom and power. Human standards of status, nobility, strength, and wisdom no longer apply, the apostle argues. Indeed, the God who created the world out of nothing again "chose what is low and despised in the world,

Ruins of a temple at Corinth, site of one of Christianity's first churches

things that are not, to reduce to nothing things that are" (1 Cor 1:28). God has chosen to give people life through the death of Jesus, who thereby became the embodiment of "wisdom from God, and righteousness and sanctification and redemption" (1 Cor 1:30).

Nothing about the heart of Christian faith can be understood without clearly realizing the centrality of the message of the cross. Thus, Paul says, when he first came to the Corinthians, he offered them nothing "except Jesus Christ, and him crucified" (1 Cor 2:2).

According to the grace of God given to me, like a skilled master builder I laid a foundation, and someone else is building on it.   1 COR 3:10

The problems of division in Corinth, Paul believes, stem from the fact that the Christians are still relying on the competitive values and self-promotion that are common in the world around them but are alien to the values of their faith. They see themselves as spiritually wise and mature, but Paul assures them that the message of the cross that he has proclaimed to them is indeed profound divine wisdom "taught by the Spirit" and understood by "those who are spiritual" (1 Cor 2:13, 15). Their divisions and allegiances to human teachers show such a failure to comprehend the core of the message that the apostle feels driven to an ironical and tragic conclusion: "I could not speak to you as spiritual people, but rather as people of the flesh, as infants in Christ" (1 Cor 3:1).

But again, ironically, their problem is not that they have evaluated themselves too highly but rather too lowly. They see their status and position as personal achievement and thus feel elevated by aligning themselves under seemingly important and powerful teachers such as Paul or Apollos. But Paul emphasizes that both he and Apollos are simply servants of God with particular commissions to fulfill and with no status to impart to anyone. They are builders laying the foundation and erecting communities of faith that are God's temple. But only God's spirit dwelling among the people makes it holy.

If the Christians at Corinth can escape the competitive wisdom of the age and "become fools so that you may become wise" (1 Cor 3:18), they will learn that their true status as believers is a far higher calling than being subordinate to any teacher. Paul challenges them to see that "all things are yours, whether Paul or Apollos or Cephas or the world or life or death or the present or the future—all belong to you, and you belong to Christ, and Christ belongs to God" (1 Cor 3:21-23).

For though you might have ten thousand guardians in Christ, you do not have many fathers. Indeed, in Christ Jesus I became your father through the gospel. 1 COR 4:15

The Corinthians' behavior, Paul believes, shows that they are living too much with the irrelevant, reversed values of the culture around them and have not allowed the Gospel to turn their vision right side up. They need to see leaders such as Paul or Apollos not as rival centers of personal or political power but as servants to whom God has assigned roles of responsibility as "stewards of God's mysteries" (1 Cor 4:1). Paul's duty is to be trustworthy before the Lord, not before any group of human judges—including the Corinthians.

The Corinthians are certainly excited by what they have experienced in their new faith as they feel the power of many spiritual gifts. But they have come to treat these experiences as though they are personal achievements rather than gifts from God. Indeed, they evidently interpret their experiences as demonstrations that they have already attained the life of the world to come, reigning as kings, spiritually self-sufficient and without responsibility to serve others. Paul uses deeply ironic language to try to bring the Corinthians to their senses. From the world's point of view, represented by their self-centered understanding of their experiences, the life of the apostles is like that of men "sentenced to death" in a public spectacle. "We are fools for the sake of Christ, but you are wise in Christ," Paul chides, pricking their bubble of self-importance. "We are weak, but you are strong" (1 Cor 4:9, 10). The very apostles whom the Corinthians cite to give themselves status live lives of service that embody the cross of Christ. They look forward to the coming age, but now define their lives by the self-sacrifice of Jesus: "hungry and thirsty . . . poorly clothed . . . beaten and homeless . . . weary from the work of our own hands. When reviled, we bless; when persecuted, we endure; when slandered, we speak kindly" (1 Cor 4:11-13).

Paul realizes how sharply his challenge may cut the hearts of the Corinthians, and he concludes with words of tenderness, calling them his "beloved children." Paul is in a unique relationship to them as their "father through the gospel," and he has the responsibility to help them turn from the arrogant talk of power that has so distorted their understanding of their faith, and to direct them toward the reality of power in a life of service such as the apostles manifest. "I appeal to you, then," he declares, "be imitators of me" (1 Cor 4:14-16).

For though absent in body, I am present in spirit; and as if present I have already pronounced judgment in the name of the Lord Jesus. 1 COR 5:3-4

The depth of the misunderstanding in Corinth becomes more obvious as Paul turns to a specific problem. In Paul's first, now lost, letter to them, he had urged the Corinthians "not to associate with sexually immoral persons" (1 Cor 5:9). Their peculiar distortion of their faith has evidently led the Corinthians to interpret Paul's instruction to mean that they should cut themselves off from sinful nonbelievers and thus isolate their community. But—and this is a big exception—they believe that they themselves are already experiencing the world to come, and thus conventional laws of morality can be suspended within their community. Therefore, when one man among them begins "living with his father's wife [his divorced or widowed stepmother]" (1 Cor 5:1), a practice condemned by both Jewish and Gentile law and thus scandalous to the society, the church does not discipline him but defends him, evidently on the grounds of spiritual freedom. "You are arrogant!" Paul says in astonishment. "Should you not rather have mourned, so that he who has done this would have been removed from among you?" (1 Cor 5:2).

Paul insists that this man be formally excluded from their community, handed over to Satan, so that through the experience of this discipline "his spirit may be saved in the day of the Lord" (1 Cor 5:5). Paul is even more concerned,

An 18th-century Italian painter imagined Paul preaching at Corinth among ruins more typical of his own period than that of the apostle.

however, with the attitude of the church toward willful sin among their members. He applies the message about the cross to this situation by comparing Jesus to the lamb sacrificed at Passover, a time when every Israelite home has to be cleansed of all forms of yeast, which he compares to their sin and boasting: "Let us celebrate the festival, not with the old yeast, the yeast of malice and evil, but with the unleavened bread of sincerity and truth" (1 Cor 5:8).

As for nonbelievers outside their community, Paul urges the Corinthians not to judge them or avoid interacting with them "since you would then need to go out of the world" (1 Cor 5:10), but also not to allow them to judge matters of dispute within the church community by bringing lawsuits against each other. The community needs to show enough wisdom to be able to deal with disputes among the believers. Indeed, the severity of the disputes shows that a spirit of competition and individualism is weakening the Christian community: "To have lawsuits at all with one another is already a defeat for you. Why not rather be wronged? Why not rather be defrauded? But you yourselves wrong and defraud—and believers at that" (1 Cor 6:7-8).

Paul may have entered Corinth via this shop-lined road from the port; in the background, the 2,000-foot-high rock on which stood the city's acropolis.

"All things are lawful for me," but not all things are beneficial. "All things are lawful for me," but I will not be dominated by anything. 1 COR 6:12

The Corinthians evidently justify their actions by using the slogan, "All things are lawful for me." This statement was likely drawn from pronouncements about Christian freedom that Paul himself had made to them (for example, Rom 6:15; Gal 2:19). But some in Corinth have interpreted freedom to mean that any action, from fraud to fornication, is permitted; to them, Christianity offers not freedom from sin but freedom to sin.

Paul affirms freedom from the domination of law, but insists that the message of the cross and the experience of the Holy Spirit must define a Christian's actions. Each one needs to realize that sexual relations with a prostitute is totally unacceptable because "your body is a temple of the Holy Spirit" and "you were bought with a price" (1 Cor 6:19, 20)—the price of Christ's death. In teaching them about proper sexual relations, Paul urges husbands and wives to be mutually concerned for the needs of the other. They should not practice sexual abstinence, as some rigorists among the Corinthians are evidently doing, "except perhaps by agreement for a set time" (1 Cor 7:5) for spiritual purposes.

Early Christian symbols: Eucharistic bread and a fish for the name Jesus

In response to a question in a letter (also lost) from the Corinthians, Paul commends to them the single life that he himself has followed, but indicates that it requires "a particular gift from God" (1 Cor 7:7) to remain single and maintain self-control and purity. Paul teaches that it is completely acceptable for Christian men and women to marry and rear families. But he believes that the church faces a time of "impending crisis" so severe that he associates it with the end of the age, as "the present form of this world is passing away" (1 Cor 7:26, 31). In such a crisis, Paul tells the Corinthians, it is better not to make major changes in their relationships by getting married or going through other transitions: "it is well for you to remain as you are" (1 Cor 7:26). Paul evidently believes that the final judgment of the righteous and unrighteous is at hand.

Now concerning food sacrificed to idols: we know that "all of us possess knowledge." Knowledge puffs up, but love builds up. 1 COR 8:1

The topic of food sacrificed to idols seems alien to modern readers of 1 Corinthians, but the underlying issues of conscience, freedom, and loving concern for other people are perennial. Most meat sold in open markets in Corinth came from sacrifices offered in various Greek temples in the city. Such meat was forbidden to Jews both because it was not kosher and because it was tainted with idolatry. For Gentiles who became believers, the same meat was also unacceptable because it reminded them too powerfully of their former lives as pagans. Some Corinthian Christians insisted on eating the meat, however, because of their knowledge that the pagan gods had no existence and could not affect the meat in any way.

As before, Paul agrees with their slogan but parts company with the Corinthians on its application. More important than the arrogant assertion of individual knowledge, he says, is the practice of love that strengthens the whole community. Love recognizes the tender consciences of other believers and knows that no one ever does right by going against conscience. Love takes care not to exercise liberty in such a way as to hurt others; otherwise, knowledge and liberty, valuable as they are, become destructive as well as sinful: "By your knowledge those weak believers for whom Christ died are destroyed" (1 Cor 8:11).

Paul shows that in his own ministry he has given them an example of voluntarily limiting the exercise of freedom in order to benefit others. As the apostle who founded the church in Corinth, he has every right to expect that the Corinthians will financially support his work. Instead, he has labored as a craftsman (at Corinth Paul lived and worked with fellow tent makers Aquila and Priscilla) in order to support himself and thus offers "the gospel free of charge" (1 Cor 9:18). Indeed, he has adapted himself in every imaginable way to the varied cultures he has encountered in order to help people hear the message he brings: "I have become all things to all people, that I might by all means save some" (1 Cor 9:22).

No testing has overtaken you that is not common to everyone. God is faithful, and he will not let you be tested beyond your strength, but with the testing he will also provide the way out so that you may be able to endure it.
1 COR 10:13

*S*ome of the Corinthians evidently believe that they do not need to worry about hurting each other because their participation in the rites of baptism and the Lord's Supper gives them complete protection from the effects of sin. Paul uses the examples of ancient Israel to warn against such overconfidence: "So if you think you are standing, watch out that you do not fall" (1 Cor 10:12). God will indeed strengthen them in the face of temptation, but they must not minimize the struggle. The Lord's Supper, the apostle is forced to remind them, is "a sharing in the blood of Christ" and "the body of Christ" (1 Cor 10:16) and must not be used to defend actions that contradict the sacrificial love of Jesus. Therefore, they must take issues of conscience such as that concerning food sacrificed to idols with all seriousness and exercise their freedom and knowledge in a way that genuinely builds up the whole community: "Do not seek your own advantage, but that of the other" (1 Cor 10:24).

Thus, they may exercise their liberty and knowledge fully within the framework of love: "So, whether you eat or drink, or whatever you do, do everything for the glory of God" (1 Cor 10:31).

Examine yourselves, and only then eat of the bread and drink of the cup. For all who eat and drink without discerning the body, eat and drink judgment against themselves. 1 COR 11:28-29

*P*aul next turns to two practical topics within the church at Corinth. The first deals with the head coverings worn by men and women in the assembly. Appropriate head coverings conveyed to people of that day a sense of reverence, order, and propriety; the flouting of custom brought shame, a sense of immorality, and scandal. The specific problem has to do with women who are exercising their spiritual gifts by praying and prophesying publicly in the assemblies. In both Jewish synagogues and Greek or Roman assemblies, such public participation by women was practically unknown and was considered scandalous. Paul deals with the problem by urging both men and women not to defy convention but show that they recognize propriety and honor the sensibilities of others by wearing the head coverings defined by tradition. Then both men and women may exercise the call to pray and prophesy as the spirit leads them.

More serious for Paul are the abuses that have accumulated around the Lord's Supper as it is practiced in Corinth. The Lord's Supper is evidently celebrated by the Christians there as part of a larger meal. But so much division and competition has marred the Corinthian community that one group will be feasting while poorer members go hungry. Such a situation shows "contempt for the church of God" (1 Cor 11:22) and humiliates the poor.

Paul had to remind the Corinthians of the meaning of the Lord's Supper, depicted here in a 15th-century French Bible.

*The resurrection of the dead; a
late-12th-century gilded copper enamel*

Paul reminds the Corinthians of the tradition he has taught them of Jesus instituting the supper on the night he was betrayed. He called the bread his body and the cup his blood, and thus in the Lord's Supper Christians "proclaim the Lord's death until he comes" (1 Cor 11:26). It is crucial, therefore, that in participating in the supper, the Corinthians discern the fact that they are the body of Christ and must be united in caring for each other.

*Now there are varieties of gifts, but the same Spirit;
and there are varieties of services, but the same Lord.*
1 COR 12:4-5

The next major section of Paul's letter deals with the gifts of the Holy Spirit, gifts of grace that the Corinthians have experienced with such delight in their new faith. It is one of the great ironies of their situation that even the most positive and powerful element of their experience has been turned to destructive effect by their divisions and internal competition. They have focused on the gift of ecstatic speech—speaking "in tongues" (1 Cor 12:30)—as the most important gift, and evidently denigrate those who do not share that experience.

Paul emphasizes that the gifts of the Holy Spirit show great variety but come from a single source; all come from "the same Spirit . . . the same Lord . . . the same God" (1 Cor 12:4-6). Every believer receives some particular "manifestation of the Spirit for the common good" (1 Cor 12:7), and there is no place for competition among believers. Together the believers form "the body of Christ" (1 Cor 12:27), and like a body they have many parts with many different functions and each with its own importance. As Paul lists some of the Holy Spirit's varied gifts, he places speaking in tongues near the bottom in importance—after teaching, helping, healing, and leading—and urges the Corinthians to "strive for the greater gifts" (1 Cor 12:31).

But neither greater nor lesser gifts have any meaning, Paul proclaims, except within the sphere of love—"the more excellent way" (1 Cor 12:31). Even if one person can combine every spiritual gift and virtue—tongues, prophecy, understanding, knowledge, faith, generosity, even martyrdom—all the rest will amount to nothing if love is missing.

Love is divine power manifested not in exalted mystic experiences but in everyday life. It shows itself in patience and kindness, in avoiding boasting, arrogance, selfishness, and resentment. It believes, hopes, and endures without fail.

The Corinthians think that in their ecstatic experiences they feel the power of the age to come. Not so, Paul says. Spiritual gifts are manifestations only for this age, aids to our limited, childish capacities. Only "faith, hope, and love" truly last, and "the greatest of these," giving meaning to all the others, "is love" (1 Cor 13:13).

*Pursue love and strive for the spiritual gifts, and
especially that you may prophesy.*   1 COR 14:1

Paul sees some of the Corinthians' misperceptions of the Holy Spirit's work in the fact that they give greater prominence in their assemblies to speaking in ecstatic tongues than to prophecy. For Paul, both are valid manifestations of the Holy Spirit, but they have very different purposes. Speaking in tongues is a private ecstatic experience that cannot genuinely be shared since "those who speak in a tongue do not speak to other people but to God; for nobody understands them" (1 Cor 14:2). By contrast prophecy is aimed at sharing God's will in a practical way with the whole community: "Those who prophesy speak to other people for their upbuilding and encouragement and consolation" (1 Cor 14:3). Tongues have their place in private devotions, Paul suggests, but in the assembly of believers "I would rather speak five words with my mind, in order to instruct others also, than ten thousand words in a tongue" (1 Cor 14:19).

The assembly is not to be a place for divisive competition in showing off impressive or mysterious gifts; it must be focused on effective guidance for believers and clear and convincing teaching to outsiders so that they will understand all that is said and "bow down before God and worship him, declaring, 'God is really among you'" (1 Cor 14:25).

In order for their assemblies to be effective in building up the church, Paul urges, "all things should be done decently and in order" (1 Cor 14:40). The impulse of the Holy Spirit should not be used as an excuse for confusion and disorder. Speaking in tongues should be limited. Prophets should speak one at a time and not compete with each other. Women who are using their new freedom to disrupt the assembly with challenging questions to their husbands and other men should ask the questions at home and not disturb the assembly. "Let all things be done," Paul says, "for building up" (1 Cor 14:26).

Listen, I will tell you a mystery! We will not all die, but we will all be changed, in a moment, in the twinkling of an eye, at the last trumpet. For the trumpet will sound, and the dead will be raised imperishable, and we will be changed. 1 COR 15:51-52

In the final section of his letter, Paul returns to the core of the Gospel to draw out its meaning for Christian hopes beyond this life. He stresses that the fundamental proclamation is the story "that Christ died for our sins in accordance with the scriptures, and that he was buried, and that he was raised on the third day in accordance with the scriptures, and that he appeared to Cephas [Peter], then to the twelve" (1 Cor 15:3-5). Last of all, Paul confirms, the risen Jesus appeared to him, "as to one untimely born" (1 Cor 15:8).

Paul is dismayed, however, that some of the Corinthians have given up the hope of a future resurrection, perhaps because of their belief that the age to come is already present in their experiences or because of a distaste for the idea of bodily resurrection. For Paul, the meaning of Jesus' resurrection is as the beginning of a great drama—"the first fruits" (1 Cor 15:20) of the future resurrection of all be-

lievers. To undermine hope in the future resurrection is to deny Jesus' resurrection and reduce the Gospel to powerless futility. "If for this life only we have hoped in Christ," Paul reflects, "we are of all people most to be pitied" (1 Cor 15:19).

Paul helps the Corinthians envision the cosmic drama of the divine war against futility and death. In his resurrection Jesus won the decisive battle, but his victory will not be complete until the final resurrection when "the last enemy to be destroyed is death" (1 Cor 15:26).

Paul assures the Corinthians that the resurrection is not a resuscitation of the physical body, of flesh and blood, but a transformation into an imperishable spiritual body appropriate for the glory of God's eternal kingdom. The oppressive power and pain of death are removed when "death has been swallowed up in victory" (1 Cor 15:54).

Paul concludes his letter to the Corinthians by reporting his plans to return to Achaia to visit them and by urging them to participate in raising funds to help poor Christians in Jerusalem. After final greetings, he blesses them: "The grace of the Lord Jesus be with you. My love be with all of you in Christ Jesus" (1 Cor 16:23-24).

The 15th-century German artist Stephan Lochner vividly portrayed the Last Judgment, with Mary and the beloved disciple John flanking Jesus as he directs the righteous into a temple (left), while the wicked are driven to the underworld (right).

THE SECOND LETTER OF PAUL TO THE CORINTHIANS

*A*fter Paul sent 1 Corinthians, the situation in the Greek city changed and Paul's relations with the Christians there deteriorated. Evidently, new missionaries arrived in Corinth, ones who disagreed with Paul's message and methods and worked hard to turn the community against him. The trip to Corinth that Paul was planning at the end of 1 Corinthians turned out to be a very "painful visit" (2 Cor 2:1) that he did not wish to repeat. When he returned to Ephesus, Paul wrote the Corinthians a severe letter "out of much distress and anguish of heart and with many tears" (2 Cor 2:4). He sent his coworker Titus to Corinth so that he could learn if there was hope of reconciliation. The first part of 2 Corinthians overflows with the sense of comfort and joy that Paul experienced when Titus met him in Macedonia with the news that the Corinthians had wholly turned away from their opposition to Paul and longed to be reconciled with him.

As a whole, 2 Corinthians is marked by a number of abrupt changes of topic and mood that have caused many biblical scholars to suggest that the document contains portions of more than one letter from Paul to Corinth. After all the joy and comfort of the first half of the letter, the final four chapters contain an intense defense against certain false apostles who have undermined Paul's proclamation of the Gospel by claiming that he is not an apostle at all. The section is addressed, however, to the congregation as a whole, whom Paul rebukes for accepting deceitful teachers. Many students of 2 Corinthians believe that rather than imagining Paul's relations with the Corinthians had collapsed after he wrote chapters 1-9, it is better to understand chapters 10-13 as the heart of that otherwise lost severe letter Paul had written with many tears before his final reconciliation with the Corinthians. Other distinct sections of the letter include 2 Corinthians 8-9, which concerns a collection for the poor in Jerusalem, and 2 Corinthians 6:14-7:1, which some believe reflects the content of Paul's initial letter to Corinth mentioned in 1 Corinthians 5:9.

The apostle Paul portrayed as a contemplative elder by Rembrandt (1609-1669)

Blessed be the God and Father of our Lord Jesus Christ, the Father of mercies and the God of all consolation, who consoles us in all our affliction. 2 COR 1:3-4

*P*aul quickly strikes the theme of consolation following the opening of his letter. In place of the usual thanksgiving for the recipients, he praises God for the experience of consolation that he can share with the Corinthians after a storm of conflict and suffering. Paul's time in Ephesus has been difficult. He has "fought with wild animals" (1 Cor 15:32), faced rioting mobs (Acts 19:23-41), and become "so utterly, unbearably crushed" that he "despaired of life itself" (2 Cor 1:8). In the midst of these experiences, and after sending 1 Corinthians across the Aegean Sea, Paul had journeyed to Corinth. But there, instead of receiving a welcome, he faced rejection, evidently instigated by new teachers who had come into the church and undermined both Paul's authority as an apostle and the Gospel he preached.

Now, Paul looks back with sorrow and relief on that painful visit and its aftermath. He had threatened to return shortly to confront the situation but changed his mind and decided to write a letter "out of much distress and anguish of heart" (2 Cor 2:4). That decision proved wise, since Paul's letter and the missionary work of Titus brought about a reconciliation with the alienated Corinthians.

But now Paul wants to reflect on the meaning of this conflict in relation to the nature of his apostleship and the character of the Gospel he preaches. Paul faces a genuine quandary. How can he defend himself and the message of the cross that he passionately proclaims, without falling into the same competitive and self-promoting spirit that he knows is so destructive and that he has urged the Corinthians to avoid? It is important to Paul that he has behaved toward the Corinthians "with frankness and godly sincerity, not by earthly wisdom but by the grace of God" (2 Cor 1:12). If he has successfully defeated those who oppose him but at the same time undermined the Gospel of grace that he conveys from Jesus, his efforts will have done far more damage than good among those to whom he ministers.

All of us, with unveiled faces, seeing the glory of the Lord as though reflected in a mirror, are being transformed into the same image from one degree of glory to another; for this comes from the Lord, the Spirit.   2 COR 3:18

In reflecting on his defense, Paul first raises the question of competence or sufficiency as an apostle. How can competence be demonstrated or judged? Those who oppose Paul in Corinth have evidently claimed to be more competent than he as teachers, apostles, and interpreters of scripture, and they apparently show letters of recommendation from other churches to attest their competence.

Paul begins by describing himself and his coworkers as Christ's prisoners of war, led through the streets in triumph while the fragrance of incense from the procession wafts through the watching crowd. Whether the fragrance portends life or death depends on the will of the conqueror, not the power of the captives. They are not peddlers hawking God's message by their skillful pitch, but are more like ambassadors whose entire power and competence comes from the Lord they represent.

As for letters of recommendation, Paul has none but the Corinthians themselves, who have come to their new life of faith in Christ through his preaching. Thus they have become "a letter of Christ, prepared by us, written . . . with the Spirit of the living God . . . on tablets of human hearts" (2 Cor 3:3).

Paul stresses that a true apostle has no competence of himself but is empowered for his work by God: "Our competence is from God, who has made us competent to be ministers of a new covenant" (2 Cor 3:5-6). Just as God gave a reflection of his glory to Moses as he brought the old covenant to the people, so to an even greater extent God shows his glory and power in the ministry of the new covenant of the Spirit. Not only the apostles are touched by God's power, but "all of us, with unveiled faces, seeing the glory of the Lord" are transformed. It was generally believed that humans were changed by divine encounters.

But we have this treasure in clay jars, so that it may be made clear that this extraordinary power belongs to God and does not come from us.   2 COR 4:7

Paul endured many forms of persecution, physical danger, opposition, and indignity during his ministry. Why did he not simply quit and live a comfortable life as a craftsman without such threats?

Since it is by the grace of God that he is in such a ministry, Paul reflects, "We do not lose heart" (2 Cor 4:1). He is confident that the origin of his ministry and its outcome depend on God's creative power and must not be compromised by human attempts to direct the result by cunning or deceit; rather, as he says, "by the open statement of the truth we commend ourselves to the conscience of everyone in the sight of God" (2 Cor 4:2).

Just as God has chosen to reveal his power in the paradoxical weakness and suffering of Jesus' crucifix-

ion, so it is God's choice that true apostleship is shown not in the strength of the apostle but in his weakness. He must be a clay jar that contributes nothing of its own to the value of the "treasure" it holds, namely, the "extraordinary power" of the Gospel that "belongs to God" (2 Cor 4:7). Just as life comes through Jesus' death, so the apostle's work must embody the death of Jesus in order that the life of Jesus may be experienced by those he teaches: "Death is at work in us, but life in you" (2 Cor 4:12).

Paul is confident that by embodying in his ministry the message of the crucifixion, he can know that he will share in the power of Jesus' resurrection. That knowledge transforms his perspective on his troubles so that he can never lose heart: "This slight momentary affliction is preparing us for an eternal weight of glory beyond all measure, because . . . what can be seen is temporary, but what cannot be seen is eternal" (2 Cor 4:17-18). The apostle's ministry, his competence to fulfill it, the power of his message, his strength and eternal hope in the midst of weakness and suffering—all are from God, Paul says, "who has given us the Spirit as a guarantee" (2 Cor 5:5).

So if anyone is in Christ, there is a new creation: everything old has passed away; see, everything has become new!
2 COR 5:17

The power of the God who is working in his ministry makes Paul extremely conscious of the seriousness of his task. He is not commending himself but wants the Corinthians to see that the work

PAUL'S MISSIONS TO CORINTH

A widely held view of Paul's missions and letters to Corinth observes the following chronology. But as in any such historical hypothesis, other reconstructions can be defended.

A.D. 50-51 Paul founds the church in Corinth.

52-55 Paul preaches in Ephesus.

52 Paul sends a letter to Corinth (1 Cor 5:9, now lost but perhaps included in 2 Cor 6:14-7:1).

53 The Corinthians send a letter of questions to Paul (1 Cor 7:1).

53-54 Paul writes 1 Corinthians.

54 New missionaries in Corinth turn the church against Paul.

54 Paul makes a "painful visit" (2 Cor 2:1) to Corinth.

54 Paul writes a severe letter (perhaps including 2 Cor 10-13) and sends Titus to Corinth.

55 Titus returns with good news (2 Cor 7:6-7).

55 Paul writes a letter of reconciliation (2 Cor 1-7) and appeal for collections (2 Cor 8-9).

56 From Corinth, Paul writes to the Romans.

of an apostle must be defined and directed by the core of the message he brings: "The love of Christ urges us on, because we are convinced that one has died for all; therefore all have died" (2 Cor 5:14). Their lives belong to Christ, who died for them, so also the way they look at the world and everyone in it. "From now on," Paul says, ". . . we regard no one from a human point of view" (2 Cor 5:16). When one fully allows the message of the cross to transform one's life, the effect is so dramatic that it is as though there were "a new creation"; the world starts over and "everything has become new!"

The apostle or Christian who appears insignificant by typical human evaluation is in fact engaged in the work of the most profound power and importance. He is an ambassador of God bringing a message of reconciliation to the world. God in Christ has done all that is necessary to make the reconciliation a reality, but he chooses to make his appeal through human messengers: "We entreat you on behalf of Christ, be reconciled to God" (2 Cor 5:20).

The role of the apostle is not to bring about the reconciliation himself—that is God's task—but simply to put "no obstacle in anyone's way" (2 Cor 6:3). Thus, Paul lists the hardships he suffers, the virtues he practices, the misunderstandings he endures, simply to allow the message of the cross a free flow through his ministry into the lives of those who hear. He lives as one who is "poor, yet making many rich; as having nothing, and yet possessing everything" (2 Cor 6:10).

For godly grief produces a repentance that leads to salvation and brings no regret, but worldly grief produces death.   2 COR 7:10

Many biblical scholars have noticed that at 2 Corinthians 6:14 the text abruptly turns to another topic—the separation of believers from interaction with nonbelievers. This remains the subject until 2 Corinthians 7:1, at which point the theme of 2 Corinthians 6:13 seems to continue without a break. This puzzling diversion has caused some to think that this section is an extract or page from the initial, now lost letter that Paul wrote to Corinth (1 Cor 5:9-13), which dealt with precisely this subject of separation from outsiders.

At 2 Corinthians 7:2, Paul returns to reflections on his ministry in light of the past conflict with the Corinthians. Now, he says, "I have great pride in you; I am filled with consolation" (2 Cor 7:4). Earlier, while waiting for Titus to return from his mission to Corinth, Paul writes,

"we were afflicted in every way—disputes without and fears within" (2 Cor 7:5). Titus arrived with consoling news that the Corinthian congregation had turned back from rejecting Paul's message and told the apostle "of your longing, your mourning, your zeal for me, so that I rejoiced still more" (2 Cor 7:7).

Thus, Paul reflects on the grief he has caused the Corinthians through the severe letter he had sent, "not because you were grieved, but because your grief led to repentance" (2 Cor 7:9). The entire process has been painful, but the outcome has produced growth and clarity for the community of believers in Corinth. Now, Paul concludes, "I rejoice, because I have complete confidence in you" (2 Cor 7:16).

We want you to know . . . about the grace of God that has been granted to the churches of Macedonia; for during a severe ordeal of affliction, their abundant joy and their extreme poverty have overflowed in a wealth of generosity on their part.   2 COR 8:1-2

Paul begins a new section by challenging the Christians in Corinth and in the whole Roman province of Achaia to participate generously in gathering a collection for poor Christians in Judea, especially in Jerusalem. Paul has been gathering this collection among the Gentile churches he established ever since his meeting with James, Peter, and John in Jerusalem. They had agreed that Paul should lead mission efforts to the Gentiles but urged him to "remember the poor" among Jewish Christians, which Paul has always been "eager to do" (Gal 2:10).

The collection was both a practical ministry to alleviate poverty and a powerful symbol of the unity of the Jewish and Gentile branches of the one faith. Paul stresses that it is the faith that produces the gift that is important. He offers the example of Christians

Paul is said to have preached from the monumental rostrum of Corinth's court of justice (above in ruins); it was under the shadow of a pagan temple on the acropolis.

in Macedonia, whose generosity in the midst of poverty flows from the fact that "they gave themselves first to the Lord" (2 Cor 8:5). Such love is a response to the grace of Jesus, who "though he was rich, yet for your sakes he became poor, so that by his poverty you might become rich" (2 Cor 8:9). Paul urges the Corinthians to welcome Titus and others who are working with him to take this collection to Jerusalem.

There must be no sense of compulsion in the gifts, Paul urges, but of intelligent reflection, faith, and joy, "for God loves a cheerful giver" (2 Cor 9:7). Like every other part of Christian life, Paul says, such giving serves to "glorify God by your obedience to the confession of the gospel of Christ and by the generosity of your sharing" (2 Cor 9:13).

Paul perusing the scriptures, a Greco-Serbian wall painting dated about 1340

ing news from Corinth since writing of his complete confidence in 2 Corinthians 7:16. Or, he may simply have added this section of alarm and rebuke onto his letter of consolation and confidence without explaining why the two stood side by side. Many students of 2 Corinthians, however, believe it is far more likely that chapters 10-13 are the heart of the severe letter that he wrote to Corinth after his painful visit there, the letter that he mentions in 2 Corinthians 2:3-4 and 7:8-12.

Three times I appealed to the Lord about this, that it would leave me, but he said to me, "My grace is sufficient for you, for power is made perfect in weakness."
2 COR 12:8-9

I myself, Paul, appeal to you by the meekness and gentleness of Christ—I who am humble when face to face with you, but bold toward you when I am away! 2 COR 10:1

*T*he mood of the letter shifts sharply at the beginning of chapter 10. All confidence in the Corinthians is gone as Paul senses tremendous danger among them coming from teachers—like him, Jewish Christians—who have used personal attacks to undermine the Gospel he has preached in Corinth. The Corinthians are submitting "readily enough," Paul says, to people who proclaim "another Jesus than the one we proclaimed . . . a different spirit from the one you received, or a different gospel from the one you accepted" (2 Cor 11:4). With sarcasm, Paul calls these teachers "super-apostles" (2 Cor 11:5) because of their claims to superior spiritual power in contrast to Paul, who, they say, writes letters that are "weighty and strong, but his bodily presence is weak, and his speech contemptible" (2 Cor 10:10). In reality, Paul says, "such boasters are false apostles, deceitful workers, disguising themselves as apostles of Christ" (2 Cor 11:13).

In the face of their claims, Paul engages in a deeply ironical bragging contest "speaking as a fool" (2 Cor 11:21). The false teachers boast of their spiritual strength, their eloquence, their commendations from other churches. "Talking like a madman," Paul says he will speak of his beatings, imprisonments, dangers, anxieties and sleepless nights: "If I must boast, I will boast of the things that show my weakness" (2 Cor 11:23, 30). If 2 Corinthians is a single unified letter, it is possible that Paul received radically disturb-

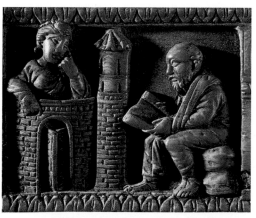

Paul reading to his legendary disciple Thekla; an 11th-century ivory carving

*P*aul continues his serious yet ironical attempt to defend the power of the Gospel without elevating himself. He talks about his own revelations and visions but, with mock modesty, attributes them to another. As for himself, he says, "a thorn was given me in the flesh, a messenger of Satan to torment me" (2 Cor 12:7). Paul never reveals the nature of this vexation, but says that God refused his prayers to remove it and instead taught him to see that God's power is "made perfect in weakness." Therefore, Paul proclaims, "I am content with weaknesses, insults, hardships, persecutions, and calamities for the sake of Christ; for whenever I am weak, then I am strong" (2 Cor 12:9, 10).

Paul expresses great fear that when he comes again to the Corinthians there will be a major confrontation. "I will not be lenient," he says, "—since you desire proof that Christ is speaking in me" (2 Cor 13:2-3). Paul promises to reflect on the character of Christ: "For he was crucified in weakness, but lives by the power of God." Similarly, Paul says, "we are weak in him, but in dealing with you we will live with him by the power of God" (2 Cor 13:4). In the hope that he "may not have to be severe" with them when he comes, Paul urges the Corinthians to "put things in order, listen to my appeal" (2 Cor 13:10, 11).

If, as many have speculated, Paul's warning is part of his severe letter, then it would appear that the Corinthians heeded his appeal and turned back to the Gospel that Paul had first preached to them. After their reconciliation, Paul traveled to Corinth again in a spirit of peace and joy and indeed wrote his powerful letter to the Romans while staying with this congregation that had caused him so much concern.

THE LETTER OF PAUL TO THE GALATIANS

Allies and sometimes adversaries, Paul (left) and Peter, as painted by Bartolommeo Vivarini (1432-c. 1491)

P*aul's letter to the Galatians, often called the Magna Carta of Christianity, defines the liberation from the Law of Moses that transformed the new sect into a world religion. Galatians addresses the most intense controversy that racked early Christianity—ethnic and religious division over whether Gentiles could be included within the church. Burning with an aggressive urgency, the letter is a clarion call to a gospel of grace and freedom.*

Although the gospels record that Jesus commissioned his apostles to "make disciples of all nations" (Mt 28:19), the book of Acts makes it clear that the disciples at first had no intention of going to any group except the Jews. Throughout the Roman Empire, Jews had long been telling Gentiles about the God of Israel. They had urged them to reject idols and serve the living God by becoming proselytes (converts) to Judaism and obeying the Law of Moses. Early believers in Jesus evidently planned a similar mission, except that they would proclaim Jesus as Israel's Messiah. Acts describes a series of incidents through which Peter and other early church leaders were divinely inspired to go against their own feelings and admit Gentiles into the fellowship of believers without becoming proselytes to Judaism (Acts 10:1-11:18).

Paul, for his part, knew that when Jesus had called him to be an apostle, he had sent him specifically to preach the Gospel to Gentiles. He was not to convert them to obedience to the Law of Moses, which Paul had followed all his life, but to offer them a message of God's grace in Jesus apart from the law, a grace available to all people including Gentiles. He had proclaimed that message effectively in the region of Galatia in central Asia Minor (Turkey)—a mission only briefly mentioned in Acts 16:6 and 18:23. In any case, after Paul's departure, other Christian teachers had come to these churches. They told the believers that Paul's message had been incomplete and inadequate. Paul had cheapened the Gospel, they said, and made its demands easy in order to win converts. They urged the Gentile believers to complete their conversion by taking on a life of obedience to the law and by accepting the rite of circumcision as God had commanded Abraham.

Paul evidently learned of the work of these teachers during or after his second tour through Galatia. He probably wrote his letter to the Galatians from Ephesus about A.D. 53, during the same general period that he was writing the letters to Corinth and before he wrote to the Romans.

I am astonished that you are so quickly deserting the one who called you in the grace of Christ and are turning to a different gospel. GAL 1:6

I n other letters Paul lavishes commendation and confidence on the addressees immediately after his greeting. For the Galatians, however, he has no such praise. He identifies himself as an apostle with a commission directly from Jesus and not from any human authority and quickly focuses on the problem at hand: "There are some who are confusing you and want to pervert the gospel of Christ" (Gal 1:7).

Paul emphatically asserts that the Gospel he has proclaimed to the Galatians is neither incomplete nor toned down in order to win human approval: There is only one Gospel, and anyone—even an angel—who proclaims "a different gospel" that contradicts the central message of that one Gospel is "accursed" (Gal 1:6, 8). To rebuild the Galatians' confidence in their original understanding, Paul recounts the dramatic transformation by which he came to know Jesus. Thus, the Galatians can see that the message he proclaimed was not "from a human source" but one received "through a revelation of Jesus Christ" (Gal 1:12).

Paul's earlier life had been set on a firm course. He was well educated and had "advanced in Judaism" beyond many of his peers because he was "far more zealous for the traditions" handed down to him. That zeal had led him into "violently persecuting the church of God and . . . trying to destroy it" (Gal 1:13, 14), in part because the church proclaimed that a man who had been crucified was the Messiah.

But God, Paul believes, had other plans for which he "had set me apart before I was born," and ultimately God "was pleased to reveal his Son to me" (Gal 1:15, 16). This revelation reversed the course of Paul's life; it confirmed that the Jesus who had been crucified was indeed God's Son, and that this message was to be proclaimed to Gentiles, such as the Galatians.

Paul had immediately obeyed his summons and begun his mission without even consulting with the disciples in Jerusalem. Only after three years did he visit Peter (Cephas) and James "the Lord's brother" (Gal 1:19) in Jerusalem and win their acceptance. In his letters Paul makes no secret of the fact that he learned many traditions about Jesus and other things from those who were believers before him. However, the apostle maintains that the core of his proclamation—that Jesus was the Messiah and Son of God, that he was crucified to atone for humanity's sins, and that the Gospel is for Gentiles as much as it is for Jews—had come directly from divine revelation.

I have been crucified with Christ; and it is no longer I who live, but it is Christ who lives in me. And the life I now live in the flesh I live by faith in the Son of God. GAL 2:19-20

In order to show how seriously he takes the issues at stake in this letter, Paul recounts two occasions in which he had stood up for the message he has proclaimed to the Galatians. About A.D. 49, 14 years after his mission to the Gentiles had begun, Paul and his coworker Barnabas went to Jerusalem along with a Gentile convert named Titus to meet with church leaders. There, Paul says, "I laid before them . . . the gospel that I proclaim among the Gentiles" (Gal 2:2). This meeting is evidently also described in Acts 15 and is sometimes called the Jerusalem conference. The main points of the two accounts are similar, though they differ in the details. Paul writes as an eyewitness participant, while Luke's account in Acts was probably written about 35 years later.

Paul describes the opposition he faced from some believers in Jerusalem who evidently objected to accepting Titus. But, Paul says, "we did not submit to them even for a moment, so that the truth of the gospel might always remain with you" (Gal 2:5). By contrast, the leaders in Jerusalem accepted the fact that God had entrusted Paul "with the gospel to the uncircumcised" (Gal 2:7). Indeed, Paul says, "James and Cephas [Peter] and John, who were acknowledged pillars . . . gave to Barnabas and me the right hand of fellowship" (Gal 2:9). They agreed that the Jerusalem leaders would head the mission to Jews while Paul and Barnabas led the mission to Gentiles. To symbolize their unity Paul and Barnabas would gather a collection to support poor believers in Judea—something Paul "was eager to do" (Gal 2:10).

On another occasion, however, things did not go so well. Peter visited Antioch and shared fellowship meals with the Gentile Christians. But when a group from the church in Jerusalem who were "of the circumcision faction" (Gal 2:12) arrived, their objections caused Peter and even Barnabas to stop eating with the Gentile converts unless they agreed to observe Jewish dietary restrictions.

For Paul, no aspect of Mosaic Law could be imposed on Gentiles as a basis for fellowship in the church. In seeking "to be justified in Christ," Paul asserts, he (and other Jewish believers) had "died to the law, so that I might live to God" (Gal 2:17, 19). Christ's crucifixion had become his own death to his old way of life. His present life is defined by his "faith in the Son of God, who loved me and gave himself for me" (Gal 2:20).

Just as Abraham "believed God, and it was reckoned to him as righteousness," so, you see, those who believe are the descendants of Abraham. GAL 3:6-7

As Paul turns to the heart of his argument, he challenges the Galatians to think about their own experience. In Paul's proclamation, "Jesus Christ was publicly exhibited as cruci-

En route to persecuting Christians in Damascus, Saul (Paul) is thrown to the ground as Jesus appears to him in a vision; a painting by Giulio Licinio (c. 1527-1584).

fied!" (Gal 3:1). When they accepted this message, they received God's Spirit; nothing had been added by their "doing the works of the law" (Gal 2:5).

If their own experience is not enough, Paul argues, the scriptures themselves point to the truth of his message. Paul first cites Genesis 15:6 to show that Abraham provides a paradigm for faith as the basis of a right relationship with God: God accepted Abraham's faith and counted it as righteousness. The promises God made to Abraham show that God always intended that Gentiles would be included in the blessings that flow from those promises. In Greek (as in Hebrew) a single word is translated either as "nations" or as "Gentiles." Thus, God's promise to Abraham is that "all the Gentiles [nations] shall be blessed in you" (Gal 3:8; Gen 18:18).

Paul notes that the law pronounces a curse on anyone who does not obey everything written there. But the Messiah, he asserts, "redeemed us from the curse of the law" by accepting for himself another of the law's curses, the one pronounced on "everyone who hangs on a tree" (Gal 3:13; Deut 21:23). By absorbing the law's condemnation in himself, Jesus made it possible for the blessings promised to Abraham to flow to all people, including the Gentiles.

In his promise to Abraham, God established the fundamental way in which he wanted to bless humanity—by a gift of undeserved grace given to one who responds in faith; the law, given centuries later, did not change God's original intention. The law was important and was certainly not "opposed to the promises of God" (Gal 3:21). But it was in an intermediary stage, revealing human sinfulness and the imprisoning "power of sin" until the Messiah arrived: "The law was our disciplinarian until Christ came, so that we might be justified by faith" (Gal 3:22, 24).

In Christ, Paul argues, the original intent of God's promise to Abraham and its broad inclusiveness are restored so that Gentiles and Jews "are all children of God through faith" (Gal 3:26). When each believer is baptized, he or she is clothed with the identity of Christ, and all racial and social barriers collapse: "There is no longer Jew or Greek, there is no longer slave or free, there is no longer male and female; for all of you are one in Christ Jesus" (Gal 3:28).

For freedom Christ has set us free. Stand firm, therefore, and do not submit again to a yoke of slavery. GAL 5:1

Paul calls the Galatians to remember that they have been pagans "enslaved to beings that by nature are not gods," but through the Gospel they have received freedom as people "known by God" (Gal 4:8-9). Ironically, they are now walking back into a slavery to religious practice that was just as destructive to their faith as their former paganism.

Paul reminds them of the enthusiastic way they had originally received him when he first preached in Galatia, even though he had been troubled by some "physical infirmity" (Gal 4:13). The nature of this infirmity is unknown. Paul had endured many beatings and had once been nearly stoned to death (2 Cor 11:23-25; Acts 14:19); any number of injuries may have plagued him. The Galatians had nevertheless welcomed him "as an angel of God" (Gal 4:14). Now Paul is perplexed by the reversal. They have been growing spiritually, but now are back at the beginning. Paul says, "I am again in the pain of childbirth until Christ is formed in you" (Gal 4:19).

Paul uses their love for scriptural interpretation by offering them an allegory of Abraham's two sons, Ishmael (born to the slave Hagar) and Isaac (born to Sarah according to God's promise). He allows Ishmael to stand for slavery to the law and flesh while Isaac stands for freedom in Christ and the Spirit. Paul urges the Galatians to claim their freedom and resist the "yoke of slavery" (Gal 5:1). If the Galatians now trust the law—expressed through the rite of circumcision—for their relationship to God, then they have stepped back from the realm of freedom and into a realm in which the law is their master. Instead, Paul urges them to recognize that what matters is not circumcision but "faith working through love" (Gal 5:6).

The fruit of the Spirit is love, joy, peace, patience, kindness, generosity, faithfulness, gentleness, and self-control. GAL 5:22-23

Paul concludes his letter by challenging the Galatians to "live by the Spirit" and not to "gratify the desires of the flesh" (Gal 5:16). As elsewhere in his writings, Paul uses "flesh" not in the sense of the physical body or as a reference to sexual appetites, but as a metaphor for the human tendency to destructive, prideful, hurtful, and faithless actions. "The works of the flesh," Paul says, are not difficult to discern, but rather "obvious," and he provides a list ranging from fornication to drunkenness and "things like these" (Gal 5:19, 21). Such destructive practices show that God is not ruling a person's life, and that person has no part in God's kingdom.

The Spirit, on the other hand, causes growth and bears his fruit in the form of a life of "love, joy, peace, patience, kindness, generosity, faithfulness, gentleness, and self-control," virtues that can flourish without any limit. Paul urges the Galatians to avoid competition with each other but rather to help "bear one another's burdens, and in this way . . . fulfill the law of Christ" (Gal 6:2). The challenge before them is serious, Paul warns: "Do not be deceived . . . you reap whatever you sow" (Gal 6:7).

The original, long lost letter ended with a paragraph handwritten in large letters by Paul—in contrast to the rest of the letter, which had been taken down by a scribe. In his closing words Paul hammers home the main themes of the letter. Boasting of keeping the commandments is useless. "May I never boast of anything," Paul says, "except the cross of our Lord Jesus Christ, by which the world has been crucified to me, and I to the world. For neither circumcision nor uncircumcision is anything; but a new creation is everything!" (Gal 6:14-15).

The letter to the Ephesians is perhaps the Bible's most elevated and visionary expression of the glory of Christian faith within the divine purpose of God. Unlike letters such as those to the Corinthians or the Galatians, Ephesians deals with no major controversy. Rather, it seeks to give readers a cosmic vision of the church and Christian life as part of the divine plan, mysterious and grand, unfolding toward the ultimate consummation of God's glory.

The letter reveals that Paul is "a prisoner" (Eph 3:1) at the time of writing. He addresses Christians in the large city of Ephesus, the Roman capital of the province of Asia (western Turkey). The small community of primarily Gentile Christians there had likely faced persecution and could easily seem powerless and insignificant in the face of the dominant Greek culture and Roman imperial power. Paul gives these Christians a new perspective on what their faith means. Paul may be in chains, and the community may be small, but the God who is revealing his purposes through them is the God who holds all time and space, all heaven and earth in his hands. Paul challenges the Ephesians to accept that vision and to recognize its reality.

The fact that the phrase "in Ephesus" is missing from the earliest copies of this letter has suggested to many who have studied it that the letter may have been intended as a circular, to be sent to a number of different churches that shared the same spiritual needs. Ephesians differs considerably in style and vocabulary from the early letters of Paul. It may, as many scholars hold, represent an evolution of his thought and language and a conscious attempt to write in a more elevated style. Others believe that these differences show that one of Paul's followers framed the letter in his name.

Assuming that Paul wrote the letter, he probably composed it during his imprisonment in Rome about A.D. 60-61. If so, he sent it to Ephesus by Tychicus along with his letter to the Colossians, which is similar to Ephesians in many points of content and style.

Paul; an early Christian mosaic portrait from St. Peter's Basilica in the Vatican

---

Blessed be the God and Father of our Lord Jesus Christ, who has blessed us in Christ with every spiritual blessing in the heavenly places. EPH 1:3

Immediately after his typical greeting, Paul plunges into the language of worship, praising God for the spiritual blessings he has bestowed on believers. In long, flowing sentences filled with wave after wave of praise for the Lord, Paul describes the cosmic drama within which the life of the believer moves. Everything flows from God's direct care for the believer, which began "before the foundation of the world," when God "destined us for adoption as his children through Jesus Christ" (Eph 1:4, 5). He accomplished this adoption by redeeming the believer through the blood of Christ, thereby showing "the riches of his grace that he lavished on us" (Eph 1:7-8).

All this is "the mystery of his will"—that is, something long hidden but now revealed. In "the fullness of time" (Eph 1:9, 10) God will bring all things in heaven and earth together in Christ. This includes the uniting of Jewish and Gentile believers into a single people who receive the Holy Spirit from God.

As Paul remembers the faith and love of his readers, he continues the attitude of worship by praying for their spiritual illumination to grasp the grand vision he has just described. He prays that the Ephesians may receive "a spirit of wisdom and revelation" to know the hope and glorious inheritance God holds for them and "the immeasurable greatness of his power for us who believe" (Eph 1:17, 19). God manifested this power when he raised Jesus from the dead, "seated him at his right hand in the heavenly places," and "made him the head over all things for the church, which is his body, the fullness of him who fills all in all" (Eph 1:21, 22-23).

For by grace you have been saved through faith, and this is not your own doing; it is the gift of God—not the result of works, so that no one may boast. EPH 2:8-9

After describing the grand sweep of God's plan, Paul describes in equally vivid terms how the believer comes to be a part of that plan. He uses two basic metaphors: the raising of the dead and the reconciliation of alienated enemies.

"You were dead," Paul reminds his readers. Because of sins and because of a life directed by "the spirit that is now at work among those who are disobedient" (Eph 2:1, 2), every person lies lifeless and helpless apart from God's grace. But God's mercy is so rich and his love so great that "even when we were dead through our trespasses," Paul says, God "made us alive together with Christ" (Eph 2:5). In Christ's resurrection, the believer is also brought to life, and in Christ's exaltation to heaven, the believer is given a place "with him in the heavenly places" (Eph 2:6). All this, Paul emphasizes, flows entirely from God's grace received through faith. None of it is accomplished by any human works. But many deeds flow from the new lives "created in Christ Jesus for good works, which God prepared beforehand to be our way of life" (Eph 2:10).

Not only did God grant life to individuals, he also broke down the barriers that keep individuals and groups separate from each other. Paul reminds his Gentile readers that they were once wholly alienated from all the covenants and promises that God had given to his chosen people. But God has now brought enemies together to his Son: "For he is our peace; in his flesh he has made both groups into one and has broken down the dividing wall, that is, the hostility between us" (Eph 2:14). Thus Jesus has created "one new humanity" so that all "have access in one Spirit to the Father" (Eph 2:15, 18).

Now to him who by the power at work within us is able to accomplish abundantly far more than all we can ask or imagine, to him be glory in the church and in Christ Jesus to all generations. EPH 3:20-21

*P*aul next turns to his own role in God's work as one who has received "the commission of God's grace" to proclaim to the Gentiles "the mystery of Christ" (Eph 3:2, 4). In earlier generations, God's will concerning the Gentiles was hidden, but now God has revealed how they are to share in his promises in Christ. "Of this gospel," Paul says, "I have become a servant according to the gift of God's grace" in order "to bring to the Gentiles the news of the boundless riches of Christ" (Eph 3:7, 8).

God's hidden plan through all the ages comes to fruition in the church that proclaims God's gracious gift of new life and reconciliation, Paul says. Through the church, God's wisdom is made manifest to all powers in heaven and earth, as it has been carried out in Jesus Christ, and

believers are granted "access to God in boldness and confidence" (Eph 3:12). Such confidence overwhelms any temptation to lose heart in the face of sufferings.

Again, Paul's vision moves him to a prayer of praise and intercession. He bows to God who is the Father of all families and offers a series of petitions for his readers. First, he prays that they may be strengthened in their "inner being with power through his Spirit" (Eph 3:16). Second, that through faith Christ may dwell in their hearts as they are "grounded in love" (Eph 3:17). Third, that they may be given the power to comprehend the vast expanse of Christ's love and genuinely to know that love. And fourth, that they "may be filled with all the fullness of God" (Eph 3:19). Such requests would be impossible except that God's power, Paul says, "is able to accomplish abundantly far more than all we can ask or imagine" (Eph 3:20).

There is one body and one Spirit, just as you were called to the one hope of your calling, one Lord, one faith, one baptism, one God and Father of all. EPH 4:4-6

*P*aul wants the Ephesians to see that a way of life flows from his vision of God's grace. He challenges them to "lead a life worthy of the calling to which you have been called" (Eph 4:1), and tells them that the life befitting such a grand vision is one of humility, gentleness, patience, and love.

God has given them life and brought them together in reconciliation in spite of ancient ethnic divisions. Now they must make every effort to "maintain the unity of the Spirit in the bond of peace" (Eph 4:3).

Elegant columned buildings once lined this street in Ephesus, the important Roman provincial city where Paul established one of the first Christian churches.

Every aspect of their religion calls them to unity; the Spirit, their Lord, their faith, their baptism, their God—all unite them.

Yes, there is diversity among them, but it is a positive diversity of gifts of grace given by Christ to his people—like a conquering general scattering gifts along the procession of his triumphal parade. His gifts of grace make some "apostles, some prophets, some evangelists, some pastors and teachers" (Eph 4:11). But all these varied gifts serve a single function, to equip believers "for the work of ministry" so that all grow toward "the unity of faith" and toward "maturity, to the measure of the full stature of Christ" (Eph 4:12, 13). Then the body of believers works together and grows in complete harmony and love.

Having established this positive standard, Paul turns to warn the Ephesians that they must completely break from their former lives as pagans "alienated from the life of God" (Eph 4:18). He challenges them to avoid all falsehood, persistent anger, stealing, evil talk, bitterness, malice, and sexual immorality. They are to be "imitators of God, as beloved children, and live in love, as Christ loved us" (Eph 5:1-2).

Be strong in the Lord and in the strength of his power. Put on the whole armor of God, so that you may be able to stand against the wiles of the devil. EPH 6:10-11

*P*aul continues his exhortation to the Ephesians to live a life shaped by the Gospel. They are to be careful in their associations and avoid people who would lead them back into the shameful practices of their former lives. They now are to "live as children of light" (Eph 5:8), with lives of open honesty, and hearts filled not with drunkenness but with songs of praise and thanksgiving to God.

Paul also challenges them to shape the relationships within their households by the values of the Gospel. Under Roman law, the household was a definite hierarchy of power with all authority residing in the father of the family. Paul begins by urging the believers to structure their households not on a hierarchy of power but on mutual submission in service to each other: "Be subject to one another out of reverence for Christ" (Eph 5:21). Wives are to serve their husbands as the church serves Jesus, out of love for him. Husbands are to love and serve their wives "just as Christ loved the church and gave himself up for her" (Eph 5:25). In the face of law and custom that gave husbands absolute power over their wives, Paul urges husbands to "love their wives as they do their own bodies" and to care for them tenderly, "just as Christ does for the church" (Eph 5:28, 29).

Paul urges children to obey their parents, repeating the commandment to honor father and mother. But he also warns fathers not to abuse their legal authority in provoking their children, but to bring them up instructed in the ways of God.

Slaves are to guide their actions not by the evils of their condition but by the devotion they have to God. Masters also must not exercise their rights to threat-

THE MANY TRIALS OF THE APOSTLE PAUL

*C*hained inside a jail cell, probably late in his life, Paul wrote to Christians in Ephesus urging them not to "lose heart over my sufferings" (Eph 3:13) or lose faith over the persecutions they were facing. Paul knew what it meant to suffer for the faith, and he was uniquely qualified to advise others on the subject. During some 10,000 miles of his traveling ministry recorded in Acts of the Apostles, Paul endured a gauntlet of attacks and misfortunes, and seemed constantly in danger.

"Five times I have received from the Jews the forty lashes minus one," the apostle once revealed. "Three times I was beaten with rods. Once I received a stoning [in Lystra, where he was left for dead]. Three times I was shipwrecked [and bitten once by a deadly snake]; for a night and a day I was adrift at sea; on frequent journeys, in . . . danger in the city, danger in the wilderness, danger at sea . . . in toil and hardship, through many a sleepless night, hungry and thirsty, often without food, cold and naked" (2 Cor 11:24-27).

Added to all this, Paul was imprisoned at least three times. During his first imprisonment, in Philippi, he was stripped, beaten with rods, and locked in stocks. Some Roman stocks were designed to force a victim's legs as far apart as possible. The torture Paul experienced in Roman jails may have deformed him; a second-century source reports that his legs were crooked. However, Paul bore all these hardships well because he believed that he was doing what Jesus wanted and that he would be rewarded with eternal life for his selfless missionary activities.

en and abuse slaves, but realize that both slave and master stand equal before God.

Finally, as Paul sits in prison guarded by Roman soldiers, he perhaps contemplates their armor and how useless such armor is in the battles against evil that really matter. He challenges the Ephesians to put on a spiritual armor for the struggle against the "powers of this present darkness" (Eph 6:12). Truth, righteousness, faith, salvation, and the good news of peace—these are the believer's defensive armor. His sword is given by the Spirit and is "the word of God" (Eph 6:17). With these, the believer can stand against the falsehood, injustice, faithlessness, destruction, and hatred that are at war with the Gospel of God's grace and love. Paul concludes his letter with a prayer that "Grace be with all who have an undying love for our Lord Jesus Christ" (Eph 6:24).

THE LETTER OF PAUL TO THE PHILIPPIANS

*J*oy in the face of intense hardship and danger is the theme of Paul's letter to the Philippians. Paul established this community of believers in the city of Philippi in Macedonia during his second missionary journey. It was the first church on the continent of Europe (Acts 16:11-34). Very soon, the believers there saw Paul facing imprisonment and beatings, and they developed a strong affection for the apostle. When Paul left Philippi, the Christian converts sent money to support his labors in nearby Thessalonica and other places (Phil 4:15).

When the Philippians heard that Paul was again in prison, they sent a man named Epaphroditus as their emissary to bring gifts to aid the apostle. Epaphroditus fell ill while he was with Paul and came close to death but recovered (Phil 2:25-27). When the emissary was able to return to Philippi, Paul wrote this letter to express his gratitude for the Philippians' kindness toward him.

Along with his words of thanks, Paul also wrote about the understanding of life that grows from his faith in Jesus and that makes it possible for him to experience joy and contentment in the midst of persecution and imprisonment. He also warns the Philippians about teachers (apparently somewhat like those he encountered in Galatia) who insist on Gentile believers practicing circumcision and observing Jewish dietary restrictions and who thereby undermine trust in the cross of Christ as the focus of God's grace.

Paul does not indicate where he was imprisoned when he wrote Philippians. Traditionally, Philippians has been treated as a letter from Rome, where Paul was confined in the period about A.D. 60-61. Paul's reference to "the whole imperial guard" (Phil 1:13) might seem to confirm Rome as Paul's location, but, in fact, the imperial guard could be found wherever a Roman provincial governor resided—for example, Ephesus, Caesarea, or Jerusalem. By the time he wrote 2 Corinthians, Paul indicated (2 Cor 11:23) that he had already been imprisoned on numerous occasions, only three of which are mentioned in Acts. It may well be, therefore, that Philippians was written during one of those earlier imprisonments, perhaps from Ephesus, as many who have studied the letter believe, or perhaps from Caesarea.

Paul visiting Peter in prison; an imaginary scene by Filippino Lippi (c. 1457-1504)

I want you to know, beloved, that what has happened to me has actually helped to spread the gospel. PHIL 1:12

*P*aul links himself with Timothy in writing this letter and addresses "all the saints" (holy ones) in Philippi. He also mentions their "bishops and deacons" (Phil 1:1)—an ecclesiastical translation of words that simply mean "overseers and servants."

As Paul begins the body of the letter, he emphasizes the joy and confidence he feels toward the Philippians, which flow from the fact that he and the Philippians have been "sharing in the gospel from the first day until now." Paul loves them because they "share in God's grace" with him, both in his "imprisonment and in the defense and confirmation of the gospel" (Phil 1:5, 7).

Paul begins to describe his situation by assuring the Philippians that his imprisonment, which they were so concerned about, "has actually helped to spread the gospel." Paul is a prisoner different from most of those held for a Roman trial. Even hardened guards have been impressed by the fact that Paul's "imprisonment is for Christ." Other Christians, far from being intimidated by Paul's punishment, now "dare to speak the word with greater boldness and without fear" (Phil 1:13, 14).

Hard experience has taught Paul that some Christian teachers do not wish him well, and indeed have tried to undermine his work and increase his suffering in prison. Still, Paul is determined to rejoice "that Christ is proclaimed in every way" (Phil 1:18).

Though Paul is confident that he will eventually be released from this particular confinement, the possibility of death holds no dread for him; he can face personal danger or threatening opponents with equanimity. He is firmly convinced that, while he lives, his life will be totally focused on Christ and that "dying is gain" because he will then "be with Christ" (Phil 1:21, 23). He urges the Philippians similarly to allow their lives to be shaped by the message of Christ so that they may stand "firm in one spirit, striving side by side with one mind for the faith of the gospel." They need this firmness, Paul says with solemnity, because God "has graciously granted you the privilege not only of believing in Christ, but of suffering for him as well" (Phil 1:27, 29).

[Jesus] did not regard equality with God as something to be exploited, but emptied himself, taking the form of a slave.
PHIL 2:6-7

Paul begins to describe the love, compassion, unity, and mutual honor and service that shine forth from the life of a community shaped by the Gospel. This life is created by a way of thinking that was shown most perfectly in Christ. Here Paul evidently quotes from a hymn or chant that he and the Philippians used in worship. Most modern translations set Philippians 2:6-11 in verse form to help the reader see the line structure of the chant. This powerful hymn is perhaps the earliest written statement of Christ's divine preexistence.

The hymn falls into two parts that describe, first, the self-emptying humiliation of Jesus and, second, his exaltation and the universal recognition of his lordship. The humiliation of Christ begins when he takes "human form" and becomes "obedient to the point of death—even death on a cross" (Phil 2:7, 8). God responds to this self-giving love by glorifying Jesus with such power and authority that every living being "in heaven and on earth and under the earth" (Phil 2:10) bows before him to recognize that he is Lord.

Paul anticipates returning to Philippi, but wants to send ahead Timothy, his most trusted coworker, and the emissary Epaphroditus, whose return to Philippi has been delayed by severe illness.

Beware of the dogs, beware of the evil workers, beware of those who mutilate the flesh! PHIL 3:2

Abruptly, Paul changes the mood of his letter in order to warn the Philippians against certain teachers whose influence can undermine the very Gospel he has presented to them. For Paul, the circumcision that they urge on the Gentiles is nothing more than mutilation, since it has no positive value and indeed weakens trust in God's grace.

Paul shows that he possesses all the credentials these Jewish Christian teachers claim and more, since he is "a Hebrew . . . a Pharisee . . . [and] as to righteousness under the law, blameless" (Phil 3:5, 6). Yet Paul has consciously emptied himself of every claim before God based on his religious standing. "I want to

know Christ and the power of his resurrection," Paul asserts, "and the sharing of his sufferings by becoming like him in his death" (Phil 3:10).

Paul urges the Philippians not to see their lives in static terms of exacting obedience to the law but as a great race or quest for a goal that is always beyond the reach of this life. They, like Paul, should not be controlled by the past but should be "straining forward to what lies ahead" (Phil 3:13), as God calls them ever higher toward Jesus.

Do not worry about anything, but in everything by prayer and supplication with thanksgiving let your requests be made known to God. PHIL 4:6-7

Paul concludes the letter with exhortations and thanksgiving. He begins by urging peace between two women, Euodia and Syntyche, who had been important coworkers as they "struggled beside me in the work of the gospel" (Phil 4:2-3). He calls on a "loyal companion" (Phil 4:3) to help them. (The word "companion" should perhaps be translated as a name, "Syzygus.")

From his prison cell Paul looks at his own life and the life he is challenging the Philippians to live. "Rejoice in the Lord always," he calls to them; "again I will say, Rejoice" (Phil 4:4). Out of such joy comes gentleness and freedom from worry, founded on the confidence that "the Lord is near" (Phil 4:5). In place of worry, Paul challenges them to build a life of prayer, in which every aspect of life is shared with God. Then "the peace of God" (Phil 4:7)—a peace more profound than anyone can explain—will stand guard over the believer's heart and mind. Paul urges the Philippians actively to engage in cultivating their minds and hearts by focusing them on "whatever is true . . . honorable . . . just . . . worthy of praise" (Phil 4:8).

The final paragraphs of the letter express Paul's gratitude that the Philippians have sent him support in his hour of need. Paul has experienced such varied circumstances throughout his ministry that he has learned "to be content with whatever I have. . . . I can do all things through him who strengthens me" (Phil 4:11, 13).

Still, Paul is very grateful for the Philippians' gifts sent through Epaphroditus because they express the love that has made this church one of the most devoted supporters of his mission. They also show, Paul says, a trust in God, who "will fully satisfy every need of yours according to his riches in glory in Christ Jesus" (Phil 4:19).

The crucifixion of Jesus, as depicted in an 11th-century English Bible

THE LETTER OF PAUL TO THE COLOSSIANS

Christ seated at the right hand of God, the dove of the Holy Spirit hovering between them; from a 15th-century French book of hours

*P*aul's months and years in prison in Caesarea and Rome gave him time for extended reflection on the meaning of the Gospel for which he was in chains. Imprisonment also forced him to continue dealing with the problems that arose in the churches he had founded through letters rather than direct visits.

The church in Colossae, about 100 miles east of Ephesus, was not established by Paul himself but by one of Paul's coworkers, Epaphras, a native of Colossae. Epaphras was evidently converted and trained by Paul, probably in Ephesus. Returning to his hometown, he preached in the region around it, including the nearby cities of Hierapolis and Laodicea in the valley of the Lycus River in western Asia Minor. Though Colossae had once been a large city, by Paul's day it had declined to a secondary market town. While Paul was imprisoned in Rome, Epaphras evidently traveled to the imperial capital with news for Paul about problems within the church at Colossae; thus, he may have been imprisoned with Paul for some period.

The letter to the Colossians was evidently written and sent at about the same time as Paul's letter to Philemon, one of the leaders of the church in Colossae. In content, Colossians is closely related to Paul's letter to the Ephesians, which was also apparently written at the same time—along with a letter to Laodicea, which is now lost. All these letters may date from the years A.D. 60-61, when Paul was imprisoned in Rome. The letters were carried by Tychicus, another of Paul's coworkers, and Onesimus, a slave of Philemon. Paul expected to be released from prison and to return to Asia Minor and visit Colossae, as he indicated to Philemon.

From Epaphras, Paul had learned of certain teachers who had come to Colossae and were corrupting the message of the Gospel by claiming to supplement the work of Christ with angelic powers, asceticism, special ceremonies, and secret knowledge that they portrayed as a philosophy (Col 2:8, 16-19). Paul counters by celebrating the all-sufficiency of Christ, in whom "the whole fullness of deity dwells bodily" (Col 2:9).

The language and expression in Colossians is sufficiently different from that in earlier letters of Paul to have led many scholars to argue that the letter was written by a disciple of Paul after his death. The differences, however, may also be accounted for by the natural development and adaptability of Paul's style and by the participation of Paul's coworkers such as Epaphras or Timothy in the process of composition.

He is the image of the invisible God, the firstborn of all creation; for in him all things in heaven and on earth were created, things visible and invisible, whether thrones or dominions or rulers or powers. COL 1:15-16

*A*fter his opening greetings, Paul effusively expresses his thanksgiving for the Christians in Colossae, emphasizing his longing that they grow to maturity in Christ. He first notes how the Gospel had produced in them faith, love, and hope—a triad of lasting Christian virtues that he also highlighted in 1 Corinthians 13:13. Paul stresses the universal scope of the Gospel and how it has been brought to them by Epaphras, one of their own, whom Paul praises

as a "beloved fellow servant" and "a faithful minister of Christ on your behalf" (Col 1:7).

Paul emphasizes his prayers for their growth "in all spiritual wisdom and understanding" so that their lives may "bear fruit in every good work" and have divine power "to endure everything with patience, while joyfully giving thanks to the Father" (Col 1:9-12). Such a life grows out of what God has already done, Paul says, when he "rescued us from the power of darkness and transferred us into the kingdom of his beloved Son" (Col 1:13).

In the beautifully poetic language of Colossians 1:15-20, Paul describes Christ's sovereignty—a passage that interpreters have often identified as a Christian hymn, similar to the song in Philippians 2:6-11. The hymn celebrates Christ as creator and sustainer of the universe, supreme over every creature. He is the head of his body, the church, and the first to conquer death. Although in Christ "all the fullness of God was pleased to dwell," Paul asserts, it was ultimately only through his human suffering—through "the blood of his cross" (Col 1:19, 20)—that he was able to reconcile all things to God and make peace.

Uniting Jews and Gentiles in a community of peace and holiness is a clear demonstration of this divine reconciliation. For this great goal, Paul says that he is glad to suffer as Christ did and to "struggle with all the energy that he powerfully inspires within me" (Col 1:29). Likewise, the Christians in Colossae can be confident that they "have the knowledge of God's mystery" and are armed against any deception by "plausible arguments" (Col 2:2-4).

When you were dead in trespasses and the uncircumcision of your flesh, God made you alive together with him, when he forgave us all our trespasses.
COL 2:13

Paul warns the Colossians against the destructive influence of some who have been propounding what they call a "philosophy" but which Paul describes as "empty deceit, according to human tradition" (Col 2:8). The precise nature of this teaching is difficult to define, since Paul describes it only indirectly, using phrases that were no doubt clearer to the addressees than to modern readers. The teaching involves special regulations about food and drink, the observance of special days of festival and sabbath rest, and some forms of asceticism or "self-abasement" (Col 2:18). Such characteristics may suggest a link to a form of Judaism similar to that ascribed to the Essenes, who are known today through the famous Dead Sea Scrolls. The false teachers depend on special revelations in visions and emphasize rites directed toward the power of angels—referred to as "rulers and authorities"—and the cosmic elements or the "elemental spirits of the universe" (Col 2:15, 20). In all these things, Paul charges, they are "puffed up without cause by a human way of thinking" (Col 2:18) and have thus lost contact with Christ.

Rigorous regulations and prohibitions evidently impress the Colossians with the seriousness of this philosophy. They apparently are attracted by strict commands—"Do not handle, Do not taste, Do not touch" (Col 2:21)—and willingly submit. Paul warns that such rules "have indeed an appearance of wisdom in promoting self-imposed piety, humility, and severe treatment of the body, but they are of no value in checking self-indulgence" (Col 2:23). Instead, Paul urges the Colossians to recognize that in their baptism into the faith they have been "buried with" Christ and "raised with him" (Col 2:12), and thus share in Christ's victory over all competing powers through his death on the cross.

If you have been raised with Christ, seek the things that are above, where Christ is, seated at the right hand of God. Set your minds on things that are above, not on things that are on earth. COL 3:1-2

Paul concludes his letter by challenging the Colossians to live day by day in a way that shows the transformation that Christ has brought about in their lives. The death and new life they have experienced must also mean the death of old practices of immorality, greed, anger, abusive language, and dishonesty. In Christ, they put on a "new self" (Col 3:10) that is like Christ and thus manifests the image of God, breaking down all barriers between races and classes. With this new self, believers are conscious that they are loved by God and respond in a life of compassion, patience, forgiveness, and love, "which binds everything together in perfect harmony" (Col 3:14).

Paul then sketches how these values affect the ways in which Christians are to act within the human relationships established by the Greco-Roman society. The small band of Christians in Colossae has no power to change the structure of Roman law, in which most relationships involved domination (husband, father, master) and dependence (wife, children, slaves). But the apostle urges believers to realize that their commitment to Christ must change their attitudes and motivations within that structure.

Paul ends with greetings from his coworkers, including "Luke, the beloved physician" (Col 4:14), and instructions to share the letter with the church in Laodicea, asking the Colossians to read his letter, now lost, to the Laodiceans. After dictating the whole letter to a scribe, Paul takes the papyrus in his own hands and adds a few final words to authenticate the document: "I, Paul, write this greeting with my own hand. Remember my chains. Grace be with you" (Col 4:18).

Luke, mentioned by Paul in Colossians, is said to have painted a portrait of the virgin Mary; a prayer book illustration dated about 1420.

THE LETTERS OF PAUL TO THE THESSALONIANS

Paul's first letter to the Thessalonians, most scholars agree, is the earliest book of the New Testament, written about A.D. 50. Paul sent the letter from Corinth in southern Greece to the community of believers in Thessalonica, the prosperous capital of the Roman province of Macedonia. In his missionary work, Paul always tried to establish churches in major cities from which the Gospel could spread to surrounding regions. Thessalonica was ideal for his purposes, since it was both a seaport and a city on the Via Egnatia, the major Roman highway between Byzantium and the Adriatic Sea.

Paul came to Thessalonica from Philippi, where he had "suffered and been shamefully mistreated" (1 Thess 2:2) by Roman authorities. He began his work in the Jewish synagogue of Thessalonica, where he argued that Jesus was the Messiah foretold by the prophets. Severe conflict arose as the synagogue split over this message, but many Gentiles who had been sympathetic to Judaism accepted Paul's message (Acts 17:1-9). Eventually, Paul's opponents organized a large crowd that stirred up the city authorities with charges that Paul was a traitor who was proclaiming Jesus as a rival to the Roman emperor. Paul escaped being arrested by hastily leaving Thessalonica and sailing down to Athens with some of his coworkers. His worry for the believers in Thessalonica, however, caused him to send Timothy back to them. When Timothy returned to Paul while he was in Corinth, the positive report he brought stimulated Paul to write 1 Thessalonians. Through this letter Paul wanted to encourage the believers who were suffering persecution and to answer their concerns about the return of Christ and the fate of some of their number who had died without seeing Jesus.

Paul's second letter to the Thessalonians was evidently written only a few months later—though some scholars argue that it is the work of another author, written at a somewhat later date. It was sent in response to news that some of the believers had been led to think that "the day of the Lord is already here" (2 Thess 2:2)—that is, that Christ had already returned, perhaps in some spiritualized sense. Faced with this misunderstanding, Paul urged the Thessalonians to recognize that though they might hope for Christ to reappear soon, the Second Coming was still in the future, and they must live their present life with a sense of responsibility and faithfulness.

Paul bearing the sword symbolizing his death by beheading; a late-15th-century Italian portrait

1 Thessalonians

Our message of the gospel came to you not in word only, but also in power and in the Holy Spirit and with full conviction. 1 THESS 1:5

Paul begins the first of his letters with a sense of relief that he has heard good news about the community of believers in Thessalonica, which he had believed was at great risk of being destroyed. There were two grave dangers. First, persecution may have threatened the believers' endurance and faithfulness; second, charges against Paul and his coworkers may have undermined their confidence in the message they had received from him. Though Paul is overjoyed that neither danger has overwhelmed them, he nevertheless speaks frankly to the believers about both dangers, in order to confirm their resolve.

In the charges, controversies, and rioting that led to Paul's flight from Thessalonica, the apostle had evidently been accused of being a charlatan philosopher—a type of street preacher well known from the literature of the time. He proclaimed a fiery message, it was being said, in order to scare people into giving him money, and then left town without caring for the people he left behind. In response to such charges, Paul calls the Thessalonian believers to remember for themselves the character that he had demonstrated among them and the kind of message he had proclaimed. God had chosen them to receive the message, which came to them "not in word only, but also in power and in the Holy Spirit and with full conviction"; and they had responded with all seriousness as they "turned to God from idols, to serve a living and true God" (1 Thess 1:9).

Paul calls them to witness that his own life has been an open book. He has never accepted any money from them, but has labored to support himself and his coworkers. And far from not caring for them, he reminds his converts, "we were gentle among you, like a nurse tenderly caring for her own children." Extending the metaphor, he adds, "We dealt with each one of you like a father with his children, urging and encouraging you" (1 Thess 2:7, 11).

In the face of their persecution, Paul reminds the Thessalonians that they are imitating Christ as well as himself and "the churches of God in Christ Jesus which are in Judea" (1 Thess 2:14), communities that have also experienced intense persecution.

As for us, brothers and sisters, when, for a short time, we were made orphans by being separated from you—in person, not in heart—we longed with great eagerness to see you face to face. 1 THESS 2:17

The way Paul had been forced to leave Thessalonica caused distress both for the believers and for himself. Paul describes how bereft he felt when he was separated from the community of believers. Paul knew that they were facing persecution; indeed, he had warned them that it would come. But he also knew that the reality of persecution was different from the expectation of it, and that the faith of new believers could be severely challenged. When Paul's

In this early-16th-century Russian painting, Jesus liberates the souls condemned to hell for Adam's sin—an event early Chrisitans believed was imminent.

attempts to arrange a return to Thessalonica were frustrated—how, it is not known—he saw the power of Satan at work. Finally, Paul says, "when I could bear it no longer, I sent [Timothy] to find out about your faith; I was afraid that somehow the tempter had tempted you and that our labor had been in vain" (1 Thess 3:5). While awaiting news from Thessalonica, Paul continues to work in Athens and then moves to Corinth, where he again meets opposition.

Timothy's return to Paul brings the good news of the Thessalonians' faith and love and assurance that their belief in the Gospel has not been undermined by charges against Paul. The news is a tremendous relief to the apostle: "We now live, if you continue to stand firm in the Lord" (1 Thess 3:8). Thus, he prays for the Thessalonians that he may come to them soon and that God will cause them to "abound in love for one another and for all" and will strengthen their "hearts in holiness" (1 Thess 3:12-13).

Paul challenges them to continue to grow in their commitment to a life pleasing to God: "For this is the will of God, your sanctification" (1 Thess 4:3). They must reject sexual immorality and exploitation but continue to grow in genuine love for each other. As members of a small community vulnerable to persecution, the believers should "behave properly toward outsiders and be dependent on no one" (1 Thess 4:12).

But we do not want you to be uninformed, brothers and sisters, about those who have died, so that you may not grieve as others do who have no hope. 1 THESS 4:13

In the final sections of his letter, Paul treats two related questions that Timothy has evidently told him are special concerns for the Thessalonians. Like all early Christians, Paul believed that Jesus could return at any time and, indeed, hoped and expected that he would do so within his own lifetime. This hope Paul has conveyed to the Thessalonians to strengthen them in the face of persecution.

But now this hope produces an emotionally charged question among the Thessalonians because some of their community have died—whether naturally or from persecution Paul does not say. What will happen to the dead? Has their existence been lost completely? Paul assures them that the death of a believer in no way destroys his hope of eternal life in Christ. Indeed, Paul states, "we who are alive, who are left until the coming of the Lord" have no advantage, but with Christ's coming all believers, living and dead, will "meet the Lord" and "will be with the Lord forever" (1 Thess 4:15, 17).

The Thessalonians are also concerned to know exactly when Christ will return. Paul reminds them that no one can know "the times and the seasons" because "the day of the Lord will come like a thief in the night" (1 Thess 5:1-2). The only thing certain is that it will be unexpected, and every prediction of it is sure to be wrong. The important thing is that believers live as "children of light" (1 Thess 5:5), who have no fear of Christ's return. God has made such a life possible by giving the believer "salvation through our Lord Jesus Christ," Paul says, "who died for us, so that whether we are awake or asleep we may live with him" (1 Thess 5:9-10).

2 Thessalonians

Therefore we ourselves boast of you among the churches of God for your steadfastness and faith during all your persecutions and the afflictions that you are enduring.
2 THESS 1:4

By the time Paul wrote 2 Thessalonians, all of his worst fears concerning the persecution in Thessalonica had become a reality. But the Christians' faith held firm. Indeed, under the challenge of persecution, Paul says, "your faith is growing abundantly, and the love of everyone of you for one another is increasing" (2 Thess 1:3). They are having to endure suffering that their opponents seem to inflict with impunity. But Paul assures them that their hardships are not the end of the story. He vividly portrays Christ's

The archangel mentioned in 1 Thessalonians 4:16 as calling souls for the Last Judgment is by tradition Michael; he is shown here in a Swiss painting dated about 1500.

triumphant return as a time when those who persecute and abuse others are punished, while God gives "relief to the afflicted" (2 Thess 1:7). This dramatic reversal will not be secret; rather, Jesus will be "revealed from heaven with his mighty angels" and will be "marveled at on that day among all who have believed" (2 Thess 1:7, 10).

With this vision in mind, Paul warns the believers against any who reinterpret or spiritualize the idea of Christ's coming so as to say that "the day of the Lord is already here" (2 Thess 2:2). Such a view may have arisen from speculations about the secret nature of Christ's coming "like a thief in the night" (1 Thess 5:2), combined with the difficulty many Greeks had in understanding the concept of resurrection. In any case, Paul emphatically states that the day of the Lord is in the future and that the present is a period during which the battle between good and evil is being waged. He uses enigmatic images for future events similar to those in apocalyptic works such as Revelation. He refers to "the rebellion," "the lawless one," and "the mystery of lawlessness" (2 Thess 2:3, 7)—terms that the Thessalonians may have at least partially deciphered, but which are obscure today. These references make the emphatic point that there are matters to attend to before the end of all things. They call for the believer to take a stand for God and against every manifestation of "the working of Satan" (2 Thess 2:9).

Finally, brothers and sisters, pray for us, so that the word of the Lord may spread rapidly and be glorified everywhere, just as it is among you. 2 THESS 3:1

In spite of these misunderstandings, Paul expresses great confidence in the Thessalonian believers, who "stand firm and hold fast to the traditions that you were taught by us" (2 Thess 2:15). But Paul warns them of the problem of idleness that seems to have been an outgrowth of their misunderstanding about Christ's return. When some accepted that "the day of the Lord is already here" (2 Thess 2:2), they apparently also concluded that all work had lost its purpose. They perhaps intended to show the seriousness of their belief, but in effect they began "living in idleness, mere busybodies, not doing any work" (2 Thess 3:11). For Paul, this is far more than an annoyance, it is a fundamental misunderstanding of Christian life and of their responsibility for each other. He reminds the Thessalonians of the example set by himself and his coworkers, how "with toil and labor we worked night and day, so that we might not burden any of you" (2 Thess 3:8). Life, with its responsibilities for love and mutual support, has not come to an end: "Brothers and sisters, do not be weary in doing what is right" (2 Thess 3:15).

Paul concludes his letter with a greeting written in his own hand as a guarantee that it is authentic and not, as he had warned them earlier, a "letter, as though from us" (2 Thess 2:2). His final words are a benediction: "The grace of our Lord Jesus Christ be with all of you" (2 Thess 3:18).

THE LETTERS OF PAUL TO TIMOTHY AND TITUS

His coworker Timothy at his side, Paul pens a message to one of his churches; a 14th-century French Bible illustration.

The two letters to Timothy and one to Titus are called the Pastoral Letters because they are brimming with sage advice on how to pastor a church. Timothy ministered to early Christians in Ephesus, and Titus to those on the island of Crete.

Though each letter claims the apostle Paul as author, many scholars doubt that he actually wrote them. The writing style and theology sound strangely unlike Paul. When the apostle spoke of faith, he meant the believer's trusting relationship with God; in the Pastorals, faith means the Christian religion. Also, some of Paul's most fervent teachings are missing, for example, the mystical union between the believer and Christ, which Paul often compared to marriage. Because of variations such as these, some scholars suggest that the Pastorals were written one or two generations after Paul—perhaps early in the second century—by a believer who borrowed Paul's name and authority to confront new problems. This was a common and accepted practice in ancient times; the opposite of plagiarism, it gave credit to someone else for material written—as much as possible—in the voice and spirit of that individual. Second-century church leaders, however, attributed the work to Paul. And the letters do discuss some of his perennial concerns, such as false teachers and rules of conduct for Christians. In addition, the letters are addressed to his well-known associates, both of whom were targets in the debate over whether non-Jewish Christians should be circumcised—Timothy, a half Jew, was circumcised; Titus, a Gentile, was not.

If Paul wrote these letters, he likely did so after the events described in Acts—otherwise the histories clash. Acts, for instance, says Timothy accompanied Paul from Ephesus to Macedonia, while 1 Timothy says the opposite: Paul left him behind. Scholars who believe Paul wrote the Pastorals argue that his story picks up where Acts leaves off, with Paul in a Roman prison. They contend that Paul was released in about A.D. 62, made a fourth missionary journey, then was arrested again and executed in Rome about A.D. 64, during Nero's persecution of Christians.

Whoever wrote the letters drew on a wealth of experience to produce insightful guidelines for public worship, selection of church leaders, and dealing with false teachers. He also warns Christians that they will inevitably face deadly persecution. But, with a moving reference to his own imminent martyrdom, the author reminds them that if they hold fast to their beliefs they will live forever and reign with Jesus.

1 Timothy

To Timothy, my loyal child in the faith: . . . . remain in Ephesus so that you may instruct certain people not to teach any different doctrine.   1 TIM 1:2, 3

The letter begins the same way that those generally acknowledged to be from Paul do—with the apostle identifying himself and his intended reader and a prayer for the reader to receive God's blessing of mercy and peace. Timothy was one of Paul's most beloved and devoted associates, one who joined the apostle's traveling entourage about A.D. 49, during Paul's second missionary journey. Timothy, son of a Gentile father and a Jewish mother, lived in Lystra, a city about 300 miles east of Ephesus.

On what may have been a fourth missionary trip, sometime after the three described in the book of Acts, Paul asks Timothy to stay in Ephesus while the apostle continues on to Macedonia, north of Greece. Timothy's task is to direct the community of believers, with special attention to protecting them from "certain people" teaching "different doctrine" (1 Tim 1:3). Paul names two of these people: Hymenaeus and Alexander, "whom I have turned over to Satan, so that they may learn not to blaspheme" (1 Tim 1:20). Paul apparently believes that Satan will plague the men with suffering, which will force them to reconsider their heretical behavior.

The specific heresy afflicting the church is hard to categorize. Among the many teachings that trouble

Paul is the preoccupation with Jewish laws. Paul argues that these laws exist not for believers but for sinners—to show them that what they are doing is wrong. Paul also warns against obsession with genealogies, which apparently tout a person's spiritual pedigree, and with embellished legends that perhaps laud family heroes. As for himself, Paul says, God "strengthened me, because he judged me faithful and appointed me to his service" (1 Tim 1:12)—thus establishing himself as a model for believers.

Clues throughout 1 and 2 Timothy lead some scholars to suggest that the false teachers in Ephesus may have been forerunners of a second-century heresy known as gnosticism (from the Greek word *gnosis*, meaning "knowledge"). This connection is made, in part, because of Paul's advice that Timothy take a stand against "contradictions of what is falsely called knowledge" (1 Tim 6:20). Gnostics drew from many religions, including Judaism and Christianity, and taught that only they had the spiritual enlightenment to interpret correctly the Bible and other writings they held sacred. Many of their teachings clashed with fundamental Christian beliefs. For example, gnostics believed that the physical world was evil and that only the spiritual world was good. This led them to reject the idea that the Son of God became a human being who suffered physical pain, died, and rose from the dead.

In every place the men should pray, lifting up holy hands without anger or argument. 1 TIM 2:8

*I*n worship, Paul says, Christians should pray for everyone—even for bad rulers. He reasons that praying for rulers will help Christians enjoy a life of peace and quiet, perhaps by converting some leaders, but certainly by adjusting the attitude of believers toward these rulers, thereby helping Christians see political leaders as people in need of God.

During worship services, Christian men are to raise their hands in prayer. Paul is not dictating the posture for prayer, but rather emphasizing the importance of praying and illustrating this by citing a common, age-old posture. Paul does, however, seem to limit the public praying to men. Women, Paul says, should "learn in silence with full submission. I permit no woman to teach or to have authority over a man" (1 Tim 2:11-12). Furthermore, he admonishes women to dress modestly. Seeming to ban jewelry, fine clothing, and attractive hairstyles, Paul cautions against allowing church meetings to become an occasion for the wealthy to show off their riches.

Paul's rule against permitting women to take an active or leading role in worship is puzzling. For in his letter to the Romans, he commends two women church leaders: Phoebe, a deacon, and Junia, an apostle (Rom 16:1, 7). In addition, both Priscilla and her husband Aquila, students of Paul, taught the famed speaker Apollos about Jesus. Some scholars say Paul's advice to Timothy is not a universal rule, but addresses a specific problem in the Ephesian

congregation—a problem similar to one in Corinth (1 Cor 14:34-35). In churches where no such problems exist, Paul places no restrictions on women leading the church. Arguing that there must have been a unique problem in Ephesus, scholars note that the plot behind some gnostic myths—to which Paul may have been referring in 1 Timothy 1:6-7—involves women oppressing men. Possibly some gnostic women in the Ephesus congregation were trying to emulate their heroines.

Equally perplexing is Paul's remark that women "will be saved through childbearing" (1 Tim 2:15). Some scholars say Paul means that women in Ephesus can ease church tensions by concentrating on their duties as wives and mothers. On the other hand, Paul could mean that women have been saved through the birth of the child Jesus, or that they will be kept physically safe during childbirth.

Whoever aspires to the office of bishop desires a noble task. 1 TIM 3:1

*O*nly two local church offices are mentioned in the New Testament: bishop and deacon. Bishop comes from a Greek word that literally means "overseer" and is sometimes translated "elder." In Greek culture, the overseer was an organization's presiding official. In early Christian churches, the bishop or elder may have been the local official in charge, though the Bible never clearly says so. Deacon means "one who serves," and is the title traditionally given

Jesus' birth, to which Paul possibly alluded in 1 Timothy, is depicted in this 15th-century Italian glazed terra-cotta lunette.

to Stephen, Philip, and several other men whose work freed the apostles to concentrate on preaching. These first deacons were charged with distributing food to the hungry in Jerusalem, but they quickly developed into respected teachers as well.

Apparently, apostles and their representatives, such as Timothy, wield authority over these local church officials, since Paul shows Timothy what to look for when appointing them. Bishops, Paul says, should be seasoned Christians capable of teaching, instead of new converts. They should have a reputation for self-control, gentleness, and hospitality. They should not be heavy drinkers or violent. And they should be able to manage their families well, "for if someone does not know how to manage his own household, how can he take care of God's church?" (1 Tim 3:5). Deacons, likewise, should be well respected and good family managers. In addition, they should first be assigned other responsibilities in the church to test their character and ability.

In later times some will renounce the faith by paying attention to deceitful spirits and teachings of demons, through the hypocrisy of liars. 1 TIM 4:1-2

By "later times" Paul means the messianic age, which began with the life and ministry of Jesus. False teachers, whom the apostle condemns as demon-led, "forbid marriage and demand abstinence from foods" (1 Tim 4:3), the latter probably referring to Jewish food restrictions. Because gnostics believed that everything in the physical world was evil, they became renowned for their ascetic restrictions that encouraged self-denial and the shunning of physical pleasures. Some gnostics, however, went to the opposite extreme. They advocated decadent lifestyles, arguing that enlightened spiritual beings such as themselves were unaffected by the physical world and should therefore feel free to wallow in all the pleasures of life. Paul tells Timothy to counter these teachings by explaining that there is nothing inherently evil about the physical world: "everything created by God is good" (1 Tim 4:4). This repeats the message the apostle Peter received in a vision that released him from Jewish food laws, which the New Testament teaches were intended only for the pre-messianic era (Acts 10:9-16). Paul also tells Timothy not to be intimidated into silence by older people who contend that they are wiser: "Let no one despise your youth, but set the believers an example in speech and conduct, in love, in faith, in purity" (1 Tim 4:12).

Do not speak harshly to an older man, but speak to him as to a father, to younger men as brothers, to older women as mothers, to younger women as sisters. 1 TIM 5:1, 2

Paul closes his first letter to Timothy with practical advice on how to deal with various groups of people in the church, followed by a moving plea to remain godly, loving, and faithful to the authentic teachings of Jesus. When correcting an older man—even a heretic—Timothy is to speak respectfully, as though addressing his own father. Likewise, he is to speak respectfully to everyone in the church.

Older widows who have no family to take care of them should be cared for by the congregation, Paul advises. But younger widows should be encouraged to remarry so they do not spend their lives "gadding about from house to house . . . not merely idle, but also gossips and busybodies" (1 Tim 5:13). Widows supported by the church become Christian workers who must exhibit many of the same qualifications as bishops and deacons. In addition, Paul says they must be at least 60 years old and willing to pledge themselves to a life of chastity while serving the church. Slaves are to serve their masters respectfully, because Paul believes that a person's conduct—especially in grim circumstances—can glorify God. So rather than call on Christians to oppose immediately and publicly an oppressive social institution, Paul advises them to act in a way that will eventually soften the hearts of the oppressors.

Some in the congregation are apparently greedy, and not aware that "the love of money is a root of all kinds of evil" (1 Tim 6:10). Paul urges his beloved friend not to pursue wealth and its associates: envy, jumping to conclusions, slander, and argument. Instead, Timothy is to seek righteousness and to remind rich believers that they have been entrusted with God's money and should therefore "be rich in good works, generous, and ready to share" (1 Tim 6:18).

2 Timothy

God did not give us a spirit of cowardice . . . . Do not be ashamed, then, of the testimony about our Lord or of me his prisoner, but join with me in suffering for the gospel. 2 TIM 1:7-8

When Paul wrote 1 Timothy and Titus, he was a free man. But now, as he writes a second letter to Timothy, he is chained like a dangerous criminal, imprisoned in a cold cell in Rome, and fully expecting to be condemned and executed soon. Scholars are uncertain when this letter was written. If Paul was freed from the Roman imprisonment that concludes the book of Acts, he likely continued his missionary trips and was arrested once again and sent to Rome. This probably occurred in the mid-60s A.D., not long after the emperor Nero accused Christians of setting the fire that destroyed two-thirds of Rome in A.D. 64. In retaliation for the mysterious fire, Nero condemned countless Christians to death by beheading, crucifixion, or as bloody entertainment in public arenas.

As Paul writes this letter—the most personal and tender in all the Bible—he sits alone with his memories. His colleagues have deserted him, perhaps realizing the hopelessness of his situation. He knows that this may be his last chance to say anything to his loyal and beloved friend. Thus, he encourages Timothy to follow his example and courageously pro-

ROMAN PERSECUTION OF THE CHRISTIANS

*Roman emperor Nero;
a marble bust made shortly
after his death in A.D. 68*

At first, Romans tolerated the emerging Christian movement, thinking that the believers represented just another group within Judaism—like the Pharisees or Sadducees. But by the summer of A.D. 64, when a fierce, nine-day fire destroyed most of Rome, killing thousands, Roman authorities knew that Christianity was a distinct, minority religion regarded with widespread distrust. The emperor Nero took advantage of this to shift blame for the fire from himself to the Christians. A rumor had spread that Nero ordered the fire to clear the way for a glorious new city and that, as the flames soared, he fiddled with glee in his palace.

The Roman historian Tacitus reported that "to suppress this rumor, Nero fabricated scapegoats—and punished with every refinement the notoriously depraved Christians." The Romans often misunderstood Christian beliefs, assuming that the Lord's Supper was a cannibalistic feast and that kisses of greeting between spiritual "brothers and sisters" was evidence of incest. The first persecution of Christians took place, Tacitus explained, to punish Christians not so much for the fire but for such shocking antisocial behavior.

Nero's persecution established a precedent. In the A.D. 90s, the emperor Domitian executed Christians for refusing to worship him as a god. The Roman governor of Turkey in 112 boasted that he summarily executed any Christian who confessed his faith.

claim the message of Jesus, even when doing so becomes dangerous. This is much more than a matter of life and death, Paul explains. It is a matter of eternal life and death: "If we have died with him [Jesus], we will also live with him; . . . if we deny him, he will also deny us" (2 Tim 2:11, 12).

Do your best to present yourself to God as one approved by him, a worker who has no need to be ashamed, rightly explaining the word of truth. 2 TIM 2:15

As Paul had done in his first letter to Timothy, he reminds the Ephesian pastor to live as a model of righteousness. This, he says, means avoiding lust, futile arguments, and counterfeit Christians, who insist they are lovers of God but whose actions reveal they are "lovers of themselves, lovers of money, boasters, arrogant, abusive, disobedient to their parents, ungrateful, unholy" (2 Tim 3:2).

All who live a godly life will suffer persecution, Paul warns from his prison cell. Even so, he pleads with Timothy to "proclaim the message; be persistent whether the time is favorable or unfavorable . . . . For the time is coming when people will not put up with sound doctrine, but having itching ears, they will accumulate for themselves teachers to suit their own desires, and will turn away from listening to the truth and wander away to myths" (2 Tim 4:2-4).

The time of my departure has come. I have fought the good fight, I have finished the race, I have kept the faith. 2 TIM 4:6-7

In a deeply moving conclusion, Paul concedes that he is about to die. But he finds comfort in knowing that he has been obedient to the Lord. For this, he expects to be rewarded with a crown of righteousness—a reference to eternal life, illustrated by the crown of wreaths given to winners of athletic competitions. Yet, like most who face death, Paul wants to be near those he loves. Only Luke remains with him. "Do your best to come to me soon" (2 Tim 4:9, 21), he twice asks Timothy, who is ministering a thousand miles away, with winter approaching. And he asks him to bring Mark, "for he is useful in my ministry" (2 Tim 4:11)—an indication that Paul has been reconciled with the follower who deserted him on his first missionary journey. The pathos builds as Paul subtly reveals he is suffering from the cold, yet wants to continue his study and letter-writing ministry as long as he can. This becomes clear when he asks Timothy to bring the cloak he left in Troas, along with his books and parchment scrolls.

As Paul ends the letter, he speaks of being spared from "the lion's mouth" (2 Tim 4:17), perhaps a metaphor for his enemies. But it is a reference that would likely remind Timothy of the many physical hardships Paul has survived: shipwrecks, beatings, and stoning. God will rescue him again, Paul writes, but this rescue will transcend the physical world "and save me for his heavenly kingdom" (2 Tim 4:18).

Titus

To Titus, my loyal child in the faith . . . . I left you behind in Crete for this reason, so that you should put in order what remained to be done, and should appoint elders in every town. TITUS 1:4, 5

During a missionary journey not among the three described in Acts, Paul evidently visits the island of Crete, south of Greece. Traveling with him is Titus, perhaps one of the first Gentiles to join his team of traveling ministers and apparently the only non-Jew to accompany him to Jerusalem in A.D. 49, when Christian leaders debated whether Gentiles should obey Jewish laws. Titus, whom Paul once entrusted with the difficult chore of confronting false teachings in Corinth and restoring the damaged relationship between Paul and the congregation there, develops into a dedicated minister. Because Titus succeeds in Corinth, Paul entrusts his seasoned colleague with another formidable challenge: establishing and organizing the church in Crete. Paul cannot do this personally because he feels obligated to press on in his travels. So he leaves Titus behind.

Paul gives his colleague much the same advice he offered to Timothy regarding selection of church leaders and the importance of standing firm against heresies. Quoting a Cretan writer, Paul warns that this assignment will be hard because the Cretan people are renowned as "liars, vicious brutes, lazy gluttons" (Titus 1:12). But Paul reminds Titus that the two of them, also, were once "despicable," yet were transformed by "God our Savior" (Titus 3:3, 4). Paul believes that God can change the infamous Cretans as well.

Teach what is consistent with sound doctrine. Tell the older men to be temperate, serious, prudent, and sound in faith, in love, and in endurance. TITUS 2:1-2

Just as Paul had advised Timothy how to minister to various groups within the Ephesian congregation, he does the same for Titus. Older men should be self-controlled, strong in the faith, and filled with love and patience. Older women should be reverent and not given to slander and heavy drinking. Young women should love their husbands and children, and be good managers of the household. Young men should live as models of integrity. And slaves should treat their masters with loyalty and respect. Paul writes that because God has made salvation available to people from all walks of life, Titus is to "declare these things; exhort and reprove with all authority. Let no one look down on you" (Titus 2:15).

Remind them to be subject to rulers . . . speak evil of no one . . . avoid quarreling . . . show every courtesy to everyone. TITUS 3:1, 2

Paul closes his letter with advice pertinent to Christians of all ages and classes. He tells Titus to teach the Cretans gentleness and humility—the same lessons Paul and Titus learned from the Holy Spirit after being baptized into the Christian faith. "I desire that you insist on these things," the apostle adds. "Avoid stupid controversies, genealogies, dissensions, and quarrels about the law, for they are unprofitable and worthless" (Titus 3:8, 9). Church members who persist in arguing over meaningless issues or bragging about their spiritual heritage (as some Jewish Christians apparently did) are to receive two warnings before being shunned by the community.

Paul's final piece of advice calls on the Cretan church to put into action everything Titus teaches them: "Let people learn to devote themselves to good works in order to meet urgent needs, so that they may not be unproductive. . . . Grace be with all of you" (Titus 3:14, 15).

By tradition, Paul was executed by beheading in Rome, a scene captured by Jacopo Robusti, called Tintoretto (1518-1594).

THE LETTER OF PAUL TO PHILEMON

*I*n the canon of the New Testament, Paul's letters are arranged in general order of their length, from Romans, the longest, to Philemon, the shortest—fewer than 350 words in 25 verses. Highly personal, but not an entirely private communication, the letter to Philemon is basically an appeal to a Christian slave owner for mercy—perhaps even freedom—for his runaway slave. If caught, runaway slaves were either executed or branded and sent back to their masters. Harboring a runaway slave was punishable by fine—though slaves claiming mistreatment could seek sanctuary at a religious shrine. Onesimus, the slave on whose behalf Paul wrote, may have sought sanctuary with the apostle; during his stay with Paul, he converted to Christianity.

In both his salutation and his closing (as well as in verses 9, 10, and 13), Paul mentions that he is a prisoner. Three imprisonments are documented in the book of Acts: at Philippi (Acts 16:23-40), at Caesarea (Acts 23:35), and at Rome (Acts 28:16-31). Problems with the chronology of Paul's missionary journeys rule out the first two as the place from which Paul was writing. A postscript in some manuscripts of the letter to Philemon says that Paul wrote it from Rome—that is, during his confinement there about A.D. 60-61. But it is unlikely that the slave from Asia Minor could have traveled as far as the imperial capital. Moreover, in Romans 15:22-24, Paul wrote that he planned to travel west to Spain, not east to Colossae as he promises in verse 22. Therefore, some suggest a fourth, unrecorded incarceration of Paul—perhaps at Ephesus, a major Christian center 100 miles west of Colossae. If this is so, a date for the letter of the late 50s is also possible.

Paul (left) sends the slave Onesimus with a letter to his master Philemon; a medieval illustration.

Paul, a prisoner of Christ Jesus, and Timothy, our brother,
To Philemon, our dear friend and co-worker.   PHILEM 1

*O*ne of Paul's closest associates in his missionary work, Timothy is also listed as a co-sender of five other letters: 2 Corinthians, Philippians, Colossians, and 1 and 2 Thessalonians. Philemon, mentioned nowhere else in the New Testament, offers his house as a church—the use of domestic structures for early Christian meetings being quite common. Of the two others to whom the letter is addressed, Apphia is perhaps Philemon's wife and Archippus his son or other close relative. Since the latter is identified elsewhere as a member of the church at Colossae (Col 4:17), that town in Asia Minor is the likely site of Philemon's house church and the place from which Onesimus fled.

I am appealing to you for my child, Onesimus, whose father I have become during my imprisonment.   PHILEM 10

*A*fter praising Philemon's love and faith, Paul gets to the point of his letter: to receive the runaway slave "no longer as a slave but more than a slave, a beloved brother" (Philem 16). A common name for a slave, Onesimus means "useful"; the apostle is playing on words by saying that formerly he was "useless," but as a convert he is now "indeed useful both to you and to me" (Philem 11).

So if you consider me your partner, welcome him as you would welcome me.   PHILEM 17

*I*n 2 Corinthians 8:23, Paul refers to his fellow missionary Titus as a partner; elsewhere (Phil 4:15) he speaks of whole churches as sharing in his work. While not specifically asking for Onesimus's emancipation, the apostle offers restitution for any wrong done by the slave—telling Philemon to "charge that to my account" (Philem 18).

I, Paul, am writing this with my own hand.   PHILEM 19

*A*lthough Paul apparently dictated most of his letters, only one of his scribes is known by name: Tertius (Rom 16:22). As he does here, Paul specifically mentions that he is the penman in 1 Corinthians 16:21, Galatians 6:11, Colossians 4:18, and 2 Thessalonians 3:17.

Epaphras, my fellow prisoner in Christ Jesus, sends greetings to you, and so do Mark, Aristarchus, Demas, and Luke, my fellow workers.   PHILEM 23

*S*ince these five individuals are also mentioned in the closing greetings of Paul's letter to the Colossians (Col 4:10-14), it is believed that the two letters were written at the same time and from the same place and sent to the same destination, Colossae.

How do believers maintain their devotion under the continual pressure of harassment and persecution that wears on their families and community year after year? An answer is given in the letter to the Hebrews, a "word of exhortation" (Heb 13:22) that seeks to encourage, strengthen, and guide a group of early Christians whose endurance is wearing thin. The author leads the readers through a series of reflections on and celebrations of the greatness and faithfulness of Jesus, in order to strengthen their confidence in a close relationship with God through his Son. He helps them to understand where their journey of faith is leading and to see their lives in relation to the faithful who have gone before them.

Little is known about the identity of the author or the recipients of this letter. The fact that the work ends like a letter and mentions Timothy, one of Paul's coworkers (Heb 13:23), led some in the early church to attribute the letter to Paul. Others, however, recognized that it was written in a style quite different from that of Paul's letters. Although the erroneous attribution to Paul helped Hebrews to be included in the scriptural canon, the letter is certainly not by Paul. The designation "to the Hebrews" represents only an early guess at the general identity of the recipients. The great interest of the writer in interpreting the Old Testament scriptures might indicate that his readers were Jewish Christians, but many Gentile Christians also shared a strong concern with the scriptures.

What can be known of the author and recipients is that they were second- or third-generation Christians (Heb 2:3), that they endured extended persecution, imprisonment, and confiscation of property (Heb 10:32-36), but that none had yet been executed for their faith, though that threat loomed (Heb 12:4). The final greeting, sent by "those from Italy" (Heb 13:24), suggests that the recipients were in Rome. Scholars' guesses as to the identity of the author have ranged from Apollos to Barnabas, Priscilla, Epaphras, and other early church leaders, but no firm case has been made for any of these. The body of the work is structured like a sermon, alternating between interpretations of scripture and words of exhortation and encouragement. The author shows considerable artistry and sophistication in using the scriptures, through which he believes the Holy Spirit speaks in a living and powerful way, to call the believers to keep "looking to Jesus the pioneer and perfecter of our faith" (Heb 12:2).

The author of Hebrews compares Christ's priesthood to Melchizedek, offering bread and wine in this late-12th-century enamel plaque.

Long ago God spoke to our ancestors in many and various ways by the prophets, but in these last days he has spoken to us by a Son, whom he appointed heir of all things, through whom he also created the worlds. HEB 1:1-2

Hebrews opens with a beautifully crafted statement of Jesus as the Son of God and the culmination of God's revelation across the ages. This description begins a long section that first establishes Jesus' divinity and then emphasizes his human identity in order to show that he can serve as a "merciful and faithful high priest" (Heb 2:17).

God's Son, says the author, is the one through whom God "created the worlds." He is the perfect and exact manifestation of "God's glory" and "God's very being" (Heb 1:2, 3). Therefore, the Son is far "superior to angels" (Heb 1:4), who, great as they are, are only messengers of God. The author quotes a series of selections from the psalms, alternating between passages that in their original context speak of the king as divinely appointed and those that speak of God. All the passages are applied to the Messiah as anointed king, divine creator, and eternal ruler. Contrast with the angels simply highlights the unique grandeur of Jesus' exalted status and the importance of taking the message of salvation through Jesus absolutely seriously: "For to which of the angels did God ever say, 'You are my Son'?" (Heb 1:5).

The author next turns to the scriptural description of human beings as "lower than the angels" but still in authority over creation with "all things under their feet" (Heb 2:7, 8; Ps 8:5-6). Such a status has not been realized for humanity at large, the author argues, but Jesus does fulfill that role as the perfect representative of humanity, for he has gone through "the suffering of death, so that by the grace of God he might taste death for everyone" (Heb 2:9). Through suffering, he became "the pioneer of their salvation," freeing humanity from being enslaved "by the fear of death" (Heb 2:10, 15). Because the Son of God, who created the world, became "like his brothers and sisters in every respect" and was "tested by what he suffered," he was able to be "a merciful and faithful high priest" on the behalf of humankind and "make a sacrifice of atonement for the sins of the people" (Heb 2:17, 18).

Christ, however, was faithful over God's house as a son, and we are his house if we hold firm the confidence and the pride that belong to hope. HEB 3:6

What later Christians called the Old Testament was to early believers simply "the scriptures." Even though the author of Hebrews believes Christ has replaced the tabernacle or temple as a place of sacrifice to God, he considers the Old Testament scriptures to be powerfully relevant to the life of early Christians. He approaches the scriptures not for historical research or curiosity, but to hear the liv-

Christians are urged in Hebrews to wait patiently, as Abraham did after receiving the promise of a son from the three angels; a late-16th-century Italian painting.

ing voice of God speaking in the present. Thus, he describes the scriptures as "the word of God," which "is living and active, sharper than any two-edged sword" and "able to judge the thoughts and intentions of the heart" (Heb 4:12).

It is in that spirit that he engages in an interpretation of Psalm 95 as a challenge to Christians. He begins with the statement that both Moses and Jesus were faithful to God's commission, though Jesus was far greater than Moses. But just as Moses' faithfulness did not keep the people of Israel from being unfaithful, so Jesus' followers must take responsibility for living faithfully and not having an "unbelieving heart that turns away from the living God" (Heb 3:12). The quotation from Psalm 95 tells how the Israelites, whom God had brought out of Egypt, were unfaithful and rebellious, and how God swore that they would never "enter my rest" (Heb 3:11), meaning the promised land. For the author of Hebrews, however, that "rest" symbolizes much more than the land of Canaan. When God speaks of "my rest," it recalls the way he rested after the days of creation and also points to the ultimate "rest" of heavenly salvation.

Thus, the example of the Israelites' failure to trust God becomes a warning and a challenge to believers. The Israelites of Moses' generation received a great message of salvation when God sent Moses to deliver them from Egypt, but they nevertheless failed to trust in God in any difficulty or new situation and repeatedly hardened their hearts and tested God. The author of Hebrews warns his readers that they are subject to the same danger. They must "exhort one another every day" so that they are not "hardened by the deceitfulness of sin" (Heb 3:13). Faithfulness is a daily matter. Thus, the challenge to Christians is "If you hear his voice, do not harden your hearts" but rather "make every effort to enter that rest, so that no one may fall through such disobedience as theirs" (Heb 4:7, 11).

For we do not have a high priest who is unable to sympathize with our weaknesses, but we have one who in every respect has been tested as we are, yet without sin. HEB 4:15

At this point, the author of Hebrews begins to elaborate in more detail on the role of Christ as high priest, the central image developed in the letter. Though the understanding of Jesus' crucifixion as a sacrifice is found in numerous places in the New Testament, only Hebrews interprets Jesus' death by portraying him as the high priest offering the sacrifice on the Day of Atonement. The understanding of Jesus as high priest joins together the two images developed in Hebrews 1-2—Christ as exalted Son of God and as representative of suffering humanity. Only by holding together both of those seemingly contradictory roles can Jesus function as "a great high priest" (Heb 4:14). Since he is both "Jesus, the Son of God," who has "passed through the heavens," and

Abraham's faith, shown by his willingness to sacrifice his son, Isaac, is offered as a model to early Christians;
the angel's intervention is depicted in this ceiling painting by Giovanni Battista Tiepolo (1696-1770).

one who "has been tested as we are, yet without sin," Jesus is able to allow humanity to approach God's "throne of grace with boldness" (Heb 4:14-16) to receive help in time of need.

A high priest, the author asserts, must be sympathetic with the people for whom he offers sacrifice, but he must also be separate from them by a special commission from God. He finds scriptural foundation for Christ's appointment in psalms that speak of the king (Messiah) as God's Son and as a "priest forever, according to the order of Melchizedek" (Heb 5:6; Ps 2:7, 110:4). Jesus' sympathy for humanity arises from "the days of his flesh" when "Jesus offered up prayers and supplications, with loud cries and tears" and "learned obedience through what he suffered" (Heb 5:7-8).

The author, however, warns his readers that much of what he wishes to explain is difficult and that they "have become dull in understanding" (Heb 5:11). He rebukes them for their lack of maturity, and challenges them to follow his lead as they together move beyond elementary teachings and "go on to perfection" (Heb 6:1) or maturity. Continued progress is imperative since, he says, "it is impossible to restore again to repentance those who have once been enlightened . . . and then have fallen away, since on their own they are crucifying again the Son of God" (Heb 6:4,6). He is confident, however, that they will persist in faith and imitate those who "inherit the promises" (Heb 6:12). These promises are absolutely secure, based on God's "unchangeable character," and thus are "a sure and steadfast anchor of the soul" (Heb 6:17, 19).

King Melchizedek of Salem, priest of the Most High God, met Abraham as he was returning from defeating the kings and blessed him. HEB 7:1

The author now turns his attention to the figure of Melchizedek as the standard for the priesthood of Christ. An obvious criticism against the interpretation of Jesus as high priest is that he was not even an ordinary priest and was from the tribe of Judah rather than Levi. (The high priesthood was limited to a select range of descendants from the tribe of Levi and the family of Aaron.) The statement of Psalm 110:4, however, provides an alternate priestly lineage for the Messiah in the figure of Melchizedek. And since Melchizedek is mentioned elsewhere in the scriptures only in the story of Abraham (Gen 14:18-20), the author examines that passage for what it says and does not say about him.

His name and title would appear to mean "king of righteousness" or "king of peace." The scriptures say nothing of him having a father or mother or of his death—all symbolically significant. Abraham, the ancestor of Levi, with an ancestor's authority over his descendants, gave a tithe to Melchizedek, suggesting that Melchizedek was even greater than Abraham.

The fact that Psalm 110 points to the Messiah as a priest after Melchizedek implies the inadequacy of the "levitical priesthood" and the Law of Moses, "for when there is a change in the priesthood, there is necessarily a change in the law as well" (Heb 7:11, 12). The levitical priesthood was limited, the author argues, by the weakness of the priests, who were sinful mortals, and the weakness of the law, which "made nothing perfect" (Heb 7:19). Now the Messiah's priesthood as described in Psalm 110 is confirmed by divine oath and given to Jesus, who is both sinless and immortal. Thus, "he holds his priesthood permanently, because he continues forever." He offered a single sacrifice "once for all when he offered himself" (Heb 7:24, 27).

The levitical priesthood and the sanctuary prescribed to Moses, the author argues, were only "a sketch and shadow of the heavenly one" (Heb 8:5). Thus, Christ's role fulfills the hopes for the "new covenant" described by Jeremiah, a covenant that "has made the first one obsolete" (Heb 8:8, 13; Jer 31:31-34).

He entered once for all into the Holy Place, not with the blood of goats and calves, but with his own blood, thus obtaining eternal redemption. HEB 9:12

In developing the contrast between the first covenant and the new covenant, the author details some of the elaborate construction of the Mosaic tabernacle. He never refers to the temple built by Solomon or the later reconstructions of the temple; his concern is strictly with the scriptural descriptions of the tent that the Israelites constructed in the wilderness (Ex 25-27, 36-38). He describes the larger room, called the Holy Place, where all priests could enter to perform their duties, and the smaller cubicle, called the Holy of Holies, where only the high priest could enter once each year on the Day of Atonement.

This arrangement was intentionally symbolic, the author argues. The Holy Place stood for the entire system of sacrificial worship under the Law of Moses, in which "sacrifices are offered that cannot perfect the conscience of the worshiper" (Heb 9:9); the Holy of Holies represented the new covenant and the unique access to God made possible through Christ. Jesus entered the sanctuary, "not with the blood of goats and calves, but with his own blood, thus obtaining eternal redemption."

Death and blood are inextricably linked to the process of establishing a covenant of purification and forgiveness. A man's last will or covenant takes effect only at death. Moses inaugurated the first covenant by sprinkling it with "the blood of the covenant"; and under Mosaic Law, "without the shedding of blood there is no forgiveness of sins" (Heb 9:20, 22). All these are symbols for heavenly realities in which Christ "has appeared once for all . . . to remove sin by the sacrifice of himself" and "to appear in the presence of God on our behalf" (Heb 9:26, 24).

Since we have a great priest over the house of God, let us approach with a true heart in full assurance of faith, with our hearts sprinkled clean from an evil conscience and our bodies washed with pure water. HEB 10:21-22

The author completes his contrast between the covenant inaugurated by Moses and the new covenant of Christ by emphasizing the perfection and permanence of the single sacrifice under the

WHY SO MANY JEWS REJECTED JESUS

Most Jews rejected Jesus for compelling reasons. Their greatest objection was to his death on a cross posted in the ground like a tree. According to Mosaic Law, "anyone hung on a tree is under God's curse" (Deut 21:23). Rather than being the Blessed One of God—a title for the Messiah—he appeared to be cursed by God. But Christians interpreted the suffering servant songs of Isaiah, about a righteous man who dies a shameful death to save others, as references to Jesus.

Jews also rejected Jesus because he did not fulfill any prophecies of a messianic king who would restore Israel's glory. Christians, however, cited prophecies not only of a dominating king but one "humble and riding on a donkey" (Zech 9:9). Prophecies of a powerful Messiah setting up an everlasting kingdom, they argued, would be fulfilled at Jesus' Second Coming. Finally, Jews could not accept Jesus as the Son of God, an apparent contradiction of their bedrock belief in only one God: "The Lord is our God, the Lord alone" (Deut 6:4). The Evangelist John addressed this problem by quoting Jesus as saying, "The Father and I are one" (Jn 10:30).

new covenant. The original covenant corresponds to the new covenant, he states, as a shadow corresponds to the object casting the shadow. The sacrifices under the law were "continually offered year after year" and served as a "reminder of sin year after year" but could never break the grip of sin, "for it is impossible for the blood of bulls and goats to take away sins" (Heb 10:1, 3-4).

Quoting a passage from Psalm 40, he argues that God did not really desire these sacrifices, but wanted the Messiah to abolish them by the single sacrifice of himself. Thus, "when Christ had offered for all time a single sacrifice for sins, 'he sat down at the right hand of God'" (Heb 10:12; Ps 110:1). By one act he "perfected for all time those who are sanctified" (Heb 10:14) and fulfilled the expectations of the new covenant that Jeremiah had described. He put his "laws in their hearts" and promised to "remember their sins . . . no more" (Heb 10:16, 17).

Through his sacrifice, Christ opened a "new and living way" into the presence of God in the Holy of Holies for every believer. Because of this reality, the author challenges the believers to sustain the "full assurance of faith," to "hold fast to the confession of our hope," and to encourage each other "to love and good deeds" (Heb 10:22-24). The confidence of salvation in Christ is sure because "he who has promised is faithful" (Heb 10:23).

On the other hand, the author warns, when one has "spurned the Son of God, profaned the blood of the covenant . . . and outraged the Spirit of grace," he learns that "it is a fearful thing to fall into the hands of the living God" (Heb 10:29, 31). The choice is clear: Believers must not be "among those who shrink back and so are lost, but among those who have faith and so are saved" (Heb 10:39).

Without faith it is impossible to please God, for whoever would approach him must believe that he exists and that he rewards those who seek him. HEB 11:6

The author turns to inspiring examples of faith to challenge Christian believers. The faith he describes is "the assurance of things hoped for, the conviction of things not seen" (Heb 11:1), which allows the faithful to persevere in the face of opposition and disappointment.

In a vivid and powerful overview of the Old Testament narrative, the author highlights characters in the scriptures from Abel onward. He especially emphasizes Abraham and Moses, but also alludes to stories throughout the historical books and even to the deaths of martyrs described in the apocryphal book of 2 Maccabees.

The theme throughout this narrative is how the faithful in the past have trusted God without obtaining the fulfillment of all their hopes. They were able to see beyond the limited confines of this world and recognize that they belonged to another homeland that they could now see only from afar. Patriarchs like Abraham, Isaac, and Jacob, he says, "confessed that they were strangers and foreigners on the earth," and desired "a better country, that is, a heavenly one" (Heb 11:13, 16). Because of their desires reaching beyond this world, "God is not ashamed to be called their God; indeed, he has prepared a city for them" (Heb 11:16).

Moses offers the greatest example of faith, for he forsook Egypt's treasures, "choosing rather to share ill-treatment with the people of God" (Heb 11:25). In every generation, the faithful have shown through their suffering that they trust the Lord's promises—these were people "of whom the world was not worthy" (Heb 11:38), he says.

Now these faithful form a great "cloud of witnesses" around the believers who must run the race of faithfulness for themselves, "looking to Jesus the pioneer

Another example of faith cited in Hebrews: the Israelites crossing the Red Sea as if it were dry land; an event depicted in a 15th-century German prayer book

and perfecter of our faith" (Heb 12:1, 2). Jesus "endured the cross" and great "hostility against himself"; his example challenges believers not to "grow weary or lose heart" (Heb 12:2, 3). Rather, they must consider their struggles as God's loving discipline through which he trains his children to know "the peaceful fruit of righteousness" (Heb 12:11).

But you have come to Mount Zion and to the city of the living God, the heavenly Jerusalem, and to innumerable angels in festal gathering. HEB 12:22

The author concludes his discourse with words of encouragement and warning, again drawing on examples from the scriptures. The believers must not treat God's promises as trivial, as Esau did to his great regret. Nor must they hear God's call as a terrifying challenge, as the Israelites did at Mount Sinai. What the faithful are part of is serious and beautiful and wonderful. It is "the city of the living God," where they stand with God the judge, with Jesus the mediator, and with all "the spirits of the righteous made perfect" (Heb 12:22, 23). The one who calls to them is the God who is a consuming fire and whose voice will shake earth and heaven to its foundations. But that destruction exists only so that God may give them "a kingdom that cannot be shaken." Before him the believers stand to "give thanks . . . with reverence and awe" (Heb 12:28).

In the final paragraphs, the author shifts more and more from the style of a sermon to that of a letter. He challenges the believers to maintain their care and love for each other. They must show hospitality for strangers and care for "those who are in prison" and "those who are being tortured" (Heb 13:3). These realities of imprisonment and physical suffering are an ever-present threat. In the face of these dangers the faithful must maintain high standards of sexual purity, freedom from greed, and trust in God.

He asks them to remember the example of their leaders who have died and to honor those who are now leading them. They must realize that their allegiance to Jesus, who was crucified in shame "outside the camp," means that in this world they will always be outsiders: "For here we have no lasting city, but we are looking for the city that is to come" (Heb 13:13, 14). Hoping to see the recipients soon, the author says farewell with a blessing, "Grace be with all of you" (Heb 13:25).

THE LETTER OF JAMES

James holding a scroll; a 12th-century fresco from a Turkish monastery

*T*he letter of James is filled with short nuggets of wisdom about how to live the Christian life. Like the book of Proverbs, James covers a wide variety of issues—from controlling the tongue, to helping the poor, to rejoicing when persecuted for the faith. For this reason, scholars have dubbed it the wisdom literature of the New Testament. The letter's most distinctive teaching is that Christian faith is more than a private spiritual experience that people can keep to themselves. With blunt language, James insists that authentic Christianity shows up in the way people live—in the positive attitude they express, the kind words they speak, and the helpful deeds they do for others. James goes so far as to declare that "faith by itself, if it has no works, is dead" (Jas 2:17).

The writer identifies himself only as James, a servant of God. But by the fourth century, church leaders claimed he was the influential brother of Jesus, who led the Jewish-Christian congregation in Jerusalem, and who served as presiding official at the first church council—the meeting that ruled that Gentiles did not have to observe Jewish laws about circumcision and food restrictions. If this is the James who wrote the letter (there are four men by that name in the New Testament), he likely did so before the Romans destroyed Jerusalem in A.D. 70; the first-century Jewish historian Josephus said Jewish leaders stoned James to death before then.

The letter of James is addressed to "the twelve tribes in the Dispersion" (Jas 1:1), a common way of referring to the people of Israel scattered throughout the Roman Empire, but in this context probably a reference to all Jews who have converted to Christianity. Another clue that James writes to Jewish Christians—rather than Gentile believers—is that he frequently mentions the Jewish law, always with reverence. He also describes the church's meeting place as an "assembly" (Jas 2:2), using a Greek word that means synagogue. Apparently, James felt that his letter would go a long way toward solving problems he believed were all too common among Jewish-Christian congregations.

My brothers and sisters, whenever you face trials of any kind, consider it nothing but joy, because you know that the testing of your faith produces endurance.
JAS 1:2

*F*rom the earliest days of the church, Jewish leaders vigorously opposed the new religion as a dangerous, heretical movement that threatened the most basic Jewish beliefs, including the conviction that there is only one God—not a trinity of Father, Son, and Holy Spirit. Jews who converted to Christianity were hunted down, flogged, jailed, and sometimes executed. In the face of such persecution, James points his readers to an idea Jesus eloquently expressed in what has become known as the Beatitudes, declarations that launch the Sermon on the Mount: "Blessed are those who are persecuted for righteousness' sake, for theirs is the kingdom of heaven" (Mt 5:10). Likewise, James tells his readers to consider hardship as an opportunity to refine and strengthen their faith, quickly assuring that anyone who withstands temptation "will receive the crown of life that the Lord has promised to those who love him" (Jas 1:12). Desire, he warns, leads to sin, and sin to death.

Let everyone be quick to listen, slow to speak, slow to anger.
JAS 1:19

*J*ames thus begins what will emerge in his letter as a crisp and detailed profile of proper Christian behavior. He believes there are distinct ways in which Christians should behave, and he wants his readers to know exactly what these are. As Christians mature in the faith, they should increasingly learn to control their tempers, bridle their tongues, rid themselves of evil influences, and be doers—not merely listeners—of the Gospel's message that God has planted in their heart. This last idea is central to the letter, and one that James will later develop with fiery emotion and stabbing sarcasm, suggesting that it represents a serious problem among his readers.

Do you with your acts of favoritism really believe in our glorious Lord Jesus Christ? JAS 2:1

James writes as an advocate for the poor, charging that they are treated as second-class citizens in the church. Rich people get the best seats, James charges, while the poor are ordered to stand at the side or sit on the floor. James, the brother of Jesus and leader of the Jerusalem church, was well acquainted with poverty because many in his congregation were poor. When the apostle Paul preached throughout the Roman Empire, he also collected offerings for "the poor among the saints at Jerusalem" (Rom 15:26).

Once again, James echoes a Beatitude from the Sermon on the Mount: "Blessed are the poor in spirit, for theirs is the kingdom of heaven" (Mt 5:3). In verse 5, however, James applies this promise not only to the "poor in spirit," or the spiritually humble, but to the physically poor believers who are humbled by their impoverished state in life. "If you show partiality," James firmly declares, "you commit sin" (Jas 2:9).

What good is it, my brothers and sisters, if you say you have faith but do not have works? JAS 2:14

The most strongly worded message in the letter is that belief in God is not enough. "Even the demons believe—and shudder," James notes. "Do you want to be shown, you senseless person, that faith apart from works is barren?" (Jas 2:20). An apparently frustrated James answers this mocking question by reminding his readers that Abraham expressed his faith by obediently agreeing to sacrifice his own son—a test of faith that God stopped at the last moment. "A person is justified by works," James concludes, "and not by faith alone" (Jas 2:24). The apostle Paul seems to disagree. He, too, points to Abraham, but argues the exact opposite. Paul contends that Abraham was justified not because of his works, but because he believed in God (Rom 4:2-3). In practice, James and Paul agree that faith and works are both essential, but the men clearly approach the issue from different perspectives. James seems to minister among undermotivated believers. Paul works among Gentile believers who think they have to obey all Jewish laws to earn their salvation. Both extremes need correcting.

If a brother is hungry, James illustrates, it is not good enough to say, "Go in peace; keep warm and eat your fill" (Jas 2:16). A person with authentic Christian faith will feed the hungry. This is exactly what Paul did by collecting offerings for Jerusalem's poor.

Not many of you should become teachers . . . for you know that we who teach will be judged with greater strictness. JAS 3:1

In a caution about pursuing the honored role of teacher in the church, James condemns two sins that often accompany the job: thoughtless words and arrogance. The tongue is small, James says, but in-credibly powerful—like a rudder that guides a massive ship to safety or disaster, or a spark that ignites oven kindling or a forest fire. "From the same mouth come blessing and cursing. My brothers and sisters, this ought not to be so" (Jas 3:10). Christians—especially teachers of Christians—should learn to speak wise and helpful words. They should also rid themselves of selfish ambition and boastfulness, which produce "disorder and wickedness of every kind" (Jas 3:16).

Whoever wishes to be a friend of the world becomes an enemy of God. JAS 4:4

James steers his readers away from the selfish values and behavior that are popular among the ungodly: envy, criticism, presumptuous self-reliance, and the pursuit of money. Unrighteous people want what they do not have, James observes, and they do whatever it takes to get it—even to committing murder. They unfairly judge and criticize neighbors. They speak as though tomorrow is a certainty, without realizing that plans made will unfold only "if the Lord wishes" (Jas 4:15). And they chase wealth that they refuse to share, failing to look ahead to the heavenly age when "your riches have rotted, and your clothes are moth-eaten. Your gold and silver have rusted, and their rust will be evidence against you, and it will eat your flesh like fire" (Jas 5:2-3).

Be patient, therefore, beloved, until the coming of the Lord. JAS 5:7

Many first-generation Christians believed that Jesus would return soon, within their lifetimes. For this reason, Paul felt compelled to rebuke Christians in Thessalonica who became so enamored with the Second Coming that they quit their jobs and were "living in idleness" (2 Thess 3:11). James, too, calls on believers to wait patiently. And in the meantime, when hardship and sickness strike, James says believers should pray for each other. The sick should also present themselves to the church elders for a ritual of anointing with oil. The ancients used oil to treat injuries, and to dedicate priests and sacred objects to the service of God. Perhaps early church leaders established this ritual to symbolize that they were releasing the sick person into the healing hands of God. "The prayer of the righteous," James explains, "is powerful and effective" (Jas 5:16). It can heal the sick, bring rain in a drought, and transform a sinner into a soul repentant, forgiven, and saved into eternal life.

Because the text lacks the traditional closing greetings, scholars have concluded that the letter of James is not an actual piece of correspondence. Rather, it is a literary form apparently adopted by the writer in order to get across the points he wished to make to his audience of troubled Jewish converts to Christianity scattered across the far-flung Roman Empire in the first century A.D.

THE TWO LETTERS OF PETER

*The two letters of Peter purport to come from the pen of Jesus'
foremost disciple, Simon (or Simeon) Peter. The apostle writes
his first letter to churches he has visited in five Roman provinces
throughout what is now Turkey. Because Christians there are
facing intense persecution, Peter writes to encourage them. Romans had
once tolerated Christianity because they thought it was one of many branches,
or denominations, of Judaism. But by the A.D. 60s, some 30 years after
Jesus' death and about the time many believe that Peter wrote this letter,
Roman officials realize Christianity is a new and separate religion. So as Rome
does with other new religions, it begins treating Christianity with suspicion,
fearing the worst: that the movement could spawn social upheaval and
empire-wide rebellion. Increasingly, Christians are ostracized and threatened.
Peter advises believers to submit to every human authority, yet be willing
to suffer for the faith, even to the death—as Jesus did. The first letter
attributed to Peter is written in refined Greek, a surprising feat for a
Galilean fisherman, and reason enough for some to doubt that Peter actually
wrote it. But the apostle admits he was assisted in the writing by Silvanus
(the Latin name for Silas; 1 Pet 5:12), most likely the same Christian who
traveled with Paul throughout the Greek-speaking world.*

*In 2 Peter, the apostle writes an open letter to all Christians after learning
he is about to die. In this letter, Peter warns believers about a group of
heretical teachers who advocate freedom from rules of morality—teachers
Peter describes as "slaves of corruption" (2 Pet 2:19). Many scholars believe
that one of Peter's followers wrote this letter—perhaps at the turn of the
first century—to use the apostle's theology and authority in confronting
new threats to the church. Disciples of deceased teachers occasionally did
this in ancient times. One clue that the letter may have been written decades
after Peter's death—which probably occurred during Nero's persecution
of Christians in A.D. 64—is that the writer categorizes Paul's letters with
"other scriptures" (2 Pet 3:16). Christian writings, however, did not start
achieving the sacred status of scripture until much later. Yet scholars who
believe Peter did write the letter argue that by the end of his life some
of Paul's letters had been in circulation for ten years or more.*

**Peter shown with the
keys to heaven; an early-
14th-century portrait
by Lippo Memmi**

1 Peter

*Blessed be the God and Father of our Lord Jesus Christ!
By his great mercy he has given us a new birth into a
living hope through the resurrection of Jesus Christ from
the dead.*   1 PET 1:3

Peter was the leader among Jesus' disciples. This
fisherman from Capernaum, about 30 miles
northeast of Jesus' hometown of Nazareth, is always
the first one named in gospel lists of the twelve. And
he often spoke on behalf of the others. Now, with
Jesus ascended into heaven, Peter becomes the principal leader and spokesman for the fledgling church.
The apostle writes from "Babylon" (1 Pet 5:13), a de-
meaning code name for Rome—capital of the empire
that controls Judea much as ancient Babylon once
did. He addresses his letter to "exiles of the Dispersion" (1 Pet 1:1) scattered throughout Asia Minor,
where Paul had planted countless churches. "Exiles
of the Dispersion" originally meant the Jews who
were deported after Babylon destroyed Jerusalem in
586 B.C. The phrase later came to mean all Jews living outside Israel. But Peter seems to use it here to
describe instantly and graphically the Christians as
spiritual foreigners in a hostile environment—just
as the exiled Jews once were.

Anti-Christian sentiment grows amid false and vicious rumors. For one, Christians are accused of being
cannibals who eat human flesh and drink human
blood. This is an allegation growing out of the ritual of communion, in which believers eat bread and
drink wine that represent the body of Jesus, sacrificed
for humanity's sins. They are also accused of holding orgies, since they meet privately in homes, and
greet one another with a "kiss of love" (1 Pet 5:14).
Writing to Christians confronted with increasing per-

secution, Peter quickly jumps from his greeting into a reminder that the faithful will experience life after death, just as Jesus has. They may first have to suffer, Peter warns, but the hardships they endure can refine their faith just as fire purifies gold. Once the trials are over, new life awaits them, "imperishable, undefiled, and unfading, kept in heaven for you" (1 Pet 1:4).

As he who called you is holy, be holy yourselves in all your conduct. 1 PET 1:15

To defuse wild accusations about Christianity and to show others what the faith is really like, Peter calls on believers to be holy. By this he means they should behave as though devoted to a righteous God. In Old Testament times, people were described as holy once they had formally dedicated themselves to serving God. Israel, for instance, became a holy nation by entering into a covenant with God, agreeing to obey him. The Israelites remained holy by observing the laws God gave Moses. When they sinned, they were cleansed and restored to holiness through heartfelt repentance and ritual sacrifices. New Testament writers teach that Jewish laws have been rendered obsolete by a new covenant God made with humanity, through Jesus. The laws of this covenant are written not on stone tablets and scrolls, but on the heart. Among these laws: "Rid yourselves . . . of all malice, and all guile, insincerity, envy, and all slander" (1 Pet 2:1). When Christians sin, they find spiritual cleansing through repentance and "the precious blood of Christ, like that of a lamb without defect or blemish" (1 Pet 1:19).

Wives . . . accept the authority of your husbands . . . . Husbands, in the same way, show consideration for your wives. 1 PET 3:1, 7

There are practical reasons why Peter encourages Christians to submit patiently to the often unfair social and political institutions that include slavery and male domination. Though Romans generally tolerate established religions, such as Judaism, they remain wary of new, unfamiliar movements that might stir up rebellion against the empire and spark insubordination in the home. Some cults, for instance, feature adulterous orgies and urge women to take control of their lives—each of which could devastate the traditional family institution, which is led by the man in Roman times. Peter wants the world to know that Christianity is not an unsavory religion, nor one that intends to

upset the customs of the day—even though by Christian standards some of the customs are unfair and need upsetting. Peter tells his beleaguered readers that this is not a time to transform society abruptly, forcing it into a Christian mold. It is a time to "conduct yourselves honorably among the Gentiles, so that, though they malign you as evildoers, they may see your honorable deeds and glorify God" (1 Pet 2:12). Wives who live righteously may win their husbands to the faith, Peter says, just as slaves may win their masters and citizens may win local officials. With this in mind, Peter tells his readers to accept the authority of human institutions.

Who will harm you if you are eager to do what is good? But even if you do suffer for doing what is right, you are blessed. 1 PET 3:13, 14

For those suffering unjustly—slaves mistreated, wives disregarded, citizens persecuted—Peter pleads with them not to repay evil with evil but to "repay with a blessing" (1 Pet 3:9). The apostle knows that some Christians will continue to suffer no matter how well they respond. When this happens, Peter says, they should accept their persecution, just as Jesus once did: "When he was abused, he did not return abuse; when he suffered, he did not threaten; but he entrusted himself to the one who judges justly" (1 Pet 2:23).

This patient and long-suffering approach to persecution had no chance of quickly changing Roman policy regarding the suspicious Christian movement. But over the centuries, one Roman at a time, Christianity transformed the Roman people. Within 300 years, it became the preferred religion within the empire.

I exhort the elders among you to tend the flock of God . . . . Do not lord it over those in your charge, but be examples to the flock. 1 PET 5:1, 3

Humility does not come naturally to many people—especially those in leadership positions. Sometimes, leaders grow to believe that they are better than the mass of followers under their care. But Peter cautions local church leaders, "clothe yourselves with humility . . . for 'God opposes the proud, but gives grace to the humble'" (1 Pet 5:5). Peter believes that the most effective leaders are those who know how to serve others. This is a lesson he learned at the Last Supper, when Jesus washed the feet of the twelve disciples. Peter had resisted, arguing that he should wash the feet of

Peter and Paul (left) present the case for Christianity to the emperor Nero; an imaginary scene from a medieval gilded enamel plaque.

Jesus instead. But in a profound call to humility, Jesus explained that he was doing this to set an example of leadership to them: "If I, your Lord and Teacher, have washed your feet, you also ought to wash one another's feet" (Jn 13:14).

Peter closes his letter by warning the people to resist the devil, God's enemy, who "like a roaring lion . . . prowls around, looking for someone to devour" (1 Pet 5:8). During Nero's reign, many Christians were fed to lions in public arenas. Yet Peter's plea to resist the devil is not a coded call to arms against Rome. Resisting the devil—and those controlled by him—means remaining steadfast in the Christian faith. The apostle reminds his readers that they are not alone; believers throughout the Roman world are suffering as well. But Peter adds that one day the sufferings will end. And no matter what has happened to the faithful, "the God of all grace, who has called you to his eternal glory in Christ, will himself restore, support, strengthen, and establish you" (1 Pet 5:10). Peter's promise is that, even in death, Christians will enjoy everlasting life.

2 Peter

[Jesus'] divine power has given us everything needed for life and godliness. 2 PET 1:3

Peter announces that his death is near. The Bible does not reveal how Peter died, but second-century stories say he was killed in Rome during the horrifying persecution under Nero in A.D. 64. Peter's second letter is like a theological will—the apostle's last words and wishes for the church. Much like Paul in 2 Timothy, Peter bequeaths the church a continuing legacy of holy living: "Make every effort to support your faith with goodness, and goodness with knowledge, and knowledge with self-control, and self-control with endurance, and endurance with godliness, and godliness with mutual affection, and mutual affection with love" (2 Pet 1:5-7).

Giving a lesson in humility, Jesus washed Peter's feet at the Last Supper; a painting by Ford Madox Brown (1821-1893).

There will be false teachers among you, who will secretly bring in destructive opinions. 2 PET 2:1

Just as Old Testament Israel had false prophets who led the people into sin, Peter warns, the church will have false teachers doing the same thing. The apostle begins speaking as though he is predicting what will happen after he dies. But he uses the present tense in verses 14-19, showing that the false teachers have already arrived. Craving sex and money, "they entice unsteady souls" (2 Pet 2:14). Peter charges that though these teachers promise freedom from the rules of common decency, they are "slaves of corruption" (2 Pet 2:19). The heretics whom Peter is describing may have been forerunners of gnosticism, which developed into an organized movement in the second and third centuries. Gnostics taught that salvation comes through secret knowledge (*gnosis* is Greek for "knowledge"), not through faith that produces godly living. Gnostics also believed that only the spiritual world is good, while the created world remains hopelessly evil. Some gnostics concluded that since they were spiritual beings with knowledge that guaranteed their salvation, they might as well enjoy all the excesses of the world. Peter counters this threat with a history lesson. He begins by telling about God punishing sinful spirit beings in heaven—angels cast from their celestial home, perhaps for taking part in Satan's revolt or for mating with human women (Gen 6:1-4; Jude 6). Peter continues by pointing to God's judgment in the Flood, at Sodom and Gomorrah, and of Balaam, a seer for hire whom the Israelites executed (Num 22:5-7, 31:8). Peter says these false teachers—former Christians—illustrate two ancient, graphic proverbs: "The dog turns back to its own vomit," and "The sow is washed only to wallow in the mud" (2 Pet 2:22).

In the last days scoffers will come . . . saying, "Where is the promise of his coming?" 2 PET 3:3, 4

If Peter wrote this letter shortly before he died during Nero's yearlong wave of persecution in A.D. 64, Christians would have been waiting more than 30 years for the return of Jesus. Already bitterly disappointed by the delay, Christians suffer further aggravation from scoffers who snidely ask what is taking Jesus so long. Peter assures them that Jesus will come in due time. Citing Psalm 90:4, Peter explains that to God, "a thousand years are like one day" (2 Pet 3:8). In addition, Peter argues, the Lord is not slow; he is patient, "not wanting any to perish, but all to come to repentance" (2 Pet 3:9).

Peter says that while Christians wait for Christ's return and God's creation of a new and eternal home for the righteous, they should cling firmly to the teachings in Paul's letters and not be fooled by teachers who twist scripture's meaning. "But grow in the grace and knowledge of our Lord and Savior Jesus Christ," he exhorts. "To him be the glory both now and to the day of eternity" (2 Pet 3:18).

*T*he three letters of John provide a rare and enlightening glimpse into what life is like for second-generation Christians at about the end of the first century. No longer are they debating whether to observe Jewish laws summarized in the book of Deuteronomy—a fiery issue for first-generation believers. Now Christians face a burgeoning movement within the church that denies Jesus came in the flesh and claims he was pure spirit. This movement—apparently an early form of gnosticism, which teaches that the physical world is evil—spawns breakaway heretical congregations that begin competing with traditional churches and luring some members away.

The first letter of John describes these separatists as "antichrists" (1 Jn 2:18), and calls on churches throughout the Roman world to hold fast to basic Christian beliefs. The second letter of John, apparently written to an individual church described as "the elect lady" (2 Jn 1), condenses the five-chapter message of 1 John into 13 verses, and urges believers to love each other and avoid false teachers. The third letter of John is a personal message to a man named Gaius, commending him for showing hospitality to visitors and condemning a dictatorial church leader named Diotrephes who refuses to receive John's representatives or to accept his authority.

The first letter is written anonymously, though clearly in the style of the Gospel of John, another anonymous work. The second and third letters, also exhibiting the Gospel's unique style, identify their writer only as "the elder." Church leaders at least as early as the second century attributed the Gospel and all three letters to the apostle John, Jesus' beloved disciple. The apostle is said to have lived to an old age, into the A.D. 90s. Yet, in the absence of any clear reference to John, and in the presence of a maturing heresy about Jesus, some scholars suspect that the Gospel and the letters were written later by students of John, perhaps about A.D. 100.

Accompanied by his symbolic eagle, the Evangelist John is shown writing one of his letters; an Italian painting dated about 1480.

1 John

God is light and in him there is no darkness at all. If we say that we have fellowship with him while we are walking in darkness, we lie.   1 JN 1:5, 6

*T*o churches suffering from shattered fellowship caused by splinter groups that have broken away, John identifies the source of unifying and lasting fellowship among believers: the Father and his Son, Jesus. Yet this is the very issue that divides the church. Most Christians embrace the teaching that Jesus is divine, a doctrine eloquently expressed throughout the Gospel of John. But some have rejected the incarnation, the idea that God became human in the person of Jesus. These dissidents believe that God and the spiritual world are good, and that humans and everything else in the created world are evil. Therefore, they maintain, a pure and holy God could not possibly have inhabited a human form. Nor could he have suffered on a cross and died. But, the separatists believe, God could look human and appear to suffer and die—just as the ancient Greek gods are said to have manifested themselves in the form of humans and even animals.

John recognizes what is at risk because of this teaching: the long-standing, fundamental belief that salvation comes through the blood shed by Jesus—a belief that people accept by faith and express in their lifestyles. Gnostics, however, contend that salvation comes through secret knowledge that only select people receive from God (*gnosis* means "knowledge"). They further contend that it is futile to try to live a holy life in a thoroughly wicked world. As a result, some gnostics earn reputations as evil people who are obsessed with money, sex, and prestige. Yet others move to the opposite extreme and shun the world, avoiding contact with others, fasting away their health, and depriving themselves of all but the barest of life's essentials.

To counter this heresy, which undermines the humanity of Jesus, John insists—with his very first sentence—that Jesus was indeed human: "We declare to you what was from the beginning, what we have heard, what we have seen with our eyes, what we have . . . touched with our hands." What John and the other disciples heard, saw, and touched was the "word of life" (1 Jn 1:1), which the Gospel of John identifies as Jesus: "The Word became flesh and lived among us" (Jn 1:14). John says that the distinguishing mark of Christians who have true fellowship with God is that they accept and live according to the fundamental teachings embodied in the life and message of Jesus. "Whoever says, 'I have come to know him,' but does not obey his commandments, is a liar" (1 Jn 2:4), John declares.

Do not love the world or the things in the world. The love of the Father is not in those who love the world.
1 JN 2:15

John is not promoting the gnostic idea that the world and everything in it is evil. He has already said, "If we confess our sins, he who is faithful and just will forgive us our sins and cleanse us from all unrighteousness" (1 Jn 1:9). Christians are purified from evil, John says, and should not sin. "But if anyone does sin, we have an advocate with the Father, Jesus Christ the righteous; and he is the atoning sacrifice for our sins" (1 Jn 2:1-2). Repentance and confession, working in conjunction with the crucifixion and the continuing advocacy of Jesus, restores a believer's purity. So when John speaks of "the world," he means everything in life that competes with a focus on God. Christians should pursue the will of God instead of chasing after the temporary and often unsatisfying pleasures that the ungodly are obsessed with: sex, physical beauty, and wealth.

Children, it is the last hour! As you have heard that antichrist is coming, so now many antichrists have come. 1 JN 2:18

"The last hour," does not mean the end of the world, or the imminent return of Jesus. It means "the age of the Messiah," the beginning of the end of God's plan to save humanity from sin. Several New Testament writers explain that this era began with the arrival of Jesus, and will continue until he returns. During this age, people can find forgiveness and salvation—not through sacrificial rituals, as in the past—but through faith in the Son of God. But also during this age, people can expect to encounter the antichrist. This term, coined by John, means "opponent of Christ" and seems to refer to an enemy of God also called "the lawless one" (2 Thess 2:3) and the "beast" (Rev 13:1).

Already, however, the church is besieged by many antichrists. These people, says John, are the dissidents who left traditional Christianity and now preach that Jesus was not the Son of God. John bluntly describes these unorthodox teachers as liars, and he urges believers to trust in the message they received "from the beginning" (1 Jn 2:24), and in the ongoing instruction they acquire from the Holy Spirit.

See what love the Father has given us, that we should be called children of God; and that is what we are. 1 JN 3:1

Dissidents confronting the church apparently disagree not only with those who believe that Jesus was human, but also with those who believe that even saved people can sin, and thereby endanger their salvation. Perhaps these dissident forerunners of gnosticism, like many of their theological heirs, believe that they are sinless in spirit, and that what they do in the physical world cannot change that. Acts of sin, as far as many gnostics are concerned, are irrelevant. John argues otherwise. He maintains that anyone who continues sinning "is a child of the devil" (1 Jn 3:8). Children of God, John adds, increasingly resemble their Father, who is pure love. John compares professing Christians who hate other believers to Cain, a bitter man who murdered his brother. Haters, like murderers, "do not have eternal life abiding in them" (1 Jn 3:15).

In this highly imaginative late-15th-century Swiss painting, John is shown preaching to King Herod and unusually attentive members of the court.

Christians are to love one another. Sounding much like the letter of James, which is noted for challenging believers to prove their faith by their actions, John pleads, "Little children, let us love, not in word or speech, but in truth and action" (1 Jn 3:18). To illustrate his point, John asks how the love of God can possibly exist in a person of financial means who sees another in need and yet refuses to help. For Christians, the perfect example of how far love should be willing to go is this: "[Jesus] laid down his life for us—and we ought to lay down our lives for one another" (1 Jn 3:16).

Beloved, do not believe every spirit, but test the spirits to see whether they are from God; for many false prophets have gone out into the world. 1 JN 4:1

The Bible identifies several ways to tell whether someone is truly speaking for God. Moses, for example, said if a prophet's prediction does not come true, the words are not from God (Deut 18:22). And a story from Israel's later history shows that a true prophet of the Lord does not contradict God's previously revealed will (1 Kgs 13). But for people in the early church, bombarded by conflicting teachings about the nature of Jesus, John provides a test appropriate for his own day: "Every spirit that confesses that Jesus Christ has come in the flesh is from God, and every spirit that does not confess Jesus is not from God" (1 Jn 4:2-3).

The false prophets John is talking about are the antichrists he mentioned earlier—probably forerunners of gnosticism, which teaches that the physical world is evil and incompatible with the perfection of the spirit realm. John directly confronts this erroneous teaching by asserting that "God sent his only Son into the world . . . . to be the atoning sacrifice for our sins." Furthermore, John adds, "God abides in those who confess that Jesus is the Son of God" (1 Jn 4:9-10, 15). Because God's spirit lives within Christians, John explains, believers can distinguish between spiritual truth and lies. With this in mind, the apostle urges his readers to trust the fundamental Christian message, which the divine spirit assures them is true.

I write these things to you who believe in the name of the Son of God, so that you may know that you have eternal life. 1 JN 5:13

Gnostics teach that they have eternal life because of secret, saving knowledge that God somehow conveys to them, perhaps through rituals or mystical experiences. John says his reason for writing is to show otherwise—that salvation comes through belief in God's Son. In 1 John 5:7-8, the apostle substantiates his claim that Jesus is God's Son by identifying three witnesses: the Spirit of truth (which John mentioned in chapter 4), the water (likely the baptism of Jesus, during which God addressed Jesus as Son), and the blood (the fatal crucifixion, which Jesus overcame through his resurrection).

John makes puzzling reference to a "mortal sin" (1 Jn 5:16). Given the context, he is probably referring to the sin of dissidents who reject Jesus and refuse to repent. They will suffer the consequences of eternal punishment in hell.

2 John

The truth that abides in us . . . will be with us forever. . . . Do not receive into the house or welcome anyone who comes to you and does not bring this teaching. 2 JN 2, 10

Traveling ministers, philosophers, and public speakers during the time of the early church often depended on the hospitality of local citizens for lodging, meals, and supplies for the road. In a brief letter to what is likely a single and beloved congregation described only as "the elect lady and her children" (2 Jn 1), John commends the people for their loyalty to the Christian faith and urges them to continue to love each other. But he also warns of "many deceivers . . . who do not confess that Jesus Christ has come in the flesh" (2 Jn 7). These are probably the dissidents of 1 John, who broke from the traditional church and began preaching a new and distorted gospel. John asks the church to shun these antichrists so as not inadvertently to help spread falsehoods about Jesus.

3 John

The elder to the beloved Gaius . . . . I was overjoyed when some of the friends arrived and testified to your faithfulness to the truth. 3 JN 1, 3

Gaius is apparently a respected and influential church leader, financially able to provide free accommodations for traveling ministers. John writes Gaius this short letter—perhaps delivered by one such minister, Demetrius (3 Jn 12)—commending him for his hospitality, and asking him to keep up his good works. "We ought to support such people," John writes, "so that we may become co-workers with the truth" (3 Jn 8).

John adds that he has written a separate letter (no longer extant) for the church, but implies that he does not expect it to get past a local church official named Diotrephes. This leader refuses to recognize John's authority or to receive his representatives. Further, Diotrephes expels from the church anyone who shows hospitality to John's colleagues. This suggests that Gaius may have to make a hard decision. If he shows hospitality to John's associates, Gaius could be excommunicated from the local congregation. John, however, assures Gaius not to worry, vowing that he himself will come and deal with the defiant church official. "Do not imitate what is evil," John advises, "but imitate what is good. Whoever does good is from God; whoever does evil has not seen God" (3 Jn 11). Promising to visit Gaius soon so they can talk "face to face" (3 Jn 14), John closes his letter with a blessing of peace.

THE LETTER OF JUDE

The judgmental and forceful letter that a Christian leader named Jude writes to churches threatened by heresy is not the gentle and beckoning letter he had planned to write. Jude says he was preparing to write about salvation. But because false teachers have intruded into the church, he feels an urgent need to warn believers that they will face God's judgment if they adopt the errant teachings. The intruders teach that Christians can sin without risking their salvation because God has already forgiven their sins—past, present, and future. And these false teachers apparently practice what they preach, by boldly indulging their lusts. In a concise sermon drawn from the Old Testament and other Jewish writings, Jude reminds his readers that God has a long and consistent history of punishing those who persistently sin.

The writer identifies himself as "Jude, a servant of Jesus Christ and brother of James" (Jude 1). Jude is short for Judas. Three men in the Bible bear this name, including the disciples Judas, the son of James, and Judas Iscariot (Lk 6:16). Only one is known to have a brother named James: Judas, the brother of Jesus (Mt 13:55). It is unlikely that Jude is an apostle, since he refers to the apostles as though he were not one (Jude 17-18). Nothing in the letter establishes when it was written, or to whom. But some scholars say the letter may be one of the earliest in the New Testament, and written by the brother of Jesus, who was likely an early church leader (1 Cor 9:5).

Jude, or Judas; a portrait by Dutch artist Anthony Van Dyck (1599-1641)

I find it necessary to write and appeal to you to contend for the faith . . . . for certain intruders have stolen in among you. JUDE 3, 4

Jude opens his letter with a greeting characteristic of early Christian letters—identifying himself and the readers (the empire-wide church) and offering a prayerful blessing from the Lord. By identifying himself as the brother of James, apparently no further authority is needed. James has risen to one of the most prominent positions in Christianity: pastor of the Jerusalem church and presiding official at the first church council.

In what almost seems an apology for the stern letter he is writing, Jude begins by saying he has been eagerly working on an encouraging letter about salvation. Instead, he feels compelled to stop and address a crucial problem caused by what appear to be traveling teachers with a distorted gospel. These intruders "pervert the grace of our God into licentiousness" (Jude 4), arguing that Christians are free to do anything they like—including committing sins—since Jesus has already died for humanity's sins. Paul, however, warns Christians in Galatia, "Do not use your freedom as an opportunity for self-indulgence, but through love become slaves to one another" (Gal 5:13). When explaining to Christians in Rome that the loving grace of God has overpowered sin, Paul bluntly adds, "Should we continue in sin in order that grace may abound? By no means! How can we who died to sin go on living in it?" (Rom 6:1-2). Yet this is exactly what the intruders are teaching.

Now I desire to remind you, though you are fully informed, that the Lord . . . destroyed those who did not believe. JUDE 5

To show convincingly that God punishes sin, Jude appeals to several stories from revered Jewish history—some from the Old Testament, others from the books of the Apocrypha, and yet others from legends. Israelites of the Exodus were not immune to God's punishment for sin, Jude reminds his readers. Nor were angels, who in the apocalyptic book of 1 Enoch are said to have left heaven to mate with human women. Jude further supports his case by appealing to a well-known legend about the devil accusing the deceased Moses of murder and trying to claim his body. The archangel Michael, in contesting Satan for the body, refused to do what the intruders of Jude's day do so flagrantly: presume to exercise the authority of God.

Have mercy on some who are wavering; save others by snatching them out of the fire. JUDE 22-23

Christians on the verge of accepting false teachings deserve and need to be rescued, Jude says. Even those who have already given in to the heresy, and have practiced sexual immorality, deserve mercy. Jude's short letter concludes with a powerful and reassuring benediction, which promises believers that God can keep them from caving in to the heresy and preserve them for heaven, where they will stand in the presence of the Lord.

*O*n the small and rocky island of Patmos, 37 miles off the coast of Turkey in the Aegean Sea, an exiled Christian prophet named John has a series of fantastic, futuristic visions. Some are beautiful, such as those depicting heaven. Others are horrible, describing blood-soaked battlefields and world-shattering cataclysm. Yet, all reassuringly confirm that John's faith is well-founded, and that Christian persecution will end and the church will emerge victorious.

John wrote to encourage Christians who were suffering intense and sometimes deadly persecution, probably late in the reign of the Roman emperor Domitian, in about A.D. 95. Domitian insisted that subjects address him as "Lord and God" and burn sacrifices in worship of him, punishing those who refused. Apparently to protect himself and his message, John wrote in the coded, highly symbolic genre known as apocalyptic literature, popular during the oppressive two centuries before and the two after Jesus. This writing style takes its name from Revelation 1:1, "revelation," or apokalypsis in the Greek language that John used. In his final, wondrous vision, John sees the fulfillment of the goal that God has been working toward throughout biblical history, since humanity's first sin: the restoration of creation as good and perfect, free of evil.

Within a few decades, during the time of the church leader Justin Martyr (about A.D. 100-165), Christians began to identify Revelation's writer as the apostle John, one of Jesus' closest disciples and, by tradition, author of the Gospel of John and the three letters of John. But about 100 years later, other Christians began to challenge this assumption, noting that in language, style, and thought, Revelation is dramatically different from the apostle's writings. Also, the John of Revelation speaks of the apostles in the past tense (Rev 21:14), never identifying himself as one. His Semitic-flavored Greek, however, suggests that John of Patmos was a Jew who emigrated from Palestine—perhaps an individual remembered only because of his notable legacy that became the closing book in the Christian Bible.

The vision of John of Patmos, author of Revelation, by the 14th-century Italian artist Jacopo Alberegno

---

The revelation of Jesus Christ . . . ; he made it known by sending his angel to his servant John. REV 1:1

John begins his book with a short, general description of what he is about to reveal—and where the revelation comes from. He is going to disclose "what must soon take place" (Rev 1:1). His source is Jesus Christ, who has sent an angel to assist him. The Old Testament prophet and apocalyptic writer Daniel also required an angel's guidance and counsel throughout a series of mysterious visions.

Revelation is intended to be read aloud in seven prominent churches in western Turkey (then the Roman province of Asia): Ephesus, Smyrna, Pergamum, Thyatira, Sardis, Philadelphia, and Laodicea. John, who identifies himself only as "your brother" (Rev 1:9), writes from nearby Patmos island—a meager ten miles long and five miles wide—where he has been exiled for talking about Jesus. In greeting the churches, John narrows his topic: the eagerly anticipated return of Jesus. "Look! He is coming with the clouds; every eye will see him" (Rev 1:7).

Then comes the first of John's many remarkable visions. He hears a roaring voice calling itself Alpha and Omega, the first and last letters of the Greek alphabet. Earlier, God had described himself in a similar way to the prophet Isaiah: "I am the first and I am the last" (Isa 44:6), the eternal ruler of all. But here the speaker is the Son of Man—Jesus Christ—equating Jesus with God the Father. Son of Man is the title Jesus preferred when describing himself, perhaps because it is the title that the prophet Daniel used when speaking of the eternally reigning Messiah, "one like a human being [son of man] coming with the clouds of heaven" (Dan 7:13).

John turns toward the voice and sees the Son of Man standing among seven lampstands, which represent the seven churches. John's description of Jesus draws on Daniel's written portrait of God. White hair visually conveys God's antiquity as the "Ancient One" (Dan 7:9). The two-edged sword elsewhere in scripture symbolizes both the word of God and judgment (Isa 49:2; Heb 4:12). In the Son's hand are seven stars, identified as angels. In fact, separate messages that John prepares for the seven churches are addressed not to the congregations, but to their angels. It is unclear if these are heavenly beings—perhaps guardian angels—or human leaders of the church.

"To the angel of the church in Ephesus write: . . . you have abandoned the love you had at first." REV 2:1,4

Whether John is writing to angelic beings who guide and protect the seven churches or to congregational leaders, the words are intended for believers to hear in a public reading. The seven leading churches may be among those to which John ministered as an itinerant prophet before he was banished to Patmos. But they may also symbolize all churches. Throughout Jewish history, the richly symbolic number seven—which John uses about 50 times in Revelation—represents completion. It was on the seventh day that God rested after finishing creation. When John writes to each church, praising its good traits and criticizing its failings, he and his readers may have understood that he was talking about the entire Christian movement. Even today,

church leaders study these seven messages in Revelation for characteristics of a godly church.

The first letter goes to Ephesus, leading city in the region, where Paul labored more than two years about a generation earlier, in the 50s A.D Though commending believers for their hard work and endurance in the face of persecution, John declares that their love is fading—perhaps their love for Jesus, for one another, or both. John's second letter is directed to Smyrna, a harbor town about 40 miles north of Ephesus and home to a large, militant group of Jews. Only Smyrna and Philadelphia receive nothing but praise and encouragement. John urges Smyrna's believers to remain fearless when they come face-to-face with death. (Perhaps among the first Smyrnans to hear this was a young man in his twenties: Polycarp, who became bishop of Smyrna. Some 60 years later, in about A.D.155, Polycarp was arrested for his faith and burned to death.)

The third letter goes to Pergamum, a thriving city of nearly 200,000 and regional center of emperor worship, which John describes as "Satan's throne" (Rev 2:13). The believers have remained faithful to God, yet they have inappropriately tolerated a sect known as the Nicolaitans. Like the ancient seer Balaam, who orchestrated the seduction of Israelites into pagan sexual rites, the Nicolaitans practice ritual sex and eat food offered to idols. John's fourth and final letter of chapter 2 is for Thyatira, an inland trading city. John chastises the otherwise faithful Christians for tolerating a false teacher he calls Jezebel. Like the Nicolaitans, this self-proclaimed Christian teacher practices ritual sex and eats food sacrificed to idols. Unless she repents, John warns, she and those who engage in sex with her will find themselves thrown onto their beds not in erotic ecstasy, but in "great distress" (Rev 2:22), possibly disease.

In this illustration from a commentary on Revelation by Beatus de Liebana of Spain, dated about 950, John of Patmos kneels before his vision of Jesus, seated beneath seven hanging lamps.

"To the angel of the church in Sardis write: . . . you have a name of being alive, but you are dead. Wake up." REV 3:1-2

Believers of Sardis, another wealthy city, are accused of being Christian in name only. Yet John reports that some believers are genuine and that their names are recorded in the "book of life" (Rev 3:5), a metaphor meaning they are citizens of God's kingdom; Moses was the first in the Bible to refer to such a heavenly book (Ex 32:32). Ancient cities often kept registers of citizens; names of the dead were deleted.

Christians in Philadelphia live up to their name—both as Christians and as Philadelphians; the town's name means "brotherly love," after the devotion of Attalus II, a former ruler of the region, for his brother. Though the church is small and feeble, John promises it will survive the coming oppression.

The seventh and final letter goes to Laodicea, a rich banking town, famous for its medical school and nearby hot springs. In brutal sarcasm, John prescribes that the Laodiceans take a dose of their own medicine—at least in its spiritual form. He diagnoses them as spiritually blind and suffering from a faith that is nauseatingly tepid. "Because you are lukewarm, and neither cold nor hot," John says, delivering the words of Jesus, "I am about to spit you out of my mouth" (Rev 3:16). Yet John adds that there is time to repent.

I looked, and there in heaven a door stood open!
REV 4:1

*A*pparently leaving his body in a trancelike state, John has a vision of being transfigured into his spiritual essence and ushered into the very throne room of God, whom John describes as shimmering with the brilliance of polished gems. With God are 24 white-robed elders, perhaps representing the 12 tribes of Israel and the 12 apostles of Jesus. Flashes of lightning and peals of thunder provide sights and sounds reminiscent of God descending to Mount Sinai to meet with Moses. Surrounding the throne on four sides are four bizarre creatures covered with eyes. In some ways, they resemble a lion, an ox, a human, and an eagle. These are reminiscent of the four-faced beings that the prophet Ezekiel describes in his vision of the heavenly throne room—each has the faces of lion, ox, human, and eagle (Ezek 1:10). What these creatures represent may have been clear to readers of John's time, but the symbolism has been lost. Their purpose, however, is clear. Day and night they praise God, singing much the same song that Isaiah reports hearing in his vision of God's throne: "Holy, holy, holy, the Lord God Almighty" (Rev 4:8; Isa 6:3).

"Who is worthy to open the scroll and break its seals?"
REV 5:2

*A*s God sits on his throne, he holds a scroll that represents his final plans for the world. The document is held in a tight roll, sealed shut not by one dried clay seal, but by seven—the numerical symbol of fullness and completion and a clue to the important contents of the scroll. An angelic herald cries loudly, asking who is worthy to break the seals and reveal God's plan. Heaven falls silent. The first sound heard is of John weeping, fearful that the scroll must remain sealed and God's plan unknown—perhaps unfulfilled. But one of the 24 elders assures John that there is among the heavens one who is worthy: "the Lion of the tribe of Judah, the Root of David" (Rev 5:5). These are Old Testament titles that point to God's Messiah, descended from the extended tribal family of Judah and Jesse's son, the great King David. The identity of this deliverer who will save the righteous becomes clear in Revelation 22:16: "It is I, Jesus, who sent my angel to you with this testimony for the churches. I am the root and

APOCALYPTIC LITERATURE

The distribution of trumpets to the seven angels; a scene from a book of apocalyptic illustrations dated about 1250

*G*od's plans *for the future are revealed— though often heavily veiled with strange and perplexing symbolism—in a genre of literature born of oppression. When the Jews returned from exile in Babylon, they did not come home as a free people. For centuries they were dominated and abused by one foreign power after another. But many Jews, and later persecuted Christians, found hope in apocalyptic writings that flourished from about 200 B.C. to A.D. 200. Using coded words and images, the writers encouraged their readers, while escaping the censorship and wrath of governing authorities. Cryptic writing was essential because of the inflammatory message the writers delivered: God will destroy the oppressors, then establish a kingdom of righteousness.*

Apocalyptic literature takes its name from the Greek word apokalypsis, *which means "revelation" —a title given to the most famous apocalyptic book in the Bible: The Revelation to John. Because of the world-shattering catastrophes predicted in Revelation, apocalypse became an English word meaning universal disaster. Daniel is the only other biblical book that is entirely apocalyptic, though Isaiah and Ezekiel have apocalyptic sections. Outside the Bible are many apocalyptic books, most of which are written by authors who assume the identity of a biblical prophet—such as Moses or Elijah—to gain a wider readership.*

Symbolism is often so thick and futuristic scenes so bizarre that it seems unlikely that even the original readers fully understood them. At times, even Daniel needs the help of an interpreting angel. Yet, the central message in Daniel and other apocalyptic works is unobscured: God will defeat evil to usher in a glorious new age.

The Four Horsemen of the Apocalypse—a conquering power, war, famine, and pestilence—crowd this canvas by the Venetian painter Jacopo Palma the Younger (1544-1628); under a hovering eagle at left, John of Patmos records the terrifying scene in the book of Revelation.

the descendant of David." John says that Jesus has seven horns and seven eyes. Horns are ancient symbols of kingly power, and eyes represent awareness of all that happens. Uncountable millions—"thousands of thousands"—praise Jesus: "Worthy is the Lamb that was slaughtered," (Rev 5:11-12). The reference is to his sacrificial death, which atones for the sins of any human being who repents.

I saw the Lamb open one of the seven seals, and I heard one of the four living creatures call out, as with a voice of thunder, "Come!"   REV 6:1

One by one, Jesus begins breaking the seven seals. The first four unleash what have become known as the Four Horsemen of the Apocalypse— riders authorized to use warfare, famine, disease, and wild animals to kill one-fourth of the planet's population. The white horse represents a conquering power; the red horse is war and bloodshed; the black horse is famine; and the pale green horse—the color of a corpse—is pestilence.

When Jesus breaks the fifth seal, spirits of martyred believers emerge from beneath an altar; at the base of the temple altar is where priests ritually pour the blood of sacrifices. The souls cry out for justice, asking how long it will be before their executioners are judged. They are given white robes, signifying their right to reside in heaven, and are told to wait a little longer, until violence and martyrdom reach the limits God has set.

Breaking of the sixth seal spawns a tremendous earthquake, followed by a series of cosmic catastrophes: The sun turns black, the moon turns red, stars drop like figs shaken from a tree, the sky disappears like a scroll being rolled up, and the contours of earth are disfigured as mountains and islands disappear. The planetary devastation sounds remarkably like that of Isaiah's description in a section known as the Isaiah Apocalypse: "The Lord is about to lay waste the earth and make it desolate, and he will twist its surface and scatter its inhabitants" (Isa 24:1).

Since apocalyptic literature is highly symbolic, these cataclysms most likely represent upheavals other than astrological and geological ones—perhaps social, political, and religious disturbances. At the tumultuous birth of the church on the day of Pentecost, Peter declared the fulfillment of Joel's prophecy: "I will pour out my Spirit upon all flesh . . . . I will show portents in the heaven above and signs on the earth below, blood, and fire, and smoky mist. The sun shall be turned to darkness and the moon to blood" (Acts 2:17, 19-20; Joel 2:28, 30-32).

In an interlude before the final seal is opened, John sees two visions assuring him that the faithful will be protected during the coming tumult. The number of those "sealed," or protected, is 144,000. This is 12 times 12,000, a number that dramatically symbolizes the entire community of God—not a single righteous person is missing. The allotment of 12,000 to each of the 12 tribes of Israel confirms the church as the spiritual heir of God's chosen people.

John's second vision shifts to a countless multitude of believers, praising Jesus and waving palm branches, as people did when Jesus rode into Jerusalem on the first Palm Sunday. One of the elders explains that these are survivors of the coming "great ordeal; they have washed their robes and made them white in the blood of the Lamb" (Rev 7:14)—their sins atoned for by Jesus' death on the cross.

When the Lamb opened the seventh seal, there was silence in heaven for about half an hour. REV 8:1

With the seventh seal broken, the scroll of God is completely unsealed, meaning his plan for the world is nearly revealed. Awe and reverential silence fill the celestial realm. Then, one after another, seven trumpets are blown, launching a new wave of catastrophes that resemble the ten plagues suffered by the Egyptians who enslaved the Israelites. In response to the first trumpet, hail, fire, and blood pelt the planet—reminiscent of Egypt's seventh plague of lethal hail and lightning. Then, a third of the sea is polluted with blood (Moses had turned the Nile into blood). Next, a star crashes to earth. Then, a mysterious darkness blots out parts of the sun, moon, and stars (Egypt suffered three days of darkness). Next comes an invasion of stinging creatures described as locusts, corresponding to Egypt's eighth plague. With scorpionlike tails and armor, these creatures may symbolize an invasion force. In fact, the catastrophe that follows—unleashed by the sixth trumpet—erupts from a massive army of 200 million. Christians in John's day may have understood some of the coded symbols behind these horrifying images, but today that code remains elusive.

Earlier, John witnessed two comforting visions before the seventh seal was broken. Now, he sees two more visions before an angel blows the seventh trumpet. As before, John is assured that God will take care of Christians living through these horrors—whatever they may be. The seventh and final trumpet begins a song of victory, declaring that God's kingdom has finally come. This fulfills the prayer Jesus taught his disciples: "Your kingdom come. Your will be done, on earth as it is in heaven" (Mt 6:10). In John's day, the kingdom of the civilized world belongs to all-conquering Rome. John may have been predicting that Rome will one day become a Christian empire, an event fulfilled about 300 years later. But the prophecy may also point beyond ancient history, into a future time when the Lord is unopposed throughout his creation.

War broke out in heaven; Michael and his angels fought against the dragon. REV 12:7

A war John witnesses in heaven seems to grow out of a familiar Greek legend about the god Apollo's birth. Apollo's pregnant mother is pursued by a serpent, which Apollo eventually kills. In John's vision, the pregnant woman seems to represent all of God's people. The 12 stars in her crown could symbolize the 12 tribes of Israel or the 12 apostles of Jesus. The dragon is Satan, as verse 9 makes clear. He is red, perhaps symbolizing violence; with seven heads, meaning clever; ten horns, powerful; and seven crowns, controlling. The celestial warfare that John describes may refer to Satan's clash with Jesus, which begins with Jesus' birth, death, resurrection, and ascension: "Her child was snatched away and taken to God and to his throne" (Rev 12:5). Since the child is safe with God, the angry dragon continues to pursue the mother—the church. But she, too, is under God's protection. At one point she grows eagle's wings and soars far away from danger. The prophet Isaiah, too, once said that those who trust in God will soar out of reach of danger: "They shall mount up with wings like eagles" (Isa 40:31).

I saw a beast rising out of the sea. REV 13:1

Two beasts appear and begin serving the dragon, previously identified as Satan. Some believe the first beast is the Roman Empire while the second is the cult that bestows divinity on the emperor and builds idols of him: "the image of the beast" (Rev 13:15). Others see in these beasts an end-of-time antichrist and a prophet accomplice. The mark of the beast—666—may be no more literal than "the seal of the living God" (Rev 7:2) on the foreheads of believers; the seal refers to God's protection, the mark of the beast refers to the doomed. John says that discovering the being represented by the diabolical 666 "calls for wisdom: let anyone with understanding calculate the number of the beast, for it is the number of a person" (Rev 13:18). Hebrew and Greek letters have numerical equivalents. Six hundred and sixty-six is the sum of the Hebrew letters for Nero Caesar, the most vicious persecutor of early Christians. Dur-

John, from behind the image of Satan in Hades, witnesses death riding a pale horse in this 14th-century French tapestry.

ing waves of intense persecution by Nero and later emperors, Christians were ostracized and boycotted—perhaps the meaning behind "No one can buy or sell who does not have the mark" (Rev 13:17) on their right hand or forehead.

Then I looked, and there was the Lamb, standing on Mount Zion! And with him were one hundred forty-four thousand. REV 14:1

Once again, interspersed between prophetic scenes of terrifying desolation are more visions intended to comfort the persecuted church. John sees Jesus standing on Mount Zion, the hill on which Jerusalem's temple was built. Surrounding Jesus are 144,000, or 12 times 12,000—a number based on the 12 tribes of Israel and symbolizing the entire, massive assembly of believers. Next, John sees angels delivering messages to earth, reporting that God's judgment is near and that Babylon has fallen. Jews had used Babylon as a code name for Rome ever since A.D. 70, when Rome did to Jerusalem what Babylon had done in 586 B.C.—burned and leveled it. The third and final vision John sees in this interlude is of angels brandishing sickles that they use to whisk across the earth, harvesting righteous souls and destroying the wicked, who are compared to grapes of God's wrath crushed in a winepress.

I heard a loud voice from the temple telling the seven angels, "Go and pour out on the earth the seven bowls of the wrath of God." REV 16:1

Earth suffers from God's final plagues—again, many of which resemble the ten plagues of Egypt. Skin sores erupt. Blood pollutes the springs, rivers, and oceans in a punishment that an angel declares fitting: "Because they shed the blood of saints and prophets, you have given them blood to drink" (Rev 16:6). Darkness covers the land. Hundred-pound hailstones pummel the ground. A tremendous earthquake levels cities. And an army east of the Euphrates River, which flows into the Persian Gulf, assembles for battle at Harmagedon (Armageddon). The name of this battle site comes from a Hebrew term meaning mountains of Megiddo, referring to a mountain pass that feeds into a sprawling valley plain in northern Israel. This pass and plain have been the site of countless major battles before and after the time of John of Patmos.

Christians debate whether these and other disasters described in Revelation should be taken literally. Some interpret them as a figurative account of the unknown devastation and horror that will precede the Second Coming of Jesus. Others take the words more literally and, for example, see Armageddon as the battle site where God will ultimately and decisively defeat the massed forces of evil.

John then witnesses the punishment of "Babylon the great, mother of whores . . . . drunk with the blood of the saints and the blood of witnesses to

The seven-headed beast that emerges from the sea (top) is slain in this illustration from an Anglo-Norman commentary on Revelation, dated about 1250.

Jesus" (Rev 17:5, 6). Rival kingdoms devour Babylon, then burn the remains; fire is a common symbol for divine punishment in Old Testament times. John gives a clue about Babylon's real identity when he reports that she is seated on seven mountains (Rev 17:9). Ancient Roman writers commonly traced Rome's origins to a settlement built on seven hills along the banks of the Tiber River. Some, however, see in Babylon an end-of-time power that God will defeat, perhaps in addition to his defeat of Rome.

I saw another angel coming down from heaven . . . . He called out with a mighty voice, "Fallen, fallen is Babylon the great!" REV 18:1, 2

In the style of an ancient taunt song, much like the prophet Isaiah's song about Tyre (Isa 23), an angel announces that Babylon has fallen. Mourning Babylon's demise are the many rulers, merchants, and sailors who have conducted lucrative business with the empire. Rome imported exotic products from all over the known world, including northern Europe, Africa, India, and China. To illustrate graphically how God will wipe Babylon off the face of the earth, a powerful angel throws a huge millstone into the sea and declares, "With such violence Babylon the great city will be thrown down, and will be found no more" (Rev 18:21).

Heaven's reaction is the opposite of earth's—a vast multitude of voices burst into song, praising God for avenging the blood of his servants. With Babylon destroyed, they sing that the time has come for "the marriage of the Lamb" (Rev 19:7). The Lamb is Jesus, the bride is the church, and the marriage is the two united at the Second Coming. Jesus establishes this analogy in his parable of the ten bridesmaids (Mt 25:1-13), which is based on the Old Testament portrayal of God as Israel's husband (Isa 54:5).

Then I saw heaven opened, and there was a white horse! Its rider is called Faithful and True, and in righteousness he judges and makes war. REV 19:11

In what may be the continuation of John's earlier reference to the battle of Armageddon, the beast assembles his forces to fight a celestial army mounted on white horses—the color symbolizing victory. Leading this army of angels is Jesus, identified by several titles intended to describe his character: Faithful and True, Word of God, King of kings and Lord of lords. His robe is dipped in blood, perhaps representing the crucifixion, which helped propel the plan of God to save humanity from sin and to restore a corrupted creation to the paradise lost.

Jesus defeats the enemy with "the sword that came from his mouth" (Rev 19:21), a symbol for the word of God and judgment. To emphasize the enemy's utter devastation, an angel calls carrion-eating birds to gorge themselves at the battlefield. The beast and prophet—perhaps the Roman Empire with its dread imperial cult, or an end-of-time antichrist and his prophet—are thrown alive into a lake of fire. This lake of eternal torment elsewhere in the New Testament is called Gehenna ("hell"), a valley outside Jerusalem where human sacrifices occasionally took place in Old Testament times. Because of its unholy reputation, the valley was turned into a constantly smoldering dump where the Jews threw their trash—and the corpses of executed criminals. In time, people began using this word to describe the place to which God sends sinners on judgment day.

Whether the battle between the beast and Jesus is meant to portray a literal clash between physical and spiritual forces remains obscure. What John's vision clearly shows, however, is that Jesus defeats all of his earthly enemies. The only enemies remaining are those of the spiritual realm, led by the dragon Satan.

I saw an angel . . . . He seized the dragon, that ancient serpent, who is the Devil and Satan, and bound him for a thousand years, and threw him into the pit. REV 20:1-3

What John witnesses next has provoked intense and continuing debate among Christians since at least the second century. John watches as the devil is bound and locked in a pit for a thousand years. During this time, martyred Christians are resurrected to rule with Jesus, though John does not say where. When the millennium is over, Satan is re-

An angel (top left) announces the fall of Babylon, a metaphor used by John to foretell the coming collapse of the Roman Empire, from which early Christians suffered so much; a 14th-century French tapestry.

Victor over Satan, the angel Michael weighs souls; from a book of hours dated about 1325.

I saw a great white throne and the one who sat on it . . . . the dead were judged according to their works.
REV 20:11, 12

With Satan defeated and condemned to eternal punishment, judgment day follows for humanity, though apparently only for the unrighteous, all of whom are now dead. The righteous dead were previously resurrected, in what John calls the "first resurrection" (Rev 20:5). Now, in what is a second resurrection, all the unrighteous dead are raised to appear before the judgment throne of God. John makes it clear that no one escapes, for he reports that the dead come from both sea and earth, or Hades, an underworld dwelling place of the dead. All individuals are judged according to the way they lived, the details of which are preserved in a celestial book. This book, the book of life, is probably only a figurative, visual image to help readers understand a spiritual truth: People will be held accountable for their actions, and judged accordingly. Those whose names do not appear in the book of life, meaning those who have chosen to reject God, are thrown into the lake of fire alongside Satan and the beast. John describes this punishment as the second death, for it follows physical death.

What the lake of fire, or hell, is like remains a disturbing mystery. John describes it as burning sulfur. Jesus confirms that sinners risk "the hell of fire" in a place outside the realm of God where there will be "weeping and gnashing of teeth"; oddly, Jesus also describes this fiery abode as "the outer darkness" (Mt 5:22, 8:12). Intensifying the mystery of this place is the awareness that John and other writers in the Bible are limited to word pictures from the physical world to describe punishment that will take place in a dimension beyond the physical.

Then I saw a new heaven and a new earth; for the first heaven and the first earth had passed away.   REV 21:1

John now sees the most wonderful vision of all— the final event in God's plan. Creation is recreated, just as Isaiah had prophesied: "I am about to create new heavens and a new earth" (Isa 65:17). Gone are all vestiges of the previous world, contaminated and damaged by humanity's sin. John helps convey this idea through the phrase, "the sea was no more" (Rev 21:1). To Jews, not a seafaring people, the ocean was a place of fearsome tumult.

Whether John sees a renewed physical creation or the spiritual world of heaven remains a matter of debate. He witnesses a new Jerusalem descending from heaven. Some Jews and Christians in ancient times believed there exists a heavenly counterpart to Jerusalem, a spiritual twin city. Some today believe this celestial city will replace the old Jerusalem. Others interpret the new Jerusalem as a metaphor representing the eternal dwelling place of God and his people. To describe in physical terms the majesty that he sees in his spiritual state, John draws on the most

leased and assembles an army, identified as Gog and Magog, which the prophet Ezekiel says are doomed enemies of Israel from the north (where most Israelite foes came from). John, however, says this particular army—"as numerous as the sands from the sea" (Rev 20:8)—is mustered from the four corners of the earth, perhaps indicating that they represent all newly recruited enemies of God's people. This mysterious army surrounds "the camp of the saints and the beloved city" (Rev 20:9), perhaps Jerusalem, or more likely a figurative description of the church. Fire from heaven consumes the invaders. Their leader, Satan, is thrown into the lake of fire forever. The long struggle between the forces of good and evil is over. God has won.

Christians interpret this passage in a wide variety of ways. Some take it literally, and teach that Jesus will return and set up a thousand-year reign on earth, either before or after the world has suffered great tribulation. Others see the present age as a metaphorical millennium, with deceased believers reigning in heaven alongside Jesus and with the church on earth spreading the Gospel, aided by the Holy Spirit, who restricts Satan. Still others look forward to what they believe will be the conversion of the entire world to Christianity, followed by an era of peace (the millennium) and the eventual Second Coming of Jesus. It is likely that Christians of John's time were equally puzzled by the reference to the millennium.

expressive imagery and symbols available. The new Jerusalem has 12 gates, perhaps emphasizing the continuity of entrance into God's community, first through the 12 tribes of Israel, then through the church established by Jesus' 12 apostles. The new Jerusalem is a huge and perfect cube, the shape of the holiest room in Jerusalem's temple—a room considered the earthly dwelling place of God. The city's gates, walls, and streets can be described only by comparing them to the world's most precious treasures: rare gems, pearls, and pure gold. Missing in Jerusalem, and unnecessary, are the temple and the sun. There is no need for a place of worship when God's people have the being they worship living among them; no longer is he invisible—now they can "see his face" (Rev 22:4). As for light, "the Lord God will be their light, and they will reign forever and ever" (Rev 22:5).

"It is I, Jesus . . . . I am the root and the descendant of David, the bright morning star. . . . Surely I am coming soon!" REV 22:16, 20

*I*n a stirring conclusion to his prophetic book, and the Christian Bible, John testifies that he witnessed everything he has reported, and that the source of his visions is none other than Jesus Christ. "Root and the descendant of David" identifies Jesus as the Messiah who was predicted by the prophets. Isaiah portrayed him as the "root of Jesse" (Isa 11:10), David's father. The "bright morning star" is the Christ himself, heralding the dawn of a new day. This description, too, is a messianic title that initially referred to David but was later applied to Jesus: "A star shall come out of Jacob, and a scepter shall rise out of Israel" (Num 24:17). Interestingly, it was the mysterious star of Bethlehem that alerted sages that a newborn king had arrived. Here, once again invoking the image of a star, Jesus declares he is coming again.

Many of the first generation of Christians apparently believed they would live to see the Second Coming. Eventually, Christian leaders began to explain that God measures time differently than humans do: "With the Lord one day is like a thousand years, and a thousand years are like one day. The Lord is not slow about his promise . . . but is patient with you, not wanting any to perish, but all to come to repentance" (2 Pet 3:8, 9). By the time John writes onto a scroll all the remarkable scenes he has witnessed some 60 years after the ascension of Jesus, it is clear that the Second Coming is not going to take place exactly as Christians had expected. Yet, believers remain certain that the event they so hope for will unfold according to the plan of the Lord. In the meantime, the fervent prayer lingering on their lips is the urgent summons that closes the Bible: "Come, Lord Jesus!" (Rev 22:20).

The Second Coming of Jesus is shown in this devotional book made for the bishop of Winchester, England, about 980.

VERSIONS OF THE BIBLE

The Hebrew (or Jewish) Bible

TORAH

Genesis
Exodus
Leviticus
Numbers
Deuteronomy

PROPHETS

Joshua
Judges
Samuel (1 & 2)
Kings (1 & 2)
Isaiah
Jeremiah
Ezekiel

The Twelve:

Hosea
Joel
Amos
Obadiah
Jonah
Micah

Nahum
Habakkuk
Zephaniah
Haggai
Zechariah
Malachi

WRITINGS

Psalms
Proverbs
Job
Song of Solomon
Ruth
Lamentations
Ecclesiastes
Esther
Daniel
Ezra-Nehemiah
Chronicles (1 & 2)

The Catholic Bible

THE OLD TESTAMENT

Genesis
Exodus
Leviticus
Numbers
Deuteronomy
Joshua
Judges
Ruth
1 Samuel
2 Samuel
1 Kings
2 Kings
1 Chronicles
2 Chronicles
Ezra
Nehemiah
Tobit

Judith
Esther (with Additions)
1 Maccabees
2 Maccabees
Job
Psalms
Proverbs
Ecclesiastes
Song of Solomon
Wisdom of Solomon
Sirach
Isaiah
Jeremiah
Lamentations
Baruch
    Letter of Jeremiah
Ezekiel

Daniel
    Prayer of Azariah and
        Song of the Three Jews
    Susanna
    Bel and the Dragon
Hosea
Joel
Amos
Obadiah
Jonah
Micah
Nahum
Habakkuk
Zephaniah
Haggai
Zechariah
Malachi

THE NEW TESTAMENT

Matthew
Mark
Luke
John
Acts of the Apostles
Romans
1 Corinthians
2 Corinthians
Galatians

Ephesians
Philippians
Colossians
1 Thessalonians
2 Thessalonians
1 Timothy
2 Timothy
Titus
Philemon

Hebrews
James
1 Peter
2 Peter
1 John
2 John
3 John
Jude
Revelation

The Protestant Bible

THE OLD TESTAMENT

Genesis
Exodus
Leviticus
Numbers
Deuteronomy
Joshua
Judges
Ruth
1 Samuel
2 Samuel
1 Kings
2 Kings
1 Chronicles

2 Chronicles
Ezra
Nehemiah
Esther
Job
Psalms
Proverbs
Ecclesiastes
Song of Solomon
Isaiah
Jeremiah
Lamentations
Ezekiel

Daniel
Hosea
Joel
Amos
Obadiah
Jonah
Micah
Nahum
Habakkuk
Zephaniah
Haggai
Zechariah
Malachi

THE NEW TESTAMENT

Matthew
Mark
Luke
John
Acts of the Apostles
Romans
1 Corinthians
2 Corinthians
Galatians

Ephesians
Philippians
Colossians
1 Thessalonians
2 Thessalonians
1 Timothy
2 Timothy
Titus
Philemon

Hebrews
James
1 Peter
2 Peter
1 John
2 John
3 John
Jude
Revelation

Abbreviations of the Books in the Bible

Acts	Acts of the Apostles	Hag	Haggai	Lam	Lamentations	Rom	Romans	2 Thess	2 Thessalonians
Am	Amos	Heb	Hebrews	Lev	Leviticus	Ruth	Ruth	1 Tim	1 Timothy
1 Chr	1 Chronicles	Hos	Hosea	Lk	Luke	1 Sam	1 Samuel	2 Tim	2 Timothy
2 Chr	2 Chronicles	Is	Isaiah	Mal	Malachi	2 Sam	2 Samuel	Titus	Titus
Col	Colossians	Jas	James	Mic	Micah	Song	Song of Solomon	Zech	Zechariah
1 Cor	1 Corinthians	Jer	Jeremiah	Mk	Mark	1 Thess	1 Thessalonians	Zeph	Zephaniah
2 Cor	2 Corinthians	Jn	John	Mt	Matthew				
Dan	Daniel	1 Jn	1 John	Nah	Nahum				
Deut	Deuteronomy	2 Jn	2 John	Neh	Nehemiah				
Eccl	Ecclesiastes	3 Jn	3 John	Num	Numbers				
Eph	Ephesians	Job	Job	Ob	Obadiah				
Esth	Esther	Joel	Joel	1 Pet	1 Peter				
Ex	Exodus	Jon	Jonah	1 Pet	2 Peter				
Ezek	Ezekiel	Josh	Joshua	Phil	Philippians				
Ezra	Ezra	Jude	Jude	Philem	Philemon				
Gal	Galatians	Judg	Judges	Prov	Proverbs				
Gen	Genesis	1 Kgs	1 Kings	Ps	Psalms				
Hab	Habakkuk	2 Kgs	2 Kings	Rev	Revelation				

Abbreviations of the Books of the Apocrypha

Add Esth	Additions to Esther	Sir	Sirach
Bar	Baruch	Song of Thr	Prayer of Azariah
Bel	Bel and the Dragon		and Song of the
Jdt	Judith		Three Jews
Let Jer	Letter of Jeremiah	Sus	Susanna
1 Macc	1 Maccabees	Tob	Tobit
2 Macc	2 Maccabees	Wis	Wisdom of Solomon

ILLUSTRATION CREDITS

The editors wish to thank Bette Duke for her map illustrations on the following pages; 17, 25, 36, 69, 76, 81, 87, 115, 142, 293, 315, 369, 372.

Picture research by Carousel Research, Inc.

Key to abbreviations used:
AKG, L: AKG, London
AR/A: Art Resource/Alinari
AR/G: Art Resource/Giraudon
AR/JM: Art Resource/The Jewish Museum, NY
AR/L: Art Resource/Erich Lessing
AR/PML: Art Resource/The Pierpont Morgan Library, NY
AR/S: Art Resource/Scala
AR/TG: Art Resource/Tate Gallery, London
AR/V&A: Art Resource/Victoria & Albert Museum, London
BAL: Bridgeman Art Library, London
BAL, NY: Bridgeman Art Library, NY
S. Halliday: Sonia Halliday Photographs
R. Nowitz: Richard T. Nowitz
Z. Radovan: Zev Radovan, Jerusalem

FRONT MATTER
Cover, Nativity, 19th century, S. Halliday; **2**, All Saints before God the Father from the book of hours of Catherine of Cleves, The Pierpont Morgan Library, New York, ms. 945, fol. 115v., AR/PML; **5**, Edward Coley Burne-Jones, Archangel Michael, Gattistock, Dorset, England, S. Halliday/Laura Lushington; **6**, Return of the spies, Canterbury Cathedral, England, S. Halliday/Laura Lushington; **7 left**, Habakkuk brings food to Daniel in the lion's den, The Pierpont Morgan Library, New York, ms. 644, fol. 260, AR/PML; **7 right**, Entry of Jesus into Jerusalem, Museo Arcivescovile, Ravenna, Italy, AR/L; **9**, Hans Memling, Angels with musical instruments, Royal Museum of Fine Arts, Antwerp, AR/S.

OLD TESTAMENT INTRODUCTION
10, Creation of the World from the Bible of Souvigny, Bibliothèque Municipal, Moulins, France, AR/G.

GENESIS
12, William Blake, The Ancient of Days, British Museum, London, BAL; **13**, Hieronymus Bosch, Garden of Eden, from The Haywain, left wing of triptych, Monasterio de El Escorial, Spain, BAL; **14**, Nicolas of Verdun, Cain slays Abel from the Verdun altar, Sammlungen des Stiftes, Klosterneuberg, Austria, AR/L; **15 bottom**, Mount Ararat, Turkey, Photo Researchers/Fred Maroon; **15 bottom left**, Birds entering the ark, San Marco, Venice, AR/S; **16 left**, Tower of Babel, Armenian manuscript, David Harris; **16 right**, Sumerian ruins, Uruk, Iraq, Bruce Coleman, Inc./Jonathan Wright; **17**, James Joseph Jacques Tissot, The caravan of Abram, Jewish Museum, New York, AR/JM; **18 left**, Lot's wife looks back, Canterbury Cathedral, S. Halliday/Laura Lushington; **18 right**, Dead Sea, Z. Radovan; **19 top**, Filippo Brunelleschi, Sacrifice of Isaac, Museo Nazionale del Bargello, Florence, AR/S; **19 bottom**, Sebastiano Ricci, Dismissal of Hagar, Galleria Sabauda, Turin, AR/S; **20**, Story of Rebecca, Duomo, Monreale, Italy, AR/S; **21**, Jean-Baptiste Jouvenet, Isaac blessing Jacob, Musée des Beaux-Arts, Rouen, AR/G; **22 top**, Jacob's ladder from the Nuremberg Bible, Private Collection, BAL; **22 bottom**, Joseph von Führich, Jacob and Rachel at the well, Österreichische Galerie, Vienna, AR/L; **23**, Giovanni Battista Tiepolo, Rachel hiding the idols, Museo Civico, Udine, BAL; **24 top**, Eugène Delacroix, Fight between Jacob and the angel, St. Sulpice, Paris, BAL/Lauros-Giraudon; **24 bottom**, Joseph in the pit, Canterbury Cathedral, S. Halliday/Laura Lushington; **26**, Raphael, Joseph fleeing Potiphar's wife, Vatican Palace, AR/S; **27**, Joseph and his brethren, Palazzo Vecchio, Florence, AR/S; **28**, Rembrandt Harmensz van Rijn, Jacob's Blessing, Staatliche Kunstsammlungen, Kassel, AKG, L; **29 left**, Pyramid of Zoser, Saqqara, Egypt, R. Nowitz; **29 right**, Semitic bedouins entering Egypt, Tomb of Chnuma-Hotep, Beni Hasan, Egypt, AR/L.

EXODUS
30, Slavery of Israel, British Library, London, AKG, L; **31**, Orazio Gentileschi, Finding the infant Moses, Museo del Prado, Madrid, AR/S; **32**, Raphael, Moses under the burning thorn bush, Vatican Palace, AKG, L; **33 top**, Moses traveling to Egypt from the Golden Haggada, British Library, London, AKG, L; **33 bottom**, James Joseph Jacques Tissot, Moses speaks to Pharaoh, Jewish Museum, New York, AR/JM; **34**, Seven plagues of Egypt from the Nuremberg Bible: Frogs; flies; boils; hail and lightning; locusts, Private Collection, BAL; **35 top**, Nicolas of Verdun, Israelites paint doorposts to ward off tenth plague, from the Verdun altar, Sammlungen des Stiftes, Klosterneuberg, Austria, AR/L; **35 bottom**, Ceramic seder plate, Jewish Museum, New York, AR/JM; **36**, Pharoah and the Exodus of the Israelites, Canterbury Cathedral, S. Halliday/Laura Lushington; **37**, Giulio Clovio, The flight from Egypt from the Farnese book of hours, Pierpont Morgan Library, New York, ms. 69, AR/PML; **38**, Master of the Holy Blood, Israelites gathering manna, Christie's Images, BAL; **39 top**, Moses receiving the Ten Commandments, Musée Condé, Chantilly, AR/G; **39 bottom**, Sinai Peninsula, David Harris; **40**, The ark of the covenant, Lincoln Cathedral, S. Halliday/Laura Lushington; **41**, The ark of the covenant, synagogue at Capernaum, S. Halliday; **42 top**, Moses dispensing the law to the people of Israel, Museo Nazionale del Bargello, Florence, AR/Nimatallah; **42 bottom**, Bronze bull, Z. Radovan; **43**, Cosimo Rosselli, Events of Exodus, Sistine Chapel, Vatican, AR/S.

LEVITICUS
44, Ram, detail from the Abraham & Isaac panel, Landesmuseum, Münster, S. Halliday/Laura Lushington; **45**, Sargon II carrying sacrificial gazelle, Musée du Louvre, Paris, AR/G; **46**, James Joseph Jacques Tissot, Moses and Joshua in the tabernacle, Jewish Museum, New York, AR/Jewish Museum; **47**, View of Mount Sinai from oasis, Israel, David Harris; **48**, Nadab and Abihu offer unholy fire and die from the Nuremberg Bible, Private Collection, BAL; **49**, Michelangelo Buonarroti, Sacrifice to God, Sistine Chapel, Vatican Palace, Vatican State, AR/S; **50**, Moses and Aaron, Westfälisches Landesmuseum, Münster, AR/L; **52**, Michelangelo Buonarroti, Moses from the tomb of Pope Julius II, S. Pietro in Vincoli, Rome, AR/S.

NUMBERS
53, Nicolas of Verdun, The spies return from the valley of Eshkol with grapes from the Verdun altar, Sammlungen des Stiftes, Klosterneuberg, Austria, AR/L; **54**, The twelve tribes of Israel encamped about the tabernacle, Calmet, Dictionary of the Bible, Mary Evans Picture Library; **55**, Code of Hammurabi, Hammurabi standing before sun-god Shamesh, Musée du Louvre, Paris, AR/G; **56**, William West, Israelites passing through the wilderness, City of Bristol Museum and Art Gallery, BAL; **57 left**, Julius Schnorr von Carolsfeld, Spies return from Canaan, AKG, L; **57 right**, Grapes, R. Nowitz; **58**, Agnolo Bronzino, Moses striking water from the rock, Capella di Eleonora, Palazzo Vecchio, Florence, BAL; **59**, Peter Paul Rubens, Moses and the Brazen Serpent, Courtauld Gallery, London, BAL; **60**, Hans Bol, Balaam's Ass, Johnny van Haeften Gallery, London, BAL; **61**, Joshua from the Winchester Bible, S. Halliday.

DEUTERONOMY
62, Moses on Mount Sinai, Musée Condé, Chantilly, France, BAL; **63**, Lucas Cranach, The Ten Commandments, Lutherhall, Wittenberg, BAL; **64**, Moses preaching to a crowd with Aaron and Joshua, S. Halliday; **65**, Sephardic boy at his bar mitzvah ceremony at the western wall, Israel, S. Halliday; **66**, Pesach seder table, Central Synagogue, London, S. Halliday/Laura Lushington; **68**, Moses on Mount Sinai, Ten Commandments, Tabernacle from the Lambeth Bible, Lambeth Palace Library, London, BAL; **69**, Kadesh-barnea, Z. Radovan; **70**, Moab Mountains, David Harris; **71**, Death of Moses from the Nuremberg Bible, Private Collection, BAL.

JOSHUA
72, Lorenzo Ghiberti, Israelites carrying the ark of the covenant, Baptistery, Florence, AR/S; **73 top**, Goffredo da Viterbo, Rahab helps the spies escape, Bibliothèque Nationale, Paris, AR/S; **73 bottom**, Jordan River, David Harris; **74**, Jean Fouquet, The fall of Jericho, Bibliothèque Nationale, Paris, BAL/Giraudon; **75**, James Joseph Jacques Tissot, Achan and his family stoned to death, Jewish Museum, New York, AR/Jewish Museum; **76**, Ruins at Jericho, David Harris; **77 top**, Capture of Ai, Israelites deceived by the Gibeonites, Pierpont Morgan Library, New York, AKG, L; **77 bottom**, Nablus, Richard T. Nowitz; **78**, Joshua and the Amorites, Wragby Church, England, S. Halliday/Laura Lushington; **79**, Joshua hangs the five kings, Bibliothèque Royale, Brussels, AKG, L.

JUDGES
82, Ehud slays Eglon, Church of St. Etienne, Mulhouse, S. Halliday/Laura Lushington; **83**, Shephelah, David Harris; **84**, James Joseph Jacques Tissot, Deborah beneath the palm tree, Jewish Museum, New York, AR/JM; **85 top**, Artemisia Gentileschi, Jael slays Sisera, Museum of Fine Arts, Budapest, AKG, L; **85 bottom**, Kishon River, David Harris; **87**, Chariot and horses, Israel Museum, Jerusalem, AR/L; **88**, Calling of Gideon and the kindling of his sacrifice; destruction of altar, people are summoned, the Midianites are overthrown, Pierpont Morgan Library, New York, AR/PML; **90**, Erasmus Quellinus II, Jephthah greeted by his daughter at Mizpah, Christie's Images, BAL; **91**, Bible Moralisée, scenes of Jephthah, Österreichische Nationalbibliothek, Vienna, AKG, L; **92**, Samson and the lion, Church of St. Etienne, Mulhouse, S. Halliday/Laura Lushington; **93**, Anthony Van Dyck, The arrest of Samson, Kunsthistorisches Museum, Vienna, BAL.

RUTH
94, Thomas Matthews Rooke, Ruth follows Naomi home to Bethlehem, Tate Gallery, London, AR/TG; **95**, Women gleaning in wheat fields in Israel, David Harris.

1 SAMUEL
96, Eli with Samuel, Church of St. Martin, Brampton, Cumbria, S. Halliday/Laura Lushington; **97**, Scenes from the book of Samuel, Pierpont Morgan Library, New York, ms. 619, fol. recto, AR/PML; **98**, Nicolas Poussin, The Plague of Ashdod, Musée du Louvre, Paris, AR/G; **99**, Ashdod with pestilence and plague; return of ark to Israelites, Pierpont Morgan Library, New York, ms. 638, fol. 21v., AR/PML; **100**, Saul destroys Nahash; Saul anoints Samuel; offering is sacrificed, Pierpont Morgan Library, New York, ms. 638, fol. 23v., AR/PML; **101**, Shiloh, David Harris; **102**, David protecting sheep; David and Goliath from Le Miroir de l'Humaine Salvation, Musée Condé, Chan-

tilly, AR/G; **103**, David returns in triumph with head of Goliath; David and Saul are met by women, Pierpont Morgan Library, New York, ms. 638, fol. 29., AR/PML; **104**, Erasmus Quellinus, Saul listening to David playing the harp, Museum of Fine Arts, Budapest, BAL; **105** top, David escapes Saul with help of Mical, Chapel of Saints and Martyrs, Canterbury Cathedral, S. Halliday/Laura Lushington; **105** bottom, Cave of Adullam, David Harris; **106**, Maerten de Vos, David and Abigail, Musée des Beaux-Arts, Rouen, AR/G; **107** left, King Saul's death, Chartres Cathedral, S. Halliday/Laura Lushington; **107** right, Mount Gilboa, Z. Radovan.

2 Samuel

108 top, David is crowned king from the Paris Psalter, Bibliothèque Nationale, Paris, AKG, L; **108** bottom, Nicolas of Verdun, Joab assassinates Abner from the Verdun altar, Sammlungen des Stiftes, Klosterneuberg, Austria, AR/L; **109**, Assassins of Ishbaal bring head to David; David is anointed king, Pierpont Morgan Library, New York, ms. 638, fol. 38v., AR/PML; **110** left, City of David, Z. Radovan; **110** right, Raphael, The Triumph of David, Vatican Palace, Vatican State, AKG, L; **111**, David slays the Philistines, Church of St. Etienne, Mulhouse, France, S. Halliday/Laura Lushington; **112** top, Wolfgang Krodel, David and Bathsheba, Kunsthistorisches Museum, Vienna, AKG, L; **112** bottom, Tapestry with story of David and Bathsheba, Chateau, Ecouen, France, AR/G; **113**, David's penance from the Paris Psalter, Bibliothèque Nationale, Paris, ms. gr. 139, fol. 135v., AKG, L; **114**, Jan Steen, Amnon and Tamor, Wallraf-Richartz-Museum, Cologne, AKG, L; **116**, Death of Absalom from the Nuremberg Bible, Private Collection, BAL; **117**, Gustave Doré, David's anguish at the death of Absalom, Archiv für Kunst & Geschichte, Berlin, AKG, L; **118**, Cornelis de Vos, King David handing the sceptre to his son, Solomon, Galerie Jan de Maere, Brussels, AKG, L.

1 Kings

119, David and Solomon, David and Abishag from Winchester Bible, S. Halliday; **120**, Bible Moralisée, scenes of Solomon, Österreichische Nationalbibliothek, Vienna, AKG, L; **121**, Bonifazio di Pitati, The Wisdom of Solomon, Galleria dell'Accademia, Venice, AKG, L; **122** top, Haggadah showing the temple in Jerusalem, Jewish Museum, Prague, ms. 240, AKG, L; **122** bottom, cherub, David Harris; **123**, Edward Coley Burne-Jones, King Solomon holding the temple, Leigh, Staffordshire, England, BAL/Ann S. Dean, Brighton; **124**, Frans Francken the elder, Solomon and the queen of Sheba, Noortman Ltd., London, BAL; **125** left, Statuette of Astarte, also called Ashtaroth, Israel, S. Halliday; **125** right, Sebastien Bourdon, Solomon making a sacrifice to the idols, Musée du Louvre, Paris, BAL/Peter Willi; **126** top, Bible Moralisée, scene of Rehoboam becoming king, Österreichische Nationalbibliothek, Vienna, AKG, L; **126** bottom, War between Asa and Baasha from the Nuremberg Bible, Private Collection, BAL; **127** top, Inscription mentioning the house of David, Dan, Z. Radovan; **127** bottom, Seal of Hoshea, Israel, S. Halliday; **128** left, Wadi Cherith, east of Jerusalem, Z. Radovan; **128** right, Pavement showing Elijah in the Wadi Cherith, Duomo, Siena, AR/S; **129**, Elijah and King Ahab, Lincoln Cathedral, S. Halliday/Laura Lushington; **130** top, Prophets of Baal on Mount Carmel, Synagogue, Dura-Europos, Z. Radovan; **130** bottom, Jehoshaphat, Church of St. Dyfnog, Llanrhaeadr, Wales, S. Halliday/Laura Lushington; **131**, Thomas Matthews Rooke, Naboth lies dead and Elijah delivers God's curse, Russel-Cotes Art Gallery and Museum, Bournemouth, BAL.

2 Kings

132, Elijah parts the waters of the Jordan, Cathedral, Lincoln, S. Halliday/Laura Lushington; **133**, Elijah ascends to heaven in a whirlwind; two boys eaten by bears from the Nuremberg Bible, Private Collection, BAL; **134**, Cornelis Engebrechtsz, The Prophet Elijah heals the Syrian captain Naaman from leprosy, Kunsthistorisches Museum, Vienna, AR/L; **136** top, Woman at window, Z. Radovan; **136** bottom, Death of Jezebel, from the Bible Historiale of Guiart Desmoulins, Private Collection, AKG, L; **137**, Antoine Coypel, Athaliah expelled from the temple, Musée du Louvre, Paris, BAL/Peter Willi; **138**, Jehu, king of Israel before King Shalmaneser III of Assyria, British Museum, London, AR/L; **139**, **a-c**, Miracle of Elisha's Tomb; Ahaz at the altar of Demascus and the people of Damascus taken captive; God's vengeance on Assyria from the Nuremberg Bible, Private Collection, BAL; **140** left, Aerial view of Lachish Tel, Israel, Israel, S. Halliday; **140** right, Sennacherib's prism, Israel Museum, Jerusalem, AR/L; **141**, Samaria under siege from Luther Bible, Bible Society, London, BAL; **143**, Eduard Bendemann, The sorrow of the Jews in exile, Wallraf-Richartz-Museum, Cologne, AKG, L.

1 Chronicles

144, Adam tilling the soil after his expulsion, Canterbury Cathedral, S. Halliday/Laura Lushington; **145**, Scenes of Saul and David, Pierpont Morgan Library, New York, ms. 619, fol. 1v, AR/PML; **146**, Coronation of King David, Pierpont Morgan Library, New York, ms. G. 25, fol. 4, AR/PML; **147**, James Joseph Jacques Tissot, Festivities in honor of David, Jewish Museum, New York, AR/JM; **148**, Nathan and King David from a Book of Hours, Private Collection, AKG, L; **149**, Tree of Jesse, Pierpont Morgan Library, New York, ms. 724, verso, AR/PML; **150**, David and the temple band, from the breviary of Isabella of Spain, British Library, London, BAL; **151**, King David, Cathedral of San Marco, Venice, AR/S.

2 Chronicles

152, The Judgment of King Solomon, Strasbourg Cathedral, AR/L; **153** top, King Solomon's stables, Megiddo, Israel, AR/L; **153** bottom, Limbourg Brothers, Solomon oversees construction of the temple; Ark of the covenant carried into the temple, from the Trés Riches Heures du Duc de Berry, Musée Condé, Chantilly, AR/G; **154** top, Giulio Clovio, Solomon and the queen of Sheba, from the Farnese Book of Hours, Pierpont Morgan Library, New York, ms. 69, fol. 39, AR/PML; **154** bottom, King Rehoboam dismisses his counselors, from the Bible Historiale of Guiart Desmoulins, Bodleian Library, Oxford, ms. Douce 211, fol. 189v., AKG, L; **155**, Shishak celebrating victory over Israelites, Karnak, Egypt, AR/L; **157** left, Stone tablet inscribed with King Uzziah's name, Z. Radovan; **157** right, Gulf of Aqaba, Z. Radovan; **158** left, Inscription at entrance to Hezekiah's tunnel, Israel Museum, Jerusalem, AR/L; **158** right, Hezekiah's tunnel, Jerusalem, AR/L; **159** top, Battle of Sennacherib, from the Bible Historiale of Guiart Desmoulins, Private Collection, AKG, L; **159** bottom, Burial of Josiah from the Nuremberg Bible, Private Collection, BAL.

Ezra

160, Rebuilding of the temple, from the Bible Historiale of Guiart Desmoulins, Private Collection, AKG, L; **161**, Julius Schnorr von Carolsfeld, The return from the Babylonian exile, Archiv für Kunst & Geschichte, Berlin, AKG, L; **162** top, Darius I enthroned, Persepolis, Iran, AR/SEF; **162** bottom, Seal of Darius I, Z. Radovan; **163** top, Cedars of Lebanon, Z. Radovan; **163** bottom, Zerubbabel, Church of St. Dyfnog, Llanrhaeadr, North Wales, S. Halliday/Laura Lushington; **164**, Gustave Doré, Rebuilding of the temple, Archiv für Kunst & Geschichte, Berlin, AKG, L; **165**, View of the walled city of Jerusalem, from Nuremberg chronicle of Hartmann Schedel, Stapleton Collection, BAL.

Nehemiah

166, Vessel in form of a lion, The Metropolitan Museum of Art, New York, Fletcher Fund, 1954. (54.3.3); **167** left, Gustave Doré, Nehemiah and his companions at the gates of Jerusalem, Archiv für Kunst & Geschichte, Berlin, AKG, L; **167** right, Golden Gate of the temple district of Jerusalem, AR/L; **168**, Ezra reading scroll, Synagogue, Dura-Europos, AR/JM; **169**, Festival of Succoth, Z. Radovan; **170** left, God separates the earth from the water, St. Florentin Church, S. Halliday/Laura Lushington; **170** right, God creates the birds and fishes, Church of La Madeleine, Troyes, S. Halliday/Laura Lushington; **171**, Temple of Jerusalem, from the commentary on the Bible of Nicolas de Lyre, Bibliothèque Municipale, Cambrai, ms. 292, vol. 3, fol. 208v., AR/G.

Esther

172, Antoine Dufour, Esther, from the Lives of Celebrated Women, Musée Dobrée, Nantes, AR/G; **173**, Gregorio Pagani, Esther before Ahasuerus, Gemäldegalerie, Kunsthistorisches Museum, Vienna, AR/L; **174**, François Langrenee, Esther and Ahasuerus, Musée des Beaux-Arts, Quimper, BAL/Giraudon; **175**, Gustave Doré, Triumph of Mordecai, Archiv für Kunst & Geschichte, Berlin, AKG, L; **176** top, Jacob Bezalel, Scroll of Esther, Jewish Museum, New York, AR/JM; **176** bottom, Sara Eydel Weissburg, Purim wall decoration, Jewish Museum, New York, AR/JM; **177**, Noisemaker with image of hanged Haman, Jewish Museum, New York, AR/JM.

Job

178, H. von Gersdorf, Job in penury being jeered by his wife, Germany, AKG, L; **179**, Job being tested by God, Bibliothèque Nationale, Paris, ms. latin 7253.15.675, fol. 4v., AR/BAL; **180**, Driving off of Job's livestock; death of Job's children; Job's wife asks him to curse God, from a book of hours, Private Collection, AKG, L; **181**, Job scratching his sores, Bibliothèque Nationale, Paris, BAL; **182** top & botttom, William Blake, Job's comforters; Job rebuked by his friends, Pierpont Morgan Library, New York, AR/PML.

Psalms

183, King David, from the Psalter of Egbert, Museo Archeologico Nazionale, Cividale, Italy Cod. 136, AR/S; **184**, Master San Francesco, Crucifixion, Musée du Louvre, Paris, AR/L; **185**, The Good Shepherd, Mausoleum of Galla Placidia, Ravenna, AR/S; **186**, Domenico Beccafumi, King David, Cathedral, Siena, AR/S; **187**, Nicolas Bataille, The Heavenly Jerusalem, Musée des Tapisseries, Angers, S. Halliday; **188**, Herbert Gustave Schmalz, The Daughters of Judah in Babylon, Christie's Images, BAL.

Proverbs

189, Solomon on the throne, from the Treatise on Devotion, Musée Condé, Chantilly, France, BAL; **191**, King Solomon dictates the Proverbs, British Library, London, Roy 15 D 111 fol. 285., BAL; **193**, Bernard van Linge, Sibylla Delphica, Wroxton Abbey, England, S. Halliday/Laura Lushington.

Ecclesiastes

194, King Solomon on his throne from the Luther Bible, Bible Society, London, BAL; **195**, The sower amongst thorns from the Poor Man's Bible window, Canterbury Cathedral, S. Halliday/Laura Lushington; **196**, The Last Judgment from the Ingeburg Psalter, Musée Condé, Chantilly, ms. 9/1695, fol. 33, AR/G.

Song of Solomon

197, Gustave Moreau, The Song of Songs: the Shulammite maiden, Private Collection, BAL/Peter Willi; **198** top, Dante Gabriel Rossetti, The Daydream, Victoria & Albert Museum, London, AR/V&A; **198** bottom, Wildflowers on Israel's Mediterranean coast, Z. Radovan.

Isaiah

199, Vision of Isaiah, Bibliothèque Municipale, Bourges, AR/G; **201**, Giulio Clovio, The Annunciation and Isaiah with King Ahaz, from the Farnese Book of Hours, Pierpont Morgan Library, New York, ms. 69, fol. 4v.-5r., AR/PML; **203**, Tree of Jesse, Victoria & Albert Museum, London, #A36-1954, AR/V&A; **204**, Capture of the city of Lachish, relief from the palace of King Sennacherib, British Museum, London, AR/L; **205**, Edward Coley Burne-Jones, Hezekiah with his sundial, from a Jesse window, Rottingdean, England, S. Halliday/Laura Lushington; **206**, Michelangelo Buonarroti, Prophet Isaiah from the Sistine Chapel, Vatican Museums and Galleries, Vatican City, Italy, BAL; **207**, Ferdinand Olivier, Jewish captivity in Babylon, Behnhaus, Lübeck, AKG, L; **208**, Francisco de Zurbaran, The Eternal Father, Museo de Bellas Artes, Seville, BAL.

Jeremiah

210, Master of the Annunciation of Aix, Prophet Jeremiah, Musée Royaux of Beaux-Arts, AKG, L; **211**, Illustration of the book of Jeremiah from the Bible Moralisée, Treasury of the Cathedral, Toledo, Spain, fol. 156, AKG, L; **212** left, Jesus drives the money changers out of the temple, Church of St. Martin's, Zillis, Switzerland, S. Halliday;

212 right, Bronze pyxis with nine shekels, AR/L; **214**, R. Weibezahl, Nebuchadnezzar destroys Jerusalem, Archiv für Kunst und Geschichte, Berlin, AKG, L; **216**, Nebuchadnezzar and Jeremiah, S. Isidoro, Leon, Spain, AKG, L; **217**, King Zedekiah is defeated and blinded, Escorial, Madrid, Spain, from the Spanish Bible, AKG, L.

LAMENTATIONS

218, Jeremiah on the ruins of the sanctuary, Judaica Collection Max Berger, Vienna, Austria, AR/L.

EZEKIEL

220, Ezekiel, Victoria & Albert Museum, London, AR/V&A; **221**, Evelyn de Morgan, By the Waters of Babylon, The De Morgan Foundation, London, BAL, NY; **222**, Ezekiel and his vision; separation of righteous and unrighteous, from the Lambeth Bible, Lambeth Palace Library, London, BAL, NY; **225**, Ezekiel's prayer from the Paris Psalter, Bibliothèque Nationale, Paris, AKG, L; **226 & 227**, Ezekiel's prophecy: destruction and restoration of Jerusalem; valley of bones, Synagogue, Dura-Europos, Z. Radovan.

DANIEL

228, Daniel in the lion's den, Church of St. Etienne, Mulhouse, S. Halliday/Laura Lushington; **229**, Master of Marradi, Nebuchadnezzar summons Daniel and his companions, Alberto Bruschi di Grassina Collection, Florence, BAL; **231**, Matthäus Merian, The feast of Belshazzar, AKG, L.

HOSEA

232 top, Hosea from the Worms Bible, British Library, London, Harley 2803, vol. I, fol. 264, BAL; **232** bottom, Hosea with Gomer from the Bible Historiale of Guiart Desmoulins, Bodleian Library, Oxford, AKG, L; **234**, Assyrian King Tiglath-pileser III, Royal Palace, Nimrud, Z. Radovan; **235**, Michael Pacher, Flight into Egypt from the Saint Wolfgang church altar, Austria, AR/L.

JOEL

236, Pinturicchio (Bernardino di Betto), Joel, Borgia Apartments, Vatican, AR/S; **237** left, Locusts, Photo Researchers/Nuridsany & Perennou; **237** right, Locusts, Photo Researchers/Gianni Tortoli.

AMOS

238, The Calling of Amos, St. Mary's Church, Shrewsbury, S. Halliday/Laura Lushington; **239**, Juan de Borgona, Amos, Museo Catedralicio, Cuenca, BAL; **240**, Ruins at Bethel, Israel, R. Nowitz.

OBADIAH

241, Melozzo da Forli, Obadiah, Sacristy of San Marco, Sanctuary of the Santa Casa, Loreto, AR/S; **242**, Petra, Jordan, Photo Researchers/Noboru Komine.

JONAH

243, Jonah swallowed by the big fish, Hessisches Landesbibliothek, Darmstadt, ms. 2505, AKG, L; **244**, Carved ivory casket with Jonah scenes, saints, etc., Museo Civicodell'Eta Cristiana, Brescia, AR/S; **245**, Scenes from the story of Jonah, Basilica, Aquileia, Italy, AR/S.

MICAH

246, Pinturicchio (Bernardino di Betto), Micah, Borgia Apartments, Vatican, AR/S; **247** left, Bethlehem at sunrise, Bethlehem, Israel, S. Halliday; **247** right, Jean Bourdichon, Nativity from a book of hours, Pierpont Morgan Library, New York, ms. 732, fol. 31v., AR/PML; **248**, E. Vuchetich, Man beating swords into plowshares, United Nations, New York, Van Bucher.

NAHUM

249, Nahum from a Latin Bible, Pierpont Morgan Library, New York, ms. 436, fol. 319 v., AR/PML; **250**, Jean-Leon Gerome, The plain of Thebes in Upper Egypt, Musée des Beaux-Arts, Nantes, AR/G.

HABAKKUK

251, Habakkuk, Manasija, AKG, L; **252**, Julius Schnorr von Carolsfeld, Habakkuk transported to Daniel in the lions' den in Babylon, Archiv für Kunst & Geschichte, Berlin, AKG, L.

ZEPHANIAH

253, Pinturicchio (Bernardino di Betto), Zephaniah, Borgia Apartments, Vatican, AR/S; **254**, Jan Massys, Lot and his daughters, Kunsthistorisches Museum, Gemäldgalerie, Vienna, AR/L.

HAGGAI

255, Haggai and Zechariah from the Bible Moralisée, Treasury of the Cathedral, Toledo, Spain, fol. 218, AKG, L; **256**, Fall and restoration of Jerusalem, Culver Pictures, Inc.

ZECHARIAH

257, Jan Provost, Zechariah, Prado Museum, Madrid, AR/S; **258**, Vision of Zechariah seeing chariots pulled by horses representing the four winds, British Library, London, Roy I E IX fol. 237v., BAL; **259**, Giotto, Entry into Jerusalem, Arena chapel, Padua, AR/S.

MALACHI

260, Frederick James Shields, Malachi, Hartlepool Museum Service, BAL; **261**, Paolo Veronese, The sermon of John the Baptist, Galleria Borghese, Rome, AR/S.

APOCRYPHA INTRODUCTION

262, Andrea Mantegna, Judith with the head of Holofernes, Gabinetto Disegni e Stampe, Florence, AKG, L.

TOBIT

264, Veit Stoss, Young Tobias with the archangel Raphael, Germanisches Nationalmuseum, Nürnberg, Germany, AR/L; **265**, Andrea del Verrocchio with Francesco Botticini, Tobias and the angels, Uffizi, Florence, AR/L; **266**, Pieter Lastman, Young Tobias and the angel, Museum of Fine Arts, Budapest, AR/L; **267**, Tobias and Sarah, Victoria & Albert Museum, London, AR/V&A; **268** top, Tobias and Sarah returning, Spilimbergo Cathedral, Italy, AR/L; **268** bottom, Giovanni Biliverti, The angel refusing Tobias' gifts, Galleria Palatina, Palazzo Pitti, Florence, AR/A; **269**, Pieter Lastman, Angel Raphael takes leave of Tobit and Tobias, Statens Museum for Kunst, Copenhagen, Denmark, AR/L.

JUDITH

270, Lucas Cranach the Elder, Judith with the head of Holofernes, Kunsthistorisches Museum, Gemäldegalerie, Vienna, AR/L; **272**, Jan van den Hoecke, Judith and Holofernes, Private Collection, Belgium, AKG, L; **273**, Michelangelo Merisi da Caravaggio, Judith and Holofernes, National Gallery of Art, Rome, AR/S; **274**, Francesco Solimena, Judith presenting the head of Holofernes, Kunsthistorisches Museum, Vienna, AR/Nimatallah.

WISDOM OF SOLOMON

275, King Solomon reading the Torah from a French Hebrew Bible and prayer book, British Library, London, add. ms. 11639, fol. 116r, AR; **277**, Flemish School, Adam and Eve after the fall with Cain and Abel, Museo Archeologico, Pamplona, Spain, AR/S.

SIRACH

278, Creation of the stars and animals from an English psalter, The Pierpont Morgan Library, New York, ms. 302, fol. 1., AR/PML; **280**, Nicolas of Verdun, God gives Moses the Ten Commandments from the Verdun altar, Sammlungen des Stiftes, Klosterneuberg, Austria, AR/L; **281**, Domenichino (Domenico Zampieri), Abraham sacrificing Isaac, Museo del Prado, Madrid, AKG, L; **282**, The Flood, Noah and his family in the ark, Pierpont Morgan Library, New York, ms. 638, fol. 2v., AR/PML; **283**, Follower of the Master of Jean Rolin II, King David praying from a French book of hours, Pierpont Morgan Library, New York, ms. 282, fol. 141., AR/PML.

BARUCH/LETTER OF JEREMIAH

284, The prophet Jeremiah, Panagia Tou Arakou Monastery, Cyprus, S. Halliday; **285**, Michelangelo Buonarroti, Prophet Jeremiah from the Sistine Chapel, Vatican Museums and Galleries, Vatican City, Italy, BAL.

ADDITIONS TO DANIEL

286, Simeon Solomon, Shadrach, Meshach and Abednego in the fiery furnace, Mallett & Sons Antiques Ltd., London, BAL; **287**, Joseph-Marie Vien, Susanna and the Elders, Musée des Beaux-Arts, Nantes, AR/G; **288**, Francesco Vanni, Stories of the chaste Susanna, Banca Monte dei Paschi, Siena, AR/S; **289**, Daniel before Bel and the Dragon from Le Miroir de l'Humaine Salvation, Musée Condé, Chantilly, AR/G.

1 MACCABEES

290, Alexander the Great from Pompeii, Casa del Faune, Pompeii, now in the Museo Archeologica Nazionale, Naples, AR/L; **291**, Greek amphora showing three participants in a footrace at the Panathenaic Games, Musée Vivenel, Compiegne, France, AR/L; **292** left, Coin of Antiochus IV, Israel Museum, Jerusalem, AR/L; **292** right, Plundering of Jerusalem in the reign of King Antiochus IV, from the Chronicles of Jean de Coucy, Bibliothèque Nationale, Paris, AKG, L; **293**, Ruins of Beth-zur, Israel, AR/L; **294**, Julius Schnorr von Carolsfeld, Judas Maccabeus defending the temple in Jerusalem, Archiv für Kunst & Geschichte, Berlin, AKG, L; **295**, Hanukkah lamp, Jewish Museum, New York, AR/Jewish Museum; **296**, Gustave Doré, Death of Eleazar, Archiv für Kunst & Geschichte, Berlin, AKG, L; **297**, Gerrit van Honthorst, Judas Maccabeus after his victory over Nicanor, Cathedral of St. Bavo, Ghent, AR/G; **298**, Rock-cut tombs of the Maccabees in Modein, Israel, AR/L; **299**, Matthäus Merian, Ptolemy VI Philometor after the battle with Alexander Balas, AKG, L; **300**, B. Elkan, The revolt of the Maccabees, Parliament Gardens, Jerusalem, Israel, Z. Radovan; **301**, Hebrew coin of the high priest John Hyrcanus II, Z. Radovan.

2 MACCABEES

302, German Hanukkah lamp, Jewish Museum, New York, AR/JM; **303**, Illustrations to the book of Maccabees, Bibliothèque Nationale, Arsenal, AKG, L; **304**, Jason's tomb in Jerusalem, Z. Radovan; **306**, Coin of Demetrius II Nicator, Z. Radovan; **307**, Matthäus Merian, Judas Maccabeus conquers the town of Caspin, AKG, L; **308**, Julius Schnorr von Carolsfeld, Judas Maccabeus' vision, AKG, L.

NEW TESTAMENT INTRODUCTION

310, Jacob Jordaens, The Four Evangelists, Musée du Louvre, Paris, AR/S.

MATTHEW

312, Girolamo da Cremona, Adoration of the Magi, Libreria Piccolomini, Duomo, Siena, AR/S; **313** top, Joseph's dream, Victoria & Albert Museum, London, AR/V&A; **313** bottom, Flight into Egypt, Pierpont Morgan Library, New York, AR/PML; **314**, Pietro Vannucci called Perugino, Baptism of Christ, Pinacoteca, Vatican Museums, Vatican State, AR/S; **316**, Christ sending out the Apostles, Pierpont Morgan Library, New York, AR/PML; **317**, Church of the Beatitudes, Sea of Galilee, R. Nowitz; **318**, Parable of the vineyards, Museo Nazionale del Bargello, Florence, AR/S; **319**, New Testament scenes, Pierpont Morgan Library, New York, AR/PML; **320**, Russian School, Christ's entry into Jerusalem, University of Liverpool Art Gallery & Collections, BAL; **321**, Jacopo Robusti, called Tintoretto, The Last Supper, Church of San Trovaso, Venice, AR/Cameraphoto-Arte, Venice; **322** top, Scenes of Judas: paid silver, betraying Christ, suicide, Victoria & Albert Museum, London, AR/V&A; **322** bottom, Saint Peter's denial, San Apollinaire Nuovo, Ravenna, AR/L; **323** top, Raphael, The Road to Calvary, Museo del Prado, Madrid, AR/S.

MARK

324, Andrea Pisano, The Baptism of Christ, Baptistery, Florence, AR/S; **325**, Marco Basaiti, Jesus calls the Sons of Zebedee, James and John, Kunsthistorisches Museum, Gemäldegalerie, Vienna, AR/L; **326**, Paralytic lowered from the roof, Jesus and an Apostle, San Apollinaire Nuovo, Ravenna, AR/L; **327**, Christ casting out the devil, Bibliothèque Sainte-Genevieve, Paris, AR/G; **328**, Salome dancing before Herod and death of John the Baptist from the Holkham Bible, British Library, London, BAL; **329**, Feeding of the five thousand from the Gospels of Henry III, Escorial, Spain, AKG, L; **330**, Fra Angelico, Transfiguration, Museo di San Marco, Florence, AR/S; **331**, Mount Tabor, site of Transfiguration, R. Nowitz; **332** left, Giotto, Cleansing of the temple, Arena chapel, Padua, BAL; **332** right, Coin of Julius Caesar, AKG, L; **333**, El Greco, Supper in the house of Simon, Chicago Art Institute, AR/S; **334**, Kiss of Judas, Pierpont Morgan Library, New York M. 190, fol. 42., AR/PML; **335**, Jean Bellegambe, Crucifixion, Museum der Bildenden Kunste, Leipzig, AKG, L.

LUKE

336 top, Annunciation, Pierpont Morgan Library, New York, AR/PML; **336** bottom, Visitation from the Playfair Book of Hours, Victoria & Albert Museum, London, AR/V&A; **337**, Paolo Veronese, Adoration of the Shepherds, Church of Saints John and Paul, Venice, AR/Cameraphoto - Arte; **338**, Albrecht Dürer, The 12-year-old Jesus in the temple, Gemäldegalerie, Dresden, AKG, L; **339**, Miraculous draught of fishes, Canterbury Cathedral, AR/Sassoonian; **340**, Cosimo Rosselli, Discourse on the mountain and healing the leper, Sistine Chapel, Vatican, AR/S; **341**, Dirk Bouts, Christ in the house of Simon the Pharisee, Staatliche Museen Preussischer Kulturbesitz, Gemäldegalerie, Berlin, AKG, L; **342**, Alessandro Allori, Christ in the house of Mary and Martha, Kunsthistorisches Museum, Vienna, AR/L; **343**, The Good Samaritan, Libreria Piccolomini, Siena, AR/S; **344**, Edward Poynter, The prodigal's return, Private Collection, AR/BAL; **345** bottom, Matthias Gerung, Lazarus and the rich man's table from Mompelgarter altarpiece, Kunsthistorisches Museum, Vienna, BAL; **346** top, Mount of Olives, R. Nowitz; **346** bottom, Rembrandt Harmensz van Rijn, Christ and the apostles at Emmaus, Musée du Louvre, Paris, AKG, L; **347**, Andrea Mantegna, Ascension, Uffizi, Florence, AR/S.

JOHN

348, Donatello, St. John the Baptist, Duomo, Siena, AR/S; **349** bottom, Master of Bartholmew Altar, Wedding feast of Cana, Musées Royaux d'Art et d'Histoire, Brussels, AKG, L; **349** bottom right, Jug, Jewish Museum, New York, AR/JM; **350**, Paolo Veronese, Christ and the Samaritan woman at the well, Kunsthistorisches Museum, Vienna, AR/L; **351**, Hendrik de Clerck, The feeding of the five thousand, Kunsthistorisches Museum, Vienna, BAL; **352** top, Christ heals a blind-born youth, Sammlungen des Stiftes, Klosterneuberg, Austria, AR/L; **352** bottom, Giovanni Domenico Tiepolo, Christ and the woman taken in adultery, Musée des Beaux-Arts, Marseilles, BAL; **353**, Good Shepherd, Greco-Roman Museum, Alexandria, AR/S; **354**, Geertgen tot Sint Jans, Resurrection of Saint Lazarus, Musée du Louvre, Paris, AR/L; **355**, Christ washing the feet of the apostles, Pierpont Morgan Library, New York, ms. 44, fol.7, AR/PML; **356**, Limbourg Brothers, Flagellation from the Trés Riches Heures du Duc de Berry, Musée Condé, Chantilly, AR/G; **357**, Crucifixion, Chartres Cathedral, AKG, L; **358**, Rogier van der Weyden, Deposition, Prado, Madrid, AR/S; **359** top, The women at the sepulchre from the Shaftsbury Psalter, British Library, London, BAL; **359** bottom, Bernardo Strozzi, Incredulity of St. Thomas, Museo de Arte, Ponce, Puerto Rico, BAL.

ACTS OF THE APOSTLES

360, Michelino da Besozzo, Ascension of Christ, Pierpont Morgan Library, New York, ms. 944, fol. 35v., AR/PML; **361**, Pieter Coecke van Aelst, The Pentecost, Museo de Santa Cruz, Toledo, Spain, AKG, L; **362**, Joshua Price, St. Peter healing the cripple at the Golden Gate, Great Witley church, S. Halliday/Laura Lushington; **363**, Vittore Carpaccio, St. Stephen preaching, Musée du Louvre, Paris, AR/S; **364**, Annibale Carracci, The stoning of St. Stephen, Musée du Louvre, Paris, AR/L; **365**, Zanobi di Benedetto Strozzi, The blinding of Saul, Museo di San Marco dell'Angelico, Florence, BAL; **366**, Konrad Witz, Freeing of St. Peter, Musée d'Art et d'Histoire, Geneva, AKG, L; **367**, Jean Fouquet, Martyrdom of St. James the Greater from the Hours of Etienne Chevalier, Musée Condé, Chantilly, AR/G; **368**, after Raphael, St. Paul's sacrifice at Lystra, Palazzo Ducale, Mantua, AR/S; **369**, Aerial view of Caesarea, S. Halliday; **370** left, The Arkadiane or main street of Ephesus, Turkey, view towards the theatre where Paul preached, AR/L; **370** right, Artemis of Ephesus, Museo Nazionale di Capodimente, Naples, AR/L; **372**, Appian way, Z. Radovan; **373**, Workshop of Pacino di Buonaguida, Martyrdoms of St. Peter and St. Paul, Fitzwilliam Museum, University of Cambridge, England, BAL, NY.

ROMANS

374, Saint Paul, Duoma, Monreale, Italy, AR/S; **375**, Catacomb chamber, Catacombs of St. Januarius, Naples, BAL; **377**, Christ with the apostles, Catacomb of Domitilla, Rome, AR/S; **378**, Samaritan woman at the well, Ipogeo di Via Latina, Rome, AR/S; **379**, Catacomb of Priscilla, The Capella Greca or cubiculum of the Fractio Panis, Catacomb of Priscilla, Rome, AR/S; **380**, Saint Paul led towards martyrdom, from the Junius Bassus Sarcophagus, Grotto Vaticano, Vatican, AR/L.

1 CORINTHIANS

381, Masaccio, Saint Paul, Museo Nazionale di S. Matteo, AR/S; **382**, Temple at Corinth, Corinth, Greece, Z. Radovan; **383**, Giovanni Paolo Panini, Ruins with the apostle Paul preaching, Hermitage, St. Petersburg, BAL; **384** top, Lechaion street in Roman Corinth, Greece, AR/L; **384** bottom, Fish and loaves of bread, Catacomb of S. Callisto, AR/S; **385**, The Last Supper from Le Miroir de l'Humaine Salvation, Musée Condé, Chantilly, AR/G; **386**, Nicolas of Verdun, Resurrection of the dead from the

Verdun altar, Sammlungen des Stiftes, Klosterneuberg, Austria, AR/L; **387**, Stephen Lochner, The Last Judgment, Wallraf-Richartz-Museum, Cologne, AKG, L.

2 CORINTHIANS

388, Rembrandt Harmensz van Rijn, The apostle Paul, Kunsthistorisches Museum, Vienna, AKG, L; **390**, Court of Justice on the forum at Corinth, Corinth, Greece, AR/L; **391** top, The apostle Paul, Church of the Ascension of Christ, AKG, L; **391** bottom, St. Paul and Thekla, British Museum, London, AR/L.

GALATIANS

392, Bartolommeo Vivarini, St. Peter and St. Paul, Chuch of Santa Maria Gloriosa dei Frari, Venice, AR/Cameraphoto-Arte; **393**, Giulio Licinio, Conversion of St. Paul, Private Collection, Venice, AR/Cameraphoto-Arte.

EPHESIANS

395, St. Paul, Grotto, St. Peter's Basilica, Vatican, AR/S; **396**, Via dei Cureti, Ephesus, Turkey, AR/SEF.

PHILIPPIANS

398, Filippino Lippi, St. Paul visiting St. Peter in prison, Brancacci Chapel, S. Maria del Carmine, Florence, AR/S; **399**, Crucifixion, from an English (Canterbury) Gospel book, Pierpont Morgan Library, New York, ms. 709, fol. 1v., AR/PML.

COLOSSIANS

400, The Trinity from the book of hours of King Charles VIII, Biblioteca Nacional, Madrid, Spain, AKG, L; **401**, Michelino da Besozzo, Luke painting the Virgin, Pierpont Morgan Library, New York, ms. 944, fol. 75v., AR/PML.

1-2 THESSALONIANS

402, Bartolomeo della Gatta, Paul, Museo Diocesano d'Arte Sacra, Volterra, AR/S; **403**, Russian icon showing the resurrection of Christ and the harrowing of hell, AKG, L; **404**, Master of the Zurich Carnation, Michael weighing the souls at the Last Judgment, Kunsthaus, Zurich, AR/G.

1-2 TIMOTHY, TITUS

405, Paul with Timothy from the Bible Historiale of Guiart Desmoulins, Ashmolean Museum, Oxford, AKG, L; **406**, Nativity of Christ on Florentine glazed terra-cotta, Christie's Images, BAL, NY; **408**, Bust of the emperor Nero, Museo Archeologico Nazionale, Naples, BAL, NY; **409**, Jacopo Robusti, called Tintoretto, The execution of Paul, Church della Madonna dell'Orto, Venice, AKG, L.

PHILEMON

410, Paul and Onesimus, British Library, London, ms. Burney 3, fol. 501v., British Library, London.

HEBREWS

411, Nicolas of Verdun, Melchizedek sacrifices bread and wine from the Verdun altar, Sammlungen des Stiftes, Klosterneuberg, Austria, AR/L; **412**, Lodovico Buti, Abraham receives the promise of the three angels, Kunsthistorisches Museum, Vienna, AR/L; **413**, Giovanni Battista Tiepolo, Abraham and the sacrifice of Isaac, Palazzo Arcivescovile, Udine, Italy, AR/S; **415**, Moses leads the children of Israel across the Red Sea from a Jewish prayer book, Staats-und Universitatsbibliothek, Hamburg, BAL.

JAMES

416, James, Monastery of Eski Gumus, Cappadocia, Turkey, S. Halliday.

1-2 PETER

418, Lippo Memmi, Peter, Musée du Louvre, Paris, AR/L; **419**, Paul and Peter before the emperor Nero, Musée des Beaux Arts, Dijon, AR/L; **420**, Ford Madox Brown, Jesus washing Peter's feet, Tate Gallery, London, AR/TG.

1-3 JOHN

421, John the Evangelist, Biblioteca Apostolica, Vatican, AKG, L; **422**, Master of the Carnations, John preaching to Herod, Kunstmuseum Bern, Switzerland, AR/SEF.

JUDE

424, Anthony Van Dyck, The apostle Judas Thaddaeus, Kunsthistorisches Museum, Vienna, AR/L.

REVELATION

425, Jacopo Alberegno, John's vision on Patmos, Galleria dell'Accademia, AKG, L; **426**, The vision of God and the commission to write from the Apocalypse by Beatus de Liebana, The Pierpont Morgan Library, New York, ms. 644, fol. 27, AR/PML; **427**, The Seventh Seal: The distribution of the trumpets to the seven angels, The Pierpont Morgan Library, New York, ms. 524, fol. 4, AR/PML; **428**, Jacopo Palma the younger, John's vision of the four horsemen of the Apocalypse, Scuola Grande di St. John the Evangelist, Venice, AKG, L; **429**, Nicolas Bataille, The opening of the Fourth Seal: Death on a pale horse followed by Hades, Musée des Tapisseries, Angers, AR/G; **430**, Apocalypse, depicting the killing of the seven-headed beast, Trinity College, Cambridge, England, BAL; **431**, Nicolas Bataille, The second angel announces the fall of Babylon, Musée des Tapisseries, Angers, AR/G; **432**, Archangel Michael weighing souls, The Pierpont Morgan Library, New York, ms. 700, fol. 2., AR/PML; **433**, The Second Coming from the benedictional of St. Aethelwold, Winchester, British Library, London, BAL.

INDEX

Page numbers in **boldface** indicate main entries or special features. Page numbers in *italics* indicate illustrations.